# Greenwich Readers

# Cognitive Functions

## Classic Readings in Representation and Reasoning

# Cognitive Functions

## Classic Readings in Representation and Reasoning

edited and introduced by

**MARK J. BROSNAN**

LECTURER IN COGNITIVE PSYCHOLOGY
SCHOOL OF SOCIAL SCIENCES
UNIVERSITY OF GREENWICH

**Greenwich University Press**

First published in 1996 by
Greenwich University Press
Unit 42
Dartford Trade Park
Butterly Avenue
Dartford
Kent DA1 1JG
United Kingdom

British Library Cataloguing-in-Publication Data
A CIP catalogue record for this book is available from the British Library

ISBN 1 874529 66 3

Designed and produced for Greenwich University Press by Angela Allwright.

# Contents

# Cognitive Functions: An Introduction

The aim of this anthology is to present the reader with the seminal research into cognitive functioning through papers focusing upon cognitive representation and reasoning. How information is represented is examined through scheme theory (including scripts) and theories positing the structure of concepts. Reasoning is examined through an investigation of a variety of reasoning processes; namely, inductive, analogical, syllogistic and deductive reasoning.

## Representation: schemata and scripts

The first set of papers looks at the hypothetical structures of memory. A (psychological) scheme is defined by the *Collins English Dictionary* as 'a mental model of aspects of the world or of the self that is structured in such a way as to facilitate the process of cognition'. The role of schemata in memory is identified through an examination of their influence upon encoding and recall in a paper by Brewer and Treyens. Subjects were asked to wait in an office until the experiment began. When subjects were taken to the laboratory for testing, they were informed that the experiment consisted of recalling items from the office that they had just been waiting in. Subjects were asked to recall items from memory and the items that would normally be expected to be in an office were typically recalled. Items that were 'recalled' but were not actually in the office (e.g., books), were identified as objects that one would typically expect to be in an office. Thus, these results imply that a cognitive representation (i.e., a schema) of a typical office was being accessed for the recall task. A specific example of a schema is a schema for a procedure, or 'a script'. A script is a representation of stereotyped event sequences. A general restaurant script (for example) might run along the lines of 'enter restaurant, be seated, read menu, order food, eat food, pay, leave restaurant'.

In the second paper Bower, Black and Turner investigate people's knowledge of routine events, such as going to the restaurant or going to the dentist. Subjects were presented with stories of these typical instances and then their recall tested. As with schemata, subjects 'recalled' non-stated information that would be expected to be present. Additionally, if part of the script was out of sequence in the story, subjects tended to recall it in its stereotypical order rather than in the order actually presented. Finally, Abelson provides an evaluation of the psychological status of the script, highlighting how these stereotypical sequences can be utilized in artificial intelligence to demonstrate an apparent 'understanding'. Abelson also describes how a script organizes comprehension of event-based situations facilitating appropriate inferences, etc. The script is argued to represent the unifying force within psychology, highlighting how similar different focuses within psychology are. 'There are not five psychologies — cognitive, social, learning, developmental, and clinical — but one psychology. The analysis of scripts and other knowledge structures based on the events of ordinary experience promotes awareness of this unity and helps to explore it' (Abelson, 1981).

## Representation: concepts and categories

The nature of cognitive structures is further examined through the research on concepts and categories. This section of papers examines the grouping of items into categories, and the cognitive representation of the categories' concepts. Categories group things that share attributes. Thus, the attributes 'has feathers' and 'has a beak' tend to occur together, this co-occurrence of attributes structuring the category 'birds'. The taxonomies of concepts are investigated in papers examining the representation of categories' component objects and parts. The notion of level is also expanded upon. For example, the concept of 'a robin' is subordinate to the concept of 'a bird'. Similarly, 'a bird' is subordinate to 'an animal' and so on. The notions of context dependency, graded structure and central tendency in concepts are additionally expounded upon along with a critical analysis of prototype theory. The representation of a category is also compared and contrasted with the representation of a script.

The work of Eleanor Rosch has been extremely influential in the research of concepts. In the first paper, 'What some concepts might not be', Armstrong, Gleitman and Gleitman replicate many of Rosch's research findings. This paper provides a comprehensive account of Rosch's work and her prototype theory. It suggests that many categories and concepts have a prototypical member. For example, a robin is considered a more typical example (or 'exemplar') of the category 'bird' than a pelican is (for example). Prototypical members share commonly occurring attributes (e.g., can fly, has feathers). Less typical birds share less of these commonly occurring attributes (e.g., an emu is untypical as it does not fly — but it is still a bird). This notion of category members sharing some attributes is likened to a family resemblance (after Wittgenstein). Just as we are not identical to our parents/siblings/children, we share some features with some family members, and other features with other family members. Armstrong, Gleitman and Gleitman reproduce experimental evidence for the existence of prototypical exemplars of concepts.

The second paper in this section examines our preferred level of abstraction in our conceptual taxonomies. People tend to communicate at what is termed the 'basic' level of abstraction (after Rosch, amongst others). For example, a far greater number of attributes for basic level items are listed by subjects (e.g., for car) than for superordinate categories (e.g., vehicle) or subordinate categories (e.g., sports car). Thus, it is argued that this level of abstraction is most informative in structuring categories, facilitating decisions of inclusion and exclusion from category membership. The basic level is the focus of the Tversky and Hemenway paper, who argue that the notion of 'parts' (i.e., a handle and a blade are parts of a screwdriver) is salient in determining the basic level. The third paper focuses on the role of context upon the defining properties of concepts. In this, Barsalou proposes that certain properties of concepts are context-independent. For example, whatever the context, our concept of a skunk invariably has the property 'unpleasant smell'. There are additionally context-dependent properties of concepts which are only 'activated' by the relevant context. For example, when evoking the concept of a basketball, rarely does the property 'floats' spontaneously spring to mind — unless appropriate context is provided. The existence of context-dependent and context-independent properties is demonstrated and the implications for a range of cognitive functions discussed. In a second paper by

Barsalou, the author examines the 'graded structure' in categories. Graded structure refers to a continuum of category representativeness from typical members (such as a robin) to atypical members (such as an emu). Barsalou compares the common taxonomic categories discussed so far (such as birds or tools) with 'goal-derived' categories. Contemplating what to buy Auntie Madge for her birthday can be seen as a goal-derived category with (appropriate present) members and (inappropriate present) non-members. In such categories, Barsalou argues that it is possible to identify an ideal. For example, the ideal for the category 'things to eat on a diet' is 'zero calories'. Barsalou's papers demonstrates that both ideals and central tendency (i.e., ideal family resemblance) determine graded structure-dependent upon context.

The final paper in this section attempts to combine the themes of this and the previous section. In both script and concept theory, the research positing relatively rigid cognitive structures has been undermined by papers indicating that a description of more fluid structures would be more appropriate. Barsalou and Sewell conclude that scripts and categories share invariant properties of abstract representations, any differences reflecting domain constraints.

## Reasoning: induction, analogies, syllogisms and deduction

Related to the notion of representation is reasoning. For example, how do we categorize novel items? This necessitates inductive reasoning and inductive judgements about natural categories. Inductive reasoning is further examined through a paper on the use of statistical heuristics in everyday inductive reasoning. Another focus of the research into reasoning is how existing knowledge within a domain can extend to a novel domain, consequently the factors facilitating analogical transfer are investigated. A classical example is using the planets circling the sun to introduce the notion of electrons circling a nucleus. Seminal papers are reproduced which identify the salient features that encourage the realization of potential analogies. Finally, deductive thinking is introduced and relationships to logic and syllogistic reasoning formulated and related to rules of inference.

The relationship between representation and reasoning is highlighted by the first paper in this section by Rips which examines how inductive judgements are made about categories. Subjects were told that one member of a category had a disease and had to estimate the proportion of other category members which had the disease. Rips found that if a typical member of the category had the disease it was more likely to be generalized to other category members than if an atypical member of the category had the disease. This paper highlights how inextricably intertwined the notions of representation and reasoning are.

Nisbett, Krantz and Kunda examine how statistical heuristics are employed in everyday inductive reasoning. For example, although receiving an A+ might represent an excellent mark, people do not infer that the student is brilliant if no one received a mark below A–. They argue that although A+ is a brilliant mark, we take into account the base rate information (i.e., performance of the class as a whole). Consequently the authors suggest that we use statistical heuristics in our inductive reasoning. They also discuss the factors that affect our statistical reasoning and the effects of training in statistics on reasoning about everyday events.

The research into analogical transfer has explored both how transfer is initiated and, once initiated, which aspects of the analogy are transferred. In the analogy given above, why is the nucleus not assumed to be intensely hot (as the sun is)? In their seminal paper 'Flowing waters or teeming crowds: mental models of electricity', Gentner and Gentner examine the effects of using either flowing water **or** teeming crowds of people as an analogy to electricity. Resistors and electric current were either mapped onto notions of narrow constrictions and water flow **or** gates and number of people (respectively). The authors then asked subjects to assess the impact of various arrangements of batteries and resistors in serial or parallel formation. The results indicated that systematic differences emerged dependent upon the original analogy. The authors conclude that, although subjects were demonstrably able to import relational structure from one domain to another, they often failed to notice and use a potential analogy. The following two papers examine which factors facilitate analogical transfer. Gentner and Toupin look at the effects of systematicity and surface similarity in school children (aged 5 to 10). Systematicity refers to the degree of explicit causal similarity between an original story and a new story. Surface similarity refers to the transparency of the analogy (e.g., using the same characters in both stories). Surface similarity strongly influenced transfer accuracy in all ages, and by 8 years old systematicity influenced transfer regardless of surface similarity. This may reflect a limitation in younger children's competence or their unfamiliarity with causal relations in the stories. Either or both of these possibilities are conceivable. Holyoak and Koh examined the effects of surface and structural similarity upon analogical transfer in adult subjects. They found that both salient structural and surface features influence spontaneous analogical transfer.

The remaining papers highlight the work of Philip Johnson-Laird upon deductive thinking and logic. The author argues that the ability to reason lies at the heart of human mentality — '*Homo sapiens* is a rational creature'. The psychology of syllogisms is discussed, starting with an introduction to syllogistic reasoning. Johnson-Laird and Steedman examined the conclusions people drew from a combination of premises (e.g., what can be concluded from 'none of the musicians are inventors' and 'all of the inventors are professors'?). The authors examine biases in conclusions, evaluating the role of analogical reasoning and heuristics. The conclusion suggests that errors occur through failure to test the full range of possible conclusions. The second paper examines the principles of inference that lie both within and outside logic. It is not 'logically valid', for example, to infer that the sun will rise tomorrow, because it has done so in the past. The logically valid area of deduction is discussed, referring to syllogistic reasoning, truth values and the 'theory of mental logic'. The effect of content upon reasoning is also incorporated to provide a comprehensive account of logical premises that are constructed into 'mental models' of the world. Johnson-Laird concludes: 'The theory of mental models accounts for nearly all the erroneous conclusions that subjects draw — on the assumption that they fail to consider all the possible models of premises'. He subsequently argues that many profoundly puzzling phenomena can be elucidated by this process of positing models.

Therein lies the essence of the research presented in this collection of papers. The cognitive functioning around representation and reasoning has hopefully been elucidated through the research presented and the models proposed. The recurrent themes of centrality and representativeness (amongst others) emphasise the interdependencies of the theory and research around representation and reasoning. It is hoped that through the presentation of these papers, the arbitrary nature of the sections has been highlighted. In this way, the collection of papers provides coverage of the crucial research into representation and reasoning that contributes to our understanding of these cognitive functions.

Seminal papers covering visual cognition, attention and memory are also available in this series (Brosnan, 1996).

Mark J. Brosnan<br>1996

## References

Brosnan, M. (Ed.) *Cognitive Processes: Readings in Visual Cognition, Attention and Memory*. Greenwich University Press, 1996.

Rosch, E. (1973) On the Internal Structure of Perceptual and Semantic Categories. In T.E. Moore (ed.) *Cognitive Development and the Acquisition of Language*. New York, Academic Press.

## Publisher's note

The contents of the readings in this anthology have been reproduced as they appear in the publications from which they are taken. In the majority of cases footnotes and bibliographic material are included, the exceptions being where they are of excessive length.

# Representation:
# Schemata and Scripts

# 1.   Role of Schemata in Memory for Places

## William F. Brewer and James C. Treyens

*A study of memory for places was carried out to examine five hypotheses about the use of schemata in memory performance: (a) that schemata determine what objects are encoded into memory; (b) that schemata act as frameworks for episodic information; (c) that schema-based information is integrated with episodic information; (d) that schemata facilitate retrieval; and (e) that schemata influence what is communicated at recall. Subjects were taken into what they thought was a graduate student's office and later were tested for memory of the room with either drawing recall, written recall, or verbal recognition. Memory scores for objects were correlated with schema expectancy and saliency ratings. Schema expectancy was positively correlated with recall and recognition. Expected objects were inferred in recall, supporting the integration hypothesis. Comparison of recall and recognition data supported the retrieval hypothesis. Analysis of the written descriptions supported the communication hypothesis. Saliency was positively correlated with recall and recognition for present objects, but was unrelated to retrieval. Saliency was negatively correlated with recognition for nonpresent objects, suggesting a metacognitive strategy in recognition of high-salient objects.*

Much current research on human memory deals with the intentional learning of linguistic materials such as words, sentences, or stories. These experiments tend to be analogs of school tasks such as remembering the names of the states or the content of a paragraph in a textbook. The present paper uses an experimental task that is intended to be more analogous to the types of incidental memory that occur in everyday life. In particular, we have chosen to focus on memory for places. We are interested in investigating the memory processes that are involved when telling someone where a particular book is on a shelf or describing someone's office after your first visit.

Recent attempts to deal with memory for stories and with perception of real-world scenes have led to the development of theories in which existing knowledge plays a crucial role (Anderson & Pichert, 1978; Bobrow & Norman, 1975; Bower, Black, & Turner, 1979; Minsky, 1975; Neisser, 1976; Piaget & Inhelder, 1973; Rumelhart, 1980; Rumelhart & Ortony, 1977; Schank & Abelson, 1977; Spiro, 1977). It seems to us that the study of memory for real-world places requires theories of a similar nature.

The representational structures in these theories (schemata, frames, scripts, plans, prototypes) will be referred to here as schemata. Schemata are knowledge structures or sets of expectations based on past experience. They exist at various levels of abstraction and vary in their structural complexity (cf. Rumelhart, 1980).

William F. Brewer and James C. Treyens: 'Role of Schemata in Memory for Places' in *COGNITIVE PSYCHOLOGY* (1981), 13, pp. 207–230. Copyright © 1981 by Academic Press, Inc.

Schema theories propose that perception, language comprehension, and memory are processes which involve the interaction of new (episodic) information with old, schema-based information. The basic assumption of schema theories is that an individual's prior experience will influence how he or she perceives, comprehends, and remembers new information.

Minsky (1975) suggests that perception is a schema-based process occurring over time which involves filling in details, collecting evidence, testing, deducing, and interpreting, on the basis of knowledge, expectations, and goals. Minsky hypothesizes that this complex process can take place rapidly because schemata already exist in memory which correspond to common environments, such as rooms. Information slots or variables in the internal structure of the schema which have not been filled with perceptual information are filled by default assignments based on stereotypic expectations derived from past experience. Kuipers' (1975) hypothetical example of room perception illustrates default assignments: if a quick perceptual scan of a room indicates that there is a clock on the wall, hands may be assigned to the internal representation by default, even though this particular clock does not have hands.

A number of schema theorists have focused directly on memory and have shown that memory performance is frequently influenced by schema-based expectations. Bartlett (1932) found that subjects' expectations and experiences distorted their recall of an unusual North American Indian folktale. Spiro (1977) found that recall of passages can be influenced by expectations based on information presented after reading the passage. Piaget and Inhelder (1973) showed that memories can be modified by schema development occurring between learning and recall. Anderson and Pichert (1978) have shown that an activated schema can aid retrieval of information in a recall task. While these studies have clearly demonstrated that schemata influence memory performance, the details of the process have not been worked out.

It appears to us that there are five fundamentally different ways in which schemata might influence memory performance: (a) they can determine what objects are looked at and encoded into memory; (b) they can act as a framework for new information; (c) they can provide schema-based information which becomes integrated with episodic information; (d) they can guide the retrieval process; and (e) they can determine what information is to be communicated at output.

*Encoding.* Minsky (1975) and Neisser (1976) have suggested that perception is guided by schemata. However, two different memory predictions are derivable from these theories. On the one hand, it might be hypothesized that subjects will spend more time looking at schema-relevant information and ignore information which does not fit into the currently active schemata. On the other hand, it might be hypothesized that subjects will only briefly glance at expected objects and spend more time looking at novel, unexpected objects. If it is assumed that looking time is directly related to how well an object is represented in memory, then the first encoding hypothesis predicts that schema-relevant information will be better remembered than unexpected information, while the second encoding hypothesis predicts that the unexpected information will be better remembered.

4

*Framework.* Schemata may serve as a framework in memory, so that schema-relevant episodic information is retained better than nonrelevant episodic information.

*Integration.* The episodic information and the schema-based information may be integrated in memory. In this case memory performance for schema-relevant information will be superior to that for nonschema information, since the memory performance for schema-relevant information is based on a mixture of new episodic information and old schema-based information. Inferences are said to occur when memory performance contains information from the schema that was not given in the episodic input. This general form of the integration model makes no claim about the degree of integration; the integration may be so complete that the subject cannot distinguish the episodic information from the schema-based information, or the two types of information may remain distinct.

*Retrieval.* Schema-based information may also be used in the process of retrieving information from memory. When individuals have been exposed to large amounts of information, they frequently retain more information than they can actually produce in a recall task. Several schema theorists (Anderson & Pichert, 1978; Lichtenstein & Brewer, 1980) have suggested that schemata are used to guide the search for information in memory; thus, information which is not related to the schema being used in retrieval will be harder to recall than information which is schema related.

*Communication.* When a subject is asked by an experimenter to recall previously presented information, the task is a form of communication between the two. If the subject's response mode is fairly open, as in a written description or narrative, then schemata can influence what information the subject gives in response. For example, Norman (1973) has pointed out that answers to questions are determined by schema-based assumptions of the answerer.

In developing an experimental paradigm to study place memory, we have chosen to study memory for rooms. This choice was based on a number of considerations. There has already been some interesting research on long-term memory for places by researchers from urban planning and geography (Downs & Stea, 1977; Lynch, 1960). These researchers have asked individuals to draw maps of towns and cities and have found a number of phenomena which appear to be the result of schema-based knowledge interacting with the information from the environment (e.g., the Boston Common is typically drawn as a rectangle, rather than as the five-sided figure it actually is). It is difficult to go beyond such observations in the study of long-term memory for public locations, since the experimenter does not have control over the characteristics of the locations involved. However, by choosing to study memory for rooms we can study place memory and yet have control over the input information. Even though rooms can easily be manipulated, they appear to be complex and meaningful enough to allow the results to be generalized to other types of real-life place memory. Finally, we wanted to study place memory in a naturalistic incidental learning situation, and using rooms made this very easy.

Given these considerations, the basic experimental paradigm used in the present research was quite simple. We designed a room to look like a graduate student's office. The subjects were taken into this room and were asked to wait there for a few minutes before the experiment began. Then, after a short time they were taken out of the experimental room and tested to determine their memory for various aspects of the room.

## Experimental room: development and rating

The experimental location studied in this paper was a room (2.73 x 1.82 x 2.08 m) which was designed to look like a graduate student's office. It contained a table with a typewriter and standard desk items. In another part of the room there was a table with a coffeepot and materials for making coffee. A third table held a Skinner box, tools, and electronic parts. There were shelves along one wall, and the other walls contained posters, a bulletin board, and a calendar. Most of the items in the room were placed there in order to make the room seem like a typical graduate-student office. However, for experimental purposes a few items not consistent with the office schema were included (e.g., a skull, a toy top) and a few items which would almost certainly be expected in such an office were deliberately omitted (e.g., books).

In order to provide objective measures of some characteristics of the experimental room, 61 objects in the room were rated on two dimensions: saliency and schema expectancy. The saliency rating was designed to indicate how noticeable an object was in the context of the room. Objects such as the skull and the Skinner box were high on this scale, while objects such as staples and an eraser were low. The schema-expectancy rating was intended to provide an index of subjects' graduate-student office schema by asking how likely the object was in the context of the room. Objects such as the desk and ceiling lights were high on this scale, while objects such as a model brain and a piece of bark were low.

Minsky's (1975) paper on the structure of everyday knowledge proposes that knowledge about rooms is organized into a "room frame." The room frame contains the information about rooms that one can be nearly certain about before encountering a particular room. Since Minsky has pointed out the theoretical importance of this type of knowledge, we were careful to include in the rating task items to test the room frame. We designated seven items to be room-frame items: walls, floor, ceiling, door, doorknob, light switch, and lights. These were chosen on a priori grounds as items that any room would almost certainly contain.

In addition to the objects actually in the room, a sample of 70 objects not in the room was chosen for rating on the same two scales. These objects were selected to vary along the full range of both scales. These items served as foils in a verbal recognition test.

The saliency rating task was carried out by 14 subjects, and the schema-expectancy rating task was carried out by 14 different subjects. Subjects were taken into the experimental office in groups of two or three and were given booklets containing the 131 objects to be rated.

The subjects in the saliency rating task were asked to rate the items on a 6-point scale with the following instructions: "Rate each object for *how noticeable the object is (or would be) in this room*. . . . Remember that some of the objects are actually in this room and some are not. If the object *is* in the room, base your rating on how noticeable that object *actually is*. If the object is *not* in the room, base your rating on how noticeable that object *would be* if it were in this room, given the general characteristics of the room." A response of 1 was defined as, "It would be *extremely unlikely* that I would notice the object," and a response of 6 was defined as, "It would be *extremely likely* that I would notice the object."

The subjects carrying out the schema-expectancy ratings were given the following instructions: "On the following pages are lists of objects (some actually in the room and some not actually in the room). Following each object is a scale from 1 to 6. We would like you to use this scale to rate each object for *how likely the objects would be to appear in a room like this. . . .* As an example, if you were in a kitchen carrying out this task, you would probably give an object such as a refrigerator a high number and an object such as a bed a low number. When making your rating *ignore whether or not the object is actually present in the room.* Simply base your rating on the likelihood that the object would occur in this room, given the general characteristics of the room." A response of 1 was defined as *"extremely unlikely* that the object would be found in a room like this," and a response of 6 was defined as *"extremely likely* that the object would be found in a room like this."

The mean saliency rating and the mean schema-expectancy rating were calculated for each of the 131 objects. The two scales are not independent. For the 61 objects present in the room, the correlation between saliency and schema expectancy is –.41; for the 70 objects not in the room, the correlation is –.69. It appears that saliency is based on two factors: a saliency intrinsic to the object and a saliency derived from its schema context. For example, a .45-caliber pistol is intrinsically more salient than a paper clip. However, an item also increases in saliency if it does not fit into the schema-based context. A spare tire is probably of intermediate intrinsic saliency, but in the context of a graduate-student office it becomes highly salient. This context effect appears to produce a portion of the negative correlation of saliency with schema expectancy. In addition, some of the negative correlation may be due to item sampling (especially for the nonpresent items). When nonpresent items of high salience are selected, few will be likely to occur in a graduate-student office, and so this intrinsic item bias will also lead to a negative correlation of saliency with schema expectancy.

Examination of the schema-expectancy scores provided considerable support for the existence of a common room schema. The subjects were in strong agreement that a room such as our experimental room is highly likely to contain a floor, a desk, a calendar, an eraser, and pencils, but is highly unlikely to contain a sewing machine or a .45-caliber pistol. The schema-extectancy data also support the a priori selection of room-frame items (items almost certain to be in a room). The six objects with the highest schema-expectancy scores were all room-frame items (door, floor, light switch, ceiling lights, walls, ceiling). The other a priori room-frame item, doorknob, was rated slightly below two strong office-frame items, desk and eraser.

The data also suggest that place schemata are not rigid preformed structures, but instead are much more flexible, utilizing the full extent of the subject's knowledge. In the present task the subjects were taken to a room in a psychology building and were asked to rate the objects in "this graduate student's office." In this context they gave high schema-expectancy ratings for experimental apparatus, worktable, and textbooks, even though it seems quite unlikely that these items would receive high expectancy scores in a rating of a generic "office" or of a different type of office, such as the office of a bank president.

The saliency ratings also showed considerable lawfulness. Subjects gave high saliency ratings to large visible objects (walls, desk), to attention-attracting objects (Playboy centerfold, skull), and to objects not fitting the graduate-student office schema (spare tire, rolling pin). Subjects gave low saliency ratings to small ordinary objects (eraser, paper clips). Overall, it appears that the rating tasks gave lawful data reflecting psychologically meaningful processes. The following experiment was designed to study the effects of schema expectancy and saliency on memory for places.

## Memory experiment

This experiment used the experimental room described above. The general procedure was designed to allow us to examine the episodic place information retained after a brief exposure to the experimental room in an unintentional setting. In order to examine different aspects of memory for the room, three groups of subjects performed different memory tasks.

### Subjects

The subjects were undergraduates fulfilling a course requirement. There was a total of 86 subjects: 30 subjects carried out written recall and then verbal recognition; 29 subjects carried out drawing recall; and 27 subjects carried out verbal recognition only. Subjects were exposed to the experimental room individually and carried out the memory tests in groups of one or two.

### Procedure for room exposure

The experimenter took the subject into the experimental wing of the Psychology Building and said, "I have to check to make sure that the previous hour's subject has completed the experiment." The experimenter then told the subject that he or she could "wait in my office." At this point the experimenter opened the door to the experimental office, turned on the lights, started a hidden stopwatch, and asked the subject to have a seat (all chairs but one had objects on top of them). The experimenter assured the subject that he would return shortly and then left the room, closing the door behind him. After 35 sec the experimenter reentered the office and asked the subject to follow him. The subject was immediately taken to a nearby seminar room where the subject was told that the real purpose of the experiment was to test his or her memory for the experimental office and then the memory task was given. Approximately 1 min elapsed between the time the subject left the experimental room and the time the subject began the memory task. The seminar room in which the memory tasks were given was quite different from the experimental office. It was a long rectangular room with two doors, a single long table, and 24 chairs.

A questionnaire given after the memory task showed that most subjects spent their time in the experimental room seated in the chair, looking around the room in order to guess what kind of person the graduate student was or to see if there were any indications as to what the experiment was going to be about. The deception appears to have been quite successful. The crucial item on the questionnaire was, " Did you think you would be asked to remember the objects in the office?" On this item, 93% of the 86 subjects responded "no."

### Recall

*Procedure.* After being taken to the conference room, the subjects given the written recall task were asked to write down what they could remember about the experimental room. The instructions stated, "We would like you to describe for us everything you can remember about the room you were just in. . . . For each object please try to give its location and as complete a description as you can provide (shape, size, color, etc.). Write your description as if you were describing the room for someone who had never seen it." Immediately after the written recall task the subjects were given a verbal recognition test. Discussion of the data from this task will be deferred until later in the paper.

Subjects given the drawing recall task were provided with an outline of the experimental office and were asked to draw in the objects they could remember from the room. The instructions stated, "We would like you to draw everything you can remember about the room on the provided floor plan. . . . Represent each object in the location you remember it, and try to draw each object's size to scale. Label each object which you draw with its name." Subjects in both recall tasks were asked to work for a minimum of 15 min and could take up to 30 min.

*Results and discussion.* Criteria were developed to classify objects mentioned in the recall protocols as present objects, frame objects, or inferred objects. For the written recall task, present objects were objects described in enough detail so that someone could take the written protocol into the room and locate the indicated object. Frame objects were the same seven frame objects included in the rating tasks (door, floor, light switch, ceiling lights, walls, ceiling, doorknob). Inferred objects were objects given in enough detail so that they could have been identified if they had been present, but were not actually in the room. The scoring criteria were essentially the same for drawing recall. A number of items in the recall protocols did not fit into these three categories and were eliminated from the analysis: (a) objects that were not in the room, but might have resulted from misidentification (birds on mobile for fish on mobile); (b) vague responses ("the other chair had something lying on it"). In addition objects that were parts of a present object (keys on typewriter) were eliminated to simplify the scoring.

In written recall, a total of 88 different objects were recalled by one or more subjects. Of these, 7 were room-frame objects, 62 were present objects, and 19 were inferred objects. The recall data for each object are given in Table 1. The mean number of frame objects recalled per subject was 3.37, the median was 3, and the range was 1 to 6. The mean number of present objects was 13.50, the median 14.5, and the range was 5 to 20. The mean number of inferred objects was 1.13, the median was 1, and the range was 0 to 4. A correlational analysis was carried out to investigate the effects of object saliency and schema expectancy on written recall. Saliency and schema-expectancy scores were available for 43 of the objects given in recall (room-frame objects and inferred objects were not included). The correlation of saliency with recall frequency and the correlation of schema expectancy with recall frequency were calculated; since saliency and schema expectancy were negatively correlated, partial correlations were also calculated. All of these correlations are given in Table 2. Examination of these correlations shows that there are clearly independent effects of saliency and schema expectancy.

**Table 1    Number of subjects recalling objects in written recall**

| Object | No. subjects[a] | Object | No. subjects[a] |
|---|---|---|---|
| Chair (next to desk) | 29 | *Filing cabinet | 3 |
| Desk | 29 | Frisbee | 3 |
| #Wall | 29 | Jar of coffee | 3 |
| Chair (in front of desk) | 24 | *Poster (in addition to | 3 |
| Poster (of chimp) | 23 |    those in room) | |
| #Door | 22 | Screwdriver | 3 |
| Table (worktable) | 22 | Snoopy picture | 3 |
| Shelves | 21 | Rotary switches | 3 |
| #Ceiling | 16 | Cactus | 2 |
| Table (with coffee) | 15 | Cardboard boxes | 2 |
| Skinner box | 14 | *Coffee cup | 2 |
| Child's chair | 12 | Computer cards | 2 |
| #Floor | 12 | Papers on bulletin board | 2 |
| #Light switch | 12 | *Pens | 2 |
| Toy top | 12 | Pot (for cactus) | 2 |
| Brain | 11 | Solder | 2 |
| Parts, gadgets (on | 11 | Vacuum tube | 2 |
|    worktable) | | *Window | 2 |
| Swivel chair | 11 | Wires | 2 |
| | | *Ball | 1 |
| Poster on ceiling | 10 | *Brain (in addition to | 1 |
| *Books | 9 |    that in room) | |
| #Ceiling lights | 9 | Brick | 1 |
| Poster (of food) | 9 | Computer surveys | 1 |
| Typewriter | 9 |    (on floor) | |
| Bulletin board | 8 | *Curtains | 1 |
| Clown light switch | 8 | *Decals on walls | 1 |
| Coffee pot | 8 | *Desk (in addition to | 1 |
| Skull | 8 |    those in room) | |
| Mobile | 7 | #Doorknob | 1 |
| Road sign | 7 | Eraser | 1 |
| Calendar | 6 | Fan | 1 |
| Wine bottle | 6 | *Glass plate (covering desk) | 1 |
| Football-player doll | 5 | Globe | 1 |
| Jar of creamer | 5 | Hole in wall (for pipe) | 1 |
| Pine (cord) | 5 | Homecoming button | 1 |
| Postcards | 5 | *Lamp | 1 |
| Tennis racket | 5 | Magazines | 1 |
| Blower fan | 4 | *Nails | 1 |
| | | Packets of sugar | 1 |
| Colored patterns | 4 | Paper (on desk chair) | 1 |
|    on ceiling lights | | Papers on shelf | 1 |
| Piece of bark | 4 | *Pencil holder | 1 |

10

**Table 1    (cont)**

| Object | No. subjects[a] | Object | No. subjects[a] |
|---|---|---|---|
| *Pencils | 1 | *Screws | 1 |
| Picnic basket | 1 | Teaspoon | 1 |
| *Pliers | 1 | *Telephone | 1 |
| Saucer | 1 | Umbrella | 1 |
| Scissors | 1 | Wrench | 1 |

*Note.* "#" indicates a frame object; "*" indicates an inferred object (i.e., an object not in the office).
[a]Maximum number of subjects = 30.

The data from drawing recall essentially replicated the findings from written recall. The correlation of the number of subjects recalling an object in drawing recall with the number recalling it in written recall is .94. Apparently, at this global level of analysis, drawing recall and written recall are roughly equivalent methods of measuring what information the subjects have picked up in their brief exposure to the room. In drawing recall a total of 77 different objects were recalled by one or more subjects. Of these, 61 were present in the office and 16 were inferred. Table 2 gives the correlations between schema expectancy, saliency, and drawing recall. The pattern of these correlations is very similar to that obtained with written recall.

**Table 2    Correlations between schema expectancy, saliency, and recall for written recall and drawing recall**

| | Recall frequency | Schema expectancy | Saliency |
|---|---|---|---|
| Written recall[a] | | | |
| Recall frequency | 1.00 | | |
| Schema expectancy | .27 (.55*)[b] | 1.00 | |
| Saliency | .47* (.64*)[c] | −.37* | 1.00 |
| Drawing recall[d] | | | |
| Recall frequency | 1.00 | | |
| Schema expectancy | .42* (.68*)[b] | 1.00 | |
| Saliency | .36* (.66*)[c] | −.43* | 1.00 |

[a] $n$ = 43 objects.
[b] Saliency partialled out.
[c] Schema expectancy partialled out.
[d] $n$ = 41 objects.
* $p < .05$.

Overall, the results in the recall tasks give strong support for the action of schemata in memory for places. The evidence for the integration of episodic information with schema-based knowledge was very clear. There were a number of inferred objects in recall, and the inferred objects for which ratings were available received high schema-expectancy scores. The power of the schema-based information on subjects' recall of the room is evident when a subject draws in a window or set of shelves that are not present. The consistency and strength of the book inference is also impressive.

11

Of the 81 different nonframe objects given in written recall, books, which were not there, were the 16th most frequently recalled objects. Of the 77 different objects given in drawing recall, books were the 12th most frequently recalled objects. It is interesting to look at inference items that were only given once in written recall. It might seem that responses at this low frequency are sporadic or random. However, several of these low-frequency inference items (pencil holder, telephone, window) were also given in drawing recall, demonstrating lawfulness in the inferences produced by the underlying office schema.

The strong positive correlation between schema expectancy and recall also shows the effect of schema information on place memory. However, the recall data taken by themselves do not distinguish between schemata operating in encoding information, as a framework for information, by integration, or in the retrieval of information. There is, however, other evidence to suggest that an encoding hypothesis cannot account for this correlation. Loftus and Mackworth (1978) and Friedman (1979) have shown that subjects examining pictures tend to spend more time looking at *nonschema* objects than at schema-related objects. This suggests that schemata do influence looking time. However, if their findings can be generalized to our more naturalistic situation, then the encoding hypothesis cannot account for our positive correlation, since as applied to the looking-time data it would predict better recall for nonschema objects than schema-related objects, i.e., a negative correlation of recall frequency and schema expectancy.

The positive correlation between saliency and recall probably reflects the amount of attention devoted to the salient objects, but given the present findings, one could also hypothesize that saliency leads to a stronger memory representation or to more efficient retrieval.

Overall, the inferences in the recall data provide clear-cut evidence for the integration of episodic information and schema-based information. Furthermore, if it is assumed that on some occasions present objects with high schema-expectancy ratings are recalled on the basis of schematic information rather than on the basis of episodic information, integration would also contribute to the positive correlation between schema-expectancy ratings and recall. However, this correlation might also be due to the office schema acting as a framework or as a retrieval mechanism. The data from the verbal recognition condition were designed to distinguish between some of the hypotheses about the use of schema-based information that were not distinguished by the recall data.

### Verbal recognition

*Procedure.* Subjects in this condition received only a verbal recognition test. After being taken out of the experimental room to the seminar room, they were given a booklet containing a list of object names. They were asked to rate each item for how certain they were that they had seen the named object in the experimental room. The instructions stated, "We would like you to indicate how certain you are that you remember seeing each object by circling one of the numbers from 1 to 6. Use 1 to indicate that you are absolutely certain that you did *not* see the object. Use 6 to indicate that you are absolutely certain that you *did* see the object. Use the numbers between 1 and 6 to indicate intermediate degrees of memory." The verbal recognition test consisted of 131 object names; 61 of the named objects had been in the experimental office and 70 had not.

*Results and discussion.* There was a strong effect of schema-based inferences in the verbal recognition data, as there had been in the recall data. Of the 51 nonframe items on the verbal recognition test with the highest recognition scores, 13 were not actually present in the room. It is clear that these 13 inferences reflect the influence of the office schema — all but one are in the top one-third of absent objects when ranked in terms of schema-expectancy scores.

In order to examine the effects of schema expectancy and saliency on verbal recognition, a series of correlational analyses was carried out. Table 3 gives the correlations of saliency and schema expectancy with verbal recognition scores for present objects (not including the room- frame objects) and for absent objects. First we will discuss the positive correlations of schema expectancy and verbal recognition for present objects. On the basis of the previous recall data, we concluded that the positive correlations of schema expectancy with drawing recall and written recall could be the result of schema-based information operating as a framework in memory, operating as a retrieval mechanism, or becoming integrated with the episodic information. In the present recognition data, the verbal recognition items themselves should serve as retrieval cues and so should eliminate any effect due to retrieval processes. Thus, it appears that we can eliminate the schema-based retrieval account of the recognition data. Therefore the positive correlation between schema expectancy and verbal recognition should be due either to schema-based information operating as a framework in memory or to schema-based information becoming integrated with episodic information from the room.

**Table 3    Correlations between mean recognition scores, schema expectancy ratings, and saliency ratings**

|  | Recognition | Schema expectancy | Saliency |
|---|---|---|---|
| | Present objects (without frame objects)[a] | | |
| Recognition | 1.00 | | |
| Schema expectancy | .21 ( .58*)[b] | 1.00 | |
| Saliency | .48* ( .69*)[c] | −.49* | 1.00 |
| | Absent objects[d] | | |
| Recognition | 1.00 | | |
| Schema expectancy | .75* ( .52*)[b] | 1.00 | |
| Saliency | −.69* (−.36*)[c] | −.69* | 1.00 |

[a] $n = 54$ objects.
[b] Saliency partialled out.
[c] Schema expectancy partialled out.
[d] $n = 70$ objects.
* $p < .05$.

The positive correlation of schema expectancy and verbal recognition for absent objects can apparently be accounted for by only one schema-based explanation. The positive correlation indicates that the subjects were more likely to state that they had seen a nonpresent object if the object was a strong member of the office schema. Since these decisions were being made for objects for which no episodic information was available, the responses must have been due totally to old schema-based knowledge, and therefore reflect the operation of the schema in integration, not as a framework or as a retrieval mechanism.

Next we will examine the correlations between saliency and verbal recognition. The positive correlation between saliency and recognition for *present objects* is probably due to increased looking time allocated to the more salient objects resulting in better memory. However, it is possible that the memory representation for salient objects is somehow simply stronger than that for nonsalient objects.

The correlation of saliency and verbal recognition scores for *absent objects* shows a qualitatively different pattern of results from that obtained for objects in the room. The correlation for objects not present in the room is negative. This suggests that when dealing with more ecologically valid memory tasks, a "simple" recognition task is not so simple. The negative correlation apparently results from the following process during the recognition task. When the subject is asked if some very salient object (e.g., a rat in a cage, or a Playboy centerfold) was in the room, the subject reasons: (a) if the object had been in the experimental room when I was there, I would have noticed it; (b) if I had noticed such a salient object, I would have remembered it; (c) I do not remember such an object; (d) thus, the object must not have been in the room. If a subject follows this reasoning process, then the *higher* the saliency of an object, the *lower* the likelihood of a false recognition response.

This I-would-have-seen-it-if-it-had-been-there phenomenon appears to be a variant of a type of inference discussed by Collins ( 1978) in a paper on reasoning in answering everyday questions. Collins calls this type of inference a lack-of-knowledge inference and states that it is very common in his data on answering everyday factual questions. Overall, the verbal recognition results support the operation of schemata in integration and the operation of a metacognitive strategy which allows subjects to avoid making false recognition responses for absent items of high saliency.

### *Verbal recognition after written recall*

*Procedure.* The subjects who provided the written recall data were given a verbal recognition test immediately afterward. Of the present objects given in the recall protocols, 80% had been included on the verbal recognition test. Thus, for many items we had data on recall and recognition for the same objects from the same subject.

*Results and discussion.* When subjects recalled an item in written recall, they almost always (96%) gave it a rating of 6 ("absolutely certain I remember seeing the object") in verbal recognition. However, they also gave ratings of 6 to many of the present objects that they had not been able to recall. In order to examine the issue of retrieval from memory, a "retrieval ratio" was developed for each object. The retrieval ratio was defined as the number of times an object was given in the recall task divided by the number of times it was given a 6 in the verbal recognition task. Thus, if 12 subjects gave an item a 6 in verbal recognition, but only 6 subjects had recalled the item on the written recall test, the retrieval ratio for that item would be .50. A high ratio (near 1.0) indicates that most subjects who gave the object a 6 in recognition also recalled the object. A low ratio (near 0) indicates that most subjects who gave the object a 6 in recognition did not recall the object. Retrieval ratios were calculated for all recalled present objects which were given ratings of 6 on the verbal recognition test by at least three subjects. A correlational analysis was carried out on the 36 items that met this criterion. The correlation of saliency and the retrieval ratio was −.04, while the correlation of schema expectancy and retrieval ratio was .56 ($p < .01$). Since the correlation of schema expectancy and saliency for this set of items was only −.19, the partial correlations with retrieval ratio were not very different from the simple correlations (.56 for expectancy and retrieval ratio with saliency partialled out, and .08 for saliency and retrieval ratio with expectancy partialled out).

The significant correlation of retrieval ratio and schema expectancy suggests that the office schema is used in the retrieval process. The near-zero correlation between retrieval ratio and saliency suggests that the retrieval process is unaffected by an object's saliency. Given that an object is in memory (as indicated by the recognition task), it is more likely to be written down in the recall task if it is related to the office schema than if it is not. A concrete example of this effect is as follows: The typewriter was ranked high in the graduate-student office schema (rank of 12.5 among present, nonframe objects) and was given in written recall by 9 of the 10 subjects who gave it a rating of 6 in verbal recognition. In contrast, the skull was ranked low in the graduate-student office schema (rank 48 for present, nonframe objects on schema expectancy) and was recalled by only 8 of the 16 subjects who gave it a rating of 6 in recognition, despite its high saliency (rank 2 for present objects). Thus, the retrieval ratio analysis provides strong evidence that the room schema is being used as a retrieval mechanism in the recall task. In all of the analyses involving verbal recognition after recall the seven room-frame items have been omitted. Comparison of recall and recognition scores for these items suggests that the recall scores were influenced by the operation of the room schema in communication, as discussed below.

### Written recall: qualitative analysis

In addition to the quantitative findings already reported, the recall protocols from the subjects in the written recall condition provided qualitative information that allowed further examination of the use of schemata in integration and in communication.

*Schemata — canonical location.* Analysis of the recall protocols suggests that the office schema contains some information about the canonical location of objects. When books are inferred, they are almost always recalled as being on the shelves, while inferred objects such as pencils and pens are almost always recalled as being on the desk. Objects that were present in the room, but not in canonical locations, tended to shift to more canonical locations in recall. For example, there was a yellow pad on the seat of the desk chair. In the written recall condition, the only subject who recalled the yellow pad recalled it as being on the desk.

*Schemata — color and shape.* The use of schema-based information could also be seen in the recall of colors. The desk in the experimental room was brown. In written recall two subjects recalled the color correctly, but four subjects recalled it as gray. There were similar effects for shape. For example, the trapezoidal worktable was recalled as being square by one of the subjects in written recall. Thus, the qualitative analysis of the recall data provides additional support for the effects of the integration of episodic information and schema-based information.

*Communication.* The qualitative analysis of the recall data provided important data on the use of schemata in determining how information about the room was communicated to their audience. In the recall instructions the subjects were asked to give each object's location "and as complete a description as you can provide (shape, size, color, etc.)." Yet, in practice, there were enormous differences across objects as to how much auxiliary information was given. Much of the variation here appears to be attributable to the subjects' use of Grice's (1975) maxim of Quantity. Grice has argued that in carrying on conversations speakers obey a maxim of Quantity, by which a speaker attempts to make the contribution as informative as required, but not more informative than required. The subject's decision to report auxiliary information in the recall protocols appears to be based on the subject's assumptions about their audience's schema-based knowledge of the room and its contents and on the application of Grice's maxim of Quantity.

*Communication — size.* There were two objects in the room that were not of canonical size (the child's chair and the worktable). Size information was given for these two objects much more frequently than for any other objects in the room. For the child's chair 67% of the 12 subjects who recalled it used a size qualifier, whereas for the normal-size chair that the subjects sat in, not one of the 29 individuals who recalled it used a size qualifier. For the worktable 82% of the responses contained a size qualifier, whereas for the desk only 17% used a size qualifier. It appears that the subjects were obeying Grice's maxim. They omitted size information for objects of usual size, since they could assume that this information was already available in their audience's office-object schemata; however, for the objects of atypical size they added the size information.

*Communication — material.* There was a similar effect for information about the materials out of which objects were constructed. The subjects never gave auxiliary information about the materials for objects such as posters, postcards, the frisbee, or the wine bottle, since they could assume schema-based knowledge concerning what materials these objects were made from. The one object in the room that was slightly deviant with respect to material was the chair the subjects sat in — it was constructed of plastic. Auxiliary information about the material was given by 55% of the subjects who recalled this chair. Auxiliary information about materials was also given fairly frequently for the other pieces of furniture. Here, it was not that the material was unusual, but that it was indeterminant (i.e., most office furniture could be constructed of either metal or wood). The rates of material qualifiers in these cases were: 24% for the desk, 25% for the desk chair, 33% for the coffee table, and 18% for the worktable.

*Communication — shape, orientation, and location.* The results were similar for the other categories of auxiliary information. Shape information was rarely given, and when it was given it was for slightly noncanonical or indeterminant objects (e.g., the chair the subjects sat in had a curved back and 14% of the subjects included that information in their recalls). Orientation information (as distinct from location) was rarely given except for the one object in the room in a highly unusual orientation — a large metal detour sign on the worktable pointing toward the ceiling. In recall, 86% of the subjects gave orientation information when recalling the sign, whereas the next highest rate of orientation information was only 22%. Location information (for present nonframe objects) was almost always given in the recall protocols (93%), presumably because the exact location of most objects is not given by the office schema.

In general, the differential rates of recall of auxiliary information appear to reflect the use of schema information in conjunction with the maxim of Quantity. Even though the instructions said to report auxiliary information, the subjects systematically omitted information that was derivable from the room and object schemata, and reported auxiliary information when it deviated from the schemata or when it was indeterminant with respect to the schemata. The subjects were asked to recall the room as if they were describing it to someone who had never seen it. The data suggest that they were able to do this quite successfully. If they had been describing the room to the experimenter, there would have been no need to tell the experimenter that the worktable was small or that the chair they had been sitting in was made of plastic, since clearly the experimenter already knew this. Instead, the schema information and maxim of Quantity were used as if the audience was an idealized average individual who knows about graduate-student offices in general, but not about this particular graduate-student office.

*Communication — negative statements.* There were 11 sentences about objects in the room which contained negatives: 3 subjects stated that the room was not large, 2 stated that there were no windows, and 6 statements occurred once — that there were no rugs, that the chair was not against the wall, that the desk was not covered with knickknacks, that the coffee table was not made of wood, that the Skinner box had no top, and that the worktable was not square. Without a theoretical construct such as the room schema, the occurrence of these negative sentences is bizarre. The subjects were instructed to write down what they had seen in the room, and thus had no apparent reason to produce any negations. However, the explanation in terms of schemata seems quite straightforward. When communicating the information about the room, the subjects were considering their audience's office schema and pointing out the nonexistence of things that the subjects thought their audience might mistakenly infer on the basis of that schema. Thus, the list of negated sentences is, in effect, an explicit list from the subjects of those aspects of the experimental room that the subjects found to deviate from their schema.

*Communication — article usage.* Another example of room and office schema information determining aspects of the recall protocols is in article usage. In traditional grammatical accounts of English (e.g., Stockwell, Schacter & Partee, 1973), the article *a* is said to be used to introduce new information into a discourse, while *the* is used anaphorically to refer to something that has already been mentioned in the

17

discourse. For example, "I saw *a* platypus. *The* platypus was running along the river bank." More recent discussions of article usage (Linde, 1975; Norman & Rumelhart, 1975) have pointed out that *a* is used to introduce something into the current shared knowledge of the speaker and hearer, while *the* is used for things that are already in the shared knowledge of the speaker and hearer. Thus, "John moved into *a* new house last year. *The* kitchen is beautiful." In this case, the speaker introduces the concept of John's house into the shared knowledge of the speaker and hearer, and then can refer to *the kitchen,* since kitchens have been introduced by the house schema.

Since English article usage is sensitive to shared knowledge, we examined the article usage in the written recall data to see if it reflected schema-based knowledge. For each present object in the written protocols, the percent usage of *the* on first mention was calculated. The results showed a clear trimodal distribution: The high-usage set consisted of 7 objects (door, 100%; doorknob, 100%; floor, 100%; ceiling, 94%; light switch, 83%; walls, 81%; lights, 44%). The low-usage set consisted of 6 objects (bulletin board, 13%; typewriter, 11%; desk, 10%; shelves, 9%; chair, 7%; coffee table, 7%). The remaining 56 objects were never introduced with *the* on first mention. These results show remarkable sensitivity to shared schema knowledge on the part of the subjects. If one were describing the experimental room to someone who has been in it, then it would be quite natural to use an introductory *the* for unexpected and highly salient objects (e.g., the skull, the road sign), since one can assume that the other individual saw them and (since there was only one object of that type in the room) there could be no confusion about what was being referred to. The recall protocols show not a single example of introductory *the* for this type of object; clearly the subjects were (as instructed) directing their recall protocols to an audience whose schemata contained no specific information about the particular experimental room the subjects had been exposed to.

Examination of the objects that fell into the high article usage set shows that once it has been established that a room is being recalled, the subjects assume that the room-frame objects are in their audience's room schema. It should be noted that the seven objects selected by the empirical criterion of high introductory *the* usage are identical with the seven a priori room-frame objects selected by the experimenters when the room was being organized and scaled. Examination of the objects that fell into the low-usage group suggests another subtle use of schema knowledge. All of these items are instances of an office schema (as distinct from a room schema). It appears that a subset of subjects makes the assumption that it is possible to assume shared knowledge about objects in the office schema when communicating about an office. Overall, the article-usage data from the written recall protocols suggest that the subjects almost always assumed in their audience the presence of a room schema, sometimes assumed the presence of an office schema, and never assumed the presence of a schema for the particular experimental room.

*Communication — omissions.* Another aspect of the use of schema information in communication is in determining what information can be omitted. Very strong schema-related information such as room-frame information appears to be frequently omitted in the written protocols. This reduced production of room-frame objects in the written recall task was shown by subtracting an object's rank in recall (for present and room-frame objects) from its rank in verbal recognition (for present and room-frame objects; data from the verbal recognition only condition). These scores were calculated for the 15 objects with the highest recognition scores. There were 9 objects with negative scores (i.e., rank in recall below that expected from rank in recognition), and 7 of these 9 were the room-frame items. This analysis indicates that the room-frame objects are written down in recall less frequently than would be expected on the basis of their recognition scores, presumably because the subjects assume the room-frame information is already known to their audience.

*Overall results.* The qualitative analysis of the written recall protocols showed the integration of episodic information and schema-based information in the production of location, color, and shape inferences. In addition, the qualitative analysis found strong effects of schema-based knowledge determining what the subjects chose to communicate to the experimenter: They reported auxiliary information that was unusual or indeterminant with respect to room and object schemata; they omitted auxiliary information given by the schemata; they explicitly denied the existence of information they thought might be mistakenly inferred on the basis of the schemata; and finally, they adjusted their article usage in accordance with the schema information they assumed was available to their audience, using the definite article to introduce objects that they assumed were shared knowledge.

## General discussion

This experiment shows that it is possible to bring the study of real-world place memory into the laboratory. The choice of an ecologically valid situation, such as the unintentional memory for rooms, has been important in theory development. Many recent discussions of schema theory have been relatively global and nonspecific. However, the complex and meaningful nature of the information available in the room led to an intricate set of empirical relations in our experiment and allowed us to be somewhat more specific in our theorizing and to show the operation of schemata on a number of different aspects of memory for places.

Our initial scaling of the office for schema expectancy and saliency uncovered a number of interesting characteristics of our subjects' perceptions of real-world places. The subjects' use of the schema-expectancy scale made it quite evident that they were relating our experimental room to their long-term knowledge of offices, e.g., they thought that pencils belonged in our office, but that a .45-caliber pistol did not. The fact that the subjects gave high schema-expectancy ratings to objects such as the experimental apparatus when they thought they were dealing with a psychology graduate-student office suggests that place schemata cannot be considered to be rigid frames, but are capable of rather subtle readjustments.

The negative correlation we found between schema expectancy and saliency suggests that both of these dimensions must be considered in an analysis of real-world places. Comparison of the ratings suggested that some objects have an intrinsic saliency, but that objects without a high intrinsic saliency are made salient if they deviate from the overall place schema.

The results of the memory experiment provided support for the operation of schemata in several quite specific aspects of place memory:

*Encoding.* Our experimental procedures provided no data on looking time per object, and so we have no evidence on the use of schemata in encoding. The work of Loftus and Mackworth (1978) and Friedman (1979) on looking at meaningful pictures suggests that schemata are involved in determining looking time. Both of these studies have found that looking time is longer for nonschema objects. The encoding hypothesis states that memory is a direct function of looking time. Therefore the looking-time data as applied to the encoding hypothesis predict that memory for low-schema objects should be better, but our basic findings are that high-schema objects show better memory performance. If the looking-time data can be generalized to our experimental paradigm of unintentional exposure to an actual room, then the use of schemata to determine looking time cannot be used to account for our memory results.

*Framework.* The results of this experiment allowed no unique test of the hypothesis that schemata can serve as a framework which preserves schema-relevant episodic information. It is possible that the positive correlations of schema expectancy with recall and with verbal recognition could result from the room schema serving as a framework to improve recall of schema-related objects from the experimental room. However, these positive correlations could also be explained by the integration of episodic information from the experimental room with old room-schema knowledge, or, for the recall data, by the use of the room schema as a retrieval mechanism. Thus, there are several findings that could support the framework hypothesis, but in each case, there is at least one other plausible hypothesis that can give an equivalent account of the data.

*Integration.* The hypothesis that memory for places is often a result of the integration of new episodic information with old schema-based information was given strong support in this experiment. In both drawing recall and written recall, the subjects recalled a number of objects that were not in the experimental room. The inferred objects were invariably high-schema-relevant objects. Thus, the recall of these items must have been due to schema-based knowledge about offices becoming integrated with the actual episodic information about the experimental room. The high positive correlation of schema expectancy and verbal recognition scores for objects that were not present in the room is also strong support for the integration hypothesis, since for objects not present, there could be no episodic information, and all of the effect must be due to old-schema knowledge. The finding that a number of items with high verbal recognition scores were not actually in the experimental room and that these items were high-office-schema items shows the power of schema information in influencing place memory.

*Retrieval.* The hypothesis that schema information can serve as a retrieval mechanism was supported by the analysis of recall and verbal recognition data for the same objects from the same subjects. Given that an item was strongly recognized in verbal recognition, it was more likely to have been written down in the recall task if it was a high-office-schema object. Thus, the office schema apparently enabled subjects to retrieve objects from memory that otherwise would have been inaccessible. Given this finding, it seems very likely that at least part of the general positive correlation of schema expectancy and recall was due to office-schema information serving as a retrieval mechanism in recall.

*Communication.* The analysis of the written recall data shows powerful effects of schemata on the communication of responses. The subjects report auxiliary information that is unusual with respect to the room schema, and tend not to write down information that they can assume is known by their audience. They adjust their article usage in accordance with the place-schema information they assume in their audience, using the definite article to introduce objects that they feel are given by the room schema.

The finding that the communication effect in our experiment is to emphasize recall of nonschema information and deemphasize the recall of information given by the schema, avoids a problem that has frequently occurred in other research. In studies of the effect of schemata on recall of narratives (Anderson & Pichert, 1978; Rumelhart, 1977; Thorndyke, 1977), the general finding is better recall of schema-relevant information. Most of these investigators have wanted to show an effect of schemata on memory, and yet with this type of material it is always possible that the schemata are operating in the communication of the recalls (i.e., the subjects choose to omit the nonschema information at recall, because they assume it is not important). Thus, in studies of the recall of narratives, the potential effects of schemata in memory are confounded with the effects of schemata in communication. In the present experimental paradigm, the subjects adopted the strategy of communicating the nonschema information and not communicating the information given by the schema. The adoption of this communication strategy by the subjects in our written recall task avoided the usual confounding of an effect of schemata in communication with the other uses of schemata and allowed us to provide more precise tests of other hypotheses.

*Saliency.* The initial scaling of the experimental office demonstrated that saliency must be distinguished from schema expectancy. It seems likely that the positive correlation between saliency and memory performance found in all three experimental conditions reflects the amount of attention devoted to the salient objects; however, other hypotheses are possible. The negative correlation of saliency with verbal recognition of absent objects suggests the operation of a powerful metacognitive strategy in recognition memory. The subjects use an I-would-have-seen-it-if-it-had-been-there strategy to avoid making false recognition responses for items of high saliency.

Overall, the results of this experiment suggest that place schemata play an important and complex role in place memory. The interaction of the schemata in various aspects of the recall process produces an interesting inverted U-shaped function of the relationship of schema expectancy and recall of objects, given that the objects are shown to be in memory by a recognition test. Objects of very high schema expectancy (e.g., roomframe objects) are not given in recall as much as might be expected, since the subjects assume that they are known to their audience. The objects of high to medium-high schema expectancy are typically recalled. The objects of low schema expectancy are not recalled as much as might be expected from their recognition scores because there are no schemata to facilitate their retrieval.

## Acknowledgements

We would like to thank Richard Anderson, Don Norman, Edward Lichtenstein, Ellen Brewer, and David Dupree for comments on an earlier draft of this paper. This research was supported in part by NIMH Grant MN 29562.

## References

Anderson, R. C. & Pichert, J. W. (1978) Recall of previously unrecallable information following a shift in perspective. *Journal of Verbal Learning and Verbal Behavior, 17*, 1–12.

Bartlett, F. C. (1932) *Rem embering.* Cambridge, England: Cambridge Univ. Press.

Bobrow, D. G. & Norman, D. A. (1975) Some principles of memory schemata. In D. G. Bobrow and A. Collins (Eds.), *Representation and understanding: Studies in cognitive science.* New York: Academic Press.

Bower, G. H., Black, J. B. & Turner, T. J. (1979) Scripts in memory for text. *Cognitive Psychology*, 11, 177–220.

Collins, A. (1978) Fragments of a theory of human plausible reasoning. In D. L. Waltz (Ed.), *Theoretical issues in natural language processing — 2.* New York: Association for Computing Machinery.

Downs, R. M. & Stea, D. (1977) *Maps in minds: Reflections on cognitive mapping.* New York: Harper & Row.

Friedman, A. (1979) Framing pictures: The role of knowledge in automatized encoding and memory for gist. *Journal of Experimental Psychology: General*, 108, 316–355.

Grice, H. P. (1975) Logic and conversation. In P. Cole and J. L. Morgan (Eds.). *Syntax and semantics,* Vol. 3, *Speech acts.* New York: Seminar Press.

Kuipers, B. J. (1975) A frame for frames: Representing knowledge for recognition. In D. G. Bobrow and A. Collins (Eds.), *Representation and understanding: Studies in cognitive science.* New York: Academic Press.

Lichtenstein, E. H. & Brewer, W. F. (1980) Memory for goal-directed events. *Cognitive Psychology*, 12, 412–445.

Linde, C. (1975) The linguistic encoding of spatial information (Doctoral dissertation, Columbia University, 1974). *Dissertation Abstracts International*, 35, 4483A. (University Microfilms No. 74–28, 512)

Loftus, G. R. & Mackworth, N. H. (1978) Cognitive determinants of fixation location during picture viewing. *Journal of Experimental Psychology: Human Perception and Performance*, 4, 565–572.

Lynch, K. (1960) *The image of the city.* Cambridge, MA: MIT Press.

Minsky, M. (1975) A framework for representing knowledge. In P. H. Winston (Ed.), *The psychology of computer vision.* New York: McGraw-Hill.

Neisser, U. (1976) *Cognition and reality.* San Francisco: Freeman.

Norman, D. A. (1973) Memory, knowledge, and the answering of questions. In R. L. Solso (Ed.), *Contemporary issues in cognitive psychology: The Loyola symposium*. New York: Wiley.

Norman, D. A. & Rumelhart, D. E. (1975) Reference and comprehension. In D. A. Norman, D. E. Rumelhart, & LNR Research Group, *Explorations in cognition*. San Francisco: Freeman.

Piaget, J. & Inhelder, B. (1973) *Memory and intelligence*. New York: Basic Books.

Rumelhart, D. E. (1977) Understanding and summarizing brief stories. In D. LaBerge and S. J. Samuels (Eds.), *Basic processes in reading: Perception and comprehension*. Hillsdale, NJ: Lawrence Erlbaum.

Rumelhart, D. E. (1980) Schemata: The building blocks of cognition. In R. J. Spiro, B. C. Bruce, and W. F. Brewer (Eds.), *Theoretical issues in reading comprehension: Perspectives from cognitive psychology, linguistics, artificial intelligence, and education*. Hillsdale, NJ: Lawrence Erlbaum.

Rumelhart, D. E. & Ortony, A. (1977) The representation of knowledge in memory. In R. C. Anderson, R. J. Spiro, and W. E. Montague (Eds.), *Schooling and the acquisition of knowledge*. Hillsdale, NJ: Lawrence Erlbaum.

Schank, R. C. & Abelson, R. P. (1977) *Scripts, plans, goals, and understanding*. Hillsdale, NJ: Lawrence Erlbaum.

Spiro, R. J. (1977) Remembering information from text: The "state of schema" approach. In R.C. Anderson, R. J. Spiro, and W. E. Montague (Eds.), *Schooling and the acquisition of knowledge*. Hillsdale, NJ: Lawrence Erlbaum.

Stockwell, R. P., Schacter, P. & Partee, B. H. (1973) *The major syntactic structures of English*. New York: Holt, Rinehart, & Winston.

Thorndyke, P. W. (1977) Cognitive structures in comprehension and memory of narrative discourse. *Cognitive Psychology, 9*, 77–110.

# 2.   Scripts in Memory for Text
## Gordon H. Bower, John B. Black
## and Terrence J. Turner

*These experiments investigate people's knowledge of routine activities (e.g., eating in a restaurant, visiting a dentist) and how that knowledge is organized and used to understand and remember narrative texts. We use the term script to refer to these action stereotypes. Two studies collected script norms: people described what goes on in detail during familiar activities. They largely agreed on the nature of the characters, props, actions, and the order of the actions. They also agreed on how to segment the low-level action sequences into constituent "scenes," suggesting a hierarchical organization in memory of the activity. Other studies investigated memory for a text narrating actions from a script. Subjects tended to confuse in memory actions that were stated with unstated actions implied by the script. This tendency increased as more related script instances were studied. Subjects also preferred to recall script actions in their familiar order; a scrambled text that presented some script actions out of order tended to be recalled in canonical order. We also investigated whether the reading time for adjacent statements in a text varied with their distance apart in the underlying script. A statement at a one-step distance was read faster than one at a two- or three-step distance; statements in the second half of a script were read faster than those in the first half. A final experiment found that goal-relevant deviations from a script were remembered better than script actions. The role of script knowledge in text memory was discussed, as was the relation of scripts to schema memory in general.*

We are interested in how people understand and remember narratives since this seems a promising way to investigate cognitive processes. A persistent problem for theories of narrative comprehension is to specify how people use their knowledge to expand upon what they are reading or hearing. Texts are usually elliptical and abbreviated, suggesting far more than they say explicitly. A conversational postulate to "avoid prolixity and boring redundancy" may force such brevity. To understand a text fully, then, a model of comprehension must have methods for expanding upon an abbreviated text. Further, the model needs an organized knowledge store surrounding the topic of the text, which serves as a base for the elaborations.

Schank and Abelson (1977) proposed their "script theory" as a partial solution to the elaboration problem. They propose that part of our knowledge is organized around hundreds of stereotypic situations with routine activities. Examples are riding a bus, visiting a dentist, placing an operator-assisted telephone call, asking for directions, and so on. Through direct or vicarious experiences, each person acquires hundreds of such cultural stereotypes along with his idiosyncratic variations. Schank and Abelson use the "term script" to refer to the memory structure a person has encoding his general knowledge of a certain situation-action routine. The script theory is a specific elaboration of the frame theory of Minsky (1975).

Gordon H. Bower, John B. Black and Terrence J. Turner: 'Scripts in Memory for Text' in *COGNITIVE PSYCHOLOGY* (1979), 11, pp. 177–220. Copyright © 1979 by Academic Press, Inc.

The parts of a script are illustrated by the restaurant script in Table 1. As with other scripts, the restaurant script has standard roles to be played, standard props or objects, ordinary conditions for entering upon the activity, a standard sequence of scenes or actions wherein one action enables the next, and some normal results from performing the activity successfully. The information surrounding any one of these roles, props, or actions is assumed to be stored at varying levels of abstraction. For example, the Server Role in the restaurant must be a human, can be a male or female, and is usually dressed "appropriately" (e.g., is not wearing a suit of armor), and so on. The Server Role may be thought of as a list of alternative feature packages, with some features obligatory (e.g., must be alive), some optional (e.g., male or female), and some with weakly-bound ranges (e.g., age and style of dress).

A person's scripts are supposedly used in several ways. First, they aid planning and execution of conventional activities. The entering conditions and normal outcomes of scripts are examined during planning; the planner selects from memory a script whose normal result matches the current goal (e.g., satisfy hunger), then tries to bring about the entering conditions so she can perform the script. Second, scripts enable understanding when the person observes or reads about someone performing another instance of a conventional activity. We shall focus on this second use of scripts.

Whenever a text mentions a script-header (e.g., "The Restaurant") or a few lines that match parts of the memory script, the reader can "instantiate" the general script by filling in its variables (or "slots") according to the details mentioned. To illustrate, consider this vignette:

> John went to a restaurant.
> He ordered lasagna.
> Later, he paid and left.

The first line activates the restaurant script. John instantiates the role of the customer and lasagna is the food ordered. Because the brief text calls forth the full script, the reader can elaborate many objects and connections that are implied but not stated. The availability of these connections is suggested by the reader's ability to answer such questions as: Did John eat? What did he eat? Did he talk to a waiter or waitress? Did he receive a bill? What for? Such elaborated connections are frequently useful in understanding later parts of the story. For example, if later in the story John is found to have tomato stains on his shirt or professes not to be hungry, readers can guess how this came about from the restaurant scene.

Our experiments investigate some psychological implications of Schank and Abelson's script theory. Experiments 1 and 2 examine the organization of people's knowledge about stereotyped activities. What actions, roles, and props do people mention and how do they group or cluster these into subscenes? Experiments 3 and 4 ask whether, in remembering a text mentioning a subset of script actions, people tend to remember numerous unmentioned parts of the underlying script. Experiment 5 examines whether in recalling a text people will tend to recall the script actions in their stereotypic order even though the actions are mentioned in another order in the text. Experiment 6 asks whether the reading of earlier actions in a script speeds up the reading and comprehension of later actions in that script. Finally, Experiment 7 examines memory for occasional events, inserted into script-based stories, which interfered with or deviated from the smooth-running of the script.

**Table 1    Theoretical restaurant script (adapted from Schank & Abelson, 1977)**

*Name: Restaurant*

| *Props:* Tables | *Roles:* Customer |
|---|---|
| Menu | Waiter |
| Food | Cook |
| Bill | Cashier |
| Money | Owner |
| Tip | |

| *Entry Conditions:* Customer hungry | *Results:* Customer has less money |
|---|---|
| Customer has money | Owner has more money |
| | Customer is not hungry |

*Scene 1: Entering*
> Customer enters restaurant
> Customer looks for table
> Customer decides where to sit
> Customer goes to table
> Customer sits down

*Scene 2: Ordering*
> Customer picks up menu
> Customer looks at menu
> Customer decides on food
> Customer signals waitress
> Waitress comes to table
> Customer orders food
> Waitress goes to cook
> Waitress gives food order to cook
> Cook prepares food

*Scene 3: Eating*
> Cook gives food to waitress
> Waitress brings food to customer
> Customer eats food

*Scene 4: Exiting*
> Waitress writes bill
> Waitress goes over to customer
> Waitress gives bill to customer
> Customer gives tip to waitress
> Customer goes to cashier
> Customer gives money to cashier
> Customer leaves restaurant

## Experiment 1: Script generation

In this experiment, we collected "free association norms" for common scripts. If subjects did not agree about the essentials of a script, we would doubt the "cultural uniformity" assumption of script theory. However, it is not a foregone conclusion that everyone would describe a continuous action stereotype in the same way, using terms at the same level of specificity. There may not be a culturally uniform level of "basic action" description for scripts, as Rosch, Mervis, Gray, Johnson, and Boyer-Braem (1976) had found for basic object categories. Groups of undergraduates were asked to write scripts about common activities. The exact instructions to them turned out to be critical. If subjects were told to "write a completely common, boring story about a lecture or doctor visit" (which is one description of a script given by Schank & Abelson, 1977), their replies were quite variable. Our subjects in fact tended to write interesting stories about boring lectures or to describe frustrations caused by boring delays in waiting to see a doctor. Therefore, we revised the instructions to emphasize the subject's task of listing the central actions in a cultural stereotype.

## Method

*Materials*. Each student generated events or actions for one situation. The five situations were attending a lecture, visiting a doctor, shopping at a grocery store, eating at a fancy restaurant, and getting up in the morning and getting off to school. Each subject received a blank sheet with appropriate instructions at the top. For example, the instructions for eliciting the lecture script were as follows:

> "Write a list of actions describing what people generally do when they go to a lecture in a course. We are interested in the common actions of a routine lecture stereotype. Start the list with arriving at the lecture and end it with leaving after the lecture. Include about 20 actions or events and put them in the order in which they would occur."

*Subjects*. The subjects were Stanford undergraduates fulfilling a course requirement for their Introductory Psychology class. We handed out different scripts to differing numbers of subjects during one mass testing session with a group of 161 students. The numbers of subjects filling out and turning in the various scripts were as follows: grocery 37, getting up 35, restaurant 33, lecture 32, and doctor 24. The data were edited and tabulated according to frequency of citation of specific events, and their associated roles and props. Paraphrases and synonyms were lumped together.

## Results

The issue is whether people agree in the actions they mention. The maximum diversity would be if all subjects generating a particular script mentioned once 20 or so completely unique events. But what is surprising is how much agreement there is in the "basic action" language that people use to describe the activities. This uniformity is reflected in how few of the events were mentioned by only one person. For example, in the restaurant script, of 730 actions mentioned in total (types times tokens), only four were completely unique (given by a single person). Similarly, the ratio of unique mentions to total events was 4/704 for Lecture, 26/814 for Grocery, 26/770 for Getting up, and 36/528 for Doctor (which had the fewest subjects and least chances for overlap). So there is at least someone who agrees with nearly every action that any subject writes for a script.

Furthermore, there is high reliability in the frequency with which particular actions of a script are mentioned. We divided each group in half and correlated the frequencies of mentioning specific actions by the two halves. The Pearson correlations were

Restaurant .88, Lecture .81, Grocery .85, Getting up .87, and Doctor .80. Thus, the frequency norms are reliable, at least with a homogeneous group like Stanford undergraduates.

Each subject mentioned a sample of very common actions along with some less common ones, presumably reflecting his experiences and speaking style. Across subjects, there was a continuous gradation in frequency of mention of particular events. We may arbitrarily designate the group's stereotype or script to be those events mentioned by more than some criterion percentage of subjects. Examining the distributions of how many actions were mentioned by varying numbers of respondents, the distributions had similar shapes with a distinct gap near 25% agreement. So we selected 25% mention as a lenient criterion for inclusion of an action in Table 2. Table 2 reports for the five situations each action mentioned by at least one-fourth the respondents. The actions are listed in the serial order in which they are usually mentioned. Two other criteria were selected at natural breaks in the percent-agreement distribution for each situation. The items in italics were more popular, falling above a criterion of 40–50% mention: actions in capitals were the most popular, having been mentioned by 55–75% of subjects (varying with scripts).

The 22 to 25 entries for the different scripts appear to capture common experiences in our culture. The actions mentioned the standard characters in the script, the usual "props" and locations for the actions. The fewer actions at the more stringent criteria also seem to be the more central or important ones of the script, with the actions in all capitals being the most important. In recent pilot work, Masling, Barsalou, and Bower collected "importance ratings" for events within scripts. The most frequently mentioned events of Table 2 were also rated as centrally important to the script. Such a high frequency-high importance event seems to correspond to what Schank and Abelson (1977, p. 45) call a "main conceptualization," an event which is essential within its scene in that subordinate actions within that scene depend upon it, often enabling or resulting from it. These main conceptualizations are likely to appear in a summary or synopsis of a script-based text. Furthermore, mention of one of these central events should act as a powerful probe to call up the script from the reader's memory.

## Discussion

The script norms in Table 2 are the main outcome of this study. There was considerable agreement in the way subjects described events. For example, people wrote "He ate his soup" rather than "He picked up his soup spoon, dipped it into the cup of soup, lifted it out, blew on it to cool it, raised it to his lips, put the spoon in his mouth. . .". Presumably people use action-summary terms or "basic-level action" terms (see Rosch *et al.*, 1976) to describe a continuum of events because they share a conversational postulate which says one ought to speak or write so as to be informative but not overly redundant (Grice, 1975). Because people know how to eat soup, it is ordinarily unnecessary and ill-mannered for a speaker to describe the steps in such detail. Perhaps it is these habits of speaking that lead our subjects into event descriptions at roughly the same basic level. Of course, a script itself is a familiar routine whose recital would normally be redundantly boring and gauche. But the experimental setting and our instructions for the generation task conveyed our interest in the subject's telling us all these normally boring details within a script.

**Table 2  Empirical script norms at three agreement levels**

| GOING TO A RESTAURANT | ATTENDING A LECTURE | GETTING UP | GROCERY SHOPPING | VISITING A DOCTOR |
|---|---|---|---|---|
| Open door | ENTER ROOM | *Wake up* | ENTER STORE | *Enter office* |
| *Enter* | *Look for friends* | Turn off alarm | GET CART | CHECK IN WITH RECEPTIONIST |
| *Give reservation name* | FIND SEAT | Lie in bed | Take out list | SIT DOWN |
| Wait to be seated | SIT DOWN | Stretch | Look at list | Wait |
| Go to table | Settle belongings | GET UP | Go to first aisle | Look at other people |
| BE SEATED | TAKE OUT NOTEBOOK | Make bed | *Go up and down aisles* | READ MAGAZINE |
| *Order drinks* | *Look at other students* | Go to bathroom | PICK OUT ITEMS | *Name called* |
| Put napkins on lap | *Talk* | Use toilet | Compare prices | Follow nurse |
| LOOK AT MENU | *Look at professor* | *Take shower* | Put items in cart | *Enter exam room* |
| *Discuss menu* | LISTEN TO PROFESSOR | *Wash face* | Get meat | Undress |
| ORDER MEAL | TAKE NOTES | *Shave* | Look for items forgotten | *Sit on table* |
| *Talk* | CHECK TIME | DRESS | Talk to other shoppers | Talk to nurse |
| Drink water | Ask questions | Go to kitchen | Go to checkout counters | NURSE TESTS |
| *Eat salad or soup* | *Change position in seat* | Fix breakfast | *Find fastest line* | Wait |
| Meal arrives | *Daydream* | EAT BREAKFAST | WAIT IN LINE | Doctor enters |
| EAT FOOD | Look at other students | BRUSH TEETH | *Put food on belt* | Doctor greets |
| Finish meal | Take more notes | Read paper | Read magazines | Talk to doctor about problem |
| *Order desert* | *Read paper* | *Comb hair* | WATCH CASHIER RING UP | DOCTOR EXAMINES |
| *Eat desert* | *Close notebook* | Get books | PAY CASHIER | Doctor asks questions |
| Ask for bill | *Gather belongings* | Look in mirror | *Watch bag boy* | Get dressed |
| Bill arrives | Stand up | Get coat | Cart bags out | Get medicine |
| PAY BILL | Talk | LEAVE HOUSE | Load bags into car | Make another appointment |
| *Leave tip* | LEAVE | | LEAVE STORE | LEAVE OFFICE |
| Get coats | | | | |
| LEAVE | | | | |

Items in all capital letters were mentioned by the most subjects, items in italics by fewer subjects, and items in small case letters by the fewest subjects.

We conceive of a standard activity like eating in a restaurant or visiting a dentist as a fuzzy concept for which there are many characteristic features but few if any defining features (see Smith, Rips, & Shoben, 1974; Rosch & Mervis, 1975; Zadah, 1965). Different instances of an activity seem to bear a "family resemblance" to one another, but they may possess no common features. For example, although eating would seem to be a general event of the restaurant script, one can be "in the restaurant script" without eating just as one can eat in many contexts besides the restaurant script (e.g., tasters, food judges). Events or actions are more or less diagnostic of a given activity or script. A diagnostic event or feature is statistically valid in the sense that its presence or absence correlates highly across situations with the presence or absence of the scriptal activity. A given script-instance should be judged as prototypical of the activity to the extent it combines highly valid features. As Rosch and Mervis have shown, the most prototypical exemplar is judged to resemble on average more other instances of the category and to bear less resemblance to instances of alternate categories. These properties of fuzzy concepts seem particularly appropriate to the notion of scripts.

The scripts of Table 2 should be useful for further experimental investigations. We have used them in investigations of memory for scripts and of comprehension of script-based texts. The scripts can be used like high-frequency association norms, much like the Battig and Montague (1969) category norms have been used in studies of word perception, priming, semantic judgments, and memory. As one example, an experiment in progress is checking to see whether a given action can be classified more rapidly as "fitting" a given script header if it is a high associate of the script. Further, one could check whether high-frequency action associates of a script are better recalled but more poorly recognized than low-frequency actions of the script. High frequency actions, if not mentioned in a text, may later attract many false-positive recognitions because they were implicitly aroused during reading the text.

## Experiment 2: Constituent structure of scripts

The events within a lengthy ordered script appear to be segmented naturally into several major chunks or constituents. The script is not an undifferentiated, linear chain, but rather seems organized into major scenes, with those composed of subsequences of actions. Thus, eating in a restaurant may have as major scenes entering, ordering, eating, paying, and leaving. But ordering requires being seated, getting and reading a menu, having a waitress come to take your order, and so on. To check our intuitions we asked subjects if they thought there was a "natural segmentation" of the lower-level action sequences in a script. If they segmented the actions into chunks, we were then interested in whether they agreed on the location of the chunk boundaries.

## Method

Ten texts were written by converting all of the actions in 10 underlying scripts into actual story statements. The texts ranged in length from 148 to 254 words. The scripts used were going to a restaurant, getting up in the morning, attending a lecture, going to a birthday party, going swimming, grocery shopping, making coffee, visiting a doctor, attending a movie, and playing football.

31

Thirty Stanford undergraduates were given a booklet containing the 10 stories, each on a different page. They were told that some people felt that each story had several natural parts; they were to read the stories, decide whether a story had some parts and, if so, identify these parts by placing a slash line in the texts marking the end of each part. They were given no hint as to how many slashes (chunk boundaries) to place in each text, if any.

## Results

The main issue is whether people agree in their chunking judgments. That is, are there locations in the stories where most people put slashes to indicate a part boundary, and other locations where very few people put slashes? We first divided the story into script action statements, since subjects only placed slashes at such clause boundaries. We tabulated the frequency of slashes (chunk boundaries) at each site. Table 3 displays these slash frequencies in brackets after each clause for two of the ten texts. To measure the agreement of the location of slashes, we divided the group in half and correlated their slash frequencies at the clause boundaries for the several story locations. The Pearson correlations for the different scripts were as follows: getting up .98, coffee .94, lecture .99, doctor .99, birthday .96, swimming .95, movie .98, football .98, shopping .96, and restaurant .98. Next, we performed chi-square tests to determine whether the distributions of slashes differed from a uniform distribution. The chi-squares for all scripts were significant, with all $p$'s < .001.

We considered how to describe the group's agreement on number and location of chunk boundaries. We examined the number and location of story constituents selected by varying numbers of people. All 10 of the scripts yielded a roughly bimodal distribution: there were a few sites between action clauses where most of the subjects placed slashes (e.g., 18 to 20 subjects); then there were many locations where few subjects placed slashes (e.g., three, four, five, and six subjects), finally, there were very few sites selected by a moderate number of subjects (e.g., 10 to 12). In nine of the 10 scripts, the one-third percentage (10 subjects) fell in a natural gap in the slash distribution, so we selected one-third as the cutoff point. By this criterion the 10 scripts each have three to five constituent boundaries. Slashes locate these major constituent boundaries in the texts of Table 3.

One guide to determining the constituents of a sentence is that "a constituent is a group of words that can be replaced by a single word without change in function and without doing violence to the rest of the sentence" (Clark & Clark, 1977, p. 48). We find that we can substitute summary-actions for our empirically derived constituents in scripts. For example, in the Doctor story given in Table 3, we can replace the first constituent by "Diane went to the doctor's office," the second by "She waited," the third by "She went through the preliminaries," the fourth by "The doctor examined her," and the fifth by "She left the doctor's office." Note that if we try to move any boundary to encompass adjacent text actions, the one-action summaries no longer fit. The other script boundaries show similar properties, so our empirically derived script boundaries fit the summary criterion of a constituent.

32

**Table 3    The chunk judgments of Experiment 2**

*The Doctor*

Diane was feeling very bad today, [0] so she decided to go see the family doctor. [7] Therefore she had her husband take her to the doctor's office. [17] / When she arrived at the doctor's office, [1] she went into the waiting room. [1] Once inside she walked over and checked in with the receptionist [0] and then sat down to wait her turn. [4] As she waived she read some old medical magazines that were on the table [0] and looked at the colorful medical posters that adorned the wall [17]/ Finally the nurse came in and called her name, [0] so she went into the examination room with the nurse. [7] The nurse closed the door and asked her to take off her clothes. [0] The nurse then weighed her and took her blood pressure. [0] When these preliminaries were completed the nurse left [7] and a short while later the doctor came in. [5] The doctor was very nice to her, so she calmed down a little bit. [15] / As the doctor started to make various examinations of her [3] she wondered what he was doing [0] and what he was finding. [5] Finally he looked directly at her and told her that she had the flu and could expect to be laid up in bed for a few days. [0] Then he wrote a prescription for some pills [0] and left [22]. / She got dressed [0] and made another appointment with the receptionist [0] on her way out of the doctor's office.

*The Restaurant*

David noticed that his stomach was emitting hunger pains, [1] so he decided to go out to a restaurant to eat. [6] Therefore he drove to the local French restaurant. [19] / He arrived at the restaurant a little before the dinner rush hour, [1] so as he entered the restaurant [0] he noticed that there were plenty of empty tables. [0] He decided to sit at a window table, [5] so he went over [0] and sat down. [20] / A waitress came up [0] and gave him a menu. [1] He carefully perused the menu [0] and decided what he wanted. [4] The waitress came back [0] and he gave her his order. [13] / After a short wait [0] during which he nibbled on bread and butter [1], his dinner arrived. [13] / He proceeded to eat the dinner with gusto. [2] The food here was really excellent [0] and not too expensive either. [16] / Finally he finished [0] and asked the waitress for the check. [9] He left the waitress a tip on the table [0] and went over to the cashier. [2] He paid the cashier [1] and went home quite satisfied.

The numbers in brackets indicate the number of subjects (out of 30) who marked those locations as boundaries between parts of the story. Slashes mark the major constituent boundary locations (i.e., those marked by 10 or more people).

## Discussion

Clearly, our subjects agreed with our intuitions that a continuous script activity can be segmented into chunks or scenes. And they agreed with one another where the scene boundaries were located in the event sequence. Thus, the script is not a linear chain of actions at one level but rather a hierarchically organized "tree" of events with several levels of subordinate actions. That activities are decomposable into a hierarchy of subactions is a recurrent theme in cognitive psychology (e.g., see Bower, 1975; Goodman, 1970; Miller, Galanter, & Pribram, 1960; Pew, 1974).

Actions may be identified with their intended goals or subgoals. From this perspective, the activity hierarchy is really a goal tree, wherein a top goal is decomposed into a series of subgoals. Thus, the top goal of eating in a restaurant script can be decomposed into the subgoals of getting inside a restaurant, sitting down and ordering, eating the food received, paying the bill, and leaving. In turn the subgoal of ordering the food can be decomposed into events of getting a menu, reading it, getting the waiter to your table and telling him what food you want. The relevance of such goal hierarchies is that they are frequently useful for answering questions about specific actions or events (see e.g., Schank & Yale A. I. Project, Note 4; Winston, 1977, p. 301 ff.). The following strategies often work:

> *Why*-questions (e.g., why did you speak to the waiter?) can often be answered by moving one level up from the queried action in the hierarchy and stating that goal (e.g., "Because I was ordering"). Repeated *Why's* may force the respondent to the top of the tree, where sits the script-entry reason (i.e., I ate to reduce hunger; and I did that to stay alive).

> *How* questions can often be answered by moving one level down in the hierarchy from the queried action, and listing its subordinate actions. Thus, "How did you order?" can be answered by "I translated the French menu, called over the waiter, and pointed to what I wanted." If the queried action has no subordinates in the tree, an acceptable answer is "I just did it," (as in answer to "How did you swallow your food?").

> *When* questions (e.g., when did you read the menu?) can be answered by referring either to the goal-activity one level up and using *while* ("While I was ordering"); or by referring to preceding and succeeding actions at the same level. Thus, we can reply "I read the menu just *after* the waiter left it on my table, and *before* I gave him my order."

Besides helping answer questions, the action hierarchy can be used by the person generating summaries of script-based texts. Any sequence of subordinate actions within a given chunk can be summarized by the superordinate action (Rumelhart, 1977; Schank & Yale A. I. Project, Note 4). Thus, "John read the menu, decided on his selection, and told the waiter what he wanted to eat" can be summarized as "John ordered."

Given this information about chunk structures in scripts, several psychological experiments would seem called for. Our own efforts along this line have been limited to date. One pilot study is that mentioned earlier by Masling, Barsalou, and Bower which had subjects rating the importance of various scenes to the goal of the script. The most important scenes within a text should be those most likely to survive in memory over a retention interval. Another pilot study of ours investigated the number of false alarms that occurred in recognition memory for unstated actions within a chunk for which either one or two other actions of that chunk were stated in a text the subject read. Contrary to expectation, the number of false alarms was lower to an unstated action when two actions within that chunk were also stated than when only one of those actions was stated. Other studies using the chunk-boundary norms could examine all-or-none recall of chunks, probe latency for recall of the "next successor" by a within-chunk vs a prior-chunk action (see Ammon, 1968), and the process of purging or clearing out of short-term memory as a sequence of script-action sentences passes over a chunk boundary (see Jarvella, 1970; 1971). Clearly more research on the topic is needed.

## Experiment 3: Script recall

Next we investigate recall of texts composed of selected lines from an underlying script.[1] The question was whether in recalling such a text subjects will use the underlying script to fill in gaps of intervening actions not explicitly mentioned in the text. We might expect some such intrusions in recall since they correspond to the familiar phenomenon of changing the working of a story when we retell it "in our own words."

The script idea gives us a way to think about paraphrases of a story. If a sequence of actions calls up an underlying script from memory which is then filled out according to the particulars of the text, then the "same story" can sometimes be retold by mentioning a different selection of its actions. If a b c d e f g represent the underlying script events and Text 1 comprises sentences instantiating a c e g, then Text 2 comprised of congruent instantiations of b d f could be judged to be an acceptable paraphrase of Text 1 despite having no events in common. Such a possibility is a consequence of conceiving of script instances as only bearing a family resemblance to one another. Similarity of two texts will probably be a systematic function of the amount and importance of their overlapping as opposed to their distinguishing features (see Tversky, 1977). It is an empirical matter to explore in detail which parts of a script-based text can be replaced or altered without changing the intuition that the second text is a paraphrase of (or closely similar to) the first. The importance of similar paraphrases for studies of memory is that we can expect the person's memory to be confused between two paraphrases of the same script, sometimes substituting or intruding in recall actions that were implied but not stated in the text.

We may expect subjects to remember for some minutes the events explicitly stated in the text. But as their "surface memory" of the text fades, they should intrude more assertions into recall which represent implications and which in theory were used to fill-in the gaps between the script actions read originally. A model for this might suppose that after reading the person has both a veridical memory for the actually read statements (in "episodic memory") and an activated and completely filled out underlying script. In immediate recall, the person merely reproduces his veridical memory. But this memory fades over time and he relies then upon the fully-completed script, which leads to unstated script actions being intruded into recall.

We were also interested in a second phenomenon which, if found, may prove harder to explain. We wondered whether we could increase the subject's belief that an unstated action had occurred in a script-based text by having him read *related* script stories in which the analogous or parallel actions were explicitly mentioned. The kind of parallel stories used are illustrated in Table 4, one for John visiting a doctor, the other for Bill

1.  Note our terminology. A *script* refers to a generic memory structure in a person's head (e.g., visiting a Health Professional). A script-based *text* or *story* is a list of sentences, read by the subject, most of which denote actions of an underlying script. A given script may be instanced by different texts (e.g., Diane visiting her doctor or dentist). An *instantiated script* is an episodic memory structure set up in the reader's head to encode and remember a particular script-based text: it is the "memory trace" of reading the story of Diane visiting her doctor.

visiting a dentist. These are different instances of an abstract script for visiting a health professional.

The actions enclosed by parentheses in Table 4 were not included in the texts read by the subjects, but are part of the Health Professional script. Notice that some of the actions left out in the Doctor text have their parallel actions explicitly stated in the Dentist text, and vice versa. For example, the Dentist text mentions nothing about Bill checking in with a receptionist whereas the Doctor text mentions that John checked in with the Doctor's receptionist. We predicted that in a memory test people would tend to recall gap-filling events left out of a script story, and they would tend to do this more if they also read other instantiations of this script which did mention the analogous actions. The experiment below tests this specific prediction, that recall intrusions of gap-fillers will increase if other instances of the same script are also read.

**Table 4    Sample texts used for Experiments 3 and 4**

| *"The Doctor"* | *"The Dentist"* |
|---|---|
| Entry: John was feeling bad today. | Entry: Bill had a toothache. |
| 1. John decided to go see the doctor. | 1. (Bill decided to go see the dentist.) |
| 2. (John arrived at the doctor's office.) | 2. Bill arrived at the dentist's office. |
| 3. (John entered the doctor's office.) | 3. (Bill entered the dentist's office.) |
| 4. John checked in with the doctor's receptionist. | 4. (Bill checked in with the dentist's receptionist.) |
| . . . | . . . |
| 7. John looked at some medical magazines. | 7. (Bill read some dental magazines.) |
| . . | . . |
| 12. (The nurse checked John's blood pressure and weight.) | 12. The dental hygenist x-rayed Bill's teeth. |
| . . . | . . . |

Sentences in parentheses were presented only during the recognition test in Experiment 4.

## Method

*Materials*. There were nine basic scripts each with about 20 actions (and thus similar to the 25% cutoff level in Experiment 1). Each script was chosen to have at least three distinctive versions, (e.g., the Health Professional script had the Doctor, Dentist, and Chiropractor versions). Hence the materials were a total of 27 specific script versions, so it was impractical to collect and analyze script norms to serve as a basis for all these materials (one would need around 30 subjects per action list for 27 action lists). Therefore these scripts were created by one of the experimenters (JB) and a colleague. We individually composed a list of common actions for each generic script, then compared our versions and reached a compromise prototype. Three stories were then written based on each script; each story was about eight lines long and represented a different instance of the script. Hence, the story pool contained nine clusters of three stories per cluster: attending a symphony, play, or movie; visiting a doctor, dentist, or chiropractor; playing a game of football, baseball, or golf; going swimming, skin diving, or surfing; getting ready in the morning to go to school, church, or work; attending a class lecture, sermon, or speech; shopping for bread, a coat, or a toaster; going to a birthday party, New Year's Eve party, or Halloween party; and making coffee, tea, or hot chocolate. Each subject read one story each for three of the nine scripts, two stories each for another three scripts (i.e., six stories), and three stories each for the other three scripts (i.e., nine stories). Hence, each subject read a total of 18 stories, presented in random order. Which story fell into which category was balanced across subjects. Each story was also given a title (e.g., The Doctor, Football, etc.).

To clarify complex relations among instantiations, the three texts for Visiting a Health Professional are given here.

### The Doctor

John was feeling bad today so he decided to go see the family doctor. He checked in with the doctor's receptionist, and then looked through several medical magazines that were on the table by his chair. Finally the nurse came and asked him to take off his clothes. The doctor was very nice to him. He eventually prescribed some pills for John. Then John left the doctor's office and headed home.

### The Dentist

Bill had a bad toothache. It seemed like forever before he finally arrived at the dentist's office. Bill looked around at the various dental posters on the wall. Finally the dental hygienist checked and x-rayed his teeth. He wondered what the dentist was doing. The dentist said that Bill had a lot of cavities. As soon as he'd made another appointment, he left the dentist's office.

### The Chiropractor

Harry woke up with a bad pain in his back again. He decided to go see a chiropractor that very day. He had to wait a long time. Finally the chiropractic assistant finished and left him, and the chiropractor himself came in. The chiropractor carefully examined Harry by feeling all the bones in his back. Eventually Harry left the chiropractor's office.

Note, the stories are about seven or eight lines long, and they share only the common entering and leaving conditions. The middle six or so actions of each story were selected without replacement from the 20 actions comprising the master Health-Professional script. A third of the subjects would read all three of these texts scattered through the study phase; a third read a randomly selected two of them; and a third read a randomly selected one of them. The same routine was followed with each of the nine master scripts.

*Procedure*. The subjects were run in groups of two to eight. As a warmup, subjects first read for 10 min a coherent narrative that was completely unrelated to the material of this experiment. They were then given reading instructions, given their story booklet for the present experiment, and had 10 min to read and study it. This study time was sufficient for all subjects to read through their 18 stories. After reading, the subjects performed an intervening task for 20 min. This task involved their recalling in writing the narrative that they had read at the beginning of the session. After that they were instructed regarding recall of the 18 scripts of this experiment. The script titles were read as cues, and subjects wrote their recall of each corresponding text on a new sheet of paper. They were given 1 min to recall each of the eight-line stories. They were asked to be accurate and to reproduce each text verbatim insofar as possible, but they were to recall the gist of an event if they could not remember it verbatim.

*Subjects*. The subjects were 18 students at California State University at Sacramento who participated to fulfill a service requirement for their Introductory Psychology course.

## Results

The recalls were scored for the presence or absence of the underlying script actions. We had no trouble deciding to which script action a given sentence in recall referred. We classified the actions in each person's recall into stated script actions, unstated script actions, and other actions that did not fit these two categories. The numbers of recalled actions falling into these three categories are displayed in Table 5. The rows of the table correspond to the conditions of one, two, or three story instances of a script.

**Table 5     Average numbers of actions recalled per script version in Experiment 3**

| | | Number of stated script actions | Number of unstated script actions | Other actions | Total actions recalled | Percent of total that are unstated script actions |
|---|---|---|---|---|---|---|
| Number of | 1 | 3.03 | 0.80 | 0.39 | 4.22 | 19 |
| script | 2 | 2.27 | 1.26 | 0.35 | 3.88 | 31 |
| versions | 3 | 2.56 | 1.16 | 0.36 | 4.08 | 28 |

Before listing statistical tests, let us recognize the current controversy over whether investigators using language materials should use fixed or mixed effect analysis of variance (ANOVA) models to test hypotheses (Clark, 1973; Wike & Church, 1976; Clark, Cohen, Smith, & Keppel, 1976). In our case, the question is whether to treat the scripts as a random sample of all scripts and thus as a random effect in the ANOVA model, or to limit the conclusions to these 18 scripts and thus treat them as a fixed effect in the ANOVA model. We report statistical tests for both models. Happily, only rarely in this paper does the test used influence the pattern of significances, and we will note whenever it does.

A first feature of the data in Table 5 is that stated script actions are recalled more than unstated script actions, which in turn are more frequent than other actions. These pairwise comparisons are statistically significant at .01 for the three- and two-instance rows, and at .05 for the one-instance row. Stated actions exceed unstated ones significantly considering the differing materials exemplifying a condition as either a fixed or random effect (using an $F$ test for a fixed effect ANOVA model or a quasi-$F$, $F'$, test for a random effect ANOVA model). So, while we may conclude that unstated script actions appear in recall in appreciable amounts, subjects nonetheless display considerable "surface memory", at least at a 20-min retention interval, since they are producing two to three times more stated than unstated actions. The data in Table 5 are raw frequencies. To convert them to percentage of script actions given, one must divide the left hand entries by the number of stated actions (eight) and the middle entries by the number of unstated actions (arbitrarily 12 here, though indeterminate in reality). Thus the proportionate reproduction of stated vs unstated actions is even more pronounced than the raw frequency results.

Next consider the influence of having read two or three script instances upon intrusion of unstated script actions (the "gap fillers" in Table 4). Since recall levels varied somewhat across conditions, we expressed the intrusions of unstated script actions as a percentage of the total recall, and entered this in the last column of Table 5. Clearly the percentage of unstated script intrusions increase when other story instances of the same script are present. Comparing the percentages of gap-fillers to all actions recalled, scripts with two story versions have many more than do scripts with one story version [$F'(1,18) = 10.68$, $p < .01$]; similarly, three story versions lead to more gap-fillers than does one story version. However, three and two do not differ in intrusion rate.

So, we may conclude that having another version of the same script mention an action increases the probability that the unmentioned analogous action is intruded in recalling a related story. We reserve theoretical discussion of this priming effect until after the results of Experiment 4 are presented. Unfortunately, the priming effect does not increase steadily as the number of script versions is increased. We have no explanation for this leveling-off.

Considering recalls of the stories having one, two, and three instances of the underlying script, it is clear that they do not differ in the number of "other actions" recalled nor in the total recall. However, the conditions differ in recall of stated actions with the one instance stories being higher. This effect is significant considering materials as a fixed effect [$F(2,30) = 4.42$, $p < .05$], but not when materials are considered as a random effect ($p > .05$).

If reliable, the lower recall of stated actions with multi-instance texts suggests several interpretations. First, because multi-instance texts create more intrusions, there are more opportunities for "output interference," whereby output of an intrusion causes forgetting of a not-yet-recalled stated action (see Roediger, 1974). Second, if people normally avoid reporting redundantly close (and therefore uninformative) actions from a script, then the increased intrusions of implied actions in the multi-instance conditions would cause increased editing out and nonrecall of nearby stated actions.

Finally, examination of the "other actions" category in recall reveals that 40% of them are superordinate actions or terms summarizing lower-level script actions. For example, if the text said "She took out the coffee pot, filled it with water, put it on the stove, . . ." a summarizing "other" statement would be "She heated some water." Such summarizing statements are expected, considering the underlying script as a hierarchical tree with the summarizing terms referring to nodes at the higher levels of the tree.

An unexpected result is that the proportion of superordinate actions among the "other actions recalled" category is over twice as great (62.5%) for the recall of the one-instance stories as for the averaged recall of the two- and three-instance stories (28.3%). This effect is statistically reliable [$F(1,5) = 19, p < .01$]. However, we have no explanation for this curiosity.

## Experiment 4: Script recognition

The recalls in Experiment 3 showed the effect of interest, namely, a fairly high intrusion rate of unstated actions from the underlying script. Moreover, this intrusion rate when recalling a story could be raised by presenting the counterpart actions in a parallel story that is a different version of the same underlying script. Our next experiment aimed to demonstrate these effects more clearly using recognition memory. In the recognition test, the subjects saw a test sentence from the underlying script and assessed how well it matched anything within the specific subset of sentences stored in memory from when they had read the text. To the extent that studying a sentence describing an action activates associated actions in the underlying script, those associated actions will later appear to have been read. This prediction arises because, during testing, the person allegedly only knows the level of activation in memory corresponding to the test proposition, but is confused about the source of this activation, whether it is due to an explicit or implicit presentation. This failure to discriminate the source of activation is one supposed cause of false-positive recognition judgments.

## Method

*Materials*. The learning materials were the same titled script stories used in Experiment 3. The presentation of the stories and the counter-balancing of materials across experimental conditions were the same as before.

*Procedure*. Subjects first read two unrelated, 600-word stories for 5 min. These stories were unrelated in content to the scripts of this experiment. Subjects then read the 18 script stories of this experiment, each with a title. They had 5 min to read these stories. They then spent 30 min writing recalls of the first two stories. Finally they were given the recognition test over the 18 script stories. The recognition test contained 16 test statements for each of the nine generic scripts (or 9 x 16 = 144 in total). These were blocked by story title. For each generic script the recognition test contained eight stated script actions, four unstated script actions, and four other actions that were false though not implausible. Typical false items mispaired actors and actions, or locations and actions, from the stories studied. When two or three story versions of the same generic script were used, the 16 recognition items were chosen evenly from the two or three stories. The subjects rated each test statement on a 7-point scale, with 1 denoting "Very sure I did not read this sentence" and 7, "Very sure I did read it."

*Subjects*. The subjects were 45 Stanford University students who were fulfilling an Introductory Psychology course requirement. They were tested in groups of two to eight.

## Results

The primary results are the average recognition ratings for the various item types. These are shown in Table 6 for stories in the one, two, and three script version conditions. A high number indicates that the subjects believed the statement had been in the texts read a half hour earlier.

**Table 6    Average recognition ratings per test item in Experiment 4[a]**

| | | Stated script actions (S) | Unstated script actions (U) | Other actions (O) | Ratio (R) |
|---|---|---|---|---|---|
| Number of script versions | 1 | 5.46 | 3.91 | 1.71 | 54.6 |
| | 2 | 5.40 | 4.62 | 1.76 | 66.3 |
| | 3 | 5.59 | 4.81 | 1.86 | 68.6 |

[a] 7 means "Sure Old" and 1 means "Sure New."

In general, ratings are highest for stated actions, intermediate for unstated script fillers, and lowest for novel false statements. These pair-wise comparisons are statistically significant at .01 within each row of Table 6; they are significant considering learning materials as either a fixed or random effect.

Comparing conditions with varying numbers of instances, recognition ratings for stated items are equivalent. So the recognition accuracy measure does not uphold the small difference between one vs two or three versions found earlier with the recall measure. There is a slight difference in ratings of False items which is significant treating learning materials as a fixed effect [$F(2,84) = 5.33, p < .01$] but not as a random effect [$F'(2,28) = 1.29, p > .10$].

The most salient difference between the different instance conditions occurs with unstated script fillers. As predicted, false-positive recognition ratings for an unstated script filler increase as more instances are put into memory. The differences in ratings on unstated script fillers for one, two, or three instances are highly significant; fixed effect ANOVA yields [$F(2,84) = 31.3, p < .001$]; random-effect ANOVA yields [$F'(2,17) = 5.35, p < .05$]. Individual comparisons show that conditions one and two differ, and one and three differ by both $F$ and $F'$ tests. However, although two and three differ at the .05 level by a fixed-effect $F$ test, they are not significant by a random-effect $F'$.

The ratio score in the last column of Table 6 scales ratings of script fillers relative to the hit rate on Stated actions and the false positive rate on Falses. The ratio score is 100 $(U–F)/(S–F)$, where S, U, and F stand for Stated trues, Unstated script fillers, and False items, respectively. The ratio scores differ reliably, mainly because the one-instance ratio is below the other two. The two- and three-instance conditions do not differ reliably in this ratio measure.

After the data were collected, we noticed that our test items for unstated script actions for two or three script instances were actually of three types. The types are illustrated by the example fillers in Table 4. One type of action confusion is shown in lines 1, 2, 4, and 7 of Table 4; it involves mixing up, say, John's arriving at the Doctor's office with Bill's arriving at the Dentist's office. False alarms to such gap fillers would reveal the person mixing up actions, objects, and actors in a simple manner. Line 3 of Table 4 illustrates the second type of action confusion. These items are script actions that were not stated in any of the story versions read. The third type of action confusion is shown in Line 12 of Table 4; here the similarity of the sentences in the two stories stems from their exemplifying the same role or function in the abstract script. For example, the abstract health-professional script has an action in which an assistant performs some preliminary procedures on the patient. An instantiation of this role for the Doctor script is "The nurse checked John's blood pressure and weight;" for the Dentist story an instantiation is "The dental hygenist checked and x-rayed Bill's teeth." Clearly, taking John's temperature has little direct similarity to x-raying Bill's teeth. Rather they are similar by virtue of the roles they play in the abstract script.

We wondered whether the effect of number of instances in increasing false alarming to gap fillers held true for all three types of recognition items. There were many more items of the first type than of the second and third; furthermore, the counterbalancing of story versions into the one-, two-, and three-instance conditions caused a marked loss of observations on any specific abstract inference. Putting aside these problems, however, we computed the average recognition ratings for the second and third types of unstated script actions mentioned above, for the one-instance condition vs the combined two- and three-instance conditions. For the direct inferences not stated in any text (second type above), the ratings for one vs two and three instances were 3.49 and 4.75, respectively (one vs two [$F(1,28) = 28.06$, $p < .01$]; one vs three [$F(1,28) = 18.15$, $p < .01$]; two vs three is not significant). For the abstract inferences (third type), the ratings for one vs two and three instances were 2.73 and 4.73, respectively (one vs two [$F(1,28) = 7.84$, $p < .01$]; one vs three [$F(1,28) = 12.11$, $p < .01$]; two vs three is not significant). There is a clear effect of other text instances on these two classes of confusion errors. The effect is as large as that obtained for simple actor-action mix-ups which comprise the majority of cases in the composite averages in Table 6. The fact that the third type of inference yields an equal-sized effect is remarkable since the basis for the similarity of two action-statements in this case is not their meaning per se but rather the abstract role they fulfill in the two scripts. In closing we would repeat that the comparison of the effect of number of instances for the three inference types is not balanced across materials, and we would be more confident if we had designed our experiment for this comparison. However, the current results suggest optimism that a properly balanced experiment would replicate the effects found here.

## Discussion

Two major results of Experiments 3 and 4 require explanation. The first is that subject intrude in recall and falsely recognize actions that are in the underlying scripts but were not stated in the texts. The second result is that these intrusions and false alarms increase if the subjects read more than one text that instances the same script. We will now contrast two models of memory for script-based texts and note whether they can account for these results. The models describe the way a script-based text interacts with a generic script in memory to create an episodic memory trace of the text. We will first discuss the representation of generic scripts and of episodic instances of them.

Figure 1 schematizes the knowledge structure for the "Visit Health Professional" script. At the top level the script has a Name (or Header), a list of Roles, Props, Entry Conditions, and Actions. The Roles would be Patient Receptionist, Professional Person, and Professional's Assistant. The Props would be an Office, Waiting Room, Magazines, Examination Room, etc. The Entry Conditions would be state descriptions such as "Patient feels bad." The Actions would be verb-based conceptualizations like "Patient Arrives at Office," "Patient Checks In With Receptionist," etc., or some representation even more abstract than these conceptualizations, such as the primitive actions suggested by Schank and Abelson (1977). The entries for the Roles, Props, Entry Conditions, and Actions in Figure 1 are enclosed in angle brackets to indicate that they are lists of constraints on whatever fills the role rather than actual instantiations of the variables.

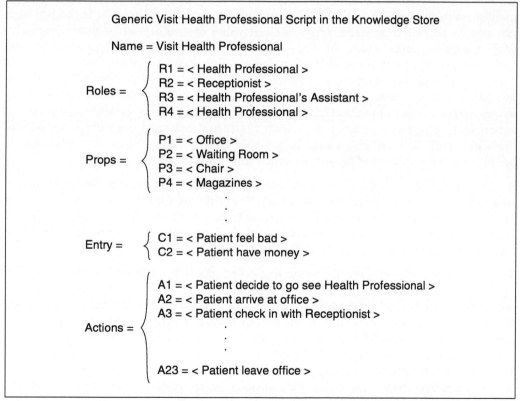

**Figure 1    Generic visit health professional script in the knowledge store**

As a person reads a script-based text that fits this Health Professional script, we assume that she sets up a new episodic memory structure to encode that particular story. We will contrast two different models of what the episodic memory contains, the

Full Copy and the Partial Copy models. To illustrate the contrast, suppose the person reads a script-based text that begins as follows:

> John was feeling ill. He arrived at Doctor Smith's office. As he waited, he read a *Family Health* magazine. Then he went into an examination room where a nurse checked his blood pressure and weight . . .

In the Full Copy model, the reading of this text allegedly causes the person to set up an episodic memory structure which is a fully instantiated version of the complete script up to and including the point of the last script statement in the text. Thus, from the sample text, the script-applying mechanism knows how several "variables" of the abstract script in Figure 1 are to be "bound" or specified. Thus, the Patient (R1) is set equal to John; the Health Professional (R4) is set equal to "Doctor Smith;" and the Assistant (R3) is set equal to "Nurse." The Receptionist (R2) is not specified but will be filled with the prototypical value (e.g., a young woman in a white uniform). The actions of the script are then filled in as fully as possible according to these bound variables or according to their prototypical values. If a script action is explicitly mentioned in the text, then that action instantiates an action variable. If the action is not mentioned, then an appropriate default value or prototypical action congruent with explicit bindings is entered. This process is shown in part by Figure 2 where we have noted the text sentences plus a few surrounding script actions. (This figure omits the role and prop variables for simplicity). To the right of each statement is a tag or marker, which is ** (two asterisks) if that script-line was in the text and which is * (one asterisk) if it was not in the text but was derived by filling in the corresponding generic action with the prototype congruent with the bound role and prop variables of this particular text. The asterisk count is the sole discriminative trace regarding which script lines were stated in the text vs which lines were derived.

A nice feature of the Full Copy model is that it can readily answer questions about script-based inferences from the stated text. If we suppose that the occurrence markers fade with time, then the person will eventually be unable to discriminate whether a script-based statement was or was not stated in the text. This explains the false positive recognition results that we found.

What about the influence on the "John at Doctor" memory of other texts such as "Bill visiting the Dentist?" According to the Full Copy theory, the "Bill visiting Dentist" text would cause another instantiation of the Health Professional script to be fully copied into episodic memory, comparable to the episodic structure in Figure 2. The new structure would have different variable bindings (e.g., "R4 = Dentist" rather than "Doctor Smith"). Unfortunately, within the Full Copy model, we have found no natural or parsimonious mechanism for creating confusions between memories of two script instances: they exist in distinct episodic compartments and do not interact. Consequently, the Full Copy model has no way to explain our second result, that other text instances of a script increase memory confusions about a given text.

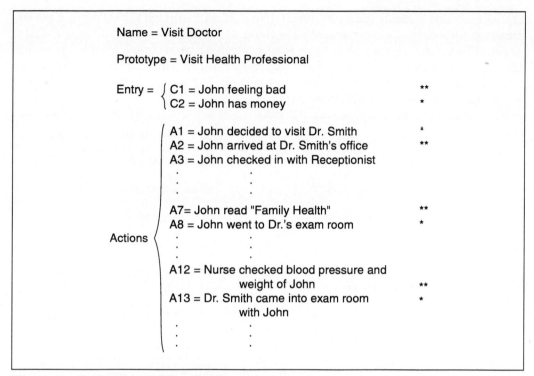

Name = Visit Doctor

Prototype = Visit Health Professional

Entry = { C1 = John feeling bad          **
          C2 = John has money            *

Actions {
A1 = John decided to visit Dr. Smith          *
A2 = John arrived at Dr. Smith's office       **
A3 = John checked in with Receptionist
    .        .
    .        .
    .        .
A7= John read "Family Health"                 **
A8 = John went to Dr.'s exam room             *
    .        .
    .        .
A12 = Nurse checked blood pressure and
        weight of John                        **
A13 = Dr. Smith came into exam room           *
        with John
    .        .
    .        .
    .        .
}

**Figure 2    Full copy model episodic memory**

A more adequate model is the Partial Copy model schematized in Figure 3. In this case, the reading of a script-based text sets up an episodic memory that leaves traces at two locations. First, the specific propositions of the texts are recorded into episodic memory structures, shown as boxes to the right in Figure 3. The unstated script actions are not instantiated at this time. Second, the abstract action corresponding to a text statement is marked in the knowledge store (to the left in Figure 3) as having been accessed and used during understanding of a text. This activation is indicated in Figure 3 by two asterisks attached to the memory node representing the abstract action. On the other hand, unstated actions of the script will be weakly activated (one asterisk) because they are part of the overall Health Professional script which has been aroused and is activating all its subordinate actions. This "top-down" activation from the script name (or header) to its subordinate actions corresponds to unconscious expectations regarding what conceptualizations the language understander is likely to encounter as the script-based text is read. In any event, stated actions are distinguished in memory from unstated script actions because (1) a copy of the stated action is in the episodic trace, and (2) the level of activation is higher on the abstract action-node corresponding to a stated action.

In such a theory, the person would be able to answer questions about the plausible truth of unstated but implied events by deriving the answer at the time of the question using the generic script and instantiating it according to the variable bindings in the episodic memory for the text. Such derived answers would take longer than directly stored answers, a result found by Reder (Note 1) and Kintsch (1974) among others. However, this difference in reaction time could be predicted by the Full Copy model if actions filled in by implication are at a weaker strength than stated actions. Therefore, the major distinguishing feature of the two models is that the Full Copy model has no simple way to account for some interfering "cross-talk" between different instantiations of the same abstract script.

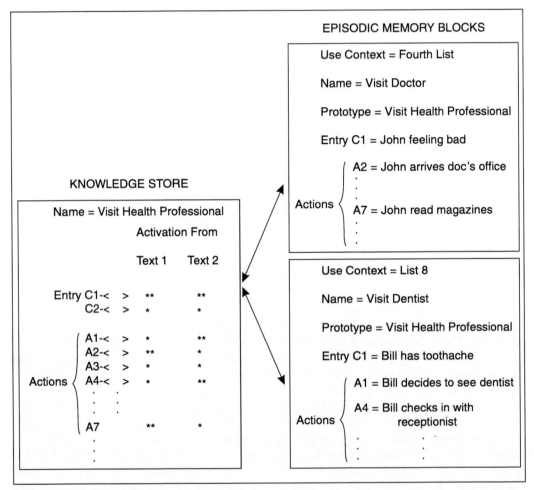

**Figure 3    Partial copy model**

In the Partial Copy model, forgetting occurs in two ways. First, the propositions represented in the episodic trace are simply "erased" or "fade away," the loss of any one propositional trace occurring in an all-or-none manner with a fixed small probability in each unit of time. This process leads to exponential decay (or spottiness) over time of the propositional traces in the text's memory block. Second, and independently of loss of the episodic propositions, the activation on the superordinate action-node in the abstract script also decays over time. The effect of the first decay process is that over time the subject will forget exactly what was stated in the script-based text, though he may be able to derive approximately what was stated from the difference in activation levels on the script-action nodes. The effect of both decay processes is to cause the person eventually to forget everything about the text he read.

In the Partial Copy theory, recognition memory is a three-stage process which is diagrammed in Figure 4. First, the memory scanner searches the appropriate episodic memory block (one of the episodic boxes in Figure 3), where it checks the test sentence for a match to the memories of the stated propositions remaining in this episodic memory block (which may be spotty from decay). If a match occurs here, then a fast, confident recognition judgment ("Yes, Old") ensues.[2] If no match occurs here, the scanner then goes up to the superordinate script-action corresponding to the test statement. If no superordinate script action corresponds to the probe, then the decision maker issues a confident "Did not read before" judgment. If a superordinate match does occur, then the scanner checks the level of activation on this node (the total number of asterisks on that line in Figure 3). If the activation here is high, that means that an instantiation of this abstract expression recently occurred in some context. Therefore, it is plausible that the text probe in fact corresponds to an action stated earlier but now forgotten. On these grounds, the decision process is likely to "accept" or "recognize" the test statement. On the other hand, if the activation on the superordinate node is low, then the test sentence should be rejected, judged to have been "not stated" in the text. The judgments given by the third stage are less confident than the judgments from the first two stages. This decision model resembles that of Atkinson and Juola (1973) except ours has more stages and its episodic and semantic memories are assumed to be searched in different orders. Hopefully there will be simplifying special cases of this complex decision model.

Let us now examine how this Partial Copy model deals with our results on memory for several instantiations of the same abstract script. Figure 3 shows an episodic memory block for the "Bill visiting Dentist" text as well as the block for the "John visiting Doctor" text. The stated propositions of two texts are recorded separately with the Prototype variable referring each instance back to the general script in the knowledge store. Note, however, each action in the Dentist text causes activation (asterisks) to accumulate at the superordinate script level in Figure 3. We suppose this activation on an action-node summates regardless of its source. This accumulation of activation occurs not only for abstract actions stated in the second instance text but also, by spreading activation, for actions not stated in either instance of the text. (These correspond to the several types of script inferences distinguished in the Results section). It is this accumulated activation on the superordinate action-node which,

2. A possible earlier stage not elaborated in Figure 4 would have the text probe first analyzed for its theme or script: and if the script of the probe is not among the active script headers, then the probe might be rejected outright. The logical complications with such a process are several: first, not all probes will activate a determinate script, so a branching decision tree must be articulated farther; second, distinctive distractions (e.g., witnessing a murder while eating) may be highly memorable parts of a text yet not be related at all to any active script from the experimental texts. Since we have no data to inform the complications created by such a "script-checking" stage, we have not inserted it in the decision process of Figure 3.

according to this theory, causes the increase in false positive responses to unstated actions as the number of related texts increases. An unstated test sentence will fail to match in the topical episodic store, will then be referred to the corresponding superordinate action, and the activation on that node is likely to be above the "acceptance" criterion if one of the other texts had recently instantiated this action. At this point, the decision maker knows only the level, not the source, of activation on the generic action node, so false positive recognitions may occur. These later-stage responses would be expected to come out more slowly and with less confidence than early-stage responses. This model predicts our result that unstated inferences receive lower recognition ratings than do tests on stated propositions.

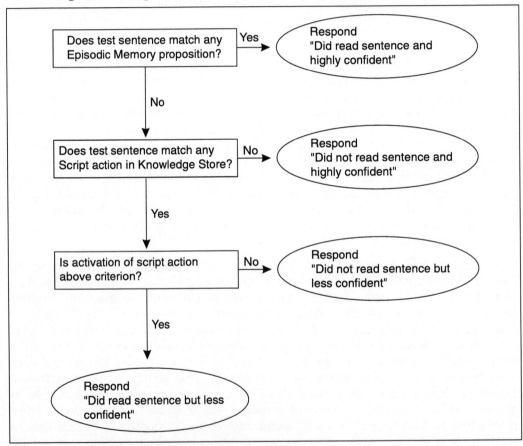

**Figure 4     Partial copy model's recognition process**

The Partial Copy model seems to provide a reasonable account of the salient features of our results. It also makes further predictions about verification latencies that seem consistent with existing data. We will, therefore, tentatively maintain the Partial Copy model. It is regrettably complex. But the data to be accounted for seem to warrant some complexities.

### Experiment 5: Script action reordering

Some scripts have strongly ordered actions, whereas others have none. The scripts used in the previous experiments (the Restaurant, the Doctor, etc.) are temporally ordered and most actions either cause or set up the preconditions for ("enable") the next action to occur.

The memory script that represents ordered actions must record this order in some manner. If this structure is used to record any text mentioning these actions anew, the process would be biased towards storing this listing in the canonical order of the script. But suppose the person must remember an arbitrarily reordered version of the Restaurant or Doctor scripts. That should prove difficult because the canonical order in memory should serve as a source of negative transfer and proactive interference against learning and recall of the reordered version. Further, the interference during recall should be in a specific direction. In trying to remember, the person should rearrange the misordered actions of the arbitrary text so that they are reproduced closer to their canonical order in the underlying script.

This ordering prediction for scripts is a special case of the general idea that stock narrative schema have ordered constituents. Thus the general story schema may have an ordering like Setting, Initiating Event Establishing Goal, Plan, Attempts, Consequence, and Resolution. Experiments have suggested that after reading misordered stories, readers are likely to remember them in their natural schematic order (see Kintsch, Mandel, & Kazminsky, 1977; Mandler, 1978: Stein & Glenn, 1978).

For comparison to learning of shuffled ordered scripts, we had subjects also learning arbitrary orders for what are naturally unordered scripts. An "unordered script" is a known set of actions or events for which there is no canonical order (in a particular subculture) — or if there is, the subject does not know it. For example, for most of us the order of events passing in review in a Veteran's Day parade is haphazard; all such parades have bands, children on bikes, dogs, policemen on horses, ladies auxiliary marchers, and so on, but to our knowledge there is no conventional order. The same is true for the scheduling of circus performers in the main ring at a circus. Since these events have no canonical order, the learning of any arbitrary order for them should be equally difficult, and there is no predictable direction for the misordering errors. Therefore, comparing memory for an arbitrary sequence of an unordered script vs an ordered script, the best recall for order (or serial position) should be for actions from ordered scripts whose position in the arbitrary sequence correspond to their position in the canonical script. Intermediate serial-position recall should occur for any actions from unordered scripts. Least accurate serial-position recall should occur for actions from ordered scripts whose position in the arbitrary sequence differs from their position in the canonical script.

A first experimental attempt to create this effect produced negative results. We scrambled all 12 actions in ordered scripts, had subjects study them, and then reconstruct their serial order from memory. Their reconstructions were almost random, with none of the predicted drift toward the canonical order. The subjects told us what was wrong with this procedure, namely, they remembered that the script actions were "all mixed up" in the to-be-learned orders, so if they forgot the presented random order they still tried to reconstruct an order which preserved the "all mixed up" property.

We avoided this task strategy in the experiment reported below by presenting the scripts predominantly in their canonical order but with a few events rather far out of order. The hope was that if subjects forgot the order, they could still use the fact that the listed actions were predominantly in their canonical order to guide their reconstruction. This reconstructive guide would help rather than hinder the directional errors of interest.

## Method

*Subjects*. The subjects were 12 Stanford undergraduates participating to fulfill a service requirement for their Introductory Psychology class. They were tested in groups of four, three, three, one, and one, sitting around a large table. The experiment took about 45 min.

*Materials*. We composed five ordered scripts and five unordered scripts, each 12 sentences long. The ordered scripts were Birthday Party, Shopping for a Coat, Playing Football, Going to a Movie, and Attending a Lecture. The unordered scripts were Cleaning House, Shopping at the Supermarket, Veteran's Day Parade, Main Ring at the Circus, and Mechanic's Check-up on Car. The Cleaning House and Birthday Party scripts were used alternately as primacy and recency buffers in the memory task, and data from them were discarded by plan. Each ordered script was paired with an unordered mate and the two scripts were yoked together in the sense of appearing close together in all input schedules. Also, an out-of-order action in the ordered script was compared in reconstruction to its yoked action presented in the same position in the unordered script.

The subjects read the 12 ordered actions in each of the 10 lists, then later tried to reconstruct all their orders. Setting aside the two lists assigned as primacy and recency buffers, the input position of the eight middle lists was counterbalanced over subjects by using four different input sequences. Thus any given list (e.g., circus) appeared in Positions 2 or 3, 4 or 5, 6 or 7, and 8 or 9 for three subjects at each position.

The position of the 12 actions within the ordered scripts was assigned by the following procedure. From the canonical order four actions were selected at random for each script to be interchanged in their positions (the other eight remained fixed in their normal positions). A Latin Square was used to produce four orders of these selected four actions: one was the normal order and the other three became unique misorderings. Each of the three misordered versions was used with four different subjects. The summed number of steps required to move all of the four interchanged actions within a story back to their canonical positions averaged 13.5. The to-be-learned order of the unordered scripts was determined by random numbers; only one order was learned by all subjects.

The 12 action statements were typed on 12 3 x 5 in. cards and a title card was placed at the front of the deck. The experimenter arranged the cards in each deck in the order to be learned by the subject using that deck.

*Procedure*. Subjects were seated and instructed that they were to study 10 ordered lists of 12 actions per list, each typed on a deck of cards with a title at the front. They were told to remember the specific order in which the cards were arranged, so that they would be able to reconstruct that order exactly when they were given the scrambled deck of cards during later testing.

Ten decks of cards were then placed before each subject in the sequence he was to study them. They were in four colors to help him keep his place as he moved from one deck to another. The subject looked at the title card at the front of a given deck for 5 sec, then turned over the cards within that deck, one at a time, studying each statement for 5 sec paced by the experimenter tapping on the table using a stopwatch. Memory for the order of the statements was emphasized.

After all 10 lists had been studied, the experimenter thoroughly shuffled each deck of 12 action statements while instructing the subject on the serial reconstruction task. The subject was to take the shuffled cards of a deck, lay the 13 cards (12 plus a title) on the table before her, rearrange the cards into the serial order she believed she had studied (guessing when necessary), and finally record on a protocol sheet her reconstructed order using random numbers on the back of the cards for identifying them. The 10 lists were reconstructed in the same sequence as they had been studied. Testing took about 30 min.

In the statistical analysis, subjects and the four scripts within each condition served as random effects, whereas the type of script (ordered or unordered) and the sequence of presentation were fixed effects. We scored each sentence on the basis of its absolute position in the reconstructed order, comparing this to its position in the studied list and, if possible, to its canonical position in the underlying script.

## Results

Comparing the probabilities that items are remembered in the same absolute position as their presentation, the predicted pattern emerges. Within ordered scripts, actions presented in their canonical location were remembered 50% at exactly that location, actions presented away from their canonical location were remembered only 18% at the presented location. For comparison, actions of the unordered (control) scripts were remembered 30% of the time at their presented position. For statistical analysis, the unordered script actions were divided into one set of four yoked to the four misordered actions in the ordered scripts and the remaining set of eight. We tested the interaction of ordered vs unordered scripts with correctly located vs mislocated actions. As the percentages above indicate, this interaction was highly significant [$F'(1.7) = 19.3$, $p < .005$]. That is, in ordered scripts, misordered actions were recalled less accurately than their yoked actions (in unordered scripts), but ordered actions were recalled more accurately than their yoked actions.

Next, we examined whether misordered actions of ordered scripts drifted back towards their canonical position during reconstruction. Each reconstructed item was given a score indicating the number of steps (serial positions) it had moved from its presented position in the direction toward its canonical location. (Movements in the opposite direction received negative signs). The summed displacements of the four misordered items towards their canonical positions averaged 6.44 steps (out of 13.5 possible), whereas the comparable sum for the unordered control items was 0.92 steps. These differ reliably [$F'(1,5) = 8.74$, $p < .05$]. Thus, the misordered items move about 48% of the distance towards their normal location in the underlying script.

We may conclude that the canonical order of a memory script helps people learn the order of any new textual instantiation which preserves the canonical order but hinders them if the new instantiation has misorderings. The script order in memory acts as a source of proactive interference or as a source for guessing when the presented order has been forgotten.

Texts that relate events out of their natural order, as we have done here, are not uncommon in literature. A storyteller is not constrained to preserve natural order in his narrative rendering. Some styles of storytelling, such as sports reporting (football, baseball), even have a standard misordering; one first tells the final score of the game, then recounts the significant events (e.g., big plays, penalties) in order of their importance, then perhaps recites the temporal succession of scoring plays. Thus, in telling some stories, we sometimes describe events in a manner other than reciting their temporal order, much as was done in the present study.

### Experiment 6: Script expectations and comprehension time

We have assumed that when an abstract script is aroused, it activates the memory nodes representing the script actions. Each such memory node is similar to a logogen (see Morton, 1969) which accepts and accumulates activation ("evidence") from prior context and from present sensory input. Activation of the overall script brings the activation level of script actions close to the firing threshold. Hence, relatively little sensory evidence directed to an action node is required in order for it to be perceived. Also, expected stimulus patterns should be identified rapidly because their logogens have been brought near firing threshold by the context alone.

The script-to-subactions activation just mentioned is a mechanism for creating generalized expectations; that is, the person expects other script actions to occur. A more refined proposal hypothesizes more specific activation local to an action node that has just been instantiated (i.e., read in the text). Specifically, this hypothesizes that the local activation caused by reading a given script action spreads to neighboring script actions in a forward direction, causing them in particular to be expected. We will call this the Local Spread hypothesis.

One method for testing this hypothesis compares the time a person takes to comprehend a sentence that is expected to one that is not. The method relies on the assumption that a sentence is perceived and understood more readily if it is expected (e.g., Haviland & Clark, 1974). The Local Spread hypothesis implies that a script line in a text should be read and comprehended more quickly if it is preceded in the text by a statement referring to an action that just precedes it in the underlying script. The text statement just preceding the target statement will be called the "priming statement" or "prime" for the target. The Local Spread hypothesis predicts that target comprehension time should be shorter the closer in the underlying script is the preceding action given as a prime and the greater the number of preceding primes.

This hypothesis and derivation was first thought of by Abelson and Reder, and they performed experiments (unpublished; Note 1) to investigate it. One experiment was inconclusive and the other gave mainly negative evidence against the Local Spread hypothesis.

We were unaware of these experiments when we planned and conducted the experiment below, looking for a distance effect. Our procedure differed from that of Abelson and Reder, and was somewhat more successful in getting the subject "farther into the scripts" before the target probe occurred.

## Method

*Materials*. The script versions used were 18 from Experiments 3 and 4, which were three instances of six different abstract scripts, each text being eight statements long. Within each text the fourth and the seventh statements served as critical test sites. These were edited to be 12 words long. The construction of the texts and the test sites relative to the underlying script are illustrated in Figure 5. Every three subjects were tested with a different selection of statements (version) from each script, comprising the columns of Figure 5. The plus marks in the columns indicate the statements presented, always in the first-to-last script order. The symbols $A_1$ through $A_{12}$ represent events of a hypothetical underlying script. The selected test sites in this instance are the sixth and eleventh elements of the underlying scripts. For different text versions the critical test sites are immediately preceded by a statement which, in the alleged underlying script, was either one, two, or three steps back ("distance"). Within a list, the priming distance at the second test site was different than that at the first site. Across the 18 lists for a given subject, the first and second sites were preceded six times each by priming sentences one, two or three steps back. The last test site was never the last line of the text or the script.

After composing these texts we used the chunk (scene) norms of Experiment 2, to score whether the priming and target actions were within the same chunk, or were one or two chunks apart. The average chunk distances for Steps 1, 2, and 3 were 0.50, 0.50, and 1.08, respectively. Thus, chunk distance increases monotonically along with number of actions between prime and target statements.

*Procedure.* The texts were presented one line at a time on a 9.5 x 7 in. cathode ray tube (Hazeltine Model 1) connected to a Nova 820 laboratory computer. The subject pressed a button as soon as she read and understood each sentence. The button press removed the sentence and 1 sec later the next sentence was displayed. Comprehension time was defined as the time from the display of a sentence to the button press removing it. Subjects were unaware that their reading time per sentence was being recorded. To provide a reason for reading the sentences, subjects were told we were interested in how people make up titles to characterize stories. Our subjects thus made up an interesting title for each text as it was read. They wrote down their title when a message signaled the end of the text. This procedure enforced a delay of 15 to 30 sec between scripts. After writing their title, to start the next text, subjects pressed the button which displayed a warning asterisk and 1 sec later the first sentence appeared. Subjects read the texts combined with the step sizes of the primes in one of 18 different orders over the experiment, with three subjects per order.

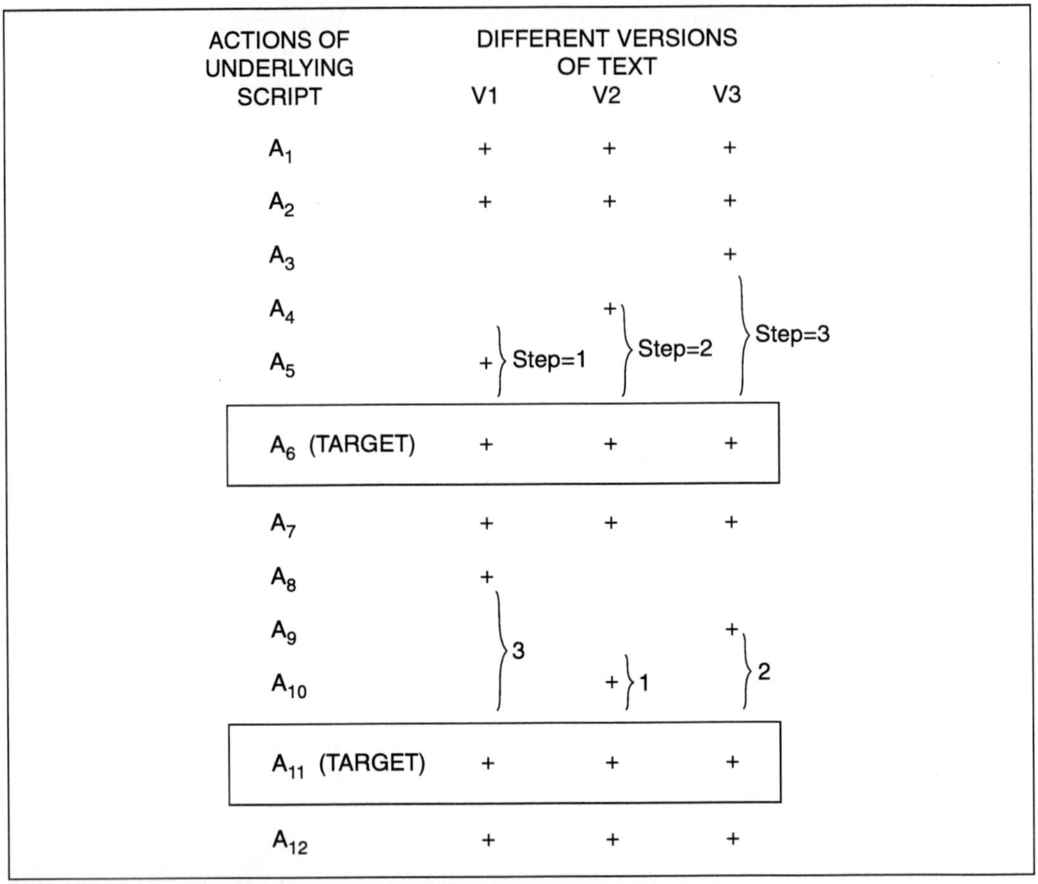

**Figure 5     Schema for materials used in Experiment 5**

*Subjects*. The subjects were 54 Stanford University undergraduates, half fulfilling an Introductory Psychology requirement and half recruited for pay. They were run in groups of one to three at separate computer terminals. Each subject sat at a table with her CRT screen about 18 in. away.

## Results

The primary result is that a Step-1 prime produced faster comprehension of the target sentence than did Step-2 and Step-3 primes. The reaction times in msec are 2600 for Step-1, 2730 for Step-2, and 2681 for Step-3. The difference in the means is statistically significant $[F(2, 106) = 3.43, p < .05]$. (Materials were nested within subjects by design so that $F$ is the correct test here even with materials as a random effect). There is a significant difference between Step-1 and Step-2 $[F(1,53) = 5.93, p < .05]$; but not between Step-3 and the other two. Inspection shows the distance effect to be small and nonmonotonic. We will return to discussing this later.

The other significant effect in the experiment is that comprehension time is slower for the later (seventh line) location (2818 msec) than for the early (fourth line) location

(2424). This is highly significant [$F(2,53) = 51.39$, $p < .001$]; however, the location effect does not interact with the priming distance effect reported above. Although the target sentences in these two locations, had been equated for number of words, we noted that they unfortunately differed in the number of syllables per sentence. In fact, when the reading time per syllable is calculated, the location effect reverses, with the first location having a comprehension time of 170 msec per syllable and the second location 152 msec per syllable [$F(1,53) = 16.71$, $p < .001$]. If syllables rather than words are the proper units for reading, this faster comprehension of the second location provides some support for the accumulation of activation across script lines.

The results show facilitation of reading at only the immediately adjacent action, without a graded effect of distance in the underlying script. While there is doubtless general activation of the whole script as individual events are read, the extra "local spread" of activation from the just-read action appears extremely local. The absence of a graded effect cannot be explained by appeal to a "chunk-distance" measure since that increases monotonically with our measure of number of intervening actions.

## Discussion

Our failure to find a graded distance effect can be interpreted in several ways. One view suggests that the failure can be laid to uncontrolled variations in literary style or conversational fittingness of the texts with increasing prime-to-target distances. Some gaps are simply too large to bridge meaningfully; others convey the wrong impression of what is going on; others sound stilted or silly. Although we tried to avoid such stylistic blemishes in our materials, we cannot guarantee that style effects were inconsequential relative to the distance effects of interest.

An alternative interpretation is that there is no graded distance effect. After hearing an action, the reader expects its immediate successor more than others, but his within-script expectations are not further differentiated than that. Apparently, the latest version of the SAM program for applying scripts to texts (see Cullingford, Note 2; Schank & Yale A. I. Project, Note 4) has a predictive mechanism that operates in just this way.

A third view of the results is to suppose that a script is such a complex web of interconnected parts that the representation of temporal distance between actions bears little relationship to the node distance between them in the network. For example, scripts often have some causal or contingent connections which bridge large temporal gaps between early events and much later events. Thus, the size of a tip the customer leaves depends upon the quality of service he received much earlier in the restaurant script; what specifically the dentist does to you depends on your specific reason for visiting him. Further, two temporally distant actions may be close in node distance because they involve the same props and actors, whereas temporally close events may be farther apart in node space in that they refer to different roles, props, and within-script locations. Taking this view of scripts, then, it is misguided to expect local spread of activation to be indexed simply by temporal distance between two events.

### Experiment 7: Remembering deviations from scripts

Although we are investigating script-based texts, we should remember that a script does not make an interesting story; in fact, it is miserably dull, containing all the predictable details of an activity. Script recital violates a conversational postulate that enjoins speakers and writers to be informative and not overly redundant. People read such boring texts only to assuage some psychology experimenter.

While actions within a script may be referred to in real stories, they serve only as a background or context within which something more interesting happens in the foreground. Thus, we may recite a restaurant script to note that while waiting for our food, a man at the next table had an epileptic seizure; or we note that when the soup arrived it had a fly in it, etc. Let us call these "interruptions" in the predictable flow of the normal script. The next experiment asks how well people remember such interruptions in comparison to the script actions.

Schank and Abelson (1977) noted several types of script interruptions called *obstacles, errors,* and *distractions*. In obstacles, some enabling condition for an imminent action is missing (e.g., You can't read the French menu), so some corrective action is taken (e.g., ask the waiter to translate for you). In errors, a script action leads to an unexpected or inappropriate outcome. For example, you order a hamburger, but the waitress brings a hot dog. The standard corrective action is to repeat the action: order the hamburger again. Distractions are unexpected events or states which set up new goals for the actor, taking him temporarily or permanently outside the script. For example, the waiter may spill soup on the customer, initiating a visit to the restroom for cleaning up.

Our intuition is that such interruptions will be remembered better than the routine script actions because they will appear subjectively more important and so will occasion more attention or deeper processing. The interruption is an unpredicted event, and so a script-based "von Restorf" effect (i.e., better memory for the surprising event) could be predicted. Further, from the viewpoint of the reader, the interruption seems to be the only "point" of the story.

Besides interruptions other extraneous statements can occur in script-based texts. These include irrelevant statements about attributes of the props or characters of the script, or the thoughts and feelings of the character which have no essential place in the causal flow of events. An irrelevancy would seem to be something that can occur in parallel with essential actions without impeding the flow of events. Thus, while looking at the menu the central character may notice the print-type, or notice the waitress' red hair, etc. Since such irrelevancies neither aid nor block the goal-directed actions of a script, we would normally expect them to be remembered very poorly. Now, there surely are some irrelevancies that refer to events or properties which, if they were experienced, would have a vivid impact, and would be well remembered (e.g., "The waitress was stark naked."). The experiment below side-steps this issue by having the irrelevancies as well as the script interruptions be relatively pallid and routine.

To summarize, then, we predict that interruptions will be remembered better than script actions and that irrelevancies will be remembered less than either.

## Method

*Materials*. Six script-based stories were written about making coffee, attending a lecture, getting up in the morning, attending a movie, visiting a doctor, and dining at a restaurant. The texts were 22 to 26 sentences long. Setting aside the first few and last few sentences, the remainder of each text was divided into three groups of five to seven actions (avoiding divisions within a chunk). In each group we inserted one irrelevant remark and one interruption. Across the three groups within a text, there was one obstacle, one error, and one distraction. Across scripts, the six possible orders of the three interruption-types occurred once each. Thus, each text contained one each of an obstacle, error, and distraction, three irrelevancies, and about 10 relevant script sections. Each story was titled, and all six were stapled into a booklet.

*Procedure*. The subjects read the booklet of six stories for 5 min total, with only general comprehension instructions. They engaged in an intervening task for about 10 min as part of another study that involved rating the comprehensibility of unrelated sentences. After the rating task, subjects were asked to recall the stories in writing as close to verbatim as possible. They were cued with each story title and given as much time as needed (maximum of 5 min per story).

*Subjects*. The subjects were 24 Stanford undergraduates either fulfilling an Introductory Psychology requirement or receiving payment. They were run in groups of two to eight.

## Results

The recall protocols were scored for presence of each text proposition (basically, clauses). The average percentages recalled were: interruptions 53%, script-actions 38%, and irrelevancies 32%. The interruptions are recalled reliably more than are the script-actions, with fixed effect $[F(1,21) = 55.26]$ and mixed effect $[F'(1,12) = 21.30$, both $p$'s $< .001]$. The script-actions are recalled somewhat better than the irrelevancies [with fixed $F(1,21) = 6.36, p < .05$ but mixed $F'(1,8) = 1.64, p > .10]$. The results are as predicted; interruptions were remembered best as though they were the point of the story, and irrelevancies were remembered poorest.

Calculating the percentages recalled of the three types of interruptions, obstacles were highest (60%), then the distractions (56%), with the errors recalled least (42%). Obstacles and distractions do not differ reliably but both are significantly higher than recall of the errors when materials are considered as a fixed effect $[F(1,21)$ for obstacles is 15.11, $p < .001$, and for distractions is 5.86, $p < .05]$. However, the differences are not significant when different scripts are considered as a random effect [obstacles $F'(1,10) = 4.83, p > .05$; and distractions $F'(1,13) = 2.69, p > .10]$. Consequently, we are uncertain whether the recall profile of types of interruptions will generalize across variations in learning materials. Although the interruptions as a whole are recalled better than the script actions as noted above, the recall of the errors does not differ reliably from the recall of the script actions $[F(1,21) = 1.56, p > .10]$.

## Discussion

Recall of interruption types was ordered in the way we expected, with obstacles and distractions being remembered better than errors. In our texts, the errors were "minor": simply incorrect outcomes of events. Obstacles, on the other hand, involved real blocks to the progress of the script; the obstacle stopped the flow of events and had to be dealt with. Distractions were interesting incidents that suspended the script's goal, and temporarily replaced it with a more pressing goal for the character.

We can speculate about how such interruptions would be recorded in the episodic memory trace of the script-based text. The main trace would be the appropriate "Partial Copy" of the underlying script (see Figure 3) with the variables bound as specified by the text. An error is an outcome with an unexpected value inserted into a standard slot in the script. It is as though a prediction of an outcome (a "slot filler") has to be replaced by a different object or value. An obstacle, and the corrective actions it causes, would also be recorded in the episodic script memory, at the script location where it occurred to frustrate a subgoal. A distraction, on the other hand, could be recorded on a separate "goal chart" (see Schank & Abelson, 1977, Ch. 5), with its actions and outcome together with a pointer to the location in the episodic script where the distraction occurred. The timing of most distractions is not linked causally to any specific point in the script (e.g., the person at the next table could have a seizure at any time). Therefore, we might expect subjects to remember the location of distractions within a script-based text more poorly than they would the location of obstacles or errors. A pilot experiment found no tendency for memory to err by mislocating distractions nearer to (rather than farther from) a scene boundary.

### General discussion

We may view our results from two perspectives. The first considers them as empirical investigations of a previously unexplored domain of semantic knowledge; the second assesses their articulation with the general script-theory of Schank and Abelson (1977).

From the empirical perspective, we have explored the properties of scripts considered as concepts about routine activities. Just as concepts like *birds* or *weapons* have culturally agreed upon attributes and instances, so do activities like *eating in a restaurant* or *visiting a doctor*. These activities have conventional roles, props, event-sequences, standard entering conditions, and standard outcomes. Not only did our subjects largely agree on what these are but also on how to segment the event sequences into constituent scenes or chunks. We found that in remembering script-based texts subjects confused what was said with what the script strongly implied. Further, subjects preferred to learn event sequences that preserved the scriptal order. In remembering a script-based text, subjects were best at recalling brief obstacles or distractions which blocked or temporarily suspended pursuit of the script goal, whereas properties or events irrelevant to that goal were least recalled. Such results serve as an opening into empirical explorations of the organization and use of script knowledge in text understanding and recall.

From the theoretical perspective, our results are generally consistent with current script theory (see Cullingford, Note 2; Schank & Abelson, 1977). Some results are not specifically addressed by script theory (e.g., how different instantiations of a script interfere with one another in memory, or how people remember texts with out-of-order actions). Further, our results do not address many problems of language processing which script theory was proposed to solve. The theoretical writings and computer-simulation programs (see Cullingford, Note 2) mainly concern the way scripts act as a predictive context for processing single sentences, for tying together sequences of sentences, and for answering questions about a text (see Lehnert, 1977). For example, for understanding single sentences, an active script will suggest the relevant meanings of ambiguous words, will help establish referents of terms, will merge referents, will fill-in unspecified roles, and will predict likely conceptualizations to follow. The psychological counterparts of such processes probably occur in real-time as sentences are comprehended, and variations in factors affecting them (e.g., the ease of establishing referents) could affect comprehension time. However, except for Experiment 6 which examined within-script gradients of expectancy, we have not investigated how scripts influence comprehension in real-time.

Our results also do not address the extensive theorizing concerning goals and plans that underlays the script concept (see Meehan, Note 3; Schank & Abelson, 1977). Goal issues arise quickly in answering *why* questions about human actors (e.g., "Why did he leave the restaurant before he'd eaten?"). It is not obvious how the methods of experimental psychology can provide much relevant information on such issues beyond that provided by intuition and common sense. In any event, we have not tried to do so here. Because we have not examined issues of real-time comprehension or of goal-based question answering, our results make contact with only a small part of script theory.

### *Unresolved issues about scripts*

Although our results have advanced the case for scripts and we find many attractive features of script theory, we would be remiss not to balance the picture by pointing out a few of the unresolved issues or critical questions about script theory. These represent conceptual puzzles that are on the research agenda.

A first question requiring some answer concerns how to elicit script knowledge. In Experiment 1 we instructed people in detail how to tell us about the major events of a routine activity and we obtained reasonable results; but the results surely will vary with the way instructions are phrased. Rather than recall, our subjects could have been asked to identify or recognize script-relevant actions from a large pool presented to them. There is little guarantee that all methods will yield the same conclusions. A problem is that recall or report methods can give only script knowledge that is accessible to conscious introspection. But just as a fish fails to report that he is surrounded by water, so do people surely have much tacit, nonintrospectible knowledge about stereotyped procedures and activities that they do not or cannot report (see Goffman, 1959 for details of unconscious social conventions). For example, traditional Japanese rarely think to mention that one takes off his shoes before entering a Japanese restaurant, though that feature immediately strikes a Westerner as unusual. Similarly, our Restaurant script does not mention when it is proper to sit at a table with a stranger, or how close the waiter stands while taking your order. In reciting a script, people assume and do not report tacit conventions regarding physical layouts and interpersonal commerce, even though such conventions are clearly exhibited when they enact the script.

This latter split between enacting vs verbalizing a script raises the more general question of how we are to decide whether someone is behaving according to a script and, if so, which script it is. Clearly someone can go through the motions of a script enactment without having the knowledge that customarily underlays its performance. Thus, an uneducated person will appear to follow eating protocol at a formal state dinner by imitating those around him, or by following instructions from his dining companion. He is using immediately available cues or rules rather than memories of prior performance or prior rules as his guide. But the cues that control behavior are rarely conspicuous, so we will frequently err in inferring whether someone is following a memory script. Furthermore, we are prone to similar errors in deciding which of several scripts someone is following. Errors are introduced by the loose relation between intentions and actions. The source of errors can be illustrated by considering cases of deceit, con-games, bluffs, and sham put-ons. In competitive situations, which many stories describe, a character may present an appearance or "front" of following one script (designed to mislead his adversary), whereas he is actually following another plan which will give him an advantage. Thus, in football, the quarterback fakes a line plunge before passing, hoping that the defenders will react to the apparent intention and leave themselves open for the pass. Such common examples show the difficulty of identifying which script someone is following from their surface behavior.

A second question about scripts concerns the level of detail that is recorded with each script, and how much of this is called forth when the script is instantiated. For example, in the Restaurant script, what kind of general and specific information is stored about the Service Person? Some features are mandatory (must be a living person), some are optional (male or female), some have a range of permissible values with a prototypical value (e.g., age, with 25–45 years), and others have a range without a clear prototype (e.g., hair color). Is all this information stored with the script and brought forth when it is instantiated? Possibly not. Rather the script may only refer to an empty waiter or waitress role, which then points to a mental "dictionary" or lexicon which holds context-free information about these concepts and their prototypes. In instantiating the script, the features of the prototype will be "loosely bound" in the sense that the text can readily replace a guessed value.

A problem with separating the script from the lexicon is that we often want the two sources to interact and exchange expectations. For example, if at lunch we discover our Server is a (nude) topless waitress, we want inferences from that to propagate back to selection of a specific track (type) for the Restaurant script, namely, that we are in a Go-Go bar. Similarly, a fast-food restaurant and a haute cuisine French restaurant have different Server prototypes. It would seem therefore that each track of a script must have an associated file of prototypical values.

Schank and Abelson (1977) introduce the idea of a *track* to refer to a distinct subclass of script situations. For example, for the eating script one has a track for eating various types of meals and snacks at McDonalds, at school, at a coffeehouse, a picnic, a hiking camp, a church benefit, an Algerian Casbah, on a train or airplane, and so on to the limits of his experience. Mention of each situation evokes memories which specify contextually appropriate prototypes for various roles, props, and events. But, one may ask, if episodic memories about track-experiences provide this information, of what value is the general Restaurant script? Presumably, the general script identifies the cluster of common or frequent features of the tracks it subsumes (e.g., there is an exchange of money for prepared food). By virtue of these clusters, to say that one ate in a restaurant is to set up many common expectations in the listener.

A third problem for script or frame theories is to account for how special or novel contexts propagate throughout the script to modify the appropriate details. For example, if we watch theater actors in a play pretend to eat in a restaurant, or if a child enacts with dolls what goes on in a restaurant (as did the preschoolers of Nelson, 1978), how does the context of that pretend world get passed along to modify this instantiation of the real-world script? We do not expect the pretend food to be hot, or the money to be real, or there to be a real kitchen off-stage, etc. The issue is to account theoretically for the way a context like "theater world" or "toy world" selectively cancels certain aspects of the script but not others. The issue is similar to how we know what properties to ascribe to a fake duck or a dollhouse.

A fourth problem for script theory (or any schema theory) is to decide at what level of abstraction the memory script is to be used and modified. For example, suppose you read a text about visiting a specific cardiologist. How are we to understand and record that text in memory? Is that an instance of the script called "visiting a cardiologist," or a doctor, or any health professional, or any professional, or any person, or the script called "going to place X and talking to person Y"? The concepts are all connected in a hierarchy, and properties true of an activity described at one level are also true of subordinate scripts in the subset tree. But when a text calls up a script from the reader's memory to begin instantiating its slots, at what level is that script?

A defensible answer is that successive clues from the text are sorted through a discrimination net to retrieve the most detailed script available in memory to encode the current text or situation. A problem with such a system is that according to schema theory the understander must commit himself to some initial schema in order to understand sentences; yet the most diagnostic information may not appear in the text until later. That is, one can be misled down "garden path" stories. When gross errors of predictions are encountered, the system must be able to discard the currently active schema, substitute another, and then try to retrieve earlier inputs and reinterpret them in terms of the newly suggested schema. Thus, what started out as an "eat-in restaurant" script may turn into an "attend political fund-raiser banquet" or a "deliver food to restaurant" script. Any strongly predictive ("top-down") understander system such as script theory must have ways to modify a current script, to reject and replace it when it becomes inappropriate.

An alternative view of the comprehension process is that the reader progressively builds up a model or image of the situation the text is about; he conjectures an initial ill-defined model from the initial sentences, then uses successive lines of the text either to fill in the empty slots of that model or to revise it dynamically (e.g., see Feldman, 1975; Collins, Brown, Larkin, 1978). In such a dynamic process, the important connections would not be specifiable in advance, the appropriate model for a text would be arrived at by successive revisions, by refinements according to constraints of the text, by applying problem solving methods rather than by selecting a preformed template from a storeroom of static scripts. This dynamic modeling approach would claim that each situation is somewhat unique, with novel combinations of features and happenings, and that it is unlikely that a limited file of scripts would "cover" or subsume many particular instances. The script-file could appear to cover many instances only by ignoring their special or deviant features, or by endlessly amending or specializing the general script to describe the unique cases (see the "weird list" of Schank & Abelson, 1977, p. 166). Perhaps it would have been more efficient to combine information from several different scripts to describe the cases directly. But then, why bother to have static scripts to do this rather than just a network of concepts?

A fifth problem for script theory is to specify an induction algorithm by which new scripts can be learned from experience. If new situations can only be understood as instances of preformed scripts (perhaps with some deviations), how then can any new script be learned? The theory now seems to encompass *specialization* as a way to learn, as when we learn the MacDonald's track as a special case of the general restaurant script. In turn, the restaurant script could be learned as a special instrument to enable the basic action of eating. Similarly, attending concerts, lectures, museums, and movies would be specialized instruments to the basic action of attending to (perceiving) something (see the semantically primitive acts enumerated by Schank, 1975, p. 40ff). This view suggests that many scripts will be clustered around the primitive action they enable. Thus, the restaurant, bar, and kitchen scripts cluster around ingestion; the bus, train, airplane, and bicycle scripts cluster around physically moving oneself, and so on. The elaboration of a given primitive action (say, eating) would seem to develop by specialization and by noting recurrent patterns of features (see, e.g., the concept learner of Hunt, Marin, & Stone, 1966). The result would be a tree or discrimination net in memory, with branches encoding different locations and styles of eating (the "tracks" of Schank & Abelson, 1977). The details of growing such a net have not been worked out.

Related to the issues of abstraction and learning, a sixth issue for script or frame theory is deciding where a new fact is to be stored and which scripts are to have access to it (see J. R. Anderson, 1976, p. 446). Suppose while at a lecture I learn that the use of saccharin sweeteners can be harmful to my health. I gain nothing by simply recording that fact in my "Lecture" script. I must record it in such manner to make it accessible to my "Bar" script to avoid drinking Thintonic, to my "Coffeehouse" script to avoid putting it in my coffee, to my "Birthday Party" script to avoid giving dietetic candies as presents to my friends, and so on. We would like the fact to be available diffusely across all relevant contexts, but that would seem difficult to achieve if it is buried in one particular script. Conceptual networks provide this sort of diffuse broadcasting of a new fact across multiple contexts. Perhaps script theory can gain some of this generality by altering facts in the lexicon (e.g., about drinks or foods that involve saccharin), so that all scripts using tokens of that lexical entry could be . modified if that value is retrieved when the script is next executed. But it is not obvious how to do this in an efficient way.

A final problem for script and frame theories is that they currently have no clear way to deal with simultaneous execution of several scripts which have strong interactions. SAM and other script implementations (Cullingford, Note 2) seem to deal with one script and motive at a time, whereas people frequently act from multiple motives and within multiple constraints. To illustrate, suppose two businessmen who are chess enthusiasts are riding together on a train to a business convention. While eating in the dining car, they play a game of chess and also negotiate a business contract with one another. These men are engaging in at least five scripts more or less at the same time (or in rapid alternation): going to a convention, riding a train, eating dinner, playing chess, and negotiating a business contract. The activities have various embedding relations to one another; the train ride is the first part of the attending convention script, the dinner script is embedded within the train script, and the chess and negotiations proceed in parallel and embedded within the dinner script.

A language understander must be able to refer an incoming sentence to the appropriate script, and this could be done reasonably well by keeping a queue of foregrounded (active) scripts to which each input would be compared for a relevant match. It would not be difficult in current script programs to interrupt a script, save your location there, go do an embedded script for a while, save your location there, return to the desired location in the first script and proceed from there for awhile, then return to the second script, and so on. What is harder to model are interactions between the goals and resource-allocations among several simultaneous scripts. Thus, the outcome of the business negotiations can influence who pays the bill for dinner, or the seller may make low-quality moves to lose in chess in hopes of influencing the business deal, or at the most delicate decision-point in the business negotiations the buyer now reveals a brilliant chess move to divert the seller's attention from the negotiations. These are cases in which a script action is performed for other than its usual reasons; they satisfy motives other than the standard ones, and along with bluffs and deceptions they comprise some of the role-taking complexities of real human commerce.

In closing this discussion, let us repeat that we consider scripts as a powerful and potentially valuable theoretical approach. The unresolved issues and theoretical puzzles raised here are not unique to script theory, but to any well-specified schema theory. We raise these issues to suggest the direction of future research.

## Acknowledgements

We wish to thank Larry Meyers, Gail Meyers, Justine Owens, and Michael Gardner for assistance with various portions of this research. This research was supported by Grant MH-13905 to the first author from the National Institutes of Mental Health. Dr. Turner was supported by a fellowship from the Australian Educational Council.

## Reference notes

1. Personal communications from Lynne Reder, March, 1977: and Bob Abelson, January, 1978.

2. Cullingford, R. E. *Script application: Computer understanding of newspaper stories.* Research Report No. 116, Department of Computer Science, Yale University, 1978.

3. Meehan, J. *The metanovel: Writing stories by computer.* Unpublished doctoral dissertation, Yale University, 1976.

4. Schank, R. C., & Yale A. I. Project. *SAM–A story understander*. Research Report No. 43, Department of Computer Science, Yale University, 1975.

## References

Ammon, P. R. (1968) The perception of grammatical relations in sentences. *Journal of Verbal Learning and Verbal Behavior, 7*, 869–875.

Anderson, I. R. (1976) *Language, memory, and thought.* Hillsdale, NJ: Lawrence Erlbaum Associates.

Anderson, R. C. (1971) The notion of schemata and the educational enterprise: General discussion of the conference. In R. C. Anderson, R. T. Spiro, & W. E. Montague (Eds.) *Schooling and the acquisition of knowledge.* Hillsdale, NJ: Lawrence Erlbaum Associates.

Atkinson, R. C. & Juola, J. R. Factors influencing speed and accuracy in word recognition. In S. Kornblum (Ed.) *Attention and performance.* IV. New York: Academic Press, 1973.

Battig, W. R. & Montague, W. E. (1969) Category norms for verbal items in 56 categories: A replication and extension of the Connecticut norms. *Journal of Experimental Psychology, 80,* Part 2, 1–46.

Bower, G. H. (1975) Cognitive psychology: An introduction. In W. K. Estes (Ed.) *Handbook of learning and cognitive processes* (Vol. 1). Hillsdale, NJ: Lawrence Erlbaum Associates.

Clark, H. H. (1973) The language-as-fixed-effect fallacy: A critique of language statistics in psychological research. *Journal of Verbal Learning and Verbal Behavior, 12,* 335–339.

Clark, H. H. & Clark, E. V. (1977) *Psychology and language.* New York: Harcourt Brace, Jovanovich.

Clark, H. H., Cohen, J., Smith. J. E. K. & Keppel, G. (1976) Discussion of Wike and Church's comments. *Journal of Verbal Learning and Verbal Behavior, 15,* 257–266.

Collins. A., Brown. J. S. & Larkin, K. M. (1978) Inference in text understanding. In R. J. Spiro, B. C. Bruce, & W. F. Brewer (Eds.), *Theoretical issues in reading comprehension.* Hillsdale, N.J.: Lawrence Erlbaum Associates.

Feldman, J. (1975) *Bad-mouthing frames.* In R. Schank & B. L. Nash-Webber (Eds.) *Theoretical issues in natural language processing.* Conference Proceedings: MIT.

Goffman, E. (1959) *The presentation of self in everyday life.* Garden City, NY: Doubleday.

Goodman. A. I. (1970) *A theory of human action.* Englewood Cliffs, NJ: Prentice Hall.

Grice, H. P. (1975) Logic and conversation. In P. Cole & J. L. Morgan (Eds.) *Syntax and semantics* (Vol. 3): *Speech acts.* New York: Seminar Press.

Haviland, S. E. & Clark. H. H. (1974) What's new? Acquiring new information as a process in comprehension. *Journal of Verbal Learning and Verbal Behavior, 13,* 512–521.

Hunt. E. B., Marin, J. & Stone, P. (1966) *Experiments in induction.* New York: Academic Press.

Jarvella, R. J. (1970) Effects of syntax on running memory span for connected discourse. *Psychonomic Science, 19,* 235–236.

Jarvella, R. J. (1971) Syntactic processing of connected speech. *Journal of Verbal Learning and Verbal Behavior, 10,* 409–416.

Kintsch, W. (1974) *The representation of meaning in memory*. Hillsdale, NJ: Lawrence Erlbaum Associates.

Kintsch, W., Mandel. T. S. & Kazminsky, E. (1977) Summarizing scrambled stories. *Memory and Cognition*, 5, 547–532.

Lehnert, W., (1977) Human and computational question answering. *Cognitive Science*, 1, No. 1, 47–73.

Mandler. J. M. (1978) A code in the node. *Discourse Processes*, 1, 14–35.

Miller, G. A., Galanter. E. & Pribram, K. H. (1960) *Plans and the structure of behavior*. New York: Holt, Rinehart & Winston.

Minsky, M. (1975) A framework for representing knowledge. In P. H. Winston (Ed.) *The psychology of computer vision,* New York: McGraw-Hill.

Morton. J. (1969) The interaction of information in word recognition. *Psychological Review*, 76, 165–178.

Pew, R. W. (1974) Human perceptual-motor performance. In B. H. Kantowitz (Ed.) *Human information processing: Tutorials in performance and cognition.* Hillsdale, NJ: Lawrence Erlbaum Assoc..

Roediger, H. L., III. (1974) Inhibiting effects of recall. *Memory and Cognition*, 2, 261–269.

Rosch, E. & Mervis, C. B. (1975) Family resemblances: studies in the internal structure of categories. *Cognitive Psychology*, 7, 573–605.

Rosch, E. R., Mervis, C. B., Gray, W. D., Johnson, D. M. & Boyer-Graem, P. (1976) Basic objects in natural categories. *Cognitive Psychology*, 8, 387–439.

Rumelhart, D. E. (1975) Notes on a schema for stories. In D. G. Bobrow & A. Collins (Eds.) *Representation and understanding: Studies in cognitive science*. New York: Academic Press.

Rumelhart, D. E. (1977) Understanding and summarizing brief stories. In D. LaBerge & J. Samuels (Eds.) *Basic processes in reading and comprehension.*

Schank. R. C. (1975) *Conceptual information processing*. Amsterdam: North-Holland.

Schank, R. C. & Abelson, R. P. (1977) *Scripts, plans, goals and understanding*. Hillsdale, NJ: Lawrence Erlbaum Associates.

Smith, E. E., Rips, L. J. & Shoben, E. I. (1974) Semantic memory and psychological semantics. In G. H. Bower (Ed.) *The psychology of learning and motivation* (Vol 8). New York: Academic Press.

Stein, N. L. & Glenn, C. G. (1978) An analysis of story comprehension in elementary school children. In R. Freedle (Ed.) *Multidisciplinary perspectives in discourse comprehension.* Hillsdale, NJ: Lawrence Erlbaum Associates.

Wike, E. L. & Church, J. D. (1976) Comments on Clark's "The language-as-fixed-effect fallacy." *Journal of Verbal Learning and Verbal Behavior*, 15, 241–255.

Winston, P. H. (1977) *Artificial intelligence*. Reading MA: Addison-Wesley.

Zadah, L. (1965) Fuzzy sets. *Information and Control*, 8, 338–353.

# 3. Psychological Status of the Script Concept

## Robert P. Abelson

*There has been growing interest within several subfields of psychology in the schematic nature of mental representations of real-world objects and events. One simple form of schema is the* script, *embodying knowledge of stereotyped event sequences. This article traces applications of the script concept in artificial intelligence, cognitive psychology, and social psychology. Scripts are compared and contrasted with related concepts such as habits, roles, and games. The suggested theoretic function of the script concept is to unify central notions in learning, developmental, clinical, social, and cognitive psychology. The present concept, while still incompletely articulated, offers encouragement toward such a unification. Areas of accumulating empirical evidence and of needed theoretical extension of the script concept are indicated.*

Recently, considerable psychological interest has developed in abstract knowledge structures or *schemata* (Cantor & Mischel, 1979; Mandler, 1978; Markus, 1977; Neisser, 1976; Nisbett & Ross, 1980; Rumelhart & Ortony, 1977; Taylor & Crocker, 1980; Tesser & Leone, 1977; Tversky & Kahneman, 1977). The concept of the schema is not new in psychology, dating back at least to Piaget (1926) and Bartlett (1932). What is new is the growing influence on the concept of developments in artificial intelligence. The recent focus in artificial intelligence is on ways to program computers to "understand" natural language texts and visual scenes by using higher order knowledge structures (frames, schemata, scripts, etc.) that embody expectations guiding lower order processing of the stimulus complex (Bobrow & Norman, 1975; Minsky, 1975; Schank & Abelson, 1977).

The schema concept has broad potential application in cognitive, social, developmental, and clinical psychology. The influence of artificial intelligence, however, creates some difficulties for psychologists because the methodology of artificial intelligence is unfamiliar and because schemata are "higher level" constructs than those traditionally employed by experimental psychologists. In this article I discuss one type of schema, the *script*. Scripts embody most of the conceptual issues raised by other types of schemata, yet are simple and well-structured enough to permit more focused analysis and experimentation.

### Scripts in artificial intelligence

A useful way to define scripts is in the context of the understanding of prose dealing with mundane events. This is the context Schank and I assumed in a previous work (Schank & Abelson, 1977). The understander is hypothesized to possess conceptual representations of stereotyped event sequences, and these scripts are *activated* when the understander can expect events in the sequence to occur in the text.

Robert P. Abelson: 'Psychological Status of the Script Concept' in *AMERICAN PSYCHOLOGIST* (1981), Vol. 36, No. 7, pp. 715–729. Copyright © 1981 by the American Psychological Association, Inc. Reprinted by permission.

A number of intuitions support these assumptions. Schank and I presented many examples suggesting the psychological reality of scripts. For example, consider the following simple story:

> John was feeling very hungry as he entered the restaurant. He settled himself at a table and noticed that the waiter was nearby. Suddenly, however, he realized that he'd forgotten his reading glasses.

Intuitively, the significance of the glasses lies in John's implied difficulty in reading the menu. No menu has been explicitly mentioned, however, raising the question of where such an expectation comes from. Our answer was that it comes from the "restaurant" script, activated at the first mention of entering the restaurant. That script contains a standard sequence of events characterizing typical activities in a restaurant from the point of view of the customer. Table 1 displays a simplified version of the *ordering scene* from this restaurant script. The odd-looking verbs in the list of actions in Table 1 are the primitive acts in Schank's (1972, 1975) Conceptual Dependency analysis.

**Table 1     The ordering scene of the restaurant script**

| Sequence of events | Action |
|---|---|
| S  MTRANS signal to W | |
| W  PTRANS W to table | S asks for the menu |
| S  MTRANS "need menu" to W | |
| W  PTRANS W to menu | |
| W  ATRANS menu to W | |
| W  PTRANS W to table | W brings the menu |
| W  ATRANS menu to S | |
| S  MTRANS food list to mind | |
| S  MBUILD choice of Food F | S decides what to order |
| S  MTRANS signal to W | |
| W  PTRANS W to table | |
| S  MTRANS "I want F" to W | S tells W |
| W  PTRANS W to C | |
| W  MTRANS (ATRANS F) to C | W tells C |
| C  DO (prepare F script) | |

*Note.* S = customer, W = waiter, F = food, and C = cook; MTRANS = mental transfer, or telling; PTRANS = physical transfer, or the moving of an object or person; ATRANS = abstract transfer, or the giving of an object from someone to someone else; and MBUILD = thinking (roughly speaking).

The successful development of computer programs for understanding simple texts that deal with scripted situations has been reported elsewhere (Schank & Abelson, 1977). In these programs, the input sentences are converted into Conceptual Dependency representation, and when a script is active, each input is examined as a possible *instantiation* of a script event or as something causally linked to one. The first script program in the Yale Artificial Intelligence Project was called SAM (for script applier mechanism; Cullingford, Note 1). It has been applied to real newspaper stories of automobile accidents as well as to the rather artificial restaurant context. Another program named FRUMP (fast reading, understanding, and memory program) takes as its input news items from the United Press International wire and outputs terse summaries of stories falling into 30 or 40 scripted categories, such as earthquakes, military invasions, diplomatic actions, and so on (DeJong, Note 2).

Several years ago I tried to apply script-related constructs in a computer simulation of the belief system of Senator Barry Goldwater (Abelson, 1973). I envisaged a computer program that could be "interviewed" about current events and respond in terms of the senator's foreign policy ideology (Abelson & Reich, 1969; Abelson, Note 3). It seemed to me that the representation of anticipated event sequences was crucial, and I tried to encode scenarios involving military threat, subversion, takeover of governments, and so on. My attempts lacked realism because the program had no representation of very concrete physical meanings. If one were to propose to the program that Fidel Castro might throw eggs at the United States, this would be accepted as a typical Communist provocation similar to the time when Latin American radicals threw eggs at then vice-president Richard Nixon in Venezuela. The program had no notion of how far and for what purpose eggs are thrown, nor of many other appropriateness relations. With the new Yale artificial intelligence programs, however, it is possible to conduct a reasonable typewritten question-and-answer session with a computer preset to respond in the fashion of either a right-wing or a left-wing belief system. Mundane realities are sorted into appropriately scripted contexts. Thus egg throwing, for example, is a possible event in a "political demonstration" script, but a country would not be accepted as a reasonable target for eggs in any script. Details of this program, called POLITICS, are provided by Carbonell (1978).

To summarize these developments, artificial intelligence workers concerned with statements about real-world events find the structures called scripts extremely useful, even indispensable. Events are seen in relation to familiar contexts rather than in isolation, with great savings in computational efficiency and in apparent "understanding."

### Scripts as cognitive structures

Some cognitive psychologists question the independent necessity of the script concept in the process of text understanding. Their argument is that the understander is almost certainly engaged in active inference processes (cf. Anderson & Ortony, 1975; Clark, 1977; Johnson, Bransford, & Solomon, 1973; Kintsch & van Dijk, 1978). However, it is not evident that understanders need to use inferential structures as extensive as scripts. Perhaps they could do as well by relying on *local inferences,* that is, on plausible expectations based on conjunctions of adjacent inputs. A type of local inference often studied by psycholinguists is the *bridging inference,* in which the reader must make implicit links explicit in order to produce connectivity in text. An example (Clark & Clark, 1977) is the following: "John had been murdered. The knife lay nearby" (p. 98). This implies that the knife was the murder weapon. It seems obvious that text understanding involves a (typically large) number of low-level inferences.

Workers in artificial intelligence are indeed aware of many types of inferences (cf. Rieger, 1975), and they are treated differently from the way scripts are treated.

Whatever the complexities of how a computer (or a human) makes inferences, one would certainly not want to say that every time an inference is made, a script is involved. The example above, for instance, ought not to invoke a "knife-murder" script. For a script to have special status as a cognitive structure, therefore, it must embody more than some simple inference rule.

Minimally, a script governs a body of inferences. The restaurant context involves the person's bundle of expectations about food prepared for and served to him or her, about menus, waiters, tips, and the paying of checks. One might perhaps think of this information as a set of *vignettes* (Abelson, 1976). In any case, a script as an expectation bundle might direct cognitive processing toward the appropriate inference. Thus, in the story about the restaurant in which John realizes he has forgotten his reading glasses, the understander can search standard restaurant events or vignettes for something involving reading. Finding "reading the menu" enables the understander to infer that John will be unable to read the menu. The details of this process are not necessarily trivial, but in this view a script is nothing more (nor less) than the simultaneous activation of a set of conceived events, any of which may become involved in local inferences. Anderson (Note 4) has recently obtained good evidence for just such a simultaneous activation process. The priming of one script event from a story leads to especially fast recognition of another script event from that story. A related effect (den Uyl & van Oostendorp, 1980) is that the priming of the script name or *header* leads to faster recognition of script events. In this "weak" concept of scripts, the order in which the events occur is immaterial. If order information is also attached to the bundle of anticipated events, then I speak of the "strong" concept of scripts.

Clearly, some stereotyped sets of events lack consistent sequencing properties. For example, a typical circus performance presents trapeze artists, a lion tamer, jugglers, and so on, but there is no necessary order to the various acts. Still, it seems appropriate to refer to the "circus" script in the weak sense of script. Weak scripts are similar to other types of cognitive schemata that do not use sequence information, such as personality prototypes (e.g., extrovert) that organize expectations about the attributes of people (Cantor & Mischel, 1977). The distinctive aspect of strong scripts is the relevance of learned associations between prior and consequent events. These associations are usually meaningful rather than rote because of causal "enablements" between script events (e.g., in order to read a menu, one must have a menu). A recent study by Black and Bern (Note 5) finds evidence for one of the many possible empirical consequences of meaningful sequential connections. Recall of paired events is better when they are connected causally rather than merely temporally.

If sequence were the only important feature of strong scripts, however, they would be too much like overlearned rote strings such as the alphabet. Even highly stereotyped real-world activities such as going to a restaurant or a laundromat admit many interruptions and interpolations from one occasion to the next. In any realistic script activation, therefore, expectations can be wrong, and the processor must be prepared to deal with script violations. Many of these issues are discussed in Schank and Abelson (1977).

In sum, a script is a hypothesized cognitive structure that when activated organizes comprehension of event-based situations. In its weak sense, it is a bundle of inferences about the potential occurrence of a set of events and may be structurally similar to other schemata that do not deal with events. In its strong sense, it involves expectations about the order as well as the occurrence of events. In the strongest sense of a totally ritualized event sequence (e.g., a Japanese tea ceremony) script predictions become infallible — but this case is relatively rare.

Evidence pertinent to hypothesized properties of scripts is accumulating rapidly. One major test of the power of scripts to organize comprehension is the *gap-filling* phenomenon. First, norms are collected on typical events in script activities such as going to the dentist. Subjects read stories of such scripted activities, with some of the normative events included and others left out. Later comes a recognition test for events actually in the story, in the script but not in the story, or in neither the script nor the story. Results by Bower, Black, and Turner (1979) and Graesser, Woll, Kowalski, and Smith (1980) show a strong tendency toward false recognition of nonmentioned script events.

The tendency to fill in the gaps in incompletely presented scripts is reminiscent of completions of implicit inferences (e.g., Johnson *et al.*, 1973) and of extrapolation from sketchy personality schemata (Cantor & Mischel, 1977). Gap filling is consistent with the hypothesis that people's long-term memory representation of a scripted situation consists of the generic script, modified by explicit memories of unusual events. This (undoubtedly oversimplified) hypothesis has been called the "script pointer plus tag" hypothesis (Graesser, Gordon, & Sawyer, 1979; see also variants in Bower *et al.*, 1979; Schank & Abelson, 1977). It harks back to the Gestalt idea of "schema plus correction (Bartlett, 1932).

Order information is not necessary for gap filling to occur, however. If false recognition of nonpresented events is based on typical script events, all that need be accessed is an unordered event collection. Other tests besides gap filling must be employed to explore the role of sequential organization.

At least three tests have been used. Bower *et al.* (1979) presented script-based stories with some events displaced from their usual sequential positions. These displaced events regressed (about half-way) toward their usual positions when subjects tried to reconstruct the order of the story events. It is clear from work by Galambos and Rips (Note 6) that subjects can agree substantially on an ordering of the events in many scripts, including the ones used by Bower *et al.* The "regression" of displaced events in memory can thus be understood as a compromise in reconstructive memory between the known typical event ordering and the actually presented atypical ordering. This effect is thus similar to the gap-filling phenomenon and is prototypical of the influence of schemata on reconstructive memory, much as Bartlett (1932) hypothesized.

Another conceivable effect of event sequencing is that it might take longer to search from a given event, through a script, to a distant event than it would take to search a nearby event. Lynne Reder and I, in an unpublished study (Abelson & Reder, Note 7), presented subjects with pairs of adjacent or separated script events and measured the time it took subjects to comprehend the second event, as a function of its separation from the first event. We failed to find an effect of separation, and Bower *et al.* (1979) in a similar test found very weak effects of separation.

This suggests that the comprehension of a given script event may not depend on a woodenheaded search through a sequential list of script events. To expect such a linear search process is probably naive. First, events in scripts differ in their *centrality* to the action flow; some events are indispensable to the script and summarize *scenes* consisting of lower level actions. "Ordering the meal" and "eating the meal," for example, are more central than are, say, "discussing the menu" and "lifting the fork." Thus, a linear search through *all* the (mostly low-level) events of a script seems a grossly inefficient process. Indeed in the original formulation of script structures (Schank & Abelson, 1977), there was explicit division of scripts into scenes, and within each scene there was a *main conceptualization* or MAINCON (Cullingford, Note 1). Certain aspects of script processing were hypothesized to be organized around MAINCONS.

There is now some experimental evidence that the centrality of events makes a difference: Central events can be verified faster as belonging to their script than can peripheral events (Galambos & Rips, Note 6), and false recognition memory for events in a script-based story tends to overrepresent central events (Abbott & Black, Note 8).

There is a second, more fundamental objection to the idea that event search in scripts is necessarily linear. It is well-known in artificial intelligence work that sequential searches through memory are inefficient. Two better search methods are the *discrimination net* and *hash coding*. The former is a tree structure governed by tests of particular attributes at each branch point (as in the game "20 Questions"). Hash coding is a device whereby the address at which to find information about an element is given by the code which symbolizes that element for the computer. (As an analogue, imagine that people's names were Dewey decimal numbers indicating where on the library shelf to find their biographies.) There is no reason why human memory searches cannot partake of these computer programming methods or of still other as yet unexplored devices.

There may still be some circumstances in which reaction time effects in script processing would be found to be proportional to event separation. An unpublished experiment by Smith (Note 9) in fact suggests this possibility — when the stimulus materials are confined to MAINCONs. But it is clear that the processing of scripted knowledge by linear sequential search is not at all obligatory, even though subjects "know" the proper ordering of events in strong scripts.

In any case, scripts are rich packages of information, and from a cognitive-experimental point of view, they are useful vehicles for testing general ideas about cognitive schemata. In addition to the research already mentioned, other recent experiments using scripted stimuli have investigated the effects of the inclusion of atypical actions (Graesser *et al.*, 1979; Graesser *et al.*, 1980), of variations in the level of abstraction at which scripts are expressed (Martin, Patterson, & Price, Note 10), and of sharedness of particular scenes between related scripts (Bower *et al.*, 1979), among other phenomena.

## Scripts as performative structures

Scripts play a double role in psychology. There are scripts in understanding and scripts in behavior. To behave a script, that is, to take a role such as customer in a restaurant, one not only must understand that such a possibility exists, but one must commit oneself to the performance of it. (I invoke the concept of *commitment* deliberately here. Starting a script performance usually entails a commitment to finish it. One does not readily leave a restaurant once seated or walk out of a dentist's office before the dentist is through.)

*Understanding* a situation can be taken to mean the cognitive retrieval of previous situations to which the present situation is similar. Appropriate behavior in the present situation is then specified by the behavior in those previous situations. This formulation is most clear for situations which over many repetitions build up an easily identified equivalence class, that is, scripts. Three conditions seem necessary for scripted behavior to occur. First, the individual must have a stable cognitive representation of the particular script. Second, an evoking context for the script must be presented. Third, the individual must *enter* the script. This third is the critical condition at the gap between cognition and behavior. It is assumed that script entry is contingent upon satisfaction of an *action rule* attached to the script representation. Consider, for example, how a person comes on a given occasion to be a patient in the dentist visit script. First, the person must know how to be a dental patient; second, there must be some stimulus making a dentist visit potentially relevant (a swollen gum, perhaps). Third, a decision must be made to undertake the visit rather than to reject or ignore the stimulus. Such a decision, since it arises fairly often, is likely to be made according to some *policy* that the individual has developed by experience, for example, "If it keeps hurting for several hours, call the dentist."

These policies or action rules are probably not necessarily consciously articulated by the individual. It does seem a reasonable hypothesis, however, that they are based on very few relevant conditions — especially if a lengthy decision process is not feasible on each occurrence of the script's evoking context. The relevant conditions for action rules might include cost, effort, mood, incentive, legitimacy, and so on, but only one or two of these would typically matter for any given script.

There is a vein of research in social psychology that is implicitly based on action rules. Before reviewing some of this literature, a further conceptual distinction is important. Situations differ in whether the evoking context for a script is self-presented or is environmentally presented. Social psychologists generally study situations in which the environment suddenly presents the options because the independent variables can be systematically manipulated. Helping behavior and conformity research spring to mind. While cases in which the individual has his or her own agenda are also important, I confine my discussion to scriptal situations in which the evoking stimuli are presented by the experimenters.

Small or apparently irrelevant variations in the situational context often make large differences in the probability of helping or conformity behavior. Helping behavior depends, among other things, on whether the helper happens to be feeling guilty (Carlsmith & Gross, 1969; Freedman, Wallington, & Bless, 1967) or is in a good mood

(Isen & Levin, 1972), on whether the weather is sunny (Cunningham, 1979), on whether there is a reason to hurry (Darley & Batson, 1973), or on how many other people are in the situation (Latané & Darley, 1970). This situational lability of behavior is theoretically troublesome for explanations based on abstract values such as altruism or social responsibility. But from a scriptal orientation, such lability is more or less what one would expect. Action rules are probably based on such simple criteria as "Can I spare the time?" or "Will I look foolish?"

Variables such as mood could of course influence behavior without entering into rules, but there are two reasons for a rule-based theory. First, the concept of rule implies a cognitive process in which the presence or absence of the triggering condition must be ascertained, and this sometimes implicates inference from observation. Thus the rule might be "If I'm in a good mood, I give money to beggars," and the inference might be "I must be in a good mood today. I said 'Good morning' to the bus driver." Theoretical emphasis on inference from self-observation is current in social psychology largely as a result of Bem's (1972) formulation and is also congenial to an artificial intelligence perspective that asks how such inferences are drawn. Second, a systematic listing of rules triggered by particular variables implies that the behaviors in question are insensitive to variations in other unstated variables. This is an important property of action rules.

An intriguing phenomenon in social psychology, the foot-in-the-door effect (Freedman & Fraser, 1966; see DeJong, 1979, for a review of later studies), can be interpreted as the experimental establishment of an action rule such that a particular variable which would otherwise control behavior no longer does so nearly as much. As the reader may recall, Freedman and Fraser (1966) demonstrated that respondents induced to comply with a small request were much more likely to comply with a larger request a few days later. This was true even if the requester was a different person asking on a different topic. In one study, for example, the initial request was that the respondent place a sticker in a window urging that California be kept beautiful and the second was that she display a large, ugly sign saying "Drive safely."

The usual explanation of the foot-in-the-door effect is that the subjects tell themselves that they did the first action because they are helpers of good causes or are generally helpful people. Thus, when the second request comes along, the respondent's self-image requires being helpful again. In the present terminology, an action rule has been learned on the first occasion, namely, "If it's a good cause, do it." The second time around, the condition is satisfied, and the person conforms again. Actually there is some uncertainty about the mediating rule. It might be "If the person asks politely, do it," or "If the person seems earnest and presentable, do it." In any case, the person carries *some* notion from the first to the second occasion, increasing the likelihood of conformity. Strikingly, this learned rule is strong enough to override for many people the onerousness of the second request. People in a no-prior-experience group who are simply asked to display the ugly sign on their lawns are quite unlikely to comply. Thus, the foot-in-the-door experience serves to shift control of the behavior from initially natural stimulus features (the size of the request) to other features that may or may not be natural (e.g., the gentility of demeanor of the interviewer).

74

Another empirical strategy has been the manipulation of the evoking stimulus to be consistent or inconsistent with a hypothesized action rule in a particular scripted situation. Langer and I adopted this strategy by varying two aspects of how an appeal for help was worded (Langer & Abelson, 1972). We varied the initial phrases of the victim to evoke or not evoke an "empathic helping" script. Later in the appeal came a detail either confirming or refuting the legitimacy of the victim's professed neediness.

In this analysis, the concern is with a knowledge structure slightly more abstract than a script (a *metascript,* to be discussed below) because some of the events are generically rather than concretely defined. But the argument proceeds similarly. If someone asks for help in a very needy manner, an empathic helping script is presumably defined. The helper knows the general outlines of what is coming next: Someone states a need, you feel sorry for the person, you help the person out, he or she thanks you and feels grateful, you say "You're welcome, it was no trouble," and you leave feeling that you've been a good Samaritan. What's the most reasonable rule for whether or not to participate in this episode? Well, so much of what goes on depends on the victim's having been truly needy (and not merely just saying so) that the script is almost unsupportable without that condition. Thus, the major action criterion ought to be the *legitimacy* of the request.

One of our helping situations was mailing a package for someone in a desperate hurry. The initial phrase meant to evoke the empathic helping script was "I'm in a terrible state." The legitimacy variable was manipulated by the victim's subsequent explanation that she either had to catch a train or had to go shopping. With the legitimate explanation, the victim was helped 80% of the time and with the illegitimate explanation, 20% of the time. This legitimacy effect was contingent upon the evoking phrase, however. When the victim's opening phrase was "Would you please do me a favor," we hypothesized that a different helping script variant having little to do with empathy would be evoked. The action rule in that case might be "If I have time, I'll do it," and would be insensitive to the legitimacy variable. The data showed 55% helping with the legitimate variant and 45% with the illegitimate variant. This 10% legitimacy differential was significantly less than the 60% differential with the empathic evocation.

Langer has continued studying the co-option of mundane behavior with sudden simple requests. One of these studies (Langer, Blank, & Chanowitz, 1978) is particularly suited to an analysis according to action rules. The situation involved a person turning over use of a photocopier to someone asking permission to interrupt. Such polite yielding can also occur at checkout counters of supermarkets, for seating on buses, and so on, and the analysis is much the same.

Langer and her associates assume that when a politely stated request is small, any other details of the request tend to be processed "mindlessly," that is, without deep attention to semantic details. When the request is large, however, the rationale for the request must be scrutinized for its legitimacy, much as in the empathic helping script. (Someone so presumptuous as to request a lengthy interruption better do so with good reason.) Figure 1 summarizes these assumptions as a simplified action rule for this situation.

The critical experimental condition in Langer *et al.*'s (1978) study was when the request was accompanied by an empty reason (p. 637): "May I use the xerox machine, because I have to make copies?" (Why else?) If the above analysis is correct, then when the request is small ("I have 5 pages"), the vapidity of the reason should not even be noticed, and yielding should occur fully as often as when a real reason is given: "May I use the xerox machine, because I'm in a rush?" However, when the request is large ("I have 20 pages"), the vapid reason should be processed and recognized as worthless, and yielding should occur no more often than when no reason is given: "May I use the xerox machine?" This delicate pattern of results was precisely what Langer *et al.* found.

Admittedly, the analysis of the action rules in these several phenomena is not well systematized, and the elicited behaviors vary in their scriptedness. Script experiments are more difficult in social than in cognitive applications because it is much harder to control the stimulus variables in the former. Nevertheless, I press on to still one more application within social psychology and some broader issues.

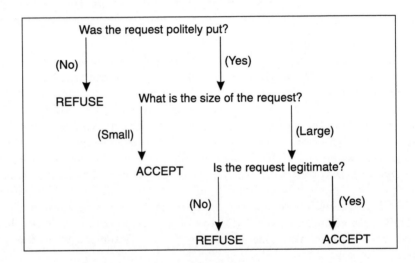

**Figure 1      An action rule for routine favors**

The observed relationship between measured attitudes and actual behaviors toward a social object has long been problematic in social psychology (see early reviews by Abelson, 1972; Wicker, 1969). Very often the correlation between attitudes and behaviors is surprisingly low, and a number of explanations for this discrepancy have been proposed. It is helpful to consider the bearing of scripted behavior on this issue. The classic study by LaPiere (1934) provides a good starting point. LaPiere and two Chinese traveling companions were received at virtually every motel and restaurant they entered. Six months after a visit, a questionnaire from LaPiere asked each establishment whether it would "welcome members of the Chinese race as guests." Ninety percent of the returns indicated *no,* demonstrating a huge discrepancy between attitude (or behavioral intention) and actual behavior.

In script terms, one would say that when the Chinese arrived, the management played standard script scenes from their role perspectives. In the restaurant, the crucial scene is "seating the customer," in the hotel, it is "registering the guest." Given very well-practiced scripts, the action rules — the policies for whether to enter the scripts — are presumably very well learned. What a hotel manager presumably checks before registering a guest is whether a room is available and the guest looks able to pay. Hotel managers (and clerks) are very well practiced at going ahead if the answers to the above are *yes* but refusing the guest politely if either answer is *no*. On the other hand, it seems quite unlikely that managers would ask themselves, "Do I feel favorable toward these potential guests?" Liking the guest is not a good action criterion if the commercial establishment is to turn a profit. Thus, attitude is manifestly not relevant for hotel (and restaurant) welcoming behavior. Even if a negative attitude exists toward a particular rare minority, this attitude (with some exceptions) is not practiced as a reason for nonaction. Emergent doubts have little chance of deflecting scripted behavior when standard action criteria are satisfied.

Of course, it is possible for an attitude to be a relevant condition for action. If you and your spouse are invited for dinner at someone's house (thus to be potential participants in the "dinner guest" script), attitude toward the hosting individuals may weigh heavily in the decision on whether to accept. Thus, attitudes can have different degrees of relevance to scripted behavior, and the degree of relevance should be predictable from the nature of the social context.

Ajzen and Fishbein (1977) have devoted a great deal of attention to the attitude–behavior dilemma (see also Fishbein & Ajzen, 1975, chap. 8). For the LaPiere (1934) case, they argue that the questionnaire referred to members of the Chinese race in general, an attitude target different from the particular (well-dressed) Chinese couple who actually visited. This same general argument is applied to scores of other cases of attitude–behavior discrepancy. Ajzen and Fishbein show that attitudes predict behavior very well when there is a close correspondence in the way that attitude and behavior are specified in their action and target components. Thus, if one wanted to predict the buying of gasohol, it would be a mistake to measure attitudes toward gasoline substitutes or even attitude (in general) toward gasohol. One would have to measure attitude toward *buying* gasohol.

The diagnosis and prescription from Ajzen and Fishbein are thus entirely methodological. To predict a particular behavior, one asks the respondent directly about that behavior. Unfortunately, this strategy leaves unexplained those very interesting cases in which general attitudes *do* predict specific behavior. Sears, Speer, and Hensler (1979) have shown that the general attitude of "symbolic racism" is a rather good predictor of opposition to school busing, which on the face of it is quite a different target object. Crosby, Bromley, and Saxe (1980) have found in reviewing empirical studies that white racial prejudice manifests itself over a broad range of interactive behaviors with blacks whenever public norms of fair treatment are not overtly violated. A totally methodological, non-theoretical solution to the attitude–behavior issue does not help much with interesting issues. Perhaps it is unfair to put it thus, but it seems to me to be like throwing out the baby and clinging to the bathwater.

A cluster of recent studies have shown that attitudes learned via direct experience with an object or issue correlate better with behavior than do attitudes learned without direct involvement. Fazio and Zanna (1978) assessed subjects' attitudes toward being in psychological experiments, along with their frequency of volunteering. For subjects who had previously been in at least four experiments, the correlation between attitude and behavior toward experiments was .42. For subjects who had been in no more than one experiment, the corresponding correlation was –.03.

Regan and Fazio (1977) have obtained similar results on two other issues, one a real campus housing crisis, the other a set of laboratory puzzle materials. Meanwhile, Snyder and Swann (1976) have shown that thinking about a general issue (affirmative action) before filling out an attitude scale results in a correlation of .58 with behavior in a later specific case, whereas without prior thought, this correlation is a mere .03. Pryor, Gibbons, Wicklund, Fazio, and Hood (1977) and several other studies reviewed by Wicklund and Frey (1980) have shown that self-awareness, manipulated by placing a mirror opposite the subject during attitude measurement, increases the attitude–behavior correlation.

These several results are not all attributable to shifts in the reliability of attitude measurements. Rather, they seem to involve the distinction between an academic attitude and a practical attitude. Snyder (Note 11), in a theoretical analysis, says that attitudes must be well organized both in their cognitive component — what they are about — and in their action component — how and when to apply them — before they can be expected to correlate well with behavior. Prior experience with the attitude object may, in the present terms, promote the formation of scripts and action rules. Thinking and self-awareness (or other forms of "consciousness raising") may make the action rules more responsive to pertinent attitudes. Thus, under some circumstances, action rules may promote attitude–behavior consistency rather than interfere with it. An action-rule and script analysis of the attitude–behavior issue is by no means the whole story, but it seems quite helpful. Further elaboration on this issue is given in Abelson (in press).

### Scripts related to other theoretical constructs

It is both a strength and a weakness of the script construct that it is reminiscent of other theoretical entities in psychology. One of these is *habit*. At the first blush, it may seem that scripts slyly sneak behaviorism in through social psychology's cognitive door. In a sense this is true, but the cognitive aspect is considerable. The difference between a script and a habit is that a script is a knowledge structure, not just a response program, and thus there is access to it symbolically as well as through direct experience.

One way symbolic factors can enter scripts is that a *modified* understanding of the script may result in modified behavior. When the veterinarian advises giving our dog a heartworm pill before chow, I try to change my dog-feeding script by adding this new step. The modification might be subtly cued. As I prepare to feed the dog my wife might remark, "I've noticed a lot of mosquitoes lately," or even, "I don't think the city sprayed the lake this year." To cope with such symbolic access to script structures, we must understand semantic inference.

An additional point is that action rules for entering scripts are a particularly fertile ground for cognitive mediation of response structures and can thus be seen as relevant to the control of habits Here, again, linguistic and conceptual structure are apt to be of greater consequence in a script theory account than in a habit theory account derivative from the animal-learning tradition. However, we should not allow ourselves to be so frozen into the adversative legacy of Hull versus Tolman, or Skinner versus his detractors, that we regard cognitive and behavioristic accounts as competing alternatives. Rather, both theoretical orientations may independently contribute to our understanding. In the last 10 years or so, there has in fact occurred a quiet theoretical convergence, with the animal-learning tradition becoming more information-process oriented (cf. Rescorla & Wagner, 1972; Wagner, 1978). In the present terms, these recent animal-conditioning models specify how stimulus features compete with one another for "criteriality" of action rules. A well-known conditioning result is that the enhancement of criteriality of one feature suppresses the criteriality of other candidate features, much as I postulated above in discussing the foot-in-the-door effect.

There are further ways in which cognitive factors can enter the otherwise stereotyped performance of scripts. The present concept of scripts does not necessarily imply total automaticity of performance and is not equivalent to Langer's (1978; Langer *et al.*, 1978; Langer & Imber, 1979; Langer & Newman, 1979) concept of "mindless" behavior. One obvious way in which "mindful" behavior enters scripts is that acts of thinking can appear explicitly in the specified event sequence. Note from Table 1 that the ordering scene in a restaurant includes the main action of deciding what to order. (This is listed in Conceptual Dependency terminology as an MBUILD, roughly equivalent to *thinking.)* While it is possible for ordering to become habituated to a single food item, there is typically a place in the script specially marked, in effect, as "Now think."

Thoughtful processing can also occur in script performance when obstacles or unusual variations occur. A script is more than just a linear list of inexorable events. In learning a script, one presumably learns variations in addition to constancies. Recent investigations have shown that children as young as age 3 or 4 begin to establish reliable and valid representations of the major events in familiar, stereotyped sequential activities such as eating lunch at nursery school (Nelson & Gruendel, 1979). Not much is known, however, about the processes by which basic script *spines* are elaborated into more complexly realistic knowledge structures. One can nevertheless make productive guesses as to what would be included in such elaborated script packages by considering what factors might make one run-through of a script different from another. The knowledge associated with each such factor could arise either through direct experience or symbolically.

In what follows I describe eight factors that embody script variations. The first factor, *equifinal actions,* indicates that several different actions may accomplish the same result. Thus, communicating an order to a waiter might be achieved by speaking the order by name, by pointing to it on the menu, or in extremity perhaps even by gestures. (A friend of mine once flapped his arms like a chicken in a restaurant in Russia.) Equifinality of different actions is already coded into the Yale artificial intelligence script representation. In Schank's (1972) system, an MTRANS, for example, can be accomplished in several ways. The script structure is noncommittal about this choice (although in a fully realistic episodic memory, the individual would presumably remember which way was personally most typical).

*Variables* are devices that imbue scripts with predictive generality. Although some object or person can be different for different script episodes, it remains constant once fixed for a given episode. In artificial intelligence jargon, there is *binding* of variables in a given script *instantiation*. The food that is ordered is the food that is served is the food that is eaten. (If not, some explanation must be given.)

Script *paths* arise when there are branch points offering alternatives to normal procedures. If the menu is on the table, for example, then signaling the waiter for the menu can obviously be skipped. The most crucial path choice is the entry path leading into the script, which I have already discussed in the section on action rules.

The fourth potential variation is *scene selection,* applying mainly to weak scripts that do not impose much sequential constraint among scenes. A restaurant allows less scene selection than does a circus or a folk dance session, and so scripts can differ on this factor.

The fifth factor is *tracks,* which are different script variants, each embodying characteristic paths, scene selections, and props not shared by other tracks. The restaurant script may be said to have a fast-food track, a standard-restaurant track, a fancy-restaurant track, and several others. There is a serious question as to whether a meal at McDonald's isn't so different from a meal at the Tour D'Argent that it is inappropriate even to call them the same script. I return to this question shortly.

The above five factors are all variations that can be anticipated in advance of a particular run-through of a particular script. But there are also unexpected sources of variation. There may be *interferences* with the proper execution of script acts, in two forms, namely, obstacles and errors (Schank & Abelson, 1977). An obstacle is something that removes a precondition for a given event. (The waiter can't give you a menu because there aren't any.) An error is the wrongful completion of a given event. (You've been served scallops instead of shrimp.) For every obstacle and error in a well-practiced script, there are one or two reasonable corrective prescriptions that allow the script to proceed. With sufficient experience with a script, a person may learn prescriptions for all common interferences, which are encoded as paths in the script (e.g., what to do if there is no menu on the table).

A *distraction* is an event of sufficient salience or importance to interrupt script action, though it does not interfere with any uniquely specified event. Examples in a restaurant would be a fire, the arrival of a long-lost friend, and so on.

Finally, *free behaviors* are those activities that may plausibly and commonly intermix with the ongoing script, such as a conversation in a restaurant (but not, e.g., throwing frisbees in a restaurant). People generally have a fairly clear conception of what behaviors are apt in particular locales (Price & Bouffard, 1974).

In sum, many factors lead one run-through of a script to be different from any other. Systematic sources of such variation are presumably learned experientially or symbolically and stored along with the script. While a behavioristic account might be possible for such a malleable "habit," it seems more natural to analyze the performance in terms of an enabling knowledge structure, namely, a script.

Another one of these "Isn't it the same as . . . ?" questions about scripts is, "Isn't it the same as role theory?" Again, there are crucial differences despite some degree of similarity. Role theory (cf. Biddle, 1979; Sarbin & Allen, 1968) tends to emphasize the web of social and institutional expectations constraining social performances, whereas a script-based theory is anchored in individual cognitive structures that may or may not mesh with the performance expectations of others. Of course, some scripts, like the restaurant script, are so consensually experienced that individual differences are not of primary importance. One can no doubt refer to the "customer role" in a restaurant. But when it comes to more abstract scripts — later discussed as metascripts — individual differences are crucial. A second departure of script theory from role theory is the "double life" of scripts as understanding and behavior structures. The argument here is similar to the one I made before when discussing habits. Ideally, scripts when well understood will have anchorage in the psychology of language and memory, an anchorage not characteristic of role theory, which has its origins in sociology. It is possible, however, that here, too, as with learning theory formulations, there may develop some motion toward an information-processing orientation. Sociologists Skvoretz, Fararo, and Axten (1980) have operationalized the role of a waiter in a restaurant in a series of *production rules* (Newell, 1973), such that a symbolic waiter can symbolically serve several symbolic customers in a reasonably realistic computer simulation of his or her comings and goings. The rules in the program correspond to the rules in the waiter's head, embodying what it means to play that role. (A set of production rules generally produces a more complex knowledge structure than that of a script, although a script could be expressed as a simple set of production rules, one of which is the action rule for starting the script.)

Another claim of theoretical overlap could come from clinical psychologists familiar with Berne (1964) and transactionalism. Scripts when generalized into metascripts (see below) are similar to what Berne calls *games*. (At least, a game is one kind of metascript.) They are also close to what Tomkins (1980) calls *nuclear scenes*. The essential insight of the clinical psychologist is that the stuff of neurosis is the repeated construction of present situations in terms of a *preemptive metaphor,* that is, an inappropriate similarity to a kernel situation from the past.

**Metascripts and other generalizations**

It is instructive to consider a script as a cognitive category and to consider various episodic instances of its performance as *members* of the category. Category theory has recently undergone a shift of orientation within cognitive psychology (Rosch, 1978; Smith, 1977) and philosophy (since Wittgenstein, 1953). The classical view that categories of objects are defined by sets of necessary and sufficient features has been challenged. Even if taxonomists could agree on the unique defining features of particular objects (which they sometimes cannot), it seems psychologically implausible that there exist well-articulated, all-or-nothing boundaries for common categories. People have trouble deciding whether a tomato is a vegetable or a fruit or deciding what the difference is between a tree and a shrub. Away from physical or biological categories, the situation may get even more fuzzy, as in the debate about what activities ought to be included in the category of "violence."

The newer theoretical view is that a category is defined not by absolutely criterial attributes, but by family resemblances among its members, just as all the siblings in a family can look somewhat similar without any single feature being common to all. Experimental subjects do not necessarily agree whether any object is definitely in a category (Is a radio "furniture"?), but there is high reliability from groups of subjects who rate *relative* degree of in-ness or out-ness. (In the furniture category, a desk is more "in" than a radio.) This judgment refers to the so-called prototypicality of objects. Rosch and Mervis (1975) have shown that to the extent an object's attributes are statistically common among other objects in the category, the object is judged more prototypical of the category.

If one regards each specific realization of a script (each dental visit, say) as an object, and the events transpiring during the episode as *attributes,* then one can regard a script as a psychological *category.* There is a family resemblance among the many realizations of a given script because they tend to share events in common, though not necessarily always the same events. The most prototypical realizations of a script are the ones that embody more of the most commonly experienced events.

This analogy can be pursued further. Categories of objects exist at various levels of abstraction. "Chairs" as a category contains subcategories like "kitchen chairs" and is itself a subcategory of the superordinate classification "furniture." Subcategories contain many low-level characteristic attributes and are highly particularized in application. Superordinates, on the other hand, are generalized in application and contain relatively few characteristic attributes (e.g., furniture is prototypically manufactured, functional, and found in living spaces).

What I have called *tracks* of scripts are the analogues of subcategories; that is, they contain many low-level particulars about events, which are slightly different from the particulars for other tracks. At the other extreme are abstractly stated scripts with a minimum of specification. These are the analogues of superordinates and are called *metascripts.* I have already cited several examples that are in effect metascripts rather than simple scripts. Structures in the original Goldwater Machine (Abelson & Reich, 1969) such as "Communist schemes to take over neutral nations" are superordinate to more detailed scripts such as military invasion, political subversion, and so forth. The "emphatic helping" script, invoked in the Langer and Abelson (1972) study, is a metascript with generically defined events like "helping out" (i.e., carrying out the plea of a victim). "Doing standard favors" (Figure 1) is similarly a metascript.

The defining feature of a metascript is that many of its scenes are specified at a higher level of abstraction than are those of a script. These abstract scenes subsume different concrete realizations. Consider, for example, the more or less parallel scripts of visiting a doctor and visiting a dentist. In each, there is a potential scene in which an assistant undertakes standard test procedures with the patient: The nurse may take blood pressure and the dental assistant, X rays. Interestingly, Bower *et al.* (1979) have shown that subjects exposed to one or the other of parallel events such as these show false confidence in having seen the companion event. The implication is that memories for script episodes are not necessarily stored with the representation for the particular script ("things that happened at the doctor's office"). Rather, memories may be stored at a metascript level ("things that happened at visits to a health professional"), promoting confusion as to which concrete script was involved.

The concept of parallel scenes can be further analyzed. Sometimes parallel scenes are almost identical, for example, the waiting room scene in the doctor's and dentist's offices. One might expect episodic-memory confusions to be maximized for events occurring in scenes which are shared among scripts; that is, memory for some event which occurred in a waiting room might not preserve whether the event was at the doctor's or at the dentist's. The existence of shared scenes between certain scripts undercuts the simple idea that all information needed for a script is necessarily stored within a closed knowledge structure privileged for that script. It is more likely that the shared knowledge is stored *outside* of the script and is made available when the script is activated. By contrast, what is likely to be permanently stored *within* a script are those scenes unique to it — for example, ordering from a menu in a restaurant. Knowledge about the details of eating by using a fork, opening one's mouth, chewing, and so on is not likely to be stored under "restaurant" as such, however, because that would be redundant with information about eating at home, at friends' houses, and so on.

Schank (1980) has recently postulated a family of knowledge structures that he calls MOPs (memory organization packets). Their function is to control the assembly of knowledge stored with various scenes into coherent sequences such as scripts or plans — or metascripts — when needed in comprehension tasks. He implicates these structures in trying to explain *reminding* — why a present experience calls a particular past experience to mind. The MOP invoked to understand the present spontaneously activates relevant past episodes. Reminding is thus theoretically linked to understanding; light can be shed on the understanding process by studying reminiscence phenomena, and vice versa.

This proposal is powerful to the degree that the nature of MOP structures can be articulated. The key problem is the categorization of episodes into similarity classes. Here I can but offer preliminary suggestions on some factors that might be involved.

Just as two or more objects are similar to the extent that they have many shared features but not many unique features (Tversky, 1977), so two or more episodes are similar to the extent they have many shared events but not many unique events. Script episodes have this critical similarity property: Separate experiences of the same script invoke a common core of events and scenes with relatively few variations. Scripts have *internal coherence.* Furthermore, scripts have potential similarity properties in relation to other scripts. Any script can in principle be compared with any other script for how many of their prototypical scenes overlap and for how many are unique. I call the resulting measure *external similarity.*

When a proposed script, however internally coherent its episodes, has high external similarity, it is not a very efficient knowledge structure. For example, "going to a hardware store" has high external similarity to "going to a sporting goods store," "going to a stationery store," and many others. While the action rules for entering these several alternatives are different, the internal scenes of each are very similar. One might well group them as the single script "going to a retail store" (with separate tracks for hardware, sporting goods, etc.).

By contrast, some scripts have not only internal coherence but also external distinctiveness. For example, a "funeral" script has scenes such as carrying the casket and filling the grave that are shared by few if any other coherent scripts. Thus "funeral" is an efficient knowledge structure, distinct from other structures. The general rule for efficiency would seem to be the maximization of the ratio of internal coherence to external similarity. This principle applies at all levels of abstraction. If there is too much external similarity at a given level, then similar structures are grouped together to increase coherence and redefine what is external. The operationalization of this general mathematical idea is not yet clear because of difficulties in defining the scope of events or scenes, but formally it might eventually lend itself to some form of hierarchical cluster analysis (e.g., Sattath & Tversky, 1977).

For any given individual, particular separate experiences contain sufficient subjective similarity to achieve coherence despite some differences in detail. The formation of individual metascripts is presumably one basis for the definition of individual differences in normal personality. It is perhaps even more so the basis for abnormal personality variations. I referred previously to Tomkins's (1980) concept of the nuclear scene. The nuclear scene is a situation that the individual experiences repeatedly, not so much by conscious intention as by seemingly being unable to avoid it.

For a nuclear scene to develop and exert an important guiding influence on an individual's behavior, it is necessary, in Tomkins's view, for the same strong emotional reaction to occur repeatedly in similar but not identical situations. The emotional component then becomes amplified, according to Tomkins, and becomes capable of connecting situations by analogy rather than by mere similarity of detail. As one of many illustrations, Tomkins cites the case of a man who as a youth was repeatedly enraged at a younger brother who in one way or another spoiled his close relationship with his mother. The nuclear scene became one of ideal communion spoiled by an ugly competitor, and remote analogies could evoke this scene. Years later, this man reported to his therapist that while driving alone one day on a lovely country highway he became suddenly and inexplicably shaken with fury at a truck that was so rude as to also use the highway.

Experimental psychologists tend to be uncomfortable with clinical examples such as the above, largely, I think, because of the great uncertainty in trying to explain the present by reference to cleverly selected incidents from the past. To a certain extent I share that discomfort, but this is not to deny that people do in fact under some conditions perceive and act upon inappropriate analogies (for the experimental creation of an inappropriate analogy, cf. Ayeroff & Abelson, 1976). The interesting thing about Tomkins's theory is its implication that it is emotional experience which turns scripts into overgeneralized metascripts.

Let us look at the role of emotion in the present theoretical terms. Feelings such as anger, pride, guilt, jealousy, and so on are conceptually very coherent (Roseman, Note 12). A sizeable set of inferences can be made from the knowledge that, say, "John is angry." A negative thing has happened to John; he blames it on someone; he regards it as unjust; he is excited, flushed, and prone to swear or lash out; he may seek revenge on the instigator; and so on. One anger experience thus has a lot of potential overlap with other anger experiences. This makes it seem plausible that scripts or metascripts might be organized around anger, for example, around the "getting angry at my boss" script or the "rage against authority" metascript. Idiographically, the class of episodes of anger toward a boss or of rage against authority might have considerable internal coherence.

The theoretical catch to such a speculation is that affects produce not only internal coherence but also external similarity. Anger at bosses may share many features with anger at salespeople, anger at spouses, anger at bureaucrats, and so forth, some of whom may be "authorities" and some not, but may have all kinds of differing situational background details. Thus, neither "anger at bosses" nor "rage against authority" is necessarily apt to be a distinctive schema — there is a substantial possibility of its blurring into other scripts and metascripts. This is one of the difficulties with case examples like Tomkins's sibling rivalry story. The observer would like to know not only what remote metaphorical connections the individual sees between present and past but also the circumstances under which the present is *not* seen like the past. What episodes don't suggest sibling rivalry to this person? What are the boundaries of the effective schema? Tomkins (1980) is not unaware of this theoretical problem, but it is a difficult one.

## Conclusion

The script concept raises and sketchily addresses a number of fundamental psychological issues: within cognitive psychology, the nature of knowledge structures for representing ordinary experience; within social psychology, the way in which social reality is constructed and how constructions of reality translate into social behavior through action rules; in learning and developmental psychology, how and what knowledge structures are learned in the course of ordinary experience; in clinical psychology, how resonances between present situations and past schemata can preempt behavior maladaptively. These are large questions that have persisted for many generations, and they are not likely to be answered simply or soon. The script approach nevertheless makes clear that the issues are highly intertwined. There are not five psychologies — cognitive, social, learning, developmental, and clinical — but one psychology. The analysis of scripts and other knowledge structures based on the events of ordinary experience promotes awareness of this unity and helps to explore it.

## Reference notes

1. Cullingford, R. (1978) *Script application: Computer understanding of newspaper stories* (Rep. No. 116). New Haven, Conn.: Yale University, Department of Computer Science.

2. DeJong, G. (1979) *Skimming stories in real time: An experiment in integrated understanding* (Rep. No. 158). New Haven, Conn.: Yale University, Department of Computer Science.

3.   Abelson, R. P. (September 1971) *The ideology machine*. Paper presented at the meeting of the American Political Science Association, Chicago.

4.   Anderson, J. (March 1980) *Cognitive units*. Paper presented at the meeting of the Society for Philosophy and Psychology, Ann Arbor, Michigan.

5.   Black, J. & Bern, H. (1980) *Causal coherence in memory for events in narratives* (Tech. Rep. No. 3). New Haven, Conn.: Yale University, Cognitive Science Program.

6.   Galambos, J. A. & Rips, L. J. (May 1979) *The representation of events in memory*. Paper presented at the meeting of the Midwestern Psychological Association, Chicago.

7.   Abelson, R. P. & Reder, L. M. (1977) *Linear ordering in scripts*. Unpublished research, Yale University.

8.   Abbott, V A. & Black, J. B. (1980) *The representation of scripts in memory* (Tech. Rep. No. 5). New Haven, Conn.: Yale University, Cognitive Science Program.

9.   Smith, E. E. (May 1981) *Studying on-line comprehension of stories*. Paper presented at the Cognitive Science Colloquium, Yale University.

10.  Martin, J., Patterson, K. & Price, R. L. (1979) *The effects of level of abstraction of a script on accuracy of recall, predictions and beliefs* (Rep. No. 520). Stanford, Calif.: Stanford University, Graduate School of Business.

11.  Snyder, M. (August 1977) *When believing means doing: A cognitive social psychology of action*. Paper presented at the meeting of the American Psychological Association, San Francisco.

12.  Roseman, I. (September 1979) *Cognitive aspects of emotion and emotional behavior*. Paper presented at the meeting of the American Psychological Association, New York City.

## References

Abelson, R. P. (1972) Are attitudes necessary? In B. T. King & E. McGinnes (Eds.), *Attitudes, conflict and social change*. New York: Academic Press.

Abelson, R. P. (1973) Structural analysis of belief systems. In R. C Schank & K. M. Colby (Eds.), *Computer models of thought and language*. San Francisco: Freeman.

Abelson, R. P. (1976) Script processing in attitude formation and decision-making. In J. S. Carroll and J. W. Payne (Eds.), *Cognition and social behavior*. Hillsdale, N.J.: Erlbaum.

Abelson, R. P. Three modes of attitude-behavior consistency. In M. Zanna, E. T. Higgins & C. P. Herman (Eds.), *Variability and consistency in social behavior: The Ontario symposium*. Hillsdale, N.J.: Erlbaum, in press.

Abelson, R. P. and Reich, C. M. (1969) Implicational molecules: A method for extracting meaning from input sentences. In D. E. Walker and L. M. Norton (Eds.), *Proceedings of the International Joint Conference on Artificial Intelligence*. Boston: Mitre Corporation.

Ajzen, I. & Fishbein, M. (1977) Attitude-behavior relations: A theoretical analysis and review of empirical research. *Psychological Bulletin, 84*, 888–918.

Anderson, R. C. & Ortony, A. (1975) On putting apples into bottles. *Cognitive Psychology, 7*, 167–180.

Ayeroff, F. & Abelson, R. P. (1976) ESP and ESB: Belief in personal success at mental telepathy. *Journal of Personality and Social Psychology, 34,* 240–247.

Bartlett, F. C. (1932) *Remembering.* London: Cambridge University Press.

Bem, D. J. (1972) Self-perception theory. In L. Berkowitz (Ed.), *Advances in experimental social psychology* (Vol. 6). New York: Academic Press.

Berne, E. (1964) *Games people play.* New York: Grove Press.

Biddle, B. J. (1979) *Role theory: Expectations, identities, and behaviors.* New York: Academic Press.

Bobrow, D. G. & Norman, D. A. (1975) *Some principles of memory schemata.* In D. G. Bobrow & A Collins (Eds.), Representation and understanding. New York: Academic Press.

Bower, G., Black, J. & Turner, T. (1979) Scripts in text comprehension and memory. *Cognitive Psychology, 11,* 177–220.

Cantor, N. & Mischel, W. (1977) Traits as prototypes: Effects on recognition memory. *Journal of Personality and Social Psychology, 35,* 38–48.

Cantor, N. & Mischel, W. (1979) Prototypes in person perception. In L. Berkowitz (Ed.), *Advances in experimental social psychology* (Vol. 12). New York: Academic Press.

Carbonell, J. G. (1978) POLITICS: Automated ideological reasoning. *Cognitive Science, 2,* 27–51.

Carlsmith. J. M. & Gross, A. E. (1969) Some effects of guilt on compliance. *Journal of Personality and Social Psychology, 11,* 232–239.

Clark, H. H. (1977) Inferences in comprehension. In D. LaBerge & S. J. Samuels (Eds.), *Basic processes in reading: Perception and comprehension.* Hillsdale, N.J.: Erlbaum.

Clark, H. H. & Clark. E V. (1977) *Psychology and language.* New York: Harcourt Brace Jovanovich.

Crosby, F., Bromley, S. & Saxe, L. (1980) Recent unobtrusive studies of black and white discrimination and prejudice: A literature review. *Psychological Bulletin, 87,* 546–563.

Cunningham, M.R. (1979) Weather, mood, and helping behavior: Quasi experiments with the sunshine Samaritan. *Journal of Personality and Social Psychology, 37,* 1947–1956.

Darley, J. M. & Batson, C. D. (1973) "From Jerusalem to Jericho": A study of situational and dispositional variables in helping behavior. *Journal of Personality and Social Psychology, 27,* 100–108.

DeJong, W. (1979) An examination of the self-perception mediation of the foot-in-the-door effect. *Journal of Personality and Social Psychology, 37,* 2221–2239.

den Uyl, M. & van Oostendorp, H. The use of scripts in text comprehension. *Poetics,* 1980, 9, 275–294.

Fazio, R. H. & Zanna, M. P. (1978) Attitudinal qualities relating to the strength of the attitude-behavior relationship. *Journal of Experimental Social Psychology, 14,* 398–407.

Fishbein, M. & Ajzen, I. (1975) *Belief, attitude, intention, and behavior: An introduction to theory and research.* Reading, Mass.: Addison-Wesley.

Freedman, J. L. & Fraser, S. C. (1966) Compliance without pressure: The foot-in-the-door technique. *Journal of Personality and Social Psychology*, 4, 195–202.

Freedman, J. L., Wallington, S. A. & Bless, E. (1967) Compliance without pressure: The effect of guilt. *Journal of Personality and Social Psychology*, 7, 117–124.

Graesser, A. C., Gordon, S. E. & Sawyer, J. D. (1979) Recognition memory for typical and atypical actions in scripted activities: Tests of a script pointer plus tag hypothesis. *Journal of Verbal Learning and Verbal Behavior*, 18, 319–332.

Graesser, A. C., Woll, S. B., Kowalski, D. J. & Smith, D. A. (1980) Memory for typical and atypical actions in scripted activities. *Journal of Experimental Psychology: Human Learning and Memory*, 6, 503–515.

Isen, A. M. & Levin, P. F. (1972) Effect of feeling good on helping: Cookies and kindness. *Journal of Personality and Social Psychology*, 21, 384–388.

Johnson, M. K., Bransford, J. D. & Solomon, S. (1973) Memory for tacit implications of sentences. *Journal of Experimental Psychology*, 98, 203–205.

Kintsch, W. & van Dijk, T. A. (1978) Toward a model of text comprehension and production. *Psychological Review*, 85, 363–394.

Langer, E. J. (1978) Rethinking the role of thought in social interaction. In J. Harvey, W. Ickes & R. Kidd (Eds.), *New directions in attribution research* (Vol. 2). Hillsdale, N.J.: Erlbaum.

Langer, E. J. & Abelson, R. P. (1972) The semantics of asking a favor. How to succeed in getting help without really dying. *Journal of Personality and Social Psychology*, 24, 26–32.

Langer, E. J., Blank, A. & Chanowitz, B. (1978) The mindlessness of ostensibly thoughtful action. *Journal of Personality and Social Psychology*, 36, 635–642.

Langer, E. J. & Imber, L. G. (1979) When practice makes imperfect: Debilitating effects of overlearning. *Journal of Personality and Social Psychology*, 37, 2014–2024.

Langer, E. J. & Newman, H. M. (1979) The role of mindlessness in a typical social psychological experiment. *Personality and Social Psychology Bulletin*, 5, 295–298.

LaPiere, R. T. (1934) Attitude versus actions. *Social Forces*, 13, 230–237.

Latané, B. & Darley, J. M. (1970) Social determinants of bystander intervention in emergencies. In J. Macauley & L. Berkowitz (Eds.), *Altruism and helping behavior*. New York: Academic Press.

Mandler, J. M. (1978) A code in the node: The use of story schema in retrieval. *Discourse Processes*, 1, 14–35.

Markus, H. (1977) Self-schemata and processing information about the self. *Journal of Personality and Social Psychology*, 35, 63–78.

Minsky, M. (1975) A framework for representing knowledge. In P. H. Winston (Ed.), *The psychology of computer vision*. New York: McCraw-Hill.

Neisser, U. (1976) *Cognition and reality*. San Francisco: Freeman.

Nelson, K. & Gruendel, J. M. (1979) At morning it's lunchtime: A scriptal view of children's dialogues. *Discourse Processes*, 2, 73–94.

Newell, A. (1973) Production systems: Models of control structures. In W. C. Chase (Ed.), *Visual information processing*. New York: Academic Press.

Nisbett, R. & Ross, L. (1980) *Human inference: Strategies and shortcomings of social judgment.* Englewood Cliffs, N.J.: Prentice-Hall.

Piaget, J. (1926) *The language and thought of the child.* New York: Harcourt, Brace.

Price, R. H. & Bouffard, D. L. (1974) Behavioral appropriateness and situational constraint as dimensions of social behavior. *Journal of Personality and Social Psychology, 30,* 579–586.

Pryor, J. B., Gibbons, F. S., Wicklund, R. A., Fazio, R. & Hood, R. (1977) Self-focused attention and self-report validity. *Journal of Personality, 45,* 513–527.

Regan, D. T. & Fazio, R. H. (1977) On the consistency between attitudes and behavior: Look to the method of attitude formation. *Journal of Experimental Social Psychology, 13,* 28–45.

Rescorla, R. A. & Wagner, A. R. (1972) A theory of Pavlovian conditioning: Variations in the effectiveness of reinforcement and nonreinforcement. In A. H. Black & W. F. Prokasy (Eds.) *Classical conditioning II: Current research and theory.* New York: Appleton-Century-Crofts.

Rieger, C. (1975) Conceptual memory. In R. C. Schank, *Conceptual information processing.* Amsterdam: North-Holland.

Rosch, E. (1978) Principles of categorization. In E. Rosch & B. B. Lloyd (Eds.), *Cognition and categorization.* Hillsdale, N.J.: Erlbaum.

Rosch, E. & Mervis, C. (1975) Family resemblances: Studies in the internal structure of categories. *Cognitive Psychology, 7,* 573–605.

Rumelhart, D. E. & Ortony, A. (1977) The representation of knowledge in memory. In R. C. Anderson, R. J. Spiro & W. E. Montague (Eds.), *Schooling and the acquisition of knowledge.* Hillsdale, N.J.: Erlbaum.

Sarbin, T. R. & Allen, V. L. (1968) Role theory. In G. Lindzey & E. Aronson (Eds.), *Handbook of social psychology* (Vol. 1). Reading, Mass.: Addison-Wesley.

Sattath, S. & Tversky, A. (1977) Additive similarity trees. *Psychometrika, 42,* 319–345.

Schank, R. C. (1972) Conceptual dependency: A theory of natural language understanding. *Cognitive Psychology, 3,* 552–631.

Schank, R. C. (1975) *Conceptual information processing.* Amsterdam: North-Holland.

Schank, R. C. (1980) Language and memory. *Cognitive Science, 4,* 243–284.

Schank, R. C. & Abelson, R. P. (1977) *Scripts, plans, goals, and understanding.* Hillsdale, N.J. Erlbaum.

Sears, D. O., Speer, L. K. & Hensler, C. P. (1979) Whites' opposition to "busing": Self-interest or symbolic politics? *American Political Science Review, 73,* 369–384.

Skvoretz, J., Fararo, T. J. & Axten, N. (1980) Role-programme models and the analysis of institutional structure. *Sociology, 14,* 49–67.

Smith, E. E. (1977) Theories of semantic memory. In W. K. Estes (Ed.), *Handbook of learning and cognitive processes* (Vol . 5). Hillsdale N.J.: Erlbaum.

Snyder, M. & Swann, W., Jr. (1976) When actions reflect attitudes: The politics of impression management. *Journal of Personality and Social Psychology, 34,* 1034–1042.

Taylor, S. E. & Crocker, J. (1980) Schematic bases of social information processing. In E. T. Higgins, C. P. Herman & M. P. Zanna (Eds.), *Social cognition: The Ontario symposium.* Hillsdale, N.J.: Erlbaum.

Tesser, A. & Leone, C. (1977) Cognitive schemas and thought as determinants of attitude change. *Journal of Experimental Social Psychology, 13,* 340–356.

Tomkins, S. (1980) Script theory: Differential magnification of affects. In H. E. Howe, Jr. & M. M. Page (Eds.), *Nebraska Symposium on Motivation* (Vol. 27). Lincoln: University of Nebraska Press.

Tversky, A. (1977) Features of similarity. *Psychological Review, 84,* 327–352.

Tversky, A. & Kahneman, D. (1977) Causal schemata in judgments under uncertainty. In M. Fishbein (Ed.), *Progress in social psychology.* Hillsdale, N.J: Erlbaum.

Wagner, A. R. (1978) Expectancies and the priming of STM. In S. Hulse, H. Fowler & W. Honig (Eds.), *Cognitive processes in animal behavior.* Hillsdale, N.J.: Erlbaum.

Wieker, A. W. (1969) Attitudes versus actions: The relationship of verbal and overt behavioral responses to attitude objects. *Journal of Social Issues, 25*(4), 41–78.

Wicklund, R. A. & Frey, D. (1980) Self-awareness theory: When the self makes a difference. In D. M. Wegener & R. R. Vallacher (Eds.), *The self in social psychology.* New York: Oxford University Press.

Wittgenstein, L. (1953) *Philosophical investigations.* New York: Macmillan.

# Representation:
# Concepts and Categories

# 4.     What Some Concepts Might Not Be

## Sharon Lee Armstrong, Lila R. Gleitman and Henry Gleitman

*A discussion of the difficulties of prototype theories for describing compositional meaning motivates three experiments that inquire how well-defined concepts fare under paradigms that are commonly interpreted to support the prototype view. The stimulus materials include exemplars of prototype categories (sport, vehicle, fruit, vegetable) previously studied by others, and also exemplars of supposedly well-defined categories (odd number, even number, female, and plane geometry figure). Experiment I, using these materials, replicated the exemplar rating experiment of Rosch (1973). It showed that both the well-defined and prototypic categories yield graded responses, the supposed hall-mark of a family resemblance structure. Experiment II, using the same sorts of stimulus materials, replicated a verification time paradigm, also from Rosch (1973). Again, the finding was that both well-defined and prototypic categories yielded results previously interpreted to support a family-resemblance description of those categories, with faster verification times for prototypical exemplars of each category. In Experiment III, new subjects were asked outright whether membership in the category of fruit, odd number, etc., is a matter of degree, or is not, and then these subjects were rerun in the Experiment I paradigm. Though subjects judged odd number, etc., to be well-defined, they provided graded responses to all categories once again. These findings highlight interpretive difficulties for the experimental literature on this topic. Part I of the discussion first outlines a dual theory of concepts and their identification procedures that seems to organize these outcomes. But Part II of the discussion argues that feature theories are too impoverished to describe mental categories, in general.*

## Introduction

Recently, psychologists have renewed their interest in mental categories (concepts) and their learning. As always, part of the basis for this rekindling of interest has to do with some apparently positive findings that seem to make a topic investigatable. In this case, what seems positive are some recent discussions of cluster concepts (as first described by Wittgenstein, 1953) and powerful empirical demonstrations of prototypicality effects by E. Rosch and others (McCloskey and Glucksberg, 1979; Mervis and Rosch, 1981; Rips, Shoben, and Smith, 1973; Rosch, 1973, 1975; Tversky and Gati, 1978; and for an excellent review of the field, see Smith and Medin, 1981). We continue in this paper discussion and interpretation of the prototypicality theory of mental categories, in light of further experimental findings we will report. To summarize at the beginning where we think these findings lead, we believe that the cluster descriptions are a less satisfactory basis for a theory of human conceptual structure than might have been hoped.

Reprinted from *COGNITION*, Vol. 13 (1983), pp. 263–308. 'What Some Concepts Might Not Be' by Sharon Lee Armstrong, Lela R. Gleitman and Henry Gleitman. Reproduced with permission from Elsevier Science–NL, Sara Burgerhartstraat 25, 1055 KV Amsterdam, The Netherlands.

## Holistic and decompositional descriptions of mental categories

The central question addressed by the work just cited has to do with everyday categories of objects. For example, over an impressively wide range of instances, people can divide the world of objects into the dogs and the nondogs. They can form and use a category that includes the poodles, the airedales, and the chihuahuas, but excludes the cats, the bears, and the pencils. The clearest demonstration that people do acquire and use such a category is that all of them, in a linguistic community, standardly use the same word, 'dog', to refer to more or less the same creatures.

In detail, we distinguish the extension of *dog* from its category (concept) and from its linguistic title. As the terms are here used, all the real and projected creatures in the world that properly fall under the category *dog* form the extension of the category *dog;* the English word 'dog' is standardly used both to refer to dogs out there (the extensions), and to the category *dog;* the category *dog* is the mental representation, whatever this will turn out to be, that fixes the conditions under which we use the word 'dog'[1].

Cognitive psychologists have asked: What are the mental bases for such categorizations; and, What is the internal structure of such categories? Related questions have traditionally been asked within philosophical and linguistic semantics: What is the relation between linguistic expressions (say, 'dog') and things in the world (say, the dogs) such that 'dog' conventionally refers to dogs?

A possible answer is that the relations between words and mental categories is simple, one-to-one, i.e., the word 'dog' refers to the category *dog,* which is unanalyzable. Such holistic theories have hardly even been considered until very recently. One reason for their unpopularity, as Fodor (1975; 1981) has discussed, is the desire to limit the set of atomic categories or elementary discriminations with which each human must be assumed to be endowed. Instead, traditional theories have assumed that only a very few of the words code unanalyzable concepts; rather, even most common words such as 'dog' are cover labels for mental categories that are themselves bundles of simpler mental categories (in this context, usually called *features, properties,* or *attributes).* Knowledge of the complex categories is then built up by recognizing that some sensible elements (simple categories) recur together in the encounters of the sensorium with the external world and so, by association, get bundled together. Maybe, for example, what we call in English 'a bird' is mentally represented as an *animal,* that *flies,* has *wings, feathers,* lays *eggs,* etc. (cf., Locke, 1968/1690). According to many proponents of feature theories, then, it is the structure of the real world as observed by the learner that gives rise to such categorizations: it is the fact that what has feathers tends to fly and lay eggs, in our world, which gives rise to (perhaps 'is') the complex category *bird.*

Despite the beguiling appearance of simplicity of semantic feature theory, this general approach looks more tangled on closer inspection. For example, our description of the possible features of *bird* has already run into a problem for actually a bird *is* an animal, *has* wings, *lays* eggs, and so forth. Not all these putatively simpler categories are related to the category *bird* in the same way. Some models of categorization that employ feature descriptions have further apparatus specifically designed to respond to such defects. For instance, the Collins and Loftus spreading activation model (1975) connects features by labelled links (such as *have, is*, etc.), thus at least acknowledging (though not explaining) the complexity of feature relations.

Another difficulty is that the empiricist program as articulated by Locke and his heirs had gained much of its explanatory force by postulating that the simple categories (or at least the nominal essences, leaving aside the unknowable real essences, cf., footnote 1) were sensory categories; that all categories, no matter how complex, could be built up as combinations of these sensory categories. It is a pretty sure bet that this strong form of the empiricist program won't work. The features (e.g., *wing*) of words that have no simple sensory description do not turn out to be noticeably more sensory than the words (e.g., 'bird') of which they are to be the features, again a point that has been made by Fodor (1975; see also Bolinger, 1965). The weaker version of this position, that recognizes nonsensory categories among the elementary ones often seems lame in practice, as the features one has to countenance to make it work grow increasingly implausible (e.g., *wing* for 'bird' but also *never married* for 'bachelor').[2]

But problems and details aside, we have just sketched the distinction between holistic theories, in which the unit of analysis is a category with scope something like that of the word itself; and feature (or decompositional) theories, in which analysis is on units more molecular than the word. We now turn to a major subdivision among the feature theories.

**The definitional view**

We take up here two major subtypes of the feature theory of mental categories (and, hence, lexical semantics): the classical *definitional* view, and the *prototype* or cluster concept view. On the definitional variant, a smallish set of the simple properties are individually necessary and severally sufficient to pick out all and only, say, the birds, from everything else in the world. Membership in the class is categorical, for all who partake of the right properties are in virtue of that equally birds; and all who do not, are not. No other distinctions among the class members are relevant to their designation as birds. For example, the familiar creature in Figure 1 is a bird because it has the feathers, the wings, and so on. But the grotesque creature of Figure 2 is no more nor less a bird despite its peculiarities, again because it exhibits the stipulated properties.

It is reasonable to ask why this definitional theory has seemed attractive for so long (see Fodor, Garrett, Walker, and Parkes, 1980, for discussion of the history of ideas on this topic and illuminating analyses, which we roughly follow here). The central reason is that this theory gives hope of explaining how we reason with words and solve the problem of compositional meaning: how the words take their meanings together in a linguistic structure, to yield the meanings of phrases and sentences. For example, programmatically, this theory has an explanation of word-to-phrase synonymy, for how 'bachelor' and 'man who has never married' could be recognized to mean the same thing. The claim is that, in the language of the mind, the category *bachelor* decomposes into its list of features, including *man* and *never married* — just the same items that occur in the semantic representation of the phrase. On this view, then, semantic interpretation is on the feature level vocabulary, not the word level vocabulary (Katz and Fodor, 1963).

**Figure 1    A prototypical bird**

**Robin**

**Figure 2    A marginal bird**

**Pelican**

The potential for explaining compositional meaning would be a formidable virtue indeed for a theory of categories; in fact, there seems little point to any theory of concepts or categorization that lacks this potentiality, for there is no way to commit to memory all the categories we can conceive, and that can be expressed by phrases (e.g., 'all the spotted ostriches on Sam's farm'). So the question now becomes: why do so many doubt the validity of the definitional view?

The only good answer is that the definitional theory is difficult to work out in the required detail. No one has succeeded in finding the supposed simplest categories (the features). It rarely seems to be the case that all and only the class members can be picked out in terms of sufficient lists of conjectured elemental categories. And eliminating some of the apparently necessary properties (e.g., deleting *feathers*, *flies*, and *eggs* so as to include the down-covered baby male ostriches among the birds) seems not to affect category membership. Generally speaking, it is widely agreed today in philosophy, linguistics, and psychology, that the definitional program for everyday lexical categories has been defeated — at least in its pristine form (cf., footnote 2; and for a very informative review of recent philosophical discussion of these issues, see Schwartz, 1979).

**The prototype view**

However, as is also well known, there is another class of feature descriptions that gives up the necessary and sufficient claim of the classical theory. This is the family resemblance description, first alluded to by Wittgenstein (1953), though he might be surprised at some of its recent guises. Wittgenstein took as an important example the word 'game'. He defied anyone to think of a definition in virtue of which all and only the possible games could be picked out. This being impossible on the face of it, Wittgenstein conjectured that *game* was a cluster concept, held together by a variety of gamey attributes, only some of which are instantiated by any one game. His analogy was to the structure of family resemblances. It is such a position that Rosch and her co-workers have adapted and refined, and brought into psychology through a series of compelling experimental demonstrations.

We can sketch the properties of such a theory by using the example of the Smith Brothers, of cough-drop fame, as shown in Figure 3. All these Brothers have features in common — the eyeglasses, the light hair, the bushy moustache, and so forth. But not all Smith Brothers have the same Smith-features, and no one criterial feature defines the family. The equal membership assumption of the definitional view is not an assumption of recent family resemblance descriptions. Instead, we can distinguish among the Smith Brothers according to the number of Smith-family attributes each embodies. The Brother at 11 o'clock in Figure 3 is a poor exemplar of *Smithness* for he has only a few of the attributes and thus will share attributes with the Jones family or the James family. But the Brother in the middle is a prototypical Smith for he has all or most of the Smith attributes. Finally, there is no sharp boundary delimiting where the Smith family ends and the Jones family starts. Rather, as the Smiths' biographers could probably tell you, the category boundary is indistinct.

**Figure 3    The Smith Brothers**

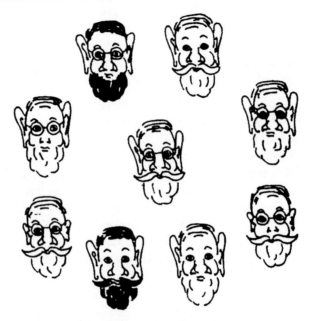

A large class of models theoretically is available that expand upon this general structure.[3] Particularly appealing is one in which the representation is "in the form of an abstract ordered set of inclusion probabilities ordered according to the internal structure of the category" (Rosch, 1975a). If we understand correctly, Rosch's idea here is that there are distinctions among the properties themselves, relative to some category. There are privileged properties, manifest in most or even all exemplars of the category; these could even be necessary properties. Even so, these privileged properties are insufficient for picking out all and only the class members, and hence a family resemblance description is still required. Prototypical members have all or most privileged properties of the categories. Marginal members have only one or a few. Possession of a privileged property from another category (e.g., the water-bound nature of whales or the air-borne nature of bats) or failure to exhibit a privileged property (e.g., the featherlessness of baby or plucked robins) may also relegate some members to the periphery.

But it should be emphasized that proponents of cluster-prototype theories of categories are not committed to defend this particular realization of such a model, nor to make detailed claims of a particular sort about the nature of the hypothesized properties themselves (as Rosch has pointed out, they may be imagelike or not, or imagelike for some concepts, less so for other concepts; see footnote 3), nor about how they are stored or accessed from memory, learned, etc. Finally, it need not be claimed that all mental categories have this structure, or this structure only, i.e., some models incorporate a paired logical and prototypical structure for single concepts (we return to discussion of this variant in the conclusions to this paper, Part I). A large variety of cluster, nondefinitional, models currently contend in the psychological literature. As

Smith and Medin (1981) elegantly describe, the models fare variously well in describing subjects' categorization behavior in various tasks. Of course, a mixed model, such as the one these latter authors finally defend, describes more of the data than any one of the other contending models, but at cost of expanding the postulated formal apparatus.

What are the virtues of this class of proposals about the organization of mental categories? To the extent that the prototype views are still componential, they still give hope of limiting the primitive basis, the set of innate concepts. If correct, they allow the empiricist program to go through in detail for the complicated concepts: in Rosch's version of the position, it is the "correlated structure of the world", the observed cooccurrence of the basic attributes out there that leads to these. Second, and most usefully, the cluster-prototype theories programmatically have an account, in terms of various available measures of feature overlap and/or feature organization, for the apparent fact that membership in a category may be graded; for example, to explain why the bird in Figure 1 seems a birdier bird than the one in Figure 2.

Moreover, there is an extensive body of empirical research that seems to provide evidence for the psychological validity of this position. For example, Table 1 shows four everyday superordinate categories — *fruit, sport, vegetable,* and *vehicle* — and some exemplars of each. (We follow Rosch's use of the term exemplar: By an exemplar we shall mean a category, e.g., *table,* that falls under some superordinate category, e.g., *furniture.* When speaking of some real table — of an extension of the category *table* — we shall use the term *instance*).

In one experiment, Rosch (1973) asked subjects to indicate how good an example each exemplar was of its category by use of an appropriate rating scale. It turns out that people will say that apples are very good examples of *fruit*, and deserve high ratings, while figs and olives are poor examplars, and deserve lower ratings. Rosch and her colleagues have interpreted such findings as evidence that membership in a category is graded, rather than all or none; and thus as suppport for a cluster-prototype theory while inconsistent with a definitional theory of the mental representation of these categories.

The robustness and reliability of these effects is not in question.[4] Prototype theorists have devised a large number of plausible paradigms, and in each shown that the same kinds of result crop up. As one more case, subjects respond faster in a verification task to items with high exemplariness ratings than to those with lower ones. That is, the verification time for 'A ROBIN IS A BIRD' is faster than the verification time for 'AN OSTRICH IS A BIRD' with word frequency controlled across the list (Rips *et al.*, 1973; Rosch, 1975a). In the face of such findings, one might well conclude, as have many cognitive psychologists, that the psychological validity of the cluster-prototype descriptions of everyday categories has been demonstrated beyond reasonable doubt.

We believe, however, that there are grounds for caution before embracing a particular interpretation of these findings. Some of the reasons have to do with the logic of the prototype position. To the extent the prototype theory is asserted to be a feature theory, it shares many of the woes of the definitional theory. For example, it is not notably easier to find the prototypic features of a concept than to find the necessary and sufficient ones. But to the extent the prototype theory is asserted not to be a feature theory — that is, to be a holistic theory — it must share the woes of that kind of theory (as pointed out by Fodor, 1975); namely, massive expansion of the primitive categorial base. (We will return in later discussion to general problems with feature theories of lexical concepts; see Discussion, Part II).

Even more damaging to prototype theories is that they render the description of reasoning with words — for example, understanding lexical entailments of the vixen-is-a-fox variety — titanically more difficult. And understanding compositional (phrase and sentence) meaning looks altogether hopeless. One reason is that if you combine, say 'foolish' and 'bird' into the phrase 'foolish bird' it is no longer a fixed matter — rather it is indeterminate — which *foolish* elements and which *bird* elements are intended to be combined. It goes almost without saying that, to fix this, one couldn't envisage the phrasal categories (e.g., *foolish bird*) to be mentally represented in terms of their own prototype descriptions, there being indefinitely many of these.[5] Speaking more generally, one need only consider such attributes as *good, tall,* and the like, and the trouble they make even for the classical view (i.e., what makes a knife a good knife is not what makes a wife a good wife; for discussion, see Katz, 1972; G. A. Miller, 1977) to realize how many millenia we are away from a useful theory of the infinitely combining lexical concepts. The problems become orders of magnitude more difficult still when the classical approach is abandoned.

In the light of these difficulties, it seems surprising that psychologists have usually been pleased, rather than depressed, by experimental findings that tend to support a cluster-prototype theory. Since we speak in whole sentences rather than in single words, the chief desideratum of a theory of categories (coded by the words) would seem to be promise of a computable description for the infinite sentence meanings. These apparent problems with a prototype theory provide some impetus to reconsider the empirical outcomes obtained by the Rosch group and others. Do these findings really commit us to the prototype theory of conceptual structure?

In the experiments we will report, we will first revisit these outcomes by extending the category types under investigation. After all, the current basis for claiming that certain categories have a prototypical, nondefinitional, feature structure is the finding of graded responses to their exemplars in various experimental paradigms. But if you believe certain concepts are nondefinitional because of graded responses to their exemplars, that must be because you also believe that if the categories *were* definitional (all-or-none) in character, and if the subjects *knew* these definitions, the graded responses would *not* have been achieved. But this remains to be shown. A necessary part of the proof requires finding some categories that *do* have definitional descriptions, and showing as well that subjects patently know and assent to these definitions; and, finally, showing that these categories do not yield the graded outcomes.[6]

Are there definitional concepts? Of course. For example, consider the superordinate concept *odd number*. This seems to have a clear definition, a precise description; namely, *an integer not divisible by two without remainder*. No integer seems to sit on the fence, undecided as to whether it is quite even, or perhaps a bit odd. No odd

100

number seems odder than any other odd number. But if so, then experimental paradigms that purport to show *bird* is prototypic in structure in virtue of the fact that responses to 'ostrich' and 'robin' are unequal should fail, on the same reasoning, to yield differential responses to 'five' and 'seven', as examples of *odd number*. Similarly, such well-defined concepts as *plane geometry figure* and *female* ought not to yield the graded response patterns that were the experimental basis for the claim that the concept *bird* has a family resemblance structure.

As we shall now show, the facts are otherwise. For graded responses are achieved regardless of the structure of the concepts, for both *fruit* and *odd number*.

## Experiment I

Experiment I asks what happens when subjects are required to rate "how good an exemplar is" as an example of a given category. In part, this experiment represents a replication of Rosch (1973), but it goes beyond it for the subjects had to rate exemplars of two kinds of categories: well-defined ones, such as *even number*, and the allegedly prototypic ones, such as *sport*.

## Method

### Subjects

The subjects were 63 University of Pennsylvania undergraduates, 22 male and 41 female, all of whom were volunteers and were native speakers of English.

### Stimuli

The stimuli were items that fell into eight categories. Four of these were prototype categories chosen from among those previously used by Rosch (Rosch, 1973; 1975a): *fruit, sport, vegetable,* and *vehicle.* Four other categories were of the kind we call well-defined: *even number, odd number, plane geometry figure,* and *female.*

Each category was represented by two sets of six exemplars each. For the prototype categories, the first sets of exemplars (set A) were those used by Rosch previously (Rosch, 1973). Their choice was determined by using norms established by Battig and Montague (1969) who asked subjects to provide exemplars of everyday categories and then computed frequencies of the responses. The choice of the six exemplars was such as to approximate the following distribution of frequencies on these norms: 400, 150, 100, 50, 15, and 4 or less. Our second sets of exemplars for prototype categories (set B) were selected according to these same criteria. Since there are no previously collected norms for the well-defined categories we used here, two sets of six exemplars were generated for each category on the basis of an intuitive ranking made by the experimenters. The eight categories with both sets of exemplars are shown in Table 1.

### Procedure

The subjects were asked to rate, on a 7-point scale, the extent to which each given exemplar represented their idea or image of the meaning of each category term. Each category name (e.g., *fruit*) was typed on a separate page. Approximately half of the subjects (31 ) rated one set of exemplars (set A) of each of the eight categories; the rest (32) rated the other sets of exemplars (set B). Within these sets, each subject was assigned randomly to a different order of the eight categories. The exemplar stimuli themselves (e.g., *apple*) were typed below their category names. They were presented in two different random orders within each category, with about half of the subjects receiving one order and the other half receiving the other order.

**Table 1 Categories, category exemplars, and exemplariness ratings for prototype and well-defined categories**

| Prototype categories | | | | Well-defined categories | | | |
|---|---|---|---|---|---|---|---|
| fruit | | | | even number | | | |
| apple | 1.3 | orange | 1.1 | 4 | 1.1 | 2 | 1.0 |
| strawberry | 2.1 | cherry | 1.7 | 8 | 1.5 | 6 | 1.7 |
| plum | 2.5 | watermelon | 2.9 | 10 | 1.7 | 42 | 2.6 |
| pineapple | 2.7 | apricot | 3.0 | 18 | 2.6 | 1000 | 2.8 |
| fig | 5.2 | coconut | 4.8 | 34 | 3.4 | 34 | 3.1 |
| olive | 6.4 | olive | 6.5 | 106 | 3.9 | 806 | 3.9 |
| sport | | | | odd number | | | |
| football | 1.4 | baseball | 1.2 | 3 | 1.6 | 7 | 1.4 |
| hockey | 1.8 | soccer | 1.6 | 7 | 1.9 | 11 | 1.7 |
| gymnastics | 2.8 | fencing | 3.5 | 23 | 2.4 | 13 | 1.8 |
| wrestling | 3.1 | sailing | 3.8 | 57 | 2.6 | 9 | 1.9 |
| archery | 4.8 | bowling | 4.4 | 501 | 3.5 | 57 | 3.4 |
| weight-lifting | 5.1 | hiking | 4.6 | 447 | 3.7 | 91 | 3.7 |
| vegetable | | | | female | | | |
| carrot | 1.5 | peas | 1.7 | mother | 1.7 | sister | 1.8 |
| celery | 2.6 | spinach | 1.7 | housewife | 2.4 | ballerina | 2.0 |
| asparagus | 2.7 | cabbage | 2.7 | princess | 3.0 | actress | 2.1 |
| onion | 3.6 | radish | 3.1 | waitress | 3.2 | hostess | 2.7 |
| pickle | 4.8 | peppers | 3.2 | policewoman | 3.9 | chairwoman | 3.4 |
| parsley | 5.0 | pumpkin | 5.5 | comedienne | 4.5 | cowgirl | 4.5 |
| vehicle | | | | plane geometry figure | | | |
| car | 1.0 | bus | 1.8 | square | 1.3 | square | 1.5 |
| boat | 3.3 | motorcycle | 2.2 | triangle | 1.5 | triangle | 1.4 |
| scooter | 4.5 | tractor | 3.7 | rectangle | 1.9 | rectangle | 1.6 |
| tricycle | 4.7 | wagon | 4.2 | circle | 2.1 | circle | 1.3 |
| horse | 5.2 | sled | 5.2 | trapezoid | 3.1 | trapezoid | 2.9 |
| skis | 5.6 | elevator | 6.2 | ellipse | 3.4 | ellipse | 3.5 |

*Under each category label, category exemplars and mean exemplariness ratings are displayed for both Set A (N = 31, shown on the left) and Set B (N = 32), shown on the right).

The specific instructions for the rating task were taken verbatim from Rosch's study (Rosch, 1975a). The following is an extract that gives the general idea of what the subjects were asked to do (The instructions from Rosch, that we repeated verbatim in our replication, do not distinguish *exemplar* from *instance*, as is obvious; for the purposes of instructing naive subjects, at least, marking the distinction seemed irrelevant):

"This study has to do with what we have in mind when we use words which refer to categories. . . Think of dogs. You all have some notion of what a 'real dog', a 'doggy dog' is. To me a retriever or a German Shepherd is a very doggy dog while a Pekinese is a less doggy dog. Notice that this kind of judgment has nothing to do with how well you like the thing... You may prefer to own a Pekinese without thinking that it is the breed that best represents what people mean by dogginess.

On this form you are asked to judge how good an example of a category various instances of the category are. . . You are to rate how good an example of the category each member is on a 7-point scale. A *1* means that you feel the member is a very good example of your idea of what the category is. A 7 means you feel the member fits very poorly with your idea or image of the category (or is not a member at all). A *4* means you feel the member fits moderately well. . . Use the other numbers of the 7-point scale to indicate intermediate judgments.

Don't worry about why you feel that something is or isn't a good example of the category. And don't worry about whether it's just you or people in general who feel that way. Just mark it the way you see it."

### Results and discussion

Our subjects, like Rosch's, found the task readily comprehensible. No one questioned or protested about doing what they were asked to do. The results on the categories and exemplars that were used by both us and Rosch (Rosch, 1973) were virtually identical, as Table 2 shows. Our subjects, like Rosch's, felt that certain exemplars are good ones for certain categories (as in *apple* for *fruit)* while others are poor (as in *olive* for *fruit).* Moreover, there was considerable agreement among subjects about which items are good and which bad exemplars. To test for such inter-subject agreement, Rosch used split-group correlations, correlating the mean ratings obtained by a randomly chosen half of the subjects with the mean ratings of the other half (Rosch, 1975a). Rosch reports split-group correlations above 0.97; our own split-group rank correlations were 1.00, 0.94, 0.89, and 1.00 for the categories *fruit, vegetable, sport,* and *vehicle,* respectively, using the same exemplars employed by Rosch (that is, our stimulus sets A). Here too, our pattern of results is essentially identical with that obtained by Rosch.

The important question concerns the results for the well-defined categories. Keep in mind that we here asked subjects, for example, to distinguish *among* certain odd numbers, *for* oddity, and common sense asserts one cannot do so. But the subjects could and did. For example, they judged *3* a better odd number than *501* and *mother* a better female than *comedienne.* The full pattern of these results is shown in Table I, which presents mean exemplariness ratings for all the exemplars of all alleged prototype and well-defined categories in our study.

What is more, just as with the prototype categories, the subjects seemed to agree as to which exemplars are good and which poor examples of the categories. To prove this point, we used the same method employed by Rosch, and calculated split-group correlations for both sets in each of the categories. The correlations are quite high.

Combining sets A and B, the median split-group rank correlations were 0.94, 0.81, 0.92, and 0.92, for *even number, odd number, female,* and *plane geometry figure,* respectively. (In retrospect, the choice of *odd number* as one of the categories was bound to cause some trouble and yield the slightly lower rank correlation just because the subjects could, and sometimes did, take the liberty of interpreting *odd* as *peculiar*; this kind of ambiguity clearly will contaminate the correlations, as McCloskey and Glucksberg, 1978, have demonstrated).

**Table 2    Comparison of mean exemplariness ratings**

|  | Rosch, 1973 | Armstrong *et al.,* 1982 |
|---|---|---|
| Fruit |  |  |
| Apple | 1.3 | 1.3 |
| Strawberry | 2.3 | 2.1 |
| Plum | 2.3 | 2.5 |
| Pineapple | 2.3 | 2.7 |
| Fig | 4.7 | 5.2 |
| Olive | 6.2 | 6.4 |
| Sport |  |  |
| Football | 1.2 | 1.4 |
| Hockey | 1.8 | 1.8 |
| Gymnastics | 2.6 | 2.8 |
| Wrestling | 3.0 | 3.1 |
| Archery | 3.9 | 4.8 |
| Weight-lifting | 4.7 | 5.1 |
| Vegetable |  |  |
| Carrot | 1.1 | 1.5 |
| Celery | 1.7 | 2.6 |
| Asparagus | 1.3 | 2.7 |
| Onion | 2.7 | 3.6 |
| Pickle | 4.4 | 4.8 |
| Parsley | 3.8 | 5.0 |
| Vehicle |  |  |
| Car | 1.0 | 1.0 |
| Boat | 2.7 | 3.3 |
| Scooter | 2.5 | 4.5 |
| Tricycle | 3.5 | 4.7 |
| Horse | 5.9 | 5.2 |
| Skis | 5.7 | 5.6 |

Taken as a whole, the results for the well-defined categories look remarkably like those that have been said to characterize fuzzy categories — those that are said in fact to be the basis on which the categories are termed nondefinitional. Just as some fruits are judged to be fruitier than others, so some even numbers seem more even than other even numbers. In addition, there is considerable inter-subject agreement about these judgments.

To be sure, there are some differences between the judgments given to exemplars of prototypic and well-defined categories. Pooling all the prototype categories, we obtain a mean exemplariness rating of 3.4, as compared to 2.5 for all the well-defined categories, (t = 18.4, df = 62, p < 0.001). This means that, overall, the subjects were more likely to judge a given exemplar of a prototype category as less than perfect than they were to render this judgment on an exemplar of a well-defined category.

One interpretation of this result is that it is a simple artifact of the way the category exemplars were selected. The prototype sets were constructed following Rosch's procedures, and included some rather unlikely exemplars (such as *skis* as an instance of *vehicle*). The lower mean ratings for the well-defined categories could have been a consequence of the fact that we made no attempt here to think of atypical exemplars. But they could also be reflections of a true difference in the category types. Maybe there is no such thing as a perfectly ghastly even number that is an even number all the same.

We did make an attempt to check the manipulability of these ratings, by developing new lists of the well-defined categories that included exemplars we thought 'atypical'. The very fact that one can consider doing this, incidentally, is further proof that there is some sense in which exemplars of well-defined categories must be rankable. For the category *female*, we replaced such stereotypical female items as *housewife* with what seemed to us more highly charged items; specifically, the new list was: *mother, ballerina, waitress, cowgirl, nun,* and *lesbian.* For the category *even number*, we substituted a list whose cardinality increased more, and at the same time which contained more and more odd digits among the even ones. Specifically, the list was: *2, 6, 32, 528, 726,* and *1154.*

We ran 20 volunteers at Wesleyan University on these new lists, using the same procedures. In fact we did get a weak increase in the means for the even numbers (the overall mean for *even number* in Experiment I was 2.4 and it increased to 2.9 for the new list, though not significantly (t = 1.51, df = 49, p < 0.10). For the category *female,* we got a surprise. It is obvious from Table 1 that the rankings of females follow a fairly strict sexism order. It was this dimension we tried to exploit in adding such items as *lesbian.* But now the mean rankings went down (to 2.8 from 2.9), not a significant difference and not in the expected direction. Perhaps the choice of new items was injudicious or perhaps there are no exemplars for *female* that fall at the lowest points on the scale.

To summarize, the central purpose of our experiment has been to show that responses to well-defined categories are graded. Graded responses to everyday concepts in precisely this experimental paradigm have heretofore been taken as demonstrating that these everyday concepts are nondefinitional. That this interpretation was too strong, *for the everyday concepts,* is shown by the fact that the formal concepts yield the same response patterns, on the same tasks. This new finding says nothing about the structure of everyday concepts for it is a negative result, pure and simple. Its thrust is solely this: to the extent it is secure beyond doubt that, e.g., *fruit* and *plane geometry figure* have different structures, a paradigm that cannot distinguish between responses to them is not revealing about the structure of concepts. A secondary point in this first experiment was that subjects may not find any even number or female quite so atypical of their categories as some fruit or some vehicle is atypical of their categories. But what has to be confronted head on is the finding that *some* even numbers are said to be *any* evener than *any* others, and that subjects are in accord on such judgments. The next experiments are designed to clarify what this strange outcome might mean.

## Experiment II

It is possible to suppose that the graded responses to all-or-none categories in the experiment just reported are epiphenomena. After all, we asked subjects to judge odd numbers for oddity, and the like. They might have been reacting to silly questions by giving silly answers. The task (rating exemplars) is a reflective one, without time and difficulty constraints, so the subjects might well have developed *ad hoc* strategies quite different from those used by subjects in previous prototype experiments, yielding superficially similar results, but arising from utterly different mental sources. To see whether such an explanation goes through, we performed another experiment, this time one in which there is a premium on speed and in which the subject is not asked explicitly to reflect on the way exemplars fit into mental category structures. This experiment again replicates prior work with prototype categories.

Rosch and others have shown that subjects respond more quickly in a category verification task given items of high as opposed to low exemplariness (Rips, Shoben, and Smith, 1973; Rosch, 1973; for general reviews see Danks & Glucksberg, 1980; Mervis & Rosch, 1981; Smith, 1978). It takes less time to verify sentences such as 'A ROBIN IS A BIRD' than sentences such as 'AN OSTRICH IS A BIRD' with word frequency controlled across the list of sentences. This result fits in neatly with the prototype view. For example, if a concept is mentally represented by a prototype, and if processing time is some function of feature matching, then one might well expect that the more features a word has in common with a prototype, the more quickly that word will be identified as a category exemplar (The varying models of fuzzy concept structure have appropriately varying accounts of why the typical exemplars are verified the faster; it is not for us to take a stand among them, but see Smith and Medin, 1981, for a lucid comparative discussion).

The present study uses the same basic verification task. But the sentences that have to be verified here include instances of both the well-defined and the alleged prototype categories. The question is whether the differential verification times that had been used as an argument for the prototype structure of categories such as *sport* or *vegetable* will be found for categories such as *even number*.

## Method

### Subjects

The subjects were ten undergraduate volunteers, 5 male and 5 female, at the University of Pennsylvania.

### Stimuli

The stimuli were 64 sentences of the form 'AN *A* IS A *B*' in which B was a category of which A was said to be an exemplar. Thirty-two of the sentences were true (e.g., 'AN

ORANGE IS A FRUIT'); 32 were false (e.g., 'AN ORANGE IS A VEHICLE'). To construct the true sentences, we used the eight categories employed in Experiment I (four prototype categories and four well-defined ones). Each of the categories had four exemplars. These varied along two dimensions: category exemplariness and word frequency. Two exemplars had previously (that is, in earlier testing) been rated to be relatively good category members and two were rated to be relatively poor (as indicated by mean ratings below and above 2.0, respectively). Following Rosch, we also controlled for word frequency (Rosch, 1973). Thus one of the two highly rated exemplars was a high frequency word, while the other was of low frequency. The same was true of the two low-rated exemplars. The word-frequencies were determined by reference to the Thorndike and Lorge (1944) and Kucera and Francis (1967) word counts. (In case you're wondering: there *are* frequency counts for some numbers in Kucera and Francis, 1967, and we limited our choices to those for which such frequency counts were available). The categories and their exemplars used in the 32 true sentences are shown in Table 3. To construct the 32 false sentences, each of the 32 exemplars was randomly paired with one of the seven categories to which it did *not* belong. There was one constraint: each category had to be used equally often; that is, four times.

**Table 3    Categories and category exemplars used in sentence verification study*§**

|  | Good exemplars | Poorer exemplars |
| --- | --- | --- |
| Prototype categories |  |  |
| fruit | orange, banana | fig, coconut |
| sport | baseball, hockey | fishing, archery |
| vegetable | peas, spinach | onion, mushroom |
| vehicle | bus, ambulance | wagon, skis |
| Well-defined categories |  |  |
| even number | 8,22 | 30,18 |
| odd number | 7,13 | 15,23 |
| female | aunt, ballerina | widow, waitress |
| plane geometry figure | rectangle | ellipse, trapezoid |

*Under each rubric (e.g., fruit, good exemplar), high-frequency exemplars are listed first, low-frequency ones second.

§The prototype exemplars were taken from Rosch (1975a). The well-defined exemplars were taken from Experiment I of this paper, and some previous pilot studies. The criterion of exemplariness was that used in Rosch's original verification study (Rosch, 1973); good exemplars had ratings of 2 or less, poorer exemplars had ratings above this.

### Procedure

The sentences were displayed on the screen of a PET microprocessor. Each trial was initiated by the subject, who pressed the space bar to indicate he or she was ready. This led to appearance of one of the 64 sentences on the screen. The trial ended when the subject pressed one of two keys to indicate 'true' or 'false'. The subjects were instructed to respond as quickly and as accurately as possible. The 64 sentences were presented twice in a different random order for each subject. The testing session was preceded by ten practice trials using other exemplars and other categories. Both the response and the reaction time were recorded by the microprocessor.

**Results and discussion**

Table 4 shows the mean verification times for the true sentences, displayed by category and by exemplariness. The data are based on correct responses only with errors excluded. Since the error rate was reasonably low (5%), this had little effect.

**Table 4    Verification times for good and poorer exemplars of several prototype and well-defined categories (in msec)**

|  | Good exemplars | Poorer exemplars |
|---|---|---|
| Prototype categories |  |  |
| fruit | 903 | 1125 |
| sport | 892 | 941 |
| vegetable | 1127 | 1211 |
| vehicle | 989 | 1228 |
| Well-defined categories |  |  |
| even number | 1073 | 1132 |
| odd number | 1088 | 1090 |
| female | 1032 | 1156 |
| plane geometry figure | 1104 | 1375 |

As the table shows, we found that exemplariness affects verification time. The better exemplars of a category were more readily identified as category members. This result was found for the prototype categories, where the mean verification times were 977 msec and 1127 msec for good and poorer exemplars respectively ($t = 2.36$, df = 9, $p < 0.05$). But it was found also for the well-defined categories, in which the mean verification times were 1074 msec and 1188 msec for good and poorer exemplars respectively ($t = 3.19$, df = 9, $p < 0.01$). An overall analysis of variance yielded a marginally significant main effect due to kind of category (members of well-defined categories required longer verification times than those of the prototype categories; $F = 3.20$, df = 1/27, $p < 0.10$) and a main effect due to exemplariness (good exemplars led to shorter verification times than poorer exemplars, $F = 12.79$, df = 1/27, $p < 0.005$). There was no trace of an interaction between these two factors ($F < 1$).

Summarizing these results, differential reaction times to verification (just like exemplariness ratings) are as reliable and often as powerful for well-defined, even mathematical, concepts as they are for the everyday concepts that seem to be ill-defined or prototypical. Moreover, this is not simply a case of subjects responding haphazardly to questions that make no sense, for such an explanation cannot account for why the subjects agreed with each other in rating and reacting. The prototype theories have ready accounts for why it takes longer to say 'yes' to 'A COCONUT IS A FRUIT' than to 'AN ORANGE IS A FRUIT', in terms of differential numbers of, or access to, features for typical and atypical exemplars of fuzzy categories. But how can such a theory explain that it takes longer to verify that '18 IS AN EVEN NUMBER' than that '22 IS AN EVEN NUMBER'?

Some have responded to these findings very consistently, by asserting that the experimental findings are to be interpreted as before: that, psychologically speaking, odd numbers as well as birds and vegetables are graded concepts. But this response to us proves only that one man's *reductio ad absurdum* is the next man's necessary truth (J. M. E. Moravcsik, personal communication). We reject this conclusion just because we could not explain how a person could compute with integers who truly believed that 7 was odder than 23. We assert confidently that the facts about subjects being able to compute and about their being able to give the definition of odd number, etc., are the more important, highly entrenched, facts we want to preserve and explain in any theory that purports to be 'a theory of the conceptual organization of the integers; particularly, of the conceptual organization of the notion odd number'. A discordant note possibly defeating such a description has been struck by the finding that some odd numbers are rated as odder than other odd numbers and verified more slowly as being odd numbers. Of all the facts about the mental structure of oddity that one would want the psychological theories to explain, however, this seems one of the least crucial and the least connected to the other facts; certainly, unimportant compared to the fact that all odd numbers, when divided by two, leave a remainder of one. Since one cannot have both facts simultaneously in the theory of the mental representation of oddity, we ourselves are prepared to give up the seeming fact that some odd numbers appear, as shown by their behavior in certain experimental paradigms, to be odder than others. As we shall later discuss, we do not give it up by saying it was no fact; rather, by saying it must have been a fact about something other than the structure of concepts. (For a theoretical treatment that turns on notions of the entrenchment and connectedness of predicates in a related way, see Goodman, 1965; and also relatedly, see Osherson, 1978, for the position that natural concepts are "'projectible' in the sense that [they] can figure in law-like generalizations that support counterfactuals" p. 265).

Reiterating, then, we hold that *fruit* and *odd number* have different structures, and yet we obtain the same experimental outcome for both. But if the same result is achieved regardless of the concept structure, then the experimental design is not pertinent to the determination of concept structure.

## Experiment III

Despite our conclusion, our subjects and previous subjects of Rosch were orderly in their response styles to these paradigms, so they must be telling us something. If not about the structure of concepts, what are they telling us about? As a step toward finding out, we now frankly asked a new pool of subjects, for a variety of the definitional and putatively prototypical concepts, to tell us straight out whether membership in the class was graded or categorical. After all, the results for Experiments I and II are puzzling only if we assume the subjects were really rating category membership (an assumption that it seems to us is made by prior investigators). But suppose the subjects are not really rating category membership; that is, suppose category exemplariness is psychologically not identical to category membership. To test this idea, we now asked subjects whether you could be a more-or-less-birdish bird, a more-or-less-odd odd number, or whether each was an all-or-none matter, as the classical theory would have it.

## Method

### Subjects

The subjects were 21 undergraduate volunteers, 10 male and 11 female, at the University of Pennsylvania, all run in individual sessions.

### Stimuli

Each subject was given two test booklets constructed in the same manner as those used for set A in Experiment I. The instructions differed, however, from those of Experiment I and were printed on a separate sheet. The two tasks are described below:

### Procedure, Task 1

The subjects were given the first booklet and asked to go through it page by page. The booklets were just like those of Experiment I. At the top of each page was typed a category name. Four of the prototype variety and four of the definitional variety were used, in fact just the categories used in Experiment I. Under each category name was typed its six exemplars; these were the set A items from Experiment I. The subjects' first task was to tell us whether they believed that membership in a given class is graded or categorical. The actual question they were posed (which they had to answer for each category by writing 'Yes' or 'No' on each page) was:

> "Does it make sense to rate items in this category for *degree of membership* in the category"?

To explain what we meant, the instruction sheet provided the following statements (on later inquiry, all subjects indicated that they had understood the question):

> "What we mean by degree of membership: It makes sense to rate items for degree of membership in a category if the items meet the criteria required for membership to a *different degree*.
>
> It does *not* make sense to rate items for degree of membership in a category if all the items meet the criteria required for membership to the *same degree;* that is, if the items are literally either in or out of the category."

### Procedure, Task 2

Having told us whether they believed that membership in the various categories is graded or categorical, the subjects were given a new task. They were presented with a second set of booklets. These contained the same categories and the same exemplars as the first booklet, except that the order of the categories (as before, each on a separate page) and the order of exemplars within categories was randomly varied. They also contained a new set of instructions that described the subjects' new task.

These new instructions first told the subjects to "disregard the previous question in answering this one. This is a new and different question". They were then asked to rate the exemplariness of each item in each category — the same task, posed with the identical instructions, that we (following Rosch) had given to the subjects in Experiment I. Their job was the same regardless of how they had performed on the first task. They had to rate the exemplariness of the category items even if they had previously stated that membership in this category is all-or-none. Thus the selfsame subject who had, say, denied that some odd numbers could be odder than others, was now asked to rate odd numbers according to which was a good example of odd numbers, which not so good, and so on, on the usual 7-point scale.

## Results and discussion

The results of Task 1 are displayed in Table 5, which shows the percentage of subjects who said that items in a given category could *not* be rated by degree of membership, that an item is either in or out with no inbetween. As the table shows, 100% felt this way about *odd number, even number,* and *plane geometry figure* and a substantial percentage (86%) felt this way about *female.* Mildly surprising is that about half of the subjects felt similarly about such presumably fuzzy categories as *fruit, vegetable, sport,* and *vehicle.*

**Table 5**   **Subjects' responses when asked: "Does it make sense to rate items in this category for degree of membership in the category?" (N = 21)**

|  | Percent of subjects who said "NO" |
| --- | --- |
| Prototype categories | |
| fruit | 43 |
| sport | 71 |
| vegetable | 33 |
| vehicle | 24 |
| Well-defined categories | |
| even number | 100 |
| odd number | 100 |
| female | 86 |
| plane geometry figure | 100 |

Notice that this result accords ill with that of Experiment I, if the latter is interpreted as a test of category structure. Subjects in Experiment I could (by hypothesis) rate exemplars of varying category types for degree of membership, but subjects in the present experiment say it is often absurd to rate for degree of membership. To solidify this result, we had to determine whether the selfsame subjects would behave in these two different ways. That is the central point of Task 2 of the present experiment, in which the subjects were asked to go back to the same categories they had just described as all-or-none and rate their members according to how good an example of this category each was. The results are shown in Table 6, which presents the mean ratings for all items on all categories. Each mean is based on the ratings of *only those subjects who had previously said 'No' when asked whether it makes sense to rate membership in this particular category.* For purposes of comparison, the table also shows the mean ratings for the same items obtained from the subjects in Experiment I.

As the table shows, there is still an exemplariness effect. *Apples* are still ranked higher than *olives,* and by subjects who say that being a fruit is a definite matter, one way or the other. By and large, the same exemplars judged to be better or worse in

Experiment I were similarly rated in Experiment III. For example, in both experiments the best two *vegetables* were *carrot* and *celery* while the worst three were *onion, parsley,* and *pickle.* The numbers *4* and *8* were still the best *even numbers,* and *34* and *106* were still the worst. As in Experiment I, these new subjects generally agreed with each other as to which exemplar is better and which worse, as shown by median split-group correlations of 0.87 and 0.98 for prototype and well-defined categories, respectively.

**Table 6    Mean exemplariness ratings**

| | Experiment I all subjects | | Experiment III subjects who said NO (out of 21) | |
|---|---|---|---|---|
| | n | $\overline{X}$ | n | $\overline{X}$ |
| *Prototype categories* | | | | |
| Fruit | | | | |
| Apple | 31 | 1.3 | 9 | 1.3 |
| Strawberry | | 2.1 | | 1.7 |
| Plum | | 2.5 | | 1.9 |
| Pineapple | | 2.7 | | 1.3 |
| Fig | | 5.2 | | 3.3 |
| Olive | | 6.4 | | 4.2 |
| Vegetable | | | | |
| Carrot | 31 | 1.5 | 7 | 1.1 |
| Celery | | 2.6 | | 1.1 |
| Asparagus | | 2.7 | | 1.4 |
| Onion | | 3.7 | | 3.1 |
| Pickle | | 4.8 | | 4.1 |
| Parsley | | 5.0 | | 3.1 |
| Sport | | | | |
| Football | 31 | 1.4 | 15 | 1.1 |
| Hockey | | 1.8 | | 1.5 |
| Gymnastics | | 2.8 | | 1.6 |
| Wrestling | | 3.1 | | 1.9 |
| Archery | | 4.8 | | 2.5 |
| Weight-lifting | | 5.1 | | 2.6 |
| Vehicle | | | | |
| Car | 31 | 1.0 | 5 | 1.0 |
| Boat | | 3.3 | | 1.6 |
| Scooter | | 4.5 | | 3.8 |
| Tricycle | | 4.7 | | 2.6 |
| Horse | | 5.2 | | 2.8 |
| Skis | | 5.6 | | 5.2 |

**Table 6    (cont)**

*Well-defined categories*

Even number

| | | | | |
|---|---|---|---|---|
| 4 | 31 | 1.1 | 21 | 1.0 |
| 8 | | 1.5 | | 1.0 |
| 10 | | 1.7 | | 1.1 |
| 18 | | 2.6 | | 1.2 |
| 34 | | 3.4 | | 1.4 |
| 106 | | 3.9 | | 1.7 |

Odd number

| | | | | |
|---|---|---|---|---|
| 3 | 31 | 1.6 | 21 | 1.0 |
| 7 | | 1.9 | | 1.0 |
| 23 | | 2.4 | | 1.3 |
| 57 | | 2.6 | | 1.5 |
| 501 | | 3.5 | | 1.8 |
| 447 | | 3.7 | | 1.9 |

Female

| | | | | |
|---|---|---|---|---|
| Mother | 31 | 1.7 | 18 | 1.1 |
| Housewife | | 2.4 | | 1.8 |
| Princess | | 3.0 | | 2.1 |
| Waitress | | 3.2 | | 2.4 |
| Policewoman | | 3.9 | | 2.9 |
| Comedienne | | 4.5 | | 3.1 |

Plane geometry figure

| | | | | |
|---|---|---|---|---|
| Square | 31 | 1.3 | 21 | 1.0 |
| Triangle | | 1.5 | | 1.0 |
| Rectangle | | 1.9 | | 1.0 |
| Circle | | 2.1 | | 1.2 |
| Trapezoid | | 3.1 | | 1.5 |
| Ellipse | | 3.4 | | 2.1 |

Another similarity to Experiment I was the fact that the mean ratings were lower for instances of the well-deflned categories than for the prototype categories. To document this point statistically, we compared overall mean ratings to exemplars of the two types. We considered only exemplars in categories that had previously been judged all-or-none. In addition, we restricted our analysis to subjects who had given such an all-or-none judgment for at least two of the prototype categories, since we wanted to have a reasonable data base for comparing ratings given to both kinds of categories and made by the same subjects. These restrictions left 12 subjects. They produced a mean rating of 1.4 for the well-defined categories and 2.3 for the prototype categories $(t = 4.4, df = 11, p < 0.001)$.

It is clear then that, even under very extreme conditions, an exemplariness effect is still found; and even for well-defined categories, and even for subjects who had said that the membership in question is all-or-none. We regard this as a strong argument that category membership is not psychologically equivalent to category exemplariness.

This is not to say that the exemplariness effect cannot be muted, for we have certainly decreased its magnitude by our various manipulations. The overall means found for the relevant categories rated in Experiment I were 3.5 and 2.6 for the prototype and well-defined categories, respectively; in Experiment III, the means are 2.3 and 1.4, as we just stated. These differences are highly significant (the two t-values are 4.3 and 7.4 respectively, with df's of 41, and p-values of less than 0.001).

This difference may indicate that the subjects genuflected slightly in Task 2 to their behavior in Task 1. The subjects as a group surely have no consciously held theory that distinguishes between class membership and exemplariness and indeed many of them may have thought their one set of responses contradicted the other. Even so, the graded responses remain, only diminished in magnitude. On the other hand, this magnitude difference may be due to differential selection, since the mean ratings here are based only on those subjects who previously said these categories are all-or-none. Such subjects may generally provide lower ratings in tests of this sort. For all we know, both factors may be involved in lowering the mean ratings in this condition, and other factors as well.

But none of this affects our main point. Superficially subjects seem to have contradicted themselves, asserting that a category is all-or-none in one condition and then regarding it as graded in the next. But as we see it, the contradiction is only apparent. The subjects responded differently because they were asked to judge two different matters: exemplariness of exemplars of concepts in the one case, and membership of exemplars in a concept in the other.

## General discussion

The results of our studies suggest that it has been premature to assign a family-resemblance structure to certain natural categories. The prior literature has shown that exemplars from various categories receive graded responses, in a variety of paradigms. But graded responses to exemplars of such categories as *fruit* do not constitute evidence for the family resemblance structure of these categories without — at minimum — a further finding: all-or-none responses to exemplars of categories that are known to have definite, all-or-none, descriptions and whose all-or-none descriptions are known to be known to the subjects. And this is precisely what we failed to find. Our subjects were tested in two of the well-known paradigms, with such categories as *odd number*. But they then gave graded responses.

These results do not suggest that categories such as *fruit* or *vehicle* are well-defined in the classical or any other sense — no more than they suggest that *odd number* is fuzzy. What they do suggest is that we are back at square one in discovering the structure of everyday categories *experimentally*. This is because our results indicate that certain techniques widely used to elicit and therefore elucidate the structure of such categories are flawed. This being so, the study of conceptual structure has not been put on an experimental footing, and the structure of those concepts studied by current techniques remains unknown.

Over and above this negative and essentially methodological conclusion, we want to know why the graded responses keep showing up, if they do not directly reflect the structure of concepts. We will now try to say something about why. Specifically, in Part I below, we will present a suitably revised description of how featural prototypes relate to concepts. This description, similar to many now in the literature of cognitive psychology, superficially seems to handle our findings rather appealingly, mitigating some of their paradoxical quality. That is the happy ending. But as the curtain reopens on Part II of this discussion, we will acknowledge that without a theory of what is to count as a 'feature' (or 'relevant dimension'), the descriptive victory of Part I was quite hollow. That is our sad ending. Part III closes with some speculations about likely directions for further investigation into concepts.

## Part I: Exemplariness and prototypes

One enormous phenomenon stands firm: subjects do give graded responses when queried, in any number of ways, about concepts. So powerful is this phenomenon that it survives even confrontation with the very concepts *(odd number)* it could not possibly illuminate or even describe. A graded view of odd numbers could not explain how we compute with integers, how we know (finally) that each integer is odd or not odd, how we know that to find out about the oddness of an integer we are quite free to look at the right-most digit only, and so forth. These facts are among those we care about most passionately, among the various oddness-competencies of human subjects. The mischievous finding of graded responses to the odd numbers makes mysterious, inexplicable, perverse, all these essential matters about the mental representation of the odds *just in case the graded findings say something about the concept of oddness.* We have concluded, therefore, and even before the findings of Experiment III were in, and bolstered the position, that the category *odd* is determined, exact, and nonfuzzy, as known to human subjects. So the question still remains to be answered: where do the graded responses come from?

In presenting the results of our experiments, we suggested that the prototype descriptions apply to an organization of 'exemplariness' rather than to an organization of 'class membership'. Perhaps the graded judgments and responses have to do with a mentally stored *identification function* used to make quick sorts of things, scenes, and events in the world. On this formulation, instances of a concept share some rough and ready list of perceptual and functional properties, to varying degrees (just as Rosch argues and as her experiments elegantly demonstrate). For example, grandmothers tend to have *grey hair, wrinkles,* a *twinkle* in their eye. Some of these properties may be only loosely, if at all, tied to the criteria for membership in the class (for example, *twinkles* for grandmotherliness) while others may be tightly, systematically, tied to the criteria for membership (for example, being *adult* for grandmotherliness). But in addition to this identification function, there will be a mentally stored *categorial description* of the category that does determine membership in it. For *grandmother,* this will be *mother of a parent.*

For some concepts, by hypothesis, there may be very little beyond the identification function that is stored in memory. For example, few, other than vintners and certain biologists, may have much in the way of a serious description of *grape* mentally represented. For other concepts, such as *grandmother,* there might be a pair of well-developed mental descriptions that are readily accessed depending on the task requirements: the exemplariness or identification function, and the sytematic categorial description, the *sense* (cf., Frege, 1970/1892). This latter seems to be essentially what Miller (1977) and some others have called the conceptual core. We adopt this term, *core*, to distinguish the systematic mental representation of the concept from yet another, third, notion, the *real essence* (cf., Kripke, 1972), or factual scientific description of natural categories, apart from the fallible mental descriptions of these. Notice that in principle, then, *gold* might have a rough and ready identification heuristic (the *yellow, glittery* stuff), a core description that is different from this at least in recognizing that all that glitters is not gold, and also a scientific description (at the present moment in the history of inorganic chemistry, atomic number such-and-such).

Even if this general position about concepts is correct, the present authors, clearly, take no stand about the nature of the conceptual cores; only, we will argue in the end that cores for the various concepts would be likely to differ massively from each other both formally and substantively. For the concepts whose internal structure seems relatively transparent, sometimes a classical feature theory seems natural, as for the kin terms. For other concepts, such as *noun* or *prime number,* it seems to us that although these concepts have substructure, that substructure cannot be featural and may not be listlike. (But see Maratsos, 1982, for the opposing idea, that lexical categories such as *noun* may be distributional feature bundles; and Bates and MacWhinney, 1982, for the view that such categories may be prototypical).

The dual position on concepts, of conceptual core and identification function, seems attractive on many grounds. Most centrally, it allows us to resolve some apparent contradictions concerning well-defined categories such as the kinship terms. To return to the present example, all it takes to be a grandmother is being a mother of a parent, but the difficulty is that all the same some grandmothers seem more grandmotherly than others. This issue is naturally handled in terms of a pair of representations: the first, the function that allows one to pick out likely grandmother candidates easily (it's probably that kindly grey haired lady dispensing the chicken soup) and the second, the description that allows us to reason from *grandmother* to *female*. In short, this dual theory seems at first glance to resolve some of the paradox of our experimental findings: subjects were able to distinguish among, e.g., the plane geometry figures or the females, simply by referring to some identification function; but when asked about membership in the class of *plane geometry figures* or *females*, they referred instead to the core description. As for the everyday concepts, such as *fruit* and *vehicle,* they too would have identification functions, whether or not for them there is also a distinct core.[7]

One could think of further reasons to be optimistic about the dual description just sketched. There even seems to be a story one could tell about how the list of identifying properties would arise necessarily as part of the induction problem for language learning. They would arise whether the properties in question were themselves part of the primitive base, or were learned. This is because a whole host of properties such as *grey hair, grandmother, kindly, elderly, female,* all or most will present themselves perceptually (or at least perceptibly) the first time you are confronted with a grandmother and introduced to her and to the word: "This is grandmother" or "This is Joey's grandmother". Favorable as this set of circumstances is, it is insufficient for learning that 'grandmother' means *a kindly grey haired elderly female* and all the more insufficient for learning that 'grandmother' means *mother of a parent*. For 'grandmother' might mean any one (or two, or three) of these properties, rather than all together. Hence, the problem that presents itself with Joey's grandmother is which among the allowable concepts (we leave aside the awesome problem of which concepts are allowable) is being coded by the term 'grandmother' that has been uttered in her presence to refer to her — is she the female in front of you, the grandmother in front of you, the grey haired one; which? Best to make a list, and wait for exposure conditions that dissociate some of these conjectures (for example, it may be helpful to meet little Howie Gabor's grandma, ZsaZsa). To the extent that certain properties occur repeatedly (e.g., *grey haired)* these remain the longer, or remain near the top of the list, as conjectures about the meaning of 'grandmother'.

If this plausible tale is part of the true story of lexical-concept attainment, a question remains. Why isn't the rough and ready attribute list torn up when it is discovered that 'grandmother' really means *mother of a parent, and chicken soup be damned?* (The discovery, to the extent this description goes through, would be that *mother of parent* is the only attribute that always is present in the 'grandmother'-utterance situation; and the discovery, insofar as this description *doesn't* go through, would be that the core is discovered in some totally different way.) The answer, as Landau (1982) and others have argued, would have to do with the sheer convenience of the identification function; it is easier, when seeking grandmothers or attempting to identify present entities, to check such a list of properties than to conduct geneological inquiries. So the list of properties that is constructed in the natural course of language learning hangs on to do a variety of identifying chores in later life. To keep matters in perspective, however, it will require quite a different organization for such kinship terms so as to reason with them — for example, as to whether some of the grandmothers could be virgins, or not. Landau has shown experimentally that even young children will switch from the one description of grandmothers to the other, as the task is changed from one of identification to one of justification.

To summarize, we have just discussed our results in terms of a dual theory of the description of concepts, one that seems to have considerable currency among cognitive psychologists today. This theory asserts that there is a core description, relevant to compositional meaning and informal reasoning; and an identification procedure that is a heuristic for picking out concept-instances in the world. In terms of this dual theory, it is not surprising that concepts of quite different kinds (at their core) all have identification functions. And it is less paradoxical by far to say that some *females* are 'better' as *females,* some *plane geometry figures* better as *figures* than others, once the role of prototypes in mental life is limited to the topic of exemplariness, removed from class membership or structure. What is more, it is not surprising that the identification functions are sometimes quite tangential to the core meanings themselves. After all, their utility does not rest on their sense, nor on the tightness of their relation to the conceptual core. Finally, such a position does not even require the belief that all concepts have a *conceptual* core, distinct from that identification function. For example, it is possible to believe with Kripke and others that the mass of everyday

117

concepts are quasi-indexical; that is, that their extensions are determined quasi-indexically by human users.

## Part II: Can we make good on the feature descriptions?

Without denying that some progress can be made by acknowledging the distinction between core and identification procedure, we would not want to paint too rosy a picture about current knowledge of concepts. We have argued so far only that our subjects' graded responses can be better understood as pertaining to a relatively unprincipled identification metric, thought to consist of a set of features prototypically organized, in the terms of one of the extant models, or some other. So understood, the role of prototypes in mental life would be more limited. For to the extent that they are understood as feature theories, both prototype theories and nonprototype theories inherit many of the difficulties of all feature theories, including the classical definitional position; namely, that the features are hard to find, organize, and describe in a way that illuminates the concepts. And this is so even if the main use — or even the only use — of prototypes is to provide an identification procedure. Alarmingly, we must return to the question whether prototype plus core has solved anything.

### A. What are the identification features?

Our prior discussion had one central explanatory aim. We wanted to hold onto the feature-list descriptions, as relevant to mental representations, in light of the orderly outcomes of the experimental literature on prototypes. At the same time, we had to find a method of preservation that encompassed our new findings for the well-defined concepts. A dual theory might accomplish these twin goals, and in fact dual theories for concepts have been widely considered recently (see, e.g., Miller, 1977; Osherson and Smith, 1981; Smith and Medin, 1981, for very interesting discussions). Even in the now limited sense, however, the featural descriptions have grave problems. For one thing, as we noted earlier (see again footnote 3), it is not obvious *how* the proposed identification schemes are to work, for the various concepts, even if we are able (a matter independently in doubt) to describe the featural substrate *on which* they are to operate.

### 1. Are there coreless concepts?

One problem concerns the extent to which the identification function approach can be pushed. Prototype theorists might be tempted to assert that the identification function for most natural concepts *is* the structure of each of these concepts. They would probably argue that for such concepts the core and identification function are essentially alike (or perhaps that those concepts have no core at all). In that case, to describe the identification function would, minutia and a few sophisticated concepts aside, be tantamount to description of the 'psychological organization' of most concepts. But things can't be quite as simple as this. For if this argument is accepted — if *apple* and *sport* and *bird* and *tiger* are nothing but heuristic identification schemes for carving up the real world — shouldn't subjects throw in the conceptual towel when asked whether a bird is still a bird even when plucked (or dewinged, or debeaked, or whatever) or a tiger still a tiger without its stripes? But on the contrary, subjects seem to be quite sanguine about having these identification features (if that

118

is what they are) removed, and even for the concepts that allegedly consist of nothing else. That is, it's not at all hard to convince the man on the street that there are three legged, tame, toothless albino tigers, that are tigers all the same. Of course the tigers are growing less prototypical, but what keeps them tigers?

A trivializing answer is that we simply haven't asked subjects to discard sufficient of these constituent tiger-features. After all, though the Cheshire cat was smug about his continuing existence, *qua* Cheshire cat, when only his smile remained, Alice was by her own admission 'disconcerted'. This question requires formal experimentation to resolve; but Komatsu (in progress), has preliminary evidence that subjects will give up most of their cherished features, while still maintaining that the tiger remains. If this is true, then whatever the case for the identification function, it is no substitute for the concept's core, even in the case of natural — family resemblance — concepts. Subjects often respond with surprise and some dismay when they are asked to describe what it is to be a *tiger,* and find they cannot. But they tend, in spite of this, to hold on to the commonsense notion that there *is* an essence, common to and definitive of *tiger,* though it is unknown to themselves; known, perhaps, to experts — biologists, maybe, for the present tiger-question (for this position, concerning the 'division of linguistic labor' between ordinary and expert users of a term, see Putnam, 1975).

## 2. *What are the identification features?*

Up to now we've assumed we know or can find out the rough-and-ready attributes by which an exemplar of a given category is to be identified — stripes for tigers, brownie-dispensing for grandmothers, and so on. But the specification of the identification function poses many problems. After all, the argument is standard and irrefutable that there's no end to the descriptions that can apply to any one stimulus or to all or some of its parts (see, for example, Quine on rabbits; 1960). All hope of an economical theory of categorization, even rough and ready categorization, is gone unless we can give an account of the feature set that learners and users will countenance. If this set is unconstrained, then the list of primitive discriminations burgeons. This argument (cf., Fodor, 1975) applies to definitional feature theories of concepts, but it applies no less to the supposed lists of identification features. Moreover, as Fodor has reminded us, the combinatorial problem that we discussed in introductory remarks for a theory of prototypical concepts arises in exactly the same way if we are to have a featural description of identification functions: it's not clear at all that the identification features for a complex concept can be inherited in any regular way from the identification features for its constituents. To use an example of Fodor's (personal communication), if you have an identification procedure for both *house* and *rich man,* this gives you no obvious productive system that yields an identification procedure for *rich man's house.* But if that is so, then the explanatory role of identification procedures is catastrophically reduced, for mainly we talk and understand more than one word at a time.

One problem at least is clear: the rough-and-ready attributes that determine whether a given item is a good or a bad exemplar differ from one category to another. In our study, the 'good' odd and even numbers were the *smaller* ones (as inspection of Table 1 shows). That makes sense, since cardinality and the notion *smallest* are surely relevant to arithmetic. But even in the domain of integers, smallness or even cardinality doesn't always enter into the prototype patterns that subjects reveal. Thus Wanner (1979) found that the prototypical prime numbers are those that go through certain heuristic decision procedures easily, and these aren't necessarily the smallest prime numbers. For example, 91 'looks primy' partly because it is odd, indivisible by 3, etc., properties that are connected only rather indirectly to primeness. When we move to a more distant domain, the relevant features are more different still. For instance, inspection of Table 1 shows that the *smallest females* are not taken to be the prototypical females. Smallness probably is not central to the female prototype even though certainly it is possible to ascertain the sizes of the females (and in fact size is even a rough distinguisher of *female* from *male,* at least for the mammals; that is, size has some cue validity in this case). As a matter of fact, we have previously remarked that it is something like a sexism metric that organizes the rankings of the female (with *mother* on the top and *comedienne* the lowest of all), as inspection of the Table also shows. None of this is really surprising, for given that the categories differ, the way in which one can identify their exemplars should surely differ too. But will we ever be able to specify how? On what limited bases? Is there any great likelihood that the list of needed identifying features will converge at a number smaller than that of the lexical items (see Fodor, 1975)?

So far as we can see, the prototype theories are not explicit, except in the claim for variability around a central value, for each concept. But that central value potentially is defined on different dimensions or features for each concept. Without stating these, there is close to no explanatory contribution in the assertion that each concept has a 'central value' in terms of feature composition, for this latter is differently composed in the case of each concept. What is likely is that 'heuristic identification schemes' like that uncovered by Wanner for spotting the prime numbers, and revealed in our experiments for spotting and ranking the odd numbers — and, quite likely, the fruits and vehicles! — are not merely matters of consulting lists of perceptual features; but something else: computation schemes, relevantly different for different concepts, in terms of which certain instances are more easily computable than others. There seems no special reason to think these schemes implicate sublexical features.

The problems we have discussed do not seem to exhaust the list of difficulties for feature list searches as identification functions — even if the features in question are just rough-and-ready ones. Suppose we knew, for *grandmother, rhubarb,* etc., the relevant features of their identification function. But surely, since this feature list is designed so that we can recognize new grandmothers, new rhubarbs, the features have to be cast in some relatively abstract form, and so must be marked also for the degree of allowable latitude on each. But allowable latitude, too, is hard to describe either in general or in particular. If (a big if) both tables and dogs are said to be identifiable by four *legs* in the same sense of legs, then what is the outside leg-to-body ratio allowed? Forty-yard legs on a two-inch body? The same for dogs and tables? Must we distinguish artifact legs from organism legs; worse, dog legs?

### B. Features and concept cores

The arguments that we reviewed above are familiar enough: once having said 'feature theory', the job is to name which features with which latitudes for which concepts.

What we argued in particular is that the difficulty of carrying out such an enterprise seems formidable even if limited to identification functions and to prototype organizations. But there is little doubt that the difficulties for a feature approach to concepts is even worse for describing the concept's core than for describing its identification function.

*1. The search for the featural substrate*

Enormous efforts have gone into the attempt to identify a featural substrate. For the most notable recent attempt, see Katz and Fodor (1963) and continuing work from Katz (1972; 1977). This enterprise was an attempt to infer the features of word meaning in terms of judgments of sentences in which the words occurred. The judgments were on such properties as synonymy, entailment, contradiction, anomaly, and so forth. For example, the judged anomaly of *I met a two year old bachelor yesterday* is a first basis for postulating a feature *adult* for *bachelor*. The approach has the great merit of tailoring the word-meaning description so that it directly serves the purposes of composing the phrase and sentence meanings, and determining the lexical and phrasal entailments. But for all its elegance, the approach has not been notoriously successful for the mass of ordinary words that, unlike the kin terms, are not so obviously definitional. In fact Fodor, Garrett, Walker, and Parkes (1980) present evidence, from sentence comprehension and verification studies, against the hypothesis that even *bachelor* literally decomposes into features, on which units comprehension is to take place. (At the opposite position, Katz, 1981, has recently argued that such psychological reactions — or even certain muddy judgments — are not the appropriate data on which to build a semantic theory, thus disconnecting formal semantics from any responsibility in accounting for human knowledge or behavior).[8]

A number of other empirical approaches to finding the feature set grew out of the traditions of experimental psychology and psychophysics. Here too the main lines of attack have been indirect. The features (or dimensions) were inferred, for example, through a factor analysis of the ratings of words on a set of polar adjectives (Osgood *et al.*, 1957) or through multidimensional scaling (Caramazza *et al.*, 1976; Rips *et al*, 1973). But the results here are somewhat disheartening for the feature set (or set of dimensions) that emerges from such manipulations is simply too impoverished to do justice to the phenomena of categorization, or lexical semantics.

*2. The attribute-listing paradigm*

It has remained for Rosch and Mervis (1975) to attack this problem head on. In effect, they asked their subjects to act as the lexicographers. Given a word, the subjects were to provide the attributes (that is, the features) that described it. This experiment has been extremely influential, and justly so for it seemed to be one of the most direct demonstrations of prototype structure.[9] But it is doubtful that it succeeded in discovering the relevant feature set for various natural concepts that others had failed to find. To document this point, we will consider the Rosch and Mervis paradigm and its usual interpretations more closely.

Rosch and Mervis' (1975) subjects were simply presented with various exemplars from a number of superordinate concepts (e.g., *chair, sofa, bed,* from the category *furniture)* and asked to list "all the attributes" they could think of for each of these items. Their rationale was straightforward: If there is a set of necessary and sufficient attributes that defines, say, *furniture,* then every item that falls under the concept *furniture* necessarily has all the required attributes. Rosch and Mervis found that "very few" (sometimes no) attributes were listed for all the items that presumably are exemplars of their superordinate categories. Given this result, the investigators concluded that the superordinate itself (e.g., *furniture)* was properly described as a family resemblance category rather than as a definitional category. We have already argued that such descriptions are more easily interpreted as pertaining to exemplariness than to category structure. But there is a prior issue that has to do with what the Rosch and Mervis task asks, for it is by no means clear that the subjects could really comply with the instructions to come up with the appropriate features that describe a given word (or concept). After all, why should one expect them to succeed where generations of lexicographers before them failed?

*a. The suppression of features:* One problem concerns the suppression of features. Suppose a subject is asked to list all the features of a given term (and suppose there are such features). Would he really list them all even if he knew them? Clearly not. Some of the reasons are quite systematic, and have to do with lexical redundancy rules. So for example most subjects don't mention *living thing* let alone *physical object* for *canary.* The features of the superordinate are simply presumed to apply to the items that fall under it, and don't have to be listed as such. For related reasons, people tend to tell you what they think you need to know, suppressing the obvious. For example, a standard dictionary defines a *zebrula* as a *cross between a zebra and a horse;* but no dictionary would ever define a *horse* as a *cross between a horse and a horse.* This could be because the lexicographer has a pretty good idea of what you know about horses, organisms, etc. What holds of lexicographers doubtless holds for subjects in attribute-listing experiments as well so the level of response, and hence the particular attributes listed, may vary from item to item. These problems are all quite obvious. Still they seem to us cause to wonder just what is happening when subjects "list the attributes".

*b. The expression of features:* An even more troublesome problem is whether the subjects could express the features anyway — again assuming such features exist, and assuming redundancy rules and context determinants, etc., will not keep the subjects from listing them all. How do we know the subject can access the features in the first place, and express them in words? For if the feature theory is the correct theory, few of the words in the language represent a feature bare. Assuming the correctness of this theory, most words must represent a bundle of features — each of which presumably is writ in Mentalese. If so, how could the subjects tell us about the features, unless each of these is expressable by one word only (which is unlikely) and that a word which carries no excess featural baggage of its own (more unlikely still)? The point is that the more the theory is correct that words are bundles of features, the less likely that the subjects' responses in whole words would be single-feature responses.

Some empirical basis for this particular worry comes from an examination of subjects' responses in an attribute-listing experiment. In a partial replication of the Rosch and Mervis study, Komatsu obtained some interesting reactions that indicate a mismatch between query (about features) and answers (in words). Take the subjects' responses to *grapefruit* and *tractor*. The subjects varied. Some said grapefruits are sweet while others said sour. Some said tractors had four wheels, while others said two wheels. To this extent the concepts *tractor* and *grapefruit* seem to vary among members of the linguistic community, much as the prototype theory would have it. But this interpretation seems shaky, just because it's not clear that *sweet* and *two wheels* are attributes of the appropriate scope. For while the subjects differed they also agreed up to a point: none of them said how many wheels a grapefruit had and none of them said how sweet a tractor was. (A tractor *can* be sweet, by the way. Taste one: it might surprise you. This means the absence of this feature can't be explained on grounds of an ontological category violation, as described by Keil, 1979. Sweetness is obviously irrelevant, of tractors; but this doesn't make it a category error). In short, the subjects seemed to share some common conceptions of the categories, but were unable to come up with the right level of description — perhaps they should have said 'bewheeled' or 'sweet/sour dimension' but they could not or would not. We conclude that even if categories are describable in terms of some featural vocabulary, it will be difficult to expose this by direct inquiry. But, as described earlier, more indirect methods have not fared much better.

*3. The sum of the features is not the whole concept*

The preceding discussion tried to highlight some difficulties in making explicit a feature account of concepts, whether fuzzy or definable. But even more damaging to such a theory is the kind of Gestalt problem that has been discussed again and again (e.g., Fodor, 1975; 1981). The simple fact is that a bird is not a sum of features, whatever these may be. All the features in the world that are characteristic of and common to all birds don't make a bird — that is, not unless these properties are held together in a bird structure. To paraphrase a famous example from Quine (used, of course, to urge a different point), without the bird-Gestalt all the bird features might as well be undetached bird parts. This is to say, though, that the crucial feature of bird is: essence of *bird*.

Symmetrically, not all feature assemblies add up to good Gestalts. An old riddle asks: What looks like a box, smells like lox, and flies? The answer is a flying lox-box. *Feathers, wings, flies, animalness* (etc.) compose on the featural view to a natural complex, *bird*. On the other hand, to the extent *lox, box,* and *flies* are features too (or bundles of features, it doesn't matter here) how come their conjunction doesn't yield a natural complex? That is, what's so funny about a flying lox-box? A good feature theory would be one that could engage this problem, it seems to us.

In addition to the fact that separable bird features don't seem to do the job in describing the bird concept, there is the question of whether proposed bird-features are, as required by a feature theory, somehow more primitive components of the concepts they describe — little meaning atoms that combine in differing ways to form the multitude of concepts in our mental world. But if so, why hasn't anyone found them? Shouldn't one expect the many words in the language to be describable by a (smaller) set of more primitive words, corresponding, however crudely, to these meaning atoms? Perhaps we should, but dictionaries seem to tell us otherwise. Most of the words in the language are defined there in terms of one another, with most words — unfamiliar ones excepted — acting as defined on some occasions and definers on others. It is as if all the words made their living by taking in each others' washing.

## Part III: Final thoughts in favor of not studying the concepts all at once, at least not now

We have been advancing a series of arguments that seem to us, taken together, to weaken the case for attribute or feature theories of at least most ordinary concepts, even if the features are to be relevant 'only' to an identification procedure. The problem is ultimately that the concepts don't seem to decompose, except into each other. There must be rich and intricate relations among the lexical concepts, to be sure, but it isn't clear that some small number of them are the basic ones. Giving up the feature story does not, as again Fodor has argued, make the job of describing compositional meaning any harder (networks of relations *among* the whole words will do the job as well or as badly).

However, giving up the idea of features makes it more difficult than ever even to envisage a *general* theory of concepts. This is because, quite possibly, a nonfeatural account of the concepts would have to countenance the huge number of natural categories (for example, those that are lexicalized in the everyday vocabulary of a natural language) each as an item in the primitive base, none of them in any natural ways arising from or reduceable to each other (Fodor, 1975).

More optimistically, we might hope for discovery of a set of *principles* — some set of interrelated rules — that, applied to our experiences with the world, would yield the variety of lexical concepts as the inevitable outcomes (see Chomsky, 1975, ch. 2, for discussion). Such principles might be general across conceptual domains (for contributions that seem to adopt this perspective, see, e.g., Garner, 1978; Markman, 1979; E. Smith and Medin, 1981; and L. Smith and Kemler, 1978). On the other hand, these principles may be different in each of the conceptual domains. Perhaps we have linguistic principles that inevitably, on exposure to linguistic data, yield such linguistic categories as *noun;* and perceptual principles of other kinds that, on exposure to, say, the visible world, yield such categories as *object* (e.g., Spelke, 1982). At any rate, positive results in these terms, even if possible, seem a long way away. For ourselves, we can only dimly envisage what kinds of principle approach to the organization of concepts might be taken. Nor can we envisage the precise sense in which generative principles of organization, for conceptual domains, might be more than terminologically different from 'features', as these latter were never made very precise by their proponents.

In the current state of affairs in cognitive psychology, we ourselves are not optimistic that a general theory of categorization, one that will answer to the serious problems (explication of functions from words to the world, and of the units that figure in phrasal meanings and in lexical entailments) is just around the corner. To the contrary, the continuing failure of the search for such units leads us to doubt whether there is a general psychological domain encompassing 'all concepts' parallel, say, to a general cognitive domain of 'all sensory experiences', 'all emotions', and so forth. In our opinion, cognitive psychology has made progress precisely where it has attempted to identify and investigate singly rich and highly structured conceptual domains. A paradigm recent example has been the study of universal grammar.

We do not think that discoveries concerning the various important conceptual domains will reveal that any of them are organized as simple feature structures. Rather, in each domain, the units, their patterning, the principles that organize them, their development, their environmental dependence, are all likely to be different and likely to be complex, rewarding serious study. As for the minor everyday concepts, such as *rhubarb, slipper, pebble, sofa,* it is possible we are fooling ourselves that the question of their single or joint structure is interesting, or fundamental to psychology. Even if it is, there may be no general theory of categorization that will subsume and therefore explain them all.

In sum, a host of thinkers have shown us that there is enormous difficulty in explicating even so simple and concrete a concept as *bird.* They've shown that the difficulty becomes greater by orders of magnitude when confronted with an abstract functional concept like *game.* Perhaps psychologists are more than a little overexhuberant in supposing it will be easier to explicate the concept *concept.*

## Acknowledgements

We are indebted to quite a large number of colleagues for discussion of the issues addressed in this paper, and for reading and commenting on prior drafts of this manuscript. Particularly, we wish to thank B. Armstrong, D. Bolinger, J. A. Fodor, J. D. Fodor, R. Gallistel, F. W. Irwin, R. Jackendoff, J. Jonides, J. Katz, L. Komatsu, B. Landau, J. Levin, J. Moravschik, E. Newport, S. Peters, M. Posner, M. Seligman, E. Shipley, E. Spelke, E. Wanner, K. Wexler, M. Williams, and an anonymous reviewer. All of us, but especially Lila Gleitman, particularly thank Scott Weinstein for his long and patient attempts to explicate the issues in philosophical semantics for us; this service, as well as reading drafts of the current paper, he has heroically extended over two years; nevertheless, he is not accountable for the manner of review of these, nor for the positions we take here, quite obviously. The work reported was funded in part by a National Institutes of Health postdoctoral Fellowship to S. L. Armstrong, and by a grant to L. R. Gleitman and B. Landau from the National Foundation of the March of Dimes. We thank these agencies for their support of this work. Felice Bedford, Manuel Ayala, and Jordan Klemes are thanked for helping us collect the data for these studies.

## Notes

1.  However, whether or not the mental category/concept 'properly' fixes the extension of the English term is left open, though this issue will come up in later discussion. It could be that there is a fact of the matter about the extension of the term unknown to the users (i.e., not given as a consequence of the structure of the mental representation). For example, on at least some views (cf., Locke, 1968/ 1690) there are *real essences* ("to be found in the things themselves", p. 288) and *nominal essences* (that "the mind makes", p. 288). Our use of concept/category, then, has to do with the nominal essences, the 'mental structure' of the concept which may or may not properly fix the extension. That is, our concept of gold may have the consequence for sorting that we pick out only certain yellow metal in the world to call 'gold', but the internal structure of the sort of thing we mean to be talking about when

125

we talk about gold may exclude some of the instances we identified as gold on the basis of their yellowness, and include some other instances that were white in appearance, but still — really — gold (see Kripke, 1972. for discussion).

2.    Recent versions of (nonfuzzy) decompositional semantics respond to some of these difficulties both by radically increasing the internal complexity of lexical entries — and thus parting company with any recognizable associationist position on mental structure — or by asserting that an appropriate semantic theory is not psychologistic anyway, but rather formal and nonempirical (Katz, 1981, and personal communication; see also Bever, 1982). Whatever the real causes of semantic structure will turn out to be, we reiterate that the present discussion is of human representation of this structure — the nominal essence. Hence the Platonic descriptions, defensible or not, are not relevant here.

3.    But we are restricting discussion to models that interpret prototype theory decompositionally rather than holistically; and featurally in particular. The major reason is that a featural interpretation is at least implicit in most of the experimental literature on prototype theory, and it is this literature that we specifically address in this paper. Nevertheless it is important to note here that some prototype theorists have a different, nonfeatural, account in mind. At the extreme, such a nondecompositional prototype theory would involve a holistic mental representation (perhaps imagistic) of a designated prototypical category member, some metric space into which other members of the category are placed, relative to the prototypical member, and some means of computing distance of members from the prototype such that the more prototypical members are those closest in the space to the prototype itself. It is hard to see how any such holistic view would allow a general theory of concepts to be stated. This is because a notion of 'general similarity', suitable for comparing all things against all other things is not likely to be found. Most nonfeatural prototype discussions, then, assume that the metric space into which category members are organized is dimensionalized in ways specifically relevant to the categories in question (e.g., comparisons of wave lengths for colors, but of lines and angles for geometric figures, etc., the dimensions of comparison now being fewer than the object types that must be compared). Osherson and Smith, 1981, have described this kind of prototype model formally, and distinguished it from the featural interpretations of prototype theory. For both types of model, these authors demonstrate that prototype theory, amalgamated with combinatorial principles from fuzzy-set theory (Zadeh, 1965), cannot account for our intuitions about conceptual combination. More to our present point, and as Osherson and Smith also point out, it is not obvious that the required designated prototypes, the dimensionalized metric space for each semantic field, or the function that computes similarity of arbitrary member to prototypical member within each field, etc., can ever be found. To us, then, the nonfeatural prototype theories escape the problems of the featural ones only by being less explicit. Moreover, whatever we say of the problems of 'features' we also assert to have closely related problems within a theory that employs 'dimensions'.

4.    This is not to say that these findings have not been questioned on methodological grounds. For example, Loftus (1975) questioned the peculiarity of some of the exemplars subjects were asked to rate: The presentation, e.g., of *foot* among the list of *weapon* exemplars might account for much of the intra-subject disagreement, generating the fuzzy outcome as a statistical artifact of these item choices (which in turn were ultimately selected from responses in an exemplar-naming task devised by Battig and Montague, 1969). But Rosch (1975b) showed that the graded responses recur in lists from which such problematical items have been removed. Furthermore, McCloskey and Glucksberg (1978) have demonstrated empirically that inter- and intra-subject variability, where each subject at each time is assumed to have a nonfuzzy definitional concept in mind, is an unlikely explanation of the graded responses.

5.  Notice that we are speaking of the combinatorial structure of the concepts (the mental representations), not of extensions. Indeed there might be a fuzzy set of foolish birds out there; but it doesn't follow that concepts, even concepts concerning foolish birds, themselves have to be fuzzy. (We particularly thank J. A. Fodor for discussion of this point). It may very well be that there are limits on humanly natural concepts, and that not all the sundry objects and events in the world fit neatly under those that we have. (For an important discussion of natural and unnatural concepts, in the sense we here intend, see Osherson, 1978). In that case, we might not be able to make a neat job of naming everything in the world. Notice that the experimental findings we have been discussing (family-resemblance type responses to exemplars and instances) would arise artifactually in case humans really do have only certain concepts, and ways of expressing these in natural language, but must willy nilly name all the gadgets in the world, whether or not these truly fit under those concepts. (See Osherson and Smith, 1981, for a formal demonstration of related problems for prototype theory in describing lexical entailments).

6.  A possibly supportive demonstration to those we will now describe, one that adopts a similar logic has appeared after the present paper was written, and we thank an anonymous reviewer for putting us on to it. Bourne (1982) reports findings from a concept learning experiment which he interprets as demonstrating that prototypelike responses can arise from sources other than "fuzzy concepts" in the subject. However, the materials used by Bourne were artificial categories, designed to be simple-featural, thus finessing the question whether natural categories are featural. Even more dffficult for his interpretations, it is ambiguous from the reported results what structure(s) the experimental subjects thought described the categories whose members they learned to identify. Nonetheless, Bourne's interpretation of his experiments and their outcomes formally parallels aspects of those we are about to report: that prototypelike responses from subjects can coexist with manifest knowledge, in the same subjects, of the logical structure of those categories. In concord with Osherson and Smith (1981), Bourne accepts something like a 'core/identification procedure' distinction as the appropriate account of the findings (for discussion of this position, see Conclusions, Part I, following).

7.  We are leaving many ends loose here, that we will try to tie up in later discussion. The present discussion is by way of a last ditch attempt to salvage a featural description of the mental concepts, in light of our experimental findings. But we have already overstated the work any feature theory we know of can do in this regard, even when viewed as a heuristic identification scheme, operating on features. Notice that having lots of odd digits or being of low cardinality doesn't really help, in any known or imaginable rough-and-ready sense, to identify odd numbers. What makes these easier than divisible by two, leaving one? A good question, one that at least limits, perhaps defeats, even the restricted role we have outlined for feature theories of conceptual structure. (We thank E. Wanner and E. Newport for pointing out these challenges to the dual feature story).

8.  A recent tradition in philosophy to which we earlier alluded supposes that for at least some terms — the natural kind terms — the systematic description (the real, not the psychologically real, essence of the terms) is the preserve of experts within the linguistic community; for example, these could be the biologists, physicists, chemists, etc., who describe *tiger, gold,* etc. in terms of scientific state-of-the-art microscopic features that correctly fix the extension of each (Putnam, 1975). An optimistic view for semantics would be that the conceptual cores are, ultimately, related to these real essences. However, Dupre (1981) gives a compelling, if depressing, discussion of the possible relations between the scientifically discoverable categories, and the mental categories underlying our lexical usages. He does this by considering how biological taxa (as developed by the biologists) map

onto ordinary language terms. He points out that the biological taxa crosscut the linguistic categories extensively; that it is not only at the margins of category boundaries that biologists and ordinary language users part company. An example cited by Dupre concerns the onion, which, as it happens, is (from an expert point of view) just one more lily. If, in general, the scientists and the speakers part company at the centers, and not only at the margins, of the categories in which they traffic, we can't look to the scientific taxonomies as explications of the natural language categories. In sum, if there is a feature set for the conceptual core (or the identification function, for that matter) we can't look to the natural scientists to do the semantic work of uncovering them for psychologists concerned with human categorization.

9. As mentioned earlier (see footnote 4), some methodological and technical objections have been mounted against this experiment. But we believe such difficulties are minor, and at any rate Rosch (1975b) has answered most of them. Even so, one problematical point is that judges intervened between the subjects' responses and the scoring. As we understand the report of the study, the judges crossed out any absurd attributes subjects listed and added some (this latter under a severe constraint) that they may have forgotten. It is a bit puzzling how to interpret the subjects' responses as filtered through this correction procedure, though it has plausibility, and though the authors report that "the changes made by the judges were infrequent". We are assuming none of these technicalities affect the reported outcomes very seriously, though subjects have on occasion been reported to be quite unruly in this procedure. For example, in a partial replication run by Komatsu (unpublished manuscript), one subject's total entry for *lettuce* was (1) throw away outside leaves, (2) eat inside leaves.

## References

Bates, E., & MacWhinney, B. (1982) Functionalist approaches to grammar in E. Wanner & L. R. Gleitman (eds.), *Language Acquisition: State of the Art*. Cambridge: Cambridge University Press.

Battig, W. R., & Montague, W. E. (1969) Category norms for visual items in 56 categories. A replication and extension of the Connecticut Category Norms. *J. exper. Psychol. Mono.*, 80, (3, pt. 2).

Bever, T. G. (1982) Some implications of the nonspecific bases of language. In E. Wanner & L. R. Gleitman (eds.), *Language Acquisition: State of the Art*. Cambridge: Cambridge University Press.

Bolinger, D. L. (1965) The atomization of meaning. *Lang.*, 41, 555–573.

Bourne, L. E., Jr. (1982) Typicality effects in logically defined categories, *Mem. Cog.*, 10 (1), 3–9.

Caramazza, A. Hersch, H., & Torgerson, W. S. (1976) Subjective structures and operations in semantic memory. *J. verb. Learn. verb. Behav.*, 15, 103–118.

Chomsky, N. (1975) *Reflections on Language,* New York: Random House.

Collins, A., & Loftus, E. F. (1975) A spreading activation theory of semantic processing. *Psychol. Rev.*, 82 (6), 407–428.

Danks, J. H., & Glucksberg, S. (1980) Experimental psycholinguistics. *An. Rev. Psychol.*, 31, 391–417.

Dupre, J. (1981) Natural kinds and biological taxa. *Phil. Rev.*, 40 (1), 66–90.

Fodor, J. A. (1975) *The Language of Thought*. Cambridge: Harvard University Press.

Fodor, J. A. (1981) *Representations*. Cambridge, Mass: MIT Press.

Fodor, J. A., Garrett, M. F., Walker, E. T., & Parkes, C. (1980) Against definitions. *Cog.*, 8 (3), 1–105.

Fodor, J. D., Fodor, J. A., & Garrett, M. F. (1975) The psychological unreality of semantic representations. *Ling. Inq.*, 6 (4),515–53.

Frege, G. (1970) On sense and reference, translated by M. Black, in P. Geach & M. Black (eds.), *Philosophical Writings of Gottlob Frege*. Oxford: Basil Blackwell, Original publication, 1892.

Garner, W. R. (1978) Aspects of a stimulus: Features, dimensions, and configurations. In E. Rosch & B. B. Lloyd (eds.), *Cognition and categorization*. Hillsdale, NJ: Erlbaum.

Goodman, N. (1965) *Fact, Fiction, and Forecast*. New York: Bobbs-Merrill.

Katz, J. J. (1972) *Semantic Theory*. New York: Harper and Row.

Katz, J. J. (1977) The real status of semantic representations. *Ling. Inq.*, 8, (3), 559–584.

Katz, J. J. (1981) *Language and Other Abstract Objects*. Totowa, NJ: Rowman and Littlefield.

Katz, J. J., & Fodor, J. A. (1963) The structure of a semantic theory. *Lang.*, 39, 170–210.

Keil, F. C. (1979) *Semantic and Conceptual Development*. Cambridge, Mass.: Harvard University Press.

Kripke, S. (1971) Identity and necessity. In M. K. Munitz (ed.), *Identity and Necessity*. New York: New York University Press.

Kripke, S. (1972) Naming and necessity. In D. Davidson & G. Harman (eds.), *Semantics of Natural Language*. Dordrecht, Holland: Reidel.

Kucera, H. K., & Francis, W. N. (1967) *Computational Analysis of Present-day American English*. Providence, RI: Brown University Press.

Landau, B. (1982) Will the real grandmother please stand up. *J. Psycholing. Res.*, 11 (2), 47–62.

Locke, J. (1968) *An Essay concerning Human Understanding*. Cleveland, Ohio: World Publishing Co. Original publication 1690.

Loftus, E. F. (1975) Spreading activation within semantic categories: Comments on Rosch's "Cognitive representation of semantic categories". *J. exper. Psychol.: Gen.*, 104 (3), 234–240.

Maratsos, M. (1982) The child's construction of grammatical categories. In E. Wanner & L. R. Gleitman, (eds.), *Language Acquisition: State of the Art*. Cambridge: Cambridge University Press.

Markman, E. M. (1979) Classes and collections: Conceptual organization and numerical abilities. *Cog. Psychol.*, 11, 395–411.

McCloskey, M., & Glucksberg, S. (1978) Natural categories: Well defined or fuzzy sets? *Mem. Cog.*, 6 (4), 462–472.

McCloskey, M., & Glucksberg, S. (1979) Decision processes in verifying category membership statements: implications for models of semantic memory, *Cog. Psychol.*, 11, 1–37.

Mervis, C. B., & Rosch, E. (1981)Categorization of natural objects. *An. Rev. Psychol.*, 32, 89–115.

Miller, G. A. (1977) Practical and lexical knowledge. In P. N. Johnson-Laird & P. C. Wason (eds.), *Thinking: Readings in Cognitive Science*. Cambridge: Cambridge University Press.

Miller, G. A., & Johnson-Laird, P. N. (1976) *Language and Perception*. Cambridge, Harvard University Press.

Osgood, C. D., Suci, G. J., & Tannenbaum, P. H. (1957) *The measurement of meaning*. Urbana: University of Illinois Press.

Osherson, D. N. (1978) Three conditions on conceptual naturalness, *Cog.*, 6, 263–89.

Osherson, D. N., & Smith, E. F. (1981) On the adequacy of prototype theory as a theory of concepts. *Cog.*, 9 (1), 35–58.

Putnam, H. (1975) *Mind, Language, and Reality: Philosophical Papers, Volume 2*. Cambridge: Cambridge University Press.

Quine, W. V. O. (1960) *Word and Object*. Cambridge: MIT Press.

Rips, L. J., Shoben, E. J., & Smith, E. E. (1973) Semantic distance and the verification of semantic relations. *J. verb. Learn. verb. Behav.*, 12, 1–20.

Rosch, E. (1973) On the internal structure of perceptual and semantic categories. In T. E. Moore (ed.), *Cognitive Development and the Acquisition of Language*. New York: Academic Press.

Rosch, E. (1975a) Cognitive representations of semantic categories. *J. exper. Psychol.: Gen.*, 104, 192–233.

Rosch, E. (1975b) Reply to Loftus. *J. exper. Psychol.: Gen.*, 104 (3), 241–243.

Rosch, E. (1978) Principles of categorization. In E. Rosch & B. B. Lloyd (eds.), *Cognition and Categorization*. Hillsdale, NJ: Erlbaum.

Rosch, E., & Mervis, C. B. (1975) Family resemblances: Studies in the internal structure of categories. *Cog. Psychol.*, 7, 573–605.

Rosch, E., Mervis, C. B., Gray, W. D., Johnson, D. M., & Boyes-Braem, P. (1976) Basic objects in natural categories. *Cog. Psychol.*, 8, 382–439.

Schwartz, S. P. (1979) Natural kind terms. *Cog.*, 7 (3), 301–315, 382–439.

Smith, E. E. (1978) Theories of semantic memory. In W. K. Estes (ed.), *Handbook of Learning and Cognitive Processes, Vol 6*. Potomac, Md.: Erlbaum.

Smith, E. E., & Medin, D. L. (1981) Categories and concepts. Cambridge: Harvard University Press.

Smith, L. B., & Kemler, D. G. (1978) Levels of experienced dimensionality in children and adults. *Cog. Psychol.*, 10, 502–532.

Spelke, E. S. (1982) Perceptual knowledge of objects in infancy. In J. Mehler, M. Garrett, & E. Walker (eds.), *On Mental Representation*. Hillsdale, NJ: Erlbaum.

Thorndike, E. L., & Lorge, I. (1944) *The Teacher's Word Book of 30,000 words*. New York: Teacher's College.

Tversky, A., & Gati, I. (1978) Studies of similarity. In E. Rosch & B. B. Lloyd (eds.), *Cognition and Categorization*. Hillsdale, NJ: Erlbaum.

Wanner, E. (1979) False identification of prime numbers. Paper presented at the 1979 meeting of *The Society for Philosophy and Psychology*, New York, N.Y.

Wittgenstein, L. (1953) *Philosophical Investigations*. New York: MacMillan.

Zadeh, L. (1965) Fuzzy sets. *Information and control*, 8, 338–53.

# 5.   Objects, Parts, and Categories

## Barbara Tversky and Kathleen Hemenway

*Concepts may be organized into taxonomies varying in inclusiveness or abstraction, such as* furniture, table, card table *or* animal, bird, robin. *For taxonomies of common objects and organisms, the basic level, the level of* table *and* bird, *has been determined to be most informative (Rosch, Mervis, Gray, Johnson, & Boyes-Braem, 1976). Psychology, linguistics, and anthropology have produced a variety of measures of perception, behavior, and communication that converge on the basic level. Here, we present data showing that the basic level differs qualitatively from other levels in taxonomies of objects and of living things and present an explanation for why so many measures converge at that level.*

*We have found that part terms proliferate in subjects' listings of attributes characterizing category members at the basic level, but are rarely listed at a general level. At a more specific level, fewer parts are listed, though more are judged to be true. Basic level objects are distinguished from one another by parts, but members of subordinate categories share parts and differ from one another on other attributes. Informants agree on the parts of objects, and also on relative "goodness" of the various parts. Perceptual salience and functional significance both appear to contribute to perceived part goodness. Names of parts frequently enjoy a duality not evident in names of other attributes; they refer at once to a particular appearance and to a particular function.*

*We propose that part configuration underlies the various empirical operations of perception, behavior, and communication that converge at the basic level. Part configuration underlies the perceptual measures because it determines the shapes of objects to a large degree. Parts underlie the behavioral tasks because most of our behavior is directed toward parts of objects. Labeling appears to follow the natural breaks of perception and behavior; consequently, part configuration also underlies communication measures. Because elements of more abstract taxonomies, such as scenes and events, can also be decomposed into parts, this analysis provides a bridge to organization in other domains of knowledge.*

*Knowledge organization by parts (partonomy) is contrasted to organization by kinds (taxonomy). Taxonomies serve to organize numerous classes of entities and to allow inference from larger sets to sets included in them. Partonomies serve to separate entities into their structural components and to organize knowledge of function by components of structure. The informativeness of the basic level may originate from the availability of inference from structure to function at that level.*

\* \* \* \* \*

Barbara Tversky and Kathleen Hemenway: 'Objects, Parts, and Categories' in *JOURNAL OF EXPERIMENTAL PSYCHOLOGY: GENERAL* (1984), Vol. 113, No. 2, pp. 169–193. Copyright © 1984 by the American Psychological Association, Inc. Reprinted by permission.

*Gallia est omnis divisa in partes tres.* Gaul as a whole is divided into three parts. How many essays, since Caesar's account of his European campaign, have begun by decomposing the subject matter into parts? Knowing the parts of a topic and their interrelationship seems to be fundamental to comprehending the topic, whether the topic is a country under siege, a scientific discipline, or an automobile in need of repair. In this article, we examine the special role of parts in determining the *basic* or preferred level of abstraction in a taxonomy.

The world is filled with an overwhelming variety of objects and living things. One of the most fundamental aspects of human thought is the ability to perceive similarities and differences in objects and organisms, and to thereby group or classify them. Grouping individuals into categories gives us a basis for treating different objects and organisms as equivalent and enables us to reduce the numbers of entities in the world to manageable proportions. Classification also allows us to infer properties of individuals from knowledge of the category and to communicate information economically by category labels. The utility of categories can be further increased by organizing them into taxonomies of inclusiveness or abstraction. The animal taxonomy is a classic example. Robins, for example, are included in the class of birds, and birds are included in the class of vertebrates. The more inclusive classes are more abstract in that the features characterizing the class are more general and less concrete. Such structures allow succinct representation of knowledge and provide powerful potential for inference.

What determines how different entities are grouped into categories, or how a general category is divided into subcategories? At one time, it was thought that category groupings were arbitrary, a matter of convention, different from culture to culture. Recent research in anthropology, linguistics, philosophy, and psychology has uncovered regularities in classification across languages and has linked characteristics of natural categories to structure in the perceived world (e.g., Berlin, 1972; Berlin, Breedlove, & Raven, 1966, 1973; Berlin & Kay, 1969; C. H. Brown, 1977, 1979; Hampton, 1979, 1981;Rosch & Mervis, 1975; Rosch, Mervis, Gray, Johnson, & Boyes-Braem, 1976). In their investigation of the internal structure of natural categories, Rosch and Mervis (1975) observed that attributes aren't evenly distributed over objects in the world; some attributes tend to co-occur with certain other attributes. For example, the attribute *has a beak* tends to co-occur with the attributes *flies, has wings, eats worms* and *builds nests*. Consequently, there are groups of entities, like birds, sharing many attributes with one another, and sharing few attributes with other entities. Rosch and Mervis showed that natural categories reflect this structure in the world: Categories group things that share attributes.

A preferred level of reference, or basic level of categorization, is a second characteristic of natural categories that has been linked to structure in the perceived world (Berlin, 1972; Berlin *et al.*, 1973; Rosch *et al.*, 1976). In essence, the basic level phenomenon is that categories at one level of specificity in a taxonomy are psychologically and linguistically more primary than more general and more specific categories. Relative informativeness has been used by Rosch *et al.* (1976) to identify the basic level. This has been operationalized as a relatively steep rise in the number of attributes listed by subjects for objects described at several levels of abstraction. For instance, subjects list very few attributes for *vehicles, furniture,* and *tools,* but list a far greater number of attributes for *car, table,* and *hammer.* Only a few additional attributes are listed for *two-door car, card table,* and *ball-peen hammer.* It has been suggested (Rosch, 1978) that basic level categories are most informative because, given our perceptual apparatus and the structure in the world, this is the level at which the natural correlations and discontinuities among features are most salient. Presumably, where informativeness is greatest, so is the inferential power of categorization.

Many empirical operations converge at the basic level in common taxonomies of objects and organisms. Basic level categories are the most general categories having members with similar and recognizable shapes; they are also the most abstract categories for which a single image can be formed for the category (Rosch *et al.,* 1976). Basic level categories are the most general categories having members that are interacted with in the same ways (Rosch *et al.,* 1976). In labeling an object, basic level terms are preferred (R. Brown, 1958; Cruse, 1977; Rosch *et al.,* 1976), and in verification, basic level labels are verified most rapidly (Murphy & Smith, 1982; Rosch *et al.,* 1976). Basic level terms tend to be the first categories named and understood by children (Mervis & Rosch, 1981), the first terms to enter a lexicon, shorter and less derived terms (Berlin, 1972; Rosch *et al.,* 1976), and contextually neutral (Cruse, 1977). The first two measures reflect our perception of objects, the next measure reflects our behavior toward objects, and the final measures reflect our communication about them. It remains to be explained why so many different and significant operations converge at the same level.

Although the basic level of reference has been defined quantitatively, there seem to be qualitative differences among the levels of abstraction in common taxonomies (Rosch *et al.,* 1976; Smith, Balzano, & Walker, 1978). Specifically, superordinate categories seem to primarily share functional features — vehicles are for transporting, and tools are for fixing. They do not seem to share perceptual features, in sharp contrast to objects belonging to the same basic level category, which appear to share both perceptual and functional features. On closer examination of the attributes listed by subjects, it appeared to us that one kind of feature especially predominates at the basic level of reference, namely, parts. Attributes listed for *screwdriver* include *handle* and *blade,* and attributes listed for *chair* include *seat, back,* and *legs.* Although object parts are portions of wholes, and therefore perceptual features, many names of parts seem to have a special status in that they are at once perceptual and functional. They refer to both a perceptually identifiable segment of an object and to a specialized function of the object. A *handle,* for instance, is typically long, thin, and of a size compatible with the human hand; a handle is used for grasping. Likewise, a *blade* is also elongated, with one of its long edges thinner and sharper than the other, it is used for cutting. Similarly, a seat is a squarish, horizontal surface, of a size and height to be compatible with humans; it is used for sitting. The other sorts of attributes generated by subjects, for instance, *red, found in water, heavy, used for fixing,* do not have this dual character. Thus part names, in contrast to names of other attributes describing objects and organisms, have two faces: one toward appearance, the other toward function.

In these studies, we garner evidence supporting the proposal that it is the psychological prevalence of parts that grants special status to the basic level; that parts underlie the distinctiveness of objects from one another at the basic level, and that parts underlie each of the types of converging operations, and thereby account for their convergence. These claims entail three predictions, to be examined empirically. First, knowledge about parts is expected to underlie the superior informativeness of the basic level. Second, because part structure is expected to underlie the natural breaks or discontinuities at the basic level, different objects at the basic level should differ on parts and share other attributes. Third, different subordinate objects belonging to the same basic level category should share parts and differ on other attributes. Following Rosch (1978), we refer to issues concerning inclusion and abstraction relations between categories as the *vertical* dimension of categorization, and to issues concerning the relations among subcategories at the same level of analysis as the *horizontal* dimension of categorization. The first prediction, then, is a prediction about representation of vertical relations among categories, and the next two predictions are about representation of the horizontal relations.

These predictions were explored for categories of plants and animals as well as for categories of common objects. Although it is difficult to identify defining characteristics of members of object categories, functional characteristics are probably at least as important as form and structure in determining membership in those categories. For example, functional *sit-on-able-ness* is at least as important a determinant of membership in the chair category as is possessing a chairlike shape. In contrast, biological categories at all taxonomic levels are morphologically based: Membership in the most general categories is determined by gross morphological features, whereas membership in the most specific categories is determined by fine structural details (Dougherty, 1978; Hunn, 1976). Because biological categories at all taxonomic ranks are morphologically based, it is not likely that basic level categories are the most general categories having members with the same parts. Members of all categories, even very general ones, probably share some parts. Even so, the extent of perceived differentiation in terms of parts and other attributes may vary with taxonomic level.

The biological categories, then, are an especially important test of our predictions because they have a part structure even at all levels of description. If we can demonstrate in biological categories a level of abstraction for which few if any, parts are listed, followed by a level for which many parts are listed, this is strong evidence for our claim that it is the psychological salience of parts that underlies the basic level of reference. Biological categories are also important because they are cultural universals and were present during the evolution of humankind in contrast to object categories, which may differ from culture to culture.

## STUDY 1: PARTS PREVAIL AT THE BASIC LEVEL

In this study, we demonstrate that the sharp increase in attributes listed from the superordinate to the basic level is accounted for by one kind of attribute listed by subjects, namely, parts. In this and subsequent studies, we follow the methods of Rosch *et al.* (1976) in many cases, reanalyzing their data by separating attributes into parts and nonparts. In reporting our results, we separate findings for object categories from findings for biological categories. One reason for this was that Rosch *et al.* did not find direct evidence for a basic level for biological categories. Another reason for treating objects separately from biological entities was the possibiiity, discussed earlier, that perceived parts would play a role in determining the basic level for objects, but not for living things.

## Object categories

### Method

#### Collection of attributes

Criteria of frequency and depictability of instances led Rosch *et al.* (1976) to select six superordinate categories (clothing, fruit, furniture, musical instruments, tools, and vehicles), three basic level categories from each superordinate, and two subordinates from each basic level category. Although *fruit* is in some sense a biological category, it can also be regarded as an object category, since it is a human defined part of a tree, engineered, packaged, and marketed much like a manufactured object. Rosch and her colleagues collected attribute norms according to a three-phase procedure described briefly here. In Phase 1, a large number of subjects were given 90 s to list attributes for each category; each subject listed attributes for categories at only one level of abstraction, and for only one category from each superordinate. In Phase 2, the attributes were tallied and every attribute listed by less than one third of the subjects was eliminated, removing idiosyncratic responses. In Phase 3, other subjects, "judges," amended the attribute lists. The judges removed attributes they felt were not true of all category members, and added attributes if they felt the attributes were true of all category members; however, they could only add an attribute if it was already included in the list. Additions and deletions made by all 7 judges were included in the final tally. These two procedures — adding and deleting attributes — made the attribute lists logically consistent, so that properties attributed to a category were also attributed to all its subcategories.

#### Separating parts from other attributes

Both the judge-amended and the nonamended attribute norms collected by Rosch *et al.* (1976) were separated into "parts" and "other attributes" according to three coinciding criteria. These norms were obtained through the good graces of Mervis and Rosch, and are used with permission. One criterion was a dictionary definition criterion. Several themes were repeated in the dictionaries we consulted. A part is one of tbe segments or portions into which something is regarded as divided; a part is less than a whole; together, parts constitute a whole. A second criterion was derived from Miller and Johnson-Laird's (1976) lucid discussion of relations that generate hierarchies. They distinguish a *taxonomic*, or *kind of* relation, from a *partonomic*, or *part of* relation. Whereas a taxonomic relation is expressed in an *is a* sentence frame, as in, A dog is an animal, a partonomic relation is expressed in a *has a* sentence frame, as in, A dog has a leg. This is not to say that all *is a* sentences express taxonomic relations or to say that all *has a* sentences express partonomic relations. However, for the attributes actually obtained, those that fit into a *has a* sentence frame were parts. Thus, the attributes *handle, teeth, blade,* and *edge,* listed for saw fit into a *has a* sentence frame, whereas *cuts* and *sharp* do not. A third criterion was the majority judgment of naive subjects who were asked to designate which of the attributes listed for 80 objects they regarded as parts. All of the attributes judges determined to be parts fit into a *has a* sentence frame, with the addition of material composition. Judges determined that attributes having an *is made of* or *is partially made of* relation to the object were also parts. These constituted only 9% of the parts attributes. The attribute *wood* listed for guitar is an example. *Wood* seems to be in lieu of *frame* or *body* in this instance and in others like it. Note here that *wood* also fits the dictionary definition of part. Additional justification for including material composition as parts comes from a separate study in which subjects, asked to list parts of objects, frequently listed parts by the materials they are made of. For example, *wood* and *metal* were commonly listed as parts of a screwdriver, instead of *handle* and *blade*. Finally, the form class of the attribute was helpful for distinguishing parts from other attributes. All of the parts listed were nouns, and most of the nouns listed were parts; the nouns that were not parts were *driver* and *passenger* for car and bus, and *chairs* for kitchen table. The nonpart attributes were adjectives *(loud, crispy, green, comfortable)* or else verb phrases or sentence fragments *(you eat on it, gives light, requires gas, lives in water)*. Attributes considered to be parts, then, refer to segments of wholes that are less than wholes: they are judged by a majority of naive informants to be parts, and they fit into a *has a* or is *made of* or is *partially made of* sentence frame.

In Table 1 the attributes from some of the categories reported in Rosch *et al.* (1976) are displayed, separated into parts and nonparts. The careful reader will notice that *keys, black keys,* and *white keys* are all listed for piano, and *legs* and *four legs* for chair. Since the judges passed on these attributes, we had no choice but to leave them in as well. Redundant attributes constituted a small portion of the attributes, and leaving them out does not change the pattern of findings.

**Table 1    Judge-amended attributes divided into parts and other attributes**

|  | Musical instrument<br>Makes sound |  |
|---|---|---|
| Guitar | Piano | Drum |
| Strings* | Keys* | Sticks* |
| Tuning keys* | Foot pedals* | Skins* |
| Neck* | Strings* | Round |
| Hole* | Legs* | Loud |
| Wood* | Lid* | Used by music groups |
| Make music | Wood* |  |
| You strum it | Black keys* |  |
| Used by music groups | White keys* |  |
|  | Makes music |  |
| Classical guitar | Upright piano | Kettle drum |
| (No additional) | (No additional) | (No additional) |
| Folk guitar | Grand piano | Bass drum |
| (No additional) | Large | (No additional) |
|  | Used in concert halls |  |

**Table 1    (cont)**

|  | Fruit | |
|---|---|---|
|  | Seeds* | |
|  | Sweet | |
|  | You eat it | |

| Apple | Peach | Grapes |
|---|---|---|
| Stem* | Pit* | Juicy |
| Core* | Skin* | Bunches |
| Skin* | Yellow-Orange | Makes wine |
| Juicy | Fuzzy | Grows on vine |
| Round | Soft |  |
| Grows on trees | Grows on trees |  |

| Delicious apple | Freestone peach | Concord grapes |
|---|---|---|
| Red | (No additional) | Purple |
| Crisp |  |  |
| Shiny |  |  |
| Tasty |  |  |

| Macintosh apple | Cling peach | Green seedless grapes |
|---|---|---|
| (No additional) | Juicy | Green |
|  | Canned | Small |

|  | Furniture | |
|---|---|---|
|  | (No attributes) | |

| Table | Lamp | Chair |
|---|---|---|
| Legs* | Light bulb* | Legs* |
| Top* | Shade* | Seat* |
| Surface* | Cord* | Back* |
| Wood* | Switches* | Arms* |
| You eat on it | Base* | Comfortable |
| You put things on it | Gives light | Four legs* |
|  | You read by it | Wood* |
|  |  | Holds people |
|  |  | You sit on it |

| Kitchen table | Floor lamp | Kitchen chair |
|---|---|---|
| Chairs | (No additional) | (No additional) |

| Dining room table | Desk lamp | Living room chair |
|---|---|---|
| Four legs* | (No additional) | Large |
|  |  | Soft |
|  |  | Cushion* |

*Note.* Judge-amended attributes selected from "Basic objects in natural categories" by E. Rosch, C.B. Mervis, W. Gray, D. Johnson, and P. Boyes-Braem, 1976, *Cognitive Psychology, 8,* pp. 435–436. Copyright 1976 by Academic Press. Adapted by permission. Lower levels include all attributes listed at higher levels. Parts are indicated by *.

## Results

### Judge-amended tallies

In order to give equal weight to each category (because some categories elicit more attributes than others), the number of part and nonpart attributes were computed for each category and averaged over categories for each level of analysis. This technique was adopted throughout the research. Overall, 58% of the attributes were parts; however, the percentage varied with taxonomic level, as predicted. Parts were infrequent at the superordinate level and frequent at the basic and subordinate levels: Only 20% of the superordinate level attributes were parts, whereas 64% of the basic level attributes were parts, and 60% of the subordinate level attributes were parts.

In Figure 1 the mean numbers of parts and other attributes in the judge-amended tally are displayed as a function of level of abstraction. For both parts and other attributes, the difference between the superordinate and basic levels is significantly larger than the difference between the basic and subordinate levels, $t(5) = 3.89, p < .01; t(5) = 3.48, p < .01$, and this disparity is more marked for parts than for other attributes, as predicted, $t(5) = 2.82, p < .01$. Also, the difference between the basic and subordinate levels is larger for other attributes than for parts, $t(5) = 2.77, p < .025$.

### Nonamended tallies

Numbers of parts and nonparts were averaged over categories for each level of abstraction, as before, to equalize the contribution of each category to the part partition. Overall, 57% of the attributes were parts; again, the proportion of parts to other attributes varied with level of abstraction. Thirty-eight percent of the superordinate level attributes were parts, 66% of the basic level attributes were parts, and 58% of the subordinate level attributes were parts.

In Figure 2 the mean numbers of parts and other attributes occurring at each level of abstraction are displayed. Subjects listed more parts at the basic level than at the subordinate level. The number of parts listed for each basic level category was significantly higher than the mean number listed for its subordinates (sign test $z = 2.58, p < .005$).

## Biological categories

### Method

#### Selection of categories

The superordinate categories used were plant and animal. The basic categories bird, fish, tree, and flower were chosen because attribute lists for 15 subordinates of each of those categories had been collected by Malt and Smith (1982), and they kindly allowed us to reanalyze their data. We asked 30 undergraduates at Stanford to rate the subordinates for familiarity, and selected 4 subordinates from each set of 15 on this basis.

#### Attribute listing

*Subjects.* In this and subsequent studies, unless noted otherwise, subjects were Stanford introductory psychology students participating for course credit, or infrequently, for pay. Subjects were run in small or large groups, and sometimes participated in other, unrelated experiments in the same session. There were 45 subjects in the present experiment; 15 subjects listed attributes for each superordinate and basic level category. In Malt and Smith's (1982) experiment there were 240 subjects, and 16 subjects listed attributes for each subordinate category. To make their data comparable to previous data, 1 of their subjects was randomly eliminated.

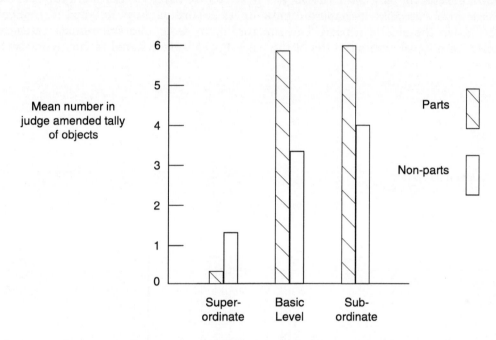

**Figure 1    Mean number of parts and other attributes listed by subjects and amended by judges for object categories at three levels of abstraction**

*Materials.* The booklets used in the present experiment were identical in format to those used by Rosch *et al.* (1976) and by Malt and Smith (1982). The booklets consisted of an instruction page, and several pages, each of which had a category label, either plant and animal or one kind of plant (tree or flower) and one kind of animal (bird or fish) at the top and was blank otherwise. Each booklet in Malt and Smith's experiment included four subordinate category labels (one kind of bird, one kind of fish, one kind of flower, and one kind of tree) as well as four unrelated basic category labels. Pages were collated in random order for each subject.

*Procedure.* The instructions were read aloud to subjects, and then the subjects were timed while they listed attributes for each category. The attributes were tallied and attributes listed by a third or more of the subjects were included in the final nonamended lists. These lists were used in the judge-amending phase. The instructions and procedure were similar to those used by Rosch *et al.* (1976). Malt and Smith (1982) also used the Rosch procedure, that they allowed subjects only 75 s per item for listing attributes.

*Judgment of attributes*

*Subjects.* Another group of 10 students judged the truth of the attributes.

The following methods were used in this and subsequent judge-amending phases.

*Materials and procedure.* Booklets consisted of an instruction page, followed by separate pages for each basic category. The attributes listed by 2 or more subjects for a basic level category, its superordinate, or its subordinates were typed in random order down the side of a page. The superordinate, basic, and subordinate category names were typed across the top of the page. Pages were collated randomly for each subject.

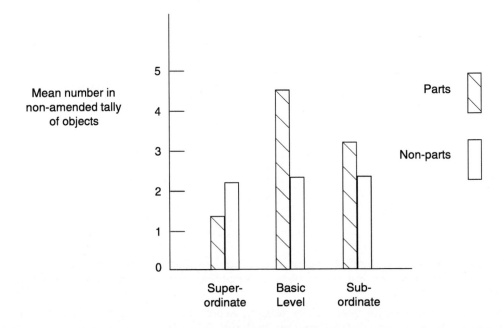

**Figure 2**   **Mean number of parts and other attributes listed by subjects for object categories at three levels of abstraction**

The experimenter read the instructions aloud to subjects while they read along silently. The instructions were very similar to those used by Rosch *et al.* (1976) and asked subjects to judge whether each attribute was true of each category listed across the top of the pages. The task was self-paced.

An attribute was included in the judge-amended norms for a category if a majority of the judges indicated possession. Logical consistency was not enforced; that is, an attribute was included for a category if a majority of the judges indicated possession, regardless of whether the attribute was included in the lists for all subcategories.

## *Results*

### *Judge-amended attribute tallies*

As before, numbers of parts and nonparts were averaged over categories at each level of analysis. Overall, 42.7% of the attributes were parts. As before, the percentage varied with taxonomic level. Forty percent of the superordinate attributes were parts, whereas 52% of the basic level attributes were parts. The proportion of parts declined to 38% for subordinate level categories. In Figure 3 the mean numbers of parts and other attributes as a function of taxonomic level are displayed. As expected, biological categories are perceived to share parts even at the superordinate level. *Stem* and *roots* were listed for plants, whereas *tail* and *eyes* were listed for animals. Some of the judge-amended norms are reported in Appendix A.

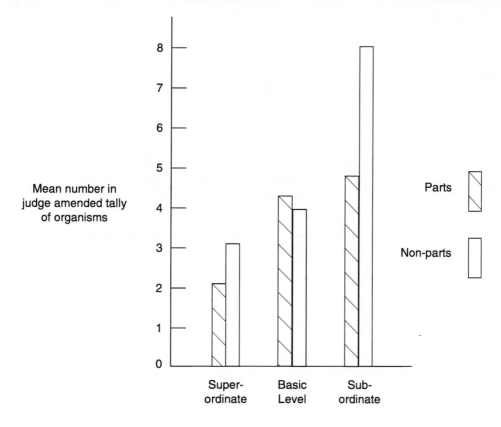

**Figure 3** **Mean number of parts and other attributes listed by subjects and amended by judges for biological categories at three levels of abstraction**

### *Nonamended attribute tallies*

Numbers of parts and nonparts were averaged over categories at each level of analysis. Overall, 49.6% of the attributes were parts. For the nonamended tallies, the variation in proportion of parts with taxonomic level is even more striking: Parts constituted only 25% of superordinates, 70% of basic level attributes, and 46% of subordinate attributes. The decrease in number of parts listed from basic level to subordinate level was significant, $t(3) = 9.52$, $p < .005$. At the superordinate level, subjects listed significantly fewer parts than other attributes, for example, plants: $t(14) = 6.44$, $p < .005$; animals: $t(14) = 2.90$, $p < .01$. The mean numbers of part and nonpart attributes listed at each taxonomic level are displayed in Figure 4.

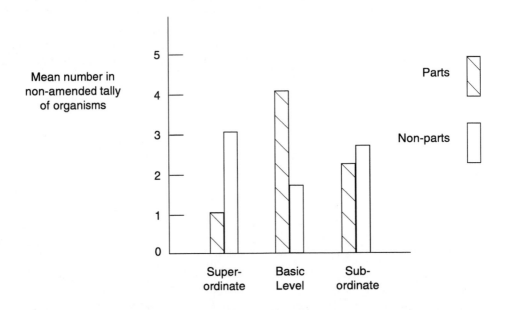

**Figure 4** **Mean number of parts and other attributes listed by subjects for biological categories at three levels of abstraction**

*Raw attribute lists*

Two analyses of the attribute lists obtained from Phase 1 shed light on the role of knowledge of parts in taxonomically organized categories. Parts were separated into modified (e.g., *red petals*) or unmodified (e.g, *petals*). Quantified parts (e.g., *two eyes*) were infrequent and were excluded from the analysis. At the superordinate and basic levels, 12% and 10% of the parts were modified, respectively, whereas at the subordinate level, 34% were modified. Although, overall, fewer parts were listed at the subordinate level than at the basic level, more than twice as many modified parts were listed at the subordinate level. This result is consistent with the hypothesis that characteristics of parts are distinctive of contrasting subordinates.

The order in which subjects list attributes should be indicative of the relative importance of the attributes for the categories. If parts are particularly salient at the basic level, they should be listed earlier than other attributes. Attribute lists for each subject were split in half by order of output, and the percentage of parts listed in each half were computed. At the superordinate level, 48.5% of the parts were listed in the first half of the output, and at the subordinate level, 53% of the parts were listed in the first half of the output. In contrast, 71% of the parts in the basic level occurred in the first half of the output. Matched pairs $t$ tests revealed a significant bias to name parts earlier for each basic level category; flower $t(14) = 5.68$, tree: $t(14) = 3.59$, fish: $t(14) = 2.83$, and bird: $t(14) = 3.31$, all $ps < .005$; no bias for either of the superordinate categories ($t < .2$); and no bias for 14 out of 16 of the subordinate categories (for 13 categories, $t < 1$; for sparrow, $t = 2.20, p < .05$; for chicken, $t = 2.70, p < .02$).

## Discussion

Parts dominate attribute lists at the basic level for amended and nonamended norms, for object and biological categories. Although parts are a minority of superordinate attributes, the majority of attributes listed at the basic level are parts. The proportion of parts listed decreases from the basic to the subordinate levels, becoming a minority of the attributes for biological categories. Only the parts attributes show the sharp rise in numbers from the superordinate to the basic level, taken as the definition of the basic level. Inclusion of other attributes attenuates this effect, especially in the biological categories. The comparison between the amended and nonamended norms is instructive. The amended norms force or encourage consistency on the tallies; attributes included in categories were also usually included for subcategories, because they were usually true of subcategories. This is consistent with the notion that more specific categories carry more information. However, the nonamended tallies tell a different story. More attributes are listed at the basic level than at the superordinate level, but fewer attributes are listed at the subordinate level than at the basic level. This drop in accessed knowledge with increasing specificity of category is completely attributable to the drop in numbers of parts listed. A desk lamp contains the same parts as a lamp, and double-knit pants contain the same parts as pants; however, subjects list fewer parts for desk lamp than lamp and fewer for double-knit pants than for pants. Moreover, a larger share of the parts listed at the subordinate level are modified parts, such as *white petals*. Because when judges amend the tallies, they add attributes (particularly parts) to the subordinate categories, we can infer that subjects know that sedans have carburetors and pine trees have trunks, even if the subordinate label fails to elicit them. Thus, the amended norms reflect the knowledge subjects have whereas the nonamended norms reflect subjects' performance in this sort of task.

What determines the sorts of attributes subjects list for objects and entities? Despite the popularity of category and attribute norms (e.g., Ashcraft, 1978; Hampton, 1979, 1981; Malt & Smith, 1982; Rosch *et al.*, 1976), their status has not received much discussion. How can we account for the failure to list parts and other attributes for objects, especially at the subordinate level of specificity, in spite of the fact that subjects judge these attributes to be true for those objects? Observation of the attribute lists suggests that in listing attributes, subjects attempt to be informative about the objects (Grice, 1975) to convey the knowledge they have about the categories. They give us good clues as to how to recognize the objects and as to what the objects are used for. Subjects also attempt to be relevant, for they do not say all they know about the objects. They tell attributes important for distinguishing the appearance or function of the object, so the smell of flowers and taste of fruit are mentioned, but not the smell or taste of clothing. They list fewer attributes at the subordinate level than at the basic level in spite of the fact that they know more attributes at the subordinate level. Subjects don't list *molecules* or *inanimate* or *cells* or *animate,* although the former two are properties of objects and the latter two are properties of living things. Subjects, then, are informative and relevant, but in the context of an implicit contrast set (see Garner, 1974; see also the discussion of contrastive field properties in Miller & Johnson-Laird, 1976). Interestingly, the implicit contrast set seems to be other objects at the same level of abstraction. More general features seem to be presupposed, and go unmentioned. So, it is more informative to mention *trunk* for tree than for pine tree, because tree contrasts with grass or bush or perhaps even more remote entities, and *trunk* is a property of trees, but not of these contrasting entities. Because the implicit contrast set for *pine tree* will include other trees, listing *trunk* is not as informative as it is shared by all trees, but listing *needles* is informative.

The parts norms (but not the nonparts norms) for biological categories establish directly that the basic level for biological categories for American college students is the level of tree, flower, fish, and bird, with plant and animal as superordinates. Previous work had shown that the level found to be basic (generic) in folk taxonomies (Berlin, 1978), namely, pine, bass, was not basic according to the Rosch *et al.* (1976) criterion. In fact, the data for object and biological categories look remarkably similar, despite the fact that biological categories are defined morphologically at all levels of abstraction, whereas superordinate object categories appear to carry functional meaning as well. Superordinate biological categories are judged to share a few parts, whereas superordinate object categories are not; however, the nonamended norms do not show this difference. For the biological categories, the basic level is less sharply defined. Inclusion of other attributes in addition to the parts attributes so attenuates the relationship of attributes to taxonomic level as to preclude establishment of a basic level for biological categories.

Although these studies have been directed at a vertical analysis of categories related by inclusiveness in a taxonomy, the results are suggestive of phenomena occurring horizontally, or between categories at the same level of analysis. We have seen that the attributes subjects list for categories are informative and relevant within an implicit contrast set, that is, characteristic and distinctive of the object in comparison to objects it is not. The prevalence of parts at the basic level suggests that, especially at that level, objects should differ from one another on the basis of parts and share other attributes. This is tested directly in the next set of studies.

### STUDY 2: BASIC LEVEL CATEGORIES DIFFER BY PARTS

To test that basic objects differ from one another by parts and share other features, we examined attribute lists for a large number of basic level entities for each of four object and two biological categories. Finding that categories at the basic level differ from one another on the basis of parts but share other attributes would indicate that the perceived natural breaks among categories at that level are between clusters of shared parts.

Because a large number of basic and subordinate categories are needed for this analysis, it could not be performed on the data from Study 1. The attributes for 20 kinds of clothing, furniture, vehicles, and weapons were generously contributed by

Rosch and Mervis (1975). Their data were collected using the three-phase procedure described earlier. These instances varied considerably in absolute frequency, production frequency (to superordinate name), and typicality vis-à-vis the superordinate category. No such lists of instances or of attributes existed for animals and plants, so we collected them. Interestingly, the six plant categories produced by our subjects (flower, tree, fern, grass, bush, vine) correspond closely to the life-form categories found in a large number of folk botanical taxonomies by Witkowski and C. H. Brown (reported in C. H. Brown, 1977). The animal categories selected were also at the life-form level as determined by cross-cultural ethnological studies (Berlin, 1978).

## Object categories

### Method

*Subjects*

The subjects were 10 naive staff persons in the Department of Psychology at Stanford who completed the booklets at their leisure.

*Materials and procedure*

Booklets were compiled according to the following procedure. Separate forms were used for each superordinate category. The 20 basic categories from a superordinate were listed at the top of each page, and the attributes from the corresponding composite attribute list were typed, in a random order, below the list of categories. The pages were collated in a different random order for each subject (with the constraint that all the pages for one superordinate always occurred together). The subjects were instructed to circle all the attributes they considered to be parts on each of the pages. They were not told what a part is: However, they were told that *ears* and *trunk* are parts of an elephant, whereas *large, gray,* and *eats peanuts* are not.

*Results and discussion*

Every attribute circled by a majority of the subjects was considered to be a part. Then, each attribute was assigned a weight equal to the number of basic level categories from the same superordinate possessing the attribute. Because of the high variability of these weights, the median (rather than the mean) weights for parts and nonparts were computed. Displayed in the top section of Table 2 are the median weights for parts and nonparts. For each category, the parts median is smaller than the nonparts median, $t(3) = 5.14, p < .01$. This result indicates that parts are more distinctive of contrasting basic categories than are nonparts, confirming our hypothesis that subjects list more parts at the basic level because parts are the distinctive features of objects at that level. Thus, parts contribute more than nonparts to the naturalness of basic level category cuts.

This result may also seem to imply that parts are working against the integrity of superordinate categories. After all, shared features are what "glue" a category together, and shared features are associated with the prototypicality of a category member (Rosch & Mervis, 1975). Because nonparts are more likely to be shared than parts, one may infer that sharing nonparts would be more predictive of prototypicality than sharing parts. To answer this question, separate family resemblance scores were computed on parts and nonparts, and each family resemblance score was correlated with typicality. The parts and the nonparts family resemblance scores correlated equally and highly with typicality, and with each other. So, although for these natural categories, parts and other attributes are equally associated with the typicality of instances of the same superordinate, only parts distinguish instances from one another.

**Table 2   Median number of basic level categories sharing parts and other attributes**

| Type of category | Median weight | |
| --- | --- | --- |
| | Parts | Other attributes |
| Object | | |
| Clothing | 3 | 5 |
| Furniture | 1 | 2 |
| Vehicles | 3 | 6 |
| Weapons | 1 | 2.5 |
| Biological | | |
| Animals | 2.5 | 4 |
| Plants | 2.5 | 3 |

## Biological categories: elicitation of instances

### *Method*

Forty-one subjects were given small booklets with a cover page that the experimenter read aloud. The rest of the booklet consisted of a page titled "Plants" and another page titled "Animals," collated in random order. The instructions informed the subjects that each page of their booklets named a kind of thing, and that they would have 60 s to write down "items people commonly give as belonging to various categories or classes." The instructions also included an example.

### *Results*

From the animals listed by 2 or more subjects, 20 animal categories were selected so that no category included another and so that the entire range of production frequency and produced genera were sampled. Thus, the list contained bee, ant, fish, snake, frog, bird, turtle, and alligator, as well as 12 mammals varying in familiarity. From the plants listed by 2 or more subjects, only six plant categories (flower, tree, fern, grass, bush, and vine) met the criteria.

## Biological categories: attribute listing

### *Method*

Ten subjects listed attributes for the six plant categories and other subjects listed attributes for the 20 animal categories. They were directed to list "characteristics and attributes that people feel are common to and characteristic of different kinds of ordinary everyday animals (plants)." The instructions also included a number of examples. To expedite collection of attribute norms, these subjects both generated and judged the truth of attributes. Malt & Smith (1982) compared attributes listed for common categories (e.g., lemon) when they were in the context of other categories from the same superordinate and when they were in the context of other categories from different superordinates. There were essentially no differences in the attributes produced in the two contexts, broad and narrow.

### Results and discussion

Those attributes listed by more than three judges were divided into parts and nonparts by the usual criteria. The median weights for parts and other attributes were computed, and are displayed in Table 2. Just as in the object categories, the median weights for nonparts are higher than the median weights for parts for biological categories, indicating that basic level plants and animals are perceived to share nonparts and to differ from one another on the basis of parts.

## STUDY 3: SUBORDINATE LEVEL CATEGORIES SHARE PARTS

Parts, more than other attributes, distinguish one basic level entity from another. Reflection on the nature of subordinate categories as well as the decrease in parts listed at the subordinate level suggest that subordinate level categories may share the same parts and differ from one another on other attributes. We next examine that conjecture, first for object categories, and then for biological categories.

### Object categories

Attribute norms for 10 subordinates from each of four basic categories, chair, table, shirt, and pants, were compiled and analyzed. These categories were used because they were the only ones for which a substantial number of familiar subordinate category labels could be found.

### Method

*Subjects*

There were 40 subjects in all; 10 subjects listed attributes for each set of subordinate categories.

*Materials*

In order to select subordinate categories, two judges (the authors) listed all the subordinate labels they could think of or find in catalogs. Brand names and unfamiliar labels were excluded from the lists. When near synonyms occurred in a list, only the more specific synonym was included. Where two labels applied to a single exemplar, one of the labels was excluded from the list whenever possible. Because many object subordinates don't form contrast sets, it was not possible to exclude all noncontrasting labels. The subordinate categories are displayed in Table 3.

Four different kinds of booklets were compiled, one for each set of subordinates. The booklets consisted of an instruction page followed by four identical forms. The 10 subordinates were listed across the top right-hand side of the forms, and blank space was left on the left-hand side for subjects to list attributes. For each attribute subjects listed, they put $x$s below the subordinates possessing the attribute.

**Table 3    Nonbiological subordinate categories**

| Pants | Shirts |
|---|---|
| Corduroy pants | Dress shirt |
| Double-knit pants | Flannel shirt |
| Flared pants | Knit shirt |
| Levi pants | Long-sleeved shirt |
| Overalls | Sweat shirt |
| Pleated pants | T-shirt |
| Riding pants | Turtleneck shirt |
| Ski pants | V-neck shirt |
| Straight-leg pants | Western shirt |
| Sweat pants | Work shirt |

| Chairs | Tables |
|---|---|
| Beanbag chair | Card table |
| Dining room chair | Coffee table |
| Director's chair | Conference table |
| Easy chair | Dining room table |
| Folding chair | Drafting table |
| High chair | End table |
| Kitchen chair | Kitchen table |
| Reclining chair | Picnic table |
| Rocking chair | Ping pong table |
| Swivel chair | Typewriter table |

*Procedure*

The written instructions were read aloud to subjects. They were asked to list "attributes, properties, and characteristics true of all the things listed across the top of the page, as well as attributes, properties, and characteristics true of only one or a few of them." Subjects worked at their own pace, listing all the attributes they could think of in 15 min.

*Scoring*

A subordinate category was considered to possess an attribute if at least 3 subjects indicated that the subordinate possessed it. The attributes were classified as parts and nonparts in the usual way. The parts were further classified as unmodified parts (called *parts*) and modified parts (e.g., *long sleeves, flat top*). Two of the parts in the lists occurred with quantifiers (i.e., *two legs, four legs*) and these parts were excluded from the tallies. Finally, a weight equal to the number of subordinates possessing an attribute was calculated for each attribute.

### Results and discussion

The median weights for parts and nonparts are given in Table 4. For each category the median parts weight is larger than the median nonparts weight. This result is significant, $t(3) = 3.70, p < .025$, and it is consistent with the other results indicating that the distinctive features of subordinate categories are nonparts. The modified parts medians were not included because so few modified parts occurred.

**Table 4    Median number of subordinate categories sharing parts, modified parts, and other attributes**

| Type of category | Median weight | | |
| | Parts | Other attributes | Modified* |
|---|---|---|---|
| Object | | | |
| Pants | 6 | 3 | |
| Shirts | 6 | 3 | |
| Chairs | 5.5 | 3 | |
| Tables | 9 | 2 | |
| Biological | | | |
| Flowers | 10 | 2 | 4 |
| Trees | 3 | 3 | 3 |
| Birds | 10 | 2 | 2 |
| Fish | 10 | 2 | 1 |

*Note.* * These numbers were inconsequential for object categories.

## Biological categories

Subordinate object categories share parts and differ from one another on other attributes. To examine the hypothesis that the distinctive features associated with biological subordinates are mostly nonparts and, to a lesser extent, modifications on parts, attribute lists for many contrasting subordinate categories were analyzed.

### *Method*

*Attribute listing*

Based on the study of familiarity of subordinates described earlier, attribute lists of Malt and Smith (1982) for the 10 most familiar subordinates from each basic category were used. The resulting set of subordinate categories is displayed in Table 5.

To match the sample size in this experiment to the sample size in the corresponding study of object subordinates, 6 of Malt and Smith's (1982) 16 subjects were randomly selected and their data were eliminated. Every attribute listed for a category by 2 or more of the remaining 10 subjects was included in the next phase of the experiment.

*Judgment of attributes*

Nine subjects judged the truth of the attributes according to the usual procedure. A subordinate was considered to possess an attribute if a majority of the 9 subjects indicated possession. A weight equal to the total number of subordinates possessing an attribute was computed for each attribute. The attributes were separated into parts and nonparts according to the usual criteria, and the parts were further separated into three classes: modified, unmodified, and quantified parts. As before, the number of quantified parts was too small to be analyzed.

151

**Table 5    Biological subordinate categories**

| Flowers | Trees |
|---|---|
| African violet | Bamboo |
| Azalea | Elm |
| Cherry blossom | Maple |
| Daisy | Oak |
| Iris | Palm tree |
| Lilac | Peach tree |
| Lily | Pear tree |
| Marigold | Pine |
| Poppy | Redwood |
| Rose | Sequoia |

| Birds | Fish |
|---|---|
| Blue jay | Carp |
| Chicken | Eel |
| Crow | Goldfish |
| Duck | Minnow |
| Hawk | Salmon |
| Mockingbird | Sardine |
| Owl | Shark |
| Pelican | Sunfish |
| Robin | Trout |
| Sparrow | Tuna |

### *Results and discussion*

The median weights for parts, nonparts, and modified parts are displayed in the bottom section of Table 4. The parts median is larger than both the nonparts median, $t(3) = 3.27$, $p < .025$, and the modified parts median, $t(3) = 2.85$, $p < .05$. The latter two medians don't differ from one another, $t(3) = .397$, *ns*. Seventy-five percent of the attributes in the norms are nonparts, 15% are parts, 9% are modified parts, and 1% are quantified parts.

On the whole, biological subordinate categories, like object subordinate categories, share parts and differ from one another on other attributes. To a certain extent, they also differ from one another in variations on parts.

### DISCUSSION OF STUDIES 1–3

Taken together, these three studies indicate that parts are significantly linked to basic level category cuts: Subjects associate few, if any, part attributes with superordinate level categories, but associate a large number of part attributes with basic level concepts. Few, if any, additional parts are associated with subordinate level categories. Most of the features shared by (subordinate) members of a basic category are parts, and most of the features distinguishing one basic category from another are parts. In contrast, the features that differentiate subordinates of a basic category are mostly nonparts. Unlike at other levels of abstraction, at the basic level parts are both (a) the features common to members of a category and (b) the features distinctive of contrasting categories. Thus, the perceived natural breaks among basic level categories occur between clusters of parts, whereas the perceived natural breaks among subordinate level categories occur between other attributes. These results extend and clarify Rosch *et al*.'s (1976) assertion that basic level categories are more effective than categories at other levels in grouping entities that share many features and separating entities that are distinguished by many features. Parts are a better index of "basicness" than are other, purely functional or perceptual attributes; in fact, these only attenuate the diagnosis of the basic level.

The predominance of parts listed at the basic level suggests, in addition to a quantitative diagnosis, a qualitative explanation of why members of basic level categories have very similar shapes, and why they are interacted with in the same ways (Rosch *et al.*, 1976). Because that is what the task demands, subjects give lists of parts, but in actuality, parts are organized in specific configurations. The configuration of parts, or structural description, determines the shape of objects to a large degree. Moreover, because they have virtually no distinctive parts, members of different subordinate categories don't have distinctive shapes. Similarly because we typically interact with the parts of an object (we grasp *handles,* sit on *seats,* push *buttons,* etc.), objects that have the same parts are interacted with in the same ways. We return to this analysis in the final discussion. But first, let us have a closer look at parts themselves.

## STUDY 4: GOODNESS OF PARTS

We have examined the role of parts in the vertical organization of categories, in distinguishing the basic or preferred level of reference. We have also examined the role of parts in the horizontal organization of categories, in distinguishing one basic level category from another. Another way of examining the horizontal role of parts is to investigate the different parts of a particular object. Until now, we have treated all parts associated with an object as equal. However, even casual perusal of the lists of parts suggests that there is variability in the "goodness" of the parts associated with an object or organism. The *trunk* of an elephant, for instance, seems to be a very good part of an elephant. It is a perceptually salient extension of the body and has functional significance for the elephant as well as for its human caretakers and perceivers. Furthermore, the trunk is a distinctive feature of an elephant, serving to distinguish elephants from other members of the animal kingdom. Similarly, the *screen* of a television is both a perceptually salient and functionally significant part of a television, as well as a part that distinguishes it from other furniture or appliances. Other parts, including many not even mentioned by our informants, seem to be less good, because they lack functional significance or perceptual salience, or object distinctiveness, or some combination of the above. For instance, optional parts, like the *cuffs* of pants or the *buttons* of a shirt lack functional significance or perceptual salience.

Goodness of parts of an object can be viewed as analogous to typicality of members of a category, in that both are ratings reflecting the perceived internal structure of elements related to a higher-level structure. In the case of goodness of parts, the relation is a partonomic, or part-whole relation, where the elements are the parts and the higher level structure is the whole object. In the case of typicality of members, the relation is a taxonomic, or class-inclusion relation, where the elements are categories at one level of abstraction and the higher order structure is a category at a higher level of abstraction. Some category members are perceived as better exemplars of the category than others (Rosch & Mervis, 1975; Mervis & Rosch, 1981); *car* is a better vehicle than *boat,* and *couch* is a better piece of furniture than *lamp.* Subjects' ratings of typicality of member have been used to describe the internal structure of categories, to reflect the fact that some members of a category are regarded as "better" than others. If the analogy holds, subjects' ratings of goodness of part should describe the internal structure of parts and reflect the fact that some parts of an object are seen as better than others.

The study reported here is an attempt to verify the intuition that parts vary in perceived goodness, that people agree on which parts are better, and that good parts are more frequently mentioned. At the moment, the notion of good part is kept vague; this is an exploratory study, and part goodness is evaluated, not manipulated. The actual ratings prompt further discussion.

## Parts listing

### *Method*

*Subjects*

The subjects were 30 students in introductory psychology at Stanford who participated for course credit.

*Materials and procedure*

The booklets were identical to those used in the attribute listing study of biological categories except that the categories differed. The categories were: apple, car, chair drum, grape, lamp, lettuce, onion, pants, piano, saw, screwdriver, shirt, and truck. Each booklet included only 7 of the 14 categories, one from each of the 7 superordinates. Each subject completed one booklet, so that 15 subjects listed parts for each category. The procedure was also identical to the procedure used in the attribute listing study of biological categories, except that subjects were asked to list parts only.

### *Results*

The parts were tallied, and each part listed by 2 or more subjects was included in the rating experiment, described next. The low criterion of mention by 2 or more subjects was adopted to increase the range of goodness of parts. This resulted in the inclusion of parts that had been excluded from previous studies. So the list of parts (with goodness ratings) included in Appendix B is not the same list as the list used in Study 1, where parts were shown to be diagnostic of the basic level.

## Goodness of parts ratings

### *Method*

*Materials*

A separate form was made for each basic category. The category label was typed at the top of the page, and the parts were listed, in random order, down the left side. Next to each part was a 7-point scale ranging from *very good part* (1) to *not a good part* (7). The pages were collated randomly for each subject. The first page had the instructions on it.

*Procedure*

The instructions were read aloud to subjects while they read along silently. They were asked to judge the goodness of each part listed for the relevant object. Subjects weren't told what a good part meant; however, they were given several examples of good and bad parts. For example, they were told that *wings* are very good parts of an airplane, and that the *floor* of an airplane isn't a good part. They were also told that *hands* are good parts of a clock, while the *back* of a clock is not. Each of the 15 subjects judged parts for all 14 basic categories.

## Results

The mean goodness rating was found for each part (see Appendix B for examples). The data for fruit are omitted from the analyses because several nonparts were inadvertently included. Intraclass correlations were computed on the ratings for each object; these reflect the degree of consensus among all 15 subjects. The correlations shown in Table 6 were good: They ranged from .21 to .66, indicating that people agree in the extent to which a given part is a good part.

**Table 6**  **Goodness ratings: agreement among subjects and correlations with frequency of mention**

| Category | Number of parts | Intraclass correlation | Pearson P-M correlation |
|---|---|---|---|
| Clothing | | | |
| Pants | 21 | .32 | .44** |
| Shirt | 16 | .24 | .21 |
| Furniture | | | |
| Chair | 16 | .33 | .50** |
| Lamp | 17 | .38 | .42* |
| Musical instruments | | | |
| Drum | 16 | .32 | .38 |
| Piano | 20 | .51 | .50** |
| Tools | | | |
| Saw | 10 | .66 | .36 |
| Screwdriver | 6 | .39 | .45 |
| Vegetables | | | |
| Lettuce | 11 | .66 | .53* |
| Onion | 6 | .35 | .09 |
| Vehicles | | | |
| Car | 48 | .25 | .42*** |
| Truck | 33 | .21 | .39** |

*p < .05. **p < .025. ***p < .01.

The mean goodness ratings were also correlated with frequency of mention of the parts. Signs were reversed so that positive correlations indicate that part goodness and frequency of mention increase together. Only 7 of the 12 correlations were significant; however, the nonsignificant correlations occurred for the items having the fewest parts. These correlations are also displayed in Table 6. The correlations indicate that the parts people listed most frequently were perceived as good parts and provide some validation for the construct, goodness of part.

Both sets of correlations are probably attenuated by including only the parts listed by subjects when asked to list parts of objects, in other words, by including mainly good and "halfway decent" parts. The lists did not include, for instance, parts of other related objects, or technical part terms, or ubiquitous parts, such as molecules. Consistent with this interpretation, the goodness ratings were highly skewed, with more parts rated toward the good end of the scale. Forty-nine percent of the parts received ratings toward the good end (ratings less than or equal to 3), but only 5% of the parts received ratings toward the poor end (ratings greater than or equal to 5).

The reader may wonder why subjects gave such high goodness ratings to *light* for lamp and to *head* for lettuce, when neither *light* nor *head* passed the criteria for inclusion in the list of parts for Study 1. We believe the explanation lies in the demand characteristic of the rating task. When confronted with *head* in a list of parts for lettuce, the subject may think something like, "Well, *head* isn't really a part of lettuce, at least not as it appears in the supermarket. So, they must mean *lettuce* as a plant, in which case, it probably has roots and a stem of sorts, so *head* would be a very important part of *lettuce*."

### *Discussion*

To a large degree, our subjects agreed on which parts are good parts of an object. Goodness ratings also predicted frequency of mention by other subjects asked to list parts of an object. The good parts, or for that matter, all the parts in these norms and in the attribute norms as well, are at the same level of analysis, the level of *seat* and *engine* and *wheel*. Subjects list parts, but not parts of parts. Appropriately configured, the parts listed form whole objects. Both perceptual salience and functional significance seem to play a role in goodness ratings. The best part of a chair is a *seat,* the best part of pants are *legs,* the best part of a saw is a *blade,* the best part of a piano is *keys,* and so on. In each of these examples, a case can be made that the best part is among the most perceptually salient and the functionally most important parts. Similarly, the parts receiving especially low ratings seem to be unimportant both to the perception of and the function of the object. The following examples illustrate this point: for lamp, the parts *gas, screws,* and *plastic;* for saw the *rust;* for lettuce, the parts *root, stem, dirt,* and *bug.* Another factor that appears to be correlated with part goodness is the prevalence of the part among the category members, or its essentialness. Optional or less essential parts, such as *stuffing* for chair and *radio* for car are viewed as less good parts than more prevalent and essential parts. Essentialness or prevalence seems to be related to functional significance; a chair without a *seat* wouldn't function as a chair, but a chair without *stuffing* would just be less comfortable. Ethnological evidence from universals in body part naming corroborate these observations (Andersen, 1978;

C. H. Brown, 1976). Body parts enjoying perceptual salience and functional significance are named earlier in the development of terminology and receive more distinctive names. A reasonable question to raise at this point would be, which contributes more to part goodness, perceptual salience, functional significance, or even frequency or essentialness. People could be asked to rate parts on each of these attributes separately, and those ratings could be correlated with goodness ratings. Examination of the goodness ratings discourages such an undertaking. Not only do perceptual salience and functional significance seem to be highly correlated themselves, but there is also an inherent ambiguity or duality in many of the part names themselves. To return to our old example, *seat* may refer to a perceptually distinct segment of a chair, but it also may refer to a distinct function.

For specially selected natural objects and for artificial objects, it seems possible to separate functional significance from perceptual salience. In artificial stimuli, there is usually no function to contend with. There is some evidence that for children, perceptual salience, particularly in the contour of an artificial object, highly determines parsing an object into its parts (Kosslyn, Heldmeyer, & Glass, 1980). Young children fail to notice parts of natural objects that are functionally significant but perceptually small (Tversky & Bassok, 1978). This suggests that perceptual salience will influence perceived goodness of part at an earlier stage of development or of knowledge acquisition than functional significance. Elsewhere (Melkman, Tversky, & Baratz, 1981) it has been argued that perceptual properties are more immediate than functional properties. Perceptual properties may be known simply from observation of a static object, but knowledge of functional significance, of behavioral properties, seems to require observation of an object in use or in motion.

Recently, there have been several interesting attempts to account for the way we parse forms into parts, usually phrased in terms of the geometry of the forms or the surface appearance of the objects (Bower & Glass, 1976; Hoffman & Richards, 1982; Kosslyn *et al.*, 1980; Palmer, 1977). Local minima in contours, changes in color or texture, "wholeness" of the part (tendency toward closed contour) have been suggested as characteristics of forms that determine parsing. Parts obtained through these perceptual principles have consequences for other tasks: They are better cues to memory for the whole form (Bower & Glass, 1976); they are more quickly identified as being part of the whole (Palmer, 1977). In recent artificial intelligence models, they have played an important role in the structural descriptions of objects (Hoffman & Richards, 1982). All of this research has explored artificial stimuli, where perceptual properties are manipulated but where functional or behavior properties are absent. The connection of parts parsing to function has only now been suggested.

Many metaphoric extensions of parts labels are evident in the list of object parts. Labels for body parts are broadly extended: many objects have *arms, legs, feet, heads,* and *bodies.* Both perceptual and functional similarity to the anthropomorphic parts affect metaphoric extensions. The arms and legs of objects, for instance, are long, thin extensions of objects, arms usually extending from the middle, legs extending at the bottom. But, arms and legs of objects also serve a similar function in objects as in people, that of support (for both) and of manipulation (for arms, viz., *arm* of a phonograph). Some object part labels seem to derive from the human parts with which they interact. *Handles* may look and function like hands, but also, they are interacted with by hands, and shirt *backs* and chair *backs* are at the rear sides of objects, but also are interacted with by the *backs* of people.

## GENERAL DISCUSSION

### Review of findings

In taxonomies of common objects and organisms, one level of reference appears to have a privileged status in many diverse cognitive tasks. This level, called the basic level (Rosch *et al.*, 1976), has been identified primarily using a quantitative index of informativeness. Our work has demonstrated a qualitative difference in categories at the basic level and has offered an explanation for the convergence of so many measures at that level. We have shown that one type of knowledge is particularly salient at the basic level, namely, knowledge about parts. Names of parts frequently enjoy a duality not apparent in other attributes, they refer both to a perceptual entity and to a functional role. The *leg* of a chair or the *handle* of a screwdriver have a particular appearance, but they also have a particular function. The prevalence of parts in subjects' attribute lists appears to be particularly diagnostic of the basic level. When asked to characterize entities at the superordinate level, subjects produce few, if any, parts, even for biological categories. Relatively many parts are produced at the basic level, the majority of attributes listed. The proportion of attributes that are parts (and, for nonamended norms, the absolute numbers) decreases at the subordinate level. Thus, part terms play a special role in the vertical organization of categories, that of distinguishing the basic level of reference. Parts play a role in the horizontal organization of categories, too. Different subordinate entities belonging to the same basic level category are perceived to share parts and to differ on other attributes. Similarly, different basic level categories are seen to share other attributes and to differ from one another on the basis of parts. So, the natural breaks among basic level categories are between clusters of parts, but the natural breaks between subordinate or superordinate level categories are not based on parts. There is a horizontal organization or internal structure to the parts belonging to a particular object, as well. Parts differ in perceived goodness. Subjects agree on which parts of an object are relatively good parts of the object, and goodness is correlated with frequency of mention. Parts that are good appear to have both functional significance and perceptual salience, such as the *leg* of pants, or the *seat* of a chair. Good parts also seem to be shared by many category members and seem to have distinctive labels. None of these variables seems to be primary; rather, their intercorrelation seems to be a fact, about the objects and organisms in the world.

### Parts and the convergence of cognitive tasks at the basic level

There is a long and growing list of cognitive tasks, reviewed earlier, that converge on the basic level. Some of these tasks reflect the appearance of objects, the way objects are perceived and represented. For instance, the basic level is the highest level of abstraction for which a generalized outline form can be recognized and the highest level for which an image can be generated. It is the level at which pictures of objects are identified most rapidly. Some of the tasks pertain to our behavior or responses to the objects, or, more teleologically, to the functions objects serve us. Thus, the basic level is the most abstract level for which motor programs directed toward the objects share elements. Some of the tasks relate to the way we label objects, to our communication about them. Thus, the basic level is the first level to be developed in the evolution of a taxonomy, and the level at which differentiations abound. Basic level terms tend to be shorter and more frequent than either more abstract or more specific terms. They are the terms first taught to and used by children.

Part configuration, we submit, forms the conceptual skeleton underlying and accounting for the convergence of so many different measures at the same level of abstraction. The configuration of parts, or structural description accounts for the shapes objects may take, thus for our perceptual representations of the appearance of objects. When we interact with objects, our behavior is typically directed toward their parts. Different parts appear to have different functions, or to elicit different behaviors. We sit on the *seat* of a chair and lean against the *back*, we remove the *peel* of a banana and eat the *pulp.* All other things being equal, entities distinguished in perception or behavior should also be distinguished in language, so breaks in communication should follow the natural breaks in perception. Our terms of reference are selected to pick out an entity in a context. Linguists have argued that basic level terms are contextually neutral (Cruse, 1977). So, saying, "Put out the dog" is fine, but when we say, "Put out the animal," we communicate something more than a simple request. Similarly, when we tell a friend we've acquired a new, pedigree, Hungarian straight-eared toy poodle, we convey something more than when we say we've gotten a new dog. Elsewhere (Tversky & Hemenway, 1983) we have argued that the ordinary context for an object is the scene in which it typically appears; scenes are, to a large degree, composed of basic level objects. So, *chairs* appear in houses and in schools and need to be distinguished from other objects appearing in those situations, particularly, other furniture. *Socks* appear in stores and houses and need to be distinguished from other objects appearing in those contexts, particularly, other clothing. Thus, parts and part configuration form a natural bridge connecting perception of objects and behavior toward them, and in turn, communication about them.

Two aspects of this argument are in need of elaboration. The first concerns the perceptual side, the second, the behavioral side. It might be argued that many of the tasks converging on the basic level concern the appearance, perception, and identification of objects, and that underlying these operations is simply the shapes of objects. Although shape undoubtedly contributes a great deal to the appearance, perception, and identification of objects, it simply does not go far enough. Shape is not unique. Objects are three dimensional and appear to have different shapes from different points of view. Many objects have moving parts and appear differently in motion. Part configuration accounts for the different shapes objects may have when viewed from different perspectives and when in motion as well. Many of the parts subjects regard as good parts of objects are enclosed parts, with no consequences for the shapes of objects. These enclosed parts, however, can affect appearance without affecting shape (e.g., the *screen* of a television set) and frequently have important functions. Will a television without a screen or a bureau without drawers be easily and reliably identified? And, only the Tin Woodsman could function without a heart. Shapes, cannot account for behavioral measures. Finally, other kinds of categories, such as scenes and events, have parts or components, but do not have shapes, so an analysis based on parts can be generalized to other hierarchies, whereas an analysis based on shape cannot. For these reasons, we believe parts and part configuration to be a more powerful theoretical concept than shape.

Others have argued that the proliferation of sensorial attributes distinguishes the basic level (Denis, 1982; Hoffmann, 1982). Of course, most sensorial attributes are parts, and most parts are sensorial, making it difficult to decide between them. The notable exceptions are internal parts, which are not sensorial, and colors, which are not parts. Would a lemon still be a lemon if it weren't yellow? If it didn't have pulp? Would a fire engine be a fire engine if it weren't red? If it didn't have an engine? Like shapes, sensorial features bear no relation to function and an account of the basic level based on sensorial features cannot be generalized to nonperceptual categories. For some tasks that depend on speeded visual recognition, there may be an advantage to color over internal parts, though for many objects and organisms, color is not a distinguishing feature at all. For other tasks, such as those that depend on function, uses, behavior, or relations to other categories, internal parts seem more important. Thus, sensorial features that are not parts may be more important in the identification procedure associated with a concept, whereas parts may be more important to the conceptual core (Smith & Medin, 1981).

Now, some comments on parts and function. The motor program norms collected by Rosch *et al.* (1976) used objects, mostly manufactured, as stimuli. These norms reflect human interaction with objects designed for human use. But, parts and function, or parts and behavior seem to be related independent of human users. Thus, the leaves and trunk of a tree have different functions for the tree, the legs and trunk of an elephant behave differently and have different functions for the elephant. Because cars are inanimate, we are less likely to talk about the function of the wheels or engine for the car, but we can say that these different parts of the car are associated with different behaviors. So we would like to argue that parts underlie function for human users, but that they are also related to functions or behaviors in a nonteleological sense, regarding the organism or object as a closed, self-contained system.

### Parts and other kinds of categories

Part configuration is especially important because of its role as a bridge between appearance and activity, between perception and behavior, between structure and function. Because structure is related to function via part configuration, part configuration underlies the informativeness of basic level categories. Is the prevalence of parts diagnostic of a privileged level in nonobject categories and hierarchies? Categories of scenes have a basic level, characterized by a proliferation of parts (Tversky & Hemenway, 1983). There is some preliminary evidence for a basic level in categories of events (Rosch, 1978; Rifkin, 1981), or scripted activities. Events, too, can be said to have parts or components. Eating at a restaurant, then, is composed of being seated, ordering food, eating, paying, and leaving. Note that the components of the restaurant script differ perceptually as well as functionally. More generally, it may be the case that perceived part structure is the basis for a privileged status in a taxonomy, that without a level of abstraction where component structure is particularly salient, there will not be a basic level of categorization where so many varied tasks and operations converge.

## Parts and principles of categorization

The basic level of reference is the starting point for building a taxonomy both phylogenetically, in a community of speakers of the same language (Berlin, 1978), and ontogenetically, in the developing speech of children (Clark, 1983; Mervis & Crisafi, 1982). There are indications that the principles of classification are not the same at other levels. Rosch and her colleagues (Rosch *et al.*, 1976) have argued that category cuts are determined by the structure of the world. Primary cuts are made at the basic level because, for this level in particular, attributes are correlated. Our work suggests that part configuration, because of its role in relating structure, function, and communication, underlies the correlated attributes or high cue validity present at the basic level. Unlike many categories at other levels, basic level categories seem to be mutually exclusive. Entities seem to belong to no more than one basic level category, though they may belong to more than one superordinate or subordinate category. Subordinate categories, in fact, seem to be designed to cross-classify members of basic object categories. So we have straight-leg pants that may or may not be denim pants and also may or may not be striped pants and even may or may not be wash-and-wear pants. Kitchen chairs may be wooden chairs and may be armless chairs and may be Breuer chairs. Moreover, in general, straight-leg pants and wooden-chairs differ from other pants and chairs only on that single feature. The principles governing the construction of subordinate categories in artifacts do not seem to be principles of mutual exclusion. Of course, biological categories are necessarily mutually exclusive, but human beings frequently destroy their elegance by using such categories as farm animals or shade trees or drought-resistant flowers or tropical fish, that cross-cut the biologically rooted categories. In a less flagrant way, superordinate categories can also violate mutual exclusion. Cars and roller skates may be vehicles as well as toys. Knives may be tools and weapons and kitchen utensils. A recorder may be a musical instrument and a toy. We do not balk at these exceptions to mutual exclusion. Not so for basic level concepts. Something isn't both a cantaloupe and a ball. It can be a cantaloupe that looks like a ball, or a ball that looks like a cantaloupe, but isn't both. Sometimes, at the boundaries, it's hard to tell the cups from the mugs or the stools from the chairs, but these are recognized as marginal examples, where both appearance and function are similar. Knives, however, are central tools and central kitchen utensils and central weapons. In folk taxonomies (Berlin *et al.*, 1973), the basic level is the first and most richly differentiated. Other levels are differentiated later, but optionally. Young children, too, appear to break up the world's objects and organisms on one level, the basic level, and show resistance, verbally and conceptually, to higher level categories that include more than one basic level category (Clark, 1983; Inhelder & Piaget, 1964). Children find part–whole relations easier than class inclusion (Markman, 1981), which may explain why their first classifications are at the basic level.

Thus, for object and biological categories, primary or basic category cuts seem to follow natural breaks in the correlational structure of attributes in the world. These breaks, we have argued, are determined by part configuration. Grouping and differentiation at other levels of abstraction need not follow the same principles as categorization at the basic level. Basic categories come first, and are based primarily on parts. Then, we form higher-order, superordinate groupings, that are typically based on function, not perception, where function is rather abstractly conceived. At the same time, we also subdivide basic level categories into more specific categories, on the basis of one (or very few) perceptual or functional features. In contrast to basic level categories, both more general and more specific categories do not have a basis in part configuration, nor do they always conform to mutual exclusivity.

## Taxonomy and partonomy

Sedans and station wagons are kinds of automobiles, while engines, wheels, and doors are parts of automobiles. Both these relations, *kind of* and *part of,* are asymmetric and transitive and can form hierarchies (Miller & Johnson-Laird, 1976). Hierarchies of kinds form the familiar object and organism taxonomies where lower levels are related to upper levels by class inclusion. Hierarchies of parts form partonomies. A familiar one is the body part partonomy, where body is divided into head, trunk, arms, and legs, and each of these is, in turn, divided into its subparts. Abstract concepts can also be represented as partonomies. In eighth-grade civics, for instance, we all learn that the government consists of legislative, judicial, and executive branches, each of which is further divided into its subcomponents. Taxonomies have been recommended for their cognitive economy (e.g., Collins & Quillian, 1969); not only do they provide a structure for a large body of knowledge, reducing the number of categories with which we ordinarily need to deal, but they also generally allow inference of properties from higher level nodes to the categories included in them. If having wheels or running on land are properties of cars, then we can infer that they will hold for any kind of car. In general, *part of* relations do not allow such inference; it is not the case that all parts of cars have wheels or run on land.

## Parts and naive induction

Part configuration seems to serve a very different role in the organization of knowledge. Put directly, part decomposition appears to be a way of relating structure to function. Our exploration of goodness of part led us to the conclusion that parts that are perceived to be good are, in general, those that enjoy both perceptual salience and functional significance. This intuition, in fact, seems to be the basis for naive induction, for initial mental models of the physical (and metaphysical) world, for intuitive science. Preliminary investigations of many phenomena are often guided by these working assumptions: that separate parts will have separate functions, that similar parts will have similar functions, that more salient parts will have more important functions, that, together, parts form an organized, integrated, functioning whole. These initial assumptions may turn out to be wrong, but they nevertheless characterize initial explorations. Biology abounds with examples where structural parts guided the search for function. Phrenology, where separate parts of the skull were assumed to have separate cognitive functions, stands as a classic example of a failure of this approach. But it was eventually replaced by neuroanatomy, which has succeeded in relating different brain structures to different cognitive functions. In his dramatic account of the revolution in microbiology, Judson (1979) showed how at many stages, new techniques for "seeing" structure and determining components led to major advances in the discovery of function. In their rudimentary, intuitive attempts to account for physical phenomena, children, too, often explain function or behavior by reference to parts, of objects, situations, or events (for instance, Bullock, Gelman, & Baillargeon, 1983). Our mental models for comprehending physical systems typically divide them into separate parts having separate functions (see examples in Anderson, 1981, and Gentner & Stevens, 1983). Designers of complex systems for human use, such as computer systems, are often explicitly advised to conform to these working assumptions, of separate parts for separate functions, of similar parts for similar functions, of large parts for important functions, and so on (Norman, 1982). Perceived part configuration, then, underlies both perceived structure and perceived function. As such, it seems to form the basis for intuitive causal reasoning and naive induction.

We began with Caesar's campaign on Gaul, with the observation that in describing or comprehending some body of knowledge or set of phenomena, we often begin by decomposing the thing to be understood into separate parts. This "divide-and-conquer" strategy is invoked not just because smaller parts are easier to deal with, but also because different parts are to be dealt with differently. Each part has a different story. How does this relate to the phenomenon of a basic level, to a preferred level of reference or abstraction, to a level more informative than others, to a level where the primary categories of objects and organisms, scenes and events are carved out? Our work has shown that one particular kind of information is more salient in the minds of people when they think about entities at the basic level, namely, information about parts. Through parts, we link the world of appearance to the realm of action. Through parts, we use structure to comprehend, infer, and predict function. This, then, seems to be the knowledge that makes the basic level the most informative level: the knowledge of function that can be inferred from structure.

## Acknowledgements

This research was supported by National Science Foundation Grant BNS 8002012 and National Institute of Mental Health Grant MH 34248 to Stanford Universty. Kathleen Hemenway was supported by a National Science Foundation Fellowship. Portions of this research were reported in a dissertation by Hemenway in partial fulfillment of the doctorate degree. Kathleen Hemenway is now at Bell Laboratories, Murray Hill, New Jersey.

We would like to express our gratitude to Barbara Malt, Edward Smith, Carolyn Mervis, and Eleanor Rosch for generously providing us with data to analyze, and to Allan Collins, Herbert Clark, Joachim Hoffman, Ellen Markman, Edward Smith, and Ewart Thomas for helpful discussion.

## References

Andersen, E S. (1978) Lexical universals in body-part terminology. In J. H. Greenberg (Ed.), *Universals of Human Language* (pp. 335–368). Stanford, CA: Stanford University Press.

Anderson, J. R (Ed.). (1981) *Cognitive skills and their acquisition.* Hillsdale, NJ: Erlbaum.

Ashcraft, M. H. (1978) Property norms for typical and atypical items from 17 categories: A description and discussion. *Memory & Cognition, 6,* 227–232.

Berlin, B. (1972) Speculations on the growth of ethnobotanical nomenclature. *Language in Society,* 1, 51–86.

Berlin, B. (1978) Ethnobiological classification. In E. Rosch & B. B. Lloyd (Eds.), *Cognition and categories* (pp. 9–26). Hillsdale, NJ: Erlbaum

Berlin, B., Breedlove, D. E. & Raven, P. H. (1966) Folk taxonomies and biological classification. *Science,* 154, 273–275.

Berlin, B, Breedlove, D. E, & Raven, P. H. (1973) General principles of classification and nomenclature in folk biology. *American Anthropologist,* 75, 214–242.

Berlin, B., & Kay, P. (1969) *Basic color terms: Their universality and evolution.* Berkeley and Los Angeles: University of California Press.

Bower, G. H. and Glass, A. (1976) Structural units and the redintegrative power of picture fragments. *Journal of Experimental Psychology: Human Learning and Memory,* 2, 456–466.

Brown, C. H. (1976) General principles of human anatomical partonomy and speculations on the growth of partonomic nomenclature. *American Ethnologist,* 3, 400–424.

Brown, C H. (1977) Folk botanical life-forms: Their universality and growth. *American Anthropologist,* 79, 317–342.

Brown, C H. (1979) Folk zoological life-forms: Their universality and growth. *American Anthropologist,* 81, 791–817.

Brown, R. (1958) How shall a thing be called? *Psychological Review,* 65, 14–21.

Bullock, M, Gelman, R., & Baillargeon, R. (1983) The development of causal reasoning. In W. Friedman (Ed.), *The developmental psychology of time* (pp. 209–254). New York: Academic Press.

Clark, E. (1983) Meanings and concepts. In J. H. Flavell & E. M. Markman (Eds.), *Handbook of child psychology: Vol. 3. Cognitive Development* (4th ed., pp. 787–840). New York: Wiley.

Collins, A. M. & Quillian, M. R. (1969) Retrieval time from semantic memory. *Journal of Verbal Learning and Verbal Behavior,* 8, 240–247.

Cruse, D. A. (1977) The pragmatics of lexical specificity. *Journal of Linguistics,* 13, 153–164.

Denis, M. (1982) Images and semantic representations. In J-F Le Ny & W. Kintsch (Eds.), *Language and comprehension* (pp. 17–27). Amsterdam: North-Holland.

Dougherty, J. W. D. (1978) Salience and relativity in classification. *American Ethnologist,* 5, 66–80.

Garner, W. R. (1974) *The processing information and structure.* Potomac, MD: Erlbaum.

Gentner, D. & Stevens A. L. (Eds.). (1983) *Mental models.* Hillsdale, NJ: Erlbaum.

Grice, H. P. (1975) Logic and conversation. In P. Cole & J. L Morgan (Eds.), *Syntax and semantics: Speech acts* (Vol. 3, pp. 41–58). New York: Academic Press, 1975.

Hampton, J. A. (1979. Polymorphous concepts in semantic memory. *Journal of Verbal Learning and Verbal Behavior,* 18, 441–461.

Hampton, J. A. (1981) An investigation of the nature of abstract concepts. *Memory & Cognition,* 9, 149–156.

Hoffman, D. D. & Richards, W. A. (1982) *Representing plane curves for recognition* (AI Memo No. 630). Cambridge, MA: MIT, Artificial Intelligence Laboratory.

Hoffmann, J. (1982) Representations of concepts and the classification of objects. In R. Klix, J. Hoffmann, & E. van der Meer (Eds), *Cognitive research in psychology: Recent approaches, designs and results* (pp. 72–89). Amsterdam: North-Holland.

Hunn, E. (1976) Toward a perceptual model of folk biological classification. *American Ethnologist, 3,* 508–524.

Inhelder. B. & Piaget, J. (1964) *The early growth of logic in the child.* New York: Norton.

Judson, H. E. (1979) *The eighth day of creation.* New York: Simon & Schuster.

Kosslyn, S. M., Heldmeyer, K. H. & Glass, A. L. (1980) Where does one part end and another begin? A developmental study. In J. Becker, F. Wilkening, & I. Trabasso (Eds.), *Information integration in children* (pp. 147–168). Hillsdale, NJ: Erlbaum.

Malt, B. C. & Smith, E. E. (1982) The role of familiarity in determining typicality. *Memory & Cognition, 10,* 69–75.

Markman, E. M. (1981) Two different principles of conceptual organization. In M. E. Lamb & A. L. Brown (Eds.), *Advances in developmental psychology* (pp. 199–236). Hillsdale, NJ: Erlbaum.

Melkman, R. Tversky, B. & Baratz, D. (1981) Developmental trends in the use of perceptual and conceptual attributes in grouping, clustering, and retrieval. *Journal of Experimental Child Psychology, 31,* 470–486.

Mervis, C. B. & Crisafi, M. A. (1982) Order of acquisition of subordinate-, basic-, and superordinate-level categories. *Child Development, 53,* 258–266.

Mervis, C. B. & Rosch, E. (1981) Categorization of natural objects. *Annual Review of Psychology, 32,* 89–115.

Mills, G. A. & Johnson-Laird, P. N. (1976) *Language and perception.* Cambridge, MA: Harvard University Press.

Murphy, G. L. & Smith, E. E. (1982) Basic-level superiority in picture categorization. *Journal of Verbal Learning and Verbal Behavior, 21,* 1–20.

Norman, D. A. (1982) Steps toward a cognitive engineering: Design rules based on analyses of human errors. *Proceedings of the conference on human factors in computer systems.* Gaithersburg, MD.

Palmer, S. E. (1977) Hierarchical structure in perceptual representation. *Cognitive Psychology, 9,* 441–474.

Rifkin, A. J. (1981) *Event categories, event taxonomies, and basic level events.* Unpublished manuscript, New York University, New York.

Rosch, E. (1978) Principles of categorization. In E. Rosch & B. Lloyd (Eds.), *Cognition and categorization* (pp. 27–48). Hillsdale, NJ: Erlbaum.

Rosch, E. & Mervis, C. B. (1975) Family resemblances: Studies in the internal structure of categories. *Cognitive Psychology, 7,* 573–605.

Rosch, E., Mervis, C. B., Gray, W., Johnson, D. & Boyes-Braem, P. (1976) Basic objects in natural categories. *Cognitive Psychology,* 8, 382–439.

Smith, E. E. & Medin, D. L. (1981) *Categories and concepts.* Cambridge, MA: Harvard University Press.

Smith, E. E., Balzano, G. J. & Walker, J. (1978) Nominal, perceptual, and semantic codes in picture categorization. In J. W. Cotton & R. L. Klatzky (Eds), *Semantic factors in cognition* (pp. 137–167) Hillsdale, NJ: Erlbaum.

Tversky, B. & Bassok, M. (1978) *What's missing?* Unpublished manuscript, Stanford University, Stanford, CA.

Tversky, B. & Hemenway, K (1983) Categories of environmental scenes, *Cognitive Psychology,* 15, 121–149.

# Appendix A

**Table A1  Attributes included in judge-amended tally for some biological categories at three levels**

| Category | Parts | Nonparts | Category | Parts | Nonparts |
|---|---|---|---|---|---|
| Animal | Tail | Moves | | | |
| | Eyes | Living | | | |
| | Eats | | | | |
| Bird | Two legs | Lays eggs | Flower | Petals | Needs carbon |
| | Wings | Living | | Stem | dioxide |
| | Feathers | Builds nests | | Leaves | Needs water |
| | Beak | Eats | | | Pretty |
| | | Moves | | | Green |
| Chicken | Two legs | Brown | Rose | Petals | Needs carbon |
| | Wings | Lays eggs | | Thorns | dioxide |
| | Feathers | Eats worms | | Stem | Needs water |
| | Beak | Living | | Leaves | Red |
| | | Eaten by humans | | | Pretty |
| | | Builds nests | | | Yellow |
| | | Eats | | | Grows on bushes |
| | | Moves | | | Colorful |
| Robin | Two legs | Chirps | | | Pink |
| | Wings | Flies | Poppy | Petals | Needs carbon |
| | Red breast | Lays eggs | | Stem | dioxide |
| | Feathers | Eats worms | | Leaves | Needs water |
| | Beak | Small | | | Pretty |
| | | Living | | | California state flower |
| | | Builds nests | | | Opium |
| | | Eats | | | White |
| | | Moves | | | Colorful |
| Fish | Tail | Moves | | | |
| | Fins | Living | | | |
| | Eyes | Eats | Tree | Bark | Green |
| | Gills | Swims | | Trunk | Needs carbon |
| | Scales | | | Wood | dioxide |
| Goldfish | Tail | Small | | Branches | Needs water |
| | Fins | Orange | | Roots | |
| | Eyes | Moves | Palm tree | Trunk | Warm climate |
| | Gills | Living | | Leaves | Green |
| | Scales | Kept in small bowl | | Coconuts | Large |
| | | Swims | | Wood | Tall |
| | | Eats | | Branches | Needs carbon |
| Salmon | Tail | Used in salads | | Branches all | dioxide |
| | Fins | Comes in cans | | at top | Needs water |
| | Eyes | Moves | | Roots | Very tall |
| | Gills | Lives in streams | | Bark | |
| | Scales | Living | Pine | Trunk | Green |
| | | Used in sandwiches | | Wood | Large |
| | | Eats | | Branches | Tall |
| | | Swim upstream | | Roots | Needs carbon |
| | | Ocean | | Needles | dioxide |
| Plant | Stem | Needs carbon | | Cones | Forest |
| | Roots | dioxide | | Bark | Needs water |
| | | Needs water | | | Fragrant |
| | | Green | | | Very tall |
| | | | | | Used for furniture |

# Appendix B

## Table B1  Selected mean goodness ratings of parts of objects

### Clothing: Pants

| Part | M | Part | M |
|---|---|---|---|
| Leg | 1.9 | Snaps | 3.9 |
| Pockets | 2.1 | Inseam | 4.0 |
| Seat | 2.2 | Hem | 4.3 |
| Zipper | 2.5 | Buttons | 4.3 |
| Material | 2.6 | Label | 4.5 |
| Crotch | 3.1 | Stitching | 4.6 |
| Waist band | 3.1 | Bell bottoms | 4.6 |
| Belt loops | 3.4 | Cuff | 4.8 |
| Belt | 3.7 | Elastic | 4.9 |
| Thread | 3.7 | Patches | 5.3 |
| Seam | 3.9 | | |

### Furniture: Chair

| Part | M | Part | M |
|---|---|---|---|
| Seat | 1.6 | Cloth, material | 3.1 |
| Arms | 1.9 | Legs | 3.3 |
| Back | 2.2 | Foot rest | 3.5 |
| Cushion | 2.3 | Leg rest | 3.5 |
| Back rest | 2.4 | Wood | 3.5 |
| Arm rests | 2.5 | Stuffing | 3.6 |
| Upholstery | 2.9 | Feet | 4.7 |
| Head rest | 3.0 | Buttons | 5.9 |

### Musical instruments: Piano

| Part | M | Part | M |
|---|---|---|---|
| Keys | 1.1 | Legs | 3.4 |
| Keyboard | 1.1 | Wood | 3.5 |
| White keys | 1.2 | Cover | 3.8 |
| Black keys | 1.5 | Lid | 4.1 |
| Music | 1.7 | Music stand | 4.3 |
| Pedals | 1.8 | Screws | 4.7 |
| Strings | 1.9 | Brand name | 4.7 |
| Hammers | 2.7 | plate | 4.7 |
| Bench | 2.9 | Hinges | 4.7 |
| Wood body | 3.0 | Wheels | 5.8 |
| Stool | 3.1 | | |

### Tools: Saw

| Part | M | Part | M |
|---|---|---|---|
| Blade | 1.1 | Handle | 2.6 |
| Sharp teeth | 1.2 | Motor | 3.3 |
| Metal blade | 1.5 | Wood (parts) | 4.0 |
| Teeth | 1.9 | Screws | 4.3 |
| Metal | 2.3 | Rust | 6.2 |

### Vegetables: Lettuce

| Part | M | Part | M |
|---|---|---|---|
| Head | 1.0 | Core | 4.5 |
| Green | 1.8 | Root | 5.3 |
| Leaf | 1.8 | Stem | 5.5 |
| Cellulose | 3.2 | Dirt | 6.5 |
| Water | 3.5 | Bug | 6.7 |
| Vein | 3.8 | | |

### Vehicles: Car

| Part | M | Part | M |
|---|---|---|---|
| Engine | 1.5 | Mirror | 2.7 |
| Steering wheel | 1.6 | Chassis | 2.7 |
| Brakes | 1.6 | Lights | 2.8 |
| Wheels | 1.9 | Axle | 2.8 |
| Seats | 1.9 | Speedometer | 2.9 |
| Tires | 2.0 | Side view mirror | 2.9 |
| Headlights | 2.1 | Radiator | 2.9 |
| Transmission | 2.1 | Hood | 3.1 |
| Gear shift | 2.1 | Horn | 3.1 |
| Windshield | 2.1 | Fender | 3.3 |
| Pedals | 2.2 | Exhaust pipe | 3.3 |
| Pistons | 2.3 | Spare tire | 3.4 |
| Carburetor | 2.3 | Roof | 3.6 |
| Fuel tank | 2.3 | Dashboard | 3.6 |
| Gasoline | 2.3 | Trunk | 3.6 |
| Battery | 2.4 | Radio | 3.7 |
| Spark plugs | 2.5 | Door handles | 3.9 |
| Rearview mirror | 2.5 | Paint | 4.0 |
| Drive shaft | 2.5 | Glove | 4.1 |
| Seat belt | 2.5 | compartment | |
| Body | 2.6 | Hubcaps | 4.4 |
| Bumpers | 2.6 | Carpeting | 4.7 |
| Window | 2.7 | Rugs | 4.8 |
| Wipers | 2.7 | Handle | 4.9 |
| Door | 2.7 | | |

# 6.   Context-independent and Context-dependent Information in Concepts

## Lawrence W. Barsalou

*It is proposed that concepts contain two types of properties. Context-independent properties are activated by the word for a concept on all occasions. The activation of these properties is unaffected by contextual relevance. Context-dependent properties are not activated by the respective word independent of context. Rather, these properties are activated only by relevant contexts in which the word appears. Context-independent properties form the core meanings of words, whereas context-dependent properties are a source of semantic encoding variability. This proposal lies between two opposing theories of meaning, one that argues all properties of a concept are active on all occasions and another that argues the active properties are completely determined by context. The existence of context-independent and context-dependent properties is demonstrated in two experimental settings: the property-verification task and judgments of similarity. The relevance of these property types to cross-classification, problem solving, metaphor and sentence comprehension, and the semantic-episodic distinction is discussed.*

Some properties in a concept seem to come to mind on all occasions. The word "skunk" usually makes people think of the property "unpleasant smell," and "rattlesnake" usually makes people think of "poisonous." In contrast, other properties in a concept rarely seem to come to mind, and when they do, it is only in relevant contexts. For example, "basketball" rarely makes people think of "floats." However, the sentence frame "Chris used X as a life preserver when the boat sank" would probably bring "floats" to mind for "basketball" when "X" is "basketball." In this paper, I propose there are two important types of properties associated with concepts: context-independent (CI) properties and context-dependent (CD) properties. CI properties are activated by the word for a concept on all occasions (e.g., "unpleasant smell" for "skunk"). CD properties are rarely if ever activated by the word for a concept and are only activated by relevant contexts in which the word appears (e.g., "floats" for "basketball").

CI properties form the core meanings of words. This is because they are activated by the respective word on all occasions, independent of contextual relevance. Barsalou and Bower (Note 1) have proposed that properties become automatically activated by a word after being frequently associated with it during processing. Frequent pairings of a word and a property cause an automatized relation between them to be established in memory (also see Shiffrin & Schneider, 1977). Barsalou and Bower (Note 1) showed that two types of properties are likely to be frequently active during the processing of

Lawrence W. Barsalou: 'Context-independent and Context-dependent Information in Concepts' in *MEMORY AND COGNITION* (1982), Vol. 10 (1), pp. 82–93. Copyright © 1982 Psychonomic Society, Inc.

a word. First, properties having high diagnosticity may often be active, since they are useful for distinguishing instances of a concept from instances of other concepts. "Gills" becomes CI for "fish" because all fish have gills and no other things do. The second type of property likely to be frequently active during the processing of a word includes properties relevant to how people typically interact with instances of the respective concept. "Edible" becomes CI for "apples" because it is central to how people typically interact with them. As shown by "edible" in relation to "apple," properties frequently relevant to human interaction can become CI even if they have low diagnosticity (i.e., "edible" is true of many other things).

CD properties are a source of semantic encoding variability. CD properties may be represented in concepts, but they are not usually activated by encoding the respective words. Rather, these properties are activated only by relevant encoding contexts in which a word appears. Semantic encoding variability is the result of different encoding contexts of a word activating different subsets of CD properties in the respective concept. This phenomenon has frequently been observed empirically (e.g., R. C. Anderson & Ortony, 1975; R C. Anderson, Pichert, Goetz, Schallert, Stevens, & Trollip, 1976; Barclay, Bransford, Franks, McCarrell, & Nitsch, 1974; Tulving & Thompson, 1973) and has been incorporated theoretically by Bower (1972) and Estes (1955, 1959). Barsalou and Bower (Note 1) suggest that CD properties are typically inactive because they have rarely, if ever, been processed simultaneously with their respective words. Hence, the associations between these properties and their respective words are weak or nonexistent. When such associations do not exist, various inference processes may be required to compute them. People may not have stored the fact that "fits in a suitcase" is a property of "flashlight," but they can certainly infer it. If a CD property comes to be frequently processed with a word, the property may change status and become CI. Although "wears horseshoes" may be CD for "horse" for people who are rarely around horses, it could become CI for someone during the course of learning to be a horseshoer.

Some properties are probably neither CI nor CD. These may sometimes be activated by a word, although not on all occasions, and may sometimes be activated by context. Such properties may occasionally be activated by a word because of random fluctuations in the amount of activation the property receives. On other occasions, however, these properties may be activated by relevant contexts. The senses of ambiguous words can similarly not be classified as strictly CI or CD. This is because they often come to mind without context, but they are also influenced by sentence contexts in which they occur (Swinney, 1979; Tanenhaus, Leiman, & Seidenberg, 1979). Nevertheless, the senses of ambiguous words can be viewed as concepts that contain CI and CD properties. Once an ambiguous word is disambiguated in context, the distinction between CI and CD properties becomes applicable to the concept converged upon. Consider "bear" in the sentence "The bear caught pneumonia." "Bear" and the sentence frame both converge on the mammalian sense of "bear." However, some of the properties activated for this sense are CI (e.g., "is furry," "can be dangerous") and some are CD (e.g., "can be sick," "has lungs"). Beyond acknowledging their existence, I will not further consider properties and word senses that are neither CI nor CD. Rather, the purposes of this paper are (1) to demonstrate the existence of CI and CD properties in concepts and (2) to consider the roles these property types play in various cognitive phenomena.

This paper addresses a particular aspect regarding the structure of concepts, namely, the accessibility of properties. Two theories of meaning take more extreme views on this aspect. Traditional views of semantics (e.g., Katz & Postal, 1964) assume that the meaning of a word contains a fixed set of semantic features applicable on all occasions on which the word is used. It appears that semantic memory models usually make a similar assumption (e.g., Glass & Holyoak, 1975; McCloskey & Glucksberg, 1979; Smith, Shoben, & Rips, 1974). In the terms of this paper, this approach argues that all of a concept's properties are CI. An opposing and more radical view of semantics (e.g., Olson, 1970) argues that the meaning of a word completely depends on the context in which the word is used. Specifically, the meaning of a word in a given context is a function of the distinctions it is supposed to convey in that context. According to this view, there may be no overlap between uses of the same word across contexts. Psychologists who have observed contextual effects on encoding have often reached a similar conclusion (e.g., Jacoby, Craik, & Begg, 1979). In the terms of this paper, this approach argues that all of a concept's properties are CD. The proposal that some of a concept's properties are CI and others are CD lies between these two theories of meaning. Consequently, evidence for the existence of CI and CD properties in concepts would have implications for theories of natural language semantics.[1]

The definitions of CI and CD properties lead to several empirical predictions. First, in a given context, all CI properties should be available and irrelevant CD properties should not. This is because CI properties are always activated by their respective words, whereas irrelevant CD properties remain inactive due to lack of contextual activation. The second prediction follows from the definition of CI properties. Since CI properties are always activated by the respective words on all occasions, they should be unaffected by contextual relevance: A CI property should be just as available in an irrelevant context as in a relevant context. This assumes that the activation of a CI property by a word maximally activates that property. The third prediction follows from the definition of CD properties. Since CD properties depend on relevant contexts for activation, they should be available in working memory for processing when the context is relevant and unavailable when the context is irrelevant. The alternative hypotheses are (1) all the properties in a concept are activated by the respective word on all occasions and (2) all the properties active in a concept are determined by context.

These hypotheses and their alternatives are contrasted in the two experiments that follow. The first experiment tests these predictions in the property verification task. The second experiment tests these predictions in judgments of similarity. Evidence from other current work is also brought to bear on these issues. Finally, the relevance of CI and CD properties to cross-classification, problem solving, metaphor and sentence comprehension, and the semantic-episodic distinction is discussed.

## Experiment 1

A version of the property-verification task was used to test the predictions following from the definitions of CI and CD properties. On each trial, subjects read a sentence containing an underlined subject noun. Several seconds later, the label for a property was presented, and subjects indicated whether or not the subject noun in the preceding sentence possessed the property.

The logic of the experiment is as follows. If the property for a trial is CI information of the subject noun, then verification time should not vary across sentence contexts. In particular, verification time should be no less when the sentence context is related to the property than when the sentence context is unrelated. This is because the property, being CI, is always activated by the subject noun itself and therefore is not dependent on context for activation. However, if the property for a trial is CD information of the subject noun, then verification time should depend on context. Specifically, verification time should be much less when the sentence context is related to the property than when the sentence context is unrelated. This is because the property, being CD, is not activated by the subject noun and therefore is dependent on context for activation. If the difference between related and unrelated contexts for CD properties is substantial (i.e., on the order of several hundred milliseconds), this would suggest that CD properties are, in fact, inactive in irrelevant contexts.

### Method

***Procedure***. Subjects looked into a modified Siliconix tachistoscope and rested their forefingers on two response buttons 7 cm apart. When prepared for a trial, subjects pressed the "start" button (positioned colinearly and midway between the two response buttons) with the same finger used to press the "true" button. After a 500-msec interval, a context sentence appeared in the top field of the tachistoscope. All sentences began with "The," followed by an underlined subject noun and a predication of the subject noun. Subjects were instructed to fully comprehend the sentence and to read it out loud. The context sentence was removed after 6 sec, and a property label immediately appeared in the bottom field; subjects did not read the label aloud. If the subject noun in the context sentence possessed the property, subjects pressed the "true" response button; otherwise, they pressed the "false" response button. For each trial, time was measured from the onset of the property to the point at which a response was detected. Subjects were instructed to respond as quickly as possible, but to avoid making errors.

Subjects received 24 practice trials and 60 test trials. There was a short break between the practice and test trials. Subjects could take a break anytime during the test trials, but they rarely did. Following the last test trial, subjects were asked a series of questions concerning their strategies.

***Subjects and Materials***. The subjects were 19 Stanford students participating for pay or course credit. One subject's data were not used because of an error rate exceeding 15% (the average error rate for the remaining subjects was 2.8%). The materials consisted of context sentences and properties, related as discussed next. Examples of the materials are shown in Table 1.

***Trues***. Thirty properties were chosen for the "true" trials; 15 were randomly assigned to the CI condition and 15 to the CD condition. The average number of syllables per property did not vary between conditions [4.06 and 4.13 for the CI and CD properties, respectively; $t(28) = .14$, $p > .30$]. For each CI property, three context sentences were constructed. Two of these contained the same subject noun, which was highly related to the property; the predicate for one of these sentences was related to the property (the related-context sentence), and the predicate for the other was unrelated (the unrelated-context sentence). Degree of relatedness was determined by the ratings of an independent group of subjects, as reported later.) The remaining context sentence contained a subject noun, weakly related to the property, and an unrelated predicate; this sentence served as a control sentence (to be explained in a moment).

Similarly, for each of the 15 CD properties, three context sentences were constructed. Two of these contained the same subject noun, which was weakly related to the property; the predicate for one of these sentences was related to the property (the related-context sentence), and the predicate for the other was unrelated (the unrelated-context sentence). The remaining sentence (the control sentence) contained a subject noun, highly related to the property, and an unrelated predicate.

A control sentence in the CI condition (having a weakly related subject noun and an unrelated predicate) served as a contrast to verify that the other two context sentences for the property had a subject noun highly related to the property. The time to verify the unrelated-context sentence (having a highly related subject noun and an unrelated predicate) should be less than that for the control sentence. Similarly, a control sentence in the CD condition (having a highly related subject noun and an unrelated predicate) served as a contrast to verify that the other two context sentences for the property had a subject noun weakly related to the property. The time to verify the unrelated context sentence (having a weakly related subject noun and an unrelated predicate) should be longer than that for the control sentence.

**Table 1    Examples of materials used in Experiment 1**

| Property | Context | Item |
|---|---|---|
| | | Context-Independent "True" Items |
| | Unrelated | The *skunk* was under a large willow |
| Has a smell | Related | The *skunk* stunk up the entire neighborhood |
| | Control | The *fire* was easily visible through the trees |
| | Unrelated | The *bank* had been built ten years ago |
| Can contain money | Related | The *bank* was robbed by three bandits |
| | Control | The *jar* was an old antique |
| | | Context-Dependent "True" Items |
| | Unrelated | The *roof* had been renovated prior to the rainy season |
| Can be walked upon | Related | The *roof* creaked under the weight of the repairman |
| | Control | The *tightrope* was high off the ground |
| | Unrelated | The *hospital* was internationally famous for its progressive techniques |
| Where cooking can occur | Related | The *hospital* was quiet when dinner was served |
| | Control | The *kitchen* had been repainted over the holidays |
| | | "False" Items |
| Has gills | | The *cheese* was growing moldy in the refrigerator |
| Can be tied in a knot | | The *refrigerator* was set to a low temperature to cool the beer |

**Table 2    Average association-to-property ratings for Experiment 1 materials**

| | A priori relatedness to property | | | | |
| | Subject nouns | | Predicates | | |
| Condition | Noncontrol* | Control | Control** | Unrelated | Related |
|---|---|---|---|---|---|
| Context-Independent | 6.80 | 3.30 | 3.00 | 3.10 | 6.60 |
| Context-Dependent | 3.18 | 6.72 | 3.22 | 2.68 | 6.25 |

*These are the subject nouns for the unrelated and related context sentences. ** Unrelated.*

Ratings were obtained to confirm the assumed relations between the subject nouns and properties, and between the predicates and properties. Of primary importance is that context be manipulated equally for the CI and CD conditions. This insures that an effect of context on CD subject nouns but not on CI subject nouns for the latency data cannot be attributed to CD materials having more relatedness for related predicates or less relatedness for unrelated predicates than the CI materials. Four judges rated the 60 subject nouns first (30 for the control and 30 for the noncontrol sentences) and the 90 predicates second (3 for each property). Subjects read either a subject noun or a predicate on one side of an index card and then flipped the card to read the property. Subjects rated how much the subject noun or predicate made them think of the property. Subjects used a scale from 1 to 7, on which 1 meant the property did not come to mind at all and 7 meant the property immediately came to mind. Within each group, the cards were randomly ordered for each subject.

An ANOVA was performed on the ratings for the subject nouns. The two factors of interest were condition (i.e., CI vs. CD) and relatedness (i.e., weakly vs. highly related). Note that for the CI materials, the nouns in the related- and unrelated-context sentences were supposed to be highly related and the nouns in the control sentences were supposed to be weakly related to their respective properties. For the CD materials, the nouns in the related- and unrelated-context sentences were supposed to be weakly related and the nouns in the control sentences were supposed to be highly related to their respective properties. The mean ratings from this analysis are shown in Table 2. There was no effect of CI/CD [$F(1,3) = 1.74$, $p > .25$], there was an effect of relatedness [$F(1,3) = 204.54$, $p < .001$], and there was no interaction between these two factors ($F < 1$). Thus the assumed difference in relatedness was substantial and equivalent for the CI and CD materials. A similar ANOVA was performed for the predicates. Again, there was no effect of CI/CD [$F(1,3)= 1.71$, $p > .25$] and no interaction of this factor with relatedness [$F(1,6) = 1.19$, $p > .25$]. The predicates for the control and unrelated-context sentences did not differ in relatedness ($F < 1$). However, the predicates for the related-context sentences were higher in relatedness than those for the unrelated-context sentences [$F(1,6) = 89.97$, $p < .001$] and those for the control sentences [$F(1,6) = 79.28$, $p < .001$]. Thus the assumed difference in relatedness was again substantial and equivalent for the CI and CD materials. Crucial to the interpretation of the latency results are the findings that (1) the related predicates for the CD materials were not higher in relatedness than those for the CI materials ($F < 1$) and (2) the unrelated predicates for the CD materials were not lower in relatedness than those for the CI materials ($F < 1$).

*Falses*. Thirty context sentence/property pairs were constructed, each context sentence having a subject noun that clearly did not possess the property. The context sentences and properties used were similar in nature to those for the "true" materials. Five of the 30 "true" context sentences presented to a subject (as discussed in the Design section) contained a subject noun and a predicate both highly related to the same property (i.e., the CI related-context sentences). Therefore, 5 of the 30 "false" context sentences also contained a subject noun and a predicate both highly related to some property; however, this was not the property actually tested (i e., for the "false" items, the subject noun could not possess the property). Creating some "false" items in this manner made it impossible for subjects to discriminate the "true" from the "false" items on the basis of subject-predicate-property relations.

*Practice items*. Twenty-four context sentence/property pairs were constructed; half were true and half were false. These items were similar in nature to the "true" and "false" test items. Also, the distribution of item types was similar to that found in the set of test items.

**Design**. Three lists were constructed. Each contained the same 30 context sentence/property pairs for the "false" items and the same 30 properties for the "true" items. The lists differed only with respect to the context sentences for the "true" properties, as discussed next.

The 15 CI properties for the "true" items were randomly divided into three groups of five properties each; the 15 CD properties were also randomly divided into three groups of five properties each. The 30 "true" context sentences in a given list consisted of (1) the control sentences from one CI group and one CD group, (2) the unrelated-context sentences from a second CI group and a second CD group, and (3) the related-context sentences from the remaining CI group and the remaining CD group. Each of the three context sentence types for each property group was instantiated in one and only one of the lists. This rotation of context sentence type through property group and list was done as randomly as possible, given the necessary constraints of a Latin square.

The 24 practice items were presented in the same random order to all subjects. The 60 test items were presented to each subject in a different, computer-generated, random order. Half the subjects used their right forefingers to press the "start" and "true" buttons and their left forefingers to press the "false" button; the other subjects had the inverse assignment. Subjects were assigned randomly to one of the six lists by hand assignment cells of the design, three subjects per cell.

### Results

Latencies for the correct true trials were analyzed as follows. Averages were computed separately across subjects and across items (i.e., properties). For each subject, the average latency was determined for each of the six subject relation by predicate relation conditions. For each property in the CI and CD conditions, the average latency was determined for each of the three predicate relations. The results for the subject averages are shown in Table 3. Separate subject relation by predicate relation ANOVAs were performed on the subject averages and item averages. The results of both analyses were combined to compute min F' planned comparisons of interest (H. H. Clark,1973).

**Table 3** **Average latencies and error rates per subject for correct true trials (Experiment 1)**

| | Predicate relation | | | | | |
|---|---|---|---|---|---|---|
| | Control (Unrelated) | | Unrelated | | Related | |
| Condition | L | % E | L | % E | L | % E |
| Context-Independent | 1335 | 11 | 1113 | 0 | 1145 | 3 |
| Context-Dependent | 1098 | 1 | 1404 | 11 | 1259 | 3 |

*Note–L = average latency; % E = error rate.*

For the CI items, the control sentences led to longer latencies than the unrelated-context sentences [min F'(1,89) = 15.80, p < .001]. For the CD items, the control sentences led to shorter latencies than the unrelated-context sentences [min F'(1,90)= 24.80, p < .001]. These two results show that (1) the subject nouns in the CI noncontrol sentences were in fact highly related to their respective CI properties, and (2) the subject nouns in the CD noncontrol sentences were in fact weakly related to their respective properties.[2]

The remaining results pertain only to the noncontrol sentences. For the CI items, there was no difference between related- and unrelated-context sentences (min F' < 1; the subject's F and item's F were also less than 1). For the CD items, related-context sentences led to shorter latencies than unrelated-context sentences [min F'(1,90) = 5.97, p < .025]. For the unrelated-context sentences, the latencies were less for the CI items than for the CD items [min F'(1,90) = 22.13, p<.001]. For the related-context sentences, there was a marginal difference between the CI and CD items [min F'(1,89) = 3.16, .10 > p > .05]; however, the subject's F was significant [F(1,34) = 9.66, p < .01], as was the item's F [F(1,56) = 4.70, p < .05]. There was a significant Subject Relation by Predicate Relation interaction for the noncontrol sentences [min F'(1,90) = 4.19, p < .05].

These data indicate that context had no effect on the CI items but had an effect on the CD items. More specifically, related contexts did not increase the priming of properties when the subject noun was highly related to the target property. However, related contexts did increase the priming of properties when the subject noun was weakly related to the property. It is not clear whether the facilitation caused by related contexts for the CD subject nouns was equivalent to the facilitation caused by the CI subject nouns themselves.

Mean latency for the correct "true" trials was 1,226 msec, and for the correct "false" trials, it was 1,253 msec. The average "true" latency for 13 of the 18 subjects was less than the average "false" latency. The average error rate per subject for all 60 test trials was 2.8%. The average error rate per subject for the 30 "true" trials was 5%, and for the 30 "false" trials, it was .6%. The average error rates per subject for the six subject relation by predicate relation cells of the design are shown in Table 3. These data, in conjunction with the latencies, indicate there was no speed-accuracy tradeoff. Notably, the most errors occurred for sentences having weakly related subject nouns and unrelated contexts. When questioned at the end of the experiment about errors on these sentences, subjects said they believed the correct response was "true" in all cases. They also indicated they had realized this almost immediately after responding "false." This suggests that CD properties in irrelevant contexts are normally inactive and that errors for these sentences occur when subjects decide to respond prior to this information's becoming active.

During the postexperimental interviews, most subjects reported not trying to guess properties before their presentation. The most common strategy involved focusing attention on the subject noun and forgetting the predicate while waiting for the property. All subjects reported either rehearsing the subject noun or focusing on it during the waiting period. Several subjects said they imaged referents of the subject nouns; several said they rehearsed the subject nouns once and then focused on them until presentation of the property. All but one subject reported that the psychological status of the predicate was either peripheral or gone from consciousness. Some subjects indicated that trying to maintain the predicate interfered with the task. In general, subjects appeared to be focusing only on the subject noun, believing this would maximize their ability to perform the verification task. Interestingly, the predicates still had an effect, as shown by the results for the CD properties.

### Discussion

These data are consistent with the distinction between CI and CD properties. Some properties are CI because their verification is unaffected by contextual relevance. Others are CD because their verifications are faster in relevant contexts than in irrelevant contexts (a facilitation of 145 msec in this experiment). These data suggest that CD properties are not activated in irrelevant contexts. Specifically, properties weakly related to subject nouns were verified 237 and 291 msec more slowly than properties highly related to subject nouns for control and unrelated sentences, respectively. It seems unlikely that differences of this size could occur if the weakly related properties were activated by their respective words. Rather, these differences may largely reflect the time it takes to activate these properties.

These results provide a functional account of property availability: Highly accessible properties of a concept are available independent of context, whereas less accessible ones are available only in relevant contexts. Conrad (1978) has also found results consistent with this account. Her task employed interference in a color-naming task as the dependent variable. On each trial subjects read a sentence and reported the ink color of a subsequent word. For "true" trials, the word in colored ink was either a highly related or weakly related property of the last word in the sentence. This factor was crossed with whether or not the sentence context made the property in colored ink relevant to the last word in the sentence. The results were analogous to those in this experiment. The amount of interference for the highly related properties was independent of contextual relevance. For the weakly related properties, however, interference occurred only when the context made the critical property relevant to the final sentence word.

177

Tabossi and Johnson-Laird (1980) also found results similar to those reported here. In a property-verification task, in which only predicate relatedness was systematically varied, subjects were faster to verify properties in relevant than in irrelevant contexts. This indicates that some of the properties must have been CD. If they had all been CI, this effect would not have occurred, given the results of the current experiment and those of Conrad (1978). Besides using contexts that primed the target property and contexts that primed no property of the target noun, Tabossi and Johnson-Laird also used contexts that primed a property of the target noun other than the target property. This third type of context led to the longest verification times. But since strength of association between the target noun and the target property was not controlled, it is not clear whether this interference effect occurred for CI properties, CD properties, or both. Nevertheless, this effect further constrains a functional account of property availability: Contexts can inhibit the activation of properties, although this may not be true of all properties.

In the current experiment and in Tabossi and Johnson-Laird's (1980) Experiment 2, the context sentences were presented 6 sec before the target properties (Conrad, 1978, did not report the details of her procedure). These experiments, therefore, are not informative at any level more specific than a functional one. This is because both automatic and conscious priming effects have been shown to occur well within 2 sec (Neely, 1977; Posner & Snyder, 1975; Swinney, 1979; Tanenhaus et al., 1979). However, Posner and Snyder's (1975) theory of attention may be an interesting way to think about property availability. They propose two types of attentional processes: (1) unconscious, automatic processes that are the result of past learning, and (2) conscious processes that are subject to capacity limitations. Although both types cause priming, conscious processes do so more slowly and interfere with other processing. Viewing property availability in this framework, the perception of a word may automatically activate its CI properties. In contrast, conscious attention may be responsible for activating relevant CD properties and for keeping both types of property active via rehearsal. (It is also possible that some CD properties are automatically activated.) Finally, focusing conscious attention away from automatically activated properties may eventually inhibit their verification.

This information processing account of property availability is consistent with the results reported here and with those of Conrad (1978): CI properties are always available because they are automatically activated by their respective words and are kept active by conscious rehearsal; CD properties are available only in irrelevant contexts because they are either automatically or consciously activated via contexts and are kept active by conscious rehearsal. This account also explains the Tabossi and Johnson-Laird (1980) interference effect: The verification of an automatically activated property may be inhibited if context focuses attention away from it.

Priming in this experiment appears at first glance to be nonadditive (cf. Foss, Cirilo, & Blank, 1979). For the CI properties, priming from the word and from the context did not add, since CI related-context sentences did not lead to faster verifications than CI unrelated-context sentences (i.e., there was no additional priming from the contexts). But in the Posner and Snyder (1975) framework, this pattern could well be additive. CI properties may receive their initial activation from encoding their respective words, this automatic activation dissipating within a few hundred milliseconds. But once these properties become active, they may receive conscious attention, which increases as automatic activation decreases. The activation of CI properties may therefore be additive in the sense that different processes are responsible for maintaining a high level of activation.

Finally, it is necessary to comment on the activation of CD properties. Functionally speaking, these properties are available in relevant but not in irrelevant contexts. But trying to explain this in information processing terms quickly becomes complex. CD properties may become available in two ways. First, they may actually be stored in a concept and be activated by contexts containing similar or associated information. Certain noun-property relations in this experiment appear to have been of this type (e.g., "snake — can be a pet"; "fingers — can be used for eating"; "frog — can be eaten"). Just how contexts activate these properties is a topic worthy of future interest. The second way CD properties can become available is via inference. Certain CD properties may not be stored in a concept but may be computed with various inference procedures (e.g., cognitive economy; Collins & Quillian, 1969; Conrad, 1972). Certain noun-property relations in this experiment may have been of the inference type for certain subjects (e.g., "basketball — can float"; "pencil — can pierce something"; "zebra — has ears"). The range and nature of these inference processes are other topics worthy of future interest. In particular, they appear to present a problem for theories of semantics, which usually try to characterize word meanings with finite sets of properties.

## Experiment 2

A much different task was used in this experiment to further demonstrate the distinction between CI and CD infommation. Subjects judged the similarity of instance pairs drawn from various categories (e.g., "desk — sofa" from "furniture"). Two types of categories, common and ad hoc, were used. Common categories are highly conventional categories, such as those studied by Rosch, Smith, and their colleagues (e.g., Rips, Shoben, & Smith, 1973; Rosch, 1975; Rosch & Mervis, 1975; Rosch, Mervis, Gray, Johnson, & Boyes-Braem, 1976; Smith *et al.*, 1974). Examples of these categories are "birds," "furniture," and "vegetables." In contrast, ad hoc categories are highly unusual categories that are rarely, if ever, used (Barsalou, Note 2). As a result, they are not well established in memory. Examples of these categories are "things that have a smell," "things that float," and "things that can be thrown."

Half the subjects received the category name prior to judging the similarity of each pair (the context condition); the remaining subjects did not receive the category names (the no-context condition). The predictions for this experiment are derived from Barsalou's (Note 2) finding that the properties shared by common category instances are usually CI, whereas the properties shared by ad hoc category instances may often be CD. For example, it is fairly obvious that carrots and broccoli share properties common to vegetables. However, it is not obvious that basketballs and logs share properties common to things that float. It follows that the similarity of pairs from ad hoc categories should be greater when these pairs are preceded by their category names than when they are not. This is because the category names activate shared properties that are normally inactive. Thus, there should be more common properties active in the context than in the no-context condition for ad hoc categories. In contrast, the similarity of pairs from common categories should not be increased by the addition of category names. This is because the shared properties are equally active with and without context. Combining the different patterns for ad hoc and common categories, the central prediction for this experiment is that there should be a Context by Category Type interaction. The difference in similarity between pairs from common and ad hoc categories should be less with context than without.

One other prediction for this experiment also follows from Barsalou (Note 2). The similarities should generally be greater for common than for ad hoc categories. This is because common categories are some of the categories having the highest intraclass similarity, whereas the exemplars of ad hoc categories often have much less in common. This effect is not relevant to the purpose of the experiment, but it is expected to occur.

### *Method*

***Materials and Design.*** Twenty common categories were selected from Battig and Montague (1969) and Rosch (1975). These categories intuitively appeared to be well-known and often used. Twenty ad hoc categories were selected that appeared to be atypical and infrequently used. Two instances were chosen from each category. The common category instances were selected such that the category properties shared by these instances appeared to be CI. The ad hoc category instances were selected such that the category properties shared by these instances appeared to be CD. Examples of the materials are shown in Table 4.

Eight judges verified that the CI properties were indeed more accessible for the common category instances than the CD properties were for the ad hoc category instances. The judges read the name of an instance on one side of an index card and then read the category name on the other side. They rated how much reading the instance name brought to mind the properties associated with the category name. The judges used a scale from 1 to 7 on which 1 meant the properties did not come to mind at all and 7 meant the properties immediately came to mind. Each judge rated only one instance per pair, to avoid priming effects between instances. So, four judges rated each instance, and each judge rated 20 common category instances and 20 ad hoc category instances. The 40 cards were randomly ordered for each judge. The mean accessibility rating for common category instances was 5.52, and for adhoc category instances, it was 2.32 [$F(1,6) = 164.39$, $p < .001$]. This indicates that there was a substantial difference in property accessibility between the common and ad hoc category materials.

Two versions of the pairs were constructed. In each version, the 40 pairs were randomly ordered, as were the two words in each pair. The pairs were typed onto two pages, 20 per page. In the context condition, the category name appeared to the left of each pair; in the no-context condition, the pairs appeared in isolation. Thus, there were four lists: two versions of the context list and two versions of the no-context list. To the right of each pair appeared the integers from 1 to 9. At the top of the page, above this block of response scales, appeared labels for the scale. Above 1 appeared "not similar at all," above 9 appeared "very similar," and above the remaining integers appeared "increasing similarity."

***Subjects and Procedure***. The subjects were 28 Stanford students participating to earn course credit. Fourteen subjects were randomly assigned to the context condition and 14 to the no-context condition. Within each of these groups, half the subjects received each version of the list. Subjects were asked to think of the thing to which each word in a pair referred. They were then to judge the similarity of these two referents. Subjects were told about the scale and asked to circle one of the numbers for each pair to indicate their judgment. Subjects in the context condition were told that each pair was preceded by the name of a category to which the words in the pair belonged.

**Table 4    Examples of materials used in Experiment 2**

| Category | Pair |
|----------|------|
| *Common categories* | |
| birds | robin-eagle |
| furniture | sofa-desk |
| kitchen utensils | cup-plate |
| beverages | coffee-milk |
| *Ad hoc categories* | |
| plunder taken by conquerors | slaves-jewelry |
| possible gifts | record album-necklace |
| taken on camping trips | flashlight-rope |
| can be a pet | raccoon-snake |

**Table 5    Effects of context and category type on average similarity (Experiment 2)**

| Conditions | Category type | |
|------------|---------------|--------|
| | Ad hoc | Common |
| Context | 3.67 | 5.28 |
| No Context | 2.52 | 5.73 |

### Results

The reliability of the mean ratings for the pairs was computed using the intraclass correlation for averages (Guilford & Fruchter, 1973). The reliability of the mean ratings was .96 for the no-context condition and .88 for the context condition.

A four-way ANOVA, context by category type by categories by subjects, was performed on the data. Since categories and subjects were both random factors, it was necessary to compute quasi-F's (H. H. Clark, 1973; Winer, 1971). The relevant means from this analysis are shown in Table 5. There was no main effect of context ($F' < 1$). However, there was a main effect of category type [$F'(1,62)=52.80$, $p<.001$], common categories exhibiting more similarity than ad hoc categories, as predicted. Most important, there was a Context by Category Type interaction [$F'(1,48)= 12.50$, $p< .001$]. The difference between common and ad hoc categories was less with context than without, as

181

predicted by the definitions of CI and CD properties. Planned comparisons were computed by performing separate ANOVAs on only the relevant data. For the ad hoc categories, the similarities were higher with context than without [$F'(1,35) = 8.31$, $p < .01$] . In contrast, the context manipulation had no effect on the similarity of common category pairs ($F' < 1$).

### *Discussion*

The presence of context reduced the difference in similarity between common and ad hoc categories by one-half. Without context, the difference was 3.21, whereas with context, the difference was 1.61. This is further support for the existence of CI and CD information. The category properties shared by ad hoc category instances were CD, since the similarity of these pairs was greater with relevant context than without. Relevant context was necessary to activate shared properties not activated by the words themselves. In contrast, the category properties shared by common category instances were CI, since the similarity of these pairs did not change across context. Relevant context was not required to activate shared properties activated by the words themselves.

Again, these results only provide support for a functional account of property availability: Some properties of a concept are available independent of context, since they are activated by the respective word, whereas others become available only in relevant contexts. Since subjects had as much time as they needed to perform their judgments, it was not possible to observe the time course of property activation. For this reason, it is not possible to test explanations based on the concepts of automatic and conscious attentional processes. However, the application of the Posner and Snyder (1975) framework to property availability, as discussed for Experiment 1, also makes sense in the context of the current experiment.

### General discussion

These experiments demonstrate the existence of CI and CD properties. CI properties were shown to be activated by their respective words independently of context. In Experiment 1, the verification of CI properties was unaffected by the relevance of sentence frames. In Experiment 2, the similarity of two concepts was not increased when a context relevant to shared CI properties was presented. In contrast, CD properties were shown not to be activated by their respective words, but only by relevant contexts in which the words appeared. In Experiment 1, the verification of CD properties was faster in relevant than in irrelevant contexts. In Experiment 2, the similarity of two concepts increased when a relevant context activated shared CD properties.

These findings have implications for theories of natural language semantics and for semantic memory models. Given the existence of CD properties, the meaning of a word is not a fixed set of properties that is activated as a whole every time the respective word is encoded. Rather, the meaning of a word also contains weakly associated and inferable properties that are inactive in irrelevant contexts and active in relevant contexts. Given the existence of CI properties, the meaning of a word is not completely determined by context. Rather, certain properties appear to be automatically activated by a word independently of context. These findings indicate that accounts of natural language semantics should include assumptions regarding (1) the accessibility of semantic properties and (2) the impact of context on the accessibility of these properties.

The remainder of this paper addresses the roles of CI and CD properties in the following cognitive phenomena: cross-classification, problem solving, metaphor, and sentence comprehension. Also discussed are implications for the semantic-episodic distinction.

### Cross-classification

Any concept is potentially cross-classifiable into an indefinitely large number of categories (see Barsalou, Note 2). For example, "chair" belongs to "furniture," "gifts," "things to sell at a garage sale," "things that can be used to hold a door open," and so on. Some of the classifications of a concept may be explicitly represented in memory (e.g., a robin is a bird) such that they can be directly accessed from the word for the concept. Many cross-classifications, however, may be implicit, in that they are not prestored but are computed by various inference processes when necessary (cf. Camp, Lachman, & Lachman, 1980). For example, there could be a process that takes any property, X, associated with a concept and infers that instances of the concept belong to the category of things that exhibit X. "Bear" can be cross-classified into things that have fur because fur is associated with bears.

Barsalou (Note 2) proposed a model of how implicit cross-classifications are computed. The model's first assumption is that for each possible classification, there is a set of criterial properties (coupled with a decision rule) used to discriminate category instances. The model's second assumption is that the properties active for a concept on a given occasion are a subset of the properties in that concept, this subset containing CI and CD properties. It follows that the implicit cross-classifications of a concept computable in a given context are those whose criterial properties are contained in the concept's active subset. Consequently, cross-classifications based on CI properties should be possible on any occasion. The category "things that are round" should be computable on all occasions for "basketball" if "round" is CI for "basketball." Cross-classifications based on CD properties should similarly be possible on occasions when these properties are active, but they should not be possible when these properties are inactive. "Things that float" should only be computable for "basketball" if a relevant context (e.g., a need for a life preserver) activates "floats" in the concept for "basketball." Barsalou (Note 2) reports data consistent with this view of cross-classification.

### Problem solving

The account of cross-classification just discussed bears upon functional fixedness in problem solving (Duncker, 1945). Functional fixedness is the phenomenon of an object's typical function preventing insight into other, less typical functions that might be more useful in a particular situation. In one problem, subjects are presented several objects and asked to use them to support a board (Duncker, 1945). Crucial to solving this problem is using a pair of pliers as a support. But since "can provide support" is not a salient function of pliers, subjects often have difficulty solving the problem. In many such cases, the salient function may be CI, whereas the less salient function may be CD. Perception of the less salient cross-classification may depend on attending to the critical object in the appropriate mental context such that the CD-based classification can be inferred. For example, the CI properties in the concept for things that could support the board might activate relevant CD properties in the representation of pliers if these two concepts were simultaneously active in memory. These CD properties could then be used to infer that "pliers" belongs to "things that could support the board."

Finding a solution to this problem may be delayed because subjects are misled by the CI properties of the critical object. For example, "to grasp something" is probably CI for "pliers." Once this property is automatically activated, subjects may rule out pliers as a possible support. Consequently, the object is not attended to in the context necessary for activating the relevant properties. When subjects get desperate, this initial classification may be discarded such that the object is more carefully scrutinized and properly classified. In support of this, Duncker (1945) and Glucksberg and Danks (1968) have found that it takes longer to solve a problem when attention is drawn to the interfering CI properties. Duncker (1945) distracted subjects by having them use the pliers to grasp something before solving the problem. Glucksberg and Danks (1968) either mentioned the word for the critical object or labeled the object with a nonsense syllable. Mentioning the word delayed solutions, presumably because hearing the word automatically activated interfering CI properties.

Sometimes the activation of CI properties may facilitate finding a solution. In the candle problem, subjects are given a candle, some matches, and a box of tacks; their task is to attach the candle to the wall and light it (Duncker, 1945). Usually it takes subjects a while to cross-classify the box as something that could contain the candle. However, Glucksberg and Weisberg (1966) found that having the experimenter label the box as "box" resulted in faster solutions than when the box of tacks was simply labeled "tacks." They argued that using "box" drew attention to an object that was otherwise obscured by what it contained. However, another factor may be involved as well. Assuming that "contains things" is CI for "box," it follows that this property should become available when subjects hear the experimenter say "box." Having this property available should then facilitate cross-classifying the box as something that could contain the candle.

### Metaphor and sentence comprehension

Ortony (1979) has proposed that metaphoricity depends on a particular type of salience imbalance. Specifically, the property brought to mind by a metaphor should have low salience for the subject and high salience for the referent of the metaphor. For "sermons are sleeping pills," the property "induces drowsiness or sleep" has low salience for "sermons," but high salience for "sleeping pills."

In many metaphors, the shared property may be CD in the subject and CI in the referent. In these cases, the CI property in the referent may automatically activate the corresponding CD property in the subject (see Glucksberg, Dial, & Bookin, Note 3). That is, the referent serves as context for the subject, activating relevant CD properties. It follows from Ortony's (1979) analysis that the best metaphors should be those in which the shared property is CD in the subject and CI in the referent. This is because these are the cases in which salience imbalance is maximized. Metaphors in which the shared property is not CD in the subject should not appear as metaphorical, since the property may come to mind for the subject outside the context of the referent.

In general, the mechanism of CI properties in one word activating CD properties in other words may be central to sentence comprehension. As shown in Experiment 1, the predicate in a sentence can bring to mind properties of the subject (e.g., the predicate in "The rag was used to start the fire" brings to mind "is flammable" for "rag"). There appear to be many other ways in which CI properties of one sentence word activate CD properties of another sentence word. For example, CI properties can bring to mind the appropriate senses of ambiguous words.[3] This occurs from direct objects to verbs. For "John ate X," the instantiation of X determines the sense of "eat" that comes to mind (e.g., consider X = soup, a sandwich, a steak, and so on). Similarly, the CI properties of a noun serve to disambiguate modifiers. For "the broken X," the instantiation of X determines the sense of "broken" that comes to mind (e.g., consider X = bowl, truck, plan, and so on). Similarly, the CI properties of an object in a prepositional phrase determine the sense of the preposition that comes to mind. For "on the X," the instantiation of X determines the sense of "on" that comes to mind [e.g., consider X = table, television, roof (where the subject is a person vs. a fly), and so on]. In general, converging on the intended meaning of a sentence may often involve selecting the properties associated with individual words that result in the most coordinated interpretation. This selection mechanism can be characterized, at least to some extent, as the activation of relevant CD properties in some words by CI properties in other words. This mechanism serves to minimize the number of words necessary for communicating all possible intended meanings. This is because it allows words to be used in many different ways, rather than requiring a different word for every possible meaning.

### The semantic-episodic distinction

Tulving (1972) proposed a distinction between episodic and semantic memories. Episodic memories represent autobiographical experiences, that is, events coded by space and time. In contrast, semantic memories represent our knowledge of the world and the meanings of words.[4] Although most investigators have not argued for physically separate memories in the brain, many have agreed that there may be different representations and processes associated with each memory type. Recently, this view has come under attack. J. R. Anderson and Ross (1980) and McKoon and Ratcliff (1979) have argued that episodic and semantic memories may be similarly represented and subject to the same processes. Barsalou and Bower (Note 1) further argue that the CI-CD distinction is problematic for the semantic-episodic distinction. If CI properties are automatized, and if practice results in automaticity, then particular processing episodes determine the accessibility of semantic memories. Similarly, CD properties are CD because there have not been many episodes in which the property and the respective word were simultaneously processed. Since the availability of semantic information depends directly on episodic information, it is not clear that two types of memories are needed when one would probably be sufficient.

Barsalou and Bower (Note 1) discuss specific ways in which particular processing episodes may affect the psychology of lexical semantics. To start with, a word can refer to different kinds of instances. "Car" can refer to cars with or without air conditioning. Consequently, the accessibility of "air conditioning" should depend on the type of car someone is used to. In general, properties of a concept not typically found for familiar referents may become CD through disuse. In contrast, properties typically encountered are more likely to become CI. Analogously, particular uses of an object may vary in accessibility. Someone who has just been to a circus may be more likely to categorize "chair" as something to fight lions with. In general, encoding a particular episode in which an object is put to atypical use may make that use more accessible, at least temporarily.

It should be pointed out that CI properties are not necessarily more semantic than CD properties. Episodes can be CI (e.g., "doberman pincher" may always activate a particular, well rehearsed episode of being bitten by one of these dogs), and semantic properties can be CD (e.g., properties that are usually irrelevant for an object, such as "floats" for "basketball"). The primary difference between CI and CD information is simply the means by which they are activated: CI information is activated by the word for a concept, whereas CD information is activated by relevant contexts in which the word is encoded. As suggested by Barsalou and Bower (Note 1), this difference in accessibility is a function of the frequency and recency of processing episodes, regardless of whether the information is an episode, a semantic feature, an affect, or some other type of information.

Finally, E. V. Clark and H. H. Clark (1979) have shown that certain innovative uses of words can result in new meanings for those words. Computing these novel meanings often requires retrieving a particular episode. Consider their example of "teapotting." Suppose someone named Max has a strange habit of rubbing a teapot on the backs of people's legs. Imagine that two people had seen Max do this before, and one of them said, "Max is in trouble, he just teapotted a policeman." The listener would compute the meaning of "teapotted" by retrieving the relevant episodes, even though he or she has never heard the word used that way. Clearly, this example illustrates the necessity of using episodic information to arrive at the speaker's intended meaning. There is no linguistic rule that could generate the exact meaning intended by the speaker in this situation. Instead, the specifics of the meaning are derived from the structure of the relevant episodes. With recurrent uses of "teapot" in this manner, however, the new meaning could eventually be abstracted away from the particulars of episodes and become CI. Thus, particular processing episodes not only enable comprehension of certain linguistic innovations but are also responsible for the respective word senses' becoming well established in memory. In general, changes in word meanings over time may often be the result of changes in the accessibility of CI and CD properties.

## Acknowledgements

This research was supported by Grant MH 13950 from the National Institute of Mental Health to Gordon H. Bower and by a National Science Foundation graduate fellowship to the author. I arn grateful to Gordon Bower for supporting this research and to Kathleen Hemenway, Brian Ross, Ronald Finke, Michael McCloskey, and an anonymous reviewer for excellent comments on earlier drafts.

## Notes

1. It should be pointed out that this proposal regarding the existence of CI and CD properties is not a theory of meaning. It simply addresses one aspect of concepts, namely, the accessibility of properties.

2. The CI control and CD unrelated-context items both have weakly related subject relations and unrelated predicate relations; analogously, the CD control and CI unrelated-context items both have highly related subject relations and unrelated predicate relations. It is not possible, however, to pool the latencies within these two sets of items, since this would make comparisons between unrelated- and related-context items impossible. The proper way to compare related and unrelated contexts is to observe latencies for the same properties under different context conditions. Pooling violates this design, since latencies for the control properties would be included in the unrelated context conditions but not in the related-context conditions.

3. As discussed earlier, these senses may not be strictly CD. Even though context is required to converge on a particular sense, many may easily come to mind in no context (Swinney, 1979; Tanenhaus *et al.*, 1979). Consequently, the primary senses of an ambiguous word may lie in the middle ground between CI and CD properties. These senses are CD in the weaker sense that they are attenuated or strengthened by context once their linguistic form has automatically activated them.

4. This use of "semantic" is nonstandard, since "semantics" is typically used to refer only to the meanings of words.

## Reference notes

1. Barsalou, L. W. and Bower, C. H. (1980) *A priori determinants of a concept's highly accessible information.* Paper presented at the annual meeting of the American Psychological Association, Montreal, September.

2. Barsalou, L. W. (1981) *Ad hoc categories and cross-classification.* Unpublished manuscript.

3. Glucksberg, S., Dial, P. C. and Bookin, H. B. (1980) *On understanding nonliteral speech: Can people ignore metaphors?* Manuscript in preparation.

## References

Anderson, J. R. & Ross. B. H. (1980) Evidence against the semantic episodic distinction. *Journal of Experimental Psychology: Human Learning and Memory,* 6, 441–466.

Anderson, R. C. & Ortony, A. (1975) On putting apples into bottles — A problem of polysemy. *Cognitive Psychology,* 7, 167–180.

Anderson, R. C., Pichert, J. W., Goetz, E. T., Schallert, D. L., Stevens, K. V. & Trollip, S. R. (1976) Instantiation of general terms. *Journal of Verbal Learning and Verbal Behavior,* 15, 667–679.

Barclay, J. R., Bransford, J. D., Franks, J. J., McCarrell, N. S. & Nitsch, K. (1974) Comprehension and semantic flexibility. *Journal of Verbal Learning and Verbal Behavior,* 13, 471–481.

Battig, W. F. & Montague, W. E. (1969) Category norms for verbal items in 56 categories: A replication and extension of the Connecticut category norms. *Journal of Experimental Psychology,* 80 (Whole No. 3, Pt. 2).

Bower, G. H. (1972) Stimulus-sampling theory of encoding variability. In A. W. Melton & E. Martin (Eds.), *Coding processes in human memory.* Washington, D.C: Winston.

Camp, C. J., Lachman, J. L. & Lachman, R. (1980) Evidence for direct-access and inferential retrieval in question-answering. *Journal of Verbal Learning and Verbal Behavior,* 19, 583–596.

Clark, E. V. & Claric, H. H. (1979) When nouns surface as verbs. Language, 55, 767–811.

Clark, H. H. (1973) The language-as-fixed-effect fallacy: A critique of language statistics in psychological research. *Journal of Verbal Learning and Verbal Behavior,* 12, 335–359.

Collins, A. M. & Quillian, M. R. (1969) Retrieval time from semantic memory. *Journal of Verbal Learning and Verbal Behavior,* 8, 240–247.

Conrad, C. (1972) Cognitive economy in semantic memory. *Journal of Experimental Psychology,* 92, 149–154.

Conrad, C. (1978) Some factors involved in the recognition of words. In J. W. Cotton & R. L. Klatzky (Eds.), *Semantic factors in cognition.* Hillsdale, N.J: Erlbaum.

Duncker, K. (1945) On problem solving. *Psychological Monographs,* 58 (Whole No. 270).

Estes, W. K. (1955) Statistical theory of spontaneous recovery and regression. *Psychological Review,* 62, 145–154.

Estes, W. K. (1959) The statistical approach to learning theory. In S. Koch (Ed.), *Psychology. A study of a science* (Vol . 2). New York: McGraw-Hill.

Foss, D. J., Cirilo, R. K. & Blank, M. A. (1979) Semantic facilitation and lexical access during sentence processing: An investigation of individual differences. *Memory & Cognition,* 7, 346–353.

Glass, A. L. & Holyoak, K. J. (1975) Alternative conceptions of semantic memory. *Cognition,* 3, 313–339.

Glucksberg, S. & Danks, J. (1968) Effects of discriminative labels and of nonsense labels upon availability of novel function. *Journal of Verbal Learning and Verbal Behavior,* 7, 72–76.

Glucksberg, S. & Weisberg, R. W. (1966) Verbal behavior and problem solving: Some effects of labeling in a functional fixedness problem. *Journal of Experimental Psychology,* 71, 659–664.

Guilford, J. P. & Fruchter, B. (1973) *Fundamental statistics in psychology and education.* New York: McGraw-Hill.

Jacoby, L. L., Craik, F. I. M. & Begg, I. (1979) Effects of decision difficulty on recognition and recall. *Journal of Verbal Learning and Verbal Behavior,* 18, 585–600.

Katz, J. J. & Postal, P. (1964) *An integrated theory of linguistic descriptions.* Cambridge, Mass: M.I.T. Press.

McCloskey, M. & Glucksberg, S. (1979) Decision processes in verifying category membership statements: Implications for models of semantic memory. *Cognitive Psychology,* 11, 1–37.

McKoon, G. & Ratcliff, R. (1979) Priming in episodic and semantic memory. *Journal of Verbal Learning and Verbal Behavior,* 18, 463–480.

Neely, J. H. (1977) Semantic priming and retrieval from lexical memory: Roles of inhibitionless spreading activation and limited-capacity attention. *Journal of Experimental Psychology: General,* 106, 226–254.

Olson, D. R. (1970) Language and thought: Aspects of a cognitive theory of semantics. *Psychological Review,* 77, 257–273.

Ortony, A. (1979) Beyond literal similarity. *Psychological Review,* 86, 161–180.

Posner, M. I. & Snyder, C. R. R. (1975) Attention and cognitive control. In R. L. Solso (Ed.), *Information processing and cognition: the Loyola symposium.* Hillsdale, N.J: Erlbaum.

Rips, L. J., Shoben, E. J. & Smith, E. E. (1973) Semantic distance and the verification of semantic relations. *Journal of Verbal Learning and Verbal Behavior,* 12, 1–20.

Rosch, E. H. (1975) Cognitive representations of semantic categories. *Journal of Experimental Psychology: General,* 104, 192–233.

Rosch, E. H. & Mervis, C. B. (1975) Family resemblances: Studies in the internal structure of categories. *Cognitive Psychology,* 7, 573–605.

Rosch, E. H., Mervis, C. B., Gray, W. D., Johnson, D. M. & Boyes-Braem, P. (1976) Basic objects in natural categories. *Cognitive Psychology,* 8, 382–439.

Shiffrin, R. M. & Schneider, W. (1977) Controlled and automatic human information processing: II. Perceptual learning, automatic attending, and a general theory. *Psychological Review,* 84, 127–190.

Smith, E. E., Shoben, E. J. & Rips, L. J. (1974) Structure and process in semantic memory: A featural model for semantic decisions. *Psychological Review,* 81,214–241.

Swinney, D. A. (1979) Lexical access during sentence comprehension: (Re)Consideration of context effects. *Journal of Verbal Learning and Verbal Behavior,* 18, 645–659.

Tanenhaus, M. K., Leiman, J. M. & Seidenberg, M. S. (1979) Evidence for multiple stages in the processing of ambiguous words in syntactic contexts. *Journal of Verbal Learning and Verbal Behavior,* 18, 427–440.

Tabossi, P. & Johnson-Laird, P. N. (1980) Linguistic context and the priming of semantic information. *Quarterly Journal of Experimental Psychology,* 32, 595–603.

Tulving, E. (1972) Episodic and semantic memory. In E. Tulving & W. Donaldson (Eds.), *Organization and memory.* New York: Academic Press.

Tulving, E. & Thompson, D. M. (1973) Encoding specificity and retrieval processes in episodic memory. *Psychological Review,* 80, 352–373.

Winer, B. J. (1971) *Statistical principles in experimental design.* New York: McGraw-Hill.

# 7. Ideals, Central Tendency, and Frequency of Instantiation as Determinants of Graded Structure in Categories

## Lawrence W. Barsalou

*Three possible determinants of graded structure (typicality) were observed in common taxonomic categories and goal-derived categories: (1) an exemplar's similarity to ideals associated with goals its category serves; (2) an exemplar's similarity to the central tendency of its category (family resemblance); and (3) an exemplar's frequency of instantiation (people's subjective estimates of how often it is encountered as a category member). Experiment 1 found that central tendency did not predict graded structure in goal-derived categories, although it did predict graded structure in common taxonomic categories. Ideals and frequency of instantiation predicted graded structure in both category types to sizeable and equal extents. A fourth possible determinant — familiarity — did not predict typicality in either common taxonomic or goal-derived categories. Experiment 2 demonstrated that both central tendency and ideals causally determine graded structure, and work showing that frequency causally determines graded structure is discussed. Experiment 2 also demonstrated that the determinants of a particular category's graded structure can change with context. Whereas ideals may determine a category's graded structure in one context, central tendency may determine a different graded structure in another. It is proposed that graded structures do not reflect invariant structures associated with categories but instead reflect people's dynamic ability to construct concepts.*

A central theme in categorization research for the last decade has been that categories possess graded structure. Instead of being equivalent, the members of a category vary in how good an example (or how typical) they are of their category (Rips, Shoben, & Smith, 1973; Rosch, 1973; 1975; Smith, Shoben, & Rips, 1974). In *birds,* for example, American college students agree that *robin* is very typical, *pigeon* is moderately typical, and *ostrich* is atypical. In addition, nonmembers of a category vary in how good a nonmember they are of the category (Barsalou, 1983). For example, *chair* is a better nonmember of *birds* than is *butterfly*. *Graded structure* refers to this continuum of category representativeness, beginning with the most representative members of a category and continuing through its atypical members to those nonmembers least similar to category members. No other variable is as important as graded structure in predicting performance on a wide range of categorization tasks (e.g., category acquisition, exemplar production, category verification). In addition, graded structure occurs in a diverse range of categories, suggesting that it may be a universal property

Lawrence W. Barsalou: 'Ideals, Central Tendency, and Frequency of Instantiation as Determinants of Graded Structure in Categories' in *JOURNAL OF EXPERIMENTAL PSYCHOLOGY: LEARNING, MEMORY, AND COGNITION* (1985), Vol. 11, No. 4, pp. 629–654. Copyright © 1985 by the American Psychological Association, Inc. Reprinted by permission.

of categories. The large body of work addressing graded structure is reviewed in Mervis and Rosch (1981), Smith and Medin (1981), and Medin and Smith (1984).

This article addresses the issue of what determines graded structure. Why are some exemplars of a category more typical than others? Two experiments examine three possible determinants of graded structure: *central tendency, ideals,* and *frequency of instantiation.* A fourth possible determinant — *familiarity* — is also briefly considered.

## Central tendency

Following the work of Rosch and Mervis (1975), there has been widespread acceptance that an exemplar's typicality depends on its *family resemblance,* where family resemblance is defined as an exemplar's average similarity to other category members and its average dissimilarity to members of contrast categories. The more similar an exemplar is to other category members and the less similar it is to members of contrast categories, the higher its family resemblance, and the more typical it is of its category. *Dog,* for example, is very similar to other members of *mammals* and not very similar to members of contrast categories (e.g., *fish, birds*). In contrast, *whale* is not as similar to other *mammals* and is highly similar to the members of a contrast category (i.e., *fish*). Consequently *dog* is more typical of *mammals* than is *whale*.

Another way to view an exemplar's family resemblance is as its similarity to central tendency (Hampton, 1979; Smith *et al.*, 1974) where central tendency refers to any kind of central tendency information about a category's exemplars (e.g., average, median, or modal values on dimensions, highly probable properties, etc.). As just discussed, an exemplar's family resemblance is defined in part as its average similarity to other category members. However its average similarity to other category members must be at least roughly the same as its similarity to their central tendency (Barsalou, 1983). This is analogous to the average difference between a number and several other numbers being the same as the difference between the first number and the average of the others. In a related manner, an exemplar's average dissimilarity to the members of contrast categories must be at least roughly the same as its dissimilarity to their central tendencies. Consequently an exemplar's family resemblance can be specified either as its average similarity and dissimilarity to category members and nonmembers, or as its similarity and dissimilarity to their central tendencies.

Although people could determine family resemblance in either of these two ways, determining family resemblance through comparisons to central tendencies may be more psychologically plausible — comparing an exemplar to central tendencies requires much fewer comparisons than comparing an exemplar to members and nonmembers. Regardless of how people actually derive family resemblance, however, similarity to central tendencies and similarity to members and nonmembers are functionally equivalent at the level of predicting typicality. Because this article primarily addresses functional relations between typicality and other variables, family resemblance and similarity to central tendencies will be assumed to be equivalent.

## Ideals

Ideals, which provide another possible determinant of graded structure, are characteristics that exemplars should have if they are to best serve a goal associated with their category. For example, an ideal for *foods to eat on a diet* is *zero calories*. The fewer calories an exemplar has, the better it serves the goal associated with its category, namely, *lose weight*. This ideal appears to determine graded structure in that exemplars with decreasing numbers of calories become increasingly good exemplars of the category. Similarly for *things to take from one's home during a fire,* finding exemplars near the ideal of *highest possible value* is relevant to the goal of *minimizing loss;* therefore this property appears to determine the category's graded structure.

Most categories probably have more than one ideal. For example, *possible restaurants to eat at* may have the ideals of *lowest possible cost, highest possible quality,* and *closest possible proximity.* The most important ideal(s) on a given occasion may depend on the goal a person is pursuing. If the goal is to have a memorable experience, then *high quality* may be most important. But if the goal is to have a quick meal, then *high quality* may succumb to *close proximity* and *low cost.*

Ideals differ from central tendency in at least two ways. First, ideals generally do not appear to be the central tendencies of their categories (although they may occasionally be). *Zero calories,* for example, is certainly not the central tendency with respect to *calories* for *things to eat on a diet;* nor is *closest possible proximity* the central tendency with respect to *distance* for *possible places to eat at.* Ideals tend to be extreme values that are either true of only a few category members or true of none at all. Instead of lying at the center of categories (as does central tendency), they generally lie at the periphery.[1]

Central tendency and ideals also differ in origin. Central tendency depends directly on the exemplars of a category, and more specifically, on the particular exemplars a person has experienced. Although people may form impressions of a category's central tendency through hearsay, they may generally acquire such information through experience with exemplars. In contrast, ideals may often be determined independently of exemplars, being acquired through the process of planning how to achieve goals before exemplars are ever encountered.

### Frequency of instantiation and familiarity

Rosch, Simpson, and Miller (1976) and Mervis, Catlin, and Rosch (1976) argued that frequency does not determine graded structure, although their tests of frequency were not very sensitive. Rosch, Simpson, *et al.* (1976) pitted family resemblance against frequency and found that only family resemblance predicted typicality. However, their design was not capable of detecting simultaneous effects of family resemblance and frequency. Consequently frequency could have had an effect, but was not detected because it was the weaker of the two factors. Mervis *et al.* (1976) found that an exemplar's word frequency in Kučera and Francis's (1967) analysis did not predict typicality. However it is by no means clear that word frequency is a good measure of how often people encounter exemplars in their everyday routines. Other measures of frequency may be better predictors of typicality.

More recent work has contradicted these initial reports, finding that familiar exemplars are perceived as more typical than unfamiliar exemplars (Ashcraft, 1978; Glass & Meany, 1978; Hampton & Gardiner, 1983; Malt & Smith, 1982).[2] Familiarity can be defined as someone's subjective estimate of how often they have experienced an entity across *all* contexts. However an alternative form of frequency that could determine graded structure is frequency of instantiation, which can be defined as someone's subjective estimate of how often they have experienced an entity as a member of a *particular category*. Whereas familiarity is a *category-independent* measure of frequency, frequency of instantiation is a *category-specific* measure of frequency. For example, people generally appear more familiar with *chair* than with *log*, having experienced *chair* more often across all contexts. However people have probably experienced *log* more often as an instantiation of *firewood*. Increases in familiarity and frequency of instantiation could both be associated with increasing typicality. Although both possible determinants receive attention here, the focus will be on frequency of instantiation, because initial inspection of categories suggested it as the more important factor.

In summary, a number of factors could determine graded structure, including central tendency, ideals, frequency of instantiation, and familiarity. Because previous work has not observed ideals and frequency of instantiation, and because previous work has generally not performed comprehensive tests of possible determinants, one of the purposes of this project was to observe all four of these possible determinants simultaneously. The focus on these factors is not meant to imply that they are the only possible determinants of graded structure. Instead it is highly likely that other factors also determine typicality. For example, Hampton and Gardiner (1983) review findings that address whether the number of properties associated with an exemplar determines its typicality. In addition, Lakoff (in press) presents a number of other possible determinants, which in at least some cases appear to be composites of the factors examined here.

## Common taxonomic and goal-derived categories

Previous work showing that central tendency and familiarity determine graded structure has focused on typicality in one particular kind of category, namely, *common taxonomic* categories (e.g., *birds, furniture, fruit*). However, because Hampton (1981) found that graded structure is not well-predicted by central tendency in some abstract categories, there is reason to believe that the generality of the previous studies is limited. The factors that determine graded structure may vary widely across categories. Consequently a second purpose of this project was to observe typicality in another kind of category, what will be referred to as *goal-derived* categories (e.g., *things not to eat on a diet, things to take from one's home during a fire, birthday presents*).

It should be noted that Barsalou (1983) found graded structure in *ad hoc* categories, which are those goal-derived categories that have been constructed to achieve a novel goal and that therefore are not well-established in memory. Once an ad hoc category is frequently used and becomes well-established in memory, however, it is no longer ad hoc by this definition (see Barsalou, 1983, pp. 224–225). Consequently goal-derived categories include both ad hoc categories and better established categories that were once ad hoc.

Of course it would be ideal to distinguish common taxonomic and goal-derived categories in terms of simple definitions. Unfortunately such definitions have not as yet been forthcoming, although it is as least possible to provide characteristic properties for each category type. One way common taxonomic and goal-derived categories generally appear to differ has to do with the "correlational structure of the environment." Correlational structure refers to the fact that properties in the physical environment are not independent; that is, a given property generally co-occurs with certain other properties but not with others. *Feathers*, for example, typically co-occurs with *wings* and *beak*, but not with *tires* and *engine*. As discussed by Rosch and Mervis (1975) and Rosch, Mervis, Gray, Johnson, and Boyes-Braem (1976), common taxonomic categories appear to circumscribe sets of things in the environment that share these clusters of co-occurring properties. Consequently these categories reflect the correlational structure of the environment. Many exemplars of *birds*, for example, share co-occurring properties that rarely occur outside the category, thereby making exemplars of this category very similar to each other and very dissimilar to nonmembers.

In contrast, goal-derived categories generally appear to violate the correlational structure of the environment. Many goal-derived categories include some members from each of several common taxonomic categories, but never all the members from a given one. *Things to take on a camping trip,* for example, includes members of *food, clothing, tools,* and so on, but it does not include all members. Because the members of these goal-derived categories are often quite dissimilar to each other and very similar to many nonmembers, they do not maximize the correlational structure of the environment. Other goal-derived categories contain subsets of one particular common taxonomic category. For example, someone with a back problem might be interested in *chairs that provide good back support.* In these cases, goal-derived categories do not maximize correlational structure because many noncategory members are highly similar to category members (e.g., *chairs that provide good back support* are very similar to *chairs that do not).* In general, because goal-derived categories do not maximize the correlational structure of the environment, they are not very salient and do not stand out as natural groups. Instead they appear to only become salient when relevant to currently pursued goals.

Another way in which common taxonomic and goal-derived categories generally seem to differ has to do with category use. Common taxonomic categories are often used for classification, whereas goal-derived categories are often used for instantiation. When classifying entities in the environment, people primarily appear to use common taxonomic categories. More specifically, people generally prefer basic level categories, which are a subset of common taxonomic categories (Jolicoeur, Gluck, & Kosslyn, 1984; Murphy & Smith, 1982; Rosch, Mervis, *et al.*, 1976; B. Tversky & Hemenway, 1984). In contrast, people primarily appear to use goal-derived categories for instantiating schema variables while achieving goals. To achieve the goal of *taking a vacation,* for example, a planner has to instantiate variables in schematic knowledge about *vacations,* such as *where to go, who to go with, how to get there, what to take,* and so on. The goal-derived categories of *places to go, people to go with, types of transportation,* and *things to pack in a suitcase* facilitate locating and selecting instantiations for these variables. In general, successfully achieving a goal requires that people bind schema variables with instantiations appropriate in the current setting. Goal-derived categories provide pools of instantiations from which instantiations can be chosen.

Although common taxonomic and goal-derived categories generally seem to differ in the extent to which they reflect correlational structure and in the way they are used, these distinctions are by no means clear-cut or defining. For example, some common taxonomic categories such as *vehicles, clothing,* and *furniture* are highly related to people's goals and may often be used for instantiation. Conversely goal-derived categories may at times be used for classification. Although these distinctions are not defining, they provide characteristic properties of common taxonomic and goal-derived categories.

**Determinants of graded structure in common taxonomic and goal-derived categories**

These general differences between common taxonomic and goal-derived categories suggest that different factors may determine their graded structures. To begin with, central tendency may be highly salient in people's representations of common taxonomic categories and thereby become the standard by which typicality is judged. Central tendency may be salient in common taxonomic categories for the following two reasons. First, because these categories generally reflect correlational structure, people may use them as a means of representing the structure of the environment. If so, then acquiring central tendency information for these categories provides *representative information* about the kinds of entities the environment contains. Central tendency information is clearly more representative than ideal information, because the former has a much higher likelihood of occurring for a category's exemplars than the latter.

A second reason central tendency information may be salient in common taxonomic categories has to do with their use. Because these categories are often used for classification, their representations may be designed to maximize classification performance. It is well-known in the category verification literature that classifying an entity proceeds faster to the extent the entity is similar to the category standard (Smith, 1978). Basing classification standards on central tendency information minimizes the average distance of category members to category standards (e.g., it is a statistical fact that the average absolute distance from all points in a set to one particular point is minimized when that point is the median; Hayes, 1973, p. 223). Therefore the average difficulty of performing classifications is minimized when the category standard contains central tendency information (as opposed to ideals). Because a primary use of common taxonomic categories is to serve classification, it would not be surprising if central tendency information were central to their representations.

In contrast, ideals may become highly salient in people's representations of goal-derived categories and thereby become the standards by which typicality is judged. Because goal-derived categories generally serve goals, their representations may contain ideals in order to maximize goal achievement. As people consider possible instantiations of a category, they can compare them to the category's ideals and thereby pick the exemplar or exemplars that will result in maximal goal satisfaction. For example, someone on a diet might compare selections on a menu to the ideals for *things to eat on a diet* in order to pick instantiations that will maximize the goal of *losing weight*.

Although central tendency may be the only determinant of graded structure for common taxonomic categories, and although ideals may be the only determinant for goal-derived categories, another possibility is that both factors determine graded structure in both category types. For example, the typicality of a particular *fruit* may be determined, not only by its similarity to central tendency information, but also by its similarity to revelant ideals (e.g., having to do with *taste* and *nutrition*). To the extent common taxonomic categories serve goals, ideals should also determine their graded structures. Analogously, to the extent central tendency information is important for the use of goal-derived categories, it should also determine their graded structures. On the basis of findings reported by Rosch and Mervis (1975) and Rosch, Simpson, *et al*. (1976), one might predict that central tendency determines graded structure in all categories.

Finally, initial inspections of categories suggested that frequency of instantiation determines graded structure to some extent in goal-derived categories but not in common taxonomic categories. Alternatively, the work of Rosch, Simpson, *et al*. (1976) and Mervis *et al*. ( 1976) suggests that frequency of instantiation should not determine graded structure in either.

## Experiment 1

This first study examined whether central tendency, ideals, and frequency of instantiation predict graded structure in goal-derived and common taxonomic categories. For each category observed, these three variables were measured for every exemplar and were then correlated with typicality. This study also observed whether central tendency, ideals, and frequency of instantiation predict how often exemplars are generated during exemplar production.

### *Method*

Nine goal-derived categories were selected that intuitively appeared to originate during goal-directed behavior as opposed to originating in the correlational structure of the environment. The common taxonomic categories were 9 of those studied by Rosch (1975). These 18 categories are shown in Table 3.

Thirty-eight subjects generated exemplars of these 18 categories after generating exemplars to each of three practice categories. Subjects received the 18 critical category names in one of two random orders. After a tape recording finished stating a name, subjects wrote down as many exemplars as they could think of in the subsequent 15-s interval. The recording then asked subjects to turn to the next page of their booklet and prepare for the next category.

The exemplars generated for each category were pooled across subjects to construct dominance orders of exemplars (as in Battig & Montague, 1969). Generated items were considered to be the same exemplar only if they were orthographically identical or differed by a minor inflection (e.g, *shirt* and *shirts; walk* and *walking).* All exemplars generated by only one subject were not used in the remainder of the experiment. However when two such exemplars were members of some superordinate not mentioned by two or more subjects, the superordinate was included (e.g., *Kung Fu* and *Karate* were combined to form *martial arts).* This occurred rarely. The number of exemplars generated by 2 or more subjects per category ranged from 9 to 24, the median being 19.83. The median for the goal-derived categories was 20.25 and for the common taxonomic categories was 19.25.

To obtain exemplar goodness judgments, subjects received the 348 exemplars blocked by category. In each of two versions, the category blocks were randomly ordered (one per page) as were the exemplars within each category. At the top of each page appeared the corresponding category name. To the right of each exemplar appeared a 9-point scale on which 1 was labeled *poor example* and 9 was labeled *excellent example.* Ten subjects circled 1 scale number for each exemplar to rate how good an example it was of its category. These instructions did not ask subjects to judge "how typical" each exemplar was because it was thought this might bias subjects towards using frequency of instantiation. "How good an example" seemed more open ended and less demanding. Although "typicality" will often be used to refer to these data out of convenience they were collected using "goodness-of-example" instructions.

To obtain frequency of instantiation judgments, subjects received the same materials as just mentioned, except the endpoints for the scale were labeled 1 for *not frequently at all* and labeled 9 for *very frequently.* Ten subjects rated each member for how frequently they thought it subjectively occurred as a category instantiation. Subjects were explicitly asked not to judge how familiar each item was but instead how frequently they thought it occurred as a member of the category.

Except for the following two changes, the materials used to collect judgments about ideals were the same as those used to collect judgments of typicality and frequency. First, the endpoints for the scale was labeled 1 for *very low amount* and labeled 9 for *very high amount.* Second, the name of a dimension occurred at the top of the page. These dimensions — which will be referred to as *ideal dimensions* — are shown in Table 3. They were picked intuitively and seemed to contain ideals that exemplars should optimally have with respect to a goal served by the respective category. The ideal for each dimension appeared to lie toward its upper end. Ten subjects rated each exemplar for its amount on its ideal dimension.[3]

It should be noted that a category could have more than one ideal or have a more important ideal than the one observed here. The goal of this study, however, was not to find the upper limit on how well ideals predict graded structure. Instead the goal was simply to determine whether ideals predict graded structure at all. Consequently the attempt to locate ideals was not exhaustive or oriented towards finding the most important ideal.

To assess the role of central tendency, a family resemblance score was obtained for each exemplar. Because an exemplar's average similarity to other exemplars is at least roughly the same as its similarity to their central tendency (as discussed earlier), these scores at least approximate how similar an exemplar is to its category's central tendency. All possible pairs of exemplars were formed for each category, with the two exemplars in each pair being randomly ordered. Two versions were formed in which pairs were blocked by category. In each, the category blocks were randomly ordered as were the pairs within each category. At the top of each page of pairs appeared the corresponding category name. To the right of each pair appeared the numbers from 1 to 9, with 1 labeled as *not similar at all* and 9 labeled as very *similar*. Six subjects circled 1 scale number to rate the similarity of each of the 3,319 pairs. Subjects were asked to think of the referent of each word in a pair and then rate the referents' similarity on the 9-point scale.

A subject's similarity judgments for pairs having the same exemplar were averaged to form its family resemblance score. All 6 subjects' family resemblance scores for the exemplar were then averaged to form its overall family resemblance score. Because Rosch and Mervis (1975) and A. Tversky ( 1977) report that similarity ratings and overlap in feature listings correlate around .90, this rating-based measure of family resemblance should be very close to the feature-based measure of Rosch and Mervis (1975).[4]

Subjects were 74 Stanford University students participating to earn either course credit or pay. A given subject provided data for only one of the five measures.

### *Results*

*Raw correlations.* An item's exemplar goodness, frequency of instantiation (referred to as *frequency* in the next three sections), and ideal dimension scores were simply averages across the 10 subjects who produced the respective data. An exemplar's family resemblance score was computed as just discussed. An exemplar's output dominance score was the number of subjects, out of 38, who had generated the exemplar. The values of these variables for each exemplar in each category are shown in the appendix.

For each of the five measures, the mean and standard deviation of the exemplar means were computed for each category. Goal-derived and common taxonomic categories did not differ on the mean or standard deviation of any measure. No differences in standard deviations indicates that differences in range between category types will not be a factor in the correlations to be reported shortly. Of more theoretical interest is that goal-derived and common taxonomic categories did not differ in the standard deviations of their family resemblance scores (the mean values were .65 and .70, respectively). This suggests that the exemplars of goal-derived categories vary as much in their similarity to one another as do the exemplars of common taxonomic categories.[5]

For each category, the 10 possible correlations between measures were computed across exemplar averages. The average values for goal-derived and common taxonomic categories are shown in Table 1. The variance of each correlation type was computed across the nine categories within each category type. These 20 variances were averaged to form a pooled estimate of the variance, and the resulting standard deviation with 160 degrees of freedom was .24. This value was used in *t* tests to determine whether average correlations differed from zero. Correlations in Table 1 whose absolute value is equal to or greater than .16 are significant at the .05 level. For the .01 and .001 levels, the corresponding values are .21 and .36, respectively. The pooled estimate of the variance was also used to test differences between means in Table 1. Differences equal to or greater than .22 are significant at the .05 level. For the .01 and .001 levels, the corresponding values are .28 and .36, respectively.

**Table 1    Average raw correlations from Experiment 1**

| Correlation | EG | CT | FOI | I |
|---|---|---|---|---|
| Goal-derived categories | | | | |
| OD | .39 | .10 | .31 | .22 |
| EG | | .38 | .72 | .70 |
| CT | | | .30 | .36 |
| FOI | | | | .56 |
| Common taxonomic categories | | | | |
| OD | .55 | .24 | .59 | .45 |
| EG | | .63 | .47 | .46 |
| CT | | | .10 | .03 |
| FOI | | | | .49 |

*Note.* The correlations are averages across categories. OD is output dominance, EG is exemplar goodness, CT is central tendency, FOI is frequency of instantiation, and I is ideals.

Most of the average correlations were significant for the goal-derived categories. Because the highest correlations were between ideals and exemplar goodness and between frequency and exemplar goodness, it appears that ideals and frequency are the determinants most central to the structure of goal-derived categories. Although central tendency (as measured by family resemblance) correlated significantly with typicality, it predicted typicality significantly less than did ideals and frequency.

Most of the average correlations were also significant for the common taxonomic categories. As predicted, central tendency predicted exemplar goodness. However ideals and frequency predicted exemplar goodness just as well for these categories (i.e., there were no significant differences between these three correlations).

As found by Barsalou ( 1983), typicality and production frequency correlated less for goal-derived than for common taxonomic categories. Better established representations in memory for common taxonomic categories may be the source of this difference. Highly familiar categories may have strong associations in memory from their category concepts to their typical examplars such that these exemplars are usually the first ones generated. Less established associations for goal-derived categories may result in generation being more random such that output dominance and typicality are not as well correlated. Consistent with this explanation is the additional finding that subjects generated exemplars at a faster rate for common taxonomic than for goal-derived categories. The average number of exemplars produced by a subject per category during the 15 s generation period was 4.28 for common taxonomic categories and 3.58 for goal-derived categories, $t(16) = 2.86$, $SE = .25$, $p < .02$.

200

*Partial correlations.* The following analysis assumed that there are three predictor variables — central tendency, ideals, and frequency — and that there are two criterion variables — exemplar goodness and output dominance. This analysis examines the possibility that some of the significant correlations discussed in the last section primarily resulted from variance shared between predictors. That is, a predictor could have correlated significantly with a criterion because it shared substantial variance with another predictor that was more strongly correlated with the criterion. For example, central tendency might have correlated with typicality in goal-derived categories because it was highly correlated with two stronger predictors, namely, ideals and frequency.

To assess the *unique* predictive power of each predictor, partial correlations were computed to remove shared variance. Of interest was how well a given predictor correlated with each criterion variable after the other two predictors had been partialed out. For each category, therefore, the second-order partial correlation was computed for each predictor, this being done separately for exemplar goodness and output dominance. The averages across categories are shown in Table 2.

**Table 2    Average second-order partial correlations from Experiment 1**

| Correlation | Original correlation | Second-order partial correlation |
|---|---|---|
| Goal-derived categories | | |
| EG–CT | .38 | .05 |
| EG–FOI | .72 | .51 |
| EG–I | .70 | .44 |
| OD–CT | .10 | −.05 |
| OD–FOI | .31 | .25 |
| OD–I | .22 | .04 |
| Common taxonomic categories | | |
| EG–CT | .63 | .71 |
| EG–FOI | .47 | .36 |
| EG–I | .46 | .45 |
| OD–CT | .24 | .24 |
| OD–FOI | .59 | .43 |
| OD–I | .45 | .26 |

*Note.* OD is output dominance, EG is exemplar goodness, CT is central tendency, FOI is frequency of instantiation, and I is ideals.

The variance for each of the six second-order partial correlations was computed across the nine categories within each category type. These 12 variances were averaged to form a pooled estimate of the variance, and the resulting standard deviation with 96 degrees of freedom was .25. This value was used in $t$ tests to determine which overall correlations differed from zero. Second-order partial correlations in Table 2 whose absolute value is equal to or greater than .16 are significant at the .05 level. For the .01 and .001 levels, the corresponding values are .21 and .27, respectively. The pooled estimate of the variance was also used to test differences between means. Differences equal to or greater than .24 are significant at the .05 level. For the .01 and .001 level, the corresponding values are .32 and .41, respectively.

For the goal-derived categories, the original relation between central tendency and typicality completely disappeared when ideals and frequency were partialed out. Central tendency accounted for no unique variance in the graded structures of goal-derived categories. Instead its apparent predictive power resulted from variance it shared with the other two predictors. Although partialing out the other predictors resulted in a loss of predicted power for ideals and frequency, each accounted for unique variance in the graded structures of goal-derived categories. Because frequency still accounted for unique variance after central tendency had been partialed out, frequency is not an artifact of central tendency as suggested by Rosch (1974).

For the common taxonomic categories, central tendency became an even better predictor of typicality after ideals and frequency were partialed out (both were suppressor variables; e.g., see Allen & Yen, 1979). In addition, central tendency was a much better predictor of typicality in common taxonomic than in goal-derived categories. It should be pointed out that this difference was not due to smaller ranges for these variables in goal-derived categories, because these ranges did not differ (as reported earlier).

Although central tendency accounted for a large amount of unique typicality variance in common taxonomic categories, ideals and frequency also accounted for significant amounts of unique typicality variance in these categories. In fact, these two second-order partials did not differ significantly from the corresponding ones for the goal-derived categories. Although ideals and frequency accounted for significant amounts of unique typicality variance in common taxonomic categories, they were significantly less predictive than central tendency.

Table 3 shows the second-order partial correlations for individual categories. Although there was much consistency within category types, categories varied substantially in their best predictors. In general, the goal-derived categories were most often structured by both ideals and frequency. However *camping equipment* and *picnic activities* were structured primarily by frequency, and *snow clothes* and *weekend entertainment* were structured primarily by ideals. Central tendency structured every common taxonomic category. However these categories differed from each other in the extent to which ideals and frequency were important. Both were important for *vehicles, birds,* and *weapons.* Frequency alone was important for *fruit,* and ideals alone was important for *clothing* and *sports.* It should be noted that failure of an ideal to predict typicality does not mean its category has no ideals, because the important ideals may not have been observed. Moreover some categories may have several ideals, all of which must be observed to estimate the role of ideals completely.

Turning to the second-order partial correlations in Table 2 for output dominance, the most important predictor for both category types was frequency. The importance of frequency for predicting output dominance is consistent with one of the oldest assumptions of memory theory: The more often two things co-occur — in this case a category concept and an exemplar concept — the more likely one is to elicit the other in a production task. The pattern of prediction varied for the two category types with regard to the other two predictors. Neither central tendency or ideals uniquely predicted output dominance for goal-derived categories, whereas both did for common taxonomic categories.[6]

**Table 3    Second-order partial correlations by categories from Experiment 1**

| Correlation | EG–CT | EG–I | EG–FOI |
|---|---|---|---|
| Goal-derived categories | | | |
| Birthday presents | .42 | .53 | .80 |
| (how happy people are to receive it) | | | |
| Camping equipment | .15 | −.12 | .66 |
| (importance to survival) | | | |
| Transportation for getting from | −.51 | .56 | .40 |
| San Francisco to New York | | | |
| (how fast it gets people there) | | | |
| Personality characteristics in people that | | | |
| prevent someone from being friends with them | −.06 | .78 | .45 |
| (how much people dislike it) | | | |
| Things to do for weekend entertainment | .34 | .43 | .08 |
| (how much people enjoy it) | | | |
| Foods not to eat on a diet | .31 | .53 | .62 |
| (how many calories it has) | | | |
| Clothes to wear in the snow | −.22 | .64 | .34 |
| (how warm it keeps people) | | | |
| Picnic activities | −.28 | .17 | .83 |
| (how much fun people think it is) | | | |
| Things to take from one's home during a fire | .29 | .47 | .41 |
| (how valuable people think it is) | | | |
| Common taxonomic categories | | | |
| Vehicles | .86 | .63 | .53 |
| (how efficient a type of transportation it is) | | | |
| Clothing | .71 | .81 | −.10 |
| (how necessary it is to wear it) | | | |
| Birds | .75 | .42 | .78 |
| (how much people like it) | | | |
| Weapons | .59 | .91 | .68 |
| (how effective it is) | | | |
| Vegetables | .69 | −.02 | .29 |
| (how much people like it) | | | |
| Sports | .74 | .53 | .11 |
| (how much people enjoy it) | | | |
| Fruit | .71 | .34 | .49 |
| (how much people like it) | | | |
| Furniture | .84 | .03 | .14 |
| (how necessary it is to have) | | | |
| Tools | .49 | .37 | .29 |
| (how important it is to have) | | | |

*Note.* Ideal dimensions are in parentheses. EG is exemplar goodness, CT is central tendency, FOI is frequency of instantiation, and I is ideals.

*The relation between typicality and the central tendencies of ideal dimensions.* If central tendency is the sole determinant of typicality, then a category's central tendency on an ideal dimension should be a better predictor of typicality than its ideal value on that dimension. More specifically, the distance of an exemplar from the central tendency of an ideal dimension should be a better predictor of typicality than its distance from the ideal value of that dimension. In *things not to eat on a diet,* for example, exemplars should become more typical as they approach the central tendency for the ideal dimension of *calories* than as they approach the ideal value of *indefinitely many.*

To test this possibility, the difference was computed between each exemplar's average rating on the ideal dimension and its category's average rating on that dimension (i.e., the average rating across all exemplars in the category). The absolute values of these differences which reflect distance from central tendency were then correlated with typicality. If exemplars become more typical as their value on an ideal dimension approximates the central tendency of the dimension — that is, as exemplars possess increasing family resemblance on that dimension — then large negative correlations between absolute differences and typicality should occur. The average correlation, however, was –.19 for the common taxonomic categories and –.01 for the goal-derived categories. The proximity of exemplars to the central tendencies of ideal dimensions does not predict typicality.

In contrast, the proximity of exemplars to the ideal values of ideal dimensions does predict typicality. Because the ideal values of these dimensions were all at their upper end, positive correlations between typicality and amount on ideal dimensions indicate that typicality is increasing as exemplars approximate ideal values. As reported earlier, the average correlation between typicality and amount on ideal dimensions was .70 for goal-derived categories and .46 for common taxonomic categories. Even after partialing out the other two predictors, increasing values on ideal dimensions still correlated substantially with typicality (.44 and .45, respectively). Ideal values on these dimensions are clearly more important to typicality than central tendencies.

*Familiarity versus frequency of instantiation.* As noted earlier, Ashcraft (1978), Glass and Meany (1978), Hampton and Gardiner (1983), and Malt and Smith (1982) all found that typicality increased as exemplars became more familiar.[7] It is therefore important to determine if familiarity entered into subjects' frequency of instantiation judgments in the current experiment. To assess the relation between familiarity and frequency of instantiation, 10 additional subjects rated each exemplar of each category on a 9-point scale for how familiar they were with that kind of thing. Subjects received the exemplar names in one of two random orders. In contrast to the procedure for rating frequency of instantiation, the exemplars were not blocked by category, and nothing was said about the categories underlying the list. The average ratings for exemplars (which are shown in the appendix) were then correlated with other measures of interest for each category, and these correlations were averaged across categories within the two category types.

The average correlation between familiarity and frequency of instantiation was greater for common taxonomic categories, .57, than for goal-derived categories, .21, $t(16) = 3.60$, $SE = .10$, $p < .01$. But both values are much less than one would expect if familiarity and frequency of instantiation measure the same thing. According to reliability theory (see Guilford & Fruchter, 1973, pp. 263–264; Barsalou & Sewell, 1984), these correlations should approximate their group reliabilities if the two measures are identical. Given that the mean group reliabilities were .89 for familiarity and .78 for frequency of instantiation, these two measures are not the same.

Regarding the prediction of typicality, familiarity was a much poorer predictor than frequency of instantiation. The average correlation between familiarity and typicality was only .03 for the goal-derived categories and only .19 for the common taxonomic categories. These correlations are much smaller than those just reported between frequency of instantiation and typicality (.72 for goal-derived categories and .47 for common taxonomic categories). Moreover when frequency of instantiation was partialed out of the correlations between familiarity and typicality, they became slightly negative, indicating that familiarity did not account for any unique variance (–.16 for goal-derived categories and –.11 for common taxonomic categories). In contrast, when familiarity was partialed out of the correlations between typicality and frequency of instantiation, the original correlations were unaffected (from .74 to .72 for goal-derived categories, and from .45 to .47 for common taxonomic categories).

Contrary to what earlier studies suggest, familiarity per se does not appear important to graded structure. Instead its relation with typicality appears to reflect variance it shares with frequency of instantiation.

**Discussion**

Although the work of Rosch and Mervis (1975) and Rosch, Simpson, *et al*. (1976) shows that central tendency can be an important determinant of graded structure, it clearly does not determine the graded structure of every category. Although central tendency (as measured by family resemblance) had a raw correlation of .38 with typicality for the goal-derived categories, it dropped to .05 when the other two predictors were partialed out. Central tendency accounted for no unique variance of its own, but only correlated with typicality initially because of variance it shared with two stronger predictors. These other predictors — ideals and frequency of instantiation — each accounted for substantial amounts of unique typicality variance in goal-derived categories.

Barsalou (1981, Experiment 1) provides a replication of this finding and also shows that it holds within specific subjects. After generating exemplars for 12 goal-derived categories, each subject provided typicality, frequency of instantiation, ideal dimension, and family resemblance judgments for the exemplars he or she generated. Correlations between the three predictors and typicality were computed individually for each subject within each category. Across subjects and categories, the average raw correlation between central tendency (as measured by family resemblance) and typicality was –.15. The highest value that the average correlation across categories ever reached for a given subject was .19, whereas the lowest value was –.58. Similar to the current experiment, ideals and frequency of instantiation correlated highly with typicality (average raw correlations across subjects of .51 and .60, respectively).

The role of central tendency clearly varies between common taxonomic and goal-derived categories. Although central tendency plays no role in the graded structures of goal-derived categories, it is clearly the most important determinant of graded structure in common taxonomic categories, correlating .71 with typicality after ideals and frequency of instantiation were partialed out. However factors besides central tendency also play roles in the graded structures of common taxonomic categories. Contrary to Mervis et al. (1976) and Rosch, Simpson, et al. (1976), frequency is important to graded structure. Frequency of instantiation accounted for as much unique variance in common taxonomic categories as in goal-derived categories. Moreover, because frequency of instantiation accounted for typicality variance even after central tendency had been partialed out, frequency is not an artifact of central tendency, as suggested by Rosch (1974). In addition, familiarity exhibited no significant relation with typicality for either the common taxonomic or goal-derived categories. Instead the important form of frequency appears to be frequency of instantiation. The more often exemplars are subjectively perceived in the context of their category, the more typical they become of it.

Ideals also accounted for significant amounts of unique variance in common taxonomic categories. In fact, ideals were as important in common taxonomic categories as they were in goal-derived categories. Although central tendency is the most important determinant of graded structure in common taxonomic categories, the structure of these categories also seems to depend on goals these categories serve. Because the ideal dimension of *how effective it is* had a second-order partial of .91 with typicality in *weapons*, goal-related information is clearly central to this category's graded structure. Similarly, the concept for *vehicles* appears to contain goal-related information regarding *efficiency*, and the concepts for *sports*, *birds*, and *fruit* appear to contain goal-related information regarding *enjoyment*.

These data indicate that graded structure is not a fixed product of central tendency. Ideals and frequency of instantiation also play significant roles in determining the graded structures of categories. Consequently the origins of graded structure are much more complex than has so far been credited by previous work. This flexibility is underlined by the fact that individual categories vary substantially in the combination of factors that determines their graded structure (see Table 3).

In a related study, Barsalou and Sewell (1985) found a similar pattern of results for category verification. Analogous to the current study, central tendency predicted verification time in common taxonomic categories but not in goal-derived categories, whereas frequency of instantiation was the best predictor in goal-derived categories. Although ideals and familiarity correlated with verification time in both category types, they did so primarily through variance shared with central tendency and frequency of instantiation. Because this pattern of results for category verification is similar to the one just reported for typicality, it appears that similar processes may underlie these two categorization tasks.

Finally, it should be noted that the experiment by Barsalou and Sewell (1985), along with the one just reported, both suffer from the following limitation. Because only one ideal was observed for each category, and because each ideal was picked intuitively, these experiments only show that ideals are related to typicality; they do not provide accurate estimates of the strength of this relation (although they do provide minimum estimates). It is likely that more careful and exhaustive sampling would provide ideals that predict typicality to a higher extent than has been observed so far.

### Experiment 2

Because the previous study was correlational, referring to ideals, central tendency, and frequency of instantiation as determinants of graded structure has been somewhat unjustified. If these factors are indeed determinants of graded structure, they must be shown to be causes of it.

Actually, Rosch and Mervis (1975) and Rosch, Simpson, *et al.* (1976) found in experimental studies with artificial categories that central tendency (as measured by family resemblance) causally determined graded structure. Although Rosch, Simpson, *et al.* (1976) also reported that frequency did not causally determine graded structure, their experimental design was not capable of detecting simultaneous effects of central tendency and frequency. However when central tendency and frequency are orthogonally manipulated in an experimental setting such that they can be detected simultaneously, both causally determine typicality (Barsalou, 1981, Experiment 3, which is the same as Experiment 2a in Barsalou, 1984). So far, no experiments have shown that ideals are causal determinants of graded structure. One purpose of this next experiment, therefore, was to examine whether ideals also causally determine typicality.

A second purpose of this experiment was to examine whether the determinants of a category's graded structure depend on the context in which the category is processed. Instead of there being a fixed determinant responsible for a category's graded structure on all occasions, different contexts may engender the use of different determinants such that the category's graded structure changes. For example, some contexts may engender the use of central tendency, whereas others may engender the use of ideals.

Subjects acquired two artificial categories whose exemplars each contained a person's last name (e.g., *Davis)* associated with five things they like to do in their spare time (e.g., *go horseback riding, jog daily, collect antiques, cook Chinese food, meditate).* Two variables structured each category. First, each category varied along a *defining dimension.* All members of one category *jogged,* and all members of the other category *read the newspaper.* Within each category, exemplars varied in the extent to which they jogged or read the newspaper (i.e., their *amount* on the defining dimension). Exemplars either jogged (read the newspaper) *daily, weekly,* or *monthly.* The second way in which exemplars varied was in how similar they were to the central tendency of their respective category, having either a high, medium, or low number of their category's characteristic activities. Categories were constructed such that amount on the defining dimension and similarity to central tendency were orthogonally manipulated.

The central manipulation in this experiment was how subjects were induced to perceive the defining dimensions. Subjects in the *related dimension* condition were told that exemplars who *jogged* belonged to the category of *physical education teachers* and that exemplars who *read the newspaper* belonged to the category of *current events teachers*. Because most people believe that physical education teachers ideally should be physically fit and that current events teachers ideally should be well-read, it was expected that these beliefs about ideals would determine graded structure. The more often a physical education teacher jogged (e.g., daily versus weekly versus monthly), the more typical that exemplar should be of its category; and the more often a current events teacher read the newspaper, the more typical that exemplar should be of its category. For each category, people should use an ideal obtained from stereotypes to determine graded structure. Because subjects may focus on how well exemplars approximate these ideals, they may not abstract each category's central tendency (although ideals and central tendency could simultaneously determine graded structure because they were manipulated orthogonally).

Subjects in the *unrelated dimension* condition were told that the category defined by one dimension contained *Q programmers* (i.e., people who program in the Q programming language) and that the category defined by the other dimension contained *Z programmers*. Because subjects probably do not have any beliefs about what constitutes ideal Q and Z programmers, it was unlikely that ideals would determine typicality for these subjects. Increasing (or decreasing) values on the defining dimensions should not determine typicality because subjects have no reason to assume that one value on a defining dimension is any more ideal than they others (e.g., there is no obvious ideal value for how often a Q programmer should jog). In addition, the spare time activities that constituted each exemplar were chosen so as not to be meaningfully related to computer programming in general. Consequently exemplars also did not vary in how ideal they were of all computer programmers. Because subjects could not use ideals to structure the categories, it was expected that they would instead abstract the central tendencies of these categories and use them to determine graded structure.

One other between subjects manipulation was included. Half the subjects performed a *relevant processing* task, and half performed an *irrelevant processing* task. Relevant processing required that subjects learn to discriminate members of the two categories from one another, where the defining dimensions and central tendencies of the category provided information relevant to performing discrimination. Irrelevant processing required that subjects decide which of two members of the *same* category were better suited to achieve some peripheral goal. The defining dimensions and central tendencies were irrelevant to these decisions, which were always based on other activities of the exemplars. It was expected that irrelevant processing would attenuate the extent to which ideals determined typicality in the related dimension condition and the extent to which central tendency determined typicality in the unrelated dimension condition. Because subjects need not focus on defining dimensions and central tendencies to perform the irrelevant processing task, they should not abstract this information.

### Method

*Materials.* Two categories of nine exemplars were formed. Each exemplar had a common surname (e.g., *Davis, Wilson, Adams*) associated with five activities they do in their spare time (e.g., *dance, renovate houses, write poetry, go to movies, read the newspaper daily*). Each category had a defining dimension: All members of one category *jogged*, and all members of the other category *read the newspaper*. Three members of each category performed their defining activity *daily*, three performed it *weekly*, and three performed it *monthly*. Each category possessed three characteristic activities, each of which occurred for six category members and for no nonmembers. These activities were not correlated with one another or with values on the defining dimensions. Exemplars varied in how similar they were to the central tendency of their category, with an exemplar's similarity to its category's central tendency being the number of characteristic activities it possessed. Three exemplars in each category possessed all three characteristic activities, three possessed two, and three possessed one. For each level of similarity to central tendency, one exemplar had a *daily* value on the defining dimension, one had a *weekly* value, and the other had a *monthly* value (i.e., similarity to central tendency and amount on the defining dimension were orthogonally manipulated). Except for the defining and characteristic activities, no activity occurred more than once in a category. Finally, one activity for each exemplar was an *irrelevant processing* activity (to be described in a moment). There were nine such activities each occurring twice, once for one exemplar in each category. Only these activities occurred in both categories. Two versions of the materials were formed in which surnames and spare time activities were randomly assigned to the stimulus structure, within the constraints of the design.

In the related dimension condition, the category defined by *jogging* was called *physical education teachers* and the category defined by *reading the newspaper* was called *current events teachers*. In the unrelated dimension condition the categories were called *Q programmers* and *Z programmers*.

*Acquisition procedure.* Subjects were asked to imagine they were being trained at a personnel agency to find teachers for high schools and were told that people's spare time activities predict the courses they are good at teaching. Subjects in the relevant processing condition were told they would learn to discriminate one category from the other on the basis of their spare time activities. Subjects in the irrelevant processing condition were told their personnel agency already had pools for each kind of teacher and that their job was to find someone from a particular pool who would be good at teaching a *special interest course*.

On each acquisition trial, subjects in the relevant processing condition received one description from each category, followed by a request to choose the one that belonged to a particular category (e.g., "Choose the better teacher of programming language Q"). Subjects in the irrelevant processing condition received two descriptions from the *same* category, followed by a request to choose the one better able to teach a special interest course (e.g., "Choose the Q programmer better able to teach *how to cook Indian food)*. The irrelevant processing activity of the correct exemplar was always related to the topic of the special interest course (e.g., *invests in real estate* was the irrelevant processing activity of an exemplar who would be good at teaching a special interest course on *how to invest in gold)*. As described earlier, the irrelevant processing activities were never defining or characteristic of their category. Because an exemplar was the correct choice on more than one trial, it was always chosen to teach a different special interest course on each occasion. So if *invests in real estate* were an exemplar's irrelevant processing activity, that exemplar might be chosen to teach *how to invest in stocks* on one trial, *how to invest in gold* on a second trial, and *how to invest in bonds* on a third trial. Each of the 18 exemplars served as the target exemplar on three trials in all conditions.

Subjects performed the experiment in individual booths. On the table before them was a stack of 54 cards (one for each trial) and a response sheet. A tape recording paced all aspects of the experiment. At the start of each trial, the recording stated the trial number. Subjects read the request on the top card, decided which exemplar was correct, and wrote that person's initial on the response sheet next to the trial number (i.e., the name for each exemplar had a unique initial). Twelve seconds after the trial number was stated, the recording provided the correct name. For the next 7 s, subjects studied the correct exemplar's spare time activities. At the end of this period, the recording instructed subjects to turn the card over and, 3 s later, stated a spare time activity. Subjects had 3 s to decide if this was one possessed by the correct exemplar and circled *yes* or *no* on their response sheet. The choice of the probe was random with the constraints that: (a) on true trials, the probe was only true of the target, and (b) on false trials, it was not true of either the target or the contrast stimulus. The probe task served to insure that subjects encoded every activity for each exemplar.

For relevant processing, each category was correct on 50% of the trials, and for irrelevant processing, each category was used on 50% of the trials. Orthogonally varied with the target category were whether the target was on the left or the right, and whether the answer to the probe task was true or false. The contrast stimuli (i.e., the nontarget stimuli for each trial) were randomly chosen with the constraints that each exemplar occurred as a constrast three times, and no exemplar was the constrast for a given target more than once. The 54 trials were randomly ordered for each of two versions with the constraint that an exemplar was never the target on two or more consecutive trials. Prior to the 54 trials, all subjects briefly studied a page showing all 18 exemplars blocked by category to develop an initial impression of the categories.

*Test procedure.* Following acquisition, subjects performed three additional tasks. First, they provided paced typicality ratings. Subjects were asked to imagine they were teaching another employee about the two populations of teachers. As they considered each exemplar, they were to tell the other person how good an example it was of its category on the basis of experience acquired during the learning phase of the experiment. Each subject received the nine exemplars of each category blocked and in a different random order. Every 12 s, a recording instructed subjects to read a new card and rate the exemplar on it for 'how good an example it was of its category." The card for each exemplar contained both its surname and its five activities. Subjects used a scale from 1 to 7, where 1 meant the exemplar was a *poor example* and 7 meant it was *excellent*. Only one exemplar was ever visible at a time to a subject.

Subjects' second task was to *rank* exemplars by typicality. Subjects were able to observe all 18 exemplars at once and had as much time as they needed.

Subjects' third task was to fill out a questionnaire. They described their strategies for the typicality tasks and the activities they thought were characteristic of each category.

*Subjects.* Fifty-four Stanford University students participated for either credit plus pay or for pay only. Subjects participated in groups of one to four, and each session lasted about 1 hr and 15 min. Six subjects' data were discarded because of equipment failure. Six subjects were randomly assigned to each of the eight between-subjects conditions created by crossing the dimension relatedness, processing type, and version factors.

## Results

*Typicality.* Because the same pattern of significant effects occurred for the ratings and rankings, only the rating data are reported. An analysis of variance (ANOVA) was performed on the ratings in which the factors were ideals (i.e., amount on the defining dimensions), central tendency (i.e., number of characteristic properties), dimension relatedness, processing type, and version. The relevant means are shown in Table 4.

**Table 4    Average exemplar goodness ratings from Experiment 2**

| Condition | Central tendencey | | | Ideals | | |
|---|---|---|---|---|---|---|
| | Low | Medium | High | Low | Medium | High |
| Unrelated dimension | | | | | | |
| Relevant processing | 4.24 | 4.99 | 5.44 | 4.96 | 4.79 | 4.92 |
| Irrelevant processing | 4.44 | 4.71 | 5.11 | 4.88 | 4.51 | 4.88 |
| Average | 4.34 | 4.85 | 5.28 | 4.92 | 4.65 | 4.90 |
| Related dimension | | | | | | |
| Relevant processing | 4.58 | 4.51 | 4.72 | 3.89 | 4.47 | 5.46 |
| Irrelevant processing | 4.06 | 4.08 | 4.76 | 3.81 | 4.03 | 5.07 |
| Average | 4.32 | 4.30 | 4.74 | 3.85 | 4.25 | 5.26 |

*Note.* The scale is from 1 to 7, where 1 is for *poor examples*, and 7 is for *excellent examples*.

Overall, ideals and central tendency both affected typicality, $F(2, 80) = 20.58$, $MS_e = 1.03$, $p < .001$ and $F(2, 80) = 20.16$, $MS_e = .85$, $p < .001$, respectively. However each factor interacted with dimension relatedness. Ideals interacted with dimension relatedness, $F(2, 80) = 18.01$, $MS_e = 1.03$, $p < .001$, having a significant effect in the related dimension condition, $F(1, 80) = 69.49$, $MS_e = 1.03$, $p < .001$, but having no effect in the unrelated dimension condition, $F(1, 80) = .01$, $MS_e = 1.03$, $p > .25$. This indicates that ideals determined typicality only when the defining dimensions were related to subjects' stereotypes for the categories. Central tendency interacted with dimension relatedness in the converse manner, $F(2, 80) = 3.83$, $MS_e = .85$, $p < .025$, having a larger effect in the unrelated dimension condition, $F(1, 80) = 37.42$, $MS_e = .85$, $p < .001$, than in the related dimension condition, $F(1, 80) = 7.47$, $MS_e = .85$, $p < .01$. This indicates that similarity to central tendency played a stronger role in determining typicality when subjects did not have ideals for the categories. The significant effect of central tendency in the related dimension condition was entirely attributable to the irrelevant processing condition, $F(1, 80) = 10.38$, $MS_e = .85$, $p < .01$. The fact that there was no effect of central tendency in the relevant processing condition, $F(1, 80) = .42$, $MS_e = .85$, $p > .25$, demonstrates that central tendency may play no role in determining graded structure under some conditions.

Taken together, these results demonstrate that (a) ideals, as well as central tendency, can causally determine graded structure, (b) the determinants of a particular category's graded structure can vary with context, and (c) multiple determinants can simultaneously determine graded structure in a particular category (e.g., for irrelevant processing subjects in the related dimension condition).

Irrelevant processing did not attenuate the effects of ideals and central tendency as expected. It it not clear why having subjects focus on irrelevant information did not reduce the effects of these variables on typicality. Irrelevant processing subjects may have had sufficient exposure to exemplars during acquisition to abstract central tendencies; and they may have later used ideals at testing when they appeared relevant to the categories.

There were unpredicted interactions between central tendency and ideals, $F(4, 160) = 6.44, MS_e = .44, p < .001$, and between processing type, dimension relatedness, and central tendency, $F(2, 80) = 3.27, MS_e = .85, p < .05$. These may have resulted in some way from two further significant interactions involving version.

*Acquisition performance.* Performance on both the choice and probe tasks was excellent. For each, an analysis of variance (ANOVA) was performed on subjects' error percentages, transformed as suggested by Winer (1971). The average error rate for the choice task was .038. The only effect was a marginally significant interaction between central tendency and dimension relatedness, $F(2, 80) = 2.81, MS_e = .01, .10 > p > .05$. Subjects in the unrelated dimension condition made fewer errors as similarity to central tendency increased, but subjects in the related dimension condition did not. This further supports the conclusion that central tendency was more important for subjects in the unrelated dimension condition than for subjects in the related dimension condition. For the probe task, the average error rate was .064, and there were no significant effects.

*Questionnaire.* Perhaps because of the ease with which people ascribe traits to behaviors, 36 subjects mentioned assimilating the categories to personality stereotypes. When asked to describe their strategies or the characteristic spare-time activities of each category, these subjects described a category in the context of a stereotype. In general, the stereotypes that subjects adopted stemmed from the defining dimensions. Categories defined by *jogs* were assimilated to physically oriented stereotypes, whereas categories defined by *reads the newspaper* were assimilated to culturally and socially oriented stereotypes.

There was a substantial difference between the reports of subjects in the related and unrelated dimension conditions. Of the 24 subjects in the unrelated dimension condition, 14 reported using central tendency when judging typicality, and 1 reported using ideals. Of the 24 subjects in the related dimension condition, 2 reported using central tendency, and 19 reported using ideals. Subjects were not probed directly about specific strategies but volunteered them in response to an open-ended question about the strategies they used. These strategies were distributed evenly over the relevant and irrelevant processing conditions and are clearly consistent with the rating data in Table 4.

## *Discussion*

These results demonstrate that ideals as well as central tendency can causally determine graded structure. When subjects were aware of ideals for the categories, an exemplar's similarity to the relevant ideal determined its typicality. These results even go so far as to suggest that ideals may be a more important determinant of graded structure than is central tendency. When subjects were aware of ideals for the categories, central tendency either had no effect (in the relevant processing condition) or had a smaller effect (in the irrelevant processing condition).

These results also show that the determinants of a particular category's graded structure depend on the context in which the category is perceived. In some contexts, ideals may determine a category's graded structure; whereas in others, central tendency may determine a different graded structure. In addition, ideals and central tendency can simultaneously determine a category's graded structure, as shown by the results for irrelevant processing subjects in the related dimension condition. This is consistent with the results from Experiment 1 in which ideals, central tendency, and frequency of instantiation simultaneously determined graded structure in some categories.

## General discussion

These studies indicate that graded structure is a complex and dynamic phenomenon. It is not the case that a single determinant, such as central tendency, is responsible for the graded structure of all categories. Instead at least two other factors — ideals and frequency of instantiation — also play major roles in determining graded structure. It is also not the case that the graded structure of a category remains constant across contexts. As shown by Experiment 2, ideals may determine a category's graded structure in one context, and central tendency may determine a different graded structure in another.

Findings further demonstrating such flexibility have been reported by Roth and Shoben (1983) and Barsalou and Sewell (1984). Roth and Shoben (1983) varied a category term's linguistic context and found that its typical referents varied across contexts. *Animals,* for example, had different graded structures when it appeared in "Stacy volunteered to milk the *animal* whenever she visited the farm" and "Fran pleaded with her father to let her ride the *animal.*" Whereas *cow* and *goat* were typical in the first context, *horse* and *mule* were typical in the second. Barsalou and Sewell (1984) found that the graded structures of both common taxonomic and goal-derived categories shifted substantially when people took various points of view while judging typicality. For example, American undergraduates believe that *robin* and *eagle* are typical exemplars of birds from the point of view of the average American citizen, but believe that *swan* and *peacock* are typical from the point of view of the average Chinese citizen. Although both studies demonstrate flexibility in graded structure, neither examines the determinants responsible for such shifts. Consequently it is not clear whether such flexibility results from changes in ideals, central tendency, frequency of instantiation, or other determinants.

Most important, such flexibility indicates that graded structure does not reflect some invariant property of categories — there do not appear to be invariant structures that underlie categories. Instead such flexibility suggests that people's perception and structuring of categories is a highly dynamic and context-dependent process.

One way to explain dynamic graded structures begins by assuming that people have a highly creative ability to construct concepts, where concept refers to the information that represents a category (e.g., a prototype). As suggested by Barsalou (in press), people may not retrieve the same concept from long-term memory everytime they deal with a particular category. Instead they may construct a diverse variety of concepts in working memory to represent a particular category across different situations such that the concept used to represent a category is rarely, if ever, the same. According to this view, long-term memory does not contain invariant concepts. Instead it contains generic and episodic information from which concepts are constructed. Although some information about a category may always be incorporated into a concept (context-independent information), other information may only be incorporated in relevant contexts (context-dependent information). As suggested by Barsalou (1982), context-independent and context-dependent information provide stability and instability, respectively, for the concepts that represent a particular category. Barsalou (in press) outlines a general theory of how concepts are constructed in working memory from information in long-term memory.

Dynamic graded structures may simply reflect this highly creative ability to construct concepts. Assuming that an exemplar's typicality increases as it becomes more similar to the concept for its category (Barsalou, 1983; Hampton, 1979; Smith *et al.*, 1974), graded structure will change with different concepts. As the information comprising a concept changes, different exemplars will be highly similar to the concept such that the ordering of exemplars by typicality changes. For example, as a category is perceived in the context of different goals, different ideals may be incorporated into its concept. If different exemplars best approximate these ideals, then different exemplars will be typical in the respective contexts. Similarly the central tendency of a category may vary across contexts, with different exemplars being highly similar to these different central tendencies. For example, the central tendencies of *animals* on the dimensions of *size* and *ferocity* may be higher when viewing the category from a forest ranger's point of view than from a pet store owner's point of view. As a result, different exemplars will be typical from these two perspectives. In general, graded structure may largely reflect people's current concept of a category, and to the extent this concept changes, their graded structure will change.

It appears, however, that another factor is also important for graded structure. As found in Experiment 1, frequency of instantiation is an important predictor of typicality. One explanation of this finding is that exemplars seem to occur frequently in a category because they possess properties that occur often across the category's exemplars (Rosch, 1974). This property frequency explanation of graded structure, however, is equivalent to the central tendency explanation; both assume typicality increases as exemplars become more similar to the characteristic properties of their category. But if frequency of instantiation ratings were based on central tendency, then they should not predict typicality after central tendency is partialed out. As found in Experiment 1, however, partialing out central tendency only slightly diminished the substantial predictive power of frequency of instantiation.

Because frequency of instantiation's role in graded structure does not seem to depend on central tendency information in the concept for a category, another explanation is that it depends on frequency information stored with exemplars. More specifically, information may be stored with exemplars that in some way reflects how often they have been encountered in the context of their category. When people estimate an exemplar's typicality, such information may be accessed and be incorporated into judgments of typicality. To the extent an exemplar has a high frequency of instantiation in a category, it is perceived as typical.

This use of frequency further complicates our understanding of people's sensitivity to frequency. It is well known that people acquire information without much effort that allows them to estimate how often they have encountered particular items (see the reviews by Hasher & Zacks, 1979; Hintzman, 1976). This kind of frequency is analogous to familiarity in Experiment 1, which reflects an exemplar's category-independent frequency. However people also appear sensitive to other kinds of frequency. First, Alba, Chromiak, Hasher, and Attig (1980) and Barsalou and Ross (in press) have shown that people acquire information without much effort that allows them to estimate how often a superordinate category has been instantiated by different exemplars (superordinate frequency). Second, Hintzman and Block (1971) have shown that people acquire information without much effort that allows them to estimate how often an item has occurred in each of several lists. This latter kind of frequency is analogous to frequency of instantiation, which is how often an exemplar has occurred in each of several categories. Similar to how familiarity, superordinate frequency, and list frequency are acquired, frequency of instantiation may also be acquired in the course of everyday experience without much effort. Such information may later become available when exemplars are accessed and may affect processing during tasks such as typicality judgments.

In general, it appears that there are many different kinds of information available for people to use when judging typicality. People can incorporate various ideals and central tendencies into category concepts when making typicality judgments, and they can also incorporate information reflecting frequency of instantiation that may be stored with exemplars. Given that more than one of these factors often predicted graded structure in Experiment 1 (see Table 3), it appears that people may often simultaneously incorporate several kinds of information into their judgments of typicality. And given that these factors varied widely in the extent to which they predicted graded structure, it also appears that people have the ability to differentially weight these sources of information.

But what determines the information used to structure a particular category on a particular occasion? What conditions determine whether ideals, central tendency, frequency of instantiation, or other factors are used to generate graded structure? And what determines the relative weighting of the information chosen?

As suggested earlier, ideals may become important when categories are used in the context of achieving goals. Little if anything, however, is known about how goals and ideals are actually related, and much remains to be learned about how goals generate ideals. Ideals may also be important in other ways. For example Lakoff (in press) suggests that people may at times use "paragons" to represent categories (e.g., *Babe Ruth* with respect to *baseball players*). Certain exemplars may become paragons because they closely approximate ideals associated with their respective categories. In general, little if any attention has been given to the role of ideals in human knowledge. Instead, because most theories of knowledge are normative in spirit, the representations they use only include central tendency and frequency information (e.g., as in prototype, exemplar, and schema theories). Given the importance of goals in human behavior, however, ideals may also be central to knowledge. If so, then future theories of knowledge should incorporate them.

Although central tendency has received more attention than ideals, much remains to be learned about it as well. For example, it is not clear why central tendency determines graded structure in common taxonomic categories but not in goal-derived categories (as found in Experiment 1). Two possibilities suggested earlier were as follows. First, central tendency may be important for common taxonomic categories because these categories provide information about the structure of the environment. By including central tendency information in the concepts for these categories, people establish representative information about the kinds of entities in the environment. Second, central tendency may be important for common taxonomic categories because it maximally facilitates classification. By representing these categories with their central tendencies, people minimize the average distance from exemplars to classification standards. Central tendency may not be important for goal-derived categories because these categories are not used to provide information about the structure of the environment and because these categories are not regularly used for classification.

Two other factors may also result in central tendency becoming important to graded structure. First members within common taxonomic categories generally bear a strong perceptual similarity to one another. As noted by Rosch, Mervis, *et al.* (1976), members within basic level categories share a common shape; and as noted by B. Tversky and Hemenway (1984), members within basic level categories share the same parts in the same configuration. Perceptual similarity also appears to occur in subordinate and superordinate common taxonomic categories, even though it does not seem to be as compelling as in basic level categories. In contrast, goal-derived categories often possess little if any perceptual similarity (e.g., *things to take on a camping trip*). For some reason, people may be more apt to acquire the central tendencies of categories that contain high perceptual similarity.

Another reason central tendency may only be acquired for common taxonomic categories is because people may be much more familiar with them than with goal-derived categories. If much exposure to a category is necessary for its central tendency to be abstracted, then central tendency may only be acquired for common taxonomic categories. If this is correct, then sufficient experience with a goal-derived category should result in the abstraction and use of its central tendency.[8]

In conclusion, it appears that the human conceptual ability is extremely dynamic. As shown by Experiment 1, people incorporate various kinds of information into concepts (e.g., central tendency and ideals), such that different kinds of information determine typicality in different categories. Moreover people construct different concepts for the same category in different contexts, tailoring concepts to represent the demands of current situations (Experiment 2; Barsalou & Sewell, 1984; Roth & Shoben, 1983). Not only do people represent well-established categories in a dynamic and context-dependent manner, they also construct new concepts for new categories that serve new goals (i.e., ad hoc categories; Barsalou, 1983). As further discussed in Barsalou (in press), these observations suggest that a fundamental characteristic of the human cognitive system is its ability to construct context-dependent representations in working memory from a large knowledge base in long-term memory to meet the constraints of specific situations.

## Acknowledgements

The research in this article was supported by Grant MH 13905 from the National Institute of Mental Health to Gordon Bower, a National Science Foundation Graduate Fellowship to the author, and Experimental Training Grant MH 15757-02 from the National Institute of Mental Health to Stanford University. Parts of this article were drawn from a doctoral dissertation submitted to Stanford University (Barsalou, 1981) and an Emory Cognition Project Technical Report (Barsalou, 1984).

I am grateful to Gordon Bower for supporting this project and to Gordon Bower, Herbert Clark, Ellen Markman, and David Rumelhart for direction during its initial development. I am also grateful to Douglas Medin for his comments on every written form of this research and for his guidance in developing it. In addition, this article has benefited from the comments of Jeffrey Farrar, James Hampton, Barbara Malt, Gregory Murphy, Brian Ross, David Sewell, and several anonymous reviewers.

## Notes

1.  Ideals are not always the most extreme values possible on a dimension. Exemplars of *clothes to wear in the snow*, for example, vary along the dimension of *how warm they keep people*, with the ideal not being *as warm as possible* (which could be fatal) but being instead *as much warmth as is necessary for survival and comfort*. This ideal, however, is probably not the central tendency of the category.

2.  McCloskey (1980) also reported effects of familiarity on conceptual processing, but his work primarily addressed the role of a category term's familiarity instead of an exemplar term's familiarity, which is of interest here.

3.  Some of these ideal dimensions could actually be composites of several ideal dimensions. For example, the ideal dimension for *birds* (i.e., *how much people like it*) could depend on the more specific dimensions of *how colorful it is, how melodic its song is,* and so on.

4.  It should be noted that this measure of family resemblance does not reflect an exemplar's dissimilarity to members of contrast categories. However Rosch and Mervis (1975) did not include dissimilarity to nonmembers in some of their studies and yet found that similarity to members alone often did an excellent job of predicting typicality (i.e., correlations around .90). So although the measure used here does not reflect dissimilarity to nonmembers, it should indicate at least to some extent whether family resemblance predicts graded structure.

5. An alternative explanation is that subjects maintain a constant distribution of similarity ratings for each category such that the distribution of family resemblance scores also remains constant.

6. In further analyses, central tendency, ideals, frequency of instantiation, and familiarity (to be discussed in a moment) were regressed upon typicality and output dominance for each category type in stepwise multiple regressions. For typicality in common taxonomic categories, significant factors entered in the order of central tendency, ideals, and frequency of instaniation to account for 64% of the variance. For typicality in goal-derived categories, significant factors entered in the order of frequency of instantiation, ideals, and familiarity to account for 69% of the variance (central tendency never entered). For output dominance in common taxonomic categories, significant factors entered in the order of frequency of instantiation, ideals, and central tendency to account for 37% of the variance. For output dominance in goal-derived categories, the only significant factor was frequency of instantiation, which accounted for 5% of the variance.

7. It should be noted that Hampton and Gardiner's (1983) operationalization of familiarity is perhaps closer to what is meant by "frequency of instantiation" here. More specifically, Hampton and Gardiner had subjects judge the familiarity of exemplars while they were blocked together in the context of their categories. As will be seen in this next analysis, making frequency judgments about exemplars varies systematically as a function of whether these judgments are made in the context of categories (frequency of instantiation) or not in the context of categories (familiarity).

8. I am grateful to Edward J. Shoben for suggesting this possibility.

## References

Alba, J. W., Chromiak, W., Hasher, L. & Attig, M. S. (1980) Automatic encoding of category size information. *Journal of Experimental Psychology: Learning Memory, and Cognition*, 6, 370–378.

Allen, M. J. & Yen, W. M. (1979) *Introduction to measurement theory*. Monterey, CA: Brooks/Cole.

Ashcraft, M. H. (1978) Property norms for typical and atypical items from 17 categories: A description and discussion. *Memory & Cognition*, 6, 227–232.

Barsalou, L. W. (1981) *Determinants of graded structure in categories*. Unpublished doctoral dissertation, Stanford University.

Barsalou, L. W. (1982) Context-independent and context-dependent information in concepts. *Memory & Cognition*, 10, 82–93.

Barsalou, L. W. (1983) Ad hoc categories. *Memory & Cognition*, 11, 211–227.

Barsalou, L. W. (1984) *Determinants of graded structure in categories* (Tech. Rep. No. 4). Atlanta, GA: Emory Umversity, Emory Cognition Project.

Barsalou, L. W. (in press) The instability of graded structure: Implications for the nature of concepts. To appear in U. Neisser (Ed.), *Concepts reconsidered: The ecological and intellectual bases of categories*. Cambridge: Cambridge University Press.

Barsalou, L. W. & Ross, B. H. (in press) The roles of automatic and strategic processing in sensitivity to superordinate and property frequency. *Journal of Experimental Psychology: Learning, Memory and Cognition*.

Barsalou, L. W. & Sewell, D. R. (1984) *Constructing representations of categories from different points of view* (Tech. Rep. No. 2). Atlanta, GA: Emory University, Emory Cognition Project.

Barsalou, L. W. & Sewell, D. R. (1985) *The relation between determinants of category verification and determinants of graded structure in common taxonomic and goal-derived categories.* Manuscript in preparation.

Battig, W. E. & Montague, W. E. (1969) Category norms for verbal items in 56 categories: A replication and extension of the Connecticut category norms. *Journal of Experimental Psychology Monographs*, 80, 3, Pt 2.

Glass, A.L. & Meany, P.J. (1978) Evidence for two kinds of low-typical instances in a categorization task. *Memory & Cognition*, 6, 622–628.

Guilford, J.P. & Fruchter, B. (1973) *Fundamental statistics in psychology and education.* New York: McGraw-Hill.

Hampton, J.A. (1979) Polymorphous concepts in semantic memory. *Journal of Verbal Learning and Verbal Behavior*, 18, 441–461.

Hampton, J.A. (1981) An investigation of the nature of abstract concepts. *Memory & Cognition*, 9, 149–156.

Hampton, J.A. & Gardiner, M.M. (1983) Measures of internal category structure: A correlational analysis of normative data. *British Journal of Psychology*, 74, 491–516.

Hasher, L. & Zacks, R.T. (1979) Automatic and effortful processes in memory. *Journal of Experimental Psychology: General*, 108, 356–388.

Hayes, W.L. (1973) *Statistics for the social sciences.* New York: Holt, Rinehart and Winston.

Hintzman, D.L. (1976) Repetition and memory. In G.H. Bower (Ed.), *The psychology of learning and motivation* (Vol. 10). New York: Academic Press.

Hintzman, D.L. & Block, R.A. (1971) Repetition and memory: Evidence for a multiple-trace hypothesis. *Journal of Experimental Psychology*, 88, 297–306.

Jolicoeur, P., Gluck, M.A. & Kosslyn, S.M. (1984) Pictures and names: Making the connection. *Cognitive Psychology*, 16, 243–275.

Kučera, H. & Francis, W.N. (1967) *Computational analysis of present-day American English.* Providence, RI: Brown University Press.

Lakoff, G. (in press) *Women, fire and dangerous things: What categories tell us about the nature of thought.* Chicago: University of Chicago Press.

Malt, B.C. & Smith, E.E. (1982) The role of familiarity in determining typicality. *Memory & Cognition*, 10, 69–75.

McCloskey, M. (1980) The stimulus familiarity problem in semantic memory research. *Journal of Verbal Learning and Verbal Behavior*, 19, 485–502.

Medin, D.L. & Smith, E.E. (1984) Concepts and concept formation. *Annual Review of Psychology*, 35, 113–138.

Mervis, C.B., Catlin, J. & Rosch, E. (1976) Relationships among goodness-of-example, category norms, and word frequency. *Bulletin of the Psychonomic Society*, 7, 283–294.

Mervis, C.B. & Rosch, E. (1981) Categorization of natural objects. *Annual Review of Psychology*, 32, 89–115.

Murphy, G.L. & Smith, E.E. (1982) Basic-level superiority in picture categorization. *Journal of Verbal Learning and Verbal Behavior*, 21, 1–20.

Rips, L.J., Shoben, E.J. & Smith, E.E. (1973) Semantic distance and the verification of semantic relations. *Journal of Verbal Learning and Verbal Behavior*, 12, 1–20.

Rosch, E.H. (1973) On the internal structure of perceptual and semantic categories. In T.E. Moore (Ed.), *Cognitive development and the acquisition of language*. New York: Academic Press.

Rosch, E.H. (1974) Universals and cultural specifics in human categorization. In R. Breslin, W. Lonner, & S. Bochner (Eds.), *Cross-cultural perspectives on learning*. London: Sage Press.

Rosch, E.H. (1975) Cognitive representations of semantic categories. *Journal of Experimental Psychology: General*, 104, 192–233.

Rosch, E.H. & Mervis, C.B. (1975) Family resemblances: Studies in the internal structure of categories. *Cognitive Psychology*, 7, 573–605.

Rosch, E.H., Mervis, C.B., Gray, W.D., Johnson, D.M. & Boyes-Braem, P. (1976) Basic objects in natural categories. *Cognitive Psychology*, 8, 382–439.

Rosch, E.H., Simpson, C. & Miller, R.S. (1976) Structural bases of typicality effects. *Journal of Experimental Psychology: Human Perception and Performance*, 2, 491–502.

Roth, E.M. & Shoben, E.J. (1983) The effect of context on the structure of categories. *Cognitive Psychology*, 15, 346–378.

Smith, E.E. (1978) Theories of semantic memory. In W.K. Estes (Ed.), *Handbook of learning and cognitive processes* (Vol. 6). Potomac, MD: Erlbaum.

Smith, E.E. & Medin, D.L. (1981) *Categories and concepts*. Cambridge, MA: Harvard University Press.

Smith, E.E., Shoben, E.J. & Rips, L.J. (1974) Structure and process in semantic memory: A featural model for semantic decisions. *Psychological Review*, 81, 214–241.

Tversky, A. (1977) Features of similarity. *Psychological Review*, 84, 327–352.

Tversky, B. & Hemenway, K. (1984) Objects, parts, and categories. *Journal of Experimental Psychology: General*, 113, 169–193.

Winer, B.J. (1971) *Statistical principles in experimental design*. New York: McGrawHill.

# Appendix

Output dominance (OD) and the average scores for exemplar goodness (EG), central tendency (CT), frequency of instantiation (FOI), ideals (I), and familiarity (FAM) are shown below for the exemplars of the nine goal-derived and the nine common taxonomic categories in Experiment 1. The measures are defined in the method of Experiment 1, and the exemplars are ordered within each category by their values for exemplar goodness.

## Birthday Presents

| Exemplar | OD | EG | CT | FOI | I | FAM |
|---|---|---|---|---|---|---|
| Clothing | 17 | 7.9 | 3.029 | 7.7 | 6.9 | 8.2 |
| Party | 2 | 7.3 | 3.616 | 7.2 | 6.4 | 7.4 |
| Jewelry | 10 | 7.2 | 4.522 | 5.3 | 5.8 | 7.7 |
| Dinner | 2 | 6.9 | 3.254 | 6.5 | 5.6 | 8.6 |
| Watch | 4 | 6.6 | 4.246 | 4.6 | 6.2 | 7.2 |
| Cake | 4 | 6.3 | 2.928 | 7.0 | 4.5 | 7.8 |
| Card | 5 | 6.3 | 3.268 | 7.5 | 4.7 | 6.3 |
| Flowers | 3 | 6.3 | 3.464 | 5.4 | 5.9 | 6.7 |
| Perfume | 4 | 6.0 | 3.565 | 5.0 | 5.7 | 6.4 |
| Money | 12 | 5.9 | 3.464 | 7.1 | 7.1 | 7.9 |
| Record | 7 | 5.8 | 3.565 | 5.4 | 5.2 | 7.6 |
| Camera | 2 | 5.6 | 3.819 | 4.2 | 6.1 | 5.6 |
| Book | 6 | 5.5 | 3.247 | 6.4 | 5.4 | 9.0 |
| Gold | 2 | 5.3 | 3.304 | 3.6 | 7.4 | 7.3 |
| Sports equipment | 2 | 5.3 | 3.420 | 6.0 | 6.7 | 4.5 |
| Booze | 2 | 5.1 | 3.290 | 4.5 | 5.8 | 5.9 |
| Tie | 2 | 4.9 | 3.247 | 3.0 | 3.8 | 4.0 |
| Toy | 5 | 4.9 | 3.341 | 6.1 | 4.6 | 5.0 |
| Game | 3 | 4.6 | 3.899 | 5.6 | 4.5 | 6.2 |
| Nic nac | 2 | 4.1 | 3.587 | 5.3 | 3.6 | 3.8 |
| Car | 5 | 4.0 | 2.638 | 2.6 | 8.8 | 8.6 |
| Appliance | 2 | 3.8 | 3.087 | 3.0 | 6.8 | 5.8 |
| Candy | 2 | 3.1 | 3.514 | 3.7 | 3.4 | 8.3 |
| Art | 3 | 2.8 | 3.660 | 2.4 | 4.8 | 6.0 |

## Camping Equipment

| Exemplar | OD | EG | CT | FOI | I | FAM |
|---|---|---|---|---|---|---|
| Sleeping bag | 26 | 8.8 | 3.140 | 8.5 | 7.1 | 4.7 |
| Tent | 34 | 7.7 | 3.737 | 5.8 | 4.3 | 3.4 |
| Flashlight | 4 | 7.5 | 4.009 | 7.0 | 6.9 | 5.1 |
| Matches | 5 | 7.4 | 3.263 | 7.9 | 7.6 | 6.0 |
| Backpack | 10 | 7.0 | 3.553 | 7.4 | 5.3 | 3.9 |
| Food | 3 | 6.9 | 3.237 | 8.5 | 8.6 | 9.0 |
| Lantern | 7 | 6.7 | 4.158 | 6.0 | 5.1 | 2.5 |
| Knife | 2 | 6.2 | 3.719 | 7.8 | 8.3 | 7.0 |
| Canteen | 4 | 6.1 | 4.272 | 7.0 | 6.6 | 3.5 |
| Camping stove | 14 | 6.0 | 4.974 | 6.5 | 3.1 | 2.2 |
| Ground cover | 2 | 5.8 | 3.105 | 5.3 | 4.2 | 3.5 |
| Utensils | 2 | 5.6 | 4.947 | 6.0 | 3.4 | 6.9 |
| Pots | 3 | 5.2 | 4.421 | 4.7 | 2.7 | 6.7 |
| Fuel | 2 | 4.8 | 3.167 | 5.8 | 4.5 | 5.7 |

## Camping Equipment (*continued*)

| Exemplar | OD | EG | CT | FOI | I | FAM |
|---|---|---|---|---|---|---|
| Can opener | 2 | 4.4 | 4.106 | 4.8 | 4.3 | 5.6 |
| Pans | 2 | 4.3 | 4.263 | 5.3 | 2.8 | 6.6 |
| Camping vehicle | 2 | 4.1 | 3.404 | 4.6 | 1.9 | 2.8 |
| Camping shoes | 3 | 3.5 | 2.316 | 4.9 | 5.3 | 3.4 |
| Dried food | 2 | 3.5 | 2.561 | 4.1 | 5.1 | 4.5 |
| Equipment to keep flies away | 2 | 2.6 | 2.526 | 3.4 | 1.8 | 3.1 |

## Transportation for Getting From San Francisco to New York

| Exemplar | OD | EG | CT | FOI | I | FAM |
|---|---|---|---|---|---|---|
| Airplane | 36 | 9.0 | 3.500 | 8.4 | 9.0 | 7.6 |
| Car | 31 | 6.6 | 4.792 | 7.5 | 7.1 | 8.6 |
| Train | 26 | 6.2 | 3.958 | 4.7 | 6.0 | 4.2 |
| Bus | 21 | 4.3 | 4.479 | 4.4 | 5.5 | 5.4 |
| Motorcycle | 3 | 3.3 | 4.250 | 4.0 | 5.4 | 3.5 |
| Bike | 9 | 2.5 | 3.833 | 2.1 | 2.8 | 5.1 |
| Hitch hike | 8 | 2.1 | 3.875 | 3.2 | 3.3 | 2.0 |
| Boat | 12 | 2.0 | 2.688 | 2.0 | 2.3 | 5.1 |
| Walking | 3 | 1.2 | 3.333 | 1.2 | 1.0 | 7.4 |

## Things to Do for Weekend Entertainment

| Exemplar | OD | EG | CT | FOI | I | FAM |
|---|---|---|---|---|---|---|
| Parties | 19 | 8.3 | 4.333 | 7.4 | 7.6 | 7.7 |
| Skiing | 2 | 8.0 | 3.720 | 5.1 | 7.1 | 3.8 |
| Drinking | 3 | 7.1 | 3.894 | 5.7 | 7.6 | 6.3 |
| Go to the beach | 12 | 7.1 | 4.576 | 7.8 | 8.1 | 5.5 |
| Movies | 19 | 6.9 | 3.901 | 7.4 | 6.0 | 6.9 |
| Go to the city | 2 | 6.7 | 4.076 | 5.5 | 6.0 | 6.2 |
| Play sports | 5 | 6.5 | 4.500 | 8.2 | 7.3 | 5.9 |
| Camping | 2 | 6.4 | 4.015 | 4.5 | 6.9 | 3.8 |
| Concerts | 3 | 6.4 | 4.060 | 6.0 | 6.6 | 6.9 |
| Sports events | 2 | 6.2 | 4.205 | 7.1 | 7.4 | 5.8 |
| Dinner at restaurants | 5 | 5.8 | 4.098 | 5.5 | 6.4 | 7.0 |
| Sex | 4 | 5.7 | 3.667 | 5.5 | 7.8 | 7.5 |
| Dancing | 7 | 5.4 | 4.273 | 6.2 | 6.6 | 6.5 |
| Picnics | 5 | 4.9 | 4.621 | 4.7 | 7.1 | 5.7 |
| Softball | 4 | 4.7 | 3.712 | 5.6 | 5.9 | 4.3 |
| Eating | 3 | 4.5 | 4.273 | 6.4 | 5.8 | 8.9 |
| Swimming | 2 | 4.5 | 3.826 | 6.5 | 5.3 | 5.9 |

## Things to Do for Weekend Entertainment
### (continued)

| Exemplar | OD | EG | CT | FOI | I | FAM |
|---|---|---|---|---|---|---|
| Walks | 3 | 4.1 | 3.523 | 4.6 | 4.4 | 7.4 |
| Sleep | 3 | 4.0 | 2.697 | 7.1 | 6.8 | 9.0 |
| Drives | 2 | 3.8 | 3.371 | 4.6 | 6.0 | 7.1 |
| Tennis | 3 | 3.8 | 3.705 | 5.1 | 6.2 | 6.3 |
| Watch TV | 7 | 3.3 | 2.993 | 6.7 | 5.7 | 8.0 |
| Work | 2 | 2.0 | 1.795 | 3.9 | 1.9 | 8.7 |

## Picnic Activities

| Exemplar | OD | EG | CT | FOI | I | FAM |
|---|---|---|---|---|---|---|
| Bar-be-queing | 2 | 8.5 | 3.563 | 8.0 | 7.0 | 4.8 |
| Eating | 22 | 8.2 | 3.917 | 8.4 | 7.4 | 8.9 |
| Laying in the grass | 2 | 7.1 | 4.281 | 7.7 | 6.1 | 5.3 |
| Softball | 9 | 7.1 | 4.531 | 7.0 | 6.7 | 4.3 |
| Talking | 2 | 7.1 | 4.250 | 8.3 | 7.3 | 8.5 |
| Frisbee | 20 | 7.0 | 4.406 | 7.1 | 7.4 | 3.5 |
| Drinking | 5 | 6.6 | 3.594 | 7.0 | 7.1 | 6.3 |
| Volleyball | 9 | 6.5 | 4.281 | 4.8 | 6.1 | 5.3 |
| Play games | 3 | 6.4 | 5.240 | 7.5 | 6.1 | 6.5 |
| Hiking | 2 | 6.2 | 3.573 | 6.3 | 7.3 | 3.8 |
| Football | 6 | 5.8 | 4.261 | 6.2 | 6.2 | 5.8 |
| Dealing with insects | 3 | 5.7 | 2.750 | 4.2 | 2.2 | 4.2 |
| Suntanning | 3 | 5.7 | 4.250 | 7.0 | 6.8 | 6.6 |
| Swimming | 9 | 5.5 | 4.240 | 6.9 | 6.0 | 5.9 |
| Baseball | 4 | 5.3 | 4.313 | 5.7 | 5.2 | 4.7 |
| Sex | 3 | 3.9 | 3.875 | 2.3 | 7.6 | 7.5 |
| Sleeping | 2 | 2.5 | 3.010 | 2.5 | 4.0 | 9.0 |

## Personality Characteristics in Others That Prevent You From Being Friends With Them

| Exemplar | OD | EG | CT | FOI | I | FAM |
|---|---|---|---|---|---|---|
| Asshole | 2 | 8.2 | 5.739 | 8.2 | 8.1 | 6.3 |
| Phony | 2 | 7.9 | 4.333 | 7.1 | 6.5 | 4.9 |
| Obnoxious | 2 | 7.8 | 5.804 | 5.8 | 7.0 | 6.0 |
| Bitchy | 3 | 7.4 | 5.580 | 6.7 | 7.7 | 7.1 |
| Unfriendly | 4 | 6.7 | 5.218 | 6.6 | 7.7 | 4.9 |
| Hostile | 2 | 6.5 | 5.529 | 5.8 | 7.0 | 4.7 |
| Untruthful | 2 | 6.5 | 3.290 | 6.3 | 7.1 | 5.3 |
| Mean | 5 | 6.4 | 5.102 | 6.2 | 6.7 | 4.4 |
| Egotistical | 2 | 6.3 | 5.486 | 5.7 | 7.4 | 6.0 |
| Snobish | 5 | 6.1 | 5.297 | 7.6 | 6.0 | 5.4 |
| Selfish | 4 | 6.0 | 5.406 | 5.6 | 6.0 | 5.3 |
| Complaining | 2 | 5.9 | 4.833 | 6.7 | 5.8 | 7.5 |
| Cocky | 2 | 5.7 | 4.848 | 5.1 | 5.9 | 5.4 |
| Humorless | 3 | 5.7 | 4.181 | 5.7 | 5.3 | 2.3 |
| Bad temper | 2 | 5.6 | 4.971 | 6.3 | 5.5 | 5.5 |
| Foul-mouthed | 2 | 5.4 | 4.406 | 5.3 | 5.2 | 5.3 |
| Jealous | 3 | 5.4 | 4.297 | 4.9 | 4.7 | 5.9 |
| Mentally ill | 3 | 5.3 | 2.326 | 3.7 | 5.7 | 5.1 |
| Showy | 2 | 4.8 | 4.536 | 4.4 | 5.1 | 4.2 |

## Personality Characteristics in Others That Prevent You From Being Friends With Them
### (continued)

| Exemplar | OD | EG | CT | FOI | I | FAM |
|---|---|---|---|---|---|---|
| Narrow-minded | 3 | 4.7 | 4.355 | 6.1 | 5.2 | 5.8 |
| Aggressive | 5 | 4.4 | 5.087 | 5.0 | 4.1 | 6.6 |
| Loud | 3 | 4.4 | 5.051 | 4.8 | 3.9 | 7.0 |
| Sarcastic | 2 | 4.3 | 5.094 | 3.7 | 4.7 | 6.5 |
| Too quiet | 3 | 3.5 | 2.275 | 3.7 | 2.6 | 4.2 |

## Foods Not to Eat on a Diet

| Exemplar | OD | EG | CT | FOI | I | FAM |
|---|---|---|---|---|---|---|
| Chocolate | 5 | 8.2 | 4.444 | 7.0 | 6.5 | 7.6 |
| Ice cream sundaes | 3 | 8.2 | 4.659 | 7.2 | 8.1 | 7.1 |
| Candy | 16 | 8.0 | 4.476 | 6.7 | 7.3 | 8.3 |
| Pie | 2 | 8.0 | 4.738 | 7.0 | 7.7 | 5.3 |
| Sugar | 2 | 8.0 | 4.540 | 7.0 | 7.0 | 6.4 |
| Cookies | 4 | 7.8 | 5.079 | 6.9 | 6.8 | 7.1 |
| Cake | 13 | 7.6 | 5.135 | 6.9 | 7.3 | 7.8 |
| Pastry | 2 | 7.6 | 5.468 | 6.8 | 7.5 | 5.7 |
| Ice cream | 19 | 6.9 | 4.683 | 6.4 | 7.4 | 8.3 |
| French fries | 4 | 6.4 | 4.294 | 6.4 | 7.4 | 6.6 |
| Pasta | 2 | 6.1 | 4.849 | 5.9 | 5.9 | 5.5 |
| Potato chips | 2 | 5.9 | 4.326 | 6.7 | 6.6 | 6.3 |
| Spaghetti | 2 | 5.9 | 4.222 | 6.1 | 5.3 | 6.7 |
| Pizza | 3 | 5.7 | 4.318 | 6.5 | 5.5 | 7.1 |
| Butter | 2 | 5.4 | 3.897 | 6.4 | 6.3 | 6.6 |
| Starches | 2 | 5.4 | 5.691 | 6.7 | 6.8 | 4.0 |
| Bread | 8 | 4.9 | 4.913 | 3.8 | 5.5 | 6.7 |
| Hamburgers | 3 | 4.5 | 3.539 | 6.4 | 4.8 | 6.5 |
| Potatoes | 10 | 3.8 | 4.397 | 4.9 | 6.1 | 5.9 |
| Salt | 3 | 3.3 | 2.675 | 5.8 | 4.5 | 6.5 |
| Cheese | 2 | 2.9 | 3.429 | 3.9 | 5.4 | 7.4 |
| Meat | 3 | 2.2 | 3.389 | 5.2 | 4.4 | 7.6 |

## Things to Take From One's Home During a Fire

| Exemplar | OD | EG | CT | FOI | I | FAM |
|---|---|---|---|---|---|---|
| Children | 2 | 9.0 | 3.140 | 8.9 | 9.0 | 7.2 |
| Other people | 5 | 9.0 | 3.184 | 8.2 | 9.0 | 8.6 |
| Family | 7 | 8.6 | 3.184 | 8.9 | 8.5 | 8.1 |
| Important documents | 8 | 7.5 | 3.921 | 6.0 | 6.3 | 5.2 |
| Pets | 10 | 7.4 | 3.439 | 6.0 | 6.3 | 6.6 |
| Prized personal possessions | 3 | 7.2 | 4.895 | 6.0 | 7.0 | 7.8 |
| Money | 20 | 7.0 | 3.974 | 5.9 | 6.2 | 7.9 |
| Valuables | 3 | 7.0 | 4.877 | 6.4 | 7.0 | 6.1 |
| Dogs | 2 | 6.9 | 3.351 | 7.1 | 6.6 | 7.0 |
| Cats | 2 | 6.7 | 3.211 | 4.3 | 5.7 | 5.7 |
| Family records | 4 | 5.3 | 3.921 | 4.7 | 5.2 | 4.2 |
| Jewelry | 8 | 5.2 | 4.228 | 4.5 | 5.8 | 7.7 |

## Things to Take From One's Home During a Fire (*continued*)

| Exemplar | OD | EG | CT | FOI | I | FAM |
|---|---|---|---|---|---|---|
| Pictures | 9 | 4.5 | 4.035 | 3.8 | 4.7 | 8.3 |
| Camera | 2 | 4.1 | 4.018 | 3.7 | 2.3 | 5.6 |
| Memorabilia | 3 | 4.1 | 3.886 | 4.4 | 5.0 | 5.7 |
| Clothes | 9 | 4.0 | 3.088 | 3.7 | 3.4 | 8.5 |
| Stereo | 2 | 3.4 | 3.641 | 3.2 | 4.1 | 7.6 |
| Blankets | 3 | 2.7 | 2.649 | 3.2 | 3.3 | 7.1 |
| TV | 2 | 1.9 | 3.807 | 2.7 | 3.0 | 8.2 |
| Food | 2 | 1.2 | 2.289 | 3.0 | 2.2 | 9.0 |

## Clothes to Wear in the Snow

| Exemplar | OD | EG | CT | FOI | I | FAM |
|---|---|---|---|---|---|---|
| Down jacket | 8 | 8.2 | 5.178 | 6.4 | 7.7 | 6.7 |
| Mittens | 8 | 7.2 | 3.792 | 6.6 | 6.1 | 5.0 |
| Thermal underwear | 11 | 7.1 | 4.126 | 5.8 | 8.0 | 5.1 |
| Boots | 22 | 6.7 | 3.386 | 6.4 | 6.4 | 6.7 |
| Sweater | 11 | 6.7 | 4.813 | 6.4 | 5.3 | 7.2 |
| Coat | 4 | 6.6 | 5.146 | 8.0 | 7.0 | 7.1 |
| Ski jacket | 3 | 6.6 | 5.438 | 6.6 | 7.7 | 5.0 |
| Socks | 5 | 6.6 | 3.917 | 7.2 | 6.5 | 6.6 |
| Parka | 3 | 6.5 | 5.104 | 6.0 | 7.3 | 3.8 |
| Snow pants | 4 | 6.5 | 4.271 | 5.6 | 6.4 | 3.8 |
| Jacket | 12 | 6.4 | 5.167 | 8.1 | 6.8 | 7.6 |
| Cap | 4 | 6.2 | 3.802 | 6.3 | 5.6 | 3.8 |
| Hat | 17 | 6.2 | 3.761 | 6.5 | 4.4 | 4.6 |
| Scarf | 9 | 5.7 | 4.011 | 4.2 | 5.1 | 4.5 |
| Ski boots | 2 | 5.3 | 3.698 | 6.0 | 5.9 | 3.9 |
| Ski suit | 3 | 4.6 | 4.802 | 4.7 | 7.4 | 3.9 |
| Jeans | 2 | 2.9 | 3.823 | 6.4 | 2.9 | 7.9 |

## Birds

| Exemplar | OD | EG | CT | FOI | I | FAM |
|---|---|---|---|---|---|---|
| Robin | 16 | 8.4 | 5.413 | 6.4 | 5.9 | 2.7 |
| Bluejay | 10 | 7.9 | 5.102 | 6.8 | 6.3 | 3.2 |
| Sparrow | 14 | 7.8 | 4.935 | 7.2 | 4.2 | 3.1 |
| Blackbird | 2 | 7.6 | 5.174 | 5.9 | 3.3 | 2.2 |
| Bluebird | 3 | 7.6 | 5.268 | 4.5 | 5.8 | 3.0 |
| Parakeet | 6 | 7.2 | 4.674 | 5.8 | 5.5 | 1.8 |
| Parrot | 6 | 7.2 | 4.261 | 4.0 | 6.5 | 2.3 |
| Seagull | 3 | 7.2 | 3.812 | 7.7 | 5.3 | 2.8 |
| Canary | 5 | 7.1 | 4.739 | 4.4 | 5.8 | 2.2 |
| Eagle | 14 | 7.1 | 3.913 | 4.2 | 8.1 | 2.9 |
| Hummingbird | 4 | 6.7 | 3.667 | 6.5 | 7.0 | 2.1 |
| Pigeon | 3 | 6.3 | 4.681 | 7.4 | 3.9 | 3.2 |
| Hawk | 8 | 6.2 | 3.812 | 5.7 | 7.2 | 2.2 |
| Cardinal | 2 | 5.8 | 5.094 | 3.1 | 5.3 | 3.4 |
| Dove | 5 | 5.3 | 4.696 | 5.8 | 7.9 | 1.6 |
| Oriole | 4 | 5.1 | 5.145 | 2.2 | 5.7 | 1.6 |
| Falcon | 3 | 4.6 | 4.174 | 3.2 | 7.2 | 2.7 |
| Condor | 2 | 4.4 | 3.406 | 2.7 | 6.4 | 2.2 |

## Birds (*continued*)

| Exemplar | OD | EG | CT | FOI | I | FAM |
|---|---|---|---|---|---|---|
| Finch | 5 | 3.8 | 4.920 | 2.7 | 5.2 | 1.5 |
| Chicken | 2 | 3.7 | 2.776 | 6.2 | 3.3 | 8.2 |
| Pelican | 2 | 3.7 | 2.638 | 4.3 | 4.8 | 2.5 |
| Thrush | 2 | 3.4 | 4.971 | 1.5 | 4.4 | 2.1 |
| Ostrich | 3 | 2.4 | 2.174 | 2.2 | 4.5 | 1.9 |
| Penguin | 2 | 2.4 | 2.051 | 2.6 | 6.5 | 2.2 |

## Vegetables

| Exemplar | OD | EG | CT | FOI | I | FAM |
|---|---|---|---|---|---|---|
| Green beans | 3 | 7.6 | 4.358 | 6.9 | 6.2 | 5.1 |
| Spinach | 8 | 7.4 | 4.367 | 5.1 | 3.5 | 5.2 |
| Corn | 6 | 7.3 | 3.667 | 7.0 | 8.0 | 7.0 |
| Carrot | 18 | 7.2 | 3.900 | 6.4 | 7.2 | 5.3 |
| Zucchini | 6 | 7.2 | 4.708 | 4.6 | 4.8 | 4.9 |
| Peas | 7 | 7.1 | 3.975 | 5.3 | 5.8 | 4.6 |
| Broccoli | 10 | 6.7 | 4.492 | 4.7 | 3.7 | 6.0 |
| Lettuce | 17 | 6.6 | 4.192 | 7.4 | 7.4 | 6.4 |
| Squash | 3 | 6.6 | 4.667 | 4.9 | 3.5 | 3.6 |
| Asparagus | 4 | 6.5 | 4.050 | 5.0 | 4.0 | 3.6 |
| Cauliflower | 4 | 5.8 | 3.875 | 3.7 | 3.6 | 5.3 |
| Cucumber | 6 | 5.7 | 4.192 | 3.8 | 5.1 | 5.1 |
| Celery | 9 | 5.5 | 4.267 | 6.2 | 6.3 | 5.6 |
| Cabbage | 2 | 5.4 | 4.108 | 3.1 | 3.0 | 4.8 |
| Tomato | 14 | 5.1 | 2.992 | 7.1 | 7.1 | 6.2 |
| Artichoke | 3 | 4.6 | 3.650 | 3.3 | 4.8 | 2.6 |
| Potato | 5 | 4.5 | 3.433 | 7.5 | 8.0 | 6.6 |
| Avocado | 4 | 3.8 | 3.158 | 4.6 | 5.8 | 2.6 |
| Beans | 2 | 3.7 | 3.892 | 6.0 | 5.6 | 4.6 |
| Onions | 2 | 3.4 | 2.983 | 5.3 | 5.0 | 4.9 |
| Sprouts | 2 | 3.4 | 3.725 | 3.9 | 5.4 | 4.8 |

## Sports

| Exemplar | OD | EG | CT | FOI | I | FAM |
|---|---|---|---|---|---|---|
| Football | 33 | 8.9 | 4.755 | 7.7 | 6.8 | 5.8 |
| Baseball | 23 | 7.9 | 4.382 | 6.1 | 6.5 | 4.7 |
| Basketball | 21 | 7.9 | 4.118 | 6.5 | 7.1 | 4.4 |
| Soccer | 14 | 7.9 | 4.402 | 4.7 | 6.5 | 3.8 |
| Tennis | 17 | 7.1 | 4.108 | 5.7 | 6.6 | 6.3 |
| Hockey | 4 | 6.8 | 4.313 | 3.5 | 4.2 | 2.4 |
| Skiing | 4 | 6.6 | 2.971 | 5.0 | 8.1 | 3.8 |
| Track | 3 | 6.0 | 3.784 | 5.0 | 4.2 | 4.8 |
| Gymnastics | 2 | 5.4 | 3.598 | 3.7 | 3.9 | 3.4 |
| Rugby | 2 | 5.4 | 4.441 | 2.7 | 4.2 | 2.2 |
| Swimming | 18 | 5.3 | 3.441 | 7.0 | 5.4 | 5.9 |
| Softball | 4 | 5.2 | 4.324 | 6.3 | 6.5 | 4.3 |
| Wrestling | 2 | 4.9 | 3.990 | 2.6 | 2.8 | 2.1 |
| Jogging | 4 | 4.6 | 3.814 | 5.2 | 4.9 | 5.0 |
| Golf | 2 | 4.1 | 3.167 | 4.8 | 5.1 | 2.5 |
| Martial arts | 2 | 4.1 | 3.020 | 2.8 | 4.1 | 2.6 |
| Horseback riding | 2 | 3.4 | 2.490 | 3.3 | 6.5 | 5.2 |
| Badminton | 3 | 3.3 | 3.647 | 2.9 | 4.0 | 3.4 |

## Fruit

| Exemplar | OD | EG | CT | FOI | I | FAM |
|---|---|---|---|---|---|---|
| Apple | 32 | 8.7 | 4.491 | 7.0 | 7.8 | 6.5 |
| Orange | 32 | 8.4 | 4.565 | 7.6 | 8.0 | 6.8 |
| Strawberries | 12 | 8.1 | 4.426 | 7.3 | 7.8 | 5.6 |
| Banana | 19 | 7.1 | 3.435 | 7.3 | 6.9 | 5.3 |
| Pear | 14 | 6.8 | 4.611 | 4.0 | 5.9 | 4.5 |
| Peach | 10 | 6.2 | 5.121 | 5.7 | 5.8 | 5.3 |
| Pineapple | 3 | 6.2 | 3.639 | 5.2 | 6.2 | 5.1 |
| Plum | 2 | 6.2 | 5.009 | 4.6 | 4.7 | 4.4 |
| Apricot | 2 | 6.1 | 4.898 | 4.9 | 4.9 | 4.0 |
| Nectarine | 2 | 5.9 | 4.843 | 4.4 | 5.5 | 3.6 |
| Tangerine | 4 | 5.9 | 4.556 | 4.3 | 4.7 | 4.0 |
| Grapes | 10 | 5.7 | 4.370 | 6.1 | 7.3 | 6.0 |
| Cherry | 11 | 5.1 | 4.824 | 5.9 | 6.9 | 4.7 |
| Watermelon | 5 | 5.1 | 2.908 | 5.8 | 6.7 | 5.4 |
| Berries | 2 | 4.7 | 4.389 | 4.2 | 5.6 | 3.9 |
| Lemon | 2 | 4.1 | 3.611 | 5.4 | 3.3 | 6.1 |
| Blueberries | 3 | 4.0 | 4.361 | 3.2 | 4.7 | 4.1 |
| Raisins | 2 | 3.3 | 3.722 | 5.3 | 5.0 | 4.5 |
| Tomato | 4 | 2.0 | 2.111 | 4.3 | 6.2 | 6.2 |

## Tools

| Exemplar | OD | EG | CT | FOI | I | FAM |
|---|---|---|---|---|---|---|
| Hammer | 35 | 8.9 | 4.042 | 8.1 | 7.8 | 4.9 |
| Screwdriver | 25 | 8.2 | 4.570 | 8.5 | 8.6 | 4.6 |
| Pliers | 5 | 7.6 | 3.681 | 7.1 | 7.7 | 4.4 |
| Wrench | 22 | 7.3 | 3.847 | 8.0 | 6.9 | 4.0 |
| Saw | 14 | 6.6 | 3.403 | 5.7 | 7.0 | 3.3 |
| Drill | 7 | 5.4 | 4.083 | 5.1 | 5.0 | 3.0 |
| Philips screwdriver | 2 | 5.4 | 3.958 | 6.6 | 7.0 | 4.3 |
| Shovel | 2 | 5.2 | 3.250 | 5.4 | 6.9 | 3.5 |
| Chisel | 2 | 4.5 | 4.722 | 2.7 | 3.3 | 1.6 |
| Socket wrenches | 2 | 4.5 | 3.653 | 6.3 | 5.4 | 1.7 |
| Nails | 5 | 4.4 | 2.917 | 7.4 | 6.5 | 5.5 |
| Crowbar | 2 | 4.1 | 4.153 | 4.3 | 4.3 | 1.6 |
| Knife | 3 | 3.1 | 4.000 | 5.3 | 6.3 | 7.0 |

## Furniture

| Exemplar | OD | EG | CT | FOI | I | FAM |
|---|---|---|---|---|---|---|
| Couch | 22 | 7.8 | 4.454 | 6.9 | 5.5 | 6.8 |
| Chair | 30 | 7.7 | 4.815 | 7.4 | 6.0 | 6.9 |
| Sofa | 10 | 7.6 | 4.491 | 5.3 | 5.0 | 5.9 |
| Dresser | 6 | 7.4 | 4.352 | 6.7 | 5.9 | 6.2 |
| Easy chair | 2 | 7.1 | 4.334 | 5.0 | 3.5 | 5.9 |
| Table | 27 | 7.1 | 5.130 | 8.4 | 5.8 | 7.1 |
| Desk | 13 | 6.8 | 4.768 | 7.9 | 6.0 | 7.6 |
| Coffee table | 5 | 6.4 | 4.676 | 6.6 | 3.9 | 5.1 |
| Dining table | 2 | 6.3 | 4.639 | 6.0 | 5.7 | 6.3 |
| Bed | 18 | 6.1 | 4.222 | 7.7 | 8.6 | 8.9 |
| Rocking chair | 2 | 5.7 | 4.083 | 4.4 | 2.4 | 4.6 |
| Stool | 5 | 4.7 | 4.213 | 3.9 | 3.7 | 4.2 |

## Furniture (*continued*)

| Exemplar | OD | EG | CT | FOI | I | FAM |
|---|---|---|---|---|---|---|
| Cabinet | 3 | 4.2 | 4.352 | 5.4 | 5.4 | 5.8 |
| Bed stand | 2 | 4.1 | 4.722 | 5.7 | 3.4 | 4.6 |
| Lamp | 13 | 3.5 | 2.871 | 7.6 | 7.5 | 7.2 |
| TV | 4 | 3.2 | 2.796 | 6.5 | 4.2 | 8.2 |
| Rug | 2 | 2.5 | 2.102 | 6.3 | 3.8 | 5.7 |
| Refrigerator | 2 | 2.4 | 2.509 | 6.7 | 8.0 | 7.9 |
| Stereo equipment | 2 | 2.1 | 2.806 | 6.3 | 5.2 | 7.4 |

## Clothing

| Exemplar | OD | EG | CT | FOI | I | FAM |
|---|---|---|---|---|---|---|
| Pants | 28 | 8.4 | 4.746 | 8.4 | 8.0 | 7.4 |
| Shirt | 28 | 8.2 | 5.000 | 7.5 | 7.4 | 7.9 |
| Blouse | 6 | 7.8 | 4.746 | 3.7 | 7.1 | 7.5 |
| Jeans | 3 | 7.7 | 4.404 | 8.0 | 6.3 | 7.9 |
| Dress | 13 | 7.5 | 4.307 | 3.6 | 6.3 | 7.2 |
| Underwear | 14 | 6.7 | 4.149 | 7.7 | 7.0 | 7.7 |
| Sweater | 4 | 6.6 | 4.886 | 5.2 | 5.2 | 7.2 |
| T-shirt | 2 | 6.5 | 4.526 | 6.4 | 5.2 | 6.5 |
| Trousers | 2 | 6.3 | 4.675 | 6.5 | 6.7 | 6.5 |
| Skirt | 0 | 5.9 | 4.237 | 3.6 | 5.9 | 6.2 |
| Shorts | 5 | 5.3 | 4.176 | 7.1 | 4.2 | 6.4 |
| Bra | 2 | 4.9 | 3.956 | 3.3 | 4.8 | 8.1 |
| Jacket | 6 | 4.8 | 4.456 | 5.7 | 4.4 | 7.6 |
| Shoes | 21 | 4.8 | 2.921 | 7.7 | 6.4 | 8.6 |
| Coat | 3 | 4.7 | 4.928 | 5.8 | 5.2 | 7.1 |
| Socks | 22 | 4.0 | 3.518 | 7.4 | 4.4 | 6.6 |
| Tie | 7 | 3.1 | 3.211 | 3.8 | 2.3 | 4.0 |
| Belt | 2 | 2.6 | 3.377 | 6.0 | 3.4 | 6.5 |
| Gloves | 2 | 2.1 | 3.088 | 1.8 | 1.7 | 5.7 |
| Hat | 9 | 2.1 | 3.079 | 3.5 | 2.5 | 4.6 |

## Weapons

| Exemplar | OD | EG | CT | FOI | I | FAM |
|---|---|---|---|---|---|---|
| Gun | 33 | 8.6 | 4.192 | 6.4 | 7.3 | 3.2 |
| Pistol | 2 | 8.5 | 3.725 | 6.4 | 6.8 | 3.4 |
| Bomb | 6 | 7.9 | 4.000 | 4.4 | 7.7 | 3.1 |
| Rifle | 3 | 7.8 | 3.808 | 5.8 | 6.9 | 2.3 |
| Nuclear bomb | 4 | 7.4 | 3.608 | 3.6 | 9.0 | 3.6 |
| Nuclear missle | 2 | 7.3 | 3.633 | 4.2 | 8.7 | 3.0 |
| Missile | 4 | 7.0 | 4.017 | 3.5 | 8.0 | 2.7 |
| Hand grenade | 3 | 6.4 | 3.708 | 2.7 | 7.0 | 1.6 |
| Bazooka | 2 | 5.9 | 3.775 | 3.9 | 7.5 | 1.5 |
| Switchblade | 3 | 5.6 | 3.933 | 5.8 | 4.6 | 1.4 |
| Sword | 4 | 4.9 | 3.992 | 5.0 | 4.0 | 2.0 |
| Knife | 29 | 4.8 | 3.908 | 7.4 | 4.9 | 7.0 |
| Bow and arrow | 3 | 3.9 | 3.692 | 3.7 | 3.7 | 2.9 |
| Cannon | 2 | 3.5 | 3.642 | 3.3 | 6.6 | 2.0 |
| Spear | 2 | 3.2 | 4.217 | 2.8 | 3.1 | 2.2 |
| Stick | 10 | 2.9 | 3.858 | 5.8 | 2.1 | 3.9 |
| Axe | 2 | 2.8 | 3.458 | 3.2 | 3.7 | 2.3 |

Weapons (*continued*)

| Exemplar | OD | EG | CT | FOI | I | FAM |
|---|---|---|---|---|---|---|
| Hands | 2 | 2.8 | 2.958 | 5.5 | 3.2 | 8.6 |
| Chain | 4 | 2.7 | 2.975 | 5.1 | 3.3 | 5.1 |
| Jet | 3 | 2.3 | 3.150 | 2.8 | 5.1 | 5.8 |
| Rocks | 2 | 2.1 | 3.317 | 5.3 | 1.8 | 3.9 |

Vehicles

| Exemplar | OD | EG | CT | FOI | I | FAM |
|---|---|---|---|---|---|---|
| Car | 31 | 9.0 | 5.563 | 8.4 | 6.1 | 8.6 |
| Truck | 14 | 6.9 | 4.646 | 6.4 | 5.8 | 3.9 |
| Bus | 11 | 6.6 | 4.094 | 5.1 | 6.5 | 5.4 |
| Sports car | 3 | 6.4 | 4.885 | 6.0 | 4.8 | 6.1 |
| Porsche | 2 | 6.3 | 4.854 | 5.9 | 5.7 | 5.7 |
| VW | 2 | 6.2 | 4.927 | 6.8 | 5.2 | 4.2 |
| Camaro | 3 | 6.1 | 5.042 | 6.5 | 5.2 | 4.2 |
| Motorcyle | 15 | 5.7 | 4.052 | 6.2 | 6.3 | 3.5 |
| Mustang | 2 | 5.6 | 5.177 | 6.8 | 5.5 | 5.3 |
| Plane | 11 | 5.5 | 2.135 | 6.6 | 7.8 | 7.4 |
| Jeep | 3 | 5.4 | 4.709 | 4.1 | 5.4 | 4.7 |
| Bike | 24 | 4.3 | 3.084 | 6.7 | 5.4 | 5.1 |
| Train | 8 | 4.3 | 3.271 | 3.5 | 7.0 | 4.7 |
| Moped | 6 | 3.7 | 3.521 | 3.7 | 5.9 | 4.4 |
| Boat | 7 | 3.3 | 2.209 | 6.3 | 4.1 | 5.1 |
| Tractor | 2 | 3.2 | 3.458 | 1.7 | 2.5 | 2.0 |
| Skateboard | 3 | 1.4 | 1.875 | 4.9 | 3.9 | 3.3 |

# 8.    Contrasting the Representation of Scripts and Categories

Lawrence W. Barsalou and Daniel R. Sewell

*Recent findings have suggested that script actions are not sequentially organized in memory. Instead investigators have argued that (1) the positions of actions within scripts are represented by temporal properties stored with actions, this being analogous to how properties represent the size, color, and other characteristics of exemplars in categories, and (2) actions are organized by centrality in scripts, this being analogous to how exemplars are organized by typicality in categories. To compare the representation of scripts and categories, this study observed timed production of script actions and category exemplars. Subjects generated actions from scripts either in whatever order they came to mind, from most to least central, from first to last, or from last to first. Subjects generated exemplars from categories either in whatever order they came to mind, from most to least typical, from smallest to largest, or from largest to smallest. The results clearly demonstrated that script actions are sequentially organized in memory and that properties are not the means by which script actions are normally ordered during production. The results are also not consistent with the view that ease of production simply depends on the efficiency of retrieval strategies. It is concluded that scripts and categories share invariant properties of abstract representations and that their differences reflect constraints associated with their respective domains.*

Common activities such as *going to a restaurant* and *doing laundry* are often composed of actions that typically occur in the same order. Because people encounter these activities so often, they have knowledge, not only of each activity's typical actions, but also of the *typical sequence* in which they occur. For example, Bower, Black, and Turner (1979) and Galambos and Rips (1982) found that people agree substantially on the order in which actions are supposed to occur. Bower *et al.* also found that when people are presented with script actions in the wrong order, they rearrange them to their typical order during recall even after being instructed to recall them in their presented order. Related results have been found by Kintsch, Mandel, and Kozminsky (1977), J. Mandler (1978), and Stein and Glenn (1978).

Schank and Abelson (1977) provided one account of how people represent sequence. They suggested that an action's position in a sequence is represented by its *relation* to other actions in the causal chain comprising its script. The order in which a script's actions are chained together in memory corresponds to the order in which these actions typically occur in the actual activity. As discussed shortly, the relations from action to action in a serial action chain can be viewed as associations or pathways capable of eliciting priming. We will refer to such organization as *dimensional organization*. More specifically, a body of knowledge is dimensionally organized

Lawrence W. Barsalou and Daniel R. Sewell: 'Contrasting the Representation of Scripts and Categories' in *JOURNAL OF MEMORY AND LANGUAGE* (1985), 24, pp. 646–665. Copyright © 1985 by Academic Press, Inc.

whenever its components are chained together in memory according to increasing (or decreasing) values on some dimension. For example, a script is dimensionally organized with respect to time if its actions are chained together from first to last. Similarly a category is dimensionally organized with respect to size if its exemplars are chained together from smallest to largest.[1]

According to many theories of memory (e.g., J. Anderson, 1976; Collins & Loftus, 1975), one would expect certain patterns of priming within dimensional organizations. In scripts, for example, the relation between two adjacent actions should cause the encoding of one to prime the other. In addition, priming from one action should spread beyond its adjacent actions to further actions, although the amount of priming should decrease with distance. Surprisingly, attempts to detect such priming, in what has come to be known as the "gap size literature," have not been encouraging. Bower *et al.* (1979) measured how long it took subjects to read actions in scripts and did not find that an action's reading time decreased monotonically as its distance in the script from the last action read decreased. Similar attempts by Reder and Abelson also failed (see Note 7 in Abelson, 1981). The only support this prediction has received so far was reported by Smith (discussed in Abbott, Black, & Smith, 1985), who found monotonically decreasing priming for statements at the scene level but not at the action level.

The most damaging evidence against dimensional organization in scripts comes from Nottenburg and Shoben (1980) and Galambos and Rips (1982). Nottenburg and Shoben, employing the comparative judgment task, had subjects decide which of two actions from a script (e.g., *leave tip* and *read menu*) comes earlier in the script (or comes later, depending on the instructions for that trial). They argued that subjects could perform this task in two ways. First, if scripts are dimensionally organized, subjects could search in from the ends of scripts sequentially until both actions had been retrieved such that their temporal relation could be determined. To the extent both actions are near the beginning or possibly the end of their script, and to the extent they are close together such that priming occurs, subjects should be able to reach a decision quickly.

Alternatively, Nottenburg and Shoben proposed that decisions could be reached on the basis of temporal properties that indicate how early or late actions occur in their script. In the restaurant script, for example, *early* could be stored with *read the menu*, and *late* could be stored with *leave the tip*. When judging which of two actions comes earlier, subjects choose the action with the earlier temporal property, and when judging which of two actions comes later, subjects choose the action with the later temporal property. According to this account, temporal position of script actions is represented in the same way that values for size, brightness, and other dimensions are represented as properties of physical objects.

If temporal judgment utilizes temporal properties, then, on the basis of previous findings in the comparative judgment literature, subjects should be *faster* as the temporal distance between two actions *increases* (see Banks, 1977, for a review). As temporal distance between actions increases, their temporal properties become more discriminable, and decisions can be reached more quickly. Whereas the sequential search account predicts that subjects should become faster as actions become closer together, the temporal properties account predicts that subjects should become faster as actions become farther apart. Since Nottenburg and Shoben found that subjects became faster as actions became farther apart, they concluded that temporal sequence in scripts is represented by temporal properties and not by dimensional organization.

Galambos and Rips (1982) provided further evidence that scripts do not possess dimensional organization. In one experiment, subjects received a script name followed by two actions that sometimes were from the preceding script and sometimes were not. Their task was to determine whether both actions belonged to the preceding script. For trials in which both actions were from the script, the temporal distance between actions was manipulated orthogonally to their centrality, where centrality was defined as some function of standardness, uniqueness, and other variables (Galambos, 1982). Galambos and Rips predicted that if scripts are dimensionally organized, then close actions should prime each other and be verified more quickly than far actions, holding centrality constant. Yet they observed no effect of temporal proximity and only an effect of centrality.

Galambos and Rips go on to present two views of scripts. According to the *strong view*, scripts contain actions dimensionally organized by time with no relations from script superordinates to actions. However, since this view assumes that actions can only be accessed by searching in from the ends of scripts, it predicts that time to retrieve an action should increase with its distance from the ends. Since Nottenburg and Shoben (1980) and Galambos and Rips (1982) both found that time to access actions is independent of whether they occur at the beginning, middle, or end of their respective scripts, the strong view of scripts appears unjustified. Instead people appear able to access actions directly from script superordinates, which suggests the presence of superordinate relations.

Consequently the *weak view of scripts* proposes that scripts, in addition to being organized dimensionally, are also organized by superordinate relations. Besides making inward sequential search unnecessary for the retrieval of actions, these relations provide a means of accounting for centrality effects; namely, central actions are retrieved fastest because they have the strongest superordinate relations. The problem with the weak view, however, is that dimensional organization predicts priming effects. Since Galambos and Rips did not observe priming effects, and since such effects have generally not been found in the gap size literature, Galambos and Rips (p. 279) reject the weak view: "No facilitation, no pathways; and no pathways, no scripts," where "pathways" can be taken to mean the relations that comprise dimensional organization. Galambos and Rips (similar to Nottenburg and Shoben) conclude that scripts do not possess dimensional organization, that sequence is represented by temporal properties, and that the only relations in scripts are superordinate relations varying in strength.

Such conclusions about the representation of scripts lead to another conclusion; namely, the representation of scripts is basically the same as the representation of common taxonomic categories (e.g., *fruit, birds,* and *furniture*). Although Nottenburg and Shoben (1980) and Galambos and Rips (1982) do not explicitly state this conclusion, it is consistent with and follows from two conclusions they do reach. First, they conclude that there are no sequential relations between adjacent script actions and that if scripts contain any relations at all, they are superordinate relations whose strength depends on centrality. Such structure is consistent with numerous views of how categories are represented, including Collins and Loftus (1975), Glass and Holyoak (1975), and Barsalou (1983). According to these views, exemplars are related to superordinate concepts with varying degrees of typicality, and there are no direct relations from exemplar to exemplar (although there can be indirect relations through shared properties).

Nottenburg and Shoben (1980) and Galambos and Rips (1982) reach a second conclusion from which it also follows that categories and scripts share a common representational form; namely, temporal position is represented by temporal properties stored with script actions. Such structure is again consistent with numerous views of how categories are represented, including Meyer (1970), Smith, Shoben, and Rips (1974), and McCloskey and Glucksberg (1979). According to these views, dimensional information about exemplars such as size, color, shape, function, and so on is represented as properties stored with exemplars.

It may well be that these two characteristics of category representations — superordinate relations varying in strength, and property representations of dimensional information — are also true of script representations. Indeed such assumptions seem necessary to account for the current script literature. Superordinate relations seem necessary to account for people's ability to access actions without going through adjacent actions and to account for the differential ease of accessing actions. Temporal properties seem necessary to account for scripts behaving like linear orders during comparative judgment. Possession of these two properties, however, does not for any theoretical reason preclude scripts from also having dimensional organization. As pointed out by Galambos and Rips (1982), all three properties could exist simultaneously in a representation. The problem is that no evidence has been found for this third property.

Yet it may be premature to give up on dimensional organization in scripts. First, many theorists believe that strong relations develop between two pieces of information that are processed contiguously on a regular basis (cf. J. Anderson, 1982; Crowder, 1976, Chapter 12; Schneider & Shiffrin, 1977; Shiffrin & Schneider, 1977). Although category exemplars are generally not processed contiguously and would not become related, adjacent script actions are often processed contiguously and would become related. Second, reviews of various literatures have concluded that representations vary in the extent to which they incorporate dimensional and superordinate organization. For example, G. Mandler (1979) argued on the basis of verbal learning studies that learning varies in the extent to which it utilizes these organizations, and J. Mandler (1979) argued on the basis of developmental studies that children's early knowledge varies in the extent to which it is structured by these organizations. Finally, it may be premature to abandon dimensional organization in scripts on the basis of null results. It could be that such organization exists, but that the proper techniques for detecting and measuring it have not been discovered.

One task that may be sensitive to dimensional organization is *timed production*. When someone is producing actions from a script, sequential relations between actions may facilitate retrieving them one after another in their correct temporal order. Such processing seems necessary to performing scripted behaviors efficiently, especially for scripts whose actions occur quickly (e.g., working on an assembly line). Using temporal properties under such conditions seems quite impractical. Imagine having to activate all the actions of a script —with the most central actions becoming available first — and then ordering them by temporal properties prior to producing them. It seems much more efficient to use a dimensional organization of actions to facilitate their deployment from memory.

Consequently the current experiment used timed production to detect possible dimensional organization in scripts. Since the findings of Nottenburg and Shoben (1980) and Galambos and Rips (1982) suggest that scripts and categories share a common representational form, we also observed production from categories. To the extent scripts and categories are similarly represented, the same pattern of data should occur for both, just as it has so far in previous studies.

On each trial, subjects received a script or a category name. During the subsequent 20 s, subjects generated as many actions (from scripts) or exemplars (from categories) as possible. The primary dependent measure was how many actions or exemplars were generated in the 20-s period. Prior to each trial, subjects were instructed to generate actions or exemplars in one of four manners. In the *unconstrained* conditions, subjects were instructed to generate actions and exemplars in the order in which they came to mind. This condition primarily provided a baseline for the other conditions, although the order in which subjects generated actions and exemplars was also of interest.

In the *centrality* and *typicality* conditions, subjects were asked to generate actions from most to least central and to generate exemplars from most to least typical. If actions are retrieved according to centrality, and if exemplars are retrieved according to typicality, then explicitly instructing subjects to retrieve actions and exemplars in this manner should not decrease production. To the extent this ordering constraint slows subjects down, however, such a decrease should be small and, most importantly, should occur to the same extent for both scripts and categories. In contrast, if production from scripts normally employs dimensional organization, centrality instructions should substantially decrease performance for scripts. Having to produce actions in this foreign order should show marked reduction in comparison to the unconstrained condition in which subjects can utilize dimensional organizations of temporal sequence.

In the *forward* conditions, subjects were asked to produce actions from the first action of the script to the last action of the script and to produce exemplars from the smallest exemplar of the category to the largest exemplar of the category. If both temporal position and size are represented by properties, then performance should show a substantial drop for both scripts and categories relative to the unconstrained conditions. This is because subjects must first access actions and exemplars via superordinate relations and then order them according to properties before producing them. In contrast, if subjects have dimensional organizations for scripts, then forward instructions should not decrease performance for scripts but only for categories.

231

In the *backward* conditions, subjects were asked to produce actions from the last action of the script to the first action of the script and to produce exemplars from the largest exemplar of the category to the smallest exemplar of the category.[2] If both temporal position and size are represented by properties, then forward and backward production should be equally difficult for scripts and categories. Since subjects must first access and then order items according to properties before producing them, the end at which they start should not matter. In contrast, if subjects have dimensional organizations for scripts, then backward generation from scripts should be slower than forward generation. This follows from a standard assumption in the memory literature that relations can be asymmetrical in strength and that the direction processed more frequently develops stronger relations. Since scripts are rarely performed in reverse, their dimensional organizations should be well established in the forward but not the backward direction.

Finally, it is necessary to address a little more carefully whether timed production is capable of detecting dimensional organization. One could argue that even though a body of knowledge may be dimensionally organized, subjects could retrieve information from it in many different ways, according to whatever *retrieval strategy* they adopt. Consider the following well-known example. People may typically have *months of the year* temporally organized in memory, but could use an alphabetic strategy to retrieve them. Consequently all we may be able to conclude from production data is which retrieval strategy subjects are using. Yet there are two reasons why production data may also provide information about underlying organization. First, if we assume that subjects are generally efficient and choose the strategy that best reflects underlying organization, then we can conclude that the strategy subjects adopted *most often* reflects underlying organization. Second, if we measure the *rate* at which information is generated, conclusions about underlying organization become even more tenable. More specifically, the rate at which retrieval strategies produce information from a representation should increase to the extent they follow its underlying organization. In general, the fastest strategy should be the one in which the underlying organization is followed as directly as possible. Not only does this minimize lengthy search transitions between nonadjacent items, it takes advantage of priming between adjacent items. For example, generating *months of the year* temporally takes advantage of priming and does not involve any search transitions between nonadjacent items. In some sense, this is an encoding specificity argument (Tulving & Thompson, 1973): if script actions are normally encoded in their correct temporal order, they should be retrieved fastest in this order.

An alternative account of differences in production rate is that such differences only reflect the *efficiency of retrieval strategies* and do not reflect underlying organization. For example, *furniture* may not be dimensionally organized either by *height* or by *height–width ratio,* but retrieving exemplars by *height* may require less computation than by *height–width ratio* and may therefore result in faster production. If efficiency of retrieval strategies is the primary determinant of production rate, however, then a strategy that is fast for scripts should also be fast for categories, and a strategy that is slow for scripts should also be slow for categories. For example, if unconstrained generation turned out to be faster than typicality generation for categories, then unconstrained generation should be faster than centrality generation for scripts (i.e., *unconstrained* > *typicality* for categories and *unconstrained* > *centrality* for scripts).[3] Similarly, if forward and backward generation are equally hard for dimensions that structure categories, then they should be equally hard for dimensions that structure scripts *(i.e., forward = backward* for both scripts and categories).

In contrast, if underlying organization is important, as assumed by the dimensional organization hypothesis, then the orderings of strategies by production rate should not be the same for scripts and categories. As discussed earlier, the dimensional organization hypothesis predicts that the ordering for scripts should be *unconstrained = forward > centrality = backward* and that the ordering for categories should be *unconstrained = typicality > forward = backward.*

The final predictions are those for the temporal properties hypothesis, which assumes that production should be fast when it can capitalize on the strength of superordinate relations, but should be slow when items must also be ordered by properties. As discussed earlier, the orderings for scripts and categories should therefore be the same; namely, *unconstrained = centrality > forward = backward* for scripts and *unconstrained = typicality > forward = backward* for categories.

## Method

### Subjects and procedure

Twenty-four Emory University undergraduates participated to earn course credit. Subjects received instruction on the four types of script generation using the script for *how to write a letter* as an example. In the *unconstrained condition,* subjects were asked "to generate actions in the order in which they come to mind." In the *centrality condition,* subjects were asked "to generate actions from the most central action to the least central action," where centrality was defined as "how important or necessary the action is to the event." In *the forward condition,* subjects were asked "to generate actions from the first action to the last action." And in the *backward condition,* subjects were asked "to generate actions from the last action to the first action."[4]

Subjects received instruction on the four types of category generation using the category of *tools* as an example. In the *unconstrained condition,* subjects were asked "to generate instances in the order in which they come to mind." In the *typicality condition,* subjects were asked "to generate instances from the most typical instance to the least typical instance," where typicality was defined as how good an example an instance was of a category. In the *forward condition,* subjects were asked "to generate instances from the smallest instance to the largest instance." And in the *backward condition,* subjects were asked "to generate instances from the largest instance to the smallest instance."

On each trial, subjects were told three things in the following order: (1) whether they were to generate actions from a script or instances from a category, (2) the type of generation they were to perform, and (3) the name of the script or category. For example, one instruction was, "Please generate actions that occur during the following activity. Generate them from the last action to the first action. The activity is going grocery shopping." Subjects were asked to generate as many actions or instances as possible within the 20-s period following the instructions for each trial. Twenty seconds was chosen on the basis of pilot data to maximize the number of items subjects generated and to minimize the chance that subjects would run out of items before the end of the period.

Subjects received three additional instructions. First, they were to generate as many items as possible, as quickly as possible. Second, they were to avoid making mistakes when having to order items in a particular way. Third, with respect to scripts, subjects were to maintain an intermediate level of abstractness in generating actions — they were not to be too specific or too general.

Prior to the sixteen test trials, subjects performed eight randomly ordered practice trials, one for each type of generation. The materials for these trials did not overlap in any way with those for the test trials. Subjects had no trouble with the practice trials, indicating they understood the instructions. Subjects performed the experiment alone in a room with the experimenter who timed and tape-recorded their protocols.

## Materials and design

The test materials were the names of eight scripts and eight categories. The scripts were ones used in recent script studies (e.g., Bower *et al.*, 1979; Galambos & Rips, 1982) whose actions are generally performed in a stereotypical order. These scripts were *doing the dishes, doing the laundry, sending someone a gift, going grocery shopping, going to a restaurant, going on vacation, visiting the dentist,* and *getting up in the morning.* The categories were common taxonomic categories frequently used in categorization studies (e.g. Rosch, 1975) whose exemplars vary widely in size. These categories were *clothing, furniture, vehicles, insects, fruit, mammals, fish,* and *vegetables.*

Two random orders of the eight categories and eight scripts mixed together were constructed. Four different assignments of generation types were then made to each order, resulting in a total of eight lists. In each list, two scripts and two categories were randomly assigned to each of the generation types. Across the four assignments to each order, every script and category was assigned once to each of the four generation types. Each of these eight lists was randomly assigned to three subjects. Consequently each subject performed each of the eight generation types twice, and across lists, each script and category was generated in each possible way equally often.

### Results

After transcribing the protocols, the following measures were computed for each subject: (1) the total number of actions generated for each script and the total number of exemplars generated for each category, (2) the number of actions or exemplars generated in each 5-s interval of each 20-s protocol, and (3) the order in which actions and exemplars were generated for each script and category. Two analyses of variance were performed on each measure, one with subjects as a random variable, and one with materials (i.e., individual scripts and categories) as a random variable. The $F$'s from these two analyses were combined in each case to form min $F'$ tests of significance (Clark, 1973). All analyses are organized around planned comparisons that tested predictions of the dimensional organization hypothesis.

## Total generation

The average number of actions and examplars generated as a function of representation and generation type is shown in Table 1. Subjects generated the same number of actions for scripts on the average, 7.12, as they generated exemplars for categories, 7.50 [min $F'(1,111) = 1.48, p > .10$; in addition, neither the subjects' nor the materials' $F$ was significant]. Having to produce phrases for actions as opposed to single words for exemplars did not cause subjects to generate fewer items for scripts than for categories.

**Table 1    Average number of exemplars/actions generated in 20 seconds**

| Representation type | | Generation instructions | | |
|---|---|---|---|---|
| | Unconstrained | Typicality/ centrality | Smallest-to-largest/ first-to-last | Largest-to-smallest/ last-to-first |
| Categories | 8.53 | 7.48 | 7.00 | 7.17 |
| Scripts | 7.65 | 6.10 | 8.17 | 6.54 |

The first planned comparison addressed the effects of centrality and typicality instructions on generation. According to the temporal properties hypothesis, people normally access both actions and exemplars via superordinate relations that vary in strength as a function of centrality and typicality. Consequently explicit instructions to generate actions and exemplars according to centrality and typicality should not reduce performance relative to the unconstrained conditions. To the extent any reduction is observed, however, it should be the same for both scripts and categories. The retrieval efficiency hypothesis makes a similar prediction, namely, that any difference between unconstrained and centrality generation for scripts should be the same as any difference between unconstrained and typicality generation for categories. In contrast, the dimensional organization hypothesis does not predict the same results for scripts and categories. Since dimensional organization is normally used to produce actions from scripts, unconstrained generation should be faster than centrality generation, since centrality generation can not utilize this structure. For categories, however, unconstrained and typicality generation should be the same, since both utilize superordinate relations.

Thus the first planned comparison tested the prediction of the dimensional organization hypothesis that centrality generation for scripts should be harder than unconstrained generation for scripts, unconstrained generation for categories, and typicality generation for categories, all three of which should be equal.[5] This prediction was supported; namely, centrality generation for scripts was significantly harder than the other three [min $F'(1,111) = 13.17, p < .001$]. Breaking this planned comparison into planned pairwise tests provided further support. For scripts, centrality generation was harder than unconstrained generation [min $F'(1,111 = 7.04, p < .01$]. In contrast, typicality generation was as easy as unconstrained generation for categories [min $F'(1,111) = 2.27, p > .10$; although the subjects' $F$ was significant, $F(1,69) = 5.97, p < .025$]. These results indicate that centrality generation from scripts was harder relative to unconstrained generation than was typicality generation from categories.

The second planned comparison addressed the effect of forward instructions, which asked subjects to generate actions from first to last and to generate exemplars from smallest to largest. According to the temporal properties hypothesis, people must first access actions and exemplars via superordinate relations and then order them according to properties before generation. Consequently forward instructions should cause a large and equal drop for both scripts and categories relative to the unconstrained conditions. The retrieval efficiency hypothesis makes a similar prediction; namely, if forward generation is harder than unconstrained generation for categories, it should also be harder than unconstrained generation for scripts. In contrast, the dimensional organization hypothesis does not predict the same results for scripts and categories. Since unconstrained and forward generation for scripts can both utilize dimensional organization, they should be equally easy. For categories, however, forward generation should be harder than unconstrained generation, since forward generation requires the additional step of ordering exemplars by size properties.

Thus the second planned comparison tested the prediction of the dimensional organization hypothesis that forward generation for categories should be harder than unconstrained generation for categories, unconstrained generation for scripts, and forward generation for scripts, all three of which should be equal. This prediction was supported; namely, forward generation for categories was significantly harder than the other three [min $F'(1,111) = 5.19, p < .025$]. Breaking this planned comparison into planned pairwise tests provided further support. For categories, forward generation was harder than unconstrained generation [min $F'(1,111) = 5.64, p < .025$]. In contrast, forward generation was no harder than unconstrained generation for scripts (min $F' < 1$); in fact, forward generation was slightly easier than unconstrained generation, although insignificantly so. These results indicate that generating exemplars from smallest to largest was difficult, whereas generating actions from first to last was not.

The third planned comparison addressed the symmetry of forward and backward generation. According to the temporal properties hypothesis, people must order actions and exemplars by properties before generating them, *regardless* of the end of the dimension at which they start. Consequently forward and backward generation should be symmetrical for both scripts and categories. The retrieval efficiency hypothesis makes a similar prediction, namely, if forward and backward generation are equally hard for categories, they should also be equally hard for scripts. In contrast, the dimensional organization hypothesis does not predict symmetrical results for the two strategies. For scripts, forward generation can utilize dimensional organization and should therefore be faster than backward generation, which can not. For categories, however, forward and backward generation should be equally slow, since both require that exemplars be ordered by properties.

Thus the third planned comparison tested the prediction of the dimensional organization hypothesis that forward generation for scripts should be easier than backward generation for scripts, forward generation for categories, and backward generation for categories, all three of which should be equal. This prediction was supported; namely, forward generation from scripts was significantly easier than the other three [min $F'(1,111) = 7.19, p < .01$]. Breaking this planned comparison into planned pairwise tests provided further support. For scripts, forward generation was easier than backward generation [min $F'(1,111) = 7.82, p < .01$]. In contrast, forward generation was the same as backward generation for categories (min $F' < 1$). Although forward and backward generation were symmetrical for categories, they were asymmetrical for scripts.

### *Time course of generation*

The average number of actions and exemplars generated in each 5-s interval of the 20-s production period are shown in Figure 1 as a function of representation and generation type.

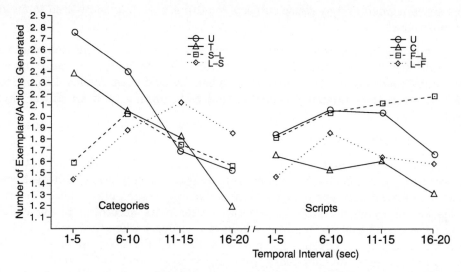

**Figure 1**    **Average number of actions generated during each 5-s interval. The results are shown for categories as a function of unconstrained generation (U), typicality generation (T), generation from smallest-to-largest (S–L), and generation from largest-to-smallest (L–S). The results are shown for scripts as a function of unconstrained generation (U), centrality generation (C), generation from first-to-last (F–L), and generation from last-to-first (L–F).**

In two of the category conditions — unconstrained generation and typicality generation — the number of exemplars decreased steadily across intervals. More specifically, both of these conditions showed a significant linear decrease in the number of exemplars generated over time [min $F'(1,568) = 23.41, p < .001$, and min $F'(1,568) = 15.84, p < .001$, respectively].

In contrast, production rate in the remaining six conditions — forward and backward generation for categories, and all four generation types for scripts — was generally constant across intervals. Subjects tended to produce about the same number of actions or exemplars in each 5-s interval. This was supported by tests for linear trends in either direction being insignificant for all six conditions. In addition, none of the differences between adjacent intervals was significant for any of these six conditions.

These results suggest that subjects produced an initial burst of typical exemplars for categories via superordinate relations during unconstrained and typicality generation. But once subjects reported the exemplars accessed in this initial burst, their ability to retrieve additional exemplars proceeded at an increasingly slower rate (cf. Graesser & G. Mandler, 1978). Since the same pattern occurred in the unconstrained and typicality conditions, it appears that subjects naturally generated exemplars according to typicality when they were unconstrained. Similar findings have been reported by Barsalou (1981, 1983, 1985) and Mervis, Catlin, and Rosch (1976). In contrast, constraining subjects to generate exemplars in an unnatural order (i.e., from smallest to largest and from largest to smallest) eliminated this initial burst of information from categories. Unnatural constraints may either cause exemplars to be retrieved in a more serial fashion or may cause subjects to output exemplars activated in an initial burst more slowly.

When generating actions from scripts, no evidence for initial bursts was observed in any condition. This suggests that even when subjects were not constrained by experimental instructions, they nevertheless constrained their retrieval to producing actions in the correct temporal order instead of beginning with an initial burst of central actions.

### Determinants of output position

One goal of this next analysis was to identify the strategies that subjects in the unconstrained conditions used to generate actions and exemplars. Of interest was the extent to which subjects generated actions according to temporal position for scripts and the extent to which subjects generated exemplars according to typicality for categories. A second goal was to observe subjects' accuracy when they were constrained to generating actions and exemplars in a particular order. For example, when subjects were required to generate exemplars from largest to smallest, how well did they do?

To perform this analysis, it was first necessary to obtain values for each action's centrality and temporal position and for each exemplar's typicality and size. All the actions generated for each script and all the exemplars generated for each category were pooled across subjects. This resulted in a list for each script of every unique action generated and a list for each category of every unique exemplar generated. Two versions of these materials were created in which the individual lists were blocked by scripts and categories. Within each version, the scripts and categories appeared in different random orders within blocks, and the actions within scripts and the exemplars within categories appeared in different random orders. Half of the booklets for each version presented the scripts before the categories, and half presented the categories before the scripts, resulting in four sets of materials.

Twenty-four Emory University undergraduates ranked the items within each script by centrality and within each category by typicality. Another twenty-four ranked the items within each script by temporal position and within each category by size. Within each group of subjects, each of the four materials sets was judged by six subjects.

Average centrality and temporal position were computed for each action in each script across subjects, and average typicality and size were similarly computed for each exemplar in each category. Three correlations were computed for each of the 384 protocols (16 for each of the 24 subjects) across only those actions or exemplars in the protocol. For scripts, the correlations were between (1) output position and centrality, (2) output position and temporal position, and (3) centrality and temporal position. For categories, the correlations were between (1) output position and typicality, (2) ouput position and size, and (3) typicality and size. An item's output position was simply its ordinal position in its protocol. The three correlations for each protocol were converted to Fisher $z$ scores prior to performing representation type by category type by correlation type ANOVAs upon them. The average Fisher $z$ scores obtained from these analyses were then transformed back into the correlations shown in Table 2.

**Table 2    Average correlations for categories and scripts**

| Generation instructions | Correlation | | |
|---|---|---|---|
| | Output position-typicality | Output position-size | Typicality-size |
| Categories | | | |
| Unconstrained | .27 | .01 | −.22 |
| Typicality | .77 | −.10 | −.22 |
| Smallest-to-largest | .17 | .85 | .32 |
| Largest-to-smallest | .12 | −.90 | −.22 |
| | Output position-centrality | Output position-temporal position | Centrality-temporal position |
| Scripts | | | |
| Unconstrained | .64 | .82 | .65 |
| Centrality | .57 | .43 | .64 |
| First-to-last | .59 | .94 | .66 |
| Last-to-first | −.70 | −.92 | .74 |

*Categories.* The average correlation between typicality and output position for the unconstrained condition (.27) indicates that typicality was related to the order in which subjects generated exemplars when unconstrained, although the relationship was certainly not strong. Barsalou (1981, Experiment 1) found the same value (.27) between the order in which individual subjects generated exemplars and their individual typicality rankings of those exemplars. The correlation between output order and typicality increased significantly to .77 when subjects were asked to generate exemplars from most to least typical [min $F'(1,220) = 11.62$, $p < .001$]. This indicates that subjects in the unconstrained condition could have generated exemplars according to typicality much more than they actually did.

Regarding the correlations between output position and size, the average correlation for the unconstrained condition (.01) clearly indicates that size was irrelevant to how subjects generated exemplars (cf. Henley, 1969). Subjects can generate exemplars according to size, however, as is shown by the correlations for the forward and backward conditions (.85 and −.90, respectively). The increase from the unconstrained condition to each of these two conditions was significant [min $F'(1,220) = 32.58$, $p < .001$; min $F'(1,220) = 43.41, p < .001$]. Output position and size correlated equally well for the forward and backward conditions (min $F' < 1$).[6] Finally, the correlations between typicality and size were generally small and varied somewhat across conditions.[7]

*Scripts.* The average correlation between centrality and output position for the unconstrained condition (.64) indicates that centrality was highly related to the order in which subjects generated actions when unconstrained. Centrality, however, was also highly related to temporal position (.65), which in turn was highly related to output position (.82). Consequently the relation between centrality and output position could have resulted from centrality being highly related to temporal position, which was the better predictor of output position. To assess the unique predictive power of centrality and temporal position for output position more carefully, partial correlations were computed. Notably, partialing out temporal position from the correlation between centrality and output position reduced this correlation to .26. In contrast, partialing out centrality from the correlation between temporal position and output position only reduced this correlation to .69. Temporal position clearly accounted for much more unique variance in the prediction of output position than did centrality. Interestingly the unique contribution of centrality to output position for scripts (.26) was very similar to how well typicality predicted output position for categories (.27) in the unconstrained condition. This suggests that centrality and typicality normally play an equal role in the retrieval of information from both scripts and categories.

The average correlation between centrality and output order did not differ significantly in the unconstrained and centrality conditions. Subjects in these two conditions did not generate actions identically, however, since the correlation between temporal position and output position was significantly less in the centrality condition [min $F'(1,220) = 9.86$, $p < .01$]. When generating actions according to centrality, subjects appeared to use a strategy not as constrained by temporal position to locate central actions, suggesting that subjects may have relied more heavily on superordinate relations than usual. As can be seen from Table 1, however, this strategy substantially reduced the rate at which subjects generated actions. Centrality was also correlated with output position for the forward and backward conditions. This relationship, however, resulted from the strong relationship between centrality and temporal position found in all conditions.[8]

Finally, the relation between temporal position and output position was significantly higher in the forward and backward conditions than in the unconstrained condition [min $F'(1,220) = 6.94$, $p < .01$; min $F'(1,220) = 4.25$, $p < .05$], indicating that subjects were not maximizing their potential to order actions temporally in the unconstrained condition. Subjects were as accurate at temporally ordering actions in the backward condition as in the forward condition (min $F' < 1$), although they were much slower during backward generation (see Table 1).

## Discussion

Although previous studies have failed to find support for dimensional organization in scripts, each analysis in the current study provided evidence for such structure. To begin with, production was fastest when actions were generated in their normal temporal sequence. This suggests that scripts are dimensionally organized in memory by time and that retrieval is fastest when it takes advantage of this structure. Since subjects were slower to retrieve actions according to centrality, it does not appear that superordinate relations provide the primary means of accessing information from scripts during production.

Categories do not appear to be dimensionally organized by *size* in the same way that scripts are by *time*. Generating exemplars from categories according to *size* was difficult regardless of whether exemplars were generated from smallest to largest or from largest to smallest. This pattern is what would be expected when information is not organized by a particular dimension; namely, forward and backward generation should be equally difficult when both require that exemplars be ordered by properties prior to production. Most importantly, this pattern should have also occurred for scripts if they were not dimensionally organized.

This pattern of results is not consistent with the view that differences in production rate simply reflect differences in the efficiency of retrieval strategies. If this view were correct, then retrieval strategies that were hard (or easy) for scripts should have also been hard (or easy) for categories. However centrality generation was harder for scripts than typicality generation was for categories (relative to unconstrained generation). In addition, forward and backward generation were both difficult for categories, whereas only backward generation was difficult for scripts. Such differences suggest that production of script actions is fastest when they are retrieved in the order in which they are normally encoded (Tulving & Thompson, 1973).

It should be noted, however, that the slowest conditions were proportionally not that much slower than the fastest conditions. For example, even though centrality and backward generation were slower than forward generation for scripts, they were not that much slower. This suggests that certain retrieval strategies may be effective even though they do not match normal encoding conditions (R. Anderson & Pichert, 1978).

The data for time course of generation also provided evidence for dimensional organization in scripts. When generating exemplars from categories, subjects produced initial bursts of exemplars in the unconstrained and typicality conditions, followed by decreasing rates of production. During these initial bursts, subjects appeared to be accessing typical exemplars with strong superordinate relations. In contrast, the rate of production for unconstrained generation from scripts remained constant across generation intervals. If scripts were only structured by superordinate relations, then initial bursts of information should have occurred in the unconstrained condition as they did for categories. The flatness of the unconstrained function for scripts suggests that subjects were accessing actions one at a time in their temporal order throughout the generation period. In addition, this function for the unconstrained condition was very similar to the function for the forward condition, further suggesting that subjects were accessing actions according to temporal sequence in both.

The correlational data provided further evidence for dimensional organization in scripts. In the unconstrained condition for scripts, temporal position correlated .82 with output position and only dropped to .69 when the effect of centrality was partialed

241

out. In contrast, centrality correlated .64 with output position but dropped to .26 when temporal position was partialed out. Temporal position was clearly a much better predictor of output position than was centrality, suggesting that subjects used a temporally organized structure to retrieve actions instead of using superordinate relations.

Finally, Haberlandt and Bingham (1984) and Fivush and J. Mandler (in press) have also recently found evidence for dimensional organization in scripts, but in paradigms very different from the one observed here. In addition, Klahr, Chase, and Lovelace (1983) have recently found evidence for dimensional organization in the alphabet, which could be construed as a very simple script. The failure of previous studies to detect dimensional organization in scripts appears to have resulted from using tasks that are not affected by such organization.

### Properties of abstract representations

These data, along with those from other script studies, show that there are both similarities and differences between scripts and categories. We next review five ways in which scripts and categories are similar at a general level of analysis, yet are different at a more specific level.

*Superordinate relations.* Most accounts of categorization typically assume that people's representations of categories possess superordinate relations between exemplars and superordinate concepts. Such relations provide access to exemplars during production (e.g., Barsalou, 1983; Mervis *et al.*, 1976), during the encoding of material to be remembered (e.g., Barsalou, 1983; Bousfield, 1953; G. Mandler, 1967), and during verification of exemplars as category members (Collins & Loftus, 1975; Glass & Holyoak, 1975).

As shown by Nottenburg and Shoben (1980) and Galambos and Rips (1982), scripts also possess superordinate relations. Such relations enable people to access actions directly from script superordinates without going through adjacent actions.

As pointed out by Abbott *et al.* (1985), however, the superordinate relations structuring categories and scripts are not the same. Whereas *inclusion* relations structure categories, *partonomy* relations structure scripts. An action is not an instance of a scene, nor is a scene an instance of script. Instead actions are parts of scenes, which are parts of scripts. So although scripts and categories both have superordinate relations, they differ in the type of superordinate relations they have.

*Graded structure.* Barsalou (1983, 1985, in press) suggests that graded structure is a universal property of categories; namely, every category appears to have some exemplars that are more typical than others. So far, no categories have been discovered that do not have this property. Even well-defined categories such as *odd numbers* have graded structure (Armstrong, Gleitman, & Gleitman, 1983).

As shown by Galambos (1982) and Galambos and Rips (1982), an analogous property exists in scripts; namely, actions vary in how central they are to their respective script. Because superordinate relations are inclusion relations in categories but are partonomy relations in scripts, however, typicality and centrality are not the same thing. Whereas typicality in categories represents how good an example an instance is of a superordinate concept, centrality in scripts represents how good a part each action is of its script.

Categories and scripts also differ in what determines their graded structure. While family resemblance (Rosch & Mervis, 1975) and ideals (Barsalou, 1985) determine graded structure in categories, these factors seem irrelevant to graded structure in scripts. Conversely, while distinctiveness determines graded structure in scripts (Galambos, 1982), this factor seems irrelevant to graded structure in categories. Although the determinants of graded structure in categories and scripts may generally differ, *frequency* appears to determine graded structure to some extent in both (see *frequency of instantiation* in Barsalou, 1985, and *standardness* in Galambos, 1982).

*Hierarchical organization and a basic level.* It is perhaps impossible to find any account of categorization that does not assume, at least to some extent, that categories possess hierarchical organization; namely, categories can be nested in one another via inclusion relations (e.g., Collins & Quillian, 1969; Glass & Holyoak, 1975; Smith *et al.*, 1974). Although such organization has been shown not to be strictly hierarchical (Collins & Loftus, 1975; Conrad, 1972; Hampton, 1982; Smith *et al.*, 1974), category organization usually appears to contain some form of higher-order clustering.

Scripts have also been viewed as hierarchical structures. Scripts decompose initially into scenes, which in turn decompose into actions (e.g., Abbott *et al.*, 1985; Bower *et al.*, 1979; Schank & Abelson, 1977; but see J. Mandler & Murphy, 1983). Even though categories and scripts may both have hierarchical organization, it again should be noted that inclusion relations underly such organization in categories, whereas partonomy relations underly such organization in scripts.

Within their hierarchical organizations, both categories and scripts appear to have a *basic level.* That is, there appears to be a level of abstraction within both kinds of hierarchies that is processed more efficiently than other levels. For categories, Rosch, Mervis, Gray, Johnson, and Boyes-Braem (1976) and Murphy and Smith (1982) have found that categories at an intermediate level of abstraction are the preferred way of labeling objects. For scripts, Abbott *et al.* (1985) have found that statements at an intermediate level of abstraction are the preferred way of describing scripted events.

*Property representations of dimensional information.* As discussed earlier, most theories of categories assume that dimensional information about exemplars is represented by properties. At issue has been whether the temporal positions of script actions are represented in a similar manner. Because comparative judgment for scripts yields the standard effects found for linear orders, it appears that temporal properties are stored with actions. Consequently dimensional information appears to be stored as properties for both categories and scripts, making them both capable of behaving like linear orders in comparative judgment (Galambos & Rips, 1982; Nottenburg & Shoben, 1980).

Perhaps the main difference between scripts and categories on this point has to do with the particular dimensions represented. As pointed out by Keil (1979), ontologically different dimensions apply to actions and objects (e.g., temporal position versus size).

It remains to be seen whether the properties for these different dimensions are represented in different ways. On the basis of the current comparative judgment literature, it appears they are not.

*Dimensional organization.* The central issue of this paper has been whether the actions in scripts are organized by temporal sequence, and the results obtained indicate that they are. Such organization has the desirable quality of enabling people to produce script actions in their correct order with a minimal amount of search. There is no reason to believe, however, that such organization precludes simultaneous representations of temporal position by temporal properties. Similarly dimensional organization does not preclude simultaneous hierarchical organization. All three kinds of structure appear necessary to account for the empirical literature on scripts.

In contrast, people do not appear to have dimensional organizations that structure categories by size. Yet there is no reason categories could not also be organized dimensionally. For example, people who stock produce at grocery stores may have dimensional organizations for fruit and vegetables with respect to the order in which they appear on the shelves. By having to stock fruit and vegetables in the same spatial and temporal orders day after day, it would not be surprising if dimensional organizations are acquired for fruits and vegetables to represent these occupational invariants and to maximize work performance.

In principle, scripts and categories both have the potential for dimensional organization. To the extent people frequently process actions or exemplars according to some dimension, they should acquire a dimensional organization for that dimension. This suggests that if people never processed a script's actions in a particular order they would never acquire a dimensional structure for temporal position in that script (e.g., see the Bower *et al.*, 1979, discussion of "unordered scripts," pp. 202–206). In addition, it should be possible to develop several dimensional structures for a given script or category. This suggests that a script's actions could be organized according to other dimensions while simultaneously being organized according to temporal sequence. For example, someone on an assembly line who puts together a device would probably develop a script for that task in which actions are ordered according to temporal sequence. Yet that person might also develop a different ordering of actions relevant to troubleshooting faulty devices. For example, he or she might develop an ordering of actions by how *likely* they were to have been performed incorrectly. Following such an ordering during troubleshooting would optimize going back and locating the result of an improperly performed action.

Although scripts and categories both have the potential for dimensional organization, scripts differ from categories in that they almost always seem to be structured by temporal position. In contrast, categories rarely seem to possess dimensional structures, and when they do, they do not seem to show much consistency in the dimensions represented. This difference may simply reflect the fact that behavior is rarely structured by dimensions, except in the case of scripts with respect to temporal order.

### Object partonomies and script taxonomies

As has been assumed so far, objects are hierarchically organized by inclusion relations into the categories that comprise object taxonomies, and actions are hierarchically organized by partonomy relations into the scenes that comprise script partonomies. It is important to note, however, that objects are associated with partonomies (e.g., the parts comprising a car) and that scripts can be organized into taxonomies (e.g., the taxonomy of scripts for entertainment activities).[9] Interestingly, object partonomies and script taxonomies both appear to have the same general properties as object taxonomies and script partonomies. Each appears to contain superordinate relations, to contain graded structure, to be hierarchically organized with a basic level, to have property representations of dimensional information, and to have the potential for dimensional organization. At a more specific level, however, object partonomies appear to differ from script taxonomies in some of the same ways in which script partonomies differ from object taxonomies. One difference appears to be that object partonomies are dimensionally organized by *spatial position* analogous to the way in which script partonomies are dimensionally organized by *time*. For example, parts of objects often appear to be dimensionally organized from *left-to-right* or from *top-to-bottom,* such that generation of parts may be fastest when retrieval follows these dimensions. In contrast, script taxonomies, similar to object taxonomies, may be primarily structured by superordinate relations and not by dimensions.

Markman's (1981) developmental work on *collections* (another kind of partonomy) provides an interesting way of viewing the presence of dimensional organization in partonomies and its absence in taxonomies. In general, scripts and other partonomies may be easier for children to learn than taxonomies (Nelson & Greundel, 1981) because partonomies are dimensionally organized.

## Conclusion

At a general level of analysis, scripts and categories have similar properties. Both possess superordinate relations, graded structure, hierarchical organization with a basic level, property representations of dimensional information, and the potential for dimensional organization. Yet at a more specific level of analysis, scripts and categories differ on each count. Although each possesses superordinate relations, the kind of relation varies. Although each possesses graded structure, the determinants of such structure vary. Although each possesses hierarchical organization, such organization is realized as partonomies in scripts and as taxonomies in categories. Although each has property representations of dimensional information, the ontology of these dimensions differs. And although each has the potential for dimensional organization, such organization seems to occur primarily for scripts as opposed to categories.

One way to view these two levels of analysis is that properties at the more general level are invariant properties of the abstract representations that comprise much of human knowledge. These properties occur for both scripts and categories and stand a decent chance of occurring for other types of representation as well. It seems reasonable that the abstract representation of any domain could potentially contain superordinate relations, graded structure, hierarchical organization with a basic level, property representations of dimensional information, potential for dimensional organization, and probably other invariant properties as well. Differences between representations at a more specific level, such as the presence or absence of dimensional organization, may primarily reflect constraints associated with particular domains.

## Acknowledgements

This work was supported by an Emory University Research Grant and by National Science Foundation Grant IST-8308984 to the first author. We are grateful to Mark Warner for assisting with data analysis and to Arthur Graesser, Jeffrey Farrar, Douglas Medin, Gregory Murphy, Eugene Winograd, and an anonymous reviewer for helpful comments.

## Notes

1. As discussed later, a script that is dimensionally organized can also be *hierarchically* organized. In fact, many theorists who propose that scripts are dimensionally organized also propose that they are hierarchically organized (e.g., Abbott, Black, & Smith, 1985; Schank & Abelson, 1977). In addition, we by no means assume that only a *single* sequence of actions comprises a script. As noted by Schank and Abelson (1977), a script may contain many different tracks for the many different situations to which it applies (e.g., the restaurant script may contain tracks for eating at a fast food restaurant or for eating at a very expensive restaurant). In general, we assume that a script contains a tremendous amount of information about a type of activity and that only a subset applies in a given situation. Similar to most other work on scripts, however, we have focused on the prototypical action sequence associated with a script that comes to mind when no specific contextual details are specified.

2. The assignment of *forward* and *backward* to the size dimension was somewhat arbitrary, since one direction is not clearly preferred over the other as appears to be the case for the temporal dimension in scripts. *Forward* was assigned to the smallest-to-largest direction, however, to maintain consistency with the markedness literature (cf. Clark & Clark, 1977).

3. We are assuming that typicality generation from categories and centrality generation from scripts are basically the same strategy, since both require that items be retrieved from a representation according to their dominance or accessibility (as determined by the strengths of their superordinate relations).

4. "Activity" was used in the instructions instead of "script" because we thought "activity" would be clearer to subjects and less likely to bias them toward generating actions according to temporal position in the unconstrained and centrality conditions. In addition, the examples provided both for scripts and categories were designed to avoid biasing subjects' performance.

5. Unconstrained generation for scripts and unconstrained generation for categories were weighted as being equal in this and subsequent comparisons because unconstrained generation from scripts and unconstrained generation from categories were equal [min $F'(1,111) = 1.48, p > .10$; in addition, neither the subjects' nor materials' $F$ was significant].

6. When statistical tests were performed on average Fisher $z$ scores corresponding to correlations in Table 2 that were negative, the absolute values of these scores were used. This enabled comparing correlations for their absolute size independent of sign.

7. Regarding this variation, typicality and size were negatively correlated in the unconstrained, typicality, and backward conditions, but were positively correlated in the forward condition. One explanation is based on the assumption that the most typical exemplars of a category are those possessing many average values of the category, including *average* size (see Rosch & Mervis, 1975; Barsalou, 1985). It follows that large exemplars should become increasingly typical as they become smaller in size (as they approach their category's average value) and that small exemplars should become increasingly typical as

they become larger in size (as they approach the average value). Consequently the negative correlations in the unconstrained, typicality, and backward conditions may indicate that subjects were generating large exemplars, whereas the positive correlation in the forward condition may indicate that subjects were generating small exemplars. This explanation is further supported by the fact that backward subjects were asked to begin at the large end of the size scale, whereas forward subjects were asked to begin at the small end.

8.  As suggested by Arthur Graesser, these high positive correlations between centrality and temporal position may stem from preparatory actions at the beginning of scripts being less central than achievement actions toward the end (cf. Miller, Galanter, & Pribram, 1960). It should be pointed out that Galambos (1982) generally found that centrality and output position were *not* correlated. Since Galambos sampled only 12 actions from each script, whereas we included every unique action generated across subjects, the difference in observed correlations may reflect differences in sampling procedures.

9.  We are grateful to Arthur Graesser for bringing this to our attention.

## References

Abbot, V., Black, J.B. & Smith, E.E. (1985) The representation of scripts in memory. *Journal of Memory and Language*, 24, 179–199.

Abelson, R. P. (1981) Psychological status of the script concept. *American Psychologist*, 36, 715–729.

Anderson, J. R. (1976) *Language, memory, and thought.* Hillsdale NJ: Erlbaum.

Anderson, J. R. (1982) Acquisition of cognitive skill. *Psychological Review*, 89, 369–406.

Anderson, R. C. & Pichert, J.W. (1978) Recall of previously unrecallable information following a shift in perspective. *Journal of Verbal Learning and Verbal Behavior*, 17, 1–12.

Armstrong, S. L., Gleitman, L. R. & Gleitman, H. (1983) What some concepts might not be. *Cognition*, 13, 263–308.

Banks, W. P. (1977) Encoding and processing of symbolic information in comparative judgments. In G. Bower (ed.), *The psychology of learning and motivation* (Vol. 11). New York: Academic Press.

Barsalou, L. W. (1981) *Determinants of graded structure in categories.* Unpublished doctoral dissertation, Stanford University.

Barsalou, L. W. (1983) Ad hoc categories. *Memory & Cognition*, 11, 211–227.

Barsalou, L. W. (1985) Ideals, central tendency, and frequency of instantiation as determinants of graded structure in categories. *Journal of Experimental Psychology: Learning, Memory and Cognition*, 11, 629–654.

Barsalou, L. W. (in press) The instability of graded structure: Implications for the nature of concepts. In U. Neisser (ed.), *Concepts reconsidered: The ecological and intellectual bases of categories.* Cambridge: Cambridge Univ. Press.

Bousfield, W. A. (1953) The occurrence of clustering in the recall of randomly arranged associates. *Journal of General Psychology*, 49, 229–240.

Bower, G. H., Black, J. B. & Turner, T. J. (1979) Scripts in memory for text. *Cognitive Psychology*, 11, 177–220.

Clark, H. H. (1973) The language-as-fixed-effect fallacy: A critique of language statistics in psychological research. *Journal of Verbal Learning and Verbal Behavior*, 12, 335–359.

Clark, H. H. & Clark, E. V. (1977) *Psychology and language*. New York: Harcourt Brace Jovanovic.

Collins, A. & Loftus, E. E. (1975) A spreading activation theory of semantic processing. *Psychological Review*, 82, 407–428.

Collins, A. & Quillian, M. R. (1969) Retrieval time from semantic memory. *Journal of Verbal Learning and Verbal Behavior*, 8, 240–247.

Conrad, C. (1972) Cognitive economy in semantic memory. *Journal of Experimental Psychology*, 92, 149–154.

Crowder, R. G. (1976) *Principles of learning and memory*. Hillsdale, NJ: Erlbaum.

Fivush, R. & Mandler, J. M. (in press) Developmental changes in the understanding of temporal sequence. *Child Development*.

Galambos, J. A. (1982) *Normative studies of six characteristics of our knowledge of common activities*. (Cognitive Science Tech. Rep. No. 14). New Haven: Yale University.

Galambos, J. A. & Rips, L. S. (1982) Memory for routines. *Journal of Verbal Learning and Verbal Behavior*, 21, 260–281.

Glass, A. L. & Holyoak, K. J. (1975) Alternative conceptions of semantic memory. *Cognition*, 3, 313–339.

Graesser, A. C. & Mandler, G. (1978) Limited processing capacity constrains the storage of unrelated sets of words and retrieval from natural categories. *Journal of Experimental Psychology: Human Learning & Memory*, 4, 86–100.

Haberlandt, K. & Bingham, G. (1984) The effect of input direction on the processing of script statements. *Journal of Verbal Learning and Verbal Behavior*, 23, 162–177.

Hampton, J. A. (1982) A demonstration of intransitivity in natural categories. *Cognition*, 12, 151–164.

Henley, N. M. (1969) A psychological study of the semantics of animal terms. *Journal of Verbal Learning and Verbal Behavior*, 8, 176–184.

Keil, F. C. (1979) *Semantic and conceptual development*. Cambridge, MA: Harvard Univ. Press.

Kintsch, W., Mandel, T. S. & Kozminsky, E. (1977) Summarizing scrambled stories. *Memory & Cognition*, 5, 547–552.

Klahr, D., Chase, W. G. & Lovelace, E. A. (1983) Structure and process in alphabetic retrieval. *Journal of Experimental Psychology: Learning, Memory, and Cognition*, 9, 462–477.

Mandler, G. (1967) Organization and memory. In K. W. Spence & Janet T. Spence (Eds.), *The psychology of learning and motivation: Advances in research and theory* (Vol. 1). New York: Academic Press.

Mandler, G. (1979) Organization, memory, and mental structures. In C. R. Puff (Ed.), *Memory organization and structure*. New York: Academic Press.

Mandler. J. M. (1978) A code in the node. *Discourse Processes*, 1, 14–35.

Mandler, J. M. (1979) Categorical and schematic organization in memory. In C. R. Puff (Ed.), *Memory organization and structure*. New York: Academic Press.

Mandler, J. M. & Murphy, C. M. (1983) Subjective estimates of script structure. *Journal of Experimental Psychology: Learning, Memory, and Cognition*, 9, 534–543.

Markman, E. (1981) Two different principles of conceptual organization. In M. E. Lamb & A. L. Brown (Eds.), *Advances in developmental psychology* (Vol. 1). Hillsdale, NJ: Erlbaum.

McCloskey, M. & Glucksberg, S. (1979) Decision processes in verifying category membership statements: Implications for models of semantic memory. *Cognitive Psychology*, 11, 1–37.

Mervis, C. B., Catlin, J. & Rosch, E. (1976) Relationships among goodness-of-example, category norms, and word frequency. *Bulletin of the Psychonomic Society*, 7, 283–284.

Meyer, D. E. (1970) On the representation and retrieval of stored semantic information. *Cognitive Psychology*, 1, 242–299.

Miller, G. A., Galanter, E. & Pribram, K. H. (1960) *Plans and the structure of behavior*. New York: Holt, Rinehart & Winston.

Murphy, G. L. & Smith, E. E. (1982) Basic level superiority in picture categorization. *Journal of Verbal Learning and Verbal Behavior*, 21, 1–20.

Nelson, K. & Greundel, J. (1981) Generalized event representations: Basic building blocks of cognitive development. In M. E. Lamb & A. L. Brown (Eds.), *Advances in developmental psychology* (Vol. 1). Hillsdale, NJ: Erlbaum.

Nottenburg, G. & Shoben, E. J. (1980) Scripts as linear orders. *Journal of Experimental Social Psychology*, 16, 329–347.

Rosch, E. (1975) Cognitive representations of semantic categories. *Journal of Experimental Psychology: General*, 104, 192–233.

Rosch, E. & Mervis, C. B. (1975) Family resemblance and studies in the internal structure of categories. *Cognitive Psychology*, 7, 573–605.

Rosch, E. H., Mervis, C. B., Gray, W. D., Johnson, D. M. & Boyes-Braem, P. (1976) Basic objects in natural categories. *Cognitive Psychology*, 8, 573–605.

Schank, R. C. & Abelson, R. P. (1977) *Scripts, plans, goals, and understanding*. Hillsdale, NJ: Erlbaum.

Schneider, W. & Shiffrin, R. M. (1977) Controlled and automatic human information processing: I. Detection, search, and attention. *Psychological Review*, 84, 1–66.

Shiffrin, R. M. & Schneider, W. (1977) Controlled and automatic human information processing: II. Perceptual learning, automatic attending, and a general theory. *Psychological Review*, 84, 127–190.

Smith, E. E., Shoben, E. J. & Rips, L. J. (1974) Structure and process in semantic memory: A featural model for semantic decisions. *Psychological Review*, 81, 214–241.

Stein, N. L. & Glenn, C. G. (1978) An analysis of story comprehension in elementary school children. In R. Freedle (Ed.), *Multidisciplinary perspectives in discourse comprehension*. Hillsdale, NJ: Erlbaum.

Tulving, E. & Thompson, D. M. (1973) Encoding specificity and retrieval processes in episodic memory. *Psychological Review*, 80, 352–373.

# Reasoning: Induction, Analogies, Syllogisms and Deduction

# 9. Inductive Judgments about Natural Categories

## Lance J. Rips

*The present study examined the effects of semantic structure on simple inductive judgments about category members. For a particular category (e.g.,* mammals*), subjects were told that one of the species (e.g.,* horses*) had a given property (an unknown disease) and were asked to estimate the proportion of instances in the other species that possessed the property. The results indicated that category structure — in particular, the typicality of the species — influenced subjects' judgments. These results were interpreted by models based on the following assumption: When little is known about the underlying distribution of a property, subjects assume that the distribution mirrors that of better-known properties. For this reason, if subjects learn that an unknown property is possessed by a typical species (i.e., one that shares many of its properties with other category members), they are more likely to generalize than if the same fact had been learned about an atypical species.*

Gaps in our knowledge of facts force us to rely on inductive methods in determining the truth or probability of certain statements. One, by now traditional, way of studying inductive strategies experimentally is through concept attainment tasks, which have been claimed to provide a direct analogue of inductive reasoning (Hunt, Marin, & Stone, 1966; Trabasso, Rollins, & Shaughnessy, 1971). The basis of the analogy is that in concept formation paradigms, as in inductive reasoning, tentative hypotheses are advanced on the basis of preliminary evidence. These hypotheses are strengthened by confirming evidence or are revised in the light of contradictory evidence. Of course, thus broadly construed, induction is mirrored not only in concept attainment, but also in many other paradigms, for example in problem-solving, decision-making, and tachistoscopic recognition. Nevertheless, it is concept attainment that is most often cited as the counterpart of inductive reasoning.

However, Rosch (1975) has noted that concept attainment paradigms may differ critically from other inductive situations. Most concept attainment studies employ logical combinations of binary attributes so that the resulting concept has well-defined boundaries. A concept so defined has an all-or-none structure, in the sense that no instance is a better exemplar of the concept than any other. Natural language concepts, on the other hand, do possess internal structure, and in many cases this is due to their relationships with other concepts. To illustrate, the best examples of mammals seem to be those instances that are least like members of the contrasting categories, birds and fish; the worst examples are those like platypuses or whales that share important attributes of the contrasting concepts. The effects, in terms of long reaction times to verify sentences like *A whale is a mammal,* have been extensively documented (Rosch, 1973; Rips, Shoben, & Smith, 1973; Sanford & Seymour, 1974; Smith, Shoben & Rips, 1974; and Wilkins, 1971)

Lance J. Rips: 'Inductive Judgments about Natural Categories' in *JOURNAL OF VERBAL LEARNING AND VERBAL BEHAVIOR* (1975), 14, pp. 665–681. Copyright © 1975 by Academic Press, Inc.

To study inductive decisions about natural categories, we must incorporate these categories directly in our experimental paradigm. All inductive situations, however, require at least three components: (a) a set of instances, (b) some property which could consistently be possessed by the instances, and (c) an initial specification of those instances known to have the property. We can then require a subject to make some judgment about those instances *not* already known to have the property. To these minimal requirements, we can add a further restriction. We limit ourselves to cases in which the set mentioned in (a) is composed of natural kinds (e.g. *birds, fruit, furniture*). Some thought must also be given to the type of property in (b). If the property is some well-known feature of the instances, then subjects' inductive judgments may reflect little more than their real world knowledge about this specific case. An alternative is to invent a nonsense property about which the subject can have no knowledge at all. However, it may prove difficult to convince subjects to accept the task and to use what they know about the structure of the category in making their decisions. The property we require should force subjects to consider the nature of the category without, so to speak, giving away the answer.

Towards these ends, the experiments presented below made use of the following procedure. Subjects read a problem concerning animal species inhabiting a small island. The problem listed the names of the species (e.g., *robins, geese,* and *hawks)*, together with the fact that the number of animals in each was approximately the same. The problem then stated that all of the animals in one of the species (e.g., all of the robins) had a new type of communicable disease. Subjects were then asked to estimate, for each of the other species, the proportion of animals that also had the disease. We can let the *Given Instance* denote that species said to have the disease, and the *Target Instances* those species about which estimates must be made.

With the exceptions noted below, the species were chosen from the Rips *et al.* (1973) scaling solutions for bird and mammal instances. These configurations had been derived by having subjects rate the similarities of each of the pairwise combinations of instances, together with the similarity of each instance to its superordinate categories *(mammal* and *animal* for the mammal instances, and *bird* and *animal* for the bird instances). These similarity ratings were then submitted to Carroll and Chang's (1970) INDSCAL program, producing the two-dimensional solutions shown in Figure 1. In Experiment I most of the instances were taken from the solution for birds in Panel a, while in Experiments II–III, most of the instances were mammals drawn from Panel b.

These configurations allow us to predict subjects' estimates on the basis of critical distances within the space. Three distance measures, in particular, are considered here: the distance between the Given Instance and the Target Instance, $d(G, T)$; the distance between the Given Instance and its immediate superordinate category, $d(C, G)$; and the distance between the Target Instance and the superordinate category, $d(C, T)$. To illustrate, take the case in which *robin* serves as Given Instance and *hawk* is among the Target Instances. The three critical distances then measure the sides of the triangle connecting *robin, hawk,* and *bird* in Figure 1a, with $d(G, T)$ the distance between *robin* and *hawk*, $d(C, G)$ the distance between *bird* and *robin*, and $d(C, T)$ the distance between *bird* and *hawk*. The distance between *robin* and *hawk* is an index of the judged similarity of these items. If subjects assume that the disease is more likely to spread among similar species and base their judgments on this criterion then we should expect a negative correlation between $d(G, T)$ and mean estimates. The use of interitem distances to predict generalization of responses has precedence in earlier studies like those of Shepard (1957), Shepard and Chang (1963), and Rumelhart and Abrahamson (1973); however, the use of scaled distances between an item and its superordinate category requires some explanation. Following Rips *et al.* (1973) and Smith *et al.* (1974), we associate these category-instance distances with the typicality of the instance with respect to the category. These distances seem to reflect our intuitions about which instances are most representative, and correlate with norms of judged typicality collected by Rosch (see Rips *et al.*, 1973). In addition, they correlate with subjects' reaction times to decide whether two instances (e.g., *robin* and *hawk)* belong to the same category (Rips *et al.*, 1973; Shoben, Note 1). In short, these distances seem to measure how well each instance fits into the structure of the category, and since we are concerned with the effect of category structure on subjects' judgments, the distances $d(C, G)$ and $d(C, T)$ may prove useful to us.

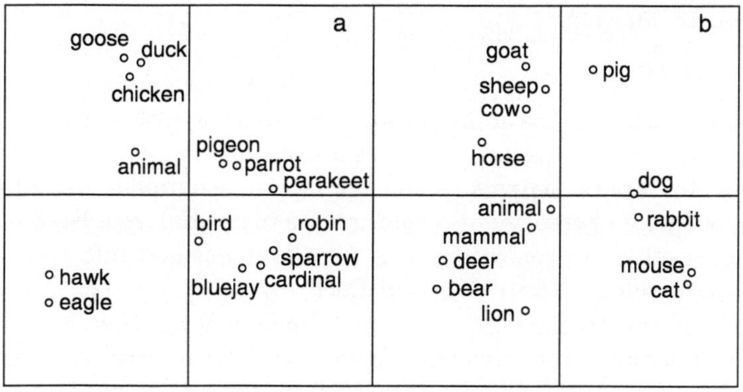

**Figure 1    Multidimensional scaling solutions for birds (panel a) and mammals (panel b)**

## Experiment I

### *Method*

Subjects read a typewritten sheet that asked them to imagine a small island containing only eight species of animals: *sparrows, robins, eagles, hawks, ducks, geese, ostriches,* and *bats.* The first six of these items, referred to as *critical items,* had been chosen from the configuration of birds in Figure 1a. The last two items, *ostriches* and *bats,* were included to emphasize the range of typicality among the eight species. Although seven of the eight species were bird instances, the word *bird* was not used in the statement of the problem situation. The eight items were listed for a subject in one of two random orders, a forward or a reversed sequence.

The problem designated one of the six critical items as the Given Instance: Subjects were told that scientists had recently discovered that all of the members of this species had a new type of contagious disease. Each subject received only one Given Instance, and each group of subjects was assigned to one of the six possible Given Instances. Finally, subjects were asked to estimate, for each of the seven Target Instances, the proportion of animals that had the disease.[1] These estimates were made on a scale from 0 to 100 %, with the stipulation that the percentage judgments should not all be equal. Subjects wrote their estimates in blanks next to the appropriate terms, which were listed in the same random order used in the statement of the problem. The different orders were crossed with the six experimental groups, producing 12 versions of the problem.

## Subjects

All 71 subjects were members of a class on human memory at Stanford University. The problem was administered in a single 20-min interval during one of the regular class meetings. At this point in the course, subjects were presumably not aware of the issues with which the experiment was concerned. The 12 versions of the problem were distributed at random to class members, and each experimental group contained between 11 and 13 subjects.

## Results and discussion

We are interested mainly in the ability of the three distance measures, $d(G, T)$, $d(C, G)$, and $d(C, T)$, to predict subjects' inductive estimates. As a preliminary step, data involving the instances *ostrich* and *bat* were excluded, leaving 30 Given Instance–Target Instance treatment combinations to be analyzed. Each of the subjects' estimates (expressed as a proportion) was then transformed into radians, using the procedure recommended by Snedecor and Cochran (1967, pp. 327–329). Means were taken for each of the treatments, and these means were then converted back to proportions by applying the inverse transformation. These corrected means are shown in Figure 2 superimposed on the scaling solution, with each panel representing the data for one of the six Given Instances (indicated by a filled circle). Within each panel, mean estimates are displayed next to the appropriate Target Instance (open circles). The contours represent predictions from a model to be discussed below.

Which of the three distance measures provides the best predictions of subjects' judgments? A separate regression analysis was performed on the means for each of the seven possible subsets of these measures, and the resulting regression equations are shown in Table 1. In comparing the equations in this table, notice first that all four of the best-fitting equations contain a term with $d(G, T)$ the distance between the Given and Target Instances, attesting to the importance of this factor in predicting subjects' estimates. However, the highest correlations are obtained in equations which also contain $d(C, G)$, the typicality of the Given Instance. We can assess the contribution of $d(C, G)$, as well as $d(C, T)$, by examining some of the partial correlations: With the effect of $d(G, T)$ controlled, $d(C, G)$ correlates significantly with the estimates ($r(27) = -.47, p < .05$), while there is no significant correlation for $d(C, T)$ ($r(27) -.26, p > .10$). Similarly, when both $d(G, T)$ and $d(C, T)$ are partialed out, a significant correlation with $d(C,G)$ remains ($r(26) = -.44, p < .05$), but when $d(G, T)$ and $d(C, G)$ are partialed out, the correlation of $d(C,T)$ is only .19 ($df = 26, p > .10$).

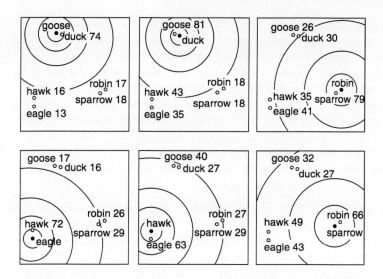

**Figure 2**  Corrected mean estimates and predictions for critical items, Experiment I. (Given Instances are designated by filled circles, Target Instances by open circles. Contours represent predicted estimates of 80, 60, 40, and 20%, from the smallest to the largest contour, on the basis of the exponential model. See text)

**Table 1**  Regression equations, Experiment I

| Equations and standard errors of coefficients[a] | R | df | F |
|---|---|---|---|
| (a) $y = .775 - .0061\, d(G,T)$<br>(.0006) | .89 | 1, 28 | 110.22** |
| (b) $y = .513 - .0029\, d(C,G)$<br>(.0024) | .22 | 1, 28 | 1.44 |
| (c) $y = .229 + .0014\, d(C,T)$<br>(.0025) | .11 | 1, 28 | <1 |
| (d) $y = .912 - .0061\, d(G,T) - .0028\, d(C,G)$<br>(.0005)  (.0010) | .92 | 2, 27 | 71.92** |
| (e) $y = .669 - .0061\, d(G,T) + .0016\, d(C,T)$<br>(.0006)  (.0016) | .90 | 2, 27 | 58.03** |
| (f) $y = .462 - .0027\, d(C,G) - .0009\, d(C,T)$<br>(.0025)  (.0025) | .23 | 2, 27 | <1 |
| (g) $y = .851 - .0061\, d(G,T) - .0026\, d(C,G) + .0010\, d(C,T)$<br>(.0005)  (.0010)  (.0010) | .92 | 3, 26 | 48.30** |

[a] Standard errors are in parentheses below corresponding coefficient.
** $p < .01$.

These results suggest that the similarity of the two instances and the typicality of the Given, but not the Target, Instances play some part in subjects' reasoning. That is, the best account of the data is given by the equation containing both $d(G, T)$ and $d(C, G)$, and this equation accounts for 84.2 % of the variance among the means. It is also possible to test the fit of this equation by comparing the residual variance among the means against the within-cell error variance. However, since the error variance is best calculated on the radian scale, the regression equation was recomputed using means on the same scale. The resulting equation accounts for 82.8 % of the variance. The $F$-ratio for treatments is reduced from 5.49 ($df = 29,325$; $p<.01$) to 1.01 ($df = 27,322$; $p > .10$) by regression. Thus the two-variable equation accounts for most of the systematic variance among the means.

One possible explanation for these results is that a subject uses the typicality of the Given Instance to decide what subset of the species might contract the disease. Presented with an item like *robin* as the Given Instance, a subject decides that the disease is one that any bird could get since robins are typical of the entire class of birds. On the other hand, presented with *duck* as the Given Instance, a subject assumes that the disease is limited to only a subset of bird species, perhaps only to the class of fowls, of which ducks are typical members. Given these boundaries, subjects can then decide what proportion of animals in each of the species have the disease using the overall similarity between these Target Instances and the Given Instance. Such a pattern of reasoning should be reflected by negative correlations for $d(G,T)$ and $d(C,G)$, just as we have found.

It is easy to see why this heuristic should be employed. A representative instance, by definition, is one that shares many important properties with the other instances in its class. If we learn that such an instance possesses some new property, then we assume that this property, too, is shared by other instances. This may be a two step process: The new property may be assumed to be based on other well-known properties of the typical instance which are, in fact, widely shared. Therefore, the new property itself, or at least susceptibility to it, should be common to many instances of the set.

However, the generality of our conclusions concerning subjects' inductive strategies is limited by the choice of stimulus items. Experiment II is an attempt to extend these findings to a second semantic domain.

## Experiment II

### Method

While the procedure duplicates that of Experiment I, this time the six critical instances were drawn from the configuration of mammal items shown in Fig 1b. These six instances were *horse, deer, lion, dog, mouse,* and *pig,* and to this set were added two outliers, *chicken* and *bat.* However, only the first six items served as Given Instances. Again, there were six groups of subjects, each group assigned to one of the six Given Instances. Within each group approximately half of the subjects received the instances listed in one random order, while the other half received the reversed order.

The 197 subjects were members of an introductory psychology class at Stanford University, and the problem was administered to them during a class in which they were engaged in filling out a variety of questionnaires unrelated to the present experiment. The different versions of the problem were distributed at random, and between 26 and 37 subjects served in each of the six groups.

### Results and discussion

As in Experiment I, we are especially concerned with the correlation between the three distance factors and subjects' estimates of the proportion of animals that have the disease. Since mammal instances were used, the relevant distances were taken from Fig 1b; in particular, the typicality measures, $d(C,G)$ and $d(C, T)$, represent the distance between *mammal* and the Given and Target Instances, respectively. Corrected mean estimates are shown in Figure 3.

The pattern of results closely parallels that of Experiment I, as can be seen from a comparison of Tables 1 and 2. The two equations providing highest correlations contain terms with the inter-instance distance, $d(G, T)$, and the distance representing the typicality of the Given Instance, $d(C, G)$. The equation containing just these two variables accounts for 43.2 % of the variance among the means. Although significant (see Table 2), this represents a smaller proportion of the variance than in Experiment I, due to a smaller correlation between $d(G, T)$ and subjects' estimates ($r = -.55$. compared to $r = -.89$ in Experiment I).

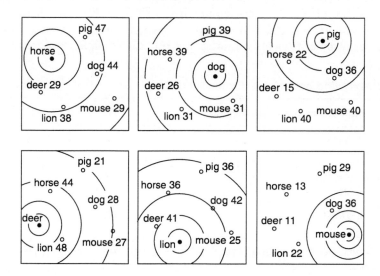

**Figure 3** **Corrected mean estimates and predictions for critical items, Experiment II**

This in turn appears to be due to the position of the critical instances within the configurations. In Experiment I, the six instances were clustered in three widely separated pairs (i.e., *robin–sparrow, hawk–eagle,* and *duck–goose*), while in the present experiment the items are more homogeneously scattered in the space, restricting the range of $d(G, T)$. The correlation coefficient equals $-.73$ when a correction is made for this restriction (McNemar, 1949, p. 126). There is little difference in range for the $d(C, G)$ factor in the two experiments, and with the effects of $d(G, T)$ partialed out, the correlations between $d(C, G)$ and the mean estimates are nearly identical: $-.43$ in Experiment II, compared to $—.47$ in Experiment I ($df = 27, p < .05$ in both cases). The equation containing $d(G, T)$ and $d(C, G)$ can be tested by comparing the residual variance after regression to the within-cell variance, as in Experiment I. In this case, $F$ is reduced from 3.20 ($df = 29,955; p <.01$) to 1.89 ($df = 27,952; p < .01$). Despite the reduction, the residual variance is still significant due to the large sample size used in this experiment.

The typicality of the Target Instance does not appear to be an important factor in these data, again mirroring the results of Experiment I. There is no significant correlation of $d(C,T)$ with the mean estimates, and no significant partial correlations when either, or both, of the other factors are controlled, $F < 1$ in all cases. The difference in the importance of the two typicality variables, $d(C, G)$ and $d(C, T)$, is worth noting, since it implies an asymmetry in subjects' judgments. For example, these results suggest that if a subject receives a typical item (e.g., *horse*) as Given Instance and a less typical item (e.g., *mouse*) as Target, his estimate will be larger than if *mouse* served as Given Instance and *horse* as Target. These results may mean that the typicality of the Target plays no role in subjects' reasoning, but it is possible that the experimental paradigm itself obscures its effect. In particular, $d(C, T)$ has varied within subjects in Experiments I and II, but $d(C, G)$ varied between subjects. Perhaps if subjects are aware of the variation of typicality among Targets, they compensate for it, eliminating the effect.

**Table 2     Regression equations, Experiment II**

| Equations and standard errors of coefficients[a] | $R$ | $df$ | $F$ |
|---|---|---|---|
| (a) $y = .498 - .0029\ d(G,T)$<br>    $\quad(.0008)$ | .55 | 1, 28 | 12.25** |
| (b) $y = .484 - .0040\ d(C,G)$<br>    $\quad(.0014)$ | .48 | 1, 28 | 8.51** |
| (c) $y = .318 + .0001\ d(C,T)$<br>    $\quad(.0016)$ | .01 | 1, 28 | <1 |
| (d) $y = .593 - .0024\ d(G,T) - .0030\ d(C,G)$<br>    $\quad(.0008)\qquad\quad(.0012)$ | .66 | 2, 27 | 10.28** |
| (e) $y = .458 - .0031\ d(G,T) + .0013\ d(C,T)$<br>    $\quad(.0008)\qquad\quad(.0014)$ | .57 | 2, 27 | 6.54** |
| (f) $y = .518 - .0041\ d(C,G) - .0007\ d(C,T)$<br>    $\quad(.0014)\qquad\quad(.0014)$ | .49 | 2, 27 | 4.26** |
| (g) $y = .574 - .0025\ d(G,T) - .0029\ d(C,G) - .0005\ d(C,T)$<br>    $\quad(.0008)\qquad\quad(.0013)\qquad\quad(.0013)$ | .66 | 3, 26 | 6.68** |

[a] Standard errors are in parentheses below corresponding coefficient.
** $p < .01$.

To check this possibility, a pilot study was run in which the roles of the two typicality variables were reversed, with $d(C, G)$ varying within and $d(C, T)$ varying between subjects; that is, subjects in each group received seven Given Instances and a single Target Instance. In all other respects, the pilot study was identical to Experiment II. It was hypothesized that if the effect of typicality appears only when it functions as a between-subjects variable then the effect of $d(C, G)$ should be eclipsed while the effect of $d(C,T)$ should be enhanced. But while the results of the experiment showed the usual effects of $d(G,T)$, neither of the typicality variables contributed significantly to the regression. These results should perhaps be treated with caution because of the small sample size ($N = 45$, compared to 71 and 197 in the first two experiments). Nevertheless, the suggestion is that lack of an effect for $d(C, T)$ in the earlier experiments was not simply due to its use as a within-subjects variable.

However, we must still explain why there was no effect of $d(C, G)$ in the pilot study. One possibility is as follows: In explaining the results of Experiment I, we assumed that subjects used the typicality of the Given Instance to decide what subset of the animals was able to contract the disease. If the Given Instance was a typical bird (or mammal), then all of the birds (mammals) could catch the disease; if the Given Instance was atypical, then only a subset of very similar instances could have it. Now, in the pilot study, subjects were told that each of the species in turn had the disease. Although the subjects were admonished to treat each item independently, it may have proved difficult for them to do so, and as a result, they may have concluded that any of the species could contract the disease. If so, subjects no longer needed to rely on the typicality of the Given Instance; consequently, there would be no effect of $d(C,G)$. Of course, a subject may not have drawn such a conclusion at the time he was doing the first few subproblems. Nevertheless, the tendency might have been sufficient to reduce the effect of $d(C, G)$.

This line of reasoning suggests the following experiment: We can replicate the procedure of Experiments I and II, allowing subjects to use only a single Given Instance. This time, however, we can include the information that any of the species on the island is able to contract the disease. If the explanation just offered is correct we would expect results similar to those obtained in the pilot experiment. This prediction is tested in Experiment III.

## Experiment III

The aim of the present study is to demonstrate that merely informing subjects that all instances are able to acquire a property (in this case, a new disease) is sufficient to eliminate any effect of typicality. Toward this end, there were two groups in the experiment: an Uninformed group who received a problem identical to that used in Experiment II, and an Informed group, who received a problem containing the additional information that "scientists know that any of the other animals could also contract the disease.' At the end of the instructions, a final sentence reminded subjects that any of the species could get the disease. There were no other differences between the two groups.

## Method

The procedure in this study was basically the same as that of Experiment II. Within both the Informed and Uninformed groups, there were six subgroups, corresponding to the six possible Given Instances. The set of predominantly mammal items, used in Experiment II, formed the Given and Target Instances in the present experiment. As a procedural nicety, each subject received a new random permutation of the Target Instances.

The problem was administered to 136 subjects during a single hour-long session in which they also completed a number of other questionnaires. Subjects were randomly assigned to conditions, 71 serving in the Uninformed group and 65 in the Informed group. Within the Uninformed group, there were between 11 and 13 subjects in each subgroup; within the Informed group, there were between 10 and 12 subjects. These students were all members of an introductory psychology class, and participated to fulfil a course requirement.

## Results and discussion

Consider first the results from the Uninformed group in Figure 4 and Table 3. These results are quite similar to those of Experiment II. For $d(G, T)$, the correlation with subjects' estimates is $-.50$, and for $d(C, G)$ the correlation is also $-.50$ ($df = 28, p < .01$). These values are roughly comparable to those of Experiment II: $-.55$ and $-.48$, respectively.

In addition, the effects of these two variables are independent, in that partialing out either variable leaves a significant correlation for the other, the partial correlations being $-.44$ ($df = 27, p < .05$).

In line with the earlier findings, the typicality of the Targets is an unimportant factor in these data. The correlation between $d(C,T)$ and subjects' estimated proportions is $-.005$, $F < 1$. Partialing out either $d(G, T)$ or $d(C, G)$, or both of these distance variables, yields no significant correlations for $d(C, T)$, $F < 1$ in all cases. The equation containing $d(G,T)$ and $d(C,G)$ accounts for 39.8% of the variance. Tested against the within mean square, the residuals are reduced from $F(29,325) = 2.42$ ($p < .01$) to $F(27,322) = 1.55$ ($p > .05$). Again the equation accounts for much of the systematic variance among the means, even though overall percentage of variance accounted for is moderate.

We can compare these results with those for the Informed subjects. The corrected means for these subjects are shown in Figure 5, and the regression equations in Table 4. Of these equations, only that containing $d(G, T)$ approaches significance, but it accounts for only 9% of the variance. The corresponding correlation, $-.30$, is about the same as that found in the pilot study, $-.33$.

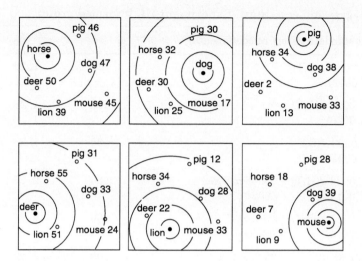

**Figure 4** **Corrected mean estimates and predictions for critical items, Experiment III, Uninformed group**

**Table 3** **Regression equations, Experiment III, uninformed group**

| Equations and standard errors of coefficients[a] | R | df | F |
|---|---|---|---|
| (a) $y = .518 - .0036\ d(G,T)$<br>$\quad\quad\quad(.0012)$ | .50 | 1, 28 | 9.16** |
| (b) $y = .532 - .0057\ d(C,G)$<br>$\quad\quad\quad(.0018)$ | .50 | 1, 28 | 9.40** |
| (c) $y = .304 - .0001\ d(C,T)$<br>$\quad\quad\quad(.0021)$ | .01 | 1, 28 | <1 |
| (d) $y = .660 - .0029\ d(G,T) - .0046\ d(C,G)$<br>$\quad\quad\quad(.0011)\quad\quad\quad(.0018)$ | .63 | 2, 27 | 8.92** |
| (e) $y = .474 - .0038\ d(G,T) + .0014\ d(C,T)$<br>$\quad\quad\quad(.0012)\quad\quad\quad(.0019)$ | .51 | 2, 27 | 4.79* |
| (f) $y = .593 - .0059\ d(C,G) - .0012\ d(C,T)$<br>$\quad\quad\quad(.0020)\quad\quad\quad(.0020)$ | .51 | 2, 27 | 4.82* |
| (g) $y = .652 - .0029\ d(G,T) - .0045\ d(C,G) - .0002\ d(C,T)$<br>$\quad\quad\quad(.0012)\quad\quad\quad(.0018)\quad\quad\quad(.0018)$ | .63 | 3, 26 | 5.73** |

[a] Standard errors are in parentheses below corresponding coefficient.
* $p = <.05$.
** $p < .01$.

**Table 4    Regression equations, Experiment III, informed group**

| Equations and standard errors of coefficients[a] | $R$ | $df$ | $F$ |
|---|---|---|---|
| (a) $y = .506 - .0021\ d(G,T)$ <br> $\quad\quad\quad (.0012)$ | .30 | 1, 28 | 2.78 |
| (b) $y = .393 - .0003\ d(C,G)$ <br> $\quad\quad\quad (.0020)$ | .03 | 1, 28 | <1 |
| (c) $y = .416 - .0009\ d(C,T)$ <br> $\quad\quad\quad (.0020)$ | .08 | 1, 28 | <1 |
| (d) $y = .488 - .0022\ d(G,T) + .0006\ d(C,G)$ <br> $\quad\quad\quad (.0013) \quad\quad\quad (.0020)$ | .30 | 2, 27 | 1.38 |
| (e) $y = .507 - .0020\ d(G,T) - .0001\ d(C,T)$ <br> $\quad\quad\quad (.0013) \quad\quad\quad (.0020)$ | .09 | 2, 27 | 1.34 |
| (f) $y = .439 - .0005\ d(C,G) - .0010\ d(C,T)$ <br> $\quad\quad\quad (.0021) \quad\quad\quad (.0021)$ | .09 | 2, 27 | <1 |
| (g) $y = .484 - .0022\ d(G,T) + .0006\ d(C,G) + .0001\ d(C,T)$ <br> $\quad\quad\quad (.0014) \quad\quad\quad (.0022) \quad\quad\quad (.0022)$ | .30 | 3, 26 | <1 |

[a] Standard errors are in parentheses below corresponding coefficient.

None of the simple correlations or partial correlations for $d(C,G)$ and $d(C,T)$ even approaches conventional significance levels; $F < 1$ in all cases. This is not due to a simple ceiling effect for Informed subjects' estimates, since the mean of these estimates is only 38.1%.

In summary, the differing patterns of results for the Informed and Uninformed groups fulfil the predictions made above. Data from the Uninformed group parallel those of the first two experiments, while for the Informed group the results conform more closely to those of the pilot study. The effect of informing subjects, then, is to lower correlations between the distance variables and subjects' estimate. However, the reduction is not a uniform one: We can contrast the effects of $d(G, T)$ and $d(C, G)$ for Informed and Uninformed subjects by comparing the equations containing these two variables (see Tables 3 and 4). The coefficients for the $d(G, T)$ terms are approximately equal $t(54) = .412, p > .10$, while the difference between the coefficients for $d(C, G)$ is marginally significant, $t(54) = 1.93, .05 < p < .10$. In the latter case, the coefficient is significantly different from zero only for the Uninformed subjects: $t(27) = 2.55, p < .05$ for Uninformed subjects; $t(27) = .30, p > .10$ for Informed subjects. Thus informing subjects that all instances are susceptible to the property eliminates their reliance on the typicality of the Given Instance.

Of the problems faced by the two groups of subjects, that of the Uninformed group seems closer to actual inductive situations. Given a relatively unknown property like that used in the present studies, it is unlikely that the ability of each instance to acquire the property would already be known. Therefore, in inductive situations like this one, we would ordinarily expect typicality effects to occur. However, there may be certain situations similar to that of the Informed subjects. If the property is one whose distribution is already known, we would expect much less reliance on the typicality of the given information.

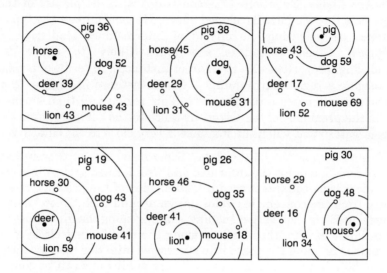

**Figure 5    Corrected mean estimates and predictions for critical items, Experiment III, Informed group**

## Some simple models for inductive judgments

Up until now we have used linear regression equations to decide which of the three distance factors predict subjects' inductive estimates. However, linear equations may not provide the best model for these data. To see this, consider the limiting cases for the measures $d(G, T)$ and $d(C, G)$. Distance $d(G, T)$ is zero when the Given and Target Instances are identical. This is the case in which a subject is asked to estimate the proportion of sick animals in the Given species. Since the subject is told that all of these animals have the disease, we trivially expect estimates of 100 %.[2] As $d(G, T)$ becomes larger, subjects' estimates become smaller, approaching zero for very large distances. Turning now to $d(C, G)$, we can imagine the situation in which the Given Instance is actually the category name itself. That is, subjects are told that all the birds have the disease, and are then asked to estimate the proportion of the various bird species which have the disease. Here, too, the trivial prediction is that all of the estimates should be 100%. As distance $d(C, G)$ increases, the proportions should decrease, at least for the subjects of Experiments I and II, and the Uninformed subjects of Experiment III, for the reasons given above.

These considerations suggest an equation like (1) as a model for the inductive data:

$$\text{Estimated proportion of animals} = \exp\left[-\,\alpha d(G, T)\, d(C, G)\right], \qquad (1)$$

where $\alpha$ is the only free parameter. The exponential form of this equation conforms to earlier work by Shepard (1957) and Rumelhart and Abrahamson (1973), who use exponentials of distances to predict subjects' responses to other types of tasks. More important, this equation allows us to predict the estimated proportions with a single parameter, instead of the three parameters needed for the linear equation with $d(G, T)$ and $d(C,G)$. And finally, Equation (1) is consistent with the picture of the inductive reasoning process that we have developed above. We can think of the typicality of the Given Instance as weighting the effects of interinstance similarity, presumably because typical Given Instances are more likely to share the crucial (disease-producing) properties with the Target Instances. In terms of a visual analogy, we might imagine a region surrounding a Given Instance in Figure 1a or b within which all the animals possess the property. This region will then shrink or expand depending on the proximity of the Given Instance to the category (*bird* or *mammal*), reaching its largest extent when the instance is very close to the category.

How well does this equation fit the data? Separate values of $\alpha$ were estimated for Experiments I and II, and for the Informed and Uninformed groups in Experiment III using a nonlinear least-squares procedure. Some idea of the predictions of this model can be gained from the concentric circles drawn around each Given Instance in Figs. 2–5. The model predicts that Target Instances falling along the innermost circle should receive an estimate of 80%, those falling along the next largest circle all estimate of 60%, each contour dividing the space into successive intervals whose width represents a difference of 20% in predicted estimates. These predictions can be compared to the obtained means, shown next to the Target Instances. The contours were derived by substituting the appropriate value (e.g., 80 for the smallest circle) on the left side of Equation (1), and solving the resulting equation for $d(G, T)$.

Table 5 lists root mean square deviation (RMSD) and percentage variance-accounted-for (PVA) by these exponential equations, as well as the comparable statistics for the linear equations containing $d(G, T)$ and $d(C, G)$. For Experiments I and II and for the Uninformed group in Experiment III the exponential equations seem to fit nearly as well as the linear ones, despite the fact that fewer parameters are used. Larger differences appear for the Informed group in Experiment III, where we would expect the exponential model to provide poor fits to the data since $d(C, G)$ is not an effective variable. A linear equation can compensate for this by lowering the coefficient associated with $d(C, G)$, but Equation (1) cannot, since the two distance measures are not separately weighted.

**Table 5    Comparison of four models in terms of percentage of variance accounted for and root mean square deviation**

| | Linear model | | Exponential model | | Distinctiveness model | | Bayesian model | |
|---|---|---|---|---|---|---|---|---|
| | PVA | RMSD | PVA | RMSD | PVA | RMSD | PVA | RMSD |
| Experiment I | 84.2 | 7.9 | 83.4 | 11.8 | 80.2 | 11.2 | 59.6 | 13.7 |
| Experiment II | 43.2 | 7.3 | 41.7 | 11.7 | 32.6 | 10.8 | 41.6 | 10.0 |
| Experiment III | | | | | | | | |
| Uninformed subjects | 39.8 | 10.4 | 38.6 | 12.5 | 22.4 | 13.3 | 33.6 | 12.9 |
| Informed subjects | 9.3 | 11.8 | 4.5 | 18.2 | 6.2 | 15.6 | 2.4 | 20.3 |

We can assess the fit of the equations from this model by comparing the residual variance to the within-cell variance, as we did for the linear model. However, in this case the test must be somewhat inexact since the within-condition variance is best calculated on the radian scale, while the means predicted by the model are proportions. As a compromise, both predicted and observed means were transformed back to radians, and the residual variance of the observed means on this scale was $F$-tested against the within mean square. For Experiment I, the $F$-ratio for treatments is reduced from 5.49 to 1.00 ($df = 28,324$) for the variance not accounted for by the model. For Experiment II the change is from 3.20 to 1.87 ($df = 28,954$), which is still significant at the .01 level due to the large sample size. For the Uninformed group in Experiment III, $F$ is reduced from 2.42 to 1.49, ($df=28,324$; $p >.05$). As we might suspect, there is no significant treatment effect to begin with for the Informed group in Experiment III, $F(29,295) = 1.36$, $p > .05$, and this $F$ value is reduced slightly to 1.33. In short, the model appears to account for most of the systematic variance among the treatment means. Only in Experiment II is there a significant portion of the variance that is not accounted for by the model.

### An alternative based on stimulus distinctiveness

In the model just discussed, we have interpreted the distance $d(C, G)$ as a measure of the typicality of the Given Instance. Typicality, in turn, can be interpreted in terms of the number of important properties that an instance shares with other category members, with typical instances sharing many of its properties and atypical instances sharing few. A somewhat similar notion can be defined with respect to the distinctiveness of the category members. That is, distinctive instances should be those that share few properties with others, and for the reasons outlined above, should produce smaller estimates when used as Given Instances in the present experiments.

Stimulus distinctiveness has been used by Murdock (1960) to explain serial position effects and more recently by Trabasso and Riley (1975) to explain the speed and accuracy with which transitive inferences can be made. While these earlier studies used only unidimensional stimuli, it seems possible to adapt the distinctiveness concept by means of distances within a multidimensional space like Figures 1a or b. As a first attempt, we can define the distinctiveness of a Given Instance as the sum of the distances between it and the other critical items divided by the sum of all the distances between pairs of critical items. This index of distinctiveness can be substituted for $d(C, G)$ in Equation (1), yielding the following equation:

Estimated proportion of animals =

$$
\exp\left[-\alpha d(G,T)\, \frac{\sum\limits_{T} d(G,T)}{\sum\limits_{G}\sum\limits_{T} d(G,T)}\right]. \tag{2}
$$

This equation has the advantages of Equation (1) and, in addition, uses only a single type of distance measure, $d(G, T)$.

As in the case of Equation (1), separate values of $\alpha$ were estimated for each experiment, and the resulting PVA and RMSD are displayed in Table 5. These values indicate that Equations (1) and (2) do about equally well in describing subjects' judgments, a conclusion that might have been expected from the similar intuitions on which they are based. Nevertheless, it may be possible in future experiments to distinguish between these models as presently formulated.

### An alternative based on Bayes' Theorem

In a pilot experiment, using approximately the same materials and procedure as Experiment I, subjects were asked to provide some justification for the estimates that they gave. Most of these explanations were "symmetric" in the sense that they involved factors like the similarity of two animals or their proximity on the hypothetical island. Factors like these obviously cannot account for the dependence of the judgments on whether an exemplar was a Given Instance or a Target. A small minority of explanations, however, did invoke "asymmetric" factors, for example, the predator–prey relationship or the differential ability of the species to contract disease. The first of these explanations seems unlikely to account for the data. Since animals that are prey for others would presumably be more likely to spread disease, these species should produce higher estimates when they served as Given Instances. In fact, the relationship appears to be the reverse. Especially for mammals, the species most likely to be preyed upon tend to be less typical, and we have seen that it is more typical species that produce an increase in subjects' estimates.

The explanation based on prior probabilities of animals contracting the disease has some plausibility, and a model embodying this idea can be constructed by use of Bayes' Theorem. If $X$ and $Y$ are two of the instances, then

$$P(X \backslash Y) = \frac{P(Y \backslash X)\, P(X)}{P(Y)}, \tag{3}$$

where $P(X \backslash Y)$ is the probability of Target $X$ animals having the disease when $Y$ serves as Given Instance, $P(Y \backslash X)$ is the probability of Target $Y$ animals having the disease when $X$ serves as Given, and $P(X)$ and $P(Y)$ are the prior probabilities for the two instances. Assuming that subjects' estimates of proportions of animals with the disease will be equal to the relevant probability, we should be able to predict these estimates using Equation (3).

While $P(Y \backslash X)$ can be obtained from the data, $P(X)$ and $P(Y)$ cannot. For this reason, a group of 12 subjects was asked to provide these priors. (The subjects were graduates or postdoctoral fellows in psychology and were unaware of the purpose of the experiment.) Two problems were presented to each subject, one problem using the predominantly mammal instances, the other using the predominantly bird instances. The problems themselves were identical in all but one respect to those of Experiments I and II: After describing the inhabitants of the island, the problem stated only that "scientists had discovered a new type of communicable disease on the island." No Given Instance was specified. Subjects were then asked to try to estimate the percentage of animals in each group that had the disease. Half of the subjects received the mammal problem first. An arcsine transformation was applied to each estimate, means were taken across subjects, and the resulting means transformed back to proportions. These transformed means served as the estimates for *P(X)* and *P(Y)* in Equation (3).

Table 5 lists PVA and RMSD for predictions from the Bayesian model, and these statistics can be compared to those from the earlier models. It appears that while this model does fairly well at predicting the results for Experiment II and for the Uninformed group in Experiment III, it does somewhat less well than the previous models for the other experimental groups. That the model does poorly for the Informed group in Experiment III is not surprising; here, the prior probabilities should have been equated, since subjects were told that all of the species could contract the disease. On the other hand, the failure of the model to predict the results of Experiment I is more informative. Recall that Experiment I employed bird exemplars while Experiments II and III used mammal exemplars. If we correlate mean estimates of the priors with the typicality measure used above, we find a higher correlation for mammal than for bird instances ($r_s$ = .77 versus −.37). Thus when the priors correlate with typicality (as for the mammal instances in Experiment II) the Bayesian model does quite well; however, when these measures are relatively uncorrelated, the earlier models do much better at predicting subjects' estimates. This provides support for the view that typicality (or distinctiveness), rather than subjects' belief about the prior likelihoods is the crucial variable in induction situations like this one.

There is a related alternative that we can also consider here. According to this alternative, the data of Experiments I–III might be explained simply by similarities among the species. The asymmetries in the data, discussed above, may be artifactual, due to our use of the wrong measure of similarity. Instead of using overall similarity, as measured by distance within the multidimensional space, we should consider some other measure of similarity, perhaps similarity with respect to susceptibility to disease. If this "true" measure were employed, the effects of typicality might vanish. This theory makes one prediction that is easily tested. If all that matters is similarity between instances (of whatever type), then given any two instances, subjects' estimates should be approximately the same, regardless of which is the Target and which the Given Instance. We can test for this by correlating the two estimates for each pair of instances, and comparing these correlations with those obtained with $d(G, T)$. For Experiment I and II, the correlations between the estimates were .76 and .36, respectively; for the Uninformed and Informed groups, the correlations are .20 and .01. In each case the correlations are lower than those obtained using the distance measure $d(G, T)$, the comparable correlations being −.89, −.55, −.50, and −.30. Furthermore, when the symmetric estimates are partialed out, a significant correlation with $d(C, G)$ remains for Experiments I and II and for the Uninformed group in Experiment III, just as we found above.

## General discussion

We noted initially that studies of concept attainment provided only limited insight into inductive reasoning. Part of this failure was ascribed to the use of artificial concepts, concepts not well-integrated in the structure of language. Most inductive situations involve concepts that are shaped by, and learned in terms of, their interplay with other concepts in the semantic system of a language. For these reasons, the experiments reported here used the more naturalistic concepts studied previously by Henley (1969), Rips *et al.* (1973), and Rumelhart and Abrahamson (1973). The aim of these experiments was to discern whether the structure of these categories, particularly the representativeness of the various instances, would influence subjects' inductive judgments. The results of these experiments provided an affirmative answer. These results indicated that when subjects know little about the distribution of a property across category instances, they assume that the distribution follows that of more common properties. If a new property is known to belong to a typical instance, subjects assume that it will belong to less typical instances as well, for properties of typical instances tend to be widely shared. Conversely, if the property is known to belong to atypical instances, subjects are hesitant to assume that it could belong to more typical ones, since, by definition, many of the important properties of atypical instances are idiosyncratic (Experiments I and II). However, if subjects are provided with information about the distribution of the property, the reliance on typicality disappears, as in Experiment III (Informed group).

A number of other investigators have recently turned to more naturalistic situations in examining inductive reasoning (e.g., Abelson & Kanouse, 1966; Kanouse, 1971; Collins, Warnock, Aiello, & Miller, 1975). Most relevant to the present study are a recent series of experiments by Kahneman and Tversky (Kahneman & Tversky, 1972, 1973; Tversky & Kahneman, 1971, 1973). These experiments demonstrate that categorical or numerical predictions are often in fundamental disagreement with normative statistical considerations. Instead, predictions are based on informal heuristics, particularly the ease with which the predicted event can be brought to mind (availability) and the similarity of the event to the evidence at hand (representativeness). For example, when subjects are asked to assess the likelihood that a personality sketch describes a person in some field of graduate study, estimates are based on the similarity of the description to subjects' prototypes of graduate students in that field. Information is ignored concerning the base-rate frequencies of students in various fields (Kahneman & Tversky, 1973). The present findings are consistent with those of Kahneman and Tversky. In this case, subjects employ a representativeness heuristic to make decisions about the relations between category members. Failure of the Bayesian model to predict the results of Experiment I is also consistent with the view that base-rate frequencies are not crucial determinants of subjects' judgments.

In both the studies of Kahneman and Tversky and those presented here, representative instances permit inductive generalizations to be made more easily than do less representative ones. This can be compared to Goodman's (1955) theory that those predicates which are "well-entrenched" in natural language carry greater inductive weight than poorly entrenched predicates. One explanation of the representativeness or entrenchment of predicates is the possibility that the more representative ones pick out sets of objects that are perceptually salient. As evidence for this possibility, Rosch (Heider, 1972) showed that "focal" colors which are best entrenched in English and other languages, are also better remembered in long-term and short-term memory tasks by Dani tribesmen, whose language lacks names for chromatic colors. Rosch argues that these results can be explained on the hypothesis that focal colors are more salient perceptually than other exemplars and are thus easier to learn.

However, there is an obvious limit to an explanation of induction by means of perception. Inductive inferences occur not only at the level of colors and shapes but also at the level of abstract predicates such as *honesty* or theoretical predicates like *second-order isomorphism*. It seems that the predicates we adopt for inductive judgments are those that best fit in our total conceptual scheme or, in scientific contexts, our total theoretical framework (Scheffler, 1963). Thus entrenchment is a bottom-up process (based on perceptual mechanisms) and top-down as well (based on consistency with other well established terms). This process can explain the structure of categories like those used here. While the boundaries for animal categories are partially determined by perceptual factors (see Berlin, 1973), in modern taxonomies many adjustments of these boundaries have been made. Thus, perception groups whales and dolphins with other fish-looking things, while theoretical considerations dictate that they be classed with mammals. The conflict between perception and theory makes these instances outliers among mammals, leaving as central instances those exemplars with common perceptual and theoretical properties. The effects of this structure has been demonstrated in the preceding experiments.

## Acknowledgements

Thanks are due to G. H. Bower, D. Burke, H. H. Clark, D. Føllesdal, J. G. Greeno, J. Huttenlocher, W. D. Marslen-Wilson, R. N. Shepard, E. A. C. Thomas, H. Wainer, and especially to Edward Smith for comments on a preliminary version of this paper. Part of the research reported here was supported by United States Public Health Service Grant MH-19705 and by a grant from the Spencer Foundation.

## Notes

1. The Given Instance also appeared among the list of Target Instances that the subject had to estimate. Since subjects had been told that all of the Given Instances had the disease, the estimates for these instances were uniformly high and are not considered in the analyses that follow.

2. As noted earlier, this condition was actually present in the experiment and as expected, estimates were near 100%. Including these data in the analysis would probably improve the fit of the exponential model vis-a-vis the linear model. For consistency these data have been omitted in fitting both models.

## References

Abelson, R. P. & Kanouse, D. E. (1966) Subjective acceptance of verbal generalizations. In S. Feldman (Ed.), *Cognitive consistency: Motivational antecedents and behavioral consequents.* New York: Academic Press.

Berlin, B. (1973) Folk systematics in relation to biological classification and nomenclature. *Annual Review of Ecology and Systematics,* 4, 259–271.

Carroll, J. D. & Chang, J. J. (1970) Analysis of individual differences in multidimensional scaling via an *n*-way generalization of "Eckart-Young" decomposition. *Psychometrika,* 36, 283–319.

Collins, A., Warnock, E. H., Aiello, N. & Miller, M. L. (1975) Reasoning from incomplete knowledge. In D. G. Bobrow & A. M. Collins (Eds.), *Representation and understanding.* New York: Academic Press.

Goodman, N. (1955) *Fact, fiction, and forecast.* New York: Bobbs-Merrill.

Heider, E. R. (1972) Universals in color naming and memory. *Journal of Experimental Psychology,* 93, 10–20.

Henley, N. M. (1969) A psychological study of the semantics of animal terms. *Journal of Verbal Learning and Verbal Behavior,* 8, 176–184.

Hunt, E. B., Marin, J. & Stoner, P. (1966) *Experiments in induction.* New York: Academic Press.

Kahneman, D. & Tverskey, A (1972) Subjective probability: A judgment of representativeness. *Cognitive Psychology,* 3, 430–454.

Kahneman. D. & Tversky, A. (1973) On the psychology of prediction. *Psychological Review,* 80, 237–251.

Kanouse, D. E. (1971) Language, labeling, and attribution. In E. E. Jones, D. E. Kanouse, H. H. Kelley, R. E. Nisbett, S. Valins, & B. Weiner (Eds.) *Attribution: Perceiving the causes of behavior.* Morristown, New Jersey: General Learning Press.

McNemar, Q. (1949) *Psychological Statistics.* New York: Wiley.

Murdock, B. B., Jr. (1960) The distinctiveness of stimuli. *Psychological Review,* 67, 16–31.

Rips, L. J., Shoben, E. J. & Smith, E. E. (1973) Semantic distance and the verification of semantic relations. *Journal of Verbal Learning and Verbal Behavior,* 12, 1–20.

Rosch, E. (1973) On the internal structure of perceptual and semantic categories. In T. E. Moore (Ed.) *Cognitive development and the acquisition of language.* New York: Academic Press.

Rosch, E. (1975) Universals and cultural specifics in human categorization. In R. Brislin, S. Bochner & W. Lonner, (Eds.), *Cross-cultural perspectives on learning.* London: Sage Press.

Rumelhart, D. E. & Abrahamson, A. A. (1973) A model for analogical reasoning. *Cognitive Psychology,* 5, 1–28.

Sanford, A. J. & Seymour, P. H. K. (1974) Semantic distance effects in naming superordinates. *Memory and Cognition,* 2, 714–720.

Scheffler, I. (1967) *The anatomy of inquiry.* New York: Knopf.

Shepard, R. N. (1957) Stimulus and response generalization: A stochastic model relating generalization to distance in psychological space. *Psychometrika,* 22, 325–345.

Shepard, R. N. & Chang, J. J. (1963) Stimulus generalization in the learning of classification. *Journal of Experimental Psychology,* 65, 94–102.

Smith, E. E., Shoben, E. J. & Rips, L. J. (1974) Structure and process in semantic memory: A featural model for semantic decision. *Psychological Review,* 81, 214–241.

Snedecor, G. W. & Cochran, W. G. (1967) *Statistical methods.* Ames: Iowa State University Press.

Trabasso, T. & Riley, C. A. (1975) On the construction and use of representations involving linear order. In R. L. Solso (Ed.), *Information processing and cognition: The Loyola Symposium.* Hillsdale, N.J.: Lawrence Erlbaum Associates.

Trabasso, T., Rollins, H. & Shaughnessy, E. (1971) Storage and verification stages in processing concepts. *Cognitive Psychology*, 2, 239–289.

Tversky, A. & Kahneman, D. (1971) Belief in the law of small numbers. *Psychological Bulletin*, 76, 105–110.

Tversky, A. & Kahneman, D. (1973) Availability: A heuristic for judging frequency and probability. *Cognitive Psychology*, 5, 207–232.

Wilkins, A. T. (1971) Conjoint frequency, category size, and categorization time. *Journal of Verbal Learning and Verbal Behavior*, 10, 382–385.

**Reference note**

1.  Shoben, E. J. (1974) *The verification of semantic relations in a same-different task: An asymmetry in semantic memory*. Unpublished manuscript, Stanford University.

# 10. The Use of Statistical Heuristics in Everyday Inductive Reasoning

## Richard E. Nisbett, David H. Krantz, Christopher Jepson and Ziva Kunda

*In reasoning about everyday problems, people use statistical heuristics, that is, judgmental tools that are rough intuitive equivalents of statistical principles. Statistical heuristics have improved historically and they improve ontogenetically. Use of statistical heuristics is more likely when (a) the sample space and the sampling process are clear, (b) the role of chance in producing events is clear, or (c) the culture specifies statistical reasoning as normative for the events. Perhaps because statistical procedures are part of people's intuitive equipment to begin with, training in statistics has a marked impact on reasoning. Training increases both the likelihood that people will take a statistical approach to a given problem and the quality of the statistical solutions. These empirical findings have important normative implications.*

It can be argued that inductive reasoning is our most important and ubiquitous problem-solving activity. Concept formation, generalization from instances, and prediction are all examples of inductive reasoning, that is, of passing from particular propositions to more general ones or of passing from particular propositions to other particular propositions via more general ones.

Inductive reasoning, to be correct, must satisfy certain statistical principles. Concepts should be discerned and applied with more confidence when they apply to a narrow range of clearly defined objects than when they apply to a broad range of diverse and loosely defined objects that can be confused with objects to which the concept does not apply. Generalizations should be more confident when they are based on a larger number of instances, when the instances are an unbiased sample, and when the instances in question concern events of low variability rather than high variability. Predictions should be more confident when there is high correlation between the dimensions for which information is available and the dimensions about which the prediction is made, and, failing such a correlation, predictions should rely on the base rate or prior distribution for the events to be predicted.

Because inductive reasoning tasks are so basic, it is disturbing to learn that the heuristics people use in such tasks do not respect the required statistical principles. The seminal work of Kahneman and Tversky has shown that this is so and, also, that people consequently overlook statistical variables such as sample size, correlation, and base rate when they solve inductive reasoning problems. (See surveys by Einhorn & Hogarth, 1981; Hogarth, 1980; Kahneman, Slovic, & Tversky, 1982; Nisbett & Ross, 1980.)

Richard E. Nisbett, David H. Krantz, Christopher Jepson and Ziva Kunda: 'The Use of Statistical Heuristics in Everyday Inductive Reasoning' in *PSYCHOLOGICAL REVIEW* (1983), Vol. 90, No. 4, pp. 339–363.

The above research on *nonstatistical heuristics* has been criticized on several grounds. Some critics have maintained that evolution should be expected to produce highly efficacious and generally correct principles of reasoning and that the research may therefore be misleading in some way (Cohen, 1979; Dennett, 1978, 1981, Note 1; Lycan, 1981). Others have maintained that the research does not demonstrate that people fail to apply correct inferential rules but rather that (a) it is the researchers themselves who are mistaken about the correct inferential rules (Cohen, 1981), (b) subjects have been misled by illusionary circumstances of little general significance beyond the laboratory (Cohen, 1981; Lopes, 1982; Dennett, Note 1), or (c) people's general inferential goals are such that at least some violations of statistical principles should be regarded as a form of *satisficing,* or cost-effective inferential shortcuts (Einhorn & Hogarth, 1981; Miller & Cantor, 1982; Nisbett & Ross, 1980).

We offer a different perspective on the incorporation of statistical principles into inductive reasoning, one that rejects the preceding criticisms but is, at the same time, fairly sanguine about people's statistical reasoning. Workers in the Kahneman and Tversky tradition have focused primarily on (a) establishing that people fail to respond to important statistical variables for a wide range of problems and (b) examining the inferential principles that people seem to rely on in solving such problems. There has been no comparable systematic effort to determine whether people do respond to statistical variables, either for problems that are easier than those examined to date or for problems of a different kind than those examined.

If it could be shown that people sometimes do reason using explicitly statistical principles, then the work to date on inductive reasoning, and the criticism of that work, would be cast in a different light. Rather than asking why the failures occur or whether the failures are real, it would seem more fruitful to ask questions such as the following. What factors encourage statistical reasoning and what factors discourage it? For what kinds of events and for what kinds of problems is statistical reasoning most likely to be used? Does purely formal training modify the untutored heuristics of everyday inductive reasoning? In addition, accusations that the work to date rests on a kind of experimental sleight of hand or that people are deliberately and advisedly setting aside statistical principles in favor of quicker and generally satisfactory procedures would seem less plausible. Instead, it would seem more likely that there are just difficulties — surprisingly severe difficulties to be sure but difficulties merely — in people's use of statistical principles for inductive reasoning.

In this article we first summarize the recent work establishing failures to reason statistically. We then review anecdotal and experimental evidence indicating that people do sometimes reason statistically. Next we present original experimental work indicating some of the factors that influence statistical reasoning. Then we summarize research suggesting that people's ability to reason statistically about everyday life problems is affected by training in formal statistics. Finally, we speculate on the normative implications of people's ability and trainability for statistical reasoning.

### Statistical problems and nonstatistical heuristics

In a succession of studies over the past decade, Kahneman and Tversky have shown that much inductive reasoning is nonstatistical. People often solve inductive problems by use of a variety of intuitive heuristics — rapid and more or less automatic judgmental rules of thumb. These include the representativeness heuristic (Kahneman & Tversky, 1972, 1973), the availability heuristic (Tversky & Kahneman, 1973), the anchoring heuristic (Tversky & Kahneman, 1974), and the simulation heuristic (Kahneman & Tversky, 1982). In problems where these heuristics diverge from the correct statistical approach, people commit serious errors of inference.

The representativeness heuristic is the best studied and probably the most important of the heuristics. People often rely on this heuristic when making likelihood judgments, for example, the likelihood that Object A belongs to Class B or the likelihood that Event A originates from Process B. Use of the heuristic entails basing such judgments on "the degree to which A is representative of B, that is, by the degree to which A resembles B" (Tversky & Kahneman, 1974, p. 1124). In one problem, for example, Kahneman and Tversky (1972) asked subjects whether days with 60% or more male births would be more common at a hospital with 15 births per day, or at a hospital with 45 births per day, or equally common at the two hospitals. Most subjects chose the latter alternative, and the remainder divided about evenly between 15 and 45. The law of large numbers requires that, with a random variable such as sex of infant, deviant sample percentages should be less common as sample size increases. The representativeness heuristic, however, leads subjects to compare the similarities of the two sample proportions to the presumed population proportion (50%); because the two sample proportions equally resemble the population proportion, they are deemed equally likely. The data indicate that, for this problem at least, most subjects used the representativeness heuristic and very few subjects used the law of large numbers.

In another demonstration, Kahneman and Tversky (1973) studied the prediction of an outcome for a target person based on various characteristics of that person or based on scores from various predictor tests. Subjects used the representativeness heuristic: In general, they predicted whichever outcome was most similar to the target person's characteristics or scores. For instance, in predicting the grade point average (GPA) for a target person who is in the 90th percentile on a predictor test, about the same results are obtained — that is, prediction of a GPA well above average — whether the predictor is the score on a test of sense of humor (which subjects do not regard as very diagnostic of GPA), the score on a test of mental concentration, or the GPA itself (!). Such predictions diverge from those that would be obtained from statistical considerations in which the average accuracy of prediction would be taken into account. Subjects do not seem to realize that if accuracy is very limited, then it is far more probable that the target person's outcome will be equal to the modal outcome (or near the mean of the unimodal symmetric distribution) than that it will take some relatively unusual value that happens to match the characteristics on the predictor. This is the statistical principle of regression to the mean, or base rate.

Other investigations have confirmed and expanded the list of statistical failings documented by Kahneman and Tversky. The failings seem particularly clear and particularly important in people's reasoning about social behavior. Nisbett and Borgida (1975), for example, showed that consensus information, that is, base rate information about the behavior of a sample of people in a given situation, often has little effect on subjects' attributions about the causes of a particular target individual's behavior. When told that most people behaved in the same way as the target, subjects shift little or not at all in the direction of assuming that it was situational forces, rather than the target's personal dispositions or traits, that explain the target's behavior. In a typical experiment, Nisbett and Borgida (1975) told subjects about a study in which participants heard someone (whom the participants believed to be in a nearby room) having what seemed to be an epileptic seizure. Subjects' predictions about whether a particular participant would quickly help the "victim" were unaffected by the knowledge that most participants never helped or helped only after a long delay. Similarly, subjects' causal attributions about the behavior of a participant who never helped the "victim" were unaffected by consensus information. Subjects were just as likely to say that the participant's personality was responsible for his behavior when they knew that most other participants were similarly unhelpful as when they assumed that most other participants helped with alacrity.

Nisbett and Ross (1980) maintained that people fail to apply necessary statistical principles to a very wide range of social judgments. They claimed that people often make overconfident judgments about others based on small and unreliable amounts of information; they are often insensitive to the possibility that their samples of information about people may be highly biased; they are often poor at judging covariation between events of different classes (e.g., "Are redheads hot-tempered?"); and both their causal explanations for social events and their predictions of social outcomes are often little influenced by regression or base rate considerations.

## Statistical heuristics

### Selective application of statistical reasoning

The foregoing work indicates that nonstatistical heuristics play an important role in inductive reasoning. But it does not establish that other heuristics, based on statistical concepts, are absent from people's judgmental repertoire. And indeed, if one begins to look for cases of good statistical intuitions in everyday problems, it is not hard to find some plausible candidates.

Even when judgments are based on the representativeness heuristic, there may be an underlying stratum of probabilistic thinking. In many of the problems studied by Kahneman and Tversky, people probably conceive of the underlying process as random, but they lack a means of making use of their intuitions about randomness and they fall back on representativeness. In the maternity ward problem, for example, people surely believe that the number of boys born on any particular day is a matter of chance, even though they rely on representativeness to generate their subjective sampling distributions. But consider the following thought experiment: If someone says, "I can't understand it; I have nine grandchildren and all of them are boys," the statement sounds quite sensible. The hearer is likely to agree that a causal explanation seems to be called for. On the other hand, imagine that the speaker says, "I can't understand it; I have three grandchildren and all of them are boys." Such a statement sounds peculiar, to say the least, because it seems transparent that such a result could be due just to chance — that is, there is nothing to understand. Such an intuition is properly regarded as statistical in our view.

The contrast between the statistical intuition in our anecdote and subjects' use of the representativeness heuristic in the maternity ward problem illustrates the selectivity with which people apply statistical concepts. The failure to do so in the maternity ward problem may be due to the use of "60%" in the problem, which evokes comparison between 60% and 50% and thence the dependence on the similarity judgment in choosing an answer. It may also be due to lack of concrete experience in thinking about samples in the range 15–45. As Piaget and Inhelder (1951/1975) put it, people seem to have an intuitive grasp of the "law of *small* large numbers," even though they may not generalize the intuition to large numbers.

People also seem to have an ability to use base rates for selected kinds of problems. Consider the concepts of *easy* and *difficult* examinations. People do not infer that a student is brilliant who received an A+ on an exam in which no one scored below A– nor that the student is in trouble who flunked a test that was also failed by 75% of the class. Rather, they convert the base rate information (performance of the class as a whole) into a location parameter for the examination (easy, . . . , difficult) and make their inference about the particular student in terms of the student's relative position compared to the difficulty of the exam. Indeed, laboratory evidence has been available for some time that base rates are readily utilized for causal attributions for many kinds of abilities and achievements (Weiner *et al.* 1972).

As Nisbett and Ross (1980) suggested, one suspects that many lay concepts and maxims reflect an appreciation of statistical principles. It seems possible, for example, that people sometimes overcome sample bias by applying proverbs such as "Don't judge a book by its cover" or "All that glitters is not gold." Perhaps people sometimes even manage to be regressive in everyday predictions by using concepts such as "beginner's luck" or "nowhere to go but up/down."

There is one inductive reasoning task in particular for which there is good reason to suspect that statistical intuitions are very frequently applied. This is *generalization from instances* — perhaps the simplest and most pervasive of everyday inductive tasks. People surely recognize, in many contexts at least, that when moving from particular observations to general propositions, more evidence is better than less. The preference for more evidence seems well understood as being due to an intuitive appreciation of the law of large numbers. For example, we think that most people would prefer to hold a 20-minute interview rather than a 5-minute interview with a prospective employee and that if questioned they would justify this preference by saying that 5 minutes is too short a period to get an accurate idea of what the job candidate is like. That is, they believe that there is a greater chance of substantial error with the smaller sample. Similarly, most people would believe the result of a survey of 100 people more than they would believe that of a survey of 10 people; again, their reason would be based on the law of large numbers.

As we shall see, there is reason to believe that people's statistical understanding of the generalization task is deeper still. People understand, at least in some contexts, that the law of large numbers must be taken into account to the degree that the events in question are uncertain and variable in a statistical sense. Thus they realize that some classes of events are very heterogeneous; that is, the events differ from one another, or from one occasion to another, in ways that are unpredictable, and it is these classes of events for which a large sample is particularly essential.

### *Randomizing devices and the ontogeny of statistical reasoning*

Where do people's selective statistical intuitions come from? An extremely important series of studies by Piaget and Inhelder (1951/1975) suggests that the intuitions may arise in part from people's understanding of the behavior of random generating devices. Statistical reasoning is of course very commonly applied in our culture to the behavior of such mechanisms. Piaget and Inhelder showed that statistical intuitions about random devices develop at an early age. They conducted experiments in which children were shown various random generating devices and then were asked questions about them. The devices included different-colored marbles on a tilt board, coin tosses, card draws, a spinner, and balls dropped through a funnel into a box with a varying number of slots. Children were shown the operation of these devices and then were asked to predict outcomes of the next operation or set of operations and to explain why particular outcomes had occurred or could or could not occur. The work showed that even children less than 10 years old used the concept of chance and understood the importance of sequences of repeated trials.

In one study, for example, Piaget and Inhelder (1951/1975) spun a pointer that could stop on one of eight different-colored locations. The young children they studied (in general, those less than 7 years old) did not initially recognize their complete inability to predict the pointer's stopping place.

> He knows quite well that he is not likely to be able to predict the color on which the bar will stop, but he does believe in the legitimacy of such a prediction and tries to guess the result. . . . The child oscillates quickly between two solutions . . . Either the bar will have the tendency to come back to a color on which it has already stopped, or it will, on the contrary, stop on the colors not yet touched (p. 61).

At this stage the children did not recognize the equivalent chances of the various stopping places, and when the pointer was made to stop at one color repeatedly (by using a magnet) they found nothing unusual in this. A satisfactory causal explanation usually was forthcoming: for example, "the pointer got tired."

By around the age of 7, the Piaget and Inhelder subjects began to understand the chance nature of the pointer's behavior. After a few demonstrations, they quickly came to doubt the predictability of single trials and came to see the distribution of possibilities and their equivalence. Between the ages of 7 and 10, their subjects came to understand the importance of repeated trials and long run outcomes.

> E: If I spun it ten or twenty times, could there be one color at which it
> never stopped?
> S (age 7): Yes, that could happen. That would happen more often if we
> did it only ten times rather than twenty (p. 75).
> E: Will it hit all the colors or not?
> S (age 10 years, 7 months): It depends on how long we spin it.
> E: Why?
> S: Because if we spin it often, it will have more chances of going
> everywhere (p. 89).

How does the child come to have an understanding of the concept of chance during this period? Piaget and Inhelder argue that *the child's understanding of uncertainty grows out of the child's understanding of physical causality.* To the very young child with little understanding of the causal mechanisms that produce outcomes in a physical system, every outcome is a "miracle" — that is, unanticipated — and, paradoxically, once the outcome has occurred, the child believes that it can be explained. As the child comes to understand, in terms of concrete operations, the causal mechanisms that produce outcomes, the child begins to recognize which sorts of outcomes are predictable (and explainable) and which are not. The outcomes that are not predictable are gradually understood to obey certain *non-causal rules.* In particular, the child comes to recognize some cases of the law of large numbers, for example, that the likelihood of any given outcome occurring is greater with a large number of trials than with a smaller number.

By the age of 11 or so, many children have — in addition to a clear conception both of fully deterministic systems and of random generating devices — a good understanding of nonuniform probability distributions. These are partially random systems in which causal factors are at work making some of the possible outcomes more likely than others. The child comes to learn that even though individual events are uncertain in such a system, aggregate events may be highly predictable. In such a probabilistic system, the child grasps the relevance to prediction of the base rate, that is, the distribution and relative frequency of the various outcomes.

This latter point is well illustrated by children's understanding of a device that allows balls to be dropped through a hole into one of a number of slots or bins beneath. Here the chances of a ball dropping into one slot versus another can be made quite unequal by the physical set-up. It is easy to build the device, for example, so that most balls drop into middle bins and fewer drop in the side bins, generating a crude bell curve. Children under 7 generally fail to use this distribution as a basis of prediction. Although they slowly come to recognize that central positions will collect more balls than peripheral ones, they cannot generalize this fact from a box with a particular number of slots to another box with a different number; they do not expect symmetry between slots that are equidistant from the center; and they do not recognize the role of the law of large numbers in making the central slots particularly favored over a long series of trials. All of these intuitions, in contrast, come easily to many 12-year-olds.

We may speculate that the older child's statistical conceptualization of the behavior of randomizing devices serves as the basis for a similar conceptualization of other kinds of events that may be seen as variable and uncertain. We discuss later just what characterizes events where an analogy to randomizing devices can be seen versus those where it cannot be seen.

### The intellectual history of statistical reasoning

The cultural history of statistical reasoning appears to parallel in some interesting respects the developmental course described by Piaget and Inhelder (1951/1975). This history has been traced by Hacking in his book *The Emergence of Probability* (1975). Hacking points out that although random generating devices have been used at least since Biblical times, the modern concept of probability was invented rather suddenly in the 17th century. This was true despite the popularity of games of chance in antiquity and the existence of sophisticated mathematics. (Hacking notes that someone with only a modest knowledge of modern probability could have won all Gaul in a week!)

Paradoxically, the major factor underlying the sudden emergence of the modern concept of probability was the change to a deterministic understanding of the physical world. In the Renaissance, the task of science was understood not primarily as a search for the causal factors influencing events but as a search for signs as to the meaning of events. These signs were clues and portents strewn about by the benign Author of the Universe. This sort of understanding of events encouraged a heavy reliance on the representativeness heuristict. The Renaissance physician, for example, adhered to the *doctrine of signatures*. This was the "belief that every natural substance which possesses any medicinal virtue indicates by an obvious and well-marked external character the disease for which it is a remedy, or the object for which it should be employed" (John Paris, cited in Mill, 1843/1974, p. 766). The representativeness heuristic thus could be derived as a rule of inference from the principle that the Author of the Universe wanted to be helpful in our attempts to understand the world.

A quite different way of understanding events became predominant in the 17th century. This was a new "mechanistic attitude toward causation" (Hacking, 1975, p. 3). Just as the development of concrete operations helps the child to recognize the irreducible ignorance and uncertainty that is left as a residue after causal analysis of a randomizing device, so the new attitude toward causation helped 17th century scientists appreciate the nature of uncertainty in probabilistic systems. "Far from the 'mechanical' determinism precluding an investigation of chance, it was its accompaniment . . . this specific mode of determinism is essential to the formation of concepts of chance and probability" (Hacking, 1975, p. 3)

### Summary

In short, there is good reason to believe that people possess *statistical heuristics* — intuitive, rule-of-thumb inferential procedures that resemble formal statistical procedures. People apply these heuristics to the behavior of random generating devices at a fairly early age. The formal understanding of statistical principles — that is, of the rules governing the behavior of randomizing devices — increases at least until adolescence. The use of such heuristics, both individually and culturally, seems related to the growth of causal understanding of the physical world and to attempts to extend this causal understanding, by analogy, to wider domains. Although we know little at present of the growth in the child's or adolescent's ability to apply statistical heuristics to events other than those produced by randomizing devices, it seems clear that such growth does take place. Adults who are untutored in formal statistics seem to reason statistically about a number of events other than those produced by randomizing machines — such as performance on tests, sports, weather, and accident and death risks. In addition, it is hard to imagine that people could conduct the most basic of inferential tasks, namely, generalization from instances, without the application of at least a rudimentary version of a law-of-large-numbers heuristic.

## Factors that affect statistical reasoning

Despite ontogenetic and historical growth in the ability to reason statistically, contemporary adults do not reason statistically about a wide range of problems and event domains that require such reasoning, and they often do not do so even if they have substantial training in formal statistics (Tversky & Kahneman, 1971). Why is this? What factors make it dificult to apply statistical heuristics when these are required, and what factors can make it easier? Three factors that seem important are implicit in the preceding discussion.

### *Clarity of the sample space and the sampling process*

Randomizing devices are usually designed so that the sample space for a single trial is obvious and so that the repeatability of trials is salient. The die has six faces and can be tossed again and again; the pointer can stop on any of eight sectors and can be spun over and over. Clarity of sample space makes it easier to see what knowledge is relevant. For randomizing devices, the most relevant knowledge is often just the observation of symmetry of the different die faces, spinner sectors, and so forth. The salience of repeatability makes it easier to conceptualize one's observations as a sample.

In the social domain, sample spaces are often obscure, and repeatability is hard to imagine. For example, the sample space consisting of different degrees of helpfulness that might be displayed by a particular person in a particular situation is quite obscure, and the notion of repetition is strained. What is it that could be repeated? Placing the same person in *different* situations? Or *other* people in the same situation? The probability that Person P will exhibit Behavior B in Situation S is abstract and not part of the inductive repertoire of most people most of the time. Even though people recognize the possibility of errors in their judgments of social situations, they do not try to construct probability models; rather, they rely on the representativeness heuristic.

### *Recognition of the operation of chance factors*

A second major factor encouraging the use of statistical heuristics is the recognition of the role of chance in producing events in a given domain or in a particular situation. We have already seen how Piaget and Inhelder (1951/ 1975) describe the recognition of chance in the operation of randomizing devices. The child comes to recognize the limitations of causal analysis for a spinner and the consequent residual uncertainty about the production of events. Something like the same transparent indeterminism exists for other sorts of events as well, even those involving human beings. For example, statistical understanding of some types of sports is undoubtedly facilitated by the manifestly random component in the movement of the objects employed: "A football can take funny bounces." The random component probably does not have to be physical in order for people to recognize it. It is possible to recognize the unpredictability of academic test performance by repeated observations of one's own outcomes. Even with one's own efforts and the group against which one is competing held constant, outcomes can vary. One may even recognize that one's performance on particular occasions was particularly good or poor because of accidents: "I just happened to reread that section because Jill never called me back"; "It was very noisy in the study area that night so I didn't get a chance to review my notes."

In contrast, cues as to randomness in the production of events are much subtler for other kinds of events, especially for many social ones. When we interview someone, what signs would let us know that a particular topic got explored just by chance or that the person seems dour and lackluster because of an uncharacteristic attempt to appear dignified rather than because of a phlegmatic disposition? In addition, as Einhorn and Hogarth (1978) have pointed out, the gatekeeping function of the interview may serve to prevent us from recognizing the error variance in our judgments: The great talent of some people not hired or admitted may never be observed. Daniel Kahneman (Note 2) has suggested to us that the "interview illusion" exists in part because we expect that brief encounters with a living, breathing person ought to provide a "hologram" of that person rather than merely a sample of the person's attributes and behaviors. In most situations, cues as to the fact that an interview ought to be regarded as a sample from a population, rather than a portrait in miniature, are missing. The same may be true for visits to a city, country, or university. One of us long believed that reports of raininess in England were greatly exaggerated because he once stayed in London for 10 days and it only drizzled twice!

### *Cultural prescriptions*

A third factor that may contribute to the use of statistical heuristics is a cultural or subcultural prescription to reason statistically about events of a given kind. Although Piaget and Inhelder focused on developmental changes in the ability to reason statistically about randomizing devices, from a historical perspective it is the young child's ability to reason statistically at all about such devices that is remarkable. It seems implausible that a medieval European child would have reasoned in such a sophisticated way as the Piaget and Inhelder subjects. Statistical reasoning is the culturally prescribed way to think about randomizing devices in our culture, and this general approach undoubtedly trickles down to children. Similarly, statistical reasoning has become (or is becoming) the norm for experts in many fields — from insurance to medical diagnosis — and is rapidly becoming normative for the lay novice as well in such domains as sports and the weather. Models of statistical reasoning abound for sports in particulars, as the two examples below indicate.

> Baseball's law of averages is nothing more than an acknowledgement that players level off from season to season to their true ability — reflected by their lifetime averages. A .250-hitter may hit .200 or .300 over a given period of time but baseball history shows he will eventually level off at his own ability ("Law of Averages," 1981).

> The musky tends to be a deep water fish. Most fishing success is in shallow water, but . . . this misleading statistic [is probably accounted for in part by the fact that] sheer statistical chance dictates that fish will come from the waters receiving the most man hours of fishing pressure. Shallow water fishing for muskies is very popular, and very few fishermen work them deep (Hamer, 1981).

The statistical spirit embodied in these quotations reaches many fans. Thus, it is commonplace to hear lay people endorse the proposition that "On a given Sunday any team in the NFL can beat any other team." (Compare with "On a given Sunday, any parishioner's altruism can exceed that of any other parishioner"!)

In our view, these three factors — clarity of the sample space and the sampling process, recognition of the role of chance in producing events, and cultural prescriptions to think statistically — operate individually and, perhaps more often, together to increase people's tendencies to apply statistical heuristics to problems that require a statistical approach. If these factors are genuinely important determinants of people's ability to reason statistically, then it should be possible to find support for the following predictions.

In cases where the sample space is clear and the possibility of repetition is salient, people will respond appropriately to statistical variables. In particular, in the task of generalizing from instances, where the sample space is a clear dichotomy and the sampling process is just the observation of more members of a clearly defined population, (a) people will generalize more cautiously when the sample size is small and when they have no strong prior belief that the sampled population is homogeneous, and (b) people can be influenced to generalize more or less readily by manipulations that emphasize the homogeneity or hetrogeneity of the sampled population.

The following predictions should hold both for generalization and for other, more complex, inferential tasks: (a) Manipulations designed to encourage recognition of the chance factors influencing events should serve to increase statistical reasoning. (b) People who are highly knowledgeable about events of a given kind should be more inclined than less knowledgeable people to apply statistical reasoning to the events — because both the distributions of the events and the chance factors influencing the events should be clearer to such people. (c) People should be disinclined to reason statistically about certain kinds of events that they recognize to be highly variable and uncertain — notably social events — because the sample spaces for the events and the chance factors influencing the events are opaque. (d) Training in statistics should promote statistical reasoning even about mundane events of everyday life because such training should help people to construct distributional models for events and help them to recognize "error," or the chance factors influencing events.

**Generalizing from instances**

Generalization from observed cases is the classic concern of philosophers and other thinkers who are interested in induction. A number of instances of Class A are observed, and each of them turns out to have Property B. Possible inferences include the universal generalization *all A's have B*, or the near universal *most A's have B,* or at least the relinquishing of the contrary generalization, namely, *most A's do not have B.*

The untrammeled employment of the representativeness heuristic would lead people to make the above inferences from quite small numbers of instances, and, indeed, this is often found, both anecdotally and in laboratory studies (Nisbett & Ross, 1980, pp. 77-82). On the other hand, philosophers since Hume have puzzled about how these generalizations can be logically justified, even when very large numbers of instances are observed. The puzzle has been compounded by the fact that sometimes it seems correct to generalize confidently from a few instances. Hume (1748/1955) wrote, "[Often, when] I have found that . . . an object has always been attended with . . . an effect . . . I foresee that other objects which are in appearance similar will be attended with similar effects" (p. 48). The problem is that only sometimes do we draw such a conclusion with confidence. "Nothing so like as eggs, yet no one, on account of this appearing similarity, expects the same taste and relish in all of them" (p. 50). Mill (1843/1974), a century later, phrased the problem like this: "Why is a single instance, in some cases, sufficient for a complete induction, while in others myriads of concurring instances, without a single exception known or presumed, go such a very little way towards establishing a universal proposition?" (p. 314).

The statistical advances since Mill's time make it clear that a large part of the answer to his question has to do with beliefs about the variability or *homogeneity* of certain kinds or classes of events (cf. Thagard & Nisbett, 1982). Generalization from a large sample is justified in terms of one's beliefs that the sampling itself is homogeneous (i.e., that the distribution of possible sample statistics is the same as would be predicted by random sampling). And generalization from a small sample or resistance to generalization, even from a large sample, are justified in terms of prior beliefs about the homogeneity or heterogeneity of objects or events of a certain kind with respect to a property of a certain kind. If, for example, the object is one of the chemical elements and the property is electrical conductivity, then one expects homogeneity: All samples of the element conduct electricity or none do. But if the object is an animal and the property is blueness, one's prior belief does not favor homogeneity so strongly; color may or may not vary within a particular species.

In other words, there are cases where use of the representativeness heuristic is justified in terms of beliefs about homogeneity, which in turn may be soundly based on individually or culturally acquired experience with kinds of objects and kinds of properties. For other cases, simple representativeness cannot be justified, and there are indeed cases, as Mill claimed, in which a strong prior belief in *heterogeneity* properly prevents acceptance of a generalization even after quite large numbers of instances have been observed.

We attempted to demonstrate, in a laboratory study of judgment, that people do in fact temper the use of representativeness to a greater or lesser degree depending on beliefs about the variability of a kind of object with respect to a kind of property.

### Study 1: Beliefs about homogeneity and reliance on the law of large numbers

In this study, we simply guessed at the prevailing beliefs about homogeneity. We tried to obtain different degrees of heterogeneity by using conductivity of metals, colors of animals, and so on. Subjects were told of one instance or of several instances of a sampled object having a particular property and were asked to guess what percentage of the population of all such objects would have the property. The sample sizes used were 1, 3, or 20; in the latter cases, all 3 or all 20 of the objects had the property in question. We anticipated that subjects would generalize more readily from a given number of instances when the kind of object was perceived as homogeneous with respect to the kind of property than when the kind of object was perceived as heterogeneous with respect to the kind of property.

## Method

Subjects were 46 University of Michigan students of both sexes who were enrolled in introductory psychology. (As sex did not affect any of the dependent variables in this or any of the other studies, it will not be discussed further.) Eighty-five percent of the subjects had taken no statistics courses in college. The questionnaire was presented as one of several in a study on judgment. It read as follows for the $N = 1$ condition:

> Imagine that you are an explorer who has landed on a little known island in the Southeastern Pacific. You encounter several new animals, people, and objects. You observe the properties of your "samples" and you need to make guesses about how common these properties would be in other animals, people or objects of the same type.

> Suppose you encounter a new bird, the shreeble. It is blue in color. What percent of all shreebles on the island do you expect to be blue?

(This and the subsequent questions were followed by

> "_____ percent. Why did you guess this percent?")

> Suppose the shreeble you encounter is found to nest in a eucalyptus tree, a type of tree which is fairly common on the island. What percent of all shreebles on the island do you expect to nest in eucalyptus trees?

> Suppose you encounter a native, who is a member of a tribe he calls the Barratos. He is obese. What percent of the male Barratos do you expect to be obese?

> Suppose the Barratos man is brown in color. What percent of male Barratos do you expect to be brown (as opposed to red, yellow, black or white)?

> Suppose you encounter what the physicist on your expedition describes as an extremely rare element called floridium. Upon being heated to a very high temperature, it burns with a green flame. What percent of all samples of floridium found on the island do you expect to burn with a green flame?

> Suppose the sample of floridium, when drawn into a filament, is found to conduct electricity. What percent of all samples of floridium found on the island do you expect to conduct electricity?

The questionnaires for the $N = 3$ condition and the $N = 20$ condition were identical except that they specified larger samples of each object. For example, the first shreeble item for the $N = 3$ condition read as follows:

> Suppose you encounter a new bird, the shreeble. You see three such birds. They are all blue in color. What percent of all shreebles on the island do you expect to be blue?

The reasons subjects gave for guessing as they did were coded as to their content. There were three basic sorts of answers: (a) references to the homogeneity of the kind of object with respect to the kind of property, (b) references to the heterogeneity of the kind of object with respect to the kind of property — due to the different properties of subkinds (e.g., male vs. female), to some causal mechanism producing different properties (e.g., genetic mistakes), or to purely statistical variability (e.g., "where birds nest is sometimes just a matter of chance"), and (c) other sorts of answers that were mostly based on representativeness or that were mere tautologies. Two independent coders achieved 89% exact agreement on coding category.

## Results

Any one element is presumed by scientists to be homogeneous with respect to most properties. At the other extreme, most human groups are highly heterogenous among themselves in many attributes, including body weight. If educated lay people share these beliefs and if they reason statistically, then (a) they should exercise more caution in generalizing from single cases when heterogeneity is expected than when homogeneity is expected and (b) large $N$ should be important primarily in the case of populations whom subjects believe to be heterogeneous with respect to the property in question.

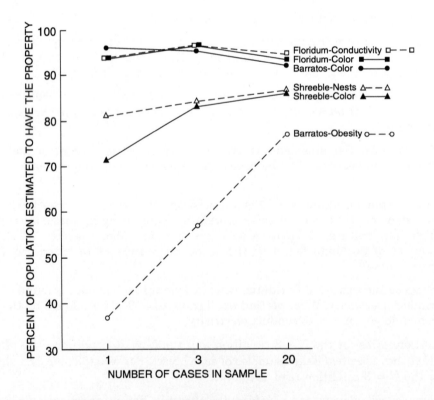

**Figure 1**   **Percentage of each population estimated to have the sample property as a function of number of cases in the sample.**

Figure 1 presents subjects' estimates of the percentage of each population having the property associated with the sample as a function of sample size presented. It may be seen that subjects are quite willing to generalize from even a single instance of green-burning or electricity-conducting floridium and also from a single, brown, Barratos tribesman. The modal estimate for $N = 1$ (as well as for $N = 3$ and $N = 20$) in all of these cases is 100%. In contrast, generalizations are less extreme for even 20 instances of blue shreebles or eucalyptus-nesting shreebles or 20 obese Barratos. The $t(31)$ contrasting $N = 1$ for floridium attributes and Barratos color with $N = 20$ for shreeble attributes and Barratos obesity is 3.00; $p < .01$.[1]

Subjects' explanations for their estimates fully justify this pattern of inferences. It may be seen in Table 1 that subjects reported believing that elements are homogeneous with respect to color and conductivity and that tribes are homogeneous with respect to color. In contrast, subjects rarely expressed the belief that there is homogeneity for the other kinds of populations and properties and instead expressed belief in heterogeneity of one sort or another for these objects and properties. Figure 1 shows that it is only for these latter cases that subjects reasoned statistically in the sense that they were more willing to assume that the population resembles the sample when $N$ is larger. $N$ affects the estimates of the obesity of Barratos and the color of shreebles ($p < .001$ and $p = .11$, respectively). In addition, a total of 10 subjects complained on one or more problems that the $N$ was too small to give a good estimate. For nine of these subjects, the complaints were about one or more of the three problems where populations were presumed to be heterogeneous with respect to the property in question, whereas for only one subject was the complaint about a problem for which subjects in general believed populations to be homogeneous with respect to properties (exact $p = .02$).

Finally, an internal analysis of the Table 1 data for each question showed that those subjects who believed the population to be homogeneous with respect to the property estimated that a higher percentage of the population was like the sample than did those subjects who believed the population was heterogeneous with respect to the property. The lowest $t$ resulting from the six comparisons yielded $p < .05$.

### Study 2: *Manipulating the salience of distribution parameters*

Study 1 established that people can apply statistical reasoning to one of the most basic of inferential tasks. It also established that beliefs about variability of the class of events in question can mediate the statistical reasoning. One other study in the literature made similar points. Quattrone and Jones (1980) proposed a version of the present view that beliefs about variability influence inductive generalizations in their important study on perception of ingroups versus outgroups. They hypothesized that "an observer's tendency to generalize from the behavior of a specific group member to the group as a whole is proportional to the observer's perception of the group's homogeneity" (p. 141). Because people are more familiar with the members of groups to which they happen to belong, they will recognize "the group's general variability, the extent to which its members . . . differ from one another when viewed over all dimensions" (p. 141). Because people are less familiar with outgroups, they are at liberty to assume that their members are relatively uniform. Thus people may generalize more readily from observations of the behavior of outgroup members than from observations of the behavior of ingroup members.

**Table 1**  **Number of subjects giving each type of reason and percentage of population estimated to have the property**

| | Reason | | | | | |
|---|---|---|---|---|---|---|
| | Homogeneity | | Tautology | | Heterogeneity | |
| Object and property | *n* | % | *n* | % | *n* | % |
| Shreeble | | | | | | |
| Color | 6 | 95 | 17 | 83 | 22 | 75 |
| Nests | 8 | 96 | 19 | 84 | 19 | 78 |
| Barratos | | | | | | |
| Obesity | 5 | 79 | 10 | 62 | 31 | 53 |
| Color | 31 | 98 | 7 | 94 | 8 | 80 |
| Floridium | | | | | | |
| Color | 31 | 97 | 9 | 91 | 6 | 82 |
| Conductivity | 31 | 98 | 7 | 92 | 8 | 82 |

To test this hypothesis, Quattrone and Jones (1980) showed Princeton and Rutgers University undergraduates videotapes of male students who were allegedly serving as partipants in psychology experiments. These students were asked to make choices such as to wait for a few minutes by themselves versus in the company of others or to listen to rock music versus classical music. Half of the subjects at each campus believed they were viewing Princeton men, and half believed they were viewing Rutgers men. After seeing the choice of one participant, subjects were asked to predict what the 100 participants in the study did. Quattrone and Jones found greater generalization from the participants' behavior to outgroup members than to ingroup members. Thus, Princeton subjects generalized more strongly to the behavior of the Rutgers population after observing the choice of the "Rutgers" participant than they did to the Princeton population after observing the choice of the "Princeton" participant.

If, as both we and Quattrone and Jones assume, generalizations about groups from the behavior of its members are mediated by assumptions about variability of group members, then it should be possible to manipulate those assumptions and therefore to influence the degree of generalization. People are inclined to think of (their own) university populations as being immensely variable — what with caftans here and exotic accents there, football players here and budding physicists there. In fact, however, university populations are not as heterogeneous as one might casually presume. Most students, even at multiversities, are, after all, bright young middle-class people of fairly homogeneous geographic and ethnic backgrounds. It seems possible that, if subjects were required to contemplate the central tendencies of their university populations before observing choice behavior like that presented to Quattrone and Jones's subjects, they might generalize more. This possibility was examined in Study 2.

## Method

The procedure used by Quattrone and Jones (1980) was followed almost exactly, except that subjects were told that the videotapes were either of University of Michigan or of Ohio State University students, and half of the subjects were exposed to a central-tendency manipulation before viewing the videotapes. Subjects were 115 University of Michigan undergraduates of both sexes enrolled in introductory psychology. They participated in small groups, seated around a table facing a .53-m (21-inch) video monitor. Subjects were told that the investigators were "studying how people make judgments about people — working from actual information they have about people to guesses about other aspects of people. One of our major interests is in how students perceive students at (their own/another) university."

At this point the central-tendency manipulation was delivered to experimental subjects, who were told that "we will be asking you several questions about students at (the University of Michigan/Ohio State University)" and were given the appropriate central-tendency questionnaire. Control subjects began viewing videotapes immediately.

The central-tendency questionnaire consisted of three questions that we expected would influence subjects' conceptions of the variability of a student population. Subjects were asked to "please list what you would guess to be the 10 most common majors at (the University of Michigan/Ohio State University)" and next to list the five most common ethnic group backgrounds and the five most common religious backgrounds at that university. Answering these questions might be expected to prompt subjects to recognize that the student body is not all that heterogeneous: Most students are, after all, white Prostestants concentrated in a limited number of relatively popular majors.

Subjects viewed the Quattrone and Jones videotapes.[2] They were introduced as having been made during psychology experiments conducted at the University of Michigan or at Ohio State University. In each of the three tapes a male participant was shown being confronted with a decision, and he then chose one of two alternative behaviors offered. In the first scenario, a target person had to choose between waiting alone or waiting with other subjects while his experimenter fixed a machine. In the second scenario, the choice was between listening to classical music or listening to rock music during an experiment on auditory perceptual sensitivity. In the third scenario, the choice was between solving mathematical problems or solving verbal problems during an experiment on the effects of noise on intellectual performance. As the order in which scenarios were presented had no effect in the Quattrone and Jones study, it was held constant in our study.

The procedure was the same for each scenario. Subjects watched the target person being given instructions and being asked to make his decision. At this point the tape was turned off and subjects were asked to predict the target person's decision on a 21-point scale that had endpoints labeled with the two relevant options. The tape was then turned on again and subjects observed the participant make his decision. Half of the subjects saw the participants in the three scenarios make one set of decisions, and half saw the complementary set. Thus, subjects in Set A saw the target persons choose

(a) to wait alone, (b) to listen to classical music, and (c) to solve mathematical problems. Subjects in Set B saw targets choose (a) to wait with others (b) to listen to rock music, and (c) to solve verbal problems.

The dependent variable of interest consisted of the subjects' estimates of how many out of 100 participants in each of the three experiments chose each of the two options. (For the sole purpose of replication, subjects were also asked to indicate what they would have done and who they liked as people more — those who would prefer Option A or those who would prefer Option B.)

### Results

Figure 2 presents subjects' generalizations about the University of Michigan and Ohio State University populations for control subjects and for subjects exposed to the central-tendency manipulation. *Generalization* is defined as the difference between population estimates for subjects presented with Set A choices versus those for subjects presented with Set B choices. The higher this index is, the more a group of subjects was influenced in their estimates by the behavior of the particular subject they witnessed. The index sums across all three types of choices, but the trends were the same for each of the three problems.

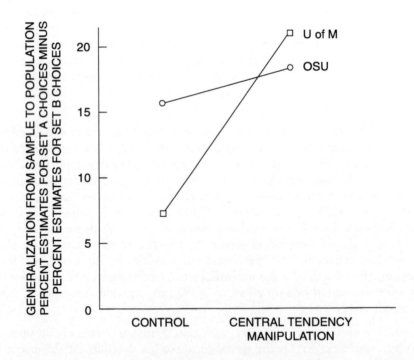

**Figure 2** **Generalization from sample to population as a function of campus population and central-tendency manipulation. (U of M = University of Michigan; OSU = Ohio State University.)**

The difference between the control groups exposed to Ohio State University participants versus those exposed to University of Michigan participants provides a replicaton of the Quattrone and Jones finding. The magnitude of the difference is very similar to that found by them, though for our smaller sample it is only marginally significant, $F(1, 50) = 2.76, .05 < p < .10)$.

The effect of the central-tendency manipulation was to increase the degree of generalization from the sample, $F(1, 107) = 4.23, p < .05)$. It may be seen that the effect was largely due to the behavior of the University of Michigan group. This is not surprising because the judgments about the Ohio State students may have already incorporated central tendencies in the form of an outgroup stereotype. This explanation should be viewed with caution, however, inasmuch as the interaction failed to reach statistical significance.

Both findings provide support for the contention that concurrent representations of population variability mediate inductive generalizations. Familiarity with one's own group results in less willingness to generalize for them than for another group, although forced contemplation of central tendencies results in more willingness to generalize, at least for the familiar ingroup.

One other study, by Silka (1981), shows the importance for inductive reasoning of people's focus on variability versus central tendency. She asked subjects to examine a series of numerical values that were said to represent the mental health of several individuals. Some subjects were asked to remember the average of the values, and some were asked to remember the range. When subjects were asked 1 week later, to assess the degree of change represented by a new value, subjects who had been asked to remember the average were more likely to infer that there had been a genuine change than those who had been asked to remember the range. The implication of Silka's finding, together with those of Study 2, is that inferences about continuity and change, and inductive reasoning generally, may be in part a function of arbitrary encoding and retrieval factors that accidentally emphasize either the homogeneity or the heterogeneity of events.

### Study 3: Manipulating the salience of chance factors

Study 2 establishes that manipulations of the salience of distributional parameters can influence subsequent generalizations. It should also be possible to influence generalizations by manipulating the salience of chance factors. One potentially interesting way of doing this would be to highlight for subjects the degree to which evidence about an object should properly be regarded as a sample from the population of the object's attributes. Such a reminder ought to prompt subjects to reason more statistically, deemphasizing evidence from smaller samples and placing greater weight on evidence from larger samples.

Borgida and Nisbett (1977) argued that people often ignore the judgments of others when choosing between two objects and substitute their own initial impressions of the objects as the sole basis of choice. People do this in part because they do not recognize the relevance of the law of large numbers when reasoning about events of the personal preference kind. When the objects are multifaceted and complex, however, the law of large numbers is applicable in two ways: (a) The reactions of other people to the object, especially if they are based on more extensive contact with the object than one has had oneself, generally should be a useful guide to choice (though, of course, it is possible to construct cases where other people's reactions would not be useful). (b) One's own experience with the object, especially if it is brief or superficial, may be a poor guide to choice because of the error that plagues any small samples, even those that happen to be our own.

It seemed likely that if people were made explicitly aware of the role of chance in determining the impression one may get from a small sample, they might place less faith in a small personal sample and more faith in a large sample based on other people's reactions.

### Method

Subjects were 157 University of Michigan students of both sexes who were enrolled in introductory psychology classes. Eighty-seven percent had taken no statistics courses in college. Subjects participated in small groups. They were presented with two versions of the following problem.

> David L. was a senior in high school on the East Coast who was planning to go to college. He had compiled an excellent record in high school and had been admitted to his two top choices: a small liberal arts college and an Ivy League university. David had several older friends who were attending the liberal arts college and several who were attending the Ivy League university. They were all excellent students like himself and had interests similar to his. The friends at the liberal arts college all reported that they liked the place very much and that they found it very stimulating. The friends at the Ivy League university reported that they had many complaints on both personal and social grounds and on educational grounds.

> David initially thought that he would go to the smaller college. However, he decided to visit both schools himself for a day.

> He did not like what he saw at the private liberal arts college: Several people whom he met seemed cold and unpleasant; a professor he met with briefly seemed abrupt and uninterested in him; and he did not like the "feel" of the campus. He did like what he saw at the Ivy League university: Several of the people he met seemed like vital, enthusiastic, pleasant people; he met with two different professors who took a personal interest in him; and he came away with a very pleasant feeling about the campus. Please say which school you think David should go to.

> 1. He should definitely go to the liberal arts college.
> 2. He should probably go to the liberal arts college.
> 3. It's a toss-up.
> 4. He should probably go to the Ivy League university.
> 5. He should definitely go to the Ivy League university.
> Please indicate why you made the recommendation you did.

The remaining subjects were presented with an identical problem except that the possibilities for error in David L.'s sample were highlighted by having him draw up a list of all the things that *might* be seen on the two campuses and then selecting randomly from among them for his actual schedule. The following was added to the second paragraph of the no-cue version.

> He proceeded systematically to draw up a long list, for both colleges, of all the classes which might interest him and all the places and activities on each campus that he wanted to see. From each list, he randomly selected several classes and activities to visit, and several spots to look at (by blindly dropping a pencil on each list of alternatives and seeing where the point landed).

Open-ended responses to the probe question were coded (by a blind coder) as to whether subjects justified their choice by showing any recognition of the statistical questions involved — either the dubiousness of David L.'s impressions because of the quantity of his evidence or the superiority of his friends' testimony because of their greater experience. There was 90% agreement among coders as to the assignment of an answer to the statistical versus nonstatistical categories.

### Results

When there was no sampling cue pointing to the probabilistic nature of David L.'s personal evidence base, 74% of the subjects recommended that David L. should go to the Ivy League university, which his friends didn't much like but where he enjoyed his day. When the sampling cue was present, this dropped to 56% ($\chi^2 = 5.38$, $p < .025$). Moreover, subjects in the probabilistic-cue condition were much more likely to refer to statistical considerations having to do with the adequacy of the sample. Fifty-six percent of probabilistic-cue subjects raised statistical questions in their open-ended answers, whereas only 35% of subjects in the no-cue condition did so ($p < .01$). Thus, when subjects are prompted to consider the possibilities for error that are inherent in a small sample of events, they are likely to shift to preference for large indirect samples over small personal ones, and their open-ended answers make it clear that it is statistical considerations that prompt this shift.

The findings of Study 3 are extremely ironic in that subjects are more likely to reject the superior personal evidence in the probabilistic cue condition than to reject the inferior personal evidence in the control condition. This is because the same circumstances that serve to make the evidence superior in the probabilistic-cue condition also serve to make salient the extreme heterogeneity of the event population to be estimated and the small size of the personal sample of those events. It is important to note that when Study 3 is run with a "within" design, subjects assess the relative value of the personal evidence correctly; that is, they generally rate the quality of evidence in the probabilistic-cue condition as superior to that in the control condition. In two slightly different within-design follow-ups to Study 3, subjects rated the probabilistic-cue sample as being superior to the sample in the control version. In one of the follow-ups (where subjects read the control problem and rated the quality of the personal evidence, then read the cue paragraph and compared the quality of the evidence there with the control version) four times as many subjects preferred the probabilistic-cue evidence as preferred the control evidence. In the other follow-up (where subjects actually acted as subjects in the control condition and then were shown the cue version), 40% more subjects preferred the probabilistic-cue evidence than preferred the control evidence.

## Expertise and statistical reasoning

### Study 4: Recognition of a regression effect in sports and acting

The studies we have just described indicate that subjects reason statistically when they recognize the heterogeneity of the events in question and the samplelike nature of their evidence about the events. If people are capable of learning from experience that events of a given kind are heterogenous and are produced in part by chance, then it should be possible to show that greater expertise in a domain is associated with a greater tendency to reason statistically in that domain. The two domains we selected to test this proposition were sports and acting. We anticipated that experience with sports would facilitate recognition of a regression effect in sports and that experience with acting would facilitate recognition of a regression effect in acting. Subjects were told about a small sample of extreme behavior followed by a larger sample of less extreme behavior. It was anticipated that inexpert subjects would generalize from the small sample and then would be obligated to give a causal explanation for the discrepancy between the small sample and the large sample. Expert subjects were expected to generalize less and to recognize that the discrepancy could be due to chance factors making the small sample appear extreme.

### Method

Subjects were the same as those in Study 3. The problem presented to them was one of several in a study described as being aimed at finding out "how people go about explaining and predicting events under conditions of very limited information about the events." Subjects were given one of two nearly identically worded problems. One concerned a football coach who usually found that the most brilliant performers at tryout were not necessarily the best players during the football season, and the other concerned a repertory company director who usually found that the most brilliant performers at audition were not necessarily the best actors during the drama season. The full text of the football version is presented below.

> *Football*. Harold is the coach for a high school football team. One of his jobs is selecting new members of the varsity team. He says the following of his experience: "Every year we add 10–20 younger boys to the team on the basis of their performance at the try-out practice. Usually the staff and I are extremely excited about the potential of two or three of these kids — one who throws several brilliant passes or another who kicks several field goals from a remarkable distance. Unfortunately, most of these kids turn out to be only somewhat better than the rest." Why do you suppose that the coach usually has to revise downward his opinion of players that be originally thought were brilliant?

The acting version of the problem was almost identical except that it was about Susan, the director of a student repertory company, who gets excited about "a young woman with great stage presence or a young man who gives a brilliant reading."

Subjects were asked which of the following explanations they preferred for the fact that the coach/director usually had to revise downward his or her opinion of the brilliant performers. The second alternative is the statistical one, suggesting that the explanation is simply that the tryout performances were uncharacteristically good for the "brilliant" performers.

1. Harold was probably mistaken in his initial opinion. In his eagerness to find new talent, he exaggerates the brilliance of the performances he sees at the try-out.

2. The brilliant performances at try-out are not typical of those boys' general abilities. They probably just made some plays at the try-out that were much better than usual for them.

3. The boys who did so well at try-out probably could coast through the season on their talent alone and don't put out the effort necessary to transform talent into consistently excellent performance.

4. The boys who did so well at try-out may find that their teammates are jealous. They may slack off so as not to arouse envy.

5. The boys who did so well at try-out are likely to be students with other interests. These interests would deflect them from putting all their energies into football.

Wording was altered very slightly for the acting version: "Boys" became "actors" and "try-out" became "audition."

Experience in sports was assessed by asking subjects whether they had played any organized team sports in high school or college. Those who had were defined as experienced. Experience in acting was defined as having had "more than a bit part" in a play in high school or college.

### Results

It may be seen in Table 2 that experience affects the likelihood of preferring a statistical explanation for both the football version of the problem and the acting version. Most of the subjects with athletic team experience (a majority) preferred the statistical explanation for the football problem, whereas most of the subjects without team experience preferred one of the other, deterministic explanations. Most of the subjects with acting experience (a small minority) preferred the statistical explanation for the acting problem, whereas most of the subjects without acting experience preferred one of the deterministic explanations.

We do not wish to infer from these results that experience in a domain will make statistical explanations more salient for *every* kind of problem. Expertise brings a recognition of the causal factors at work in a domain as well as a recognition of the remaining uncertainty. When the problem can be approached with this expert causal knowledge, the expert may give answers that are less statistical, at least in form, than those of the novice. We may speculate that expertise reduces reliance on the representativeness heuristic, which encourages unreflective assumptions that the future will resemble the past and that populations will resemble samples, and substitutes either statistical reasoning or reasoning in accordance with well-justified causal rules.

**Table 2**  **Percentage of experienced and inexperienced subjects who preferred the statistical explanation for the football and the acting problems**

| Problem | Subjects | | $\chi^2$ | $p$ |
|---|---|---|---|---|
| | Experienced | Inexperienced | | |
| Football | | | 3.10 | .10 |
| % | 56 | 35 | | |
| N | 52 | 26 | | |
| Acting | | | 5.18 | .025 |
| % | 59 | 29 | | |
| N | 17 | 62 | | |
| Both versions | | | 10.60 | .001 |
| % | 57 | 31 | | |
| N | 69 | 88 | | |

We should note also that it is possible that the tendency of experts to reason statistically may have less to do with knowledge of variability and uncertainty than with a subcultural norm for them to do so. The statistical answer may simply look more like a familiar, standard answer to the experts than to the nonexperts. For a correlational study such as Study 4, it is not easy to disentangle the undoubtedly related factors influencing statistical reasoning.

**Domain specificity of inductive rules**

One of the major implications of the present viewpoint is that there should be a substantial degree of domain specificity of statistical reasoning. Its use should be rare for domains where (a) it is hard to discern the sample space and the sampling process, (b) the role of chance in producing events is unclear, and (c) no cultural prescription for statistical reasoning exists. We have noted that many of the studies showing people's failures in statistical reasoning examined judgments about events characterized by one or more of these factors. We have also noted that some of people's few demonstrated successes in statistical reasoning have been observed for people's reasoning about sports and academic achievements that seem to be characterized by clearer distributions for events, a more obvious role of chance, and, probably, cultural prescriptions as well. These observations were made across studies, across tasks, and across subject populations, however.

To demonstrate that the same subjects dealing with the same tasks in the same experiment are more likely to reason statistically for some events characterized by uncertainty than for others, Jepson, Krantz, and Nisbett (in press) presented subjects with two broad classes of problems. The first class of problems dealt with events that are assessable by objective means, such as abilities, achievements, and physical illness. The second class dealt with events that are assessable only by subjective means, for example, personal preferences among objects, assessments of leadership potential, and judgments about the need for sexual fidelity in relationships. It was reasoned that, in general, it is relatively easy to apply statistical reasoning to objective events because one is likely to have some idea of their distributions (or to be able to guess what the distributions might look like because the units of measurement and the sample space are likely to be relatively clear). In general, also, the role of chance is likely to be relatively transparent for those objectively assessable events that in fact have been observed under repeated, relatively fixed conditions. Finally, cultural prescriptions to reason statistically probably exist for many such events. In contrast, none of these things is true for most events that can be assessed only by subjective means. The first problem below is an example of the Jepson et al. *objective* problems; the second is an example of the *subjective* problems.

### Championship selection problem

Two sports fans are arguing over which sport — baseball or football — has the best (most accurate) playoff system. Charlie says that the Super Bowl is the best way of determining the world champion because, according to him, "the seven games of the World Series are all played in the home cities of the two teams, whereas the Super Bowl is usually played in a neutral city. Since you want all factors not related to the game to be equal for a championship, then the Super Bowl is the better way to determine the world championship." Which procedure do you think is a better way to determine the world champion — World Series or Super Bowl? Why?

### Class selection problem

It is the first week of the winter term. Henry has signed up for five classes, but plans to take only four. Three of these classes he knows he wants, so he must decide between the other two. Both are on subjects interesting to him. The student course evaluations indicate that Course A is better taught. However, he attended the first meeting of both classes this week, and found Course B's session more enjoyable. Which class should he take and why?

Subjects wrote open-ended answers to problems of each type. These were coded as to whether they reflected the use of statistical principles — chiefly the law of large numbers or the regression principle — or not. An example of a nonstatistical answer for the championship problem is the following: "Super Bowl, because of neutral ground and also a one shot deal. Either you make it or break it — one chance. The pressure is on to perform the team's best." An example of a statistical answer is the following: "World Series is better. Anyone can get lucky for one game, but it is harder to be lucky for four. Besides, being home or away is part of the game, you don't play on neutral ground during the season." An example of a nonstatistical answer for the class-choice problem is the following: "He's got to choose for himself." An example of a statistical answer is: "You can't tell from one time — thus a survey that is over a longer range is better. Although Henry's idea of a good class could be different from most students."

299

Statistical answers were much more common for problems about objective events than for problems about subjective events. Forty-one percent of the answers for the former were statistical; the range of mean percentage statistical answers across problems was 30%–93%. Only 12% of the answers to subjective problems were statistical; the range was 5%–16%.

The results also showed that subjects were consistent in their tendency to give statistical answers. Those who gave statistical answers for any given problem were more likely to give them for any other. This tendency was correlated with both verbal and mathematical scores on the Scholastic Aptitude Test.

The results of the Jepson *et al.* (in press) study show that the same subjects in the same context answering the same general kind of problem are more likely to give statistical answers for a set of problems dealing with abilities than for a set dealing with more subjective attributes. The results do not rule out the possibility that it is problem structure or the exact nature of the required statistical rule that produces the difference among problems rather than their content. To control for this, Fong, Krantz, and Nisbett (Note 3) developed five separate problem structures for which somewhat different versions of the law of large numbers were required to produce the most appropriate statistical solution. For example, in one structure a small personal sample of events had implications that were different from those of a large sample collected by someone else (as in the class-choice problem above). Subjects were asked to indicate which sample was the better guide to action and why. Another structure presented a simple regression problem in which subjects were asked to explain why an extreme outcome for a small sample was not maintained in a larger sample. For each problem structure, two or more problem versions were constructed, some dealing with objective events and others with subjective ones. With structure and required rule type thus controlled, there was still a marked difference in the percentage of statistical answers for the two kinds of events.

It should be noted that an alternative explanation still exists even for the Fong *et al.* (Note 3) results. This is the possibility that statistical answers are not as appropriate for the subjective problems as for the objective problems. This objection is not readily answerable with our present level of knowledge about the uncertainty of events. We can only urge our view that statistical answers were fully appropriate for all problems because all problems involved high degrees of uncertainty. But it must be acknowledged that other people having the relevant statistical training might not agree.

### The effects of training in statistics on reasoning about everyday events

Perhaps the most important implication of the present view is that statistical reasoning about everyday events should be highly trainable. A major reason for optimism is that, as we have just demonstrated, people's intuitive reasoning skills include strategies that may be called statistical heuristics. Formal training in statistics, therefore, should represent less a grafting on of procedures than a refinement of preexisting ones. Formal training seems likely to improve reasoning for three distinct, but mutually supportive, reasons.

1. *Training in statistics is apt to facilitate the recognition of event distributions and their statistical parameters.* It can be difficult to apply rules such as the law of large numbers unless the units of evidence can be identified and, hence, the sample space and distribution of the event units. It seems likely that training in statistics could provide quite general skills in construing evidence in such a way that it can be properly unitized, the sample space identified, and parameters recognized. Training in probability theory, especially in permutations and combinations, should be particularly likely to be helpful in this regard as should test theory, which requires the student to recognize, for example, the different reliability of tests composed of different numbers of units — items, trials, occasions, and so on. But ordinary inferential statistics also introduces a fair amount of instruction in unitizing evidence: In order to measure the corn yield of a type of seed, for example, it is necessary to measure the yield for some unit of sampling (individual plot, individual farm, etc.). Statistics courses should also make it easier for people to think usefully about parameters of distributions — about central tendencies and about dispersion.

2. *Training in statistics is apt to facilitate the recognition of the role of chance in producing events.* A major concept of parametric statistics is that of error. Every inferential test features an estimate of error, and much of statistical training centers on questions of allocation of effects to the systematic category versus the random category. It seems possible that the focus on the concept of error in statistics might heighten the salience of uncertainty in daily life. A second major concept that might be helpful in recognizing uncertainty is the formal notion of sampling. This might be of general use in construing evidence as a (possibly small and inaccurate) sample from a (possibly heterogeneous) population.

3. *Training in statistics is apt to improve the clarity and accessibility of statistical rules and should expand the repertoire of statistical rules.* In effect, statistics training should hone intuitive heuristics into more precise tools. It seems clear that without training some statistical rules are poorly understood at any level of abstraction and in any context. Rules of covariation assessment and some versions of the regression principle are particularly difficult and may not even be represented in most people's intuitive repertoire. But even relatively intuitive rules such as the law of large numbers have nearly limitless corollaries and implications, some of which may be much easier to discern with formal training. Although people understand the "law of small large numbers," they may not be able to extend the principle to numbers of nonexperiential magnitudes without formal training. It may be the lack of a fully formal understanding of the law of large numbers that prevents people from applying it in the maternity ward problem, for example, where the sample sizes involved (15 and 45) are not often represented in people's everyday experience of sampling and variability.

The evidence indicates that statistical training does indeed have profound effects on people's reasoning about everyday life events. In one series of studies, Krantz, Fong, and Nisbett (Note 4) examined four groups of subjects differing widely in educational level. Subjects, who were college students with or without statistical training, graduate students with a fair amount of statistical training, or PhD level scientists with several years of training, were presented with one of a pair of restaurant problems. In each problem, a protagonist experienced a truly outstanding meal on the first visit to a restaurant but was disappointed on a repeat visit. The subjects were asked to explain, in writing, why this might have happened. A subject's explanation was classified as nonstatistical if it assumed that the initial good experience was a reliable indicator that the restaurant was truly outstanding and attributed the later disappointment to a definite cause, such as a permanent or temporary change in the restaurant (e.g., "Maybe the chef quit") or a change in the protagonist's expectation or mood. The explanation was classified as statistical if it suggested that meal quality on any single visit might not be a reliable indicator of the restaurant's overall quality (e.g., "Very few restaurants have only excellent meals; odds are she was just lucky the first time"). Statistical explanations were coded as to how articulate they were in indicating that a single visit may be regarded as a small sample and, hence, as unreliable. Explanations were thus coded as falling into one of three categories: (1) nonstatistical, (2) poor statistical, and (3) good statistical. The frequencies in each of these categories were used to define two dependent variables: *frequency* of statistical answers, defined as the proportion of responses in Categories 2 and 3, and *quality* of statistical answers, defined as the proportion of Category 2 and 3 answers that were Category 3.

The two versions of the restaurant problem differed. The probabilistic-cue version included a random mechanism for selects from the menu: The protagonist did not know how to read a Japanese menu and selected a meal by blindly dropping a pencil on the menu and observing where the point lay. The other version had no such cue. Within each group tested, half of the subjects received the cue and half did not.

The effects of training on both dependent measures were dramatic. College students without statistical training almost never gave an answer that was at all statistical unless the problem contained the probabilistic cue, in which case about half of the answers were statistical. In contrast, more than 80% of the answers of PhD-level scientists were statistical, whether or not there was a cue. Quality of statistical answers also depended on level of training. Only 10% of the statistical answers by untrained college students were rated as good, whereas almost 80% of the statistical answers by PhD-level scientists were rated as good. It is interesting that although the presence of the probabilistic cue was very important in determining whether less trained subjects would give a statistical answer, it did not affect the quality of statistical answers for subjects at any level of training. Apparently probabilistic cues can trigger the use of statistical heuristics, but they do not necessarily improve the quality of answers: the appropriate skills must be in the individual's repertoire to insure good quality.

The preceding study confounds training and native mathematical ability, but subsequent studies both avoid the confounding with ability and show that statistical training influences inductive reasoning outside the classroom and laboratory. Krantz *et al.* (Note 4) conducted a telephone "survey of opinions about sports." Subjects were males who were enrolled in an introductory statistics course and who admitted to being at least somewhat knowledgeable about sports. One hundred subjects were randomly selected and surveyed during the first 2 weeks of the term they were enrolled in statistics. Another 93 students were surveyed at or near the end of the term. In addition to filler questions on NCAA rules and NBA salaries, subjects were asked questions for which a statistical approach was relevant, as in the example below.

> In general the major league baseball player who wins Rookie of the Year does not perform as well in his second year. This is clear in major league baseball in the past ten years. In the American League, 8 rookies of the year have done worse in their second year; only 2 have done better. In the National League, the rookie of the year has done worse the second year 9 times out of 10.

> Why do you suppose the rookie of the year tends not to do as well his second year?

Most subjects answered this question in a nonstatistical way, invoking notions like "too much press attention" and "slacking off." Some subjects answered the question statistically (e.g., "There are bound to be some rookies who have an exceptional season; it may not be due to any great talent advantage that one guy has over the others — he just got a good year").

The statistics course increased the percentage of statistical answers and also increased the quality of statistical answers. The course also markedly influenced both the frequency and the quality of statistical answers to another question asking subjects to explain why .450 batting averages are common the first 2 weeks of the baseball season but are unheard of as a season average. In all, the course had a significant effect on three of the five questions asked.

Finally, Fong et al. (Note 3) showed that even a very brief training procedure can suffice to affect markedly subjects' answers to problems about everyday events. There were two major elements in their training package: One covered formal aspects of sampling and the law of large numbers and the other showed how to use sampling notions as a heuristic device in modeling problems. In the sampling instruction, subjects received definitions of population and sample distributions, a statement of the law of large numbers, and a demonstration (by drawing colored gumballs from a glass vase) that a population distribution is estimated more accurately, on the average, from larger samples. The modeling, or mapping, instruction consisted of three problems (in the general style of the restaurant problem and similar to the subsequent test problems), each followed by a written solution that used the law of large numbers and emphasized the analogy between amount of evidence and size of sample.

There were four major conditions: a control group given no instruction and three experimental groups — one given sampling training only, one given mapping training only, and one given both types of training. The subjects were adults and high school students. The test consisted of 15 problems. Five of these had clear probabilistic cues, five dealt with objective attributes such as abilities or achievements, and five dealt with subjective judgments. Training effects were marked for all three problem types, for both the frequency of statistical answers and the quality of statistical answers. Sampling training and mapping training were about equally effective, and in combination they were substantially more effective than either was alone. A particularly encouraging finding is that training showed no domain specificity effects. In a companion study, Fong et al. (Note 3) showed that it made no difference to performance whether mapping training had been on probabilistic-cue problems, objective attribute problems, or subjective judgment problems. The latter finding suggests that training on specific problem types can be readily abstracted to a degree sufficient for use on widely different problem types.

The work on training should not be taken to indicate that a statistical education is sufficient to guarantee that people will avoid errors in inductive reasoning. Kahneman and Tversky (1982; Tversky & Kahneman, 1971, 1983) have shown repeatedly that statistical expertise provides no such guarantee against errors. On the other hand, it should also be noted that courses in statistics do not emphasize ways to use statistical principles in everyday life. Were they to do so, one might see much larger differences between the educated and the uneducated than we have found.

## Normative considerations

People can apply statistical reasoning to a wide range of problems of an everyday life sort. The use of statistical reasoning seems to be increased by greater clarity about the sample space and the sampling process, by recognition of the role played by chance, and by cultural prescriptions to apply statistical reasoning. As a consequence, statistical reasoning appears to be more prevalent for events that are assessed by objective means than for events that are assessed only subjectively. People apply statistical reasoning more frequently and more aptly after formal training in statistics.

Exactly what is the content of lay statistical heuristics? What is the range of problems to which they can be applied? Which statistical principles are well entrenched in the repertoire of formally untutored people and which are not represented or even counterintuitive? Is there an improvement or a worsening of statistical reasoning as one moves from laboratory studies of reasoning to studies of *in vivo* reasoning about analogous problems in their appropriate ecological context? Exactly how much improvement in people's ability to reason statistically could be expected from traditional formal education in statistics? How could educational practices be improved so as to amplify the real world consequences of training?

We refrain from speculating about these questions, despite their importance, because they are fundamentally empirical in nature. It would be more appropriate for us to sketch the normative implications of the work to date rather than to try to be prescient about future matters of fact. We have addressed many of the normative implications of the previous work on limits elsewhere (Krantz, 1981; Nisbett, 1981; Nisbett, Krantz, Jepson, & Fong, 1982; Stich & Nisbett, 1980; Thagard & Nisbett, 1983), and we have addressed at some length some of the normative implications of our work on individual differences (Jepson, Krantz, & Nisbett, in press), but it would be useful to summarize the general normative implications of the work presented in this review.

### Ecological representativeness of problems showing errors

One criticism of the literature showing errors in inductive reasoning has been to argue that they are the result simply of examining people's judgment about particular kinds of problems, and in a particular kind of context, where judgments are particularly likely to be fallible (e.g., Cohen, 1981; Dennett, 1981; Lopes, 1982). The tenor of this criticism is that the studies show more about the cleverness of experimenters than they do about the real world failures of lay people.

The accusation that psychologists have been devising parlor tricks, which people are susceptible to in the laboratory context but either do not encounter or could solve in real world contexts, seems less plausible in view of the research reported here. First, for each problem we have reported, some of the subjects showed by their answers (and often by the rationales for their answers, subsequently elicited) an appreciation of the statistical principles that in previous work other subjects failed to appreciate. It seems more reasonable to explain the success of some of our subjects by saying that they are more skilled at statistical reasoning than the other subjects rather than to explain it by saying that they saw through the experimenters' tricks. Second, the factors that make statistical reasoning more or less likely, for example, recognition of heterogeneity and of the role played by chance, do not sound like factors that make people more or less dupable by experimenters but rather like factors that make the appropriateness of statistical reasoning more or less obvious. Third, statistical training markedly influences answers to the sort of problems we studied. This suggests that it is not problem- or context-produced illusions that make people unable to solve statistical problems but simply lack of statistical knowledge.

## "Satisficing" in decision making and inductive reasoning

Since Simon's (1957) important work on decision making, it has been a standard part of normative analysis to point out that, because of time pressures and other constraints, it may be quite sensible for people to depart from formal decision models. This corner-cutting practice is called *satisficing* (in distinction to the presumed *optimizing* that would result from the formal procedures). This same defense is often applied to people's failures to reason statistically (Einhorn & Hogarth,1981; Miller & Cantor, 1982; Nisbett & Ross, 1980). People who study inductive reasoning seem to have presumed that normatively correct inductive reasoning is usually more laborious and time-consuming than is purely intuitive inductive reasoning, just as formal decision making is usually more time consuming than is intuitive decision making. The present work makes it clear that this presumption cannot be imported uncritically into the realm of inductive reasoning. Exclusively causal reasoning and the search for values on putatively relevant causal factors can be extraordinarily laborious. Statistical reasoning, once it is mastered, can be very rapid, even automatic. We found it striking, for example, to contrast the answers given over the telephone by subjects in the sports survey by Krantz *et al*. (Note 4). Some subjects doggedly persisted in causal explanations for problems such as the rookie of the year, sophomore slump ("Well, the success goes to their heads . . . and there's pressure to keep up the performance after the great first year . . . and . . ."), which did not seem to satisfy even the subjects who were generating them. Other subjects generated quick, crisp statistical explanations ("They just happened to have a first year that was better than their lifetime average") that still left them free to explore possible causal explanations.

It is also important to note that one has very little sense of subjects' *choosing* inferential strategies when one reads such protocols, in the sense that people may choose a formal decision-making strategy over an intuitive one. Rather, subjects either seem to spontaneously pursue a statistical approach or they do not. Formal decision-making procedures involve novel and counterintuitive practices such as drawing tree diagrams and multiplying probability and utility assessments. On the

305

other hand, many statistical procedures, as we have shown, have their simpler intuitive counterparts in the equipment of everyday thought. There is no reason to presume that these will be any more cumbersome to use or will require any more conscious deliberation to access than will other intuitive approaches. Similarly, training in formal statistics may produce automatic, nonreflective transfer to everyday problems in a way that formal decision training would not.

## Evolution and inductive reasoning

Many people have responded to the work demonstrating inferential errors by assuming that the errors are either exaggerated or that they are the incidental by-product of some overwhelmingly useful inferential procedure that happens to go astray under ecologically rare circumstances. This is essentially the argument from design, and several philosophers have endorsed it. (See, e.g., Cohen, 1979; Dennett, 1978, 1981, Note 1; Lycan, 1981; Einhorn & Hogarth, 1981, have presented several very compelling arguments against the design view, and we shall not repeat them here.)

Endorsement of the evolutionary, or design, view requires a rather static, wired-in assumption about the nature of inferential procedures. Philosophers are not alone in making this assumption, it should be noted. Psychologists who are wont to presume unlimited plasticity in social behavior often seem to presume complete rigidity in inferential rules, as if these could be influenced at most by maturation. In our view, there are few grounds for such a presumption. Whatever may be true for deduction, there are good grounds for assuming that inductive procedures can be changed. Renaissance physicians adhered to the doctrine of signatures, an inductive system with both descriptive and procedural components. Modern physicians have curtailed the scope of the representativeness heuristic in their daily inferential lives. (Although it is still relied on in interviews of applicants to medical schools. See Dawes, 1980, for a description of the doctrine of signatures at work in the admissions process for American universities.) Sophisticated causal analysis and statistical reasoning will eventually result in the further curtailment of simple intuitive heuristics, for physicians and for everyone else.

Although we see no merit in an evolutionary defense of the inferential behaviors that happen to characterize American college students in the latter part of the 20th century, we see a powerful argument in the work we have reviewed for the role of cultural evolution. It does not require unusual optimism to speculate that we are on the threshold of a profound change in the way that people reason inductively. The range of events that scientists can think about statistically has been increasing slowly but in a decided, positively accelerated fashion at least since the 17th century. The work of Kahneman and Tversky may be regarded as the most recent and one of the most dramatic inflection points on that curve.

We believe that, with a lag in time, lay people have been following a similar curve of ever-widening application of statistical reasoning. Most people today appreciate entirely statistical accounts of sports events, accident rates, and the weather; also, we found many subjects who gave statistical explanations even for subjective events such as disappointment about meals served by a restaurant; and Piaget's young subjects reasoned about the behavior of randomizing devices with a sophistication that seems quite unlikely for people of earlier centuries. Will our own descendants differ as much from us as we do from Bernoulli's contemporaries?

## Acknowledgements

The research reported here was supported by Grants BNS79-14094 and BN575-23191 from the National Science Foundation. We are indebted to Lee Ross and Amos Tversky for their invaluable advice. We thank Geoffrey T. Fong for his assistance and criticism, and we thank Nancy Cantor, Robyn Dawes, Hillel Einhorn, Robin Hogarth, John Holland, Keith Holyoak, Nancy Pennington, Michael Shafto, Stephen Stich, and Paul Thagard for comments on an earlier version of the manuscript. Sara Freeland provided able editorial assistance.

## Notes

1. All $p$ values are based on two-tailed tests unless otherwise indicated.

2. We are indebted to George Quattrone for making these available.

## Reference notes

1. Dennett, D. C. (1983) *True believers: The intentional strategy and why it works.* Unpublished manuscript, Tufts University.

2. Kahneman, D. (1982) Personal communication.

3. Fong, G. I, Krantz, D. H. and Nisbett, R. E. (1983) *Improving inductive reasoning through statistical training.* Unpublished manuscript, University of Michigan.

4. Krantz, D. H., Fong, G. T. and Nisbett, R. E. (1983) *Formal training improves the application of statistical heuristics to everyday problems.* Unpublished manuscript, Bell Laboratories, Murray Hill, New Jersey.

## References

Borgida, E. & Nisbett, R. E. (1977) The differential impact of abstract vs. concrete information on decisions. *Journal of Applied Social Psychology*, 7, 258–271.

Cohen, L. J. (1979) On the psychology of prediction: Whose is the fallacy? *Cognition*, 7, 385–407.

Cohen, L. J. (1981) Can human irrationality be experimentally demonstrated? *Behavioral and Brain Sciences*, 4, 317–331.

Dawes, R. M. (1980) You can't systemize human judgment: Dyslexia. *New Directions for Methodology of Social and Behavioral Science*, 4, 67–78.

Dennett, D. C. (1978) *Brainstorms*. Montgomery, Vt.: Bradford Books.

Dennett, D. C. (1981) Three kinds of intentional psychology. In R Healey (Ed.), *Reduction, time and reality*. Cambridge, England: Cambridge University Press.

Einhorn, H. J. & Hogarth, R. M. (1978) Confidence in judgment: Persistence of the illusion of validity. *Psychological Review*, 87, 395–416.

Einhorn, H. & Hogarth, R. M. (1981) Behavioral decision theory: Processes of judgment and choice. *Annual Review Psychology*, 32, 53–88.

Hacking, I. (1975) *The emergence of probability*. New York: Cambridge University Press.

Hamer, C. (1981) *"Good-fishin'!"* (2nd ed.).St.Paul, Minn.: P.F., Inc.

Hogarth, R. M. (1980) *Judgement and choice.* New York: Wiley.

Hume, D. (1955) *An inquiry concerning human understanding.* Indianapolis, Ind.: Bobbs-Merrill. (Originally published, 1748.)

Jepson, C., Krantz, D. H. & Nisbett, R E. Inductive reasoning: Competence or skill? *Behavioral and Brain Sciences,* in press.

Kahneman, D., Slovic, P. & Tversky, A. (1982) *Judgment under uncertainty. Heuristics and biases.* New York: Cambridge University Press.

Kahneman, D. & Tversky, A. (1972) Subjective probability: A judgment of representativeness. *Cognitive Psychology*, 3, 430–454.

Kahneman, D. & Tversky, A. (1973) On the psychology of prediction. *Psychological Review*, 80, 237–251.

Kahneman, D. & Tversky, A. (1982) On the study of statistical intuitions. *Cognition*, 11, 237–251.

Krantz, D. H. (1981) Improvements in human reasoning and an error in L. J. Cohen's, *Behavioral and Brain Sciences*, 4, 340–341.

Law of averages a reality for ballplayers. *Los Angeles Times.* June 7, 1981, Part 3, p. 6.

Lopes, L. L. (1982) Doing the impossible: A note on induction and the experience of randomness. *Journal of Experimental Psychology*, 8, 626–636.

Lycan, W. G. (1981) "Is" and "ought" in cognitive science. *Behavioral and Brain Sciences*, 4, 344–345.

Mill, J. S. (1974) *A system of logic ratiocinative and inductive.* Toronto, Ontario, Canada: University of Toronto Press. (Originally published, 1843.)

Miller, G. A. & Cantor, N. (1982) Book review of Nisbett, R., & Ross, L. Human inference: Strategies and shortcomings of social judgment. *Social Cognition*, 1, 83–93.

Nisbett, R. E. (1981) Lay arbitration of rules of inference. *Behavioral and Brain Sciences*, 4, 349–350.

Nisbett, R. E. & Borgida, E. (1975) Attribution and the psychology of prediction. *Journal of Personality and Social Psychology*, 32, 932–943.

Nisbett, R. E., Krantz, D. H., Jepson, C. & Fong, G. T. (1982) Improving inductive inference. In D. Kahneman, P. Slovic, & A. Tversky (Eds.) *Judgment under uncertainty: Heuristics and biases.* New York: Cambridge University Press.

Nisbett, R. E. & Ross, L. (1980) *Human inference: Strategies and shortcomings of social judgment.* Englewood Cliffs, N.J.: Prentice-Hall.

Piaget, J. & Inhelder, B. (1975) *The origin of the idea of chance in children.* New York: Norton. (Originally published in 1951.)

Quattrone, G. A. & Jones, E. E. (1980) The perception of variability within in-groups and out-groups: Implications for the law of large numbers. *Journal of Personality and Social Psychology*, 38, 141–152.

Silka, L. (1981) Effects of limited recall of variability on intuitive judgments of change. *Journal of Personality and Social Psychology*, 40, 1010–1016.

Simon, H. A. (1957) *Models of man: Social and rational.* New York: Wiley.

Stich, S. & Nisbett, R. E. (1980) Justification and the psychology of human reasoning. *Philosophy of Science*, 47(2) 188–202.

Thagard, P. & Nisbett, R. E. (1982) Variability and confirmation. *Philosophical Studies*, 42, 379–394.

Thagard, P. & Nisbett, R. E. (1983) Rationality and charity. *Philosophy of Science*, 50, 250–267.

Tversky, A. & Kahneman, D. (1971) Belief in the law of small numbers. *Psychological Bulletin*, 76, 105–110.

Tversky, A. & Kahneman, D. (1973) Availability: A heuristic for judging frequency and probability. *Cognitive Psychology*, 5, 207–232.

Tversky, A. & Kahneman, D. (1974) Judgment under uncertainty: Heuristics and biases. *Science*, 185, 1124–1131.

Tversky, A. & Kahneman, D. (1983) Extensional vs. intuitive reasoning: The conjunction fallacy in probability judgment. *Psychological Review*, 90, 293–315.

Weiner, B., Frieze, I., Kukla, A., Reed, L., Rest, S. & Rosenbaum, R. M. (1972) Perceiving the causes of success and failure. In E. E. Jones, D. E. Kanouse, H. H. Kelley, R. E. Nisbett, S. Valins, & B. Weiner(Eds.), *Attribution: Perceiving the causes of behavior.* Morristown, NJ: General Learning Press.

# 11.   Flowing Waters or Teeming Crowds: Mental Models of Electricity

## Dedre Gentner and Donald R. Gentner

*Question:* When you plug in a lamp and it lights up, how does it happen?

*Subject Delta:* . . . basically there is a pool of electricity that plug-in buys for you . . . the electricity goes into the cord for the appliance, for the lamp and flows up to — *flows* — I think of it as flowing because of the negative to positive images I have, and also because . . . a cord is a narrow contained entity like a river.

Analogical comparisons with simple or familiar systems occur often in people's descriptions of complex systems, sometimes as explicit analogical models, and sometimes as implicit analogies, in which the person seems to borrow structure from the base domain without noticing it. Phrases like "current being routed along a conductor," or "stopping the flow" of electricity are examples.

In this paper we want to explore the conceptual role of analogy. When people discuss electricity (and other complex phenomena) in analogical terms, are they thinking in terms of analogies, or merely borrowing language from one domain as a convenient way of talking about another domain? If analogies are to be taken seriously as part of the apparatus used in scientific reasoning, it must be shown that they have real conceptual effects.

There are two lines of observational evidence (aside from the protocol cited) for the proposition that analogies can have genuine effects on a person's conception of a domain. First, analogies are often used in teaching, as in the following introduction to electricity (Koff, 1961).

> The idea that electricity flows as water does is a good analogy. Picture the wires as pipes carrying water (electrons). Your wall plug is a high-pressure source which you can tap simply by inserting a plug. . . . A valve (switch) is used to start or stop flow.

Thus, educators appear to believe that students can import conceptual relations and operations from one domain to another.

A more direct line of evidence is that working scientists report that they use analogy in theory development. The great astronomer Johannes Kepler wrote (quoted in Polya, 1973): "And I cherish more than anything else the Analogies, my most trustworthy masters. They know all the secrets of Nature, and they ought to be least neglected in Geometry [p. 12]." The Nobel Prize lecture of nuclear physicist Sheldon Glashew

(1980) makes constant reference to the analogies used in developing the theory of the unified weak and electromagnetic interactions:

> I was lead to the group SU(2) x U(1) by analogy with the approximate isospin-hypercharge group which characterizes strong interactions....

> Part of the motivation for introducing a fourth quark was based on our mistaken notions of hadron spectroscopy. But we also wished to enforce an analogy between the weak leptonic current and the weak hadronic current. . . .

These kinds of remarks are strongly suggestive of the conceptual reality of generative analogy. But people's understanding of their own mental processes is not always correct. It could be that, despite these introspections, the underlying thought processes proceed independently of analogy and that analogies merely provide a convenient terminology for the results of the process. This hypothesis, the Surface Terminology hypothesis, contrasts with the Generative Analogy hypothesis that analogies are used in generating inferences.

Our goal is to test the Generative Analogy hypothesis: that conceptual inferences in the target follow predictably from the use of a given base domain as an analogical model. To confirm this hypothesis, it must be shown that the inferences people make in a topic domain vary according to the analogies they use. Further, it must be shown that these effects cannot be attributed to shallow lexical associations; e.g., it is not enough to show that the person who speaks of electricity as "flowing" also uses related terms such as "capacity" or "pressure." Such usage could result from a generative analogy, but it could also occur under the Surface Terminology hypothesis.

The plan of this paper is to (1) set forth a theoretical framework for analogical processing, called structure-mapping; (2) use this framework to explore the analogies people use in the domain of electronic circuitry, based on evidence from introductory texts and from interviews; (3) present two experimental studies that test the Generative Analogy hypothesis; and finally, (4) discuss the implications of our findings for a general treatment of analogy in science.

## A structure-mapping theory of analogical thinking

Just what type of information does an analogy convey? The prevailing psychological view rejects the notion that analogies are merely weak similarity statements, maintaining instead that analogy can be characterized more precisely (Miller, 1979; Ortony, 1979; Rumelhart & Abrahamson, 1973; Sternberg, 1977; Tourangeau & Sternberg, 1981; Verbrugge & McCarrell, 1977). We argue in this section that analogies select certain aspects of existing knowledge, and that this selected knowledge can be structurally characterized.

An analogy such as

1. The hydrogen atom is like the solar system

clearly does not convey that *all* of one's knowledge about the solar system should be attributed to the atom. The inheritance of characteristics is only partial. This might suggest that an analogy is a kind of weak similarity statement, conveying that only some of the characteristics of the solar system apply to the hydrogen atom. But this characterization fails to capture the distinction between literal similarity and analogical relatedness. A comparable literal similarity statement is

2. There's a system in the Andromeda nebula that's like our solar system.

The literal similarity statement (2) conveys that the target object (The Andromeda system) is composed of a star and planets much like those of our solar system, and further, that those objects are arranged in similar spatial relationships and have roughly the same kind of orbital motion, attractive forces, relative masses, etc. as our system.

Like the literal comparison, the analogy (statement 1) conveys considerable overlap between the relative spatial locations, relative motions, internal forces, and relative masses of atom and solar system; but it does *not* convey that the objects in the two domains are similar. One could argue with the literal statement (2) by saying "But the star in the Andromeda system isn't yellow and hot" if the star happened to be a white dwarf. To argue with the analogical statement (1) by saying "But the nucleus of the atom isn't yellow and hot" would be to miss the point. The analogy, in short, conveys overlap in relations among objects, but no particular overlap in the characteristics of the objects themselves. The literal similarity statement conveys overlap both in relations among the objects and in the attributes of the individual objects.[1]

The analogical models used in science can be characterized as structure-mappings between complex systems. Such an analogy conveys that like relational systems hold within two different domains. The predicates of the base domain (the known domain) — particularly the relations that hold among the objects — can be applied in the target domain (the domain of inquiry). Thus, a structure-mapping analogy asserts that identical operations and relationships hold among nonidentical things. The relational structure is preserved, but not the objects.

In such a structure-mapping, both domains are viewed as systems of objects[2] and predicates. Among the predicates, we must distinguish between object attributes and relationships. In a propositional representation, the distinction can be made explicit in the predicate structure: *Attributes* are predicates taking one argument, and *relations* are predicates taking two or more arguments. For example, COLLIDE (x,y) is a relation, whereas RED (x) is an attribute. We will use a schema-theoretic representation of knowledge as a propositional network of nodes and predicates (cf. Miller, 1979; Rumelhart, 1979; Rumelhart & Norman, 1975; Rumelhart & Ortony, 1977; Schank & Abelson, 1977). The nodes represent concepts treated as wholes and the predicates express propositions about the nodes. The predicates may convey dynamic process information, constraint relations, and other kinds of knowledge (e.g. de Kleer & Sussman, 1978; Forbus, 1982; Rieger & Grinberg, 1977). Figure 1 shows the structure-mapping conveyed by the atom/solar system analogy. Starting with the known base domain of the solar system, the object nodes of the base domain (the sun and planets) are mapped onto object nodes (the nucleus and electrons) of the atom. Given this correspondence of nodes, the analogy conveys that the relationships that hold between the nodes in the solar system also hold between the nodes of the atom: for example, that there is a force attracting the peripheral objects to the central object; that the peripheral objects revolve around the central object; that the central object is more massive than the peripheral objects; and so on.

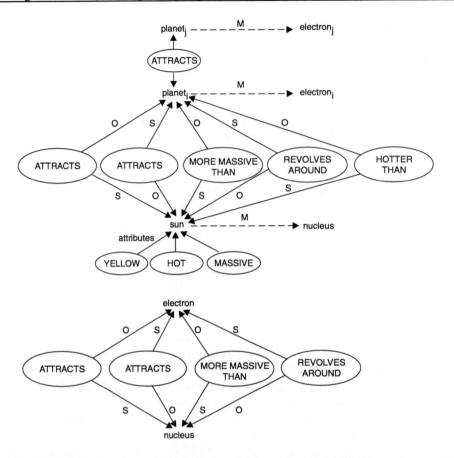

**Figure 1** **Representations of knowledge about the solar system and the hydrogen atom, showing partial identity in the relational structure between the two domains.**

*Notes*: S = subject; O = Object; M denotes mapping to a different system.

### Structure-mapping: interpretation rules

Assume that the hearer has a particular propositional representation of a known domain B (the *base* domain) in terms of object nodes $b_1, b_2, \ldots, b_n$ and predicates such as A, R, R'. Assume also a (perhaps less specified) representation of the domain of inquiry (the *target* domain) in terms of at least some object nodes $t_1, t_2, \ldots, t_m$. Then a structure-mapping analogy maps the nodes of B into the nodes of T:

$$M: b_i \longrightarrow t_i$$

The hearer derives analogical predications by applying predicates valid in the base domain B to the target domain T, using the node substitutions dictated by the mapping:

$$M: [R(b_i, b_j)] \longrightarrow [R(t_i, t_j)]$$

where $R(b_i, b_j)$ is a relation that holds in the base domain B. These analogical predications are subject to two implicit structural rules:

1. *Preservation of relationships.* If a relation exists in the base, then predicate the same relation between the corresponding objects in the target:

$$M: [R(b_i, b_j)] \longrightarrow [R(t_i, t_j)]$$

In contrast, attributes (one-place predicates) from B are not strongly predicated in T:

$$[A(b_i)] \not\longrightarrow [A(t_i)]$$

2. *Systematicity.* Sets of interconstraining relations are particularly important in explanatory analogy. Therefore, a relation that is dominated by a potentially valid higher-order relation is more strongly predicated than an isolated relation. For example, in the following expression, relations $R_1$ and $R_2$ are each dominated by the higher order relation $R'$ that connects them. To the extent that any of these relations can be validly imported into the target, the strength of predication of the others is increased.

$$M: [R' (R_1 (b_i, b_j), R_2 (b_k, b_l))] \longrightarrow$$

$$[R' (R_1 (t_i, t_j), R_2 (t_k, t_l))]$$

*Preservation of relationships.* Assertion (1) states that relational predicates, and not object attributes, carry over in analogical mappings. This differentiates analogy from literal similarity, in which there is also strong attribute overlap. This follows from the central assertion that analogical mappings convey that identical propositional systems apply in two domains with dissimilar objects. For example, in the solar system model of the atom, the ATTRACTS relation and the REVOLVES AROUND relation between planet and sun are carried across to apply between electron and nucleus, whereas the separable *attributes* of the base objects, such as the color or temperature of the sun, are left behind. Mass provides a good illustration: The *relation* "MORE MASSIVE THAN" between sun's mass and planet's mass carries over, but not the absolute mass of the sun. We do not expect the nucleus to have a mass of $10^{30}$ kilograms, any more than we expect it to have a temperature of 25,000,000 °F.

*Systematicity.* Assertion (2) states that predicates are more likely to be imported into the target if they belong to a system of coherent, mutually constraining relationships, the others of which map into the target. These interconnections among predicates are explicitly structurally represented by higher-order relations between those predicates (e.g.. Smith, in preparation). One common higher-order relation is CAUSE; for example, CAUSE ($R_1$ , $R_2$) expresses a causal chain between the lower-order relations $R_1$ and $R_2$. Focusing on such causal chains can make an analogical matcher more powerful (Winston, 1981).

Figure 2 shows the set of systematically interconnected relations in the Rutherford model, a highly systematic analogy. Notice that the lower-order relations — DISTANCE (sun, planet), REVOLVES AROUND (planet, sun), etc. — form a connected system, together with the abstract relationship ATTRACTIVE FORCE (sun, planet). The relation MORE MASSIVE THAN (sun, planet) belongs to this system. In combination with other higher-order relations, it determines which object will revolve around the other. This is why MORE MASSIVE THAN is preserved while HOTTER THAN is not, even though the two relations are, by themselves, parallel comparisons. HOTTER THAN does not participate in this systematic set of interrelated predicates. Thus, to the extent that people recognize (however vaguely) that gravitational forces play a central role in the analogy they will tend to import MORE MASSIVE THAN, but not HOTTER THAN, into the target.

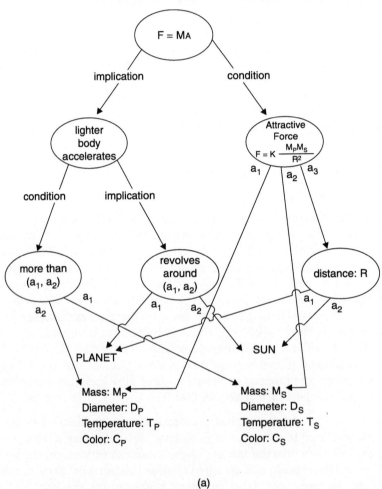

(a)

**Figure 2**  **More detailed representation of knowledge about (a) the solar system and (b) the atom, showing partial identity in the higher-order relational structures between the two domains.**

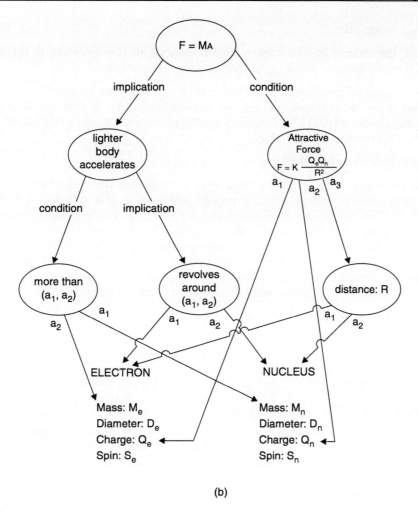

(b)

**Figure 2    (Cont)**

The systematicity rule aims to capture the intuition that explanatory analogies are about systems of interconnected relations. Sometimes these systems can be mathematically formalized. Some of the interrelations within this solar system are described in this equation:[3]

$$F_{grav} = Gmm'/R^2 \tag{1}$$

This equation embodies a set of simultaneous constraints on the parameters of the objects, where m is the mass of the sun, m' is the mass of the planet, G is the gravitational constant, and $F_{grav}$ is the gravitational force. For example, if $F_{grav}$ decreases while the masses are constant, then the distance R between the sun and the planet must increase. Equation (1) summarizing the interrelations in the base maps into a corresponding target equation:

$$F_{elec} = -qq' / R^2 \qquad\qquad (2)$$

where q is the charge on the proton, q' the charge on the electron, R the distance between the two objects, and $F_{elec}$ is the electromagnetic force.[4]

All these analogical predications are attempted predications, to use Ortony's (1979) term; they must be checked against the person's existing knowledge of the target domain. But the structural bias for relationality and systematicity provides an implicit guide to which predications to check.

## Two analogies for electricity

The domain of simple electricity is ideal for investigating the role of analogy. It is a familiar phenomenon; everyone in our society knows at least a little about it. Further, it is tractable: We can define ideal correct understanding. Yet because its mechanisms are essentially invisible, electricity is often explained by analogy. Moreover, because no single analogy has all the correct properties, we can compare different analogies for the same target domain. Finally, a great advantage of electronics is that, using simple combinations of circuit elements, it is easy to devise problems that require quantitative inferences that cannot be mimicked by mere lexical connections.

### *The water-flow analogy*

The analogy most frequently used to explain electricity is the water-flow analogy. We begin with this analogy, and later discuss an alternative analogy for electricity. The following passage is part of the instructions for a miniature lamp kit (Illinois Hobbycraft Inc., 1976).

### Electricity and water — an analogy

> An electrical system can be compared to a water system. Water flows through the pipes of a water system. Electricity can be considered as "flowing" through the wires of an electrical system. Wire is the pipe that electricity "flows" through. Volts is the term for electrical pressure. Milliamperes is the term for electrical "volume."

Here the base domain is a plumbing system and the object mappings are that a water pipe is mapped onto a wire, a pump or reservoir is mapped onto a battery, a narrow constriction is mapped onto a resistor, and flowing water is mapped onto electric current. What predicates is this analogy supposed to convey? Not that electricity shares object attributes with water, such as being wet, transparent, or cold to the touch. This analogy is meant to convey a system of relationships that can be imported from hydraulics to electricity. In the next passages we discuss this relational structure, first for hydraulics and then for electricity. This will serve both to explicate the analogy and to provide some insight into electricity for readers who are unfamiliar with the domain. Then we compare the hydraulic analogy with another common analogy for electricity, the moving-crowd model.

*Simple hydraulics.* We begin with a reservoir with an outlet at its base. The *pressure* of the water at the outlet is proportional to the height of water in the reservoir. (See Figure 6, following.) The *rate of flow* through any point in the system is the amount of water that passes that point per unit time. Pressure and flow rate are clearly distinguishable: Rate of flow is *how much* water is flowing, while pressure is the *force* per unit area exerted by the water. Yet there is a strong relation between pressure and flow: The rate of flow through a section is proportional to the *pressure difference* through that section. This means that the greater the height of water in the reservoir, the greater the flow rate, all else being equal.

A *constriction* in the pipe leads to a drop in pressure. Water pressure, which is high when the water leaves the reservoir, drops across the constriction. Constrictions also affect flow rate: The greater the constriction in a section, the less the flow rate through that system. Figure 3b shows the relations among flow rate, pressure and degree of constriction for a hydraulics system.

SIMPLE CIRCUIT

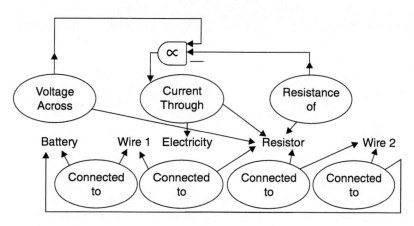

WATER SYSTEM

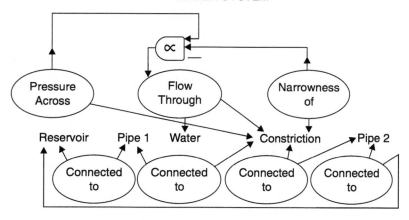

Figure 3    Representation of knowledge about (a) simple electric circuits and (b) simple hydraulic systems, showing overlap in relational structures. The relation stands for a higher-order qualitative division relation: The output (e.g., current) varies monotonically with the positive input (e.g., voltage) and negative — monotonically with the negative input (e.g., resistance).

*The analogy with electricity.* An electrical circuit is analogous to the plumbing system just described. Table 1 shows the object correspondences, as well as some of the predicates that are imported from base to target. Notice that the predicates that are shared are relational predicates: for example, that increasing voltage causes an increase in current.

**Table 1    Mappings between water flow and electricity**

| *Base–Hydraulic System* | *Target–Circuit* |
|---|---|
| *Object Mappings*: | |
| pipe | wire |
| pump | battery |
| narrow pipe | resistor |
| | |
| *Property Mappings*: | |
| PRESSURE of water | VOLTAGE |
| NARROWNESS of pipe | RESISTANCE |
| FLOW RATE of water | CURRENT |
| | (FLOW RATE of electricity) |
| | |
| *Relations Imported*: | |
| CONNECT | CONNECT |
| (pipe, pump, narrow pipe) | (wire, battery, resistor) |
| INCREASE WITH | INCREASE WITH |
| (flow rate, pressure) | (current, voltage) |
| DECREASE WITH | DECREASE WITH |
| (flow rate, narrowness) | (current, resistance) |

The first insight derivable from the analogy is the distinction between the flow rate and pressure, which maps onto an analogous distinction between current (the number of electrons passing a given point per sec) and voltage (the pressure difference through which the current moves). This aspect of the analogy is important because novices in electricity often fail to differentiate current and voltage; they seem to merge the two of them into a kind of generalized-strength notion. For example, one subject, defining voltage, says:

> . . . Volts is . . . the strength of the current available to you in an outlet. And I don't know if it means there are more of those little electrons running around or if they're moving faster; . . . .

Besides the current-voltage distinction, the analogy conveys the interrelation between current, voltage and resistance. Figure 3a shows the structural description of the circuit induced by the mapping. The batteries, wire, and resistors of an electrical circuit correspond to the reservoirs, pipes, and constriction of a plumbing system. Note the parallel interdependency relations in the two systems (Figures 3a and 3b): e.g., Electrons flow through the circuit because of a voltage difference produced by the battery, just as water flows through the plumbing system because of a pressure difference produced by the reservoir. Thus, the analogy conveys the dependency relations that constitute Ohm's Law, $V = IR$. Of course, naive users of the analogy may derive only simpler proportional relations such as "More force, more flow" and "More drag, less flow." These qualitative-proportion relationships (see Forbus, 1989) may be phenomenological primitives, in the sense discussed by diSessa.

## *The moving-crowd model*

Besides the hydraulics model, the most frequent spontaneous analogy for electricity is the moving-crowd analogy. In this analogy, electric current is seen as masses of objects racing through passageways, as in these passages from interviews:

> (1) You can always trick the little devils to go around or through. . . Because they have to do that. I mean, they are driven to seek out the opposite pole. In between their getting to their destination, you can trick them into going into different sorts of configurations, to make them work for you. . . .

> (2) If you increase resistance in the circuit, the current slows down. Now that's like a highway, cars on a highway where . . . as you close down a lane . . . the cars move slower through that narrow point.

The moving-crowd model can provide most of the relations required to understand electrical circuits. In this model current corresponds to the number of entities that pass a point per unit time. Voltage corresponds to how powerfully they push. Like the water analogy, the moving-crowd model establishes a distinction between current and voltage. Further, the moving-crowd model allows a superior treatment of resistors. In this model we can think of a resistor as analogous to a barrier containing a narrow gate. This "gate" conception of resistors is helpful in predicting how combinations of resistors will behave, as we describe in the following section. However, it is hard to find a useful realization of batteries in this model.

## Experiments on analogies for electricity

### *Rationale and overview*

The language used in the protocols suggests that people base their understanding of electronics at least in part on knowledge imported from well-known base domains. But are these true generative analogies or merely surface terminology? In order to verify that the use of a particular model leads to predictable inferences in the target domain, we performed two studies of analogical models in electronics. In Experiment 1, we elicited subjects' models of electronics and asked whether their models predict the types of inferences they make. In Experiment 2, we taught subjects different analogical models of electronics and compared their subsequent patterns of inference.

### *The four combinatorial problems*

We wished to test deep indirect inferences that could not be mimicked by surface associations. At the same time, we needed to keep our problems simple enough for novices to attempt. The solution was to ask about different combinations of simple components. There were four basic combination circuits, namely the four circuits generated by series and parallel combinations of pairs of batteries or resistors, as shown in Figure 4. For example, we asked how the current in a simple circuit with one battery and resistor compares with that in a circuit with two resistors in series, or with two batteries in parallel.

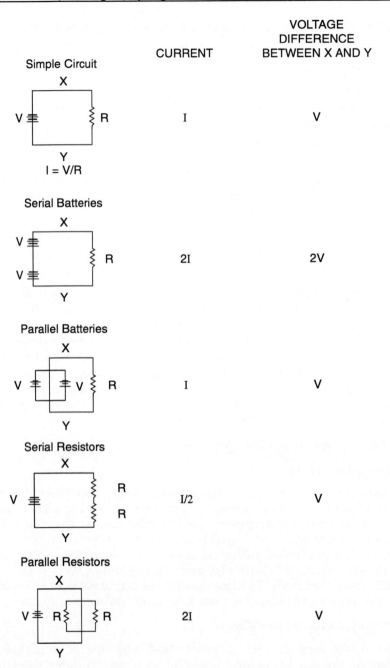

| | CURRENT | VOLTAGE DIFFERENCE BETWEEN X AND Y |
|---|---|---|
| Simple Circuit | I | V |
| Serial Batteries | 2I | 2V |
| Parallel Batteries | I | V |
| Serial Resistors | I/2 | V |
| Parallel Resistors | 2I | V |

**Figure 4**   **Current and voltage for the four combination circuits: serial and parallel pairs of batteries or resistors. A simple battery-resistor circuit is shown at top.**

322

The chief difficulty in these combination problems is differentiating between serial and parallel combinations. The serial combinations are straightforward: More batteries lead to more current and more resistors to less current. This accords with the first level of novice insight: the "More force, more flow/more drag, less flow," model, in which current goes up with the number of batteries and goes down with the number of resistors. But the parallel combinations do not fit this naive model: As Figure 4 shows, parallel batteries give the *same* current as a single battery, and parallel resistors lead to *more* current than a single resistor (always assuming identical batteries and resistors).

*Combinations of batteries.* To gain some intuition for these combinations, we return briefly to the water domain for a review of serial and parallel reservoirs. Consider what happens when two reservoirs are connected in series, one on top of the other. Because the pressure produced by the reservoirs is determined by the height of the water and the height has doubled, two reservoirs in series produce *twice* the original pressure, and thus *twice* the original flow rate. This conforms to the intuition that doubling the number of sources doubles the flow rate. However, if two reservoirs are connected in parallel, at the same level, the height of the water will be the same as with the single reservoir. Because pressure depends on *height,* not on total amount of water, the pressure and flow rate will be the same as that of the original one-reservoir system (although the capacity and longevity of the system will be greater).

Figure 5 shows the higher-order relationships comparing flow rate given parallel or serial reservoirs with flow rate in the simple one-reservoir system. The same higher-order relationships hold in the domain of electricity: The current in a circuit with two serial batteries is greater than current with a single battery. Current given two parallel batteries is equal to that given a single battery.

*Combinations of resistors.* These combinations are understood most easily through the moving-crowd model, in which resistors can be thought of as gates. In the serial case, all the moving objects must pass through two gates, one after the other, so the rate of flow should be lower than for just one gate. In the parallel case, the flow splits and moves through two side-by-side gates. Since each gate passes the usual flow, the overall flow rate should be twice the rate for a single gate. Applying these relationships in the domain of electricity,[5] we conclude that serial resistors lead to less current than a single resistor; whereas parallel resistors lead to more current.

### Predicted differences in patterns of inference

The flowing-water and moving-crowd models should lead to different patterns of performance on the four combination circuits. Both models can yield the first stage "More force, more flow/more drag, less flow" law. Where the models should differ is in the ease with which further distinctions can be perceived. Subjects with the flowing-water model should be more likely to see the difference between the two kinds of battery combinations. Subjects with the moving-crowd model should be more likely to see the difference between the two kinds of resistor combinations.

*Flowing-fluid model.* Subjects who use the flowing-fluid model should do well on the battery questions. This is because, as described earlier, serial and parallel reservoirs combine in the same manner as serial and parallel batteries; thus already-familiar combinational distinctions can be imported from the water domain. However, subjects with the fluid flow model should do less well on resistor combinations. In the hydraulic model resistors are viewed as impediments. This often leads people to adopt the "More drag, less flow" view. Here, people focus on the idea that in both parallel and serial configurations the water is subjected to *two* obstacles rather than one. They conclude that two resistors lead to less current, regardless of the configuration.

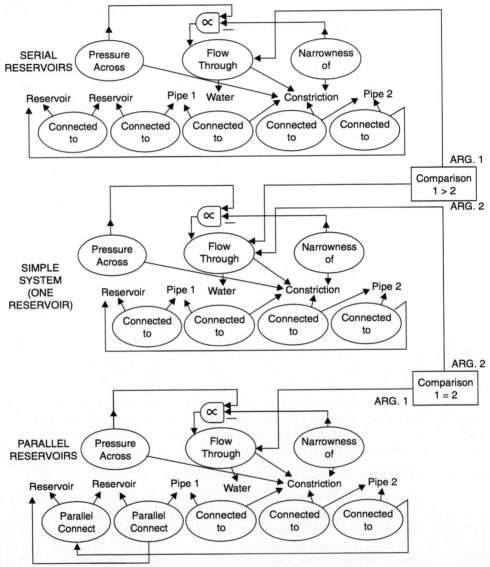

**Figure 5**   **Representation of knowledge in the hydraulic domain, showing higher-order comparison relations between rate of water flow in systems with parallel reservoirs and systems with serial reservoirs as compared with simple one-reservoir systems.**

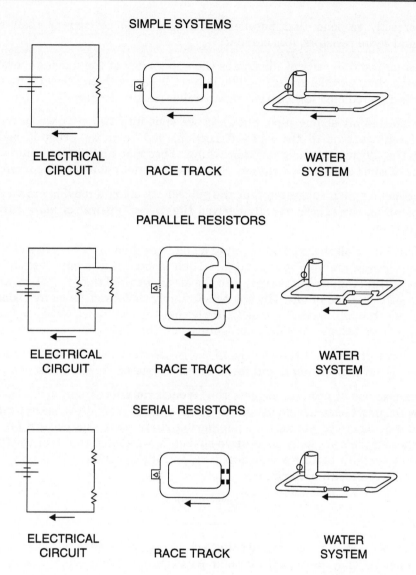

**Figure 6** **Diagrams of electrical circuits, moving-crowd tracks and hydraulic systems, showing analogous systems for simple circuits, parallel-resistors circuits and serial resistors circuits.**

*Moving-crowd model.* For subjects with the moving-crowd model, the pattern should be quite different. In this model, configurations of batteries should be relatively difficult to differentiate, since it is hard to think of good analogs for batteries with the correct serial-parallel behavior. In contrast, resistors should be better understood, because they can be seen as gates. This should lead to better differentiation between the parallel and serial configurations, as described earlier. Subjects using this model should correctly respond that parallel resistors give more current than a single resistor; and serial resistors, less current.

The following protocol excerpt illustrates the superiority of the moving-crowd model for understanding parallel resistors. The subject began with the flowing-fluid model and incorrectly predicted less current in a parallel-resistor circuit:

> We started off as one pipe, but then we split into two. . . . we have a different current in the split-off section, and then we bring it back together. That's a whole different thing. That just functions as one big pipe of some obscure description. So you should not get as much current.

The experimenter then suggested that the subject try using a moving-crowd analogy. With this model, the subject rapidly derived the correct answer of *more* current for parallel resistors:

> Again I have all these people coming along here. I have this big area here where people are milling around. . . . I can model the two gate system by just putting the two gates right into the arena just like that. . . . There are two gates instead of one which seems to imply that twice as many people can get through. So that seems to imply that the resistance would be half as great as if there were only one gate for all those people.

Figure 6 shows drawings of the analogs in the two systems, similar to those drawn by the subject. (Drawings of simple and serial-resistor systems are shown for comparison.)

These two sections of protocol suggest that models do affect inferences. The subject who drew incorrect conclusions using the water analogy later drew correct inferences using the moving-crowd analogy. The following study tests this pattern on a larger scale. If these models are truly generative analogies, we should find that the fluid-flow people do better with batteries than resistors, and the moving-crowd people do better with resistors than with batteries.

## Experiment 1

### Subjects

The subjects were 36 high school and college students, screened to be fairly naive about physical science. They were paid for their participation. Only subjects who used the same model throughout the study, as determined from their questionnaire responses, are included in the results discussed below. Also, among subjects who used a fluid-flow model, only those who correctly answered two later questions about the behavior of water systems were included. There were seven subjects who consistently used fluid-flow models and eight subjects who consistently used moving-object models. The responses of subjects who were inconsistent in their use of models were analyzed separately and are not reported here.

### Method

*Qualitative circuit comparisons.* Subjects were given booklets containing a series of questions and allowed to work at their own pace. The first page showed a simple circuit with a battery and a resistor, like the simple circuit in Figure 4. Succeeding pages showed the four series-and-parallel combination circuits (see Figure 4). They were asked to circle whether the current (and voltage) in each of the combination circuits would be greater than, equal to, or less than that of the simple battery-resistor circuit.

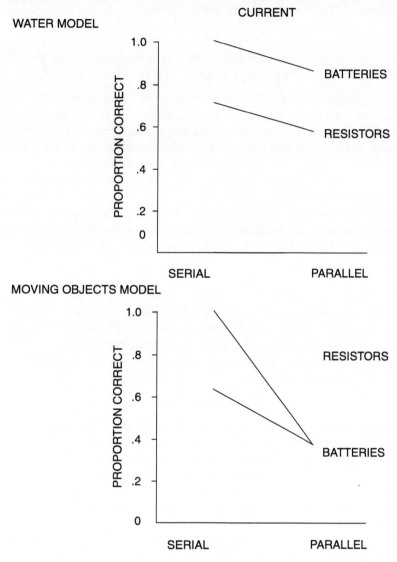

**Figure 7   Results of Experiment 1: Proportions correct, for subjects with either a water-flow model or a moving-crowd model of electricity, on serial and parallel problems for batteries and resistors.**

*Questions about models.* After the subjects gave their answers for all four combination circuits, they were asked on a separate page to describe the way they thought about electricity, in their own words. On the next page, they were given a more specific choice: For each of the four circuit problems, they were asked to circle whether they had thought about flowing fluid, moving objects, or some other view of electricity while working on the problem. On the final page of the booklet they were asked questions about the behavior of reservoirs in the water domain.

### Results

Figure 7 shows the results for subjects who reported using either the flowing-fluid analogy or the moving-crowd analogy consistently, on all four problems.

The patterns of inference are different depending on which model the subject had. As predicted, people who used the flowing-fluid model performed better on batteries than on resistors. The reverse is true for the moving-crowd people: they performed better with resistors, particularly in parallel, than with batteries. A Model X Component X Topology 2 X 2 X 2 analysis of variance was performed on the proportions of correct answers. Here Model refers to whether the subject was using a flowing-fluid or moving-crowd model of electricity; Component refers to whether the combination was of batteries or resistors; and Topology refers to whether the problem involved a serial or parallel configuration. As predicted, the interaction between Model and Component was significant; $F(1,13) = 4.53$; $p < .05$. No other effects were significant.

### Conclusions

The results of the study indicate that use of different analogies leads to systematic differences in the patterns of inferences in the target domain. Subjects with the flowing fluid model did better with batteries, while moving objects subjects did better with resistors. These combinatorial differences cannot be attributed to shallow verbal associations. These analogies seem to be truly generative for our subjects; structural relations from the base domain are reflected in inferences in the target domain.

### Experiment 2

In this study we taught subjects about electricity, varying the base domain used in the explanation. We then compared their responses to a series of questions about the target domain. Three different models of electronic circuitry were used. The first two models were versions of the hydraulic model, with fluid flow mapping onto current, pumps or reservoirs mapping onto batteries, pipes onto wires, and narrow pipes onto resistors. The two versions of this model varied according to what maps onto the battery: either a pump (Model P) or a reservoir (Model R). The third model was a moving-crowd model (Model M). In this model, current was seen as a moving crowd of mice and voltage was the forward pressure or pushiness of the mice.

The basic method was to present different groups of subjects with different models of electronics and then observe their responses to circuit problems. As in Experiment 1, the dependent measure is not merely percent correct but the pattern of responses. Each model should cause particular incorrect inferences as well as particular correct inferences. We also presented problems in the base domains. It seemed possible that subjects might have misconceptions in the base domains (such as hydraulics); in this case the knowledge available for importing into the target would deviate from the ideal knowledge.

## Predicted results

In the two hydraulics models, reservoirs (R) or pumps (P) are sources of pressure (voltage), which results in a flow of liquid (current) depending on the narrowness of the pipes (resistance). In the moving-crowd model, M, the forward pressure on the crowd (voltage), is generated by a loudspeaker shouting encouragement. This pressure creates a certain number of mice past a point per unit time (current) depending on the narrowness of the gates (resistance). Table 2 shows the correspondence among the three models.

Our major predictions were

1.  that the moving-crowd model (M) would lead to better understanding of resistors, particularly the effects of parallel resistors on current, than the hydraulics models.

2.  that the reservoir model (R) would lead to better understanding of combinations of batteries than either the moving-crowd model (M) or the pump model (P). With reservoirs, the correct inferences for series versus parallel can be derived by keeping track of the resulting height of water, as discussed earlier.

Neither the pump analog nor the loudspeaker analog has as clear a combination pattern.

**Table 2    Comparison of water flow, moving crowd, and electricity domains**

| Water flow models (R,P) | Moving crowd model (M) | Electrical circuit |
| --- | --- | --- |
| *Object mappings* | | |
| hydraulic system | race course | circuit |
| water | mice | electricity or electrons |
| pipe | wide corridor | wire |
| pump or reservoir | loudspeaker | battery |
| constriction in pipe | gate in barrier | resistor |
| *Attribute mappings* | | |
| PRESSURE OF water | PRESSURE OF mice | VOLTAGE |
| NARROWNESS OF pipe | NARROWNESS OF gate | RESISTANCE |
| FLOW OF pipe | PASSAGE RATE OF mice | CURRENT |
| *Relations between objects that hold in all domains* | | |
| pump CONNECTED TO pipe | loudspeaker CONNECTED TO corridor | battery CONNECTED TO wire |
| pipe CONNECTED TO constriction | corridor CONNECTED TO gate | wire CONNECTED TO resistor |
| *Higher-order relations that hold in all domains* | | |
| (FLOW OF water) *INCREASES WITH* (PRESSURE ACROSS constriction) | (PASSAGE RATE OF mice) *INCREASES WITH* (PRESSURE ACROSS gate) | (CURRENT) *INCREASES WITH* (VOLTAGE ACROSS resistor) |

**Table 2    (Cont)**

| Water flow models (R,P) | Moving crowd model (M) | Electrical circuit |
|---|---|---|
| (FLOW OF water) *DECREASES WITH* (NARROWNESS OF constriction) | (PASSAGE RATE OF mice) *DECREASES WITH* (NARROWNESS OF gate) | (CURRENT) *DECREASES WITH* (RESISTANCE) |
| [SUM OF (FLOW INTO point)] *EQUALS* [SUM OF (FLOW OUT OF point)] | [SUM OF (PASSAGE RATE INTO POINT)] *EQUALS* [SUM OF (PASSAGE RATE OUT OF point)] | [SUM OF (CURRENT) INTO point)] *EQUALS* [SUM OF (CURRENT OUT OF point)] |

*Relations that do not hold in all domains*

| *RATIO OF* (cross-section WIDTHS OF pipe and constrictions) is typically 100:1 | *RATIO OF* (WIDTHS OF corridor and gate) is typically 10:1 | *RATIO OF* (RESISTANCES OF resistor and wire) is typically 1,000,000:1 |

### *Method*

*Subjects.* Eighteen people participated, all either advanced high school or beginning college students from the Boston area. Subjects had little or no previous knowledge of electronics. They were paid for their participation. Due to experimenter's error, there were seven subjects in the M group, six in the P group and five in the R group.

*Procedure.* After filling out a questionnaire concerning their general backgrounds, subjects were divided into three groups, each receiving different models. The procedure was as follows:

1. *Model-teaching.* Subjects were given a brief introduction to electricity consisting of Ohm's Law ($I=V/R$) together with an explanation of one of the three models.

2. *Simple test.* All three groups were given an identical set of five simple circuit problems to calculate. In each case the circuit was a simple battery-plus resistor circuit, and subjects solved for current, voltage or resistance by applying Ohm's Law. We required that subjects solve at least four problems correctly to be included in the study.

3. *Qualitative comparisons.* Subjects were next shown diagrams of the four complex circuits (SB, PB, SR, and PR, as shown in Figure 4) along with a diagram of a simple battery-resistor circuit. For each such complex circuit, we asked subjects to compare current and voltage at several points in the circuit with that of the corresponding point in a simple circuit; e.g., they were asked whether current just before the resistors in a parallel-resistor circuit is *greater than, equal to* or *less than* the corresponding current in a simple circuit.

4. *Quantitative scaling.* Each subject received each of the four kinds of complex circuits (SB, SR, PB or PR) and filled out a series of scales indicating current and voltage at the same test points as in task (3).

5. *Drawing base given target analog.* Each subject received, for each of the four complex circuits, a sheet containing a simple base version of the standard simple system (analog of battery plus resistor); and a circuit drawing of one of the four complex circuits (SB, SR, PB or PR). They were told to draw the *base* version of the complex circuit shown.

6. *Base qualitative questions.* To test knowledge of the base system, subjects were given a picture of one of the four complex systems in the base, and answered qualitative questions about pressure and flow rate in the base system. Each sheet showed a simple system (the analog of battery plus resistor) plus a complex system (the analog of SB, SR, PB or PR). The subjects made judgments at the same points as in tasks (3) and (4).

7. *Thought questions.* Subjects were asked to write out answers to questions such as "What will happen if there is no resistor in the circuit?"; and "Do electrons go faster, slower or the same speed through the resistor as through the wire?"

### Results: Prediction 1

Results supported the first prediction, that the moving-crowd model (M) would lead to better performance on parallel-resistor problems than the water models (P and R).

Table 3    Results of Experiment 2: performance on problems involving current with parallel resistors

|  | M | P | R |
|---|---|---|---|
| Qualitative comparisons[a] | .93 | .58 | .70 |
| Quantitative scaling[b] | .71 | .50 | .40 |

[a] Proportions of responses that current in parallel-resistor circuit is greater than or equal to current in simple one-resistor circuit

[b] Proportions of responses that current in parallel-resistor circuit is greater than current in simple circuit

*Qualitative comparisons.* In the M group, 93% of the subjects answered that current given two parallel resistors would be greater than or equal to current given a single resistor, as compared with .63 for the combined P and R groups. This difference between the M group and the P and R groups combined was significant by a $X^2$ test (p < .05). Table 3 shows the results for current given parallel resistors both for the qualitative comparisons task and for the quantitative scaling task.

The pattern of M-superiority on parallel-resistor problems also obtained for voltage. The proportions of questions in which subjects (correctly) answered that the voltage in a circuit with two parallel resistors is equal to the voltage in the simple circuit with one resistor were for the M group, .86; for the P group, .42; and for the R group, .50. Again, the M group is significantly different from the combined P and R groups by a $X^2$ test (p < .025); M differs from P significantly as well (Fisher test, p < .05).

*Quantitative scaling.* The differences, though nonsignificant, were in the predicted direction, as shown in Table 3. The proportions of times subjects answered that current in a parallel-resistor circuit would exceed current given a single resistor were .71 for M, .50 for P, and .40 for R. For voltage, the proportions of times subjects answered that voltage in a parallel-resistor circuit equals that in a simple circuit were .86 for M, .83 for P and .60 for R.

### Results: Prediction 2

Our second prediction, that the R group would be superior to the M and P groups on parallel-batteries problems, was not supported.

*Qualitative comparisons.* The proportions of times subjects correctly answered that the voltage given parallel batteries is equal to the voltage given a single battery were .40 for the R group, .64 for the M group, and .33 for the P group. None of these differences was statistically significant.

For serial-battery problems, we expected less difference between the groups. This is because the correct answer — that voltage is greater in a circuit with two batteries in serial than with just one battery — is derivable from several different models, even from the naive "More force, more flow" view. The results are that the proportion of correct responses was .60 for R and .50 for P; for the M group, it was .57 (no significant differences).

*Quantitative scaling.* Again we failed to find clear evidence that the R group understood parallel-battery problems better than the P group. The proportions of correct answers (that voltage is the same for PB as for a simple circuit) were .2 for R and .33 for P. The R group did perform better on the serial battery problems: .8 of the R answers indicated more voltage with serial batteries, whereas only .33 of the P answers did so. None of these differences is significant. (This lack of significance may seem surprising; however, we had only one data point per subject.) Rather surprisingly, the M group, with .86 correct, was significantly better than the other two groups on parallel batteries ($p < .025$, $X^2$).

### Other results in the qualitative comparison and quantitative scaling tasks

There were two other significant differences. First, in the qualitative comparisons task, the P group was superior to the R group for current in a serial-resistor circuit. The proportion of times subjects correctly answered that current is lower with two serial resistors than with a single resistor was .58 for P and .10 for R ($p < .05$). There were no other significant differences on the qualitative comparison task.

The other remaining significant result is that, in the quantitative scaling problems, the R group performed better (at .40 correct) than the M group (0 correct) or P group (0 correct) on answering that current is constant everywhere in a purely serial circuit (such as SB or SR). The difference between R and P is significant ($p < .05$) as well as the difference between R and M ($p < .025$). This issue of constant steady-state current flow seems quite difficult for subjects, as discussed next.

*Subjects' knowledge of the base.* We were puzzled by the failure of Prediction 2: the finding that the R group did not excel at combinations of batteries, in spite of the seeming transparency of the corresponding combinations in the reservoir domain. One possible explanation is that, contrary to our intuitions, our subjects did not understand serial and parallel reservoirs any better than they understood serial and parallel pumps or loudspeakers. To check this possibility, we examined the subjects' answers in the base domains.

The results of the Base Qualitative Comparisons task revealed that subjects indeed failed to grasp the distinction between parallel and serial pressure sources in the base domains. Scores on the qualitative comparison problems concerning rate of flow of water or animals (analogous to current) were .35 for R, .42 for P and .32 for M. It is not surprising, then, that the R subjects failed to make correct inferences in the target domain of electricity.

Subsequent interviews have borne out the suspicion that even college-educated people fail to understand the way water behaves. They have difficulties not only with series versus parallel combinations of reservoirs or pumps, but also with the notion of steady-state flow. Current is seen not as a steady flow, constant throughout the system, but rather as a progression: flow is strong and rapid at the source and gradually weakens as it goes through the pipes, with a drastic cut-back as it goes through the constriction. Moreover, people often fail to make the distinction between flow rate and related physical variables. Many people seem to have a *generalized strength-attribute* which is a composite of velocity, pressure, force of water, and rate of flow. This strength is thought to be very high at the outset, just after the reservoir, to diminish as the water travels around the water system, and to decrease sharply at the constriction.

Similar misconceptions show up in electronics. People in interviews do appear to have a kind of composite strength attribute that is interchangeably referred to as current, voltage, velocity of the electrons, power, pressure, or force of the electrons. This strength attribute fails to obey steady-state: It decreases as the stuff flows around the circuit, with the sharpest diminution occurring at the resistor.

The subjects' misconceptions in electronics are strikingly analogous to those in hydraulics. Therefore, subjects' failure to import veridical differentiations from the base domain does not constitute evidence against the Generative Analogies hypothesis. Even a fully generative, rigorous structure-mapping process cannot produce correct distinctions in the target domain unless subjects have grasped these differentiations in the base domain. Our investigations bring home the point that an analogy is only useful to the extent that the desired relational structure is present in the person's representation of the base domain.

**Discussion**

It is an appealing notion that analogies function as tools of thought (Clement, 1981; Darden, 1980; Dreistadt, 1968; Hesse, 1966; Hoffman, 1980; Jones, in preparation; Oppenheimer, 1955). In this research we have sought to bring psychological evidence to bear on this claim.

We first noted that we find analogical references in people's spontaneous discussions of natural phenomena; for example, when a person discusses electric current in terms of traffic or in terms of flow of water. Our protocols suggest that people use analogies to help structure unfamiliar domains. The pervasiveness and generative quality of people's analogical language suggests that the analogies are used in thinking (Lakoff & Johnson, 1980; Quinn, 1981; Reddy, 1979; Schon, 1979). But to make this conclusion it must be demonstrated that the thinking truly depends on the analogy: that the analogy is more than a convenient vocabulary in which to discuss the results of independent inferential processes.

Evidence for the conceptual role of analogy comes from the introspections of creative scientists. The journals and self-descriptions of scientists from Johannes Kepler (1969; see also Koestler, 1963) to Sheldon Glashow (1980) seem to lean heavily on analogical comparisons in discovering scientific laws. Glashow's account of his use of generative analogies in nuclear physics was quoted earlier. Kepler's journals show several signs of generative analogy use. First, he makes reference to the analogy in stating his theory. Second, he appears to derive further insights from the analogy over time. Finally, as quoted earlier in this chapter, Kepler himself states that he uses analogy to further his thinking. The tempting conclusion is that, for scientists like Kepler and Glashow, analogies are genuine conceptual tools.

However, self-reports concerning psychological processes are not conclusive evidence, as Nisbett and Wilson (1977) have argued. In this research we tested the Generative Analogy hypothesis that analogy is an important source of insight by asking whether truly different inferences in a given target domain are engendered by different analogies. We chose as our target domain simple electricity, partly because it has the right degree of familiarity, and partly because there are two good, readily available base domains — flowing water and moving crowds — that support different inferences in the target domain.

To test this hypothesis, we needed to find problems for which the inferences required in the target could not be mimicked by verbal patterns, but would reflect structural relations imported from these different base domains. We chose the four combinatorial problems described earlier: serial and parallel combinations of resistors and batteries. These problems are simple enough to be posed even to a novice, yet are nontransparent enough that they require some sustained thought. We predicted that the parallel-serial distinction for batteries should be clearer using flowing fluid as the base. This is because the pressure difference between serial and parallel reservoirs can be understood in terms of height of fluid, a relatively accessible distinction. Therefore, use of the water system as a base domain should improve understanding of batteries. In contrast, the parallel-serial distinction for resistors should be more obvious using the moving-crowd base domain. In the moving-crowd model, resistors can be thought of as gates (inferior passages) rather than as obstructions. Subjects who use that model should see that parallel resistors, analogous to gates side by side, will allow more flow than a single resistor. The opportunity is there to find effects of thinking in different analogical models.

In Experiment 1, we divided subjects according to which analogy they reported using for electricity and compared their inferences about the current in our four combination problems. We found, as predicted, that subjects using the water model (given that they understood the way water behaves) differentiated batteries more correctly than resistors, and that subjects who used the moving-crowd model were more accurate for resistors than for batteries. These results support the generative analogies claim of a true conceptual role for analogical models. The pattern of inferences a subject made in the target domain did indeed match the pattern that should have been imported from the base domain.

Experiment 1 provided evidence for the Generative Analogies hypothesis for people's preexisting spontaneous analogies. Experiment 2 examined the effects of analogical models that were taught to subjects. In Experiment 2, we taught people to use one of three models and compared their subsequent patterns of inference. If people's inferential patterns varied according to the model they were taught, this would provide a second line of evidence for analogical reasoning. We found some of the predicted effects in Experiment 2. Subjects who were taught the moving-crowd analogy could differentiate parallel versus serial resistor configurations more accurately than subjects who had learned either of the water models. However, we did not find the predicted differences in ability to differentiate the two types of battery combinations.

We suspect that there are two main reasons that the results of Experiment 2 were weaker than those of Experiment 1. The first problem was that we did not screen people for knowledge of the water domain in Experiment 2. In many cases, people simply did not understand that serial reservoirs and parallel reservoirs yield different pressure in the domain of water. Because we had information concerning subjects' knowledge of the respective base domains, we were able to demonstrate that in many cases the failure of the analogical inference was due to the lack of the corresponding inference in the original base domain.

The phenomenon of mapping erroneous knowledge may be fairly widespread. Several independent researchers have reported that mental representations of physical phenomena — even among college populations — often contain profound errors. Yet, although these initial models may be fragmentary, inaccurate, and even internally inconsistent, nonetheless they strongly affect a person's construal of new information in the domain (Brown & Burton, 1975; Brown, Collins & Harris, 1978; Chi, Feltovich, & Glaser, 1981; Clement, 1981, this volume; diSessa, this volume; Eylon & Reif, 1979; Gentner, 1980, 1982; Hayes, 1978; Hollan, Williams & Stevens, this volume; Larkin, this volume; McCloskey, this volume; Miyake, 1981; Sayeki, 1981; Stevens & Collins, 1980; Stevens, Collins & Goldin, 1979; Wiser & Carey, this volume). Our research, and that of other investigators, suggests that these domain models, whether correct or incorrect, are carried over in analogical inferencing in other domains (Collins & Gentner, in preparation; Darden, 1980; Gentner, 1979; Johnson-Laird, 1980; Riley, 1981; VanLehn & Brown, 1980; Winston, 1978, 1980, 1981; Wiser & Carey, this volume).

Aside from the subjects' lack of insight in the base domain, the second problem with Experiment 2 is that the teaching sessions may have been inadequate to convince all the subjects to use the models. People simply read a one-page description of the model that they were to learn, and then began answering questions. Accepting a new model often requires considerable time and practice. The problem of convincing subjects to use a particular model did not exist in Experiment 1; subjects were sorted according to the model they reported using a priori. This possible pattern of conservatism in use of new models accords with that found in experimental studies of analogical transfer by Gick and Holyoak (1980), and Schustack and Anderson (1979). Both these studies found that, although subjects are demonstrably able to import relational structure from one domain to another, they often fail to notice and use a potential analogy. We suspect that one reason subjects may be slow to begin using a new analogy for an area is that they normally enter a study with existing models of the domain.

However, although Experiment 1 produced stronger results than Experiment 2, the results of the two experiments taken together provide clear evidence for the Generative Analogies hypothesis. People who think of electricity as though it were water import significant physical relationships from the domain of flowing fluids when they reason about electricity; and similarly for people who think of electricity in terms of crowds of moving objects. Generative analogies can indeed serve as inferential frameworks.

## Acknowledgment

This research was supported by the Department of the Navy, Office of Naval Research under Contract No. N00014-79-0338.

We would like to thank Allan Collins and Al Stevens, who collaborated on the development of these ideas, and Susan Carey, Ken Forbus, David Rumelhart, Billy Salter and Ed Smith for helpful comments on earlier versions of this paper. We also thank Molly Brewer, Judith Block, Phil Kohn, Brenda Starr and Ben Teitelbaum for their help with the research and Cindy Hunt for preparing the manuscript.

## Notes

1. An adequate discussion of literal similarity within this framework would require including a negative dependency on the number of *nonshared* features as well as the positive dependency on the numser of shared features (Tversky, 1977). However, for our purposes, the key point is that, in analogy, a structural distinction must be made between different types of predicates. In Tversky's valuable characterization of literal similarity, the relation-attribute distinction is not utilized; all predicates are considered together, as "features." This suggests that literal similarity (at least in the initial stages of study) does not require as elaborate a computational semantics as metaphor and analogy.

2. The "objects" in terms of which a person conceptualizes a system need not be concrete tangible objects; they may be simply relatively coherent, separable component parts of a complex object, or they may be idealized or even fictional objects. Moreover, often a target system can be parsed in various ways by different individuals, or even by the same individual for different purposes. [See Greeno, Vesonder & Majetic (this volume) and Larkin (this volume).] The important point is, once the objects are determined they will be treated as objects in the mapping.

3. Mathematical models represent an extreme of systematicity. The set of mappable relations is strongly constrained, and the rules for concatenating relationships are well-specified. Once we choose a given mathematical system — say, a ring or a group — as base, we know thereby which combinatorial rules and which higher-order relations apply to the base. This clarifies the process of deriving new predictions to test in the target. We know, for example,

that if the base relations are addition ($R_1$) and multiplication ($R_2$) in a field (e.g., the real numbers) then we can expect distributivity to hold: $c(a + b) = ca + cb$, or

$$R_2 [(c, R_1 (a, b))] = R_1 [R_2 (c, a), R_2 (c, b)]$$

A mathematical model predicts a small number of relations which are well-specified enough and systematic enough to be concatenated into long chains of prediction.

4.  Notice that the analogy shown in Figure 2 actually involves two different systems of mappings that do not completely overlap. Each system is dominated by a different higher-order relation. Although the *object* mappings are the same in both cases, the *attribute* mappings are different. (Recall that object attributes, like objects themselves, can be mapped onto arbitrarily *different* elements of the target, according to the structure-mapping theory: only the resulting *relations* need be preserved.)

The first system of mappings is dominated by the attractive force relation

$$(F = G\, m_1\, m_2 / R^2).$$

In this system, the mass of objects in the solar system is mapped onto the *charge* of objects in the atom. This system includes the higher-order relation that attractive force decreases with distance.

The other system is dominated by the inertial relation ($F = ma$); in this system, the *mass* of objects in the solar system maps into the *mass* of objects in the atom. This system includes the inference (expressed as a higher-order relation in Figure 2) that the less massive object moves more than the more massive object.

5.  In combinations of resistors, the key principle is that the voltage changes significantly only when current encounters a resistance. When the circuit contains two identical resistors in a row, the total voltage drop gets divided between the two resistors. Thus the voltage drop across each resistor is only half as great. As the current is proportional to the voltage drop, the current through each resistor is only half the original current. By conservation of charge, this reduced current is constant throughout the system. When the resistors are connected in parallel, each resistor has the full voltage drop across it. Therefore, current passes through each of the resistors at the original rate. This means that in the parts of the circuit where the two currents are united (before and after the resistors) the total current will thus be twice the current given one resistor.

# References

Brown, J. S. & Burton. R. R. (1975) Multiple representations of knowledge for tutorial reasoning. In D.G. Bobrow & A. Collins (Eds.), *Representation and understanding*. New York: Academic Press.

Brown, J. S., Collins, A. & Harris. G. (1978) Artificial intelligence and learning strategies. In H. F. O'Neil (Ed.), *Learning strategies*. New York: Academic Press.

Chi, M. T. H., Feltovich, P. J. & Glaser, R. (1981) Categorization and representation of physics problems by experts and novices. *Cognitive Science*. 5, 121–152.

Clement, J. (1981) Analogy generation in scientific problem solving. *Proceedings of the Third Annual Meeting of the Cognitive Science Society*. Berkeley, California.

Collins, A. M. & Gentner, D. (in preparation) Constructing runnable mental models.

Darden, L. (1980) Theory construction in genetics. In T. Nicklles (Ed.), *Scientific discovery: Case studies*. D. Reidel Publishing Co., pp. 151–170.

de Kleer, J. & Sussman, G. J. (1978) *Propagation of constraints applied to circuit synthesis.* Artificial Intelligence Laboratory, AIM-485, Cambridge, Mass.: M.I.T.

Dreistadt, R. (1968) An analysis of the use of analogies and metaphors in science. *The Journal of Psychology,* 68, 97–116.

Eylon, B. & Reif, F. (1979) *Effects of internal knowledge organization on task performance.* Paper presented at the meeting of the American Educational Research Association.

Forbus, K. D. (1982) *Qualitative process theory.* A.I.M. 664, Artificial Intelligence Laboratory, M.I.T.

Gentner, D. (1980) *The structure of analogical models in science.* Technical Report No. 4451, Bolt Beranek and Newman.

Gentner, D. (1982) Are scientific analogies metaphors? In D. S. Miall (Ed.), *Metaphor: Problems and perspectives,* Brighton, England: Harvester Press Ltd.

Gick, M. L. & Holyoak, K. J. (1980) Analogical problem solving. *Cognitive Psychology,* 12, 306–355.

Glashow, S. L. (1980) Toward a unified theory: Threads in a tapestry. Nobel prize lecture; Stockholm, December 1979. Reprinted in *Science,* 210, 1319–1323.

Hayes, P. J. (1978) *The naive physics manifesto.* Unpublished manuscript, University of Essex, Colchester.

Hesse, M. B. (1966) *Models and analogies in science.* Notre Dame, Indiana: University of Notre Dame Press.

Hoffman, R. R. (1980) Metaphor in science. In R. P. Honeck & R. R. Hoffman (Eds.), *The psycholinguistics of figurative language.* Hillsdale, N.J.: Lawrence Erlbaum Associates.

Johnson-Laird, P. N. (1980) Mental models in cognitive science. *Cognitive Science,* 4, 71–115.

Jones, R. S. (in preparation) *Physics as metaphor.*

Kepler, J. (1969) *Epitome of Copernical astronomy,* Books IV and V, Volume 1. New York: Kraus Reprint Company.

Koestler, A. (1963) *The sleepwalkers.* New York: The Universal Library, Grosset and Dunlap.

Koff, R. M. (1961) *How does it work?* New York: Doubleday.

Lakoff, G. & Johnson, M. (1980) *Metaphors we live by.* Chicago, Ill.: University of Chicago Press.

Miller, G. A. (1979)'Images and models: Similes and metaphors. In A. Ortony (Ed.), *Metaphor and thought.* Cambridge, England: Cambridge University Press, pp. 202–250.

Miyake, N. (1981) The effect of conceptual point of view on understanding. *The Quarterly Newsletter of the Laboratory of Comparative Human Cognition,* 3, 54–56.

Nisbett, R. E. & Wilson, T. D. (1977) Telling more than we know: Verbal reports on mental processes. *Psychological Review,* 84, 231–259.

Oppenheimer, R. (1955) *Analogy in science.* Paper presented at the 63rd Annual Meeting of the American Psychological Association, San Francisco, Calif.

Ortony, A. (1979) The role of similarity in similes and metaphors. In A. Ortony (Ed.) *Metaphor and Thought.* Cambridge, England: Cambridge University Press, pp. 186–201.

Polya, G. (1973) *Mathematics and plausible reasoning, Volume 1.* Princeton, N.J.: Princeton University Press.

Quinn, N. (1981) Marriage is a do-it-yourself project: The organization of marital goals. *Proceedings of the Third Annual Conference of the Cognitive Science Society.* Berkeley, Calif., pp. 31-40.

Reddy, M. J. (1979) The conduit metaphor: A case of frame conflict in our language about language. In A. Ortony (Ed.), *Metaphor and thought.* Cambridge, England: Cambridge University Press.

Rieger, C. & Grinberg, M. (1977) The declarative representation and procedural simulation of causality in physical mechanisms. *Proceedings of the Fifth International Joint Conference on Artificial Intelligence,* pp. 250–255.

Riley, M. S. (1981) *Representations and the acquisition of problem-solving skill in basic electricity/electronics.* Paper presented at the Computer-based Instructional Systems and Simulation meeting, Carnegie-Mellon University.

Rumelhart D. E. (1979) Some problems with the notion of literal meaning. In A. Ortony (Ed.) *Metaphor and thought.* Cambridge, England: Cambridge University Press.

Rumelhart D. E. & Abrahamson A. A. (1973) A model for analogical reasoning. *Cognitive Psychology,* 5, 1–28.

Rumelhart, D. E. & Norman. D. A. (1975) The active structural network. In D. A. Norman, D. E. Rumelhart and the LNR Research Group, *Explorations in Cognition.* San Francisco: W. H. Freeman & Co.

Rumelhart, D. E. & Ortony, A. (1977) Representation of knowledge. In R. C. Anderson, R. J. Spiro & W. E. Montague (Eds.), *Schooling and the acquisition of knowledge.* Hillsdale, N.J.: Lawrence Erlbaum Associates.

Sayeki, Y. (1981) "Body analogy" and the cognition of rotated figures. *Quarterly Newsletter of the Laboratory of Comparative Human Cognition,* 3, 36–40.

Schank, R. & Abelson, R. (1977) *Scripts, plans, goals, and understanding.* Hillsdale, N.J.: Lawrence Erlbaum Associates.

Schon, D. A. (1979) Generative metaphor: A perspective on problem-setting in social policy. In A. Ortony (Ed.), *Metaphor and thought.* Cambridge, England: Cambridge University Press.

Schustack, M. W. & Anderson, I. R. (1979) Effects of analogy to prior knowledge on memory for new information. *Journal of Verbal Learning and Verbal Behavior,* 18, 565–583.

Smith, B. C. (in preparation) *Computational reflection.* Doctoral dissertation, Electrical Engineering and Computer Science, M.I.T.

Sternberg, R. I. (1977) Component processes in analogical reasoning. *Psychological Review,* 84, 353–378.

Stevens, A. & Collins, A. (1980) Multiple conceptual models of a complex system. In R. E. Snow, P. Federico & W. E. Montague (Eds.), *Aptitude, learning, and instruction. Vol. 2.* Hillsdale, N.J.: Lawrence Erlbaum Associates.

Stevens, A., Collins, A. & Goldin, S. E. (1979) Misconceptions in students' understanding. *Journal of Man-Machine Studies,* 11, 145–156.

Tourangeau, R. & Sternberg. R. J. (1981) Aptness in metaphor. *Cognitive Psychology,* 13, 27–55.

Tversky, A. (1977) Features of similarity. *Psychological Review,* 84, 327–352.

VanLehn, K. & Brown, J. S. (1980) Planning nets: A representation for formalizing analogies and semantic models of procedural skills. In R. E. Snow, P. A. Federico & W. E. Montague (Eds.), *Aptitude, learning and instruction, Vol. 2.* Hillsdale, N.J.: Lawrence Erlbaum Associates.

Verbrugge, R. R. & McCarrell, N. S. (1977) Metaphoric comprehension: Studies in reminding and resembling. *Cognitive Psychology,* 9, 494–533.

Winston, P. H. (1978) Learning by creating and justifying transfer frames. *Intelligence,* 10, 147–172.

Winston, P. H. (1980) Learning and reasoning by analogy. *CACM,* 23, no. 12.

Winston, P. H. (1981) *Learning new principles from precedents and exercises: The details.* AIM 632, Artificial Intelligence Laboratory, M.I.T.

# 12. Systematicity and Surface Similarity in the Development of Analogy

## Dedre Gentner and Cecile Toupin

*This research investigates the development of analogy: In particular, we wish to study the development of systematicity in analogy. Systematicity refers to the mapping of systems of mutually constraining relations such as causal chains or chains of implication. A preference for systematic mappings is a central aspect of analogical processing in adults (Gentner, 1980, 1983). This research asks two questions: Does systematicity make analogical mapping easier? And if so, when developmentally, do children become able to utilize systematicity?*

*Children aged 5–7 and 8–10 acted out stories with toy characters. Then they were asked to act out the same stories with new characters. Two variables were manipulated: systematicity or the degree of explicit causal structure in the original stories and the transparency of the object-mappings. Transparency was manipulated by varying the similarity between the original characters and the corresponding new characters; it was included in order to vary the difficulty of the transfer task. If children can utilize systematicity then their transfer accuracy should be greater for systematic stories.*

*The results show: (1) As expected, transparency strongly influenced transfer accuracy (for both age groups, transfer accuracy dropped sharply as the object correspondences became less transparent); and (2) for the older group there was also a strong effect of systematicity and an interaction between the two variables. Given a systematic story, 9-year-olds could transfer it accurately regardless of the transparency of the object correspondence.*

## Introduction

Analogy is a central process in learning and discovery. For example, Sadi Carnot's great work on the principles of heat is pervaded by an analogy between heat and water: The "fall" of heat from high temperature to low temperature is compared to the fall of water from high elevation to low elevation. Just as Carnot used this analogy to think through the mechanical action of heat, so a student learning about heat can use the same analogy to come to understand ideas like, "The power released when heat flows between two bodies varies with the difference in temperature between them" (Buckley, 1979). But notice that to make this analogy useful the learner must focus on certain kinds of matches between the two domains (e.g., Clement, 1981, 1982; Collins & Gentner, in press; Forbus & Gentner, 1986; Kempton, in press; VanLehn & Brown, 1980). A learner who interpreted the analogy to mean that heat is wet or transparent like water might be worse off with the analogy than without it. The power of an analogy in learning is in the system of relations that can be mapped.

Dedre Gentner and Cecile Toupin: 'Systematicity and Surface Similarity in the Development of Analogy' in *COGNITIVE SCIENCE* (1986), 10, pp. 277–300. Reproduced by permission of Ablex Publishing Corporation.

Focus on systems of mutually constraining relations is a central aspect of adult competence in processing analogy (Gentner, 1980, 1983). Adults not only have the *ability* to map a system of relations, but show a marked *preference* for such mappings (Gentner & Landers, 1985). This bias towards mapping systems seem to reflect a tacit preference for coherence and mutual constraint in analogical mapping. This research asks two questions: (1) Does the presence of systematic relations make analogical mapping easier; and (2) if so, when developmentally do children become able to utilize this systematicity?

The plan of the paper is as follows. We first give a brief review of the literature on analogical development. Then we present structure-mapping and the systematicity principle. Finally, we describe our research tracing the development of systematicity in analogy.

### Development of analogy

Since children are major consumers of education, it is important to know what they do with instructional and experiential analogies. Unfortunately, there is a great deal of evidence suggesting that young children do not use analogies in the powerful systematic way that adults do. Experimental studies show a marked developmental change in children's fluency at interpreting metaphors. A 4-year-old asked, "Can a person be sweet?" answers literally: for example, "Not unless he was made out of chocolate" (Asch & Nerlove, 1960). Similarly, young children are poor at matching sentences with metaphorically related pictures (Dent, 1984; Kogan, 1975) and choosing appropriate metaphorical completions for sentences (Gardner, Kircher, Winner, & Perkins, 1975). Young children tend to produce and select attributional interpretations on nonliteral comparisons. This pattern contrasts sharply with the adult preference for relational interpretations. For example, given the comparison, "A cloud is like a sponge," 5-year-olds produce interpretations like, "Both are round and fluffy." Adults produce relational interpretations: for example, "Both can hold water for some time and then later give it back" (Gentner, 1980; Gentner & Block, 1984; Gentner & Stuart, 1983). Further, adults rate analogical comparisons as more apt when they can find relational interpretations than when they can find only attributional interpretations (Gentner & Landers, 1985). Children show no such preferences; they are equally happy with relational and attributional interpretations (Gentner, 1986). These and many other experimental results seem to indicate that the ability to perform figurative comparisons develops gradually and late (Inhelder & Piaget, 1958).

However, it has been pointed out that a number of factors enter into the assessment of metaphoric and analogical ability (Gentner, 1977; Reynolds & Ortony, 1980; Vosniadou, 1985). Young children differ from older children in their command of the vocabulary, in their knowledge of the domains, and in their pragmatic understanding of when non-literal interpretations are permissible. This means that in many situations, especially with verbal interpretation tasks, there is danger of underestimating the young child's metaphorical ability and of conflating other developmental trends with the development of true analogical ability.

In this research, we sought to develop a natural, nonintrusive measure of children's analogical ability, by using *transfer accuracy* in a mapping task as a measure of analogical performance. Before going into the task, we must lay out our basic model of analogical processing.

### Structure-mapping and systematicity

The theoretical framework for this research is the structure-mapping theory of analogy (Gentner, 1980, 1982, 1983; Gentner & Gentner, 1983). This theory describes the set of implicit rules by which people interpret analogy and similarity. An analogy is a mapping of knowledge from one domain (the base) into another (the target), according to the following rules.[1] Objects in the base are placed in correspondence with objects in the target:

$$M: b_i \rightarrow t_i.$$

Predicates are mapped from the base to the target according to the following mapping rules[2]:

1. Attributes of objects are dropped:

e.g., $[RED (b_i)] \rightarrow [RED (t_i)]$.

2. Relations between objects in the base tend to be mapped across:

e .g ., $COLLIDE(b_i, b_j) \rightarrow COLLIDE(t_i, t_j)$

3. The particular relations mapped are determined by systematicity, as defined by the existence of higher-order constraining relations which can themselves be mapped:

e.g., $CAUSE [PUSH(b_i, b_j), COLLIDE (b_j, b_k)] \rightarrow$
$CAUSE [PUSH(t_i, t_j), COLLIDE (t_j, t_k)]$.

Figure 1 shows an example analogy: the Rutherford analogy between the solar system and the hydrogen atom. Let us ask what this analogy conveys to the person hearing it for the first time. Assuming that the person has the prior knowledge about the solar system shown in the top network, the person must:

- Set up the object correspondence between the two domains: sun → nucleus and planet → electron.

- Discard object attributes, such as YELLOW (sun).

- Map base relations such as MORE MASSIVE THAN (sun, planet) to the target domain: MORE MASSIVE THAN (nucleus, electron).

- Observe systematicity: that is, discard isolated relations, such as HOTTER THAN (sun, planet), and keep systems of relations that are governed by higher-order constraining relations which can themselves be mapped.
Here, the mappable system is

CAUSE [MORE-MASSIVE-THAN (sun, planet),
REVOLVE-AROUND (planet, sun).

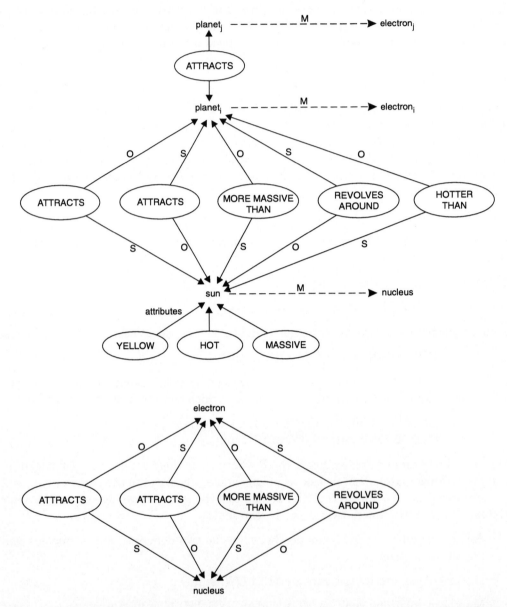

**Figure 1** **Partial depiction of the anology between solar system and hydrogen atom, showing a person's presumed initial knowledge of the solar system and the mapping of that knowledge to the atom**

*Systematicity.* Part of our understanding about analogy is that it conveys a system of connected knowledge, not a mere assortment of independent facts. The systematicity principle is included to formalize this tacit preference for coherence and deductive power in analogy. The *systematicity principle* states that a base predicate that belongs to a mappable system of mutually interconnecting relations is more likely to be imported into the target than is an isolated predicate. A *system* of relations refers to an interconnected predicate structure in which higher-order predicates enforce constraints among lower-order predicates.[3]

The systematicity principle requires a *mappable* relational chain. If the predicates, and especially the higher order relations, of the base chain are not valid in the target, then another chain must be selected. Thus, a relational chain — such as a causal chain — in the base that matches a relational chain in the target constitutes good support for its members. Winston (1982) gives an insightful demonstration of the need for such importance-dominated matching.[4]

By promoting deep relational chains, the systematicity principle operates to promote predicates that participate in causal chains and in other constraint relations. It is a structural mechanism which guarantees that the set of candidate mappings will be as interesting — in the sense that a mutually interconnected system of predicates is interesting — as the knowledge base allows.

*Ease of mapping.* Our discussion so far has been couched in terms of the implicit standards for a good analogical mapping. Empirical studies have borne out the prediction that systematicity is one of the implicit rules for a good analogical mapping. Adults focus on shared systematic relational structure in interpreting analogy. They tend to include relations and omit attributes in their interpretations of analogy, and they judge analogies as more apt if they share systematic relational structure (Gentner, 1980; Gentner & Block, 1983; Gentner & Landers, 1985; Gentner & Stuart, 1983). From this we can conclude that systematicity is a desideratum in analogy; it is one of the criteria by which an interpretation is devised and by which the analogy itself is judged.

But we want to go beyond the prior evidence here to suggest that systematicity may also play an active role in guiding the on-line mapping process. We conjecture that the presence of higher-order constraints helps guide the mapping of lower-order relations and provides a check on the correctness of the mapping. An error made in mapping a particular relation from base to target is more likely to be detected quickly if there is a higher-order relation which relates that lower-order relation to other knowledge.

To see how this could work, imagine a learner who hears the Rutherford analogy, "The atom is like the solar system," for the first time. Let us assume that the learner knows something about the solar system and little or nothing about the structure of the atom, and must map information from his model of the solar system. We contrast the case in which the learner has a systematic representation of the solar system with that in which he does not. In each case, we will assume the learner makes one mistake in mapping predicates from base to target. Then we will contrast the two cases — the *systematic knowledge* case and the *nonsystematic knowledge* case — to show how systematic knowledge enables the learner to repair mapping errors.

Figure 2 shows two representations of the solar system/atom analogy: a systematic representation (Figure 2a) and a nonsystematic representation (Figure 2b).

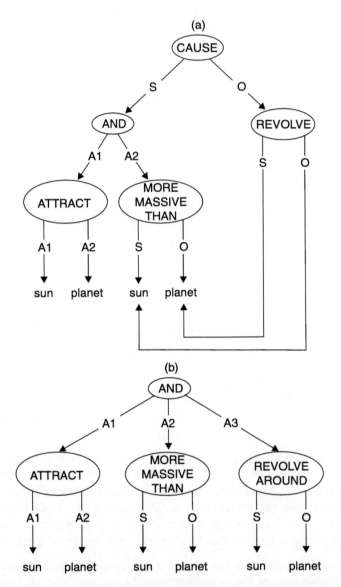

**Figure 2    More detailed depictions of a person's representations of the solar system: (a) systematic representation; (b) nonsystematic representation**

Suppose that the learner momentarily switches the objects when mapping the MORE MASSIVE THAN predicate and ends up with

MORE MASSIVE THAN (electron, nucleus).

At this point the learner is in danger of ending with a garbled and inaccurate notion of the structure of the atom. Now let us take the two cases in turn.

*Systematic knowledge case.* For the learner who has a systematic model of the base domain, there is a higher-order causal relation that can be mapped from base to target. This gives the learner a way of spotting the error. For at this point he has the following derived propositions in the target:

1. MORE MASSIVE THAN (electron, nucleus). (the incorrect mapping).
2. REVOLVE AROUND (electron, nucleus). (We assume both learners have mapped this lower order relation correctly.)
3. CAUSE [MORE MASSIVE THAN (electron, nucleus), REVOLVE AROUND (electron, nucleus).

The last assertion is the causal chain that the learner derives by plugging in his (partly erroneous) lower-order mappings to the higher order CAUSE relation. This chain can be compared to the similar causal statement that the learner knows from the base domain:

CAUSE [MORE MASSIVE THAN (sun, planet),
REVOLVE AROUND (planet, sun)].

Comparing these two chains, the learner can see an inconsistency. In the base domain, the less massive object revolves; in the target, the more massive object revolves. One way to resolve the inconsistency is to recheck the object mappings, giving the learner an opportunity to correct his error. Thus systematic knowledge of the base domain should allow the learner to detect and repair an incorrect local mapping.

*Nonsystematic knowledge Case.* The learner's derived representation of the target domain has only the two lower-order relations:

1. MORE MASSIVE THAN (electron, nucleus).
2. REVOLVE AROUND (electron, nucleus).

There is nothing to alert him to an error in mapping these relations. Without systematic structure to map from the base domain, the learner simply has a disconnected set of low-order predicates. Thus he is unlikely to notice and repair a mapping error.

Based on this reasoning, we conjecture that the presence of systematic relational structure should provide an on-line check on the correctness of the individual lower-order predicate mappings. Thus, systematicity should increase the transfer accuracy of an analogical mapping. Another factor that should be important during the on-line mapping process is the *transparency* of the object-correspondences. Transparency is defined as the ease of determining the object correspondences and predicate mappings for an analogy or similarity match. Transparency is high when surface similarity correlates well with structural similarity. There is evidence that transfer accuracy is greater for high-transparency analogies (Reed, 1985; Ross, 1986). We predict that transparency will have a strong effect on transfer accuracy. To the degree that it is easy to determine how the objects in the base correspond with the objects in the target, the transfer of predicate structure from base to target should be easier.

This line of reasoning leads us to three predictions concerning analogical mapping:

1. Transparent object-correspondences promote accurate mapping.
2. Systematic knowledge of the base domain promotes accurate analogical mapping.
3. The effect of systematicity will be stronger the more difficult (the less transparent) the analogical mapping.

### The development of systematicity

In this research, we investigated the development of systematicity in analogical mapping. We wished to discover when children become able to benefit from the presence of a system of mutually constraining relations in carrying out an analogy. To do this, we used a technique we called *cross-mapping* to vary the transparency of a set of analogical mappings. Then we gave children either systematic or nonsystematic base scenarios to map, as described below. The question was whether the degree of systematicity would affect children's ability to perform analogical transfer. If children's accuracy is improved by the presence of systematically connected knowledge structures, this is evidence that they can appreciate systematicity, whether or not they are able to articulate this appreciation explicitly. Our method was designed to avoid the confoundings inherent in requiring a verbal interpretation. The children were simply asked to act out stories using toy dolls and animals. The analogical step was that the children had to transfer a story plot from one set of characters to another. An important aspect of the methodology is that we did not require our subjects to articulate the higher-order information. Children were compared only in their accuracy at acting out the low-order event predicates, which were identical in systematic and nonsystematic stories. Thus any developmental differences in the effects of systematicity here are likely to reflect true cognitive differences, and not merely differences in facility with language.

In order to fully test the effects of systematicity, we wanted to include a wide range of mapping difficulty. This brings us to the second theoretical question addressed in the study: the effects of varying the transparency of the object-correspondence between base and target. To achieve this variation, we varied the surface similarity between the characters and the test characters. There were three levels of transparency: (1) *high transparency* — test characters look highly similar to corresponding original characters; (2) *moderate transparency* — test characters look quite different from corresponding original characters; and (3) *low transparency* — test characters look similar to non-corresponding original characters (the *cross-mapped* case). The cross-mapped case is predicted to be very difficult, because the object similarities between base and target are deliberately misleading. A given test character looks like one of the original characters, but plays a different role in the story. An example will help make the three transparency conditions clear. Suppose that in the original story the hero was a chipmunk, the hero's friend was a robin and the villain was a horse. Then the roles in the three kinds of mapping conditions might be as shown in Table 1.

The design included age and systematicity as between-subjects variables and transparency as a within-subjects variable. We predicted that children's accuracy in enacting the second story would be greatest in the high-transparency mapping condition and lowest in the low-transparency cross-mapped condition, where the natural object mappings had to be resisted. Besides this prediction, there were three questions of interest:

1. Whether transfer accuracy would be higher for systematic stories than for nonsystematic stories.
2. If so, when such systematicity effects would show up developmentally.
3. Whether systematicity would interact with mapping difficulty.

This last question is particularly interesting from our theoretical perspective. For if the presence of systematic higher order relations helps the child preserve the relational structure he/she is trying to map, then the more difficult the mapping the greater the potential benefit of systematicity.

**Table 1    Roles in three kinds of mapping conditions**

|         | Original | High     | Medium   | Low      |
|---------|----------|----------|----------|----------|
| Hero    | chipmunk | squirrel | elephant | zebra    |
| Friend  | robin    | bluebird | shark    | squirrel |
| Villian | horse    | zebra    | cricket  | bluebird |

## Method

### Subjects

The subjects were 72 children, 36 4- to 6-year-olds and 36 8- to 10-year-olds, recruited from schools and preschools in Cambridge, Massachusetts. They were randomly assigned to either the systematic or the nonsystematic condition. Approximately equal numbers of males and females were included within each of the two experimental conditions, within each age group.

### Materials

*Stories.* Nine short stories were constructed, each involving three characters and depicting a series of actions which led to a final outcome. There were two versions of each story: systematic and nonsystematic. The structure of the stories was as follows: (1) an *introductory section,* which introduced the characters; (2) an *event sequence,* with an outcome; (3) a *moral* (in systematic versions only). For each story, the event sequence was a set of 10 to 15 sentences depicting a series of events and an outcome. This section was identical in the systematic and nonsystematic story types. The story types differed only in their introductory sections and in whether they contained a moral. Table 2 shows sample stories.

For both kinds of stories, the introductory section was one or two sentences long and contained (1) some descriptive information about the protagonist (e.g., "There once was a very handsome chipmunk") and (2) some relation between the protagonist and one of the other two characters (e.g., "The chipmunk was friends with the cow"). The relation between the characters was the same in the systematic and nonsystematic story types. However, the information about the protagonist differed between the two story types. In the systematic stories, the description of the protagonist concerned a relevant habit or relational trait (e.g., "The chipmunk was very jealous"). In the nonsystematic stories the description attributed a neutral trait (e.g., "The chipmunk was very good looking"). For both systematic and nonsystematic stories, the introductory sections were designed to define the roles of the characters. This meant that, to set up a transfer test, we could simply read the child the introduction with the new character assignments; this determined the rest of the story.

**Table 2**   **Sample story, in systematic and nonsystematic versions (Systematic version includes indented material)**

---

*Setting*[a]: There once was a very jealous cat who was friends with a walrus. The cat often said to the walrus. "Don't ever play with anyone else but me."

One day the cat went away on a trip and the walrus had no one to play with. But then a seagull came to visit the walrus. He brought a wagon along and said, "Would you like to play with me and my wagon?" The walrus said, "Yes." The seagull and the walrus had a great time pulling each other around in the seagull's wagon.

When the cat came and found the walrus playing with someone else he got very angry. He shouted, "I'll never play with you again!" The cat was so angry that he jumped into the seagull's wagon. But the wagon began to roll faster down a steep hill. The cat was very scared. The seagull jumped up and chased after the wagon so the cat wouldn't crash. The seagull stopped the runaway wagon and saved the cat's life.

*Moral*[b]: In the end, the cat realized that being jealous only got him into trouble. It is better to have two friends instead of one.

---

[a] *Setting*, Nonsystematic Version: There once was a very strong cat who was friends with a walrus.

[b] *Moral* is omitted in nonsystematic version.

Aside from the difference in the introduction, the systematic stories differed from the nonsystematic stories in possessing a moral: a final sentence that expressed a moral and linked the protagonist's initial character trait to the story outcome (e.g., "The chipmunk realized that he shouldn't be so jealous, because it is better to have more friends"). No moral was added to the nonsystematic stories. The systematic stories, with a mean word length of 200 words, were somewhat longer than the nonsystematic stories (with a mean word length of 170 words), chiefly because of the presence of the moral. Half the children received systematic stories: the other half, nonsystematic stories.

*Story-telling stimuli.* Sixty-three toy dolls and animals were used to depict the characters. Of these, there were 27 pairs of animals that were independently judged by three judges to be similar looking, and 9 animals that were judged to be different looking from one another and from any of the paired animals. A small number of props were used to aid in the story telling. For each story, one or two rectangular, colored felt pieces were used to mark key locations, such as a house or road. For some stories, one or two additional toys, such as a wagon or plastic food, were used as props.

*Mapping conditions.* For each target story, three further stories were constructed using different sets of characters. These three story types reflected three mapping conditions corresponding to high, medium, or low transparency:

- S/S: Similar Characters / Similar Roles (High Transparency).

- D: Different Characters / Similar Roles (Medium Transparency).

- S/D: Similar Characters / Different Roles (Low Transparency).

In the S/S condition, the test characters looked like the characters in the original story, and they played the same role as their counterparts in the original story. In the D condition, the test characters bore no resemblance to any of the characters in the original story. In the S/D condition, the test characters resembled those in the original story, but were given different roles from their look-alike counterparts in the original story. This cross-mapped condition was predicted to be the most difficult mapping condition. Figure 3 shows an example with the S/S, D, and S/D mappings. Table 3 shows the object mappings for all nine stories.

**Table 3**  **Characters used in the stories, showing the three mapping conditions for each story**

| Story | Test | S/S | D/S | S/D |
|-------|------|-----|-----|-----|
| 1 | seal | walrus | lion | cat |
|   | penguin | seagull | giraffe | walrus |
|   | dog | cat | camel | seagull |
| 2 | goose | swan | giraffe | racoon |
|   | panda | racoon | camel | monkey |
|   | chimp | monkey | lion | swan |
| 3 | hare | rabbit | camel | bear |
|   | beaver | bear | giraffe | porcupine |
|   | mole | porcupine | lion | rabbit |
| 4 | bull | cow | shark | cricket |
|   | mule | camel | elephant | cow |
|   | ant | cricket | lion | camel |
| 5 | moose | elk | shark | medicine man |
|   | hog | pig | elephant | elk |
|   | warrior | medicine man | lion | pig |
| 6 | dragon | dinosaur | lion | unicorn |
|   | horse | unicorn | shark | eel |
|   | snake | eel | elephant | dinosaur |
| 7 | hunter | cowboy | ostrich | fly |
|   | pony | zebra | turtle | cowboy |
|   | spider | fly | giraffe | zebra |
| 8 | gorilla | orangutan | giraffe | lizard |
|   | steer | buffalo | turtle | orangutan |
|   | alligator | lizard | ostrich | buffalo |
| 9 | eagle | vulture | turtle | bobcat |
|   | hippo | rhino | giraffe | vulture |
|   | tiger | bobcat | ostrich | rhino |

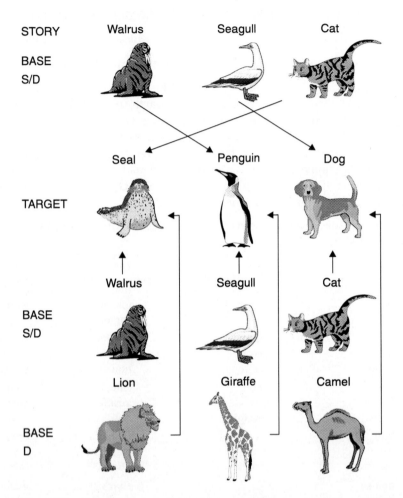

**Figure 3    Schematic examples of the three mapping conditions. Note that the contrast between the high-transparency (S/S) and low transparency (S/D) mappings is in the object correspondences**

The mapping condition could have been varied by giving all children the same base story and then varying the target story. As Table 3 shows, we decided instead to vary the original base story that the children heard. Thus, a child in the S/S condition and a child in the S/D condition would receive different original stories, but the same target story. This was done in order to achieve strict comparability on the test phase. Since the child can receive help or extra practice when necessary in acting out the original stories, any small differences in the ease of comprehension of the original stories are less likely to affect the overall results than would differences in the test stories.

Thus the base stories varied according to systematicity (systematic or nonsystematic) and mapping condition (S/S, D, or S/D), for a total of six kinds of base stories (see Table 3).

All children received three stories in each of the three mapping conditions, for a total of nine stories. The assignment of stories to mapping condition was counterbalanced across groups of children. The mapping conditions (S/S, D, and S/D) were presented in three different orders, according to a Latin square design. There were two orderings — one the reverse of the other — for the stories themselves. Thus, children were divided into 12 groups according to their Systematicity Condition, Mapping Order, and Story Order. However, the essential experimental variables were Age (2 levels, between), Systematicity (2 levels, between), and Mapping Condition (3 levels, within).

## Procedure

Children were read aloud the stories and asked to act them out with toy animals. Once they had acted out a story, they were asked to act out the same story again, only with new characters. A practice session using a four line story about two characters was used to acquaint subjects with their task. During the practice session, children were encouraged to tell the story and speak the dialogue. The experimenter demonstrated the two-fold task for the child if necessary. The experiment began once a child demonstrated the ability to perform the transfer task successfully without help. The experimental procedure was the same for each story and was divided into two parts: the *story phase* and the *test phase*.

*Story phase.* The experimenter began each story by introducing the three story characters (e.g., "Here is the moose"). The experimenter made sure that the child could correctly name the toys before proceeding. With the story characters in view, the child was then instructed to listen carefully to the story. After the experimenter finished reading the story aloud, props, including location markers, were introduced (e.g. the wheelbarrow or the lake). Some individual variation in the use of props was allowed, as long as the child used each prop consistently. The child then acted out the story, using the characters and props. If the child made omissions or errors, the experimenter corrected them and asked the child to again act out the story. Once the child demonstrated the ability to act out the original story correctly without help, the test phase began.

*Test phase.* The experimenter then asked the subject to act out the same story again, but with three new characters. The three original story characters were removed from view and the new test characters were introduced (e.g., "This is the squirrel"). Location markers, such as the lake, were left in the same position, and props were gathered and set before the subject to use. The child was then instructed to listen carefully to the beginning of the story with the names of the new characters. The experimenter read aloud the introductory section and repeated it if desired. Then the child was told to act out the rest of the story.

The stories were designed so that the introductory section set the roles of the characters in such a way as to determine the rest of the story for a child who had performed the character-mapping correctly. During the test phase, the experimenter did not provide the subject with any information regarding mapping assignments, omissions, or errors. However, the experimenter could give neutral prompts (e.g., "What happened next? " or "Who is doing that?"). In addition, the experimenter would repeat the correct name(s) of the character(s) or the introductory section on request.

The story and test phases were carried out in the same way for each story. Children were given three stories in a test session, with a 2-min distractor task of coloring or putting together a puzzle between stories. Each child participated in three test sessions, spaced at least one day apart.

*Scoring.* For each story, the sentences were grouped into six core propositions representing the major events and the outcome. The moral in the systematic stories constituted a seventh proposition that was scored separately. In scoring, propositions were treated as wholes. If an error was committed with respect to any one character or action contained in a proposition, the proposition was considered incorrect. Thus, for each subject there were six possible correct propositions per story. The same six propositions were scored for systematic and nonsystematic stories.

Three scoring procedures were used: *strict, lenient,* and *key sentence* scoring. However, since all gave the same results, we describe only the strict scoring procedure. In the strict scoring procedure, a proposition was scored as correct if the child either verbally or nonverbally depicted each of its events with the correct assignment of actors. Two types of errors were scored: omissions and incorrect answers. A proposition was scored as an omission if the subject verbally omitted any action or character contained in that proposition *and* failed to adequately demonstrate the inclusion of the action or character through nonverbal actions. A proposition was scored as incorrect if any character or action contained in that proposition was incorrectly identified both verbally and through nonverbal actions.

## Results

The results are shown in Figure 4. These results show:

1. As predicted, object-mapping transparency had strong effects on transfer accuracy for both age groups.
2. Systematicity benefited only the older group.
3. The benefits of systematicity were strongest in the most difficult mapping condition.

A 2 x 2 x 3 mixed-measures analysis of variance of Age (Between) x Systematicity (Between) x Mapping Condition (Within) showed main effects of Age, $F(1, 68) = 14.93$, $p < .001$; Systematicity, $F(1, 68) = 6.28$, $p < .05$; and Mapping Condition, $F(2, 136) = 29.01$, $p < .000001$. There was also predicted interaction between Systematicity and Mapping Condition, $F(2, 136) = 3.89$, $p < .05$.

Although both Mapping Condition and Systematicity show main effects, their developmental patterns differ. Mapping Condition shows strong effects for both age groups. As predicted, the children performed best with the easy S/S mapping, intermediate with the D mapping, and worst with the misleading S/D mapping. Planned comparisons confirmed that Mapping Condition had significant effects on both age groups.

In contrast, Systematicity showed significant effects only in the older group. For the older children, performance was significantly better on systematic stories, $t(34) = 2.48$, $p < .01$. This was not true for the younger children; they derived no significant advantage from systematic plot structure, $t(34) = 1.08$, NS.[5]

354

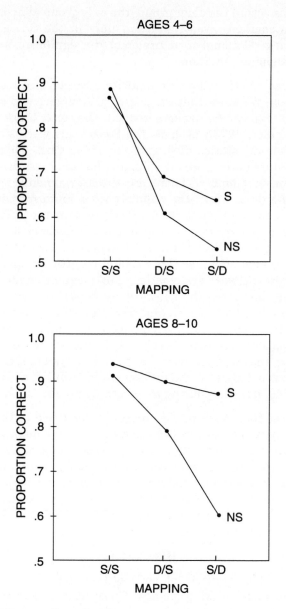

**Figure 4** **Results: Proportion of statements in the target stories correctly enacted under different conditions for 4- to 6-year olds (top graph) and 8- to 10-year-olds (bottom graph)**

The last prediction was that Systematicity should have its greatest effects on the most difficult mappings (since these are they mappings in which the children cannot rely on object similarity to perform the transfer). This prediction was confirmed by the Systematicity x Mapping Condition interaction noted above. More to the point, planned comparisons within the older group (the only group affected by Systematicity) confirmed that Systematicity was significant only in the S/D condition. Thus the presence of systematic relational structure created a significant improvement only in the most difficult mapping condition.

It might be wondered whether the systematicity advantage in transfer was simply a memory phenomenon. We know that the degree of structure and organization plays a role in how well material can be remembered (e.g., Bower & Clark, 1969; Bransford & Johnson, 1972; Mandler, 1976); perhaps the 8-year-olds were simply better able to remember the systematic stories during the mapping task. Then the systematicity advantage would tell us nothing about mapping, but only reaffirm the superiority of organized structures in memory. There are three arguments against the memory interpretation of the data. First, the children were uniformly able to perform the original story enactments — that is, the enactments using the initial set of characters. Since this, too, was a memory task, any difference in memory for the original stories should have shown up here. Recall that the transfer enactment is done immediately after the initial story enactment, so there should be little opportunity for forgetting. Second, the interaction between systematicity and mapping condition discussed in the preceding paragraph shows that the effects of systematicity were specific, rather than an across-the-board advantage. Third, and most important, all children regardless of systematicity condition performed nearly perfectly on the high-transparency transfer task. When the transfer mappings were easy, children could demonstrate nearly perfect memory for the original story in both the systematic and nonsystematic condition. Thus we conclude that the differences in transfer accuracy are not due to differential forgetting, but arise during the mapping process itself.

These results suggest that systematicity indeed plays a role in the mapping process: that children, at least by the age of 8, can use higher-order constraints to help keep the lower-order predicates straight. We found informal support for this claim in the self-corrections that the older children occasionally made. A child would begin to make an error, acting out an event with the wrong character, and then stop with a remark like, "No, wait, it's the *greedy* one who got stuck in the well, because he ate too much." These children, then, used higher-order relations to check the correctness of lower-order predicates during the mapping.

### Discussion

In this research, we found effects of both systematicity and transparency on the accuracy of children's analogical mappings. These results have implications both for theories of analogical processing and for accounts of the development of analogy and metaphor. We begin by discussing the implications for theories of analogy.

### *Systematicity in analogical mapping*

The principle of systematicity is becoming increasingly prominent in computational approaches to analogy (e.g., Burstein, 1983; Carbonell, 1983; Gentner, 1980, 1982, 1983; Gentner & Gentner, 1983; Rumelhart & Norman, 1981; Winston, 1980, 1982). Although accounts vary in detail, it is generally supposed that the presence of some kind of common higher order constraining structure is an important determinant of the utility of an analogy for learning and transfer. However, there has been little evidence about *how* systematicity enters into the analogical process. Is it simply a passive desideratum, which the learner checks after interpreting an analogy to decide which interpretation to choose and to determine how good the analogy is? This limited view of systematicity is contradicted by the present research. Our results show that systematicity enters into the mapping process itself.

In this work we go beyond structure-mapping as a competence theory — a theory of how people think an analogy *should* be mapped — and consider its implications as a performance theory. We ask what makes an analogy easy to process, and, in particular, whether systematicity plays a role in making analogical mapping easier. According to structure-mapping theory, once the base and target domains have been accessed, the mapping process involves setting up object-correspondences and carrying across predicates. This suggests that at least two factors should enter into the difficulty of the mapping process. The first is the transparency of the object-correspondences: The more similar the corresponding objects in base and target, the easier it should be to keep the mapping straight. Here, the transparency was manipulated by varying the similarity among corresponding objects of base and target. The second target is the sturdiness of the predicate structure that is to be mapped from base to target. This is where systematicity enters in. The presence of constraining higher-order relations that govern the lower-order predicates both guides the on-line mapping of lower order predicates and provides the learner with checks on the correctness of the mapping. Indeed, we saw children correct their enactments when they remembered higher order information that predicted a different event.

By this reasoning, both systematicity and transparency should facilitate analogical mapping.[6] Both these claims were verified for the 8-year-olds. We believe the same pattern of results will hold for adults. Preliminary results using an adult version of the same paradigm indicate that adults take longer to retell the story in the most difficult mapping condition — the cross mapping (S/D) case with a nonsystematic base story — than they do in the more natural conditions.

### Developmental implications and further questions

Two developmental questions were posed here:

1. Are there developmental differences in the effects of transparency of object correspondences in analogical mapping?

2. Do children change in their ability to profit from systematic relational structure in dealing with difficult correspondences?

One useful aspect of this methodology for studying development is that it allows an indirect measure of the child's ability to use systematicity. Research on development of metaphor has shown repeatedly that children do not articulate their interpretation of metaphors in the same manner as adults (Gardner, Kircher, Winner, & Perkins, 1975; Gentner & Stuart, 1983; Reynolds & Ortony, 1980; Vosniadou & Ortony, 1983; Winner, Rosenstiel, & Gardner, 1976). However, we cannot therefore infer that children are intellectually unable to perform metaphorical and analogical transfer (cf. Brown & Campione, 1985; Carey, 1984; Winner, Engel, & Gardner, 1980). There is some evidence that children can perform analogical mappings without necessarily being able to articulate all the predicates that they are mapping (Crisafi & Brown, 1983; Gardner, 1974; Gentner, 1977; Holyoak, Juin, & Billman, in press; see also Vosniadou, 1985 for a review of this issue). In the present methodology, children simply acted out stories with a new set of characters. Thus, although they were not required to verbalize the relational structure that they were carrying across, their ability to make the transfer was clear from the accuracy of their reenactment. Given that the child can act out the original story (which was in all cases true), we found:

1  Children of both ages were affected by the transparency of the object mappings.

2.  Systematicity benefited the older children.

3.  Systematicity had its greatest effect when the object mappings were most difficult.

The transparency of the object-mapping affects both younger and older children. Object similarity between base and target may well be important in determining the ease of analogical processing at all levels of development. The work of Ross (1984, 1986) and Reed (1985) suggests that even adults are greatly influenced by the degree of surface similarity between potential analogs in learning and problem-solving tasks. In developmental research on transfer tasks, the reliance of young children on surface information is well-established (Keil & Batterman, 1984; Kemler, 1983; Shepp, 1978; Smith & Kemler, 1977). Research by DeLoache (1984) provides a particularly striking demonstration of young children's reliance on surface similarity in transferring knowledge. She tested children of $2^1/_2$ to 3 years of age in a transfer-search task: An object is hidden in one space — for example, a room — and the child must find a like object in a similar space — for example, another room or a smaller scale model of the original room. She finds that the children's performance is extremely sensitive to surface similarity between the original space and the search space. Our results are compatible with DeLoache's findings in suggesting that transparency may be developmentally among the earliest determinants of ease of analogical mapping.

Systematicity, on the other hand, may make a somewhat later developmental appearance. In our research, systematicity effects were clearly present among the 8-year-olds, but not among the younger children. However, our conclusions here must be tentative; it is possible that with more sensitive methodology or different materials we could find systematicity effects earlier in development. Moreover, if indeed young children are deficient in their ability to benefit from systematicity, there are at least two different extreme interpretations, one based on developmental increases in intellectual competence and the other based on acquisition of knowledge. The competence interpretation is that younger children lack the processing ability to map whole systems of relations. Their failure to use systematicity reflects a developmental limitation in their basic competence. The knowledge-based interpretation is that the younger children had insufficient familiarity with the higher-order relations used here. Thus, even if they were intellectually able to use systematicity in mapping, they were not in position to demonstrate that ability. By this account, the difference between younger and older children found here is a novice-expert shift in the sense of Chi,

Glaser, and Reese (1982) or Larkin (1983). From what we know so far, either account or a combination could be correct.

## Acknowledgements

This research was conducted at Bolt Beranek & Newman in Cambridge, Massachusetts as part of the Center for the Study of Reading sponsored by the National Institute of Education under Contract No. 400-80-0031. The theoretical work was supported by the Office of Naval Research under Contracts No. N00014-85-K-0559, NR667-551. We thank Alicia Marcus for her help in planning and running the research and Ann Brown, Allan Collins, Judy DeLoache, Philip Johnson-Laird, Doug Medin, Brian Ross, Ed Smith, Yvette Tenney, and David Zola for their helpful discussions and comments.

## Notes

1.  Besides analogy, other kinds of similarity can be characterized by the distribution of relational and attributional predicates that are mapped. In *analogy,* only relational predicates are mapped. In *literal similarity,* both are relational predicates and object-attributes are mapped. In *mere-appearance* matches, it is chiefly object-attributes that are mapped.

2.  In general, an analogical mapping involves both *matching* existing predicates in the base target and *carrying over* further predicates from base to target. (See Falkenhainer, Forbus & Gentner ( 1986) for a description of a computer simulation of the mapping algorithm.) The proportion of matching versus carryover depends on the amount of domain knowledge: The more one knows about the target, the more matching occurs.

3.  The *order* of a relation is determined by the order of its arguments. A first-order relation is one that takes objects as its arguments. A second-order relation has at least one first-order relation among its arguments. An $n$th-order relation has at least one ($n$-1)th-order argument.

4.  A relational chain can also provide support — particularly in cases where little or nothing is known about the target domain — if it merely generates no contradictions in the target.

5.  It should be noted that there was no significant Age x Systematicity interaction in the overall analysis of variance. Therefore, it is possible that systematicity benefited both groups, but that only in the older group did the effects reach significance.

6.  Note that, although both systematicity and transparency are postulated to make analogical mapping easier, only systematicity enters into the perceived soundness of an analogy. Indeed, if the object similarity becomes too high, the comparison becomes a literal similarity match instead of an analogy.

## References

Asch, S.E. & Nerlove, H. (1960) The development of double function terms in children: An exploratory investigation. In B. Kaplan & S. Wapner (Eds.), *Perspectives in psychological theory.* New York: International Universities Press.

Bower, G.H. & Clark, M.C. (1969) Narrative stories as mediators for serial learning. *Psychonomic Science*, 14, 181–182.

Bransford, J.D. & Johnson, M.K. (1972) Contextual prerequisites for understanding: Some investigations of comprehension and recall. *Journal of Verbal Learning and Verbal Behavior*, 11, 717–726.

Brown, A.L. & Campione. J.C. (1985) Three faces of transfer: Implications for early competence, individual differences, and instruction. In M. Lamb, A. Brown, & B. Rogoff (Eds.), *Advances in developmental psychology* (Vol. 3). Hillsdale, NJ: Erlbaum.

Burstein, M.H. (1983) Concept formation by incremental analogical reasoning and debugging. *Proceedings of the International Machine Learning Workshop.* Monticello, IL: University of Illinois.

Buckley, S. (1979) *Sun up to sun down.* New York: McGraw-Hill.

Carbonell, J.G. (1983) Learning by analogy: Formulating and generalizing plans from past experience. In R.S. Michalski, J. Carbonell, & T. Mitchell (Eds.). *Machine learning.* Palo Alto, CA: Tioga.

Carey, S. (1984) Are children fundamentally different kinds of thinkers and learners than adults? In S.F. Chipman, J.W. Segal, & R. Glaser (Eds.), *Thinking and learning skills: Current research and open questions* (Vol. 2). Hillsdale, NJ: Erlbaum.

Chi, M.T.H., Glaser, R. & Reese, E. (1982) Expertise in problem solving. In R. Sternberg (Ed.), *Advances in the psychology of human intelligence* (Vol. 1). Hillsdale, NJ: Erlbaum.

Clement, J. (1981) Analogy generation in scientific problem solving. *Proceedings of the Third Annual Meeting of the Cognitive Science Society.*

Clement, J. (1982) *Spontaneous analogies in problem solving: The progressive construction of mental models.* Paper presented at the AERA, New York.

Collins, A.M. & Gentner, D. (1986) How people construct mental models. In D. Holland & N. Quinn (Eds.), *Cultural models in language and thought.* Cambridge, England: Cambridge University Press.

Crisafi, M. & Brown, A.L. (1983) *Flexible use of an inferential reasoning rule by very young children.* Paper presented at the Biennial Meeting of the Society for Research in Child Development, Detroit, MI.

Dent, C.H. (1984) The developmental importance of motion information in perceiving and describing metaphoric similarity. *Child Development*, 55, 1607–1613.

Falkenhainer, B., Forbus, K.D. & Gentner, D. (1986, August) The structure-mapping engine. *Proceedings of the Meeting of the American Association for Artifcial Intelligence,* Philadelphia.

Forbus, K. & Gentner, D. (1986) Learning physical domains: Towards a theoretical framework. In R.M. Michalski, J. Carbonell, & T. Mitchell (Eds.), *Machine learning. An artificial intelligence approach* (Vol. II). Morgan-Kaufmann.

Gardner, H. (1974) Metaphors and modalities: How children project polar adjectives onto diverse domains. *Child Development*, 45, 84–91.

Gardner, H., Kircher, M., Winner, E. & Perkins, D. (1975) Children's metaphoric productions and preferences. *Journal of Child Language*, 2, 1–17.

Gentner, D. (1977) Children's performance on a spatial analogies task. *Child Development*, 48, 1034–1039.

Gentner, D. (1980) *Metaphor as structure-mapping.* Paper presented at the meeting of the American Psychology Association, Montreal.

Gentner, D. (1983) Structure-mapping: A theoretical framework for analogy. *Cognitive Science*, 7, 155–170.

Gentner, D. (1986) *Structure-mapping in the development of metaphor*. Manuscript submitted for publication.

Gentner, D. & Gentner, D.R. (1983) Flowing waters or teeming crowds: Mental models of electricity. In D. Gentner & A.L. Stevens (Eds.), *Mental models*. Hillsdale, NJ: Erlbaum.

Gentner, D. & Landers, R. (1985) Analogical reminding: A good match is hard to find. *Proceedings of the International Conference on Systems, Man and Cybernetics*. Tucson, AZ.

Gentner, D. & Stuart, P. (1983) *Metaphor as structure-mapping: What develops* (Tech. Rep No. 5479). Cambridge, MA: Bolt, Beranek, and Newman.

Holyoak, K.J., Junn, E.N. & Billman, D.O. (1984) Development of analogical problem-solving skill. *Developmental Psychology*, 55, 2042–2055.

Inhelder, B. & Piaget, J. (1958) *The growth of logical thinking from childhood to adolescence*. New York: Basic Books.

Keil, F. & Batterman, N.A. (1984) A characteristic to defining shift in the development of word meaning. *Journal of Verbal Learning and Verbal Behavior*, 23, 221–236.

Kemler, D.C. (1983) Holistic and analytical modes in perceptual and cognitive development. In T.J. Tighe & B.E. Shepp (Eds.), *Perception cognition and development: Interactional analysis*. Hillsdale, NJ: Erlbaum.

Kempton, W. (1986) Two theories used for home heat control. In D. Holland & N. Quinn (Eds.), *Cultural models in language and thought*. Cambridge, England: Cambridge University Press.

Kogan, N. (1975) *Metaphoric thinking in children: Developmental and individual-difference aspects*. Paper presented at the Biennial Meeting of the Society for Research in Child Development, Denver, CO.

Larkin, J.H. (1983) Problem representations in physics. In D. Gentner & A.L. Stevens (Eds.), *Mental Models*. Hillsdale, NJ: Erlbaum.

Mandler, G. (1967) Organization and memory. In K.W. Spence & J.T. Spence (Eds.), *Psychology of learning and motivation* (Vol. 1). New York: Academic.

Reed, S.K. (1985) *A structure-mapping model for word problems*. Paper presented at the meeting of the Psychonomic Society, Boston.

Reed, S.K., Ernst, C.W. & Banerji, R. (1974) The role of analogy in transfer between similar problem states. *Cognitive Psychology*, 66, 436–450.

Reynolds, R.E. & Ortony, A. (1980) Some issues in the measurement of children's comprehension of metaphorical language. *Child Development*, 51, 1110–1119.

Ross, B.H. (1984) Remindings and their effects in learning a cognitive skill. *Cognitive Psychology*, 16, 371–416.

Ross, B.H. (1986) *This is like that: Object correspondences and remindings and the separation of similarity effects on the access and use of earlier problems*. Manuscript submitted for publication.

Rumelhart, D.E. & Norman, D.A. (1981) Analogical processes in learning. In J.R. Anderson (Ed.), *Cognitive skills and their acquisition*. Hillsdale, NJ: Erlbaum.

Shepp, B.E. (1978) From perceived similarity to dimensional structure: A new hypothesis about perceptual development. In E. Rosch & B.B. Lloyd (Eds.), *Cognition and categorization*. Hillsdale, NJ: Erlbaum.

Smith, L.B. & Kemler, D.G. (1977) Developmental trends in free classification: Evidence for a new conceptualization of perceptual development. *Journal of Experimental Child Psychology*, 24, 279–298.

VanLehn, K. & Brown, J.S. (1980) Planning nets: A representation for formalizing analogies and semantic models of procedural skills. In R.E. Snow, P.A. Federico & W.E. Montague (Eds.), *Aptitude, learning and instruction: Cognitive process analyses*. Hillsdale, NJ: Erlbaum.

Vosniadou, S. (1985) *On the development of metaphoric competence*. Unpublished manuscript.

Vosniadou, S. & Ortony, A. (1983) The emergence of the literal-metaphorical-anomalous distinction in young children. *Child Development*, 55, 14–161.

Vosniadou, S. & Ortony, A. (in press) Testing the metaphoric competence of the young child: Paraphrase versus enactment. *Human Development*.

Winner, E. (1979) New names for old things: The emergence of metaphoric language. *Journal of Child Language*, 6, 469–491.

Winner, E., Engel, M. & Gardner, H. (1980) Misunderstanding metaphor: What's the problem? *Journal of Experimental Child Psychology*, 30, 22–32.

Winner, E., Rosenstiel, A. & Gardner, H. (1976) The development of metaphoric understanding. *Developmental Psychology*, 12, 289–297.

Winston, P.H. (1980) Learning and reasoning by analogy. *Communications of the ACM, 23*.

Winston, P.H. (1982) Learning new principles from precedents and exercises. *Artificial Intelligence*, 19, 321–350.

# 13.    Surface and Structural Similarity in Analogical Transfer

## Keith J. Holyoak and Kyunghee Koh

*Two experiments investigated factors that influence the retrieval and use of analogies in problem solving. Experiment 1 demonstrated substantial spontaneous analogical transfer with a delay of several days between presentation of the source and target analogues. Experiment 2 examined the influence of different types of similarity between the analogues. A mechanism for retrieval of source analogues is proposed, based on summation of activation from features shared with a target problem. The results of Experiment 2 indicated that both structural features, which play a causal role in determining possible problem solutions, and salient surface features, which do not have a causal role, influence spontaneous selection of an analogue. Structural features, however, have a greater impact than do surface features on a problem solver's ability to use an analogue once its relevance has been pointed out.*

A person confronted by a novel problem can sometimes solve it by drawing an analogy to a similar problem that has a known solution. Analogy is a central form of induction used to generate inferences in pragmatically important situations (Holland, Holyoak, Nisbett, & Thagard, 1986). Analogical transfer is one factor that makes human problem solvers more flexible than current expert systems in artificial intelligence. Such systems are "brittle" in that they typically require extensive intervention by the human programmer in order to deal with relatively small changes in problem domains. An understanding of the mechanisms of human analogical transfer, in addition to providing insight into human cognition, might suggest remedies for the brittleness of mechanized problem solvers.

At a global level, analogy is used to generate knowledge applicable to a novel *target* domain by transferring knowledge from a *source* domain that is better understood. Analogical problem solving can be characterized in terms of four basic steps: (1) constructing mental representations of the source and the target; (2) selecting the source as a potentially relevant analogue to the target; (3) mapping the components of the source and target; and (4) extending the mapping to generate a solution to the target (Holyoak, 1984). These steps need not be carried out in a strictly serial order, and they may interact in many ways (e.g., the selection step may require some preliminary mapping); nonetheless, they provide a useful conceptual organization for the overall process.

Perhaps the least understood of the above four steps is the second, selecting a source analogue. Selection requires retrieval of the source analogue from memory and noticing of its relevance to the target problem. Particularly in the case of analogies between problems drawn from disparate domains, it is unclear how a problem solver

---

Keith J. Holyoak and Kyunghee Koh: 'Surface and Structural Similarity in Analogical Transfer' in *MEMORY AND COGNITION* (1987), 15(4), pp. 332–340. Copyright © 1987 Psychonomic Society, Inc.

can retrieve a potentially useful source analogue from a large knowledge base. Computational models of analogy have typically evaded this issue, either by explicitly directing the program to compare particular situations (Burstein, 1986) or by implementing a psychologically implausible exhaustive search mechanism (Winston, 1980). Carbonell (1983) suggested that retrieval of problem analogies could be facilitated by organizing the data base according to similarities in basic problem components, such as goals, starting states, and problem constraints; however, the usefulness of such a scheme has not been demonstrated by either computational or psychological evidence.

## Evidence for spontaneous use of analogies

There appear to be a variety of mechanisms by which people can potentially select plausible source analogues. In some cases source analogues are generated by systematic transformations of the target (Clement, 1982). In other cases the source will be directly provided by a teacher, as is the case, for example, when water flow is used as an analogy to elucidate the nature of electricity (Gentner & Gentner, 1983). In the present paper we will focus on the processes by which an analogist, without the intervention of a teacher, may retrieve the representation of a situation stored in memory and notice its relevance to a target problem.

The conditions under which people are likely spontaneously to make use of potential analogies are far from clear. Indeed, a consistent research finding has been that college subjects often fail to use analogies spontaneously (Gick & Holyoak, 1980, 1983; Hayes & Simon, 1977; Reed, Ernst, & Banerji, 1974). For example, Gick and Holyoak (1980, 1983) had subjects attempt to solve Duncker's (1945) radiation problem, which involves finding a way for a doctor to use X rays to destroy a stomach tumor without damaging the surrounding healthy tissue. Some groups of subjects first read a story describing an analogous military problem in which a general captured a centrally located fortress by having small units of soldiers attack simultaneously along multiple roads. When given a hint to use the prior military story, about 75% of the subjects in a typical experiment were able to generate the analogous convergence solution to the radiation problem (i.e., focusing multiple low-intensity X rays on the tumor from different directions). In contrast, only about 30% of subjects generated this solution prior to receiving an explicit hint. Given that about 10% of subjects produced the convergence solution without any analogue, this suggests that only about 20% of the subjects may have spontaneously retrieved and applied the analogy.

In fact, one could reasonably question whether there is any convincing experimental evidence that people notice analogies between problems presented in substantially remote contexts. Even in the case of analogies between problems in the same domain, such as geometry, anecdotal reports suggest that students seldom notice analogies between problems presented in different chapters of their textbook. In virtually all the experiments reported to date, the source and target analogues were presented consecutively within a single experimental session. It could be, for example, that the 20% of subjects in Gick and Holyoak's (1980, 1983) experiments who spontaneously used the analogy did so simply because they were sensitive to demand characteristics of the situation, which would surely suggest that the story and the problem immediately following might be somehow related. Spencer and Weisberg (1986) found no evidence of transfer to the radiation problem when a delay or change of context separated presentation of the source and target problems.

Perhaps the strongest evidence that analogues drawn from remote domains sometimes produce spontaneous transfer comes from studies in which multiple source analogues are provided. Gick and Holyoak (1983) had some groups of subjects first read two convergence stories (e.g., the military story described above and a fire-fighting story in which converging sources of the retardant were used to extingtush a large blaze). Other groups read a single convergence story plus a nonanalogous story. All subjects summarized each story and also wrote descriptions of how the two stories were similar. The latter task was intended to trigger a mapping between the two stories, which would have the incidental effect of leading to the induction of an explicit representation of the shared schematic structure. All subjects then attempted to solve the X-ray problem, both before and after a hint to consider the stories. Gick and Holyoak (1983) found that subjects in the two-analogue groups were significantly more likely to produce the convergence solution, both before and after the hint, than were subjects in the one-analogue groups. Since demand characteristics were presumably comparable for both sets of subjects, the advantage of the two-analogue subjects prior to the hint is evidence of spontaneous transfer.

Gick and Holyoak (1983) interpreted these and other more detailed results to indicate that induction of an explicit schema facilitates transfer. Once a person has induced a schema from initial examples, novel problems that can be categorized as instances of the schema can be solved without necessarily directly accessing representations of the initial analogues. It follows that although experiments illustrating the role of schemata demonstrate spontaneous interdomain transfer, they do not provide clear evidence of *analogical* transfer, in the sense of direct transfer from a representation of a particular prior situation to a novel problem. A major goal of the present study was to identify conditions under which spontaneous analogical transfer in fact occurs.

**Surface and structural similarity**

If two situations drawn from disparate domains have never previously been associated, there can be no direct retrieval pathway linking the two. How, then, might the target activate the source? This question pertains not only to analogical problem solving, but more generally to mechanisms by which an episode can trigger reminding of a disparate but structurally similar situation (Schank, 1982).

One possibility is that retrieval of analogies is based on *summation of activation* resulting from multiple shared features. Summation mechanisms have been proposed in many activation-based cognitive models to account for performance in tasks requiring retrieval or classification of inputs (e.g., Anderson, 1983; McClelland & Rumelhart, 1981; Thibadeau, Just, & Carpenter, 1982). The present proposal for extending the summation mechanism to account for retrieval of analogies could be implemented in various ways, and will be described in general terms. We assume that situations can be represented in terms of more elementary *features* (a term we will use in a general sense to include both properties and relations). Each feature attended to will activate memory representations of other situations that share that feature.

Shared features thus serve as retrieval cues in a content-addressable memory system. Activation from multiple shared features will summate, and if the activation level of a stored representation exceeds some threshold, that representation will become available for further processing, such as initiation of an explicit mapping process. Such a summation mechanism allows multiple weak cues to collaborate as converging evidence indicating the potential relevance of related situations stored in memory.[1]

It might seem that such a simple summation mechanism would tend to retrieve stored representations with many superficially similar features, rather than remote analogues with important shared structural components. In fact, the low rate of spontaneous transfer observed by Gick and Holyoak (1980, 1983) and others suggests that this possibility may be at least partially realized. An experiment by Gilovich (1981) provided evidence of the effect of superficial cues on the retrieval of analogues. He had subjects suggest resolutions for various hypothetical political crises, and found the subjects' suggestions were influenced by superficial resemblances between the hypothetical crises and actual historical situations. Ross (1984) found evidence that superficial similarity influences retrieval of examples in the domain of statistics problems.

In order to investigate the conditions under which people will retrieve a source analogue and notice its relevance to a target problem, in the present study we manipulated different types of similarity, which will be termed *surface* and *structural*. Following Hesse (1966) and Tversky (1977), we assume that similarity between two situations can be decomposed into identities and differences between features. The surface versus structural distinction depends on whether or not a feature is causally relevant to goal attainment. A surface dissimilarity between two situations involves what Holyoak (1984) termed a *structure-preserving* difference — a change in a feature that does not influence goal attainment. For example, in the convergence analogies investigated by Gick and Holyoak (1980), there are many differences between the fortress attacked by the general and the tumor attacked by the doctor; but because the only causally relevant aspect is that each is a centrally located target, these differences are structure preserving.

In contrast, a structural dissimilarity involves a *structure-violating* difference that alters the causal relations in the two situations. Suppose, for example, that the radiation problem stated that only one X-ray source was available. This difference would block use of multiple converging forces, and hence would violate the structure of the solution plan paralleling that which succeeded in the military story. Such a structural dissimilarity would be expected to make the analogy less useful.[2] Note that the present distinction between surface and structural features is defined in terms of the causal relationships involved in problem situations, rather than in terms of purely syntactic criteria, such as Gentner's (1983) distinction between one-place and multiplace predicates. (See Holyoak, 1985, for a critique of purely syntactic analyses of analogy.)

Ideally, a problem solver would use only the structural features of the target as retrieval cues, thus avoiding activation of superficially similar but unhelpful situations. Carbonell's (1983) proposal that situations are indexed by problem components (which constitute structural features) thus has considerable normative appeal. In practice, however, the problem solver's ability to distinguish surface from structural features will almost inevitably be imperfect, since initial understanding of the unfamiliar target problem will be impoverished. Consequently, surface features that in fact are functionally irrelevant to a solution to the target problem may affect the solution plan indirectly by influencing the selection of a source analogue, as suggested by the results of Gilovich (1981) and Ross (1984).

It should now be clear why it is generally difficult for people to spontaneously access relevant source analogues from disparate domains. The basic problem is that a remote analogue, by definition, shares few of the salient surface features of the target. To the extent that these features serve as retrieval cues, they will tend to activate competing associations that may block retrieval of more remote analogues. Conversely, the more the problem solver is able to identify and focus on the causally relevant aspects of the target problem, the greater the probability that a useful but remote analogue will be retrieved.

Once a source analogue has been retrieved, surface features should have less impact on the subsequent mapping process than will structural ones. Structure-violating differences will necessitate refinement of the initial solution plan generated by the mapping, whereas structure-preserving differences will not. Thus, surface features will tend to have a relatively greater impact on selection of a source analogue than on the subsequent mapping process. For example, it seems much easier to learn about electrical circuits by mapping them with water systems than to spontaneously link the two analogues in the first place. In contrast, structure-violating differences should diminish not only the probability of selecting the source analogue, but also the probability of using it successfully once mapping is initiated. The predicted effects of surface and structural similarity were tested in Experiment 2.

## Experiment 1

Experiment 1 was designed to demonstrate that spontaneous analogical transfer can be obtained in the absence of demand characteristics that might serve as cues to relate the source and target analogues. The basic strategy was to impose a substantial delay between presentation of the source and the target, and to alter the context in which each was presented. Establishing that spontaneous transfer can be reliably obtained is a precondition for investigating the relationship between types of similarity and transfer.

### Method

*Materials*. A new convergence analogue was written for this purpose. It was first written as a story describing a problem and its solution, and was then modified for use in Experiment 1 by deleting the solution and presenting the problem as a target for subjects to solve. The basic content of this "lightbulb story" was inspired by an analogy spontaneously mentioned in a protocol obtained earlier from a subject solving the radiation problem (Gick & Holyoak, 1980, p. 328). In this story (see Appendix), the filament of an expensive lightbulb in a physics lab was broken. The lightbulb was completely sealed, but an intense laser could be used to fuse the filament. However, at that high intensity, the glass surrounding the filament would be broken. At lower intensities the laser would not break the glass, but neither would it affect the filament. The solution was to direct multiple low-intensity lasers toward the filament from different directions. Table 1 illustrates the analogical correspondences between the lightbulb story and the radiation problem.

**Table 1    Correspondences between lightbulb story and radiation problem**

| Lightbulb story | Radiation problem |
|---|---|
| Initial State | Initial State |
| Goal: Use lasers to fuse filament | Goal: Use X rays to destroy tumor |
| Resources: Sufficiently powerful laser | Resources: Sufficiently powerful rays |
| Operators: Reduce laser intensity, move laser source, activate lasers | Operators: Reduce ray intensity, move ray source, administer rays |
| Constraint: High-intensity laser will break glass | Constraint: High-intensity rays will destroy healthy tissue |
| Solution plan: Administer low-intensity lasers from multiple directions simultaneously | Solution plan: Administer low-intensity rays from multiple directions simultaneously |
| Outcome: Filament fused by lasers | Outcome: Tumor destroyed by X rays |

Pilot data indicated that subjects who first read the lightbulb story would often spontaneously produce the corresponding convergence solution to the radiation problem. The present experiment was performed to exclude an explanation of such transfer in terms of demand characteristics.

*Design and procedure.* Two groups of subjects were tested, all of whom were currently enrolled in an introductory psychology course at the University of Michigan. The course was taught in small sections by different instructors, using various textbooks. Subjects in the analogy condition were selected from sections in which the textbook was *Psychology* by Gleitman (1981). This text contains an extensive discussion of Duncker's (1945) investigation using the radiation problem, and includes an illustrated explanation of the convergence solution (pp. 321–322). For these subjects, the textbook treatment and class discussion of the radiation problem provided an incidental context in which they learned a potential source analogue. Subjects in the control condition were selected from sections of the course using other textbooks, which did not describe the radiation problem. These subjects thus were not provided with a source analogue. Since students were assigned to sections without regard to the textbook used, there was no reason to expect analogy and control subjects to differ with respect to other factors that might influence performance.

From 3 to 7 days after the subjects in the analogy group had discussed the radiation problem in class, all subjects were brought into the lab in small groups to serve in the experiment. They were told that the experiment involved solving problems. The first problem was a version of the lightbulb story described above with the solution omitted. Subjects read the problem, which described the broken lightbulb in a physics lab, and were asked to suggest procedures by which the laser could be used to fuse the filament. They were asked to write down as many solutions as possible, and to not worry if they were unsure whether a possible solution was actually feasible. No hint was given for them to relate the problem to material in their course. When they had completed the lightbulb problem, they were given the radiation problem, stated as in Gick and Holyoak (1980), and were asked to provide possible solutions. This was done in order to ascertain whether subjects in the analogy condition had in fact learned the convergence solution to the radiation problem from their textbook.

*Subjects*. Twenty-one subjects served in the analogy condition and 10 served in the control condition. Subjects received course credit for participating in the experiment.

### Results and discussion

Of subjects in the analogy condition, 81% produced the convergence solution to the lightbulb problem, and 86% produced the convergence solution to the radiation problem. The corresponding percentages for subjects in the control group were 10% and 10%. A solution was scored as indicating convergence as long as the idea of administering lasers (or X rays) from different directions was clearly stated. Differences in solution frequencies were tested using the maximum-likelihood chi-square statistic. Subjects in the analogy group were much more likely than those in the control group to produce the convergence solution to the lightbulb problem [81% vs. 10%; $G^2(1) = 15.2, p < .001$], indicating substantial spontaneous transfer from the source analogue encountered days earlier in a textbook to the target problem. Furthermore, the analogy subjects were also much more likely than control subjects to produce the convergence solution to the radiation problem itself, confirming that they had in fact learned the solution.

The 4 subjects in the analogy group who failed to generate the convergence solution to the lightbulb problem included the 3 who failed to generate the convergence solution to the radiation problem. Most of the failures to transfer the solution from the source to the target are therefore attributable to subjects who may have failed to encode the source analogue in the first place.

### Experiment 2

The results of Experiment 1, in contrast to earlier findings, such as those of Gick and Holyoak (1980, 1983) and Spencer and Weisberg (1986), revealed a high frequency of spontaneous analogical transfer, even when a delay of several days was imposed between presentation of the source and target analogues. The most probable factor leading to greater transfer in the present study is that the lightbulb problem is in several respects more similar to the radiation problem than were the story analogues used in earlier work. One difference in similarity involves the instruments used in the analogues. A laser is obviously far more similar to X rays than an army is, providing a significant additional retrieval cue in the case of the lightbulb story. In addition, the deeper structural parallels between the lightbulb and radiation analogues make the analogy a strong one. Both cases involve a target area enclosed within a fragile "container" that is at risk from a high-intensity force. Thus, both a salient surface similarity and a relatively complete structural mapping provide retrieval cues that can connect the lightbulb and radiation analogues.

Experiment 2 was performed to investigate the influence of surface and structural similarity on analogical transfer. If spontaneous retrieval depends on summation of activation from multiple features shared by the source and target, and if both surface and structural features can serve as retrieval cues, then both types of factors should influence spontaneous transfer. However, since only structural dissimilarities actually impair the analogical mapping, structural features should have a greater impact than surface features on transfer once a hint to use the analogy is provided. These hypotheses contrast with various possible alternatives, such as that different types of similarity have equivalent effects on all steps in analogical problem solving.

## Method

*Materials*. Four story analogues to the radiation problem were written (see Appendix). These were used as source analogues, and the radiation problem was used as the target. All of the stories are variations of the lightbulb story described above. The original story is the "fragile-glass and laser" version. The other three versions were generated by varying surface and/or structural similarities to the radiation problem. To vary the surface similarity, two of the new stories employed ultrasound waves in place of lasers.[3] Since laser beams are more similar to X rays than are ultrasound waves, the surface similarity of a laser version to the radiation problem was greater than that of an ultrasound-wave version.

In order to make the effect of the ultrasound seem plausible to subjects, the nature of the damage done to the lightbulb, and therefore the repair required, were also modified in the ultrasound versions. Instead of the filament's being broken apart, it is described as fused together and the ultrasound waves are used to jar it apart. The two types of damage and repair do not seem to differ considerably in their similarity to the destruction of a tumor, but "jarring apart" seems more similar to "destroying" than does "fusing together." Thus, if any advantage is observed for a laser version over an ultrasound version as a prompt for the convergence solution, it can be attributed to the more salient difference in the similarity of instruments.[4]

The structural similarity of the stories to the radiation problem was varied by altering the constraint preventing administration of an intense force from one direction. The constraint in two of the modified versions is that none of the several machines available can generate a single force of sufficient intensity. The constraint of insufficient intensity is much less similar to that in the radiation problem than is the alternative constraint that a high-intensity force would break the surrounding glass. Although the same convergence solution is described in the insufficient-intensity versions, the convergence element of the solution is not essential, as it is in the fragile-glass versions or in the radiation problem. Among the three basic components of the convergence solution — the application of (1) multiple (2) low-intensity forces (3) from different directions — only the use of multiple machines is a necessary component in the insufficient-intensity versions. The use of low-intensity forces in this context is a simple restatement of the given fact that only low-intensity forces are available. It is not strictly necessary to focus the forces on the filament from different directions. Another possible solution would be to focus several forces on some point outside the lightbulb so as to form a single high-intensity force. This would not be a viable solution for the fragile-glass versions, since the high-intensity force would affect the glass as well as the filament. The necessity of focusing several forces in the insufficient-intensity versions arises from the physical impossibility of putting several machines in the same spatial location, and hence is implicit in the use of multiple machines. The insufficient-intensity versions thus alter a feature that influences the necessity (although not the possibility) of the stated solution. Even though the same convergence solution is provided in all four stories, the analogy with the radiation problem is structurally weaker for the insufficient-intensity than for the fragile-glass versions.

*Subjects.* Sixty-three University of Michigan undergraduates served in the experiment, with 16 in each of the fragile-glass conditions and the insufficient-intensity laser condition, and 15 in the insufficient-intensity ultrasound condition. Each subject was paid $3 for participation in a 40-min session.

*Procedure.* Subjects were told that the experiment consisted of several parts, involving story comprehension and problem solving. In the first part of the experiment, subjects were asked to read and summarize a story (one of the four lightbulb stories). All versions were presented with the title "The Broken Lightbulb." Subjects were allowed to refer back to the story while writing the summary. When the summarization task was complete, subjects were asked to solve several deductive-reasoning problems. This unrelated filler task was included to reduce demand characteristics that might cause subjects to relate the story task to the subsequent problems. A sheet with the radiation problem was then handed out, and subjects were required to write as many solutions as possible, without worrying about not having enough technical knowledge.

Finally, subjects filled out a questionnaire that asked (1) whether they had tried to use the lightbulb story to help solve the radiation problem; (2) what solution to the problem was suggested by the story (a prompt for additional solutions); and (3) whether they knew the problem and its solution prior to the experiment. The first and second questions served as a hint that the initial story might be useful in solving the problem. The hint would tend to equalize retrieval for all subjects, so that factors affecting only retrieval and not transfer would have little effect once the hint was provided.

### Results and discussion

The data were discarded for 1 subject in the insufficient-intensity laser condition, who indicated that she had known the radiation problem and the convergence solution prior to the experiment. As in Experiment 1, all solutions clearly stating that the X rays should be administered from different directions were scored as convergence solutions. Table 2A presents the percentage of subjects in each of the four conditions who generated the convergence solution prior to receiving a hint to consider the story. When the source was the "laser and fragile-glass" analogue, in which both instrument and constraint were similar to those of the radiation problem, 69% of the subjects spontaneously generated the convergence solution. Transfer was significantly impaired if *either* the surface similarity of the instrument *or* the structural constraint similarity was reduced. The ultrasound versions yielded lower solution frequencies than did the laser versions [$G^2(1) = 4.42$, $p < .05$], and the insufficient-intensity

371

versions yielded lower solution frequencies than did the fragile glass versions [$G^2(1) =$ 5.92, $p < .05$]. The factors of surface and structural similarity were approximately equal in magnitude and did not interact. If dissimilarities in both were introduced (the insufficient-intensity ultrasound version), only 13 % of the subjects spontaneously generated the convergence solution. These results indicate that both surface similarities and deeper structural commonalities aid in the retrieval and use of source analogues, as would be expected on the basis of a summation mechanism.

**Table 2    Percentage of subjects producing convergence solution (Experiment 2)**

| Structural similarity (Constraint) | Surface similarity (Instrument) | | Mean |
|---|---|---|---|
| | High (Laser) | Low (Ultrasound) | |
| A. Prior to hint | | | |
| High (Fragile glass) | 69 | 38 | 54 |
| Low (Insufficient intensity) | 33 | 13 | 23 |
| Mean | 51 | 26 | |
| B. Total (before and after hint) | | | |
| High (Fragile glass) | 75 | 81 | 78 |
| Low (Insufficient intensity) | 60 | 47 | 54 |
| Mean | 68 | 64 | |

As the data in Table 2B indicate, a different transfer pattern was observed once a hint to use the story was provided. The total percentages of subjects producing convergence solutions include subjects who generated the solution either before any hint or in response to the direct question as to what solution the story suggested. Structural dissimilarity of the constraints significantly impaired total transfer (78% for the fragile-glass versions vs. 54% for the insufficient-intensity versions) [$G^2(1) = 4.31$, $p < .05$]. In contrast, surface dissimilarity of the instruments had no effect on total transfer (68 % for the laser versions vs. 64% for the ultrasound versions) [$G^2(1) < 1$]. Thus, although surface and structural similarity had comparable effects on spontaneous transfer, only the latter had a significant impact on total analogical transfer once a hint was provided.

A further analysis was performed to provide a more direct statistical test of the differing impacts of surface and structural similarity on use of the analogy. A weighted least squares analysis was used to compare the parameters of an additive linear logit model (Grizzle, Starmer, & Koch, 1969; Wickens, in press) for the odds of solving without a hint with the parameters of a model for the odds of solving at all. The interaction of surface and structural similarity was not significant for either dependent measure, so only parameters for the two main effects were included in the models. The hypothesis that the parameters corresponding to the effect of surface similarity were identical for solutions obtained prior to the hint and for total solutions was rejected;

the value of the Wald statistic (an approximately chi-square distributed statistic) was 4.20 with 1 $df$, $p < .05$. In contrast, the hypothesis of equal parameters corresponding to structural similarity could not be rejected (Wald statistic $= 1.58$, $p > .20$).[5] The results of Experiment 2 therefore support the prediction that surface similarity will have a greater relative impact on retrieval of a source analogue than on application of an analogue once it is retrieved, whereas structural similarity has a comparable impact on both steps in analogy use.

Subjects' responses to the question of whether they had tried to use the prior story to help solve the radiation problem confirmed that both types of similarity affected spontaneous use of the analogy. As the data in Table 3 indicate, the percentage of subjects reporting use of the story decreased both when the instrument was dissimilar [$G^2(1) = 5.30$, $p < .05$] and when the constraint was dissimilar [$G^2(1) = 13.1$, $p < .001$].

**Table 3    Percentage of subjects reporting noticing of analogy (Experiment 2)**

| Structural similarity (Constraint) | Surface similarity (Instrument) | | Mean |
|---|---|---|---|
| | High (Laser) | Low (Ultrasound) | |
| High (Fragile glass) | 88 | 56 | 72 |
| Low (Insufficient intensity) | 40 | 13 | 27 |
| Mean | 64 | 35 | |

It was claimed earlier that the insufficient-intensity constraint reduces the necessity of the use of multiple directions in the solution stated in the story. Given that aspects of a story that, subjectively, seem less important tend to be omitted when subjects write summaries (e.g., Thorndyke, 1977), it follows that subjects should be less likely to mention the use of different directions when summarizing the insufficient-intensity version than when summarizing the fragile-glass version. Accordingly, the story summaries were scored for inclusion of this aspect of the convergence solution. More subjects in the fragile-glass conditions than in the insufficient-intensity conditions mentioned the use of different directions [66% vs. 30%; $G^2(1) = 8.05$, $p < .005$]. Instrument similarity had no significant effect (52 % for the laser versions vs. 45 % for the ultrasound versions).

Although subjects in the insufficient-intensity conditions tended not to mention use of different directions in their summaries, as indicated by the above results, this does not imply that they simply ignored the stated convergence solution. The summaries were also scored for inclusion of the idea of using multiple machines, which, unlike the idea of using different directions, is necessary to the viability of the convergence solution in all versions. Neither similarity factor had a significant influence on the probability of mentioning multiple machines in the summary. In particular, the probability of including this aspect of the solution did not differ between the fragile-glass and the insufficient-intensity conditions (81 % vs. 77%). The nature of the constraint thus selectively affected the perceived importance of the use of different directions. The fact that this aspect of the convergence solution was viewed as less crucial in the insufficient-intensity stories may be related to the subsequent difficulty subjects in these conditions had in developing a convergence solution to the radiation problem, even when directed to use the prior story.

## General discussion

The results of the present study begin to elucidate the conditions under which people are able to spontaneously use a known analogue stored in memory when they encounter a novel problem. Spontaneous analogical transfer is most likely to occur when the target problem shares multiple features with the source analogue. Both salient surface differences, which do not impede achievement of the critical solution, and deeper structural differences, which involve the nature of the solution constraints (Carbonell, 1983), have an impact on transfer. The results implicate a retrieval mechanism based on the summation of activation from multiple shared features that serve as retrieval cues.

Whereas both structural and surface similarities influenced the probability that an analogy would be used without an explicit hint, only structural similarity — the nature of the problem's constraint — affected subjects' ability to make use of the source analogue once its relevance was pointed out. Gentner and Landers (1985) also found evidence that superficial similarity has a greater influence on accessing than on application of analogies. Unlike surface differences, a structure-violating difference between the source and target impairs mapping and makes the analogous solution more difficult to derive, since further transformation is required to generate a solution that is viable in the target situation (Carbonell, 1983).

Clearly, the present results must be viewed as preliminary, given the narrow range of materials employed. In particular, the results should not be construed as indicating that surface features will *never* influence mapping once a source is selected. In Experiment 2, only a single change was introduced to create the surface-dissimilarity condition. It might well be that introduction of multiple surface dissimilarities would make it more difficult to map the components of the two analogues. In addition, surface differences will continue to impair transfer if the problem solver has difficulty in discriminating them from structural differences even after a source analogue is provided. This problem may be especially acute for inexperienced problem solvers. For example, in an experiment on analogical transfer performed with 6-year-olds, Holyoak, Junn, and Billman (1984) found that what appeared to be a minor surface dissimilarity between the source and target significantly decreased the percentage of children who were able to use the analogy even when told to use it. It may be that children who lack experience with a problem domain have greater difficulty than do adults in analyzing the causally relevant aspects of the source and target problems.

In general, surface dissimilarity may or may not influence mapping, but even when it does not, it may still impair retrieval. In contrast, structural dissimilarity is expected to affect both retrieval and mapping. The present results suggest that many of the basic mechanisms involved in analogical transfer operate in other memory and reasoning tasks. Retrieval by summation of activation can provide a general mechanism for flexibly accessing information in memory that is related to a novel input. According to the present view, the distinctive aspect of retrieval of interdomain analogies, as opposed to mundane associations, lies in the selection of appropriate features of the target to use as retrieval cues. A plausibly useful remote analogue will be one that shares multiple structural features with the representation of the target problem — the initial state, the goal state, and solution constraints (Carbonell, 1983). The appropriate features can be determined by knowledge of the target domain, coupled with skill in causal analysis. Studies of expertise in domains such as physics have revealed a shift from novices' problem representations based on surface features to experts' representations based on deeper structural features (e.g., Chi, Feltovich, & Glaser, 1981). It follows that experts should be better able to retrieve and use analogies from other domains. Both novices and experts may use a summation mechanism to retrieve potential analogues, but the latter will be better able to focus on causally relevant features to use as retrieval cues.

The contrast between the relatively high rates of spontaneous transfer obtained in the present experiments and the much lower rates observed in previous studies is attributable to the greater similarity of the analogues used here. It may be that presence of at least one pair of highly similar problem elements, such as X rays and lasers, is, for most people, necessary to trigger retrieval. Detection of an analogy based solely on abstract structural features may be a rare event for novice problem solvers. It should be noted, however, that transfer between problems as disparate as even the most similar pair used in the present study is beyond the competence of current expert systems in artificial intelligence. Even if such a program mimicked the expertise of both a physicist and a physician, it would lack any capacity to apply its knowledge about lasers and filaments to invent a procedure for treating tumors. The mechanisms that allow humans to select useful analogies, such as the differentiation of structural from surface features, may provide the key to designing more flexible mechanized problem solvers.

## Acknowledgements

This research was supported by National Science Foundation Grant BNS-8216068 and Army Research Institute Contract MDA903-86-K-0297. The first author held an NIMH Research Scientist Development Award, I-K02-MH00342-05. Early drafts of the paper were written while the first author was visiting the Psychology Department at Carnegie-Mellon University and the Learning Research and Development Center of the University of Pittsburgh. Patricia Cheng and Edward Smith provided useful comments on earlier drafts of the paper. A talk based on the paper was presented at the annual meeting of the Midwestern Psychological Association, May 1986, in Chicago.

## Notes

1.  The reader may have noticed that the summation-of-activation mechanism is itself an example of the convergence principle that can be used to solve Duncker's radiation problem (multiple low-intensity sources combine to achieve the threshold for some critical event). We will not speculate as to whether this similarity illustrates the analogical origin of scientific hypotheses, or is simply coincidental.

2.  Note, however, that a structure-violating difference need not render an analogy useless. For example, even with the added constraint of having only a single X-ray source available, a

kind of convergence solution could be implemented by passing the rays through a device that defocuses them and then redirects them to a new focus at the tumor site. However, the constraint dissimilarity would make it necessary to modify the solution directly analogous to that in the source analogue.

3.  The ultrasound versions were less realistic than the laser versions in that ultrasound waves will not pass through a vacuum, such as that inside a lightbulb, and hence would not, in fact, achieve the stated outcome. However, none of our subjects, most of whom were psychology majors, expressed any doubt that ultrasound waves would behave as described in the story.

4.  A further experiment was performed to control for any possible effect of varying the nature of the damage and repair. This experiment used two fragile-glass versions of the lightbulb story in which both the laser and the ultrasound beam were described as being able to "jar apart" wires in the filament that had overheated and fused together. The pattern of transfer was the same as in the experiment described here. The convergence solution to the radiation problem was spontaneously generated by 87% of the 15 subjects who read the laser version, compared to 41% of the 17 subjects who read the ultrasound version [$G^2(1)$ = 7.53, $p < .01$]. After the subjects were given a hint to use the story, however, the two conditions did not differ significantly in solution frequencies [87% for the laser version vs. 77% for the ultrasound version; $G^2(1) < 1$].

5.  We thank Tom Wickens for performing the logit analysis.

## References

Anderson, J. R. (1983) *The architecture of cognition*. Cambridge, MA: Harvard University Press.

Burstein, M. H. (1986) A model of learning by incremental analogical reasoning and debugging. In R. Michalski, J. C. Carbonell, & T. M. Mitchell (Eds.), *Machine learning: An artificial intelligence approach* (Vol. 2). Los Altos, CA: Kaufmann.

Carbonell, J. G. (1983) Learning by analogy: Formulating and generalizing plans from past experience. In R. Michalski, J. G. Carbonell & T. M. Mitchell (Eds.), *Machine learning: An artificial intelligence approach*. Palo Alto, CA: Tioga Press.

Chi, M. T. H., Feltovich, P. J. & Glaser, R. (1981) Categorization and representation of physics problems by experts and novices. *Cognitive Science*, 5, 121–152.

Clement, J. (1982, April) *Spontaneous analogies in problem solving: The progressive construction of mental models*. Paper presented at the meeting of the American Educational Research Association, New York.

Duncker, K. (1945) On problem solving. *Psychological Monographs*. 58 (Whole No. 270).

Gentner, D. (1983) Structure-mapping: A theoretical framework for analogy. *Cognitive Science*, 7, 155–170.

Gentner, D. & Gentner, D. R. (1983) Flowing waters or teeming crowds: Mental models of electricity. In D. Gentner & A. L. Stevens (Eds.), *Mental models*. Hillsdale, NJ: Erlbaum.

Gentner, D. & Landers, R. (1985, November) *Analogical access: A good match is hard to find*. Paper presented at the annual meeting of the Psychonomic Society, Boston.

Gick, M. L. & Holyoak, K. J. (1980) Analogical problem solving. *Cognitive Psychology*, 12, 306–355.

Gick, M. L. & Holyoak, K. J. (1983) Schema induction and analogical transfer. *Cognitive Psychology*, 15, 1–38.

Gilovich, T. (1981) Seeing the past in the present: The effect of associations to familiar events on judgments and decisions. *Journal of Personality & Social Psychology*, 40, 797–808.

Gleitman, H. (1981). *Psychology.* New York: Norton.

Grizzle, J. E., Starmer, C. F. & Koch, G. C. (1969) Analysis of categorical data by linear models. *Biometrika* 25, 489–504.

Hayes, J. R. & Simon, H. A. (1977) Psychological differences among problem isomorphs. In N. J. Castellan, Jr., D. B. Pisoni, & G. R. Potts (Eds.), *Cognitive theory.* Hillsdale, NJ: Erlbaum.

Hesse, M. B. (1966) *Models and analogies in science.* Notre Dame, IN: Notre Dame University Press.

Holland, J. H., Holyoak, K. J., Nisbett, R. E. & Thagard, P. R. (1986) *Induction: Processes of inference, learning, and discovery.* Cambridge, MA: MIT Press.

Holyoak, K. J. (1984) Analogical thinking and human intelligence. In R. J. Sternberg (Ed.), *Advances in the psychology of human intelligence* (Vol. 2). Hillsdale, NJ: Erlbaum.

Holyoak, K. J. (1985) The pragmatics of analogical transfer. In G. H. Bower (Ed.), *The psychology of learning and motivation* (Vol. 19). New York: Academic Press.

Holyoak, K. J., Junn, E. N. & Billman, D. O. (1984) Development of analogical problem solving skill. *Child Development*, 55, 2042–2055.

McClelland, J. L. & Rumelhart, D. E. (1981) An interactive activation model of context effects in letter perception: Part 1. An account of basic findings. *Psychological Review*, 88, 375–407.

Reed, S. K., Ernst, G. W. & Banerji, R. (1974) The role of analogy in transfer between similar problem states. *Cognitive Psychology*, 6, 436–450.

Ross, B. H. (1984) Remindings and their effects in learning a cognitive skill. *Cognitive Psychology*, 16, 371–416

Schank, R. C. (1982) *Dynamic memory.* Cambridge, MA: Cambridge University Press.

Spencer, R. M. & Weisberg, R. W. (1986) Is analogy sufficient to facilitate transfer during problem solving? *Memory & Cognition*, 14, 442–449.

Thibadeau, R., Just, M. A. & Carpenter, P. A. (1982) A model of the time course and content of reading. *Cognitive Science*, 6, 157–203.

Thorndyke, P. W. (1977) Cognitive structures in comprehension and memory of narrative discourse. *Cognitive Psychology*, 9, 77–110.

Tversky, A. (1977) Features of similarity. *Psychological Review*, 84, 327–352.

Wickens, T. (in press) *Statistical methods for frequency tables.* New York: W. H. Freeman.

Winston, P. H. (1980) Learning and reasoning by analogy. *Communications of the ACM*, 23, 689–703.

## Appendix

## Four versions of the lightbulb story

### First part, all versions

In a physics lab at a major university, a very expensive lightbulb which would emit precisely controlled quantities of light was being used in some experiments. Ruth was the research assistant responsible for operating the sensitive lightbulb. One morning she came into the lab and found to her dismay that the lightbulb no longer worked. She realized that she had forgotten to turn it off the previous night. As a result the lightbulb overheated, and [the filament/two wires in the filament] inside the bulb [had broken into two parts/fused together]. The surrounding glass bulb was completely sealed, so there was no way to open it. Ruth knew that the lightbulb could be repaired if a brief high-intensity [laser beam/ultrasound wave] could be used to [fuse the two parts of the filament into one/jar apart the fused parts]. Furthermore, the lab had the necessary equipment to do the job.

### Second part, fragile-glass versions

However, a high-intensity [laser beam/ultrasound wave] would also break the fragile glass surrounding the filament. At lower intensities the [laser/ultrasound wave] would not break the glass, but neither would it [fuse the filament/jar apart the fused parts]. So it seemed that the lightbulb could not be repaired, and a costly replacement would be required.

Ruth was about to give up when she had an idea. She placed several [lasers/ultrasound machines] in a circle around the lightbulb, and administered low-intensity [laser beams/ultrasound waves] from several directions all at once. The [beams/waves] all converged on the filament, where their combined effect was enough to [fuse it/jar apart the fused parts]. Since each spot on the surrounding glass received only a low-intensity [beam/wave] from one [laser/ultrasound machine], the glass was left intact. Ruth was greatly relieved that the lightbulb was repaired, and she then went on to successfully complete the experiment.

### Second part, insufficient-intensity versions

However, the [lasers/ultrasound machines] only generated low-intensity [beams/ waves] that were not strong enough to [fuse the filament/jar apart the fused parts]. She needed a much more intense [laser beam/ultrasound wave]. So it seemed that the light-bulb could not be repaired, and a costly replacement would be required.

Ruth was about to give up when she had an idea. She placed several [lasers/ultrasound machines] in a circle around the lightbulb, and administered low-intensity [laser beams/ultrasound waves] from several directions all at once. The [beams/waves] all converged on the filament, where their combined effect was enough to [fuse it/jar apart the fused parts]. Ruth was greatly relieved that the lightbulb was repaired, and she then went on to successfully complete the experiment.

*Note* — Differences between laser and ultrasound versions in brackets.

# 14.    The Psychology of Syllogisms

## Philip N. Johnson-Laird and Mark Steedman

Two experiments were carried out in which subjects had to draw
conclusions from syllogistic premises. The nature of their responses
showed that the figure of the syllogisms exerted a strong effect on the
accuracy of performance and on the nature of the conclusions that were
drawn. For example, premises such as "Some of the parents are scientists;
All of the scientists are drivers" tend to elicit the conclusion, "Some of the
parents are drivers" rather than its equally valid converse "Some of the
drivers are parents". In general, premises of the form $\begin{array}{l} A - B \\ B - C \end{array}$ created a
bias towards conclusions of the form A — C, whereas premises of the form
$\begin{array}{l} B - A \\ C - B \end{array}$ created a bias towards conclusions of the form C — A. The data
cast doubt on current theories of syllogistic inference: a new theory was
accordingly developed and implemented as a computer program. The
theory postulates that quantified assertions receive an analogical mental
representation which captures their logical properties structurally. A
simple heuristic generates putative conclusions from the combined
representations of premises and such conclusions are put to logical tests
which, if exhaustively conducted, invariably yield a correct response.
Erroneous responses may occur if there is a failure to test exhaustively.

*Only connect.*

— E. M. Forster

The first experimental investigation into syllogisms appears to have been carried out
about 70 years ago by Storring (see Woodworth, 1938) and since then there has been a
steady series of studies of the various factors affecting their difficulty. Yet, it is only in
the last few years that any model of the complete inferential process has been
proposed. Part of the reason for such slow progress would seem to be the baleful
influence, Aristotle excluded, of traditional logic. The scholastics recognized 64
different moods of syllogism, since the two premises and the conclusion have to be
selected from the four moods of sentence (4 x 4 x 4 = 64):

| | |
|---|---|
| (A) Universal affirmative | All A are B |
| (I) Particular affirmative | Some A are B |
| (E) Universal negative | No A are B |
| (O) Particular negative | Some A are not B, |

Philip N. Johnson-Laird and Mark Steedman: 'The Psychology of Syllogisms' in *COGNITIVE PSYCHOLOGY* (1978), 10, pp. 64–99. Copyright © 1978 by Academic Press, Inc.

where the parenthesized letters are the traditional mnemonics (derived from *Affirmo* and *Nego*). Traditional logic also admits four different "figures":

| First figure | Second figure | Third figure | Fourth figure |
|:---:|:---:|:---:|:---:|
| M — P | P — M | M — P | P — M |
| S — M | S — M | M — S | M — S |
| ─── | ─── | ─── | ─── |
| ∴ S — P | ∴ S — P | ∴ S — P | ∴ S — P |

where S denotes the subject of the conclusion, P denotes the predicate of the conclusion, and M denotes the middle term which is common to both premises but disappears in the deduction.

If there are 64 moods and four figures, it is natural to suppose that there are 64 x 4 = 256 different sorts of syllogism. This number has certainly been taken for granted by many psychologists. It is, of course, erroneous: There are twice that number of syllogisms. Logicians ignored the order of the premises and made an arbitrary decision to cast their figures so that the subject (S) of the conclusion always occurs in the second premise. Obviously, logic is not affected if S happens to occur in the first premise, e.g.,

$$S — M$$
$$M — P$$
$$\overline{\phantom{S — P}}$$
$$S — P$$

and it is worth noting that Aristotle used a set of figures that included this "deviant" case. One immediate consequence of the slavish adherence to scholastic logic is a general neglect of half the possible syllogisms, and this omission has had serious consequences for understanding the psychology of syllogisms.

Another reason for slow progress has to do with experimental technique. Rather than attempt to castigate the shortcomings of particular investigations, it will be simpler to spell out some of the desirable requirements of an experiment on syllogistic reasoning:

First, subjects should have to make a deduction in order to carry out their experimental task. The point is obvious, but the drawbacks of conventional techniques are more subtle. If the task is merely to evaluate a given syllogism as valid or invalid, a subject may carry it out without ever having to make an inference. Even a multiple choice between different putative conclusions may tend to obscure the deductive process, either because of the particular set of alternatives chosen by the experimenter or because of some idiosyncratic procedure that a subject adopts, such as working backward from conclusion to premises, guessing the most plausible conclusion, and so on.

Second, subjects should be given a representative selection of problems. It is little use seeking to draw general conclusions on the basis of, say, a dozen syllogisms when the total possible number is 512.

Third, syllogisms should be presented with a sensible, though non-controversial, linguistic content. Although a case has been made in the past for studying inference with an abstract or symbolic content, it is now known that such materials can lead to qualitative changes in performance (Wason and Johnson-Laird, 1972). A psychologist who studies reasoning with abstract materials is not so much studying a pure deduction, unsullied by his subjects' knowledge or attitudes, as a very special sort of reasoning designed to compensate for the absence of everyday content.

Fourth, in the analysis and description of results, it is crucial to consider each syllogism separately. A number of published studies present only data pooled across different figures or across different moods. Such an exposition may be appropriate for the evaluation of an author's own hypothesis, but it can render the data useless for anyone who wishes to examine an alternative theory or to construct a general model of syllogistic inference.

These four simple requirements have never been satisfied by any investigation to be found in the literature, and even some recent studies have neglected them. Our initial goals were accordingly to carry out an experiment in which subjects drew their own inferences from a reasonable selection of sensible syllogisms and to try to give an account of how they performed this task.

### Experiment 1: Valid syllogisms

The aim of the experiment was to examine our subjects' ability to make valid syllogistic deductions. The subjects were presented with pairs of syllogistic premises and asked to state in their own words what conclusion followed logically from them. This technique has a subsidiary advantage: Although there are 512 different syllogisms, there are only 64 different pairs of premises, and this reduction makes it very much more feasible to test a representative sample of problems. In the present experiment, subjects were tested with the 27 pairs of premises that yield a valid conclusion: that is, at least one of the eight possible conclusions is correct.

### Design and materials

Each subject was asked to make a deduction from the 27 pairs of premises that are shown in Table 1 with their valid conclusions italicized. The problems were presented with a sensible content of a sort unlikely to predispose subjects toward a particular conclusion. Hence, a typical pair was:

> None of the musicians are inventors
> All of the inventors are professors
> _____
> ∴    ?

The materials were mimeographed and assembled into booklets in different random orders.

### Procedure

The subjects were tested individually. They were told that they were going to take part in an investigation of the way in which people combine information in order to draw conclusions from it. They would be given a series of pairs of statements about people

381

whom they were to imagine as assembled in a room. Their task was to write down what followed from each pair of statements about the occupants of the room. The purpose of this instruction was to insulate still further the content of the problems from subjects' attitudes or expectations. The subjects were also instructed that their answers were to be based solely upon what could be deduced with absolute certainty from the premises, and it was made clear that for every problem there was always at least one such conclusion that could be drawn. The subjects were allowed as much time as they wanted in order to complete the task.

### Subjects

Twenty volunteers who were undergraduate students at University College London participated in the experiment.

### Results

The best way to illustrate the conventions that we have adopted in presenting the results is to examine in detail the actual performance on one problem. Consider the following premise pair and the 14 valid responses it evoked (we present premises and conclusions in an abstract form for ease of reading):

> All of the A are B
> All of the B are C
> ─────────────
> ∴ *All the A are C*  (seven subjects)
> ∴ *All A are C*  (five subjects)
> ∴ *The A are C*  (one subject)
> ∴ *All A are B and C*  (one subject)

These conclusions despite some superficial heterogeneity are all logically impeccable; here, and throughout the paper, we italicize valid deductions. (The last response is interesting because it is an instance of a partially digested middle term.) Since we shall be concerned only with logic and the order of terms, we shall ignore superficial variations and classify all of these responses under the same general rubric: *All A are C*. No claims about the present experiment hinge upon any more subtle distinctions in the data.

Table 1 presents the frequencies of the main responses (i.e., any response made by two or more subjects) to each of the 27 problems. Since 20 subjects participated, the residual untabulated value for any problem corresponds to those miscellaneous erroneous responses that were not made by more than one subject.

What is immediately evident from a casual inspection of Table 1 is the variation in the difficulty of the problems. With the easiest premise pair 17 out of 20 subjects produced valid deductions: with the hardest premise pair only six out of 20 subjects produced valid deductions. This aspect of the results was reinforced by the extent to which subjects agonized over conclusions: Sometimes a conclusion would emerge rapidly, sometimes only a very hesitant conclusion emerged which was often either erroneous or merely a restatement of the premises. The variation is remarkable but well established, and we will make no further comment on it at this point. There is a more important phenomenon to be considered.

**Table 1 The frequencies of the main sorts of deduction in Experiment 1[a]**

| Second premise | First premise | | | | | | | |
|---|---|---|---|---|---|---|---|---|
| | All A are B | Some A are B | No A are B | Some A are not B | All B are A | Some B are A | No B are A | Some B are not A |
| All B are C | *All A are C* 14<br>All C are A 2 | *Some A are C* 15<br>Some C are A 2 | *Some C are not A* 8<br>No C are A 5<br>Some A are C 2 | | *Some A are C* 7<br>Some C are A 3<br>All A are C 3<br>All B are A and C 5 | Some C are not A 10<br>*Some A are C* 4 | *Some C are not A* 8<br>No A are C 4 | *Some C are not A* 11<br>Some A are C 4 |
| Some B are C | | | *Some C are not A* 9<br>No A are C 3<br>No C are A 2 | | *Some A are C* 8<br>Some C are A 4 | | *Some C are not A* 12 | |
| No B are C | *No A are C* 13<br>No C are A 2<br>Some A are C 2 | *Some A are not C* 10<br>Some A are C 4 | | | Some A are not C 8<br>No C are A 3<br>No A are C 2 | Some A are not C 9<br>Some A are C 3<br>Some C are not A 2 | | |
| Some B are not C | | | | | *Some A are not C* 12<br>Some C are A 3 | | | |
| All C are B | | | | *Some A are not C* 10<br>Some C are A 2 | *All C are A* 12<br>All A are C 4 | | *No C are A* 10<br>No A are C 5 | |
| Some C are B | | | *Some C are not A* 12<br>Some C are A 3 | | *Some C are A* 16<br>Some A are C 1 | | | |
| No C are B | *No C are A* 11<br>No A are C 6 | *Some A are not C* 11<br>Some C are A 2 | | | Some A are not C 6<br>No A are C 5<br>No C are A 3 | Some A are not C 9<br>No C are A 2<br>Some A are C 2 | | |
| Some C are not B | *Some C are not A* 12<br>Some A are not C 2<br>Some C are B (sic) 2 | | | | | | | |

[a] Valid deductions are italicized. The eight columns represent the first premise in a problem, the eight rows the second premise. The maximum total for any problem is 20: Where totals are less than 20, the residuals correspond to miscellaneous errors.

When the results in each quadrant of Table 1 are examined, it is evident that there is a pronounced "figural" effect. Thus, the following examples show a highly reliable bias toward one of two equally valid conclusions:

Some A are B        All B are A
All B are C        Some C are B

∴ *Some A are C* (15 subjects)    ∴ *Some C are A* (16 subjects)
∴ *Some C are A* (2 subjects)     ∴ *Some A are C* (1 subject).

Such patterns are entirely representative: With the $\frac{A-B}{B-C}$ figure (the top left-hand quadrant), 71% of all the valid conclusions were of the form A — C, whereas with the $\frac{B-A}{C-B}$ figure (the bottom right-hand quadrant), 70% of the valid conclusions were of the form C — A. The bias is evident both in those syllogisms that permit two converse conclusions and in the ease of solution to those premises that permit only a single conclusion and not its converse. There was little if any bias in the case of the $\frac{A-B}{C-B}$ figure (53% valid conclusions of the form C — A) and no bias at all in the case of the $\frac{B-A}{B-C}$ figure. All 20 subjects had a bias toward A — C conclusions for the $\frac{A-B}{B-C}$ premises and a bias toward C — A conclusions for the $\frac{B-A}{C-B}$ premises, and hence the effect is highly significant. The effect occurs for all the relevant syllogisms except those that have only one valid conclusion which is inconsistent with the bias.

## Discussion

Why has such a striking phenomenon as the figural effect not been reported before? The answer is that the crippling effect of traditional logic has led to a neglect of syllogisms in the "unorthodox" figures: the stigma attached to such figures is, indeed, still observable in recent publications. The effect was, however, partially anticipated by Frase (1968) who observed that orthodox syllogisms in the first figure,

B — A
C — B
———
∴ C — A ,

were more often evaluated correctly than orthodox syllogisms in the fourth figure,

A — B
B — C
———
∴ C — A ,

with the other two figures yielding an intermediate performance. Doubtless, if Frase had used syllogisms with conclusions of the form A — C, the difference would have reversed and he would have established the complete figural effect. Frase explained his results by analogy with the mediational paradigms of paired-associate learning, since

384

the first figure corresponds to a "forward chain" and the fourth figure corresponds to a "backward chain", but the analogy seems to break down in the light of the full figural effect. Both Wilkins (1928) and Sells (1936) used some syllogisms in unorthodox figures, and with hindsight one can also detect some traces of a figural effect in their data.

## Experiment 2: Valid and invalid syllogisms

Although a figural effect emerged clearly from Experiment 1, we were unable to formulate a theoretical explanation of it in the absence of data from premises from which no valid deduction could be drawn. Hence, a second experiment was devised in order to try to replicate the results of the first one and to extend the technique to premises lacking valid conclusions. The experiment also allowed us to evaluate the main hypotheses about syllogistic inference, since they largely concern invalid inferences.

### Design

The aim of the experiment was to assess performance with the complete set of syllogisms, and accordingly each subject attempted to make an inference from all 64 possible pairs of premises illustrated in Table 1. This task was performed twice by every subject on two separate occasions approximately a week apart. The contents of the syllogisms were similar to those used in Experiment 1, except that a more stringent attempt was made to minimize semantic relations between the terms within each premise pair while retaining moderate plausibility for them and for any conclusion, valid or invalid. We found that the most successful way to construct premises within these constraints was to use one term denoting an occupation and two terms denoting preoccupations or interests, for example, "All of the gourmets are storekeepers. All of the storekeepers are bowlers." Two separate lists of the 64 problems were constructed. In order to create the second list, the contents of the 27 soluble problems in the first list were exchanged with those of 27 insoluble problems, and the remaining 10 insoluble problems had their contents reassigned from one problem to another at random. The subjects received one list in the first session and the other list in the second session in a counterbalanced pattern. Each list was presented in a random order.

### Procedure

The procedure was the same as in Experiment 1 except that the subjects' performance was timed and they were told to make their responses both accurately and as quickly as possible. They were also told to restrict their answers to one of the four moods or else to state that no valid conclusion followed from the premises.

### Subjects

Twenty paid volunteers, students at Teachers College, Columbia University, were tested individually in the experiment.

### Results

The results for each of the 64 problems are presented in the four tables in the Appendix. In order to simplify the presentation we shall mainly consider performance in the second test. However, the pattern of the results was with one exception (to be discussed below) very similar in both tests, as the reader may care to check, and the significant effects we report are manifest in the results from the first test.

### The effect of figure on the form of conclusions

By far the most important result is the confirmation of the figural effect. In the case of the $\begin{smallmatrix}A-B\\B-C\end{smallmatrix}$ figure there was a strong bias towards a conclusion of the form A — C, and in the case of the $\begin{smallmatrix}B-A\\C-B\end{smallmatrix}$ figure, there was a strong bias towards a conclusion of the form C — A. (The phenomenon has turned out to be easy to replicate: When audiences at universities as far afield as Chicago, New York, Edinburgh, London, Padova, and Nijmegen, were presented with appropriate syllogisms, they all showed a massive figural effect in their conclusions.) The present data are summarized in Table 2, but the results of the second test will be analyzed in more detail.

**Table 2** **The overall effect of figure on the form of conclusion in Experiment 2: the percentages of A — C and C — A conclusions as a function of the figure of the premises**

| Form of conclusion | Figure of premises | | | | | | | |
|---|---|---|---|---|---|---|---|---|
| | A —B<br>B — C | | B — A<br>C — B | | A — B<br>C — B | | B — A<br>B — C | |
| A — C | (51.2)[a] | 44.7 | (4.7) | 5.3 | (21.2) | 13.7 | (31.9) | 29.4 |
| C — A | (6.2) | 7.8 | (48.1) | 45.3 | (20.6) | 28.1 | (17.8) | 25.0 |

[a] Numbers in parentheses are from the first test.

When a syllogism has only one valid conclusion (i.e., the converse conclusion is invalid), then subjects tend to make this deduction where it is compatible with the figure of the premises, but tend to be unable to make it where it is incompatible with the figure of the premises. Thus, the following two examples of IE and EI problems illustrate the relative ease of drawing a conclusion compatible with the figure

Some A are B           No B are A

No B are C             Some C are B

∴ *Some A are not C*     ∴ *Some C are not A*

(17 subjects)        (14 subjects),

whereas the following two examples illustrate the relative difficulty of drawing a conclusion incompatible with the figure

No A are B           Some B are A

Some B are C        No C are B

∴ *Some C are not A*     ∴ *Some A are not C*

(8 subjects)         (5 subjects).

The overall differences are massive: Where valid deductions were compatible with figure, they occurred on 85% of occasions with the $\frac{A-B}{B-C}$ figure and 77.5% of occasions with the $\frac{B-A}{C-B}$ figure, but where they were incompatible with the figure they occurred on only 20% of occasions. There was not a single exception in all 90 subjects to this pattern of results. There was a comparable bias in the invalid conclusions that occurred for these problems, though the frequencies were too low for statistical comparison.

There was also a pronounced figural effect for syllogisms with two (converse) valid conclusions: 82.5% conclusions compatible with figure versus 10% incompatible with it for $\frac{A-B}{B-C}$ premises, and 77.5 versus 7.5% for $\frac{B-A}{C-B}$ premises. (The effect is present in the results of 18 subjects, absent in the results of one subject, and controverted by the results of one subject: Sign test, $p < 0.0005$, two-tailed.) It is noteworthy that in none of these syllogisms was there ever an invalid conclusion incompatible with figure.

Finally, in the case of syllogisms lacking a valid conclusion, there was a figural effect in the invalid conclusions that were drawn: 30% invalid conclusions were drawn compatible with the $\frac{A-B}{B-C}$ figure, but only 2.5% were drawn incompatible with it, and 31.5% invalid conclusions were drawn compatible with the $\frac{B-A}{C-B}$ figure but only 3.5%, were drawn incompatible with it. (This trend was also confirmed by the results of 18 subjects, disconfirmed by the results of one subject, and there was a tie for one subject.)

Turning to the other two remaining figures, there was some bias towards conclusions of the form C — A for the $\frac{A-B}{C-B}$ figure. The bias was evident in the results for premises with only one valid conclusion (67.5% correct where the required conclusion was of the form C — A, but only 30% correct where it was of the form A — C; Wilcoxon test, $p < 0.01$, two-tailed), but the bias for premises with two (converse) valid conclusions was not statistically significant (45% of the form C — A but 30% of the form A — C), and it was only very slight for premises with no valid conclusion (14% invalid conclusions of the form C — A, and 9% invalid conclusions of the form A — C). There did not appear to be any reliable bias towards one form of conclusion or the other in the case of the $\frac{B-A}{B-C}$ figure.

### The effect of figure on accuracy

There was a considerable difference in the difficulty of the problems (Cochran's $Q = 368$, with $df = 63, p < 0.001$). The difference reflects in part the figure of the premises ($\chi r^2 = 10.8, df = 3, p < 0.025$, Friedman two-way analysis of variance). Table 3 states the percentages of correct responses for the four figures both for premises with a valid conclusion and for premises without a valid conclusion.

For each $\begin{smallmatrix}A-B\\B-C\end{smallmatrix}$ problem, there is a corresponding $\begin{smallmatrix}B-A\\C-B\end{smallmatrix}$ problem: In effect, the

order of the two premises is simply reversed. The $\begin{smallmatrix}A-B\\B-C\end{smallmatrix}$ figure yielded a superior

performance for all six of the problems with valid conclusions, and the difference is statistically significant. It was evident in the data of 11 subjects, four subjects yielded data in the opposite direction, and there was no difference between the figures for the remaining five subjects (Wilcoxon test, $p < 0.05$, two-tailed). However, there is no real difference between these two figures for problems lacking a valid conclusion. Comparisons with (and between) the other two figures can only be made globally because they do not contain equivalent problems. The impression that these other two figures show a marked superiority for premises lacking a valid conclusion is borne out in the data for all but three subjects, a highly significant difference (Sign test, $p < 0.003$, two-tailed). In fact, there is an interaction here: These two figures show a greater advantage for premises lacking valid conclusions (in comparison with those having a valid conclusion) than do the first two figures (14 subjects conform to this trend, six subjects contravene it; Wilcoxon test, $p < 0.05$, two-tailed). An interesting related result concerns the proportion of times subjects respond "No valid conclusion" to premises that, in fact, permit a valid conclusion to be drawn: Table 4 presents these data for the four figures. The figure of the premises here exerted a significant effect on the propensity to respond "No valid conclusion" (Friedman two-way analysis of variance, $\chi r^2 = 9.4.\ df = 3, p < 0.05$).

**Table 3**  **The percentage of correct responses for the four figures**

|  | Figure of premises | | | | |
|---|---|---|---|---|---|
|  | $\begin{smallmatrix}A-B\\B-C\end{smallmatrix}$ | $\begin{smallmatrix}B-A\\C-B\end{smallmatrix}$ | $\begin{smallmatrix}A-B\\C-B\end{smallmatrix}$ | $\begin{smallmatrix}B-A\\B-C\end{smallmatrix}$ | Overall |
| Premises with valid conclusions | (60)[a] 68 | (50) 58 | (53) 58 | (49) 69 | (53) 64 |
| Premises with no valid conclusions | (52) 66 | (53) 64 | (71) 75 | (74) 84 | (61) 71 |
| Overall | (55) 67 | (52) 62 | (64) 68 | (60) 76 | (58) 68 |

[a] Numbers in parentheses are from the first test.

**Table 4**  **The percentages of "no valid conclusion" responses to those premises with valid conclusions in the four figures[a]**

| Figure of premises | | | |
|---|---|---|---|
| $\begin{smallmatrix}A-B\\B-C\end{smallmatrix}$ | $\begin{smallmatrix}B-A\\C-B\end{smallmatrix}$ | $\begin{smallmatrix}A-B\\C-B\end{smallmatrix}$ | $\begin{smallmatrix}B-A\\B-C\end{smallmatrix}$ |
| $(n = 6)$ | $(n = 6)$ | $(n = 6)$ | $(n = 9)$ |
| (13) 7 | (21) 18 | (22) 22 | (23) 13 |

[a] Data in parentheses are from the first test: $n$ = number of premise pairs.

## The effect of mood

Since mood has long been known to have effects on syllogistic inference, our analysis of it in the present experiment will be brief. Table 5 presents the percentages of correct responses (from the second test) pooled in terms of the mood of the premises. It is evident from the degree of variation that mood has a marked effect on performance ($\chi r^2 = 71$, $df = 9$, $p < 0.001$, Friedman two-way analysis of variance). The critical point, of course, is that the difficulty of a syllogism depends on both its figure and mood. It is evident from our discussion of the IE and EI examples in the first section of results that neither figure nor mood alone is sufficient to predict difficulty. The two variables interact. Their interaction not only determines the difficulty of a problem but also the characteristic conclusions that it elicits.

**Table 5    The percentages of correct responses on the second test in terms of the mood of the premises**

| Mood of the second premise | Mood of the first premise | | | |
|---|---|---|---|---|
| | A | I | E | O |
| A | 69 | 68 | 51 | 39 |
| I | 76 | 83 | 60 | 81 |
| E | 50 | 54 | 71 | 74 |
| O | 54 | 89 | 78 | 94 |

## The effect of content and practice

In order to simplify the analysis of the results, we have assumed that performance on the problems was independent and that the content of the problems had no systematic effect upon performance. These assumptions are in general supported by the results, for example, the consistency of the figural effect. However, there was a distinct improvement in performance from the first test to the second test. There were 58% correct responses in the first test and 68% correct responses in the second test. Nineteen out of the 20 subjects improved performance, and an improvement was registered on 44 out of the 64 premise pairs. One striking differential effect of practice concerned those pairs of premises in the $\frac{B-A}{B-C}$ figure that permit a valid conclusion to be drawn: There was an improvement from 49% correct on the first test to 69% correct on the second test, with only two subjects failing to enhance their performance on these nine problems (Sign test, $p < 0.001$, two-tailed). Much of this improvement is due to a decline in the propensity to respond "No valid conclusion" (see Table 4).

Because the responses themselves proved to be extremely revealing as well as varying considerably in their accuracy, we shall report no extensive analysis of the latency data. It is difficult to treat the latencies statistically because of the diversity of responses to many pairs of premises. Moreover, there was a very reliable correlation between latency and accuracy: Those premises that yielded many correct answers also yielded them rapidly ($\tau = 0.37$, $p < 0.0001$, two-tailed).

## The analogical theory of reasoning with quantifiers

Because the present results cast considerable doubt on current theories, our major task is to provide a satisfactory explanation of syllogistic reasoning. This explanation must account both for invalid and valid deductions because competent adults make mistakes but are capable of rational thought under optimal circumstances. Indeed, without this ability, it is difficult to see how the logic of syllogisms could have been formulated in the first place.

The central assumption of the present theory (of which a preliminary account may be found in Johnson-Laird, 1975) is that syllogistic inference is based on an *analogical* representation of the premises that captures their logical properties within its structure. The theory postulates four stages in the process of inference:

(1) a semantic interpretation of the premises,
(2) an initial *heuristic* combination of the representations of the two premises,
(3) the formulation of a conclusion corresponding to the combined representation, and
(4) a *logical* test of the initial representation which may lead to the conclusion being modified or abandoned.

As a heuristic for generating potential conclusions, the theory postulates a bias toward forming connections during the process of combining the representations of the premises. The process of logical testing involves an attempt to break links that may have been invalidly forged in this way. We now consider the four stages in more detail.

### Stage 1: The interpretation of the premises

One clue to the mental representation of quantified assertions was provided by a subject in Experiment 1. When he was asked to describe how he had performed the task, he replied, referring to a specific premise, "I thought of all the little (sic) artists in the room and imagined that they all had beekeeper's hats on." This remark provided the germ of an idea for a new hypothesis about the semantic representation of quantified assertions: *A class is represented simply by thinking of an arbitrary number of its exemplars.* Thus, a subject represents a statement such as "All the artists are beekeepers," first by imagining an arbitrary number of artists, which he takes to represent a relevant class of them, and then by tagging each of them in some way as a beekeeper. Since there may be beekeepers who are not artists, he adds an arbitrary number of such beekeepers to his representation tagging them in some way as optional. The various elements in the representation may be vivid images or abstract or verbal items. What is important is not their phenomenal content but the relations between them. Accordingly, the representation of "All the artists are beekeepers" might have the following form:

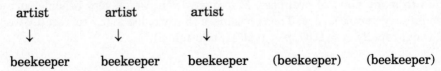

$$
\begin{array}{ccccc}
\text{artist} & \text{artist} & \text{artist} & & \\
\downarrow & \downarrow & \downarrow & & \\
\text{beekeeper} & \text{beekeeper} & \text{beekeeper} & \text{(beekeeper)} & \text{(beekeeper)}
\end{array}
$$

This is a direct analog of the logic of the assertion: There are an arbitrary number of artists tagged as beekeepers, and the parenthetical items represent the possibility of an arbitrary number of beekeepers who are not artists. The arrows stand for the semantic relation of class membership (each artist *is a* beekeeper); they are directional because we assume that it is relatively easy to traverse the link from artist to beekeeper but relatively difficult, though not impossible, to traverse it in the opposite direction. What we have in mind (and indeed actually exploit in a computer implementation of the theory) is a list-structure. The representation of each artist has stored with it the address of the corresponding representation of the beekeeper, and it is consequently easy to move from artist to beekeeper, but the representation of a beekeeper has no concomitant address of an artist, and the only way to move from beekeeper to artist is to search through all the artists until an appropriate link is found that leads back to the starting place.

Although arbitrary numbers of exemplars are involved, for convenience we will illustrate the various sorts of premise with a minimal number. An A premise, "All A are B," has the representation:

$$a \quad a$$
$$\downarrow \quad \downarrow$$
$$b \quad b \quad (b)$$

An I premise, "Some A are B," has the representation

$$a \quad (a)$$
$$\downarrow$$
$$b \quad (b)$$

which allows for the possibility that there are $a$'s which are not $b$'s and $b$'s which are not $a$'s.

An E premise, "No A are B," has the representation

$$a \quad (a)$$
$$\perp \quad \perp$$
$$b \quad b$$

where the stopped arrows indicate negative links. It is, of course, insufficient to represent negation merely by the absence of a link because subsequent processes might lead to a link being established: The broken link, $a \longrightarrow\!\!\mid b$ corresponds to a negative which prohibits a positive link between the $a$ and any $b$.

An O premise, "Some A are not B," has the representation

$$a \quad (a)$$
$$\perp \quad \downarrow$$
$$b \quad b$$

This allows for the possibility that there are $a$'s which are $b$'s, and for the possibility that no $a$'s are $b$'s: that is, when the optional $a$ is omitted, the $b$ drops out with it. There is evidence that "Some A are not B" is often taken to imply "Some A are B" (e.g., Johnson-Laird, 1970) though our representation leaves it as an option. In accordance with traditional terminology any term that has an optional element in its representation is "undistributed," otherwise it is "distributed": for example, the term A in "Some A are not B" is undistributed, whereas the term B is distributed.

### Stage 2: The heuristic combination of the representations of premises

Some heuristic is required in order to generate putative conclusions because logic cannot determine what conclusions to draw but at most whether a *given* conclusion is valid. There is evidence from other tasks for a bias toward making one-to-one matches and toward verification (see. e.g., Wason and Johnson-Laird, 1979, p. 241). Hence, we assume that in combining the premises there is a heuristic bias toward forming thoroughgoing connections between all the classes, that is, a bias toward linking up end items by way of middle items. Such premises as

> All the artists are beekeepers
> Some of the beekeepers are chemists

will be combined in such a way that the beekeepers who are chemists will be chosen from among those who are artists. Thus, the combined representation has the following sort of structure:

$$
\begin{array}{llll}
\text{All A are B} & a & a & \\
& \downarrow & \downarrow & \\
\text{Some B are } C & b & b & (b) \\
& \downarrow & & \\
& c & (c) &
\end{array}
$$

This representation readily leads to the invalid conclusion: "Some of the artists are chemists" (a conclusion that 12 subjects actually drew). With negative premises, we assume that there is the same bias toward trying to link up end items by way of the middle items, but in such a case the path will be a negative one. In general, where a path contains two positive links, it is positive; where it contains at least one negative link, it is negative; and any other path is indeterminate; for example, $a \rightarrow b$ (c), because the missing link could be positive or negative. The theory makes no assumptions about the order in which paths are constructed or assessed.

### Stage 3: The formulation of a conclusion

In order to formulate a conclusion, it is necessary to determine the nature of the paths between the end items in a representation. The logic of this process is transparent. Where there is at least one negative path, then the conclusion is of the form *Some X are nor Y*, unless there are only negative paths in which case it is of the form *No X are Y*. Otherwise, where there is at least one positive path, the conclusion is of the form *Some X are Y*, unless there are only positive paths in which case it is of the form *All X are Y.* In any other case, no valid conclusion can be drawn, that is, where there are only indeterminate paths.

Let us consider some specific examples of the initial combinations of premises and the conclusions that would be drawn from them. We have indicated the appropriate interpretation of each path in the following examples, using "+" for a positive path, "−" for a negative path, and "?" for an indeterminate path. The first example is a simple valid deduction, with one positive path and one indeterminate path:

$$
\begin{array}{cccccl}
 & & + & ? & & \\
\text{Some A are B} & & a & (a) & & \\
 & & \downarrow & & & \\
\text{All B are C} & & b & (b) & & \therefore \textit{Some A are C} \text{ (16 subjects)} \\
 & & \downarrow & \downarrow & & \therefore \textit{Some C are A} \text{ (3 subjects)} \\
 & & c & c & (c) & \\
 & & + & ? & &
\end{array}
$$

A strong figural effect is predicted because the paths are in a uniform direction; it is confirmed, and only three subjects produced the equally valid but nonoptimal conclusion. The next examples illustrate what happens when there is no optimal direction in which to establish a connection between the end items and consequently no predicted bias in the form of the conclusions:

$$
\begin{array}{cccccl}
 & & + & ? & & \\
\text{All B are A} & & a & a & (a) & \\
 & & \uparrow & \uparrow & & \therefore \textit{Some A are C} \text{ (11 subjects)} \\
\text{Some B are C} & & b & (b) & & \\
 & & \downarrow & & & \therefore \textit{Some C are A} \text{ (9 subjects)} \\
 & & c & (c) & & \\
 & & + & ? & &
\end{array}
$$

$$
\begin{array}{ccccccl}
 & & - & - & - & & \\
\text{No A are B} & & a & a & a & & \\
 & & \perp & \perp & \perp & & \therefore \textit{No A are C} \text{ (9 subjects)} \\
\text{All C are B} & & b & b & (b) & & \\
 & & \uparrow & \uparrow & & & \therefore \textit{No C are A} \text{ (6 subjects)} \\
 & & c & c & & & \\
 & & - & - & & &
\end{array}
$$

### Stage 4: The logical test of an initial representation

An initial representation is formed on the basis of a heuristic. Once it is formed, however, it is possible to bring logic to bear on it. If the heuristic is analogous to a bias toward verification, then the logical test is analogous to an attempt at falsification: It consists in trying to break the established paths between end items without doing violence to the meaning of the original premises. Thus, in the case of the example, "All the artists are beekeepers; some of the beekeepers are chemists," the initial representation tags one of the beekeepers who is an artist as a chemist in testing this representation, one can establish the link from a beekeeper that is *not* an artist to the chemists, and in this way destroy the path leading from artists to chemists. It follows that no conclusion can be read off from the modified representation. Hence, the initial representation

|  |  | + | ? |  |
|---|---|---|---|---|
| All A are B |  | $a$ | $a$ |  |
|  |  | ↓ | ↓ |  |
| Some B are C |  | $b$ | $b$ | $(b)$ |
|  |  | ↓ |  |  |
|  |  | $c$ | $(c)$ |  |
|  |  | + | ? |  |

is modified as the result of the logical test to

|  |  | ? | ? |  |
|---|---|---|---|---|
| All A are B |  | $a$ | $a$ |  |
|  |  | ↓ | ↓ |  |
| Some B are C |  | $b$ | $b$ | $(b)$ |
|  |  |  | ↓ |  |
|  |  | $c$ |  | $(c)$ |
|  |  | ? | ? |  |

from which no valid conclusion can be derived

The principles governing the testing of negative syllogisms reflect the same basic idea. The initial bias is toward establishing negative links, and testing consists in trying to break them or to establish a positive link where a negative one had prevailed, without doing violence to the meaning of the premises or creating a contradiction. Here is a typical example where an initial representation gives rise to a fallacious inference:

|  |  | − | − |
|---|---|---|---|
| No A are B |  | $a$ | $a$ |
|  |  | ⊥ | ⊥ |

No B are C $\qquad$ $b$ $\qquad$ $b$ $\qquad$ ∴ No A are C (five subjects)

$\qquad$ $\perp$ $\qquad$ $\perp$

$\qquad$ $c$ $\qquad$ $c$ $\qquad$ [∴ No C are A (two subjects)]

$\qquad$ $-$ $\qquad$ $-$

But such a representation readily permits the establishment of positive links incompatible with the initial conclusions:

$$\left(\begin{array}{cc} a & a \\ \downarrow & \downarrow \\ b & b \\ \downarrow & \downarrow \\ c & c \end{array}\right) \quad \therefore \textit{No valid conclusion (13 subjects)}$$

A truly rational subject may have to pursue a vigorous search in order to establish the correct conclusion to a pair of premises. Consider, for instance, what could happen with premises of the form: "Some A are B," "No C are B". Their initial interpretation may lead a particular subject to the following conclusion, reading the conclusion off from $c$ to $a$:

Some A are B $\qquad$ $a$ $\qquad$ $(a)$

$\qquad\qquad\qquad\qquad$ $\downarrow$

No C are B $\qquad$ $b$ $\qquad$ $(b)$ $\qquad$ ∴ No C are A

$\qquad\qquad\qquad\qquad$ $\top$ $\qquad$ $\top$

$\qquad\qquad\qquad\qquad$ $c$ $\qquad$ $c$

A test of the initial representation establishes its invalidily since both paths now become positive:

$$\begin{array}{ccc} a & (a) & (a) \\ \downarrow & & \\ b & (b) & \\ \top & \top & \\ c & c & \end{array}$$

The really prudent subject, however, would do well not simply to rely on this test, but also to try to construct a conclusion in the converse direction.

The initial representation above suggests: No A are C, but the test modifies this to:

$$\left.\begin{array}{cc} a & (a) \\ \downarrow & \\ b & (b) \\ \top & \top \\ c & c \end{array}\right) \quad \therefore \textit{Some A are not C}$$

Try as one will, this conclusion cannot be falsified. Thus, the correct answer may only be obtained after a succession of tests.

### *The logical status of the analogical theory*

The heuristic process embodied in the analogical theory is plainly outside logic. However, the test phase introduces a logical assessment of the validity of putative conclusions: If the tests are properly carried out, then any conclusion that remains will invariably be a logically valid one. Hence, the essence of the theory is that subjects are very good at drawing conclusions on heuristic grounds but generally less efficient at submitting them to logical tests.

As part of the process of developing the analogical theory, a number of different versions of it were modelled in the form of computer programs in a list-processing language, POP-2. The final model implemented a number of simplifications of the theory purely for ease of computation. However, quite unexpectedly, these modifications threw some light on the status of the theory and on the origins of the logical theory of syllogisms.

In specifying the tests to be carried out on initial representations it proved to be convenient to consider syllogisms in three basic categories: those with affirmative premises, those with an affirmative and a negative premise, and those with negative premises. With affirmative premises, it turns out that whenever one path can be broken, all of them can be broken. There was an extremely simple implementation of this principle: The relevant procedure simply looked for a middle item that was not linked to any end items, and whenever such an item was found the program indicated that no valid conclusion could be drawn. This procedure sacrifices psychological plausibility for the sake of simplicity: It cuts out a whole series of redundant processes that are likely to occur when logically naive individuals reason. However, this abstraction from actual behavior corresponds directly to one of the traditional laws of the syllogism: The middle term must be distributed at least once in a valid syllogism (see Cohen & Nagel, 1934, p. 79). With an affirmative and a negative premise, such as "Some A are B" and "No C are B," there is a similar shortcut. A prudent subject ought to test one conclusion and then, if it is invalid, test its converse. Rather than go through the whole complicated procedure illustrated above, the program merely checked whether any term distributed in a conclusion was also distributed in the representation of the premises. If there was no such correspondence, the conclusion was invalid. This procedure also corresponds to a traditional rule for syllogisms: No term may be distributed in the conclusion which is not distributed in the premises. With negative premises, it was also necessary to specify a process of forming links between the end items. The principle implemented was simply to test for the presence of a path made up of two negative links since its existence is sufficient to establish the possibility of connecting the end items with a positive link. This shortcut amounts to the traditional rule of rejecting any conclusion drawn from two negative premises. Thus, we recovered all the major laws of the syllogism merely by simplifying the operation of the psychological principles. It may not be too farfetched to imagine that the original discoverers of those laws relied in part on analogous reflections on their own processes of thought.

## An evaluation of the analogical theory

### The predictions of the theory

The analogical theory was developed in order to account for the main sorts of response that were made in the two experiments. In fact, the theory predicts a total of 213 different responses to the 64 sorts of problems, an average of 3.3 responses per problem out of the nine possible responses, and the vast majority of responses that subjects made are within this set (92% of the first test and 95% of the second test in Experiment 2; see the tables in the Appendix). The theory predicts 23 responses that were not observed, but 16 of them were predicted to be relatively rare because they were incompatible with the figure of the premises.

In order to evaluate the theory, we shall consider initially the predictions that can be based on it about the relative difficulty of responding to premises correctly. The first basis from which such predictions derive is that if an initial representation is not tested logically a conclusion based on it may be erroneous. With some premises, the process of testing does not lead to any modifications: Such problems are predicted to be relatively easy. With other premises, the process of testing does lead to a modified representation, and hence a modified conclusion: Such problems are predicted to be relatively difficult. This difference was reliably confirmed by the results of the experiments. On the second test of Experiment 2, for example, 80.4% of responses to problems where a test leads to no modification were correct, whereas only 46.5% of responses to premises where a test leads to a modified conclusion were correct; the difference was apparent in the results of all 20 subjects.

The second basis from which predictions about difficulty can be derived is the figural bias created by the directional links. The bias predicts differences in accuracy within the set of problems that are unmodified by logical testing. The easiest of these problems will be those where the conclusions can be read off the representation in either direction (their converses are valid) and those problems where the conclusions can be read off in only one direction (their converses are invalid) but in accord with the figural bias. The hardest of these problems will be those where the conclusion can be read off in only one direction but with a figure that has no bias. The percentages of correct responses were in accord with this prediction: 88.1 and 85% versus 62.5%, respectively, on the second test of Experiment 2 (Sign test, $p < 0.035$). Figural bias also leads to a prediction about accuracy within the set of problems where the logical test leads to a modified conclusion. The easiest of these problems will be those where the conclusion can be read off in accord with the figural bias, slightly harder will be those problems where there is no figural bias, and the hardest will be those where the conclusion can be read off only in the direction opposite to the figural bias. The trend was in accord with this prediction: 73.3, 50.8, and 20.0% correct responses, respectively, on the second test of Experiment 2 (Page's $L = 266.5$, $p < 0.01$).

Comparable support for the theory is evident in the data for those premises that do not permit a valid conclusion to be drawn. It is plausible to assume that the easier it is to form paths the harder it will be to appreciate that there is no valid conclusion. Hence, premises without a figural bias will be easier than premises with a figural bias. The results of the experiments bear out the prediction: 78.2% correct responses to unbiased premises, and 64.8% correct responses to biased premises (a difference reflected in the performance of 18 out of the 20 subjects). Likewise, it should be easier to destroy an erroneous initial representation when there are fewer paths to be broken, that is, when premises are particular rather than universal. With affirmative premises, the percentages of correct responses in the second test were as follows: 82.5% where both premises were particular, 47.5% where one premise was particular, and 40% where neither premise was particular (Page's $L = 260$, $p < 0.05$). With one affirmative and one negative premise, the percentages of correct responses were 85% correct where both premises were particular, and 30% where one premise was particular (a difference reflected in the performance of 19 out of the 20 subjects). With negative premises, the percentages of correct responses were 93.8% where both premises were particular, 75.6% where one premise was particular, and 71.3% where neither premise was particular (Page's $L = 263$, $p < 0.01$). The relative ease of problems with two negative premises suggests that some subjects may have learned to interpret two negative links in a path as indeterminate, the shortcut implemented in the program.

The only wholly independent data available to test the predictions of the theory are results obtained by Mazzocco, Legrenzi, and Roncato (1974). These investigators required subjects to complete symbolic syllogisms by adding a second missing premise from a multiple choice of alternatives. For example, subjects were asked to complete the syllogism:

All A's are B's

. . .
_____

∴ No A's are C's

As a matter of fact, 72% of the subjects selected "No B are C" and only 20% of the subjects selected "No C are B"; both answers are correct, but the theory predicts a figural bias toward the first one. This result is typical: As Mazzocco *et al.* report, where the given premise has the middle term as its predicate, 73% of the subjects selected a premise in which the middle term was the subject, thus creating a figure of the form

$\begin{matrix} A - B \\ B - C \end{matrix}$ , but there was no such bias where the given premise has the middle term as its subject. Although providing a missing premise is rather different from drawing a conclusion from given premises, the analogical theory is readily extended to cope with it.

We assume that a subject represents the given premise, and then attempts to add to it links appropriate to form the path demanded by the conclusion. For example, with the problem

All A's are B's

. . .
_____

∴ Some A's are not C's.

the first step is to represent the given premise

$$
\begin{array}{ccc}
\text{All A's are B's} & a & a \\
& \downarrow & \downarrow \\
& b & b \quad (b)
\end{array}
$$

and the second step is to construct the path(s) required by the conclusion:

$$
\begin{array}{ccc}
& a & a \\
& \downarrow & \downarrow \\
\therefore \text{ Some A's are not C's} \quad b & b & \quad (b) \\
& \bot & \downarrow \\
& c & (c)
\end{array}
$$

It is then necessary to formulate a premise corresponding to the new link(s): Some B's are not C's. However, the initial addition must be submitted to exactly the same process of logical testing that occurs in ordinary syllogistic reasoning in order to ensure that the new premise guarantees the validity of the given conclusion. In the present case, the test consists in establishing that the negative path can be broken without doing violence to the premises:

$$
\begin{array}{ccc}
\text{All A's are B's} & a & a \\
& \downarrow & \downarrow \\
\text{Some B's are not C's} \quad b & b & \quad (b) \\
& \downarrow & \bot \\
& c & c
\end{array}
$$

It is accordingly necessary to strengthen the negative pathways,

$$
\begin{array}{ccc}
a & a & \\
\downarrow & \downarrow & \\
b & b & (b) \\
\bot & \bot & \bot \\
c & c & c \quad,
\end{array}
$$

and this modification gives rise to the correct premise: *No B's are C's*. Problems of this sort in which an initial response is modified as a result of the logical test are predicted, of course, to be more difficult than those where the test has no effect on the initial response. In the present example, 32 out of the 50 subjects selected "Some B's are not C's" as the missing premise, and only two subjects made the correct selection of *"No B's are C's."* In general, there were 63.2% correct responses for the 10 problems unaffected by the logical test, 12.9% correct responses for the 17 problems where the test demands a modified response, and a minimal overlap between the two distributions.

There are, of course, other ways in which the analogical theory could be tested, and it is intended to investigate performance under time pressure in order to determine whether the conclusions that subjects draw correspond to those of the initial representations postulated by the theory. The final way in which we shall assess the theory is to compare it with other conjectures about syllogistic inference.

### A comparison of the analogical theory with other approaches

One of the most influential hypotheses about difficulties in syllogistic inference concerns the mood of a syllogism. The so-called "atmosphere" hypothesis proposed by Woodworth and Sells (1935) and Sells (1936) suggests that people are predisposed to accept a conclusion that is congruent in mood with the premises. The theory has been succinctly formulated by Begg and Denny (1969): Whenever at least one premise is negative, the most frequently accepted conclusion will be negative; whenever at least one premise is particular, the most frequently accepted conclusion will likewise be particular: otherwise the bias is towards affirmative and universal conclusions. Revlis (1975a,b) has developed an information-processing model that allows errors to occur in working out the joint atmosphere of the two premises. It also assumes that if the atmosphere of the premises is incongruent with a given conclusion, a subject responds that the syllogism is invalid, or else considers the next possible conclusion in a multiple-choice test. The heuristic stage of the analogical theory yields initial conclusions that happen to be largely in accord with the atmosphere of the premises. However, the two theories diverge in at least four crucial ways.

First, the atmosphere hypothesis cannot even in principle explain the figural effect.

Second, the atmosphere hypothesis is unable to account for those conclusions that do not accord with the atmosphere of premises. For example, consider the results with the following premises:

All B are A
No B are C
_____

∴ No A are C        (five subjects)
∴ No C are A        (three subjects)
- - - - - - - - - - - - - - - - - - - - - - - - - -
∴ *Some A are not C*        (seven subjects)
∴ No valid conclusion        (four subjects)

The atmosphere hypothesis predicts only the results above the dotted line; if a principle of caution is introduced then it can be made to predict *"Some A are not C"* but only at the cost of also predicting "Some C are not A." The four responses above are precisely those predicted by the analogical theory.

Third, when a subject draws a conclusion in his own words, then according to the atmosphere hypothesis he should never respond "No valid conclusion" because there is always a possible conclusion congruent with the atmosphere of the premises. Hence, the hypothesis is never able to explain the response, "No valid conclusion." The analogical theory predicts this response even in certain cases where a valid conclusion does exist (as in the example above): The results confirm that such responses are made.

Finally, it is well established that the apparent effects of atmosphere are invariably greater when a conclusion is valid than when it is invalid (see Sells, 1936; Revlis, 1975a,b; and the present results). The atmosphere hypothesis cannot, of course, explain such a phenomenon. In our view, it arises because most valid conclusions happen to be in accord with the atmosphere of the premises, and because subjects have recourse to an inferential mechanism that enables them both to make valid deductions and to refrain from drawing conclusions where none is warranted.

Another influential conjecture about the source of errors in syllogistic inference is Chapman and Chapman's (1959) theory of probabilistic inference. These authors argued that people often invalidly convert A and O statements; that is to say, "All A are B" is taken to imply "All B are A" and "Some A are not B" is taken to imply "Some B are not A." Such conversions can yield true conclusions in everyday life, and they could explain why the following syllogism is sometimes accepted as valid:

$$\text{All A are B}$$
$$\underline{\text{All C are B}}$$
$$\therefore \text{ All C are A}$$

According to the Chapmans, subjects also assume on similar probabilistic grounds that entities with a predicate in common are likely to be the same sort of thing, for example.

$$\text{Some A are B}$$
$$\underline{\text{Some C are B}}$$
$$\therefore \text{ Some C are A },$$

and that entities that lack a common predicate are likely *not* to be the same sort of thing, for example,

$$\text{Some A are B}$$
$$\underline{\text{Some C are not B}}$$
$$\therefore \text{ Some C are not A }.$$

Since the Chapmans investigated only invalid syllogisms, we cannot be entirely sure what their predictions would be for premises that permit a valid deduction. However, they do make clear predictions for 44 of our problems, comprising 37 premise pairs that permit no valid conclusions and seven premise pairs that permit valid conclusions only in unorthodox figures. The predicted response was the most frequent one in our data for only seven out of the 44 problems. Hence, their own corroboration of the theory may largely depend upon the use of symbolic materials and a multiple-choice test limited to conclusions in orthodox figures. A more explicit version of the illicit conversion hypothesis has recently been proposed by Revlis (1975a,b). Like his model based on the atmosphere effect, this model involves some assumptions additional to those proposed by the original theorists. However, even in this revised form, the conjecture does not receive very convincing support from the results of Revlis's or our experiment.

However, there is little doubt that subjects do sometimes argue from an A or an O premise to its converse, particularly with symbolic materials (Wilkins, 1928; Sells,

1936). Why should this be so? We assume that such errors arise from the forgetting of the optional unlinked elements in a representation (or even perhaps a failure to include them in the first place). Thus, an A premise of the form "All A are B" may be erroneously represented as

$$a \qquad a$$
$$\downarrow \qquad \downarrow$$
$$b \qquad b$$

from which the converse, "All B are A," can be derived. Likewise, the erroneous representation of "Some A are not B" readily yields the converse assertions. However, the fact that subjects will accept the converse of an A or an O premise as valid provides no direct evidence for a process of conversion, licit or illicit, in syllogistic inference. Moreover, if such a process readily occurred, it would eliminate the figural effect. A figure of the form $\begin{array}{c} A - B \\ B - C \end{array}$ should be just as likely to yield a conclusion of the form C — A as one of the form A — C. In developing the computer model of the analogical theory, we did at one time devise a program in which optional unlinked elements were "forgotten"; while such failures may indeed be one source of human error, they will not alone suffice to explain the experimental results. One decisive reason that led us to abandon this variant model is that it predicts far too many errors that do not occur. For example, with the premises

> All A are B
> Some C are not B,

it predicts the fallacious conclusion, No C are A. This and other similar errors for a variety of moods are seldom made.

In the case of those items that the Chapmans regarded as crucial tests between their account and the atmosphere predictions, our data fail to substantiate either approach decisively. Consider, for instance, the fate of the respective predictions for premises in the EI and IE moods, for example,

> No B are A
> Some C are B

| | | |
|---|---|---|
| Atmosphere predictions | ∴ Some A are not C | (no subjects) |
| | ∴ *Some C are not A* | (14 subjects) |
| Probabilistic predictions | ∴ No A are C | (no subjects) |
| | ∴ No C are A | (2 subjects) |

Evidently, the atmosphere theory fails to explain the bias toward *Some C are not* A, and the probabilistic theory predicts only a small minority of responses. The analogical theory, however, predicts two main responses: No C are A and *Some C are not A*. It appears to offer a more powerful explanation of syllogistic inference than either of these earlier theories.

The first explicit attempt to specify the mental processes involved in syllogistic inference is Erickson's (1974) set-theoretic model. According to Erickson, the premises are represented in forms equivalent to Euler circles. Thus, the representation of "All A are B" involves two separate mental diagrams: a circle representing set A included within a circle representing set B, and, since the two sets may be coextensive, a circle representing set A coincident with a circle representing set B. The representation of "Some A are B" requires four separate mental diagrams: set A overlapping set B, set B included in set A, set A included in set B, and set A co-extensive with set B. It is, of course, unlikely that subjects will be careful enough to consider all these possibilities, and Erickson assumes that such a failing is one source of error in inference. In particular, he assumes that "All A are B" is often treated as simply denoting that set A and set B are co-extensive. Likewise, since the combination of the representations of premises can present a considerable combinatorial problem, Erickson considers an alternative hypothesis in which subjects construct only one actual combination of representations selected at random from the total number of possibilities (each of which is assumed to be equiprobable). This procedure will invariably come up with a conclusion, and hence the model cannot predict a response of "No valid conclusion." When subjects formulate a conclusion to characterize the results of this process, they are supposed to select statements that agree with the mood of the premises; that is to say, Erickson assumes that the atmosphere effect operates at this stage. This assumption is necessary in order to account for the fact that, if not all combinations of premises are explicitly constructed, there will be occasions where a set overlap needs to be interpreted as "Some A are C" and other occasions where it needs to be interpreted as "Some A are not C."

A set-theoretic interpretation of quantified assertions has been explored by a number of psychologists (e.g., Johnson-Laird, 1970; Ceraso & Provitera, 1971; Neimark & Chapman, 1975). We find certain aspects of Erickson's (1974) model extremely plausible; indeed, the theory was put forward informally by Wason and Johnson-Laird (1972, p. 56–7). However, there are several phenomena that would seem to count against it and in favor of the analogical theory.

First, the fact that subjects readily respond "No valid conclusion" counts against Erickson's simple model in which only one combination of representations is constructed. The fact that they also make this response to premises that allow a valid conclusion counts against the full-scale model in which all combinations are constructed. Both these sorts of responses are, of course, predicted by the analogical theory.

Second, the figural effect obtained in the present experiments is a considerable embarrassment to set-theoretic representations such as Euler circles. They are symmetrical: The representation of "Some A are C" is identical to that of "Some C are A," and similarly the representation of "No A are C" is identical to that of "No C are A." The representations are quite without the directional component necessary to predict biases in the form of conclusions, and, at the very least, the theory would need to be supplemented in some way in order to account for the figural effect.

One such an assumption would be provided by Huttenlocher's finding of the importance of the grammatical subject in a variety of tasks (see, e.g., Huttenlocher and Weiner, 1971). Obviously, in the case of $\begin{array}{c}A-B\\B-C\end{array}$ premises only the A term can be maintained as the subject of the conclusion, in the case of $\begin{array}{c}B-A\\C-B\end{array}$ premises only the C term can be maintained as the subject of the conclusion, and in the case of the other two figures there can be no bias. Alternatively, the figural effect could be a consequence of the operations in working memory required to set up the initial representation of premises. In the spirit of Hunter's (1957) account of three-term series problems, we could argue that with $\begin{array}{c}A-B\\B-C\end{array}$ premises a subject encodes the first premise and can immediately add on to it a representation of the second premise: A — B, . . . , B — C, with a resulting bias toward a conclusion of the form A — C. It would be slightly harder to draw a conclusion from $\begin{array}{c}B-A\\C-B\end{array}$ premises because their middle terms are not adjacent, and so it would be necessary to recall the first premise to working memory to combine it with the second premise already there: C — B, . . . , B — A, with a resulting bias toward a conclusion of the form C — A. There are two alternative strategies for the remaining figures, and so there might well be no marked bias in their conclusions. These two explanations are not incompatible with each other. Although they could equally well be combined with the analogical or the set-theoretic theory, their addition to the latter is an *ad hoc* maneuver designed to save it from falsification, whereas their addition to the former is not really necessary.

Third, the set-theoretic theory lacks a suitable heuristic to make accurate predictions about performance when subjects draw their own conclusions from premises. Once again, we could suggest the following sort of principles: With affirmative premises, ensure that the intersections between sets are never empty, and with negative premises, ensure that the intersections between sets are always empty.

In short, it might appear that the analogical theory could be based on an Eulerian representation. However, the translation offers no gain in theoretical power and a considerable loss in flexibility. The analogical representation can easily accommodate inferences involving particular individuals:

Arthur is a Briton $\quad\quad a$

$\downarrow$

All Britons are Christians $\quad b \quad\quad (b) \quad\quad \therefore$ Arthur is a Christian

$\quad\quad\quad\quad\quad\quad\quad\quad\quad \downarrow \quad\quad \downarrow$

$\quad\quad\quad\quad\quad\quad\quad\quad\quad c \quad\quad c \quad\quad (c)$

It can accommodate inferences involving quasinumerical quantifiers:

Most fascists are authoritarians $\quad f \quad f \quad f \quad f \quad f$

$\quad\quad\quad\quad\quad\quad\quad\quad\quad\quad\quad \downarrow \quad \downarrow \quad \downarrow \quad \downarrow$

Most authoritarians are dogmatic *a*     *a*     *a*     *a*     (*a*)     (*a*)

             ↓   ↓     ↓   ↓

            *d*  *d*    *d*  *d*  (*d*)

What counts as a valid inference in this domain is more problematic because it has been relatively neglected by logicians (but see Altham, 1971). Yet it is clear that people readily make such inferences and that their knowledge of the world helps them to determine the relative sizes of classes. Thus, in the previous example the likely conclusion is, "Many fascists are dogmatic," whereas the following premises, superficially of the same form, are unlikely to elicit any conclusion: "Most geniuses are madmen." "Most madmen are in asylums." The relative sizes of the classes are entirely compatible with the representation:

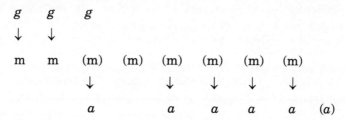

The analogical representation also accommodates multiply quantified assertions:

All the boys kissed some of the girls

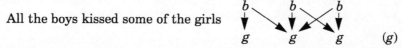

This representation demands multiple links each denoting the appropriate relation, and it cannot be translated into Euler circles. Subjects who are logically naive run into some difficulty with such assertions, but they can interpret them and make inferences from them (Johnson-Laird, 1969a,b). The analogical theory accordingly provides a uniform method of representing quantified sentences, including ones that cannot be represented by Euler circles.

### Conclusions

There are a variety of metaphors for human deductive reasoning. At one extreme, there is the idea in artificial intelligence of a uniform proof procedure in which all deductions are handled by a single rule of inference applied to assertions in a standardized format. This approach may be intelligent, but it is extremely artificial. At the other extreme there is the idea of expressing every general assertion as a rule of inference couched in the form of a procedure. Such "theorems," most notably exploited in Carl Hewitt's problem-solving theory PLANNER (see Winograd, 1972) can even take into account information specific to their content, for example, hints as to how to achieve an inferential goal. There is also the intermediary notion of so-called "natural deduction" systems in logic in which a number of content-free rules of inference are introduced in a way that permits intuitiveness to take precedence over parsimony. There can be little doubt that human beings operate with both a logic resembling a natural deduction system and content-specific rules of inference of a sort postulated in PLANNER (see Johnson-Laird, 1975, for arguments in support of both suggestions).

The theory of syllogistic inference that we have proposed differs in a number of respects from all of these approaches. It contains, of course, a simple heuristic for generating putative conclusions, a matter that falls outside the concerns of formal logic. The heuristic is epitomized by Forster's motto quoted at the head of this paper, though the connections that concerned him were of a different sort. Once a putative conclusion has been generated, it could be evaluated by a system with a single resolution rule of inference or a system with a variety of rules of inference. However, when we consider the testing procedure of the present model of syllogistic inference, it is not easy to classify it in these terms. It contains neither a single rule of inference nor a whole set of them: Rather, the rules are inherent in the way it models the entities and relations involved in a syllogism. Although it is hard to decompose this system into separate rules, its performance *can* be captured by a set of rules, the traditional rules of syllogistic inference. However, it would be misleading to think of it in these terms. We regard the difficulty, or at least lack of perspicuity, in matching it to rules of inference as an argument in favor of its psychological plausibility. If human reasoning followed a simple set of principles, the task of specifying them should have been solved long ago.

## Appendix

The detailed predictions of the analogical theory are set out in Tables 6–9, together with the results of Experiment 2. The upper pair of statements in each cell are the theory's predictions about the initial conclusions. The statements below the dotted line correspond to the conclusion, if any, forthcoming after the logical testing process. Thus, in the case of the problem "Some A are B" and "No C are B," one finds the following results

| | | |
|---|---|---|
| No A are C | (6) | 1 |
| No C are A | (3) | 7 |
| | | |
| *Some A are not C* | (3) | 7 |
| No valid conclusion | (5) | 4 , |

where *"Some A are not C"* is the result of testing "No A are C," and "No valid conclusion is the result of testing "No C are A". Numbers in parentheses correspond to the numbers of subjects making the response on the first test; other numbers are the results of the second test. Conclusions that are predicted to be relatively rare are included in parentheses; valid conclusions are italicized. In certain cases a representation is susceptible to more than one modification, for example,

|  | + | + |  |  |  |
|---|---|---|---|---|---|
| All A are B | a | a |  |  |  |
|  | ↓ | ↓ |  |  |  |
| All C are B | b | b | (b) | ∴ All A are C | (2) 2 subjects |
|  | ↑ | ↑ |  |  |  |
|  | c | c |  | ∴ All C are A | (3) 5 subjects |
|  | + | + |  |  |  |
|  | ? | + |  | - - - - - - - - - - - - - - - - - - - - - |  |
|  | a | a |  |  |  |
|  | ↓ | ↓ |  |  |  |
|  | b | b | (b) | ∴ Some A are C | (4) 3 subjects |
|  |  | ↑ | ↑ |  |  |
|  | c | c |  | ∴ Some C are A | (1) 1 subject |
|  |  | + | ? | - - - - - - - - - - - - - - - - - - - - - |  |
|  | ? | ? |  |  |  |
|  | a | a |  |  |  |
|  | ↓ | ↓ |  |  |  |
|  | b | b | (b) (b) ∴ | *No valid conclusion:* | |
|  |  |  |  | (9) 8 subjects | |
|  |  | ↑ | ↑ |  |  |
|  |  | c | c |  |  |
|  |  | ? | ? |  |  |

In such cases, the data within a cell are divided into three. The relatively few unpredicted responses that occurred with any frequency are preceded by an asterisk in the tables.

**Table 6**  The frequencies of the conclusions for A — B, B — C premises in Experiment 2, together with the mean latencies for the correct responses[a]

| Second premise | First premise A | First premise I | First premise E | First premise O |
|---|---|---|---|---|
| **A** | All A are C (16) 17<br>(Some C are A) (0) 1<br>*Some A are C (3) 1<br>(3.8) 2.9 | Some A are C (18) 16<br>(Some C are A) (1) 3<br>(4.7) 5.7 | No A are C (9) 11<br>(Some C are not A) (5) 2<br>(9.5) 10.2 | Some A are not C (5) 9<br>(Some C are not A) (2) 1<br>(12) 9 |
| **I** | Some A are C (13) 12<br>(Some C are A) (0) 0<br> · · · · ·<br>No valid conclusion (7) 8 | Some A are C (7) 3<br>(Some C are A) (0) 0<br> · · · · ·<br>No valid conclusion (13) 16<br>(4.7) 5.7 | No A are C (6) 3<br>(Some C are not A) (3) 0<br> · · · · ·<br>No valid conclusion (9) 16<br>(22.7) 8.9 | No A are C (1) 0<br>(No C are A) (0) 0<br>Some A are not C (7) 4<br>(Some C are not A) (1) 0<br> · · · · ·<br>No valid conclusion (14) 19 |
| **E** | No A are C (14) 17<br>(No C are A) (1) 1<br> · · · · ·<br>No valid conclusion (13) 16<br>(11.5) 4.4 | Some A are not C (15) 17<br>(No C are A) (3) 1<br> · · · · ·<br>No valid conclusion (3) 1<br>(3.1) 1.9 | *Some A are C (6) 8<br>(Some C are not A) (3) 0<br> · · · · ·<br>No valid conclusion (9) 16<br>(17.4) 10.3 | Some A are not C (4) 5<br>(Some C are not A) (0) 1<br> · · · · ·<br>No valid conclusion (9) 13<br>(8.4) 7.1 |
| **O** | Some A are not C (10) 4<br>(Some C are not A) (0) 0<br>(9.0) 6.7<br> · · · · ·<br>No valid conclusion (6) 5<br>(9.2) 8.2 | No A are C (2) 2<br>(No C are A) (0) 0<br>Some A are not C (10) 4<br>(Some C are not A) (0) 0<br> · · · · ·<br>No valid conclusion (10) 16<br>(7.1) 7.1 | No A are C (10) 5<br>(No C are A) (0) 2<br>Some A are not C (4) 5<br>(Some C are not A) (0) 1<br> · · · · ·<br>No valid conclusion (9) 13<br>(16.4) 6.5 | No A are C (1) 0<br>(No C are A) (0) 0<br>Some A are not C (4) 0<br>(Some C are not A) (0) 0<br> · · · · ·<br>No valid conclusion (14) 14<br>(11.7) 8.2 |

(14.5) 10.9        (7.7) 8.2

[a] Correct responses are italicized, and numbers in parentheses are from the first test and the other numbers are from the second test. Mean latencies are given in seconds. The results are set out in terms of the prediction of a model. The upper pair of statements in each cell corresponds to initial responses, and the statements below the dotted line correspond to the respective results, if any, of submitting the initial responses to the tests specified by the model. Responses that are predicted to be rare are included in parentheses. An asterisk indicates a response not predicted by the model: Only those such responses that occurred more than twice on a given test have been included, and hence the frequencies in a cell do not invariably sum to 20 (the number of subjects tested).

408

**Table 7** The frequencies of the conclusions for $\dfrac{B-A}{C-B}$ premises in Experiment 2, together with the mean latencies for the correct responses[a]

|  | First premise | | | |
|---|---|---|---|---|
| **Second premise** | **A** | **I** | **E** | **O** |
| **A** | All C are A (15) 17<br>(Some A are C) (2) 0<br>*Some C are A (2) 2<br>(5.7) 5.7 | Some C are A (14) 12<br>(Some A are C) (2) 2<br>No valid conclusion (3) 6<br>(4.4) 6.6 | No C are A (15) 13<br>(No A are C) (0) 3<br>*No valid conclusion (1) 3<br>(7.2) 7.2 | Some C are not A (15) 15<br>(Some A are not C) (0) 0<br>No valid conclusion (3) 3<br>(13.7) 10.1 |
| **I** | Some C are A (15) 18<br>(Some A are C) (3) 0<br>*No valid conclusion (2) 2<br>(6.3) 6.1 | Some C are A (9) 3<br>(Some A are C) (1) 1<br>No valid conclusion (9) 15<br>(5.5) 6.0 | No C are A (3) 2<br>(No A are C) (0) 0<br>Some C are not A (10) 14<br>No valid conclusion (5) 3<br>(9.8) 8.9 | Some C are not A (8) 3<br>(Some A are not C) (0) 1<br>No valid conclusion (9) 16<br>(7.6) 5.3 |
| **E** | No C are A (12) 9<br>(No A are C) (2) 2<br>No valid conclusion (4) 6<br>(Some A are not C) (0) 0<br>*Some C are not A (2) 3<br>(—) (—) | No C are A (4) 3<br>(No A are C) (0) 0<br>No valid conclusion (12) 8<br>(Some A are not C) (2) 5<br>*Some C are not A (2) 4<br>(38.8) 11.7 | No C are A (6) 3<br>(No A are C) (1) 2<br>No valid conclusion (11) 14<br>(11.9) 8.6 | Some C are not A (4) 2<br>(Some A are not C) (0) 0<br>No valid conclusion (13) 17<br>(15.5) 13.2 |
| **O** | Some C are not A (11) 11<br>(Some A are not C) (0) 0<br>No valid conclusion (8) 7<br>(9.2) 10.2 | Some C are not A (3) 2<br>(Some A are not C) (0) 0<br>No valid conclusion (16) 18<br>(7.2) 7.3 | No C are A (0) 0<br>(No A are C) (0) 0<br>Some C are not A (3) 5<br>(Some A are not C) (0) 0<br>No valid conclusion (16) 15<br>(12.6) 7.3 | Some C are not A (0) 3<br>(Some A are not C) (2) 1<br>No valid conclusion (17) 16<br>(7.7) 4.6 |

[a] See footnote $a$ of Table 6 for explanation of presentation of data.

**Table 8**  The frequencies of the conclusions for A — B / C — B premises in Experiment 2, together with the mean latencies for the correct responses[a]

| Second premise | First premise | | | |
|---|---|---|---|---|
| | A | I | E | O |
| **A** | All A are C (2) 2<br>All C are A (3) 5<br>Some A are C (4) 3<br>Some C are A (1) 1<br>*No valid conclusion* (9) 8<br>(7.9) 3.6 | Some A are C (4) 5<br>Some C are A (2) 5<br>*No valid conclusion* (13) 9<br>(7.2) 13.5 | No A are C (9) 9<br>No C are A (11) 6<br>*Some C are not A (0) 3<br>No valid conclusion<br>(11.7) 8.9 | Some A are not C (7) 5<br>Some C are not A (2) 6<br>*No valid conclusion* (7) 9<br>(9.6) 7.3 |
| **I** | Some A are C (4) 1<br>Some C are A (5) 4<br>*No valid conclusion* (11) 15<br>(12.1) 6.6 | Some A are C (4) 3<br>Some C are A (1) 0<br>*No valid conclusion* (15) 17<br>(3.6) 4.2 | No A are C (2) 1<br>No C are A (4) 1<br>No valid conclusion (6) 4<br>*Some C are not A* (7) 13<br>(8.0) 8.4 | No A are C (2) 2<br>No C are A (0) 0<br>*No valid conclusion* (18) 17<br>(9.5) 4.5 |
| **E** | No A are C (7) 3<br>No C are A (10) 12<br>(7.7) 9.7 | No A are C (6) 1<br>No C are A (3) 7<br>Some A are not C (3) 7<br>No valid conclusion (5) 4<br>(17.1) 10.8 | No A are C (2) 2<br>No C are A (0) 0<br>*No valid conclusion* (18) 17<br>(9.5) 7.0 | No A are C (1) 0<br>No C are A (0) 1<br>Some A are not C (2) 0<br>Some C are not A (1) 2<br>*No valid conclusion* (14) 14<br>(15.1) 7.5 |
| **O** | Some A are not C (3) 0<br>Some C are not A (9) 14<br>*No valid conclusion* (7) 6<br>(9.2) 8.2 | Some A are not C (2) 0<br>Some C are not A (3) 2<br>*No valid conclusion* (14) 18<br>(9.6) 6.4 | No A are C (1) 0<br>No C are A (0) 1<br>Some A are not C (2) 0<br>Some C are not A (1) 2<br>*No valid conclusion* (13) 17<br>(10.8) 11.5 | Some A are not C (1) 0<br>Some C are not A (1) 0<br>*No valid conclusion* (18) 20<br>(6.6) 5.8 |

[a] See footnote a of Table 6 for explanation of presentation of data.

410

**Table 9   The frequencies of the conclusions for $\begin{array}{c}B-A\\B-C\end{array}$ premises in Experiment 2, together with the mean latencies for the correct responses[a]**

|  | First premise | | | |
|---|---|---|---|---|
| **Second premise** | **A** | **I** | **E** | **O** |
| **A** | All A are C (8) 1<br>All C are A (2) 3<br>*Some A are C (4) 8*<br>*Some C are A (1) 5*<br>*\*No valid conclusion (5) 3*<br>(9.0) 8.5 | *Some A are C (11) 8*<br>*Some C are A (7) 12*<br>(6.4) 5.1 | No A are C (4) 3<br>No C are A (4) 4<br>*No valid conclusion (6) 4*<br>*Some C are not A (5) 7*<br>(9.6) 8.3 | Some A are not C (0) 1<br>*Some C are not A (12) 4*<br>No valid conclusion (3) 5<br>*\*Some A are C (3) 0*<br>(9.5) 9.5 |
| **I** | *Some A are C (12) 11*<br>Some C are A (7) 9<br>(7.9) 11.5 | Some A are C (3) 2<br>Some C are A (0) 0<br>*No valid conclusion (17) 18*<br>(3.6) 3.1 | No A are C (1) 2<br>No C are A (3) 0<br>*No valid conclusion (8) 4*<br>*Some C are not A (4) 13*<br>*\*Some A are not C (3) 0*<br>(14.2) 7.1 | Some A are not C (2) 0<br>Some C are not A (5) 1<br>*No valid conclusion (13) 19*<br>(5.9) 6.3 |
| **E** | No A are C (9) 5<br>No C are A (0) 3<br>*Some A are not C (4) 7*<br>No valid conclusion (6) 4<br>(8.5) 5.5 | No A are C (2) 1<br>No C are A (0) 3<br>*Some A are not C (9) 14*<br>No valid conclusion (8) 2<br>(11.3) 8.1 | No A are C (2) 4<br>No C are A (1) 0<br>(10.5) 7.0 | No A are C (0) 0<br>No C are A (1) 1<br>Some A are not C (15) 13<br>Some C are not A (1) 3<br>*No valid conclusion (11) 14*<br>(16.3) 14.1 |
| **O** | *Some A are not C (13) 17*<br>Some C are not A (1) 1<br>No valid conclusion (3) 1<br>(5.4) 7.9 | Some A are not C (5) 1<br>Some C are not A (0) 0<br>*No valid conclusion (14) 19*<br>(5.3) 5.5 | Some A are not C (3) 4<br>Some C are not A (1) 0<br>*No valid conclusion (14) 14*<br>(9.6) 15.6 | Some A are not C (0) 0<br>Some C are not A (1) 0<br>*No valid conclusion (19) 20*<br>(5.2) 4.3 |

[a] See footnote *a* of Table 6 for explanation of presentation of data.

## Acknowledgements

We are grateful to Janellen Huttenlocher for her very considerable advice, and to Paul Byerly, Diana Shapiro, and David Weltman for help in conducting the experiments. We also thank the editor, the anonymous referees, and Stuart Sutherland for their helpful comments on expository matters. The research was carried out, in part, with grants for scientific assistance from the Medical Research Council and the Social Science Research Council (GB).

## References

Altham, J. E. J. (1971) *The logic of plurality*. London: Methuen.

Begg. I. & Denny, J. P. (1969) Empirical reconciliation of atmosphere and conversion interpretations of syllogistic reasoning errors. *Journal of Experimental Psychology*, 81, 351–354.

Ceraso, J. & Provitera, A. (1971) Sources of error in syllogistic reasoning. *Cognitive Psychology*, 2, 400–410.

Chapman, I. J. & Chapman, J. P. (1959) Atmosphere effect re-examined. *Journal of Experimental Psychology*, 58, 220–226.

Cohen, M R. & Nagel, E. (1934) *An introduction to logic and scientific method*. London: Routledge & Kegan Paul.

Erickson, J. R. (1974) A set analysis theory of behavior in formal syllogistic reasoning tasks. In R. Solso (Ed.), *Theories in cognitive psychology: The Loyola Symposium*. Potomac, MD: Erlbaum.

Frase, L. T. (1968) Associative factors in syllogistic reasoning. *Journal of Experimental Psychology*, 76, 407–412.

Hunter, I. M. L. (1957) The solving of three-term series problems. *British Journal of Psychology*, 48, 286–298.

Huttenlocher, J. & Weiner, S. (1971) Comprehension of instructions in varying contexts. *Cognitive Psychology*, 2, 369–385.

Johnson-Laird, P. N. (1969a) On understanding logically complex sentences. *Quarterly Journal of Experimental Psychology*, 21, 1–13.

Johnson-Laird, P. N. (1969b) Reasoning with ambiguous sentences. *British Journal of Psychology*, 60, 17–23.

Johnson-Laird, P. N. (1970) The interpretation of quantified sentences. In G. B. Flores D'Arcais & W.J.M. Levelt (Eds), *Advances in psycholinguistics*. Amsterdam: North-Holland.

Johnson-Laird, P. N. (1975) Models of deduction. In R. J. Falmagne (Ed.), *Reasoning: Representation and process in children and adults*. Hillsdale, NJ: Erlbaum.

Mazzocco, A., Legrenzi, P. & Roncato, S. (1974) Syllogistic inference: The failure of the atmosphere effect and the conversion hypothesis. *Italian Journal of Psychology*, 2, 157–172.

Neimark, E. D. & Chapman, R. H. (1975) Development of the comprehension of logical quantifiers. In R. J. Falmagne (Ed.), *Reasoning: Representation and process in children and adults*. Hillsdale, NJ: Erlbaum.

Revlis, R. (1975a) Two models of syllogistic reasoning: Feature selection and conversion. *Journal of Verbal Learning and Verbal Behavior*, 14, 180–195.

Revlis, R. (1975b) Syllogistic reasoning: Logical decisions from a complex data base. In R. J. Falmagne (Ed.), *Reasoning: Representation and process in children and adults*. Hillsdale, NJ: Erlbaum.

Sells, S. B. (1936) The atmosphere effect: An experimental study of reasoning. *Archives of Psychology*, 29, 3–72.

Wason, P. C. & Johnson-Laird, P. N. (1972) *Psychology of reasoning: Structure and content*. Cambridge, MA: Harvard University Press: London: Batsford.

Wilkins, M C. (1928) The effect of changed material on the ability to do formal syllogistic reasoning. *Archives of Psychology*, 16, No. 102.

Winograd, T. (1972) *Understanding natural language*. New York: Academic Press.

Woodworth, R. S. (1938) *Experimental psychology*. New York: Holt.

Woodworth, R. S. & Sells, S. B. (1935) An atmosphere effect in formal syllogistic reasoning. *Journal of Experimental Psychology*, 18, 451–460.

# 15. Deductive Thinking: How We Reason
## Philip N. Johnson-Laird

### Introduction: what is deductive thinking?

The ability to reason lies at the heart of human mentality: *Homo sapiens* is a rational creature. There are many occasions in life that call for logical skill, and they include the evaluation of alternative courses of action; the determination of the consequences of assumptions and hypotheses; the interpretation of instructions, rules, and regulations; the pursuit of arguments and negotiations; the weighing of evidence; the solution of intellectual problems; and, above all, the governance of society and the development of science, culture, and technology. The importance of reasoning is reflected in the investment of resources in attempts to improve the ability of adults and children. These efforts include a project to raise the intelligence of the entire population of Venezuela, making use of the combined expertise of Harvard University; Bolt, Beranek, and Newman, Inc.; and many other institutions (see Nickerson, 1980). There are also numerous school projects in the United States and elsewhere dedicated to the teaching of reasoning (e.g., Lipman, 1980; Whimbey & Lochhead, 1980; Feuerstein, Rand, Hoffman, & Miller, 1980; Sternberg, 1980a), as well as a variety of books, educational materials, and instructional aids for improving inferential performance in solving problems (e.g., Covington, Crutchfield, Davis, & Olton, 1972; Wickelgren, 1974; Hutchinson, 1980). There is in comparison only a small amount of research into the nature of the processes that these projects are designed to enhance. If more were known about the psychology of reasoning, pedagogical procedures might be improved, and in some cases, they might even be abandoned as worthless.

It is, of course, no more possible to define deductive thinking than to define democracy or an electron. Such matters can be elucidated only by reference to a theory. However, it is useful to give a working definition that roughly delimits the domain of study. An inference is a systematic process of thought leading from one set of propositions to another. Typically, it proceeds from several premises to a single conclusion, though sometimes it may be an immediate step from a single premise to a conclusion; the propositions are usually expressed verbally, though in the case of some practical inferences, the premises may consist of a perceived or imagined state of affairs and the conclusion may consist of a course of action. The process of thought is based, explicitly or implicitly, on principles that establish a semantic relation between the premises and the conclusion. Different types of principles yield different types of relation, and hence inferences can be classified according to the principles or assumptions on which they are based.

A deduction is an inference that is supposedly based on principles of logic alone. The purpose of these principles is to guarantee validity, and an inference is valid if and only if the truth of its premises suffices to ensure the truth of its conclusion. If the conclusion does not follow validly from the premises, then the inference is fallacious.

Other sorts of inference depend on principles that lie outside logic. An induction is an inference based on the assumption that there are regularities in nature, for example:

> The sun has risen every day.
> Therefore, the sun will rise today.

An inference based on applied mathematics depends on the assumption that the mathematics is appropriate to the situation, for example:

> One bar of this soap costs 3 francs.
> Therefore, two bars of this soap cost 6 francs.

A statistical inference is based on principles governing probabilities, for example:

> The coin was tossed 92 times by Guildenstern.
> It came down heads every time.
> Therefore, either the coin was double-headed or Guildenstern was
> cheating.

And most of the inferences of daily life depend on general knowledge or common experience, for example:

> Mr. Norris was on the Amsterdam–Berlin Express on Tuesday evening.
> Therefore, he was not on the Orient Express.

Whenever an inference depends on more than the premises and the principles of logic, there can never be any guarantee that it is valid. That is to say, the premises could be true and the conclusion could nevertheless be false. Thus, the sun does not rise during the Arctic winter; there may be a special offer of 5 francs for the two bars of soap; Guildenstern's success with the coin could be a one-in-a-trillion chance or a miracle in which the laws of probability failed to apply; and Mr. Norris may have changed trains with the aid of a helicopter.

This chapter is restricted to the topic of deductive inference, because deduction is logically prior to any other form of inference. Thus, inductive and statistical methods could be neither developed nor applied without recourse to deduction. And commonsense inferences, as we shall see, turn out to be a special sort of deduction — which, of course, is not to say that they are invariably valid. The chapter outlines what is currently known about reasoning. Its psychological study has been, and continues to be, dominated by logic: investigators study how ordinary individuals untutored in logic make deductions that can be derived within a particular logical calculus. This strategy has arisen from a fundamental but pervasive misconception about the relation of logic to thought. The aim of the chapter is accordingly to elucidate the nature of this misconception and to exorcise logic from the mind. Rationality need not depend on a mental logic. Before this step can be taken, however, it is necessary to consider the nature of logic.

## Logic and the laws of thought

The fundamental semantic criterion of validity is that an inference is valid provided that there is no interpretation of its premises consistent with the denial of its conclusion (see Beth, 1971, p. 10). This criterion lies behind all formalizations of deduction. Aristotle, who by his own account was the first logician, observed that there are certain patterns of argument that are always valid. He was primarily interested in syllogisms, that is, arguments based on two premises containing quantifiers such as *every, some,* and *no,* and he noted that certain syllogisms are obviously valid, such as:

> Every man is an animal.
> Every animal is mortal.
> Therefore, every man is mortal.

Aristotle appreciated that it is the form of this argument, not its specific content, that renders it valid. Hence, any argument of the form:

> Every A is a B.
> Every B is a C.
> Therefore, every A is a C.

is valid. It follows, of course, that it is possible to argue validly from a false premise. Such an argument may yield a true conclusion:

> Every cat is a fish.
> Every fish is a vertebrate.
> Therefore, every cat is a vertebrate.

Alternatively, it may yield a false conclusion:

> Every cat is a fish.
> Every fish is an aquatic animal.
> Therefore, every cat is an aquatic animal.

The interrelation between truth and validity is accordingly that a valid argument leading to a false conclusion must be based on a false premise, since validity transmits the truth of its premises to the conclusion.

Aristotle discovered that there are valid syllogisms in forms that are much harder to grasp than the one above. He therefore devised procedures for transforming them into obviously valid patterns of argument, and in this way, he invented the formal discipline of logic. He seems to have regarded it as a tool for thought — as a formal device for evaluating the validity of any syllogism (see Kneale & Kneale, 1962, Ch. 2). Certain philosophers, however, have argued that logic is nothing but the laws of thought. This doctrine of "psychologism" was vigorously repudiated by Frege, the founder of modern logic (Frege, 1884/1950), but it continues to win adherents to the present day. Both Wittgenstein (1922, 3.03) and Popper (1972, p. 24) appear to have defended variants of the doctrine. The late Jean Piaget was its most distinguished psychological defender: Inhelder and Piaget (1958, p. 305) wrote, for example, "reasoning is nothing more than the propositional calculus itself." With the exception of the theory to be described presently, all current psychological theories of rational deduction assume some version of psychologism (e.g., Braine, 1978; Henle, 1962, 1978; Mayer & Revlin, 1978; Osherson, 1975b; Wason & Johnson-Laird, 1972; Youniss, 1975). The doctrine's plausibility, however, was much greater in the nineteenth century, when logic appeared to be a monolithic discipline. Thus, George Boole, the inventor of Boolean algebra, wrote a book with the title *An Investigation of the Laws of Thought, on Which Are Founded the Mathematical Theory of Logic and Probabilities* (1854). (His wife once observed that the trouble with Macbeth was that he had not acquainted himself with her husband's work.) Since we now know that it is possible to construct many different logics — that there are, for instance, an infinite number of distinct modal logics dealing with the notions of possibility and necessity (see Hughes & Cresswell, 1968) the temptation to assume that logic merely makes explicit the way we think ought to be considerably reduced.

Linguists have often drawn a distinction between an individual's tacit knowledge of the language and the way in which this knowledge is put to use in linguistic performance (Chomsky, 1965). This idea suggests the most plausible version of "psychologism": there is a logic in the mind underlying deductive competence, and the task of psychology is to establish how this tacit logical knowledge is put into practice (see Wason & Johnson-Laird, 1972, p. 2; Falmagne, 1980, for explicit versions of this thesis). The question that naturally arises is what form logic takes in the mind.

The two most important logical calculi for psychological purposes are the propositional calculus and the quantificational (or predicate) calculus. The propositional calculus is, in fact, a Boolean algebra that is interpreted in a way that roughly corresponds to the sentential behavior of such connectives as *and, or,* and *if.* It is thus a useful tool for analyzing inferences that hinge on the relations between clauses, for example:

> Richard is honest or Pat is incompetent (or both).
> Pat is not incompetent.
> Therefore, Richard is honest.

However, the connectives are treated as truth-functional; that is, they are defined by specifying the truth values of the propositions they form as a function of the truth values of the propositions they connect. The meaning of *not*, which operates on a single proposition, is defined as a truth function in the following way: a proposition of the form, not-A, is true if and only if A is false. Since a proposition is taken to be either true or else false, it follows that if A is true, not-A is false. An inclusive disjunction, A or B, as in the example above, is true if and only if A is true or B is true. Despite appearances, such definitions are not circular, because the expression "A or B" is in the language under analysis (the language of the calculus), but the rest of the sentence is in a metalanguage used for defining the semantics of that language.

The propositional calculus can be formalized by stating a set of axioms together with a set of rules of inference that enable one proposition to be derived from others. Such an axiomatic system is a formal device for proving theorems in an essentially syntactic way, that is, by deriving strings of symbols from other strings of symbols according to the rules of inference and without regard to the meaning of the symbols. Thus, in a formal system, one speaks of the *derivation* of a conclusion, not of its *validity,* which concerns the semantic interpretation of the system. There are formalizations of the propositional calculus in which a conclusion is derivable if and only if it is valid. Gödel's (1931/1965) famous theorem established that there is no such equivalence for arithmetic: in any formal calculus for arithmetic, there are always arithmetical truths that cannot be derived.

The quantificational calculus includes the propositional calculus but goes beyond it by containing a logic for quantifiers. Thus, syllogisms constitute a small suburb of this calculus. It, too, can be formalized so that a conclusion is derivable if and only if it is valid. But in one of the major logical discoveries of this century, Church (1936/1965) proved that there can be no general procedure guaranteed to determine the status of an inference. There are procedures that will determine sooner or later that an inference is valid, but there can be no procedure guaranteed to discover that an inference is invalid. Both procedures do exist for the propositional calculus, as well as for subsets of the quantificational calculus such as syllogisms, but a procedure for invalidity is impossible for the calculus as a whole.

## The theory of mental logic

The purpose of everyday inference is not to prove theorems but to pass from one proposition, or set of propositions, to another. It is therefore unlikely that there are logical axioms in the mind. If there is a mental logic, then it presumably consists of rules of inference, and the psychologist's task is to determine which rules are mentally embodied and what form they take. The simplest hypothesis is that there is just one rule of inference, which is used in a uniform way to make deductions. Such inferential systems, "uniform theorem-provers," have been implemented in computer programs devised by workers in artificial intelligence. These programs are largely motivated by a consequence of Church's (1936/1965) proof: while a program is trying to establish the validity of an inference, there is no way of knowing whether it will ultimately succeed or merely go on computing for ever. It is therefore important to cut down the time taken to discover that an inference is valid.

The theorem-proving programs make use of a single rule of inference, known as the *resolution rule,* which has the following form:

> A or B
> not-A or C
> Therefore, B or C.

It is really a combination of two familiar disjunctive rules:

> A or B         not-A or C
> not-A          A
> Therefore, B.   Therefore, C.

If not-A is the case, then B follows from the first of these rules; if A is the case, then C follows from the second of these rules. Since either A or not-A must hold, it follows that either B or C must, too. The problem with the resolution rule is to get the premises into a form in which the rule can be applied. There is no difficulty in converting *and* and *if* into truth-functionally equivalent disjunctions, but it is rather more complicated to eliminate the quantifiers. In essence, an existential quantifier *(some)* has to be translated into a special function. The assertion, "Every psychologist knows some statistical test" means that there is a function that, when it is provided with a psychologist as its argument, delivers a value consisting of a statistical test that the psychologist knows. Hence, the assertion can be represented by the formula:

> For every x, if x is a psychologist then x knows F(x)

where the value of F(x) is a statistical test. A universal quantifier can simply be dropped from an expression, since its work is done by the presence of a variable:

> If x is a psychologist then x knows F(x).

The conditional can be transformed into an equivalent inclusive disjunction:

> x is not a psychologist or x knows F(x)

and, finally, the expression can be translated into the familiar predicate-argument notation:

> Not(Psychologist(x)) or knows(x, F(x)).

In order to evaluate a simple inference, such as:

> Cyril is a psychologist.
> Every psychologist knows some statistical test.
> Therefore, Cyril knows some statistical test.

a uniform theorem-prover proceeds by way of a *reductio ad absurdum;* that is, it assumes the negation of the conclusion-to-be-proved and attempts to derive a contradiction. If a contradiction is derived, then the original conclusion must be valid. The first step is, accordingly, to express the premises and the negated conclusion in the notation that has been described:

> Psychologist(Cyril)
> Not(Psychologist(x)) or knows(x, F(x))
> Not(knows(Cyril, F(Cyril)))

The only complication about applying the resolution rule is that the relevant parts of premises need not consist of one formula and its literal negation. For example, Psychologist(Cyril) and Not(Psychologist(x)) will suffice. Granted this point, the three assertions have the following form:

> A
> not-A or C
> not-C

The resolution rule applies to the first two assertions to yield only:

> C

since there is no proposition corresponding to the B in its schema. Hence, the three assertions are reduced to two:

> C
> not-C

The resolution rule applies again in a similar way to eliminate both of these assertions. Once everything has been eliminated, the proof is complete: the absurdity of assuming the negation of the conclusion has been established, since nothing is consistent with it and the premises. Therefore, the conclusion itself follows at once:

Knows(Cyril, F(Cyril)).

Such a system of proof will always ultimately establish the validity of an inference in the quantificational calculus, but it may take a very long time. Much effort in this area of artificial intelligence has been devoted to cutting down the search time for proofs (see Meltzer, 1973; Robinson, 1965, 1979).

The resolution rule is too complicated — especially in the constraints it places on the form of the premises — to be psychologically plausible. If human reasoners have a mental logic, then it is likely to contain more than one formal rule of inference. The obvious middle ground, or so it seemed to a number of psychologists a few years ago, is an inferential system based on the method of "natural deduction" (Johnson-Laird, 1975; Osherson, 1975b; Braine, 1978). This method of formalizing logic uses no axioms (see, e.g., Kneale & Kneale, 1962, p. 538). Each logical term is instead introduced with its own rules of inference. Thus, for example, conjunction has such rules as:

$$
\frac{A \quad B}{\therefore A \& B} \qquad \frac{A \& B}{\therefore A}
$$

The first schema allows A & B to be inferred from the independent occurrence of A and B among the premises; the second schema allows A to be inferred from A & B. Inclusive disjunction has such rules as:

$$
\frac{A}{\therefore A \text{ or } B} \qquad \frac{A \text{ or } B \quad \text{not-}A}{\therefore B}
$$

The first of these schemata allows an inclusive disjunction, A or B (where B is any proposition), to be inferred from A; the second schema is the familiar disjunctive rule that we have already encountered. Conditionals are introduced with the rule of *modus ponens*:

$$
\frac{\text{If A then B} \quad A}{\therefore B}
$$

and the rule of *modus tollendo tollens*:

$$
\frac{\text{If A then B} \quad \text{not-B}}{\therefore \text{not-A}}
$$

There is a considerable difficulty in corroborating any hypothesis about mental logic. On the one hand, if subjects draw valid deductions, then, like Inhelder and Piaget (1958), a theorist can make the following sort of argument:

> If the propositional calculus is in the mind, then subjects are
> able to make such-and-such a deduction.
> Subjects are able to make this deduction.
> Therefore, the propositional calculus is in the mind.

Ironically, this argument is a well-known fallacy, "affirming the consequent," and the fact that distinguished psychologists commit it in arguing for the mental embodiment of the propositional calculus should perhaps be counted as strong *prima facie* evidence against their claim. On the other hand, if subjects make invalid deductions, then their performance is difficult to reconcile with mental logic. One sensible way to proceed is to examine the relative times taken to make different valid deductions, and to check their relation to a strong hypothesis about the form of the rules of inference. Although there are results that have been taken to corroborate mental versions of natural deduction (see Osherson, 1975a; Braine, 1978), the evidence is hardly overwhelming, and researchers have yet to confront the alternative hypothesis that there are no formal rules of inference in the mind.

**The effect of content on reasoning**

It has long been known that the content of a reasoning problem may significantly affect performance (e.g., Wilkins, 1928). One domain in which such effects have been studied intensively is inferences that hinge on a transitive relation, such as:

> Anne is better than Betty
> Betty is better than Charles.
> Therefore, Anne is better than Charles.

These inferences, which are known as *three-term series problems* or *linear syllogisms*, differ in their difficulty as a function of their form and their content. For example, the problem above is reliably easier than:

> Anne is worse than Betty.
> Betty is worse than Charles.
> Therefore, Anne is worse than Charles.

Some authors have argued that the difference is attributable to the direction in which a reasoner must work in constructing a mental array (De Soto, London, & Handel, 1965; Huttenlocher, 1968); other authors have argued that it is attributable to a difference in the semantics of such terms as *better* and *worse* (Clark, 1969; Clark & Clark, 1977). Although this controversy has never been resolved to the mutual satisfaction of the protagonists, it seems entirely possible that reasoners do build up a model of the array and that this process is affected by the semantic complexity and imageability of the relational terms (cf. Johnson-Laird, 1972; Wood & Shotter, 1973; Potts & Scholz, 1975; Trabasso, Riley, & Wilson, 1975; Shaver, Pierson, & Lang, 1974; Griggs, Townes, & Keen, 1979; Sternberg, 1980b)

Perhaps the most striking effects of content have been obtained by means of Wason's (1966) selection task. In the standard version of this task, four cards are laid out in front of a subject with the following symbols written on them: E, K, 2, and 3. The subject already knows that the cards have letters on one side and numbers on the other side. The task is to state which cards need to be turned over in order to determine the truth or falsity of the general rule:

If a card has a vowel on one side, then it has an even number on the other side.

Each card has to be considered on its own merits, and there is no question of turning over the cards in a particular order. As Wason (1966) found in his original study, and as we jointly corroborated in a number of subsequent experiments (Wason & Johnson-Laird, 1972), most subjects fail to make a completely correct selection. They choose either the card bearing the E or the cards bearing E and 2. The choice of E is correct, since if it has an odd number on its other side, the rule is false. The choice of 2 is a venial sin of commission: if it has a vowel on its other side, then the card is consistent with the rule, but, equally, if it has a consonant on its other side, it is hardly inconsistent with the rule. The significant error is the failure of the subjects to select the card with 3 on it. This is a serious sin of omission: if the card has a vowel on its other side, then the rule is false. What seems to happen is, first, that subjects are hypnotized by the instances explicitly mentioned in the rule, and, second, that they choose cards in order to verify the rule rather than to falsify it (see Johnson-Laird & Wason, 1970, for an information-processing model based on these assumptions).

Critics have argued that the selection task is a trick (Cohen, 1981), and that the task is so complicated that even the correct selections are made only by chance (Finocchiaro, 1980). Such arguments, as I have suggested elsewhere (Johnson-Laird, 1982a), are tendentious. Their motive is to defend the rationality of human deductive thought. Moreover, they lose their point in the light of the effects of content on performance.

Wason and I explored a number of changes in procedure and materials in a vain attempt to improve performance on the task until we discovered that a seemingly simple change in content produced a dramatic effect. When the subjects were presented with four cards representing journeys (i.e., a destination on one side and a mode of transport on the other) then there was a significant gain in insight (Wason & Shapiro, 1971). Hence, with the cards:

Manchester   Sheffield   Train   Car

and the general rule:

Every time I go to Manchester I travel by train.

over 60% of the subjects appreciated the need to turn over the card with *car* on it. If this card has *Manchester* on its other side, then the rule is plainly false. In a control group, only just over 12% of the subjects made the equivalent choice with the abstract materials. A further study showed that experience with realistic materials failed to transfer positively to abstract materials (Johnson-Laird, Legrenzi, & Legrenzi, 1972). In one realistic condition in this experiment, there was a set of envelopes, including one that was face down and sealed, one that was face down and unsealed, one that was face up with a 50-lire stamp on it, and one that was face up with a 40-lire stamp on it. The subjects were told that there was a general postal regulation:

If a letter is sealed, then it has a 50-lire stamp on it.

and they were asked to imagine that they were sorting letters to make sure they conformed to the regulation. Their task was to determine which envelopes it was necessary to turn over to find out whether they violated the rule. In this condition, the subjects, who were English, had no difficulty in appreciating that it was necessary to turn over the envelope with the 40-lire stamp on it. (If it was sealed, then plainly it contravened the regulation.) They performed almost as well in another realistic condition with the rule:

A letter is sealed only if it has a 5∂ stamp on it.

where again they realized that they needed to turn over an envelope with a 4∂ stamp on it to check whether it was in accordance with the regulation. But although the trials with the realistic materials alternated with trials with abstract materials, there was no apparent transfer: the subjects continued to fail to select the falsifying item.

There have been many replications of the effect of realistic materials on increased insight into the selection task (e.g., Lunzer, Harrison, & Davey, 1972; Gilhooly & Falconer, 1974; van Duyne, 1974), and variations in the type of content have been shown to yield different degrees of insight (van Duyne, 1976; Pollard & Evans, 1981). But there have also been failures to demonstrate improved performance with realistic materials (Manktelow & Evans, 1979; Reich & Ruth, 1982; Brown, Keats, Keats, & Seggie, 1980; Griggs & Cox, 1982). There are a number of factors that may account for the discrepancy . One obvious possibility is that it arises as a result of "experimenter" effects. The standard administration of the selection task is certainly open to such effects. Some of the more notable failures to obtain an effect of realistic materials occurred with group testing, and any procedure that reduces the onus on the subjects to think is likely to yield a poorer performance. However, there is at least one study that employed the optimal technique of individual face-to-face testing by a naive experimenter, and this experiment replicated the facilitating effect of a realistic rule (Pollard, 1981).

Another conjecture is that realistic materials improve performance only if the subjects can recall past experiences with the content of the rule. There are several variations on this hypothesis. At one extreme, the subjects merely have to remember the answer and do not have to reason at all (Manktelow & Evans, 1979). Responses of this sort may have occurred in certain conditions in some experiments. But the inadequacy of this version of the "memory cue" explanation is obvious from the very first results on realistic materials; subjects had surely never encountered such rules as "Every time I go to Manchester I travel by train," or "If a letter is sealed, then it has a 50-lire stamp on it." A weaker version of the hypothesis is therefore more plausible: subjects can be cued to make the correct selections by their memory for analogous rules and their counterexamples (Griggs & Cox, in press). The fact that the relation between the terms in the rule must be a familiar one supports this proposal. Thus, such rules as, "Every time I think of Ottawa I remember car" (Bracewell & Hidi, 1974) and "If I eat haddock, then I drink gin" (Manktelow & Evans, 1979) do not lead to insight into the task. Similarly, when the familiarity of the rules is manipulated, insight into the task is correlated with it. For example, with subjects in Florida, the local law, "If a person is drinking beer, then the person must be over 19" yields better performance than its unfamiliar contrapositive or converse (Cox & Griggs, 1981). A striking result with one and the same rule is that English subjects over the age of 45, who may remember the postal regulation concerning sealed envelopes, performed well in a recent replication of the envelope experiment, but subjects under the age of 45, who may never have encountered the regulation, performed no better than they did with abstract materials (Golding, 1981). However, direct personal experience of the rule is not necessary. In a study carried out by D'Andrade (cited by Rumelhart & Norman, 1981; and replicated by Mandler, 1980), the subjects had to imagine that they managed a store; they showed insight with the "sensible" principle:

> If a purchase exceeds $30, then the receipt must have the signature of the manager on the back.

but they lacked insight with an arbitrary principle. In a further replication, Griggs and Cox (1982) demonstrated a significant degree of insight with such negated rules as:

> If a purchase does not exceed $30, then the receipt must have the signature of the manager on the back.

Such a rule is the very opposite of "sensible," but perhaps its clear violation of common sense suffices, as Wason (1983) has suggested, to trigger the correct inference.

Memory is plainly important for correct performance of the selection task: no effect of content can be explained without an appeal to previous experience. What is crucial, however, is that insight into the task reflects an effect of content on the process of deduction. This phenomenon is an embarrassment to any psychological theory that assumes that generalizations are falsified by recourse to formal rules of inference. Piaget wrote, for example, that once children have attained the age of reason — the level of formal operations — they readily appreciate that a generalization of the form "if p then q" has to be tested by a systematic search for counterexamples of the form p & not-q (see Beth & Piaget, 1966, p. 181). Whatever the ultimate explanation of performance in the selection task, such a formal account is not feasible. It fails to explain the uniform failure with the arbitrary rules. What may be necessary are content–specific rules of inference (Johnson-Laird & Wason, 1977, p. 4; Rumelhalt, 1979; Wason, 1983).

## Content–specific rules of inference

The idea that there might be rules of inference framed with a specific content is similar to the familiar logical device of "meaning postulates" (Carnap, 1956). Valid inferences that depend on the meanings of words can be captured by postulates that specify the relevant semantic relations, for example:

> For every x, if x is a physicist then x is a scientist.

Such rules can be added to a statement of the semantics of a language in order to rule out certain possibilities (e.g., physicists who are not scientists). This device has recently been cut loose from theoretical semantics and taken over by both psychologists and artificial intelligencers. Inferential systems based on content-specific rules have been implemented in programs written in the programming language PLANNER (Hewitt, 1972; Winograd, 1972). Programs written in this language and its descendants have a data base consisting of a set of assertions, such as a description of the current state of affairs in some small universe of discourse. These assertions are about specific individuals, and they are represented in the standard predicate–argument notation:

(PHYSICIST ALBERT)

The programming language makes it easy to write a program for interrogating the data base and for adding new assertions to it. Such a program will return the answer, "Yes," if one asks whether Albert is a physicist, and it adds a new statement to the data base if one asserts that Albert is a mathematician. However, if an assertion takes the form of a generalization, such as:

All physicists are mathematicians

then the programming language makes it possible to write a routine that represents this assertion as a content-specific rule of inference. For instance, a procedure known as an *antecedent theorem* can be set up, which in simplified form looks like this:

(ANTECEDENT (x) (PHYSICIST x)
    ASSERT(MATHEMATICIAN x))

This procedure springs to life whenever anyone is described as a physicist and adds to the data base the information that the same individual is also a mathematician. Alternatively, the same generalization can be used in a consequent theorem:

(CONSEQUENT (x) (MATHEMATICIAN x)
    GOAL(PHYSICIST x))

This procedure acts like the addition of a general description to the data base. If the user of the program asks, "Is Albert a mathematician?" then there may be no direct assertion to that effect in the data base. The consequent theorem establishes that x is a mathematician provided that the goal of showing that x is a physicist is satisifed. If there is an assertion in the data base to the effect that Albert is a physicist, then that goal is indeed satisfied, and the program responds, "Yes."

By representing general assertions in the form of rules of inference, either for adding information to the data base when an assertion is made, or for deducing it from the data base when a question is to be answered, PLANNER-like languages allow a programmer to encode specific heuristics for achieving particular inferential goals. In place of the blind uniform procedures of the resolution method, the content of a problem may directly govern the way in which an inference is made. This aspect of performance certainly seems psychologically plausible. However, it is the programmer's task to devise the appropriate rules of inference.

There must be more to human inference than content-specific rules, because individuals do possess certain formal deductive abilities. Indeed, without such abilities they would be unable to set up appropriate content-specific rules — a fact that is often overlooked by devotees of PLANNER and its cognates, who tend to ignore the role of the programmer in setting up the inferential system in the first place. The evidence from the selection task shows that people are affected by the content of reasoning problems; it does not show that they only possess — or even possess — content-specific rules of inference.

We appear to be confronted by a dilemma. A mental logic consisting of either formal rules of inference or content-specific rules cannot explain the psychology of reasoning. It might therefore seem to be necessary to develop a theory with both sorts of rule; fortunately, there is a quite different possibility. The first clue to this approach is to be found in the answer to the following question. What determines which inferences are drawn?

If you give an ordinary intelligent individual, who knows no logic, the following premises:

> If the fuse has blown there is a short in the circuit.
> The fuse has blown.

and then ask what conclusion can be drawn, the chances are that your subject will reply:

> There is a short in the circuit.

A natural explanation for this response is that it results from the use of the *modus ponens* rule of inference:

> If A then B
> A
> --------------
> ∴ B

This answer is so seductive that it is easy to overlook a critical problem: What determined that the reasoner should have used this particular rule of inference? There are many other possibilities. For example, a rule for conjunction might have been used to derive the conclusion:

> The fuse has blown and if the fuse has blown there is a short in the circuit.

Or a rule for disjunction might have been used to derive the conclusion:

> If the fuse has blown there is a short in the circuit or the fuse has blown.

Or another rule for disjunction might have been applied to the second premise to yield the valid conclusion:

> The fuse has blown or the queen has abdicated.

Both of the last two rules might have been used to derive:

> If the fuse has blown there is a short in the circuit or the fuse has blown
> or the queen has abdicated.

There are indeed an infinite number of possible conclusions that might have been drawn, yet the majority of people settle for the one above. Of course, most of the possible conclusions are silly, but they are none the less completely valid. Hence, whatever the principles are that rule out the silly conclusions, they cannot be part of logic. Few theorists have confronted this problem. Most have been content to follow Piaget's tacit assumption that once we understand the nature of mental logic, the psychology of reasoning will have been explained. However, if there is a mental logic, it alone cannot determine what conclusions people draw from given premises.

The problem of constraining logic so that it delivers the conclusions that people actually infer has been tackled in a prescriptive way. A system is set up in which it is impossible to make the more bizarre deductions. In a natural deduction system, a distinction can be drawn between major rules of inference, such as *modus ponens,* and auxiliary rules, such as:

P

--------

∴ P or Q

One can stipulate that auxiliary rules are never used by themselves, but only as precursors to the use of a major rule (see Johnson-Laird, 1975, for this approach). Thus, it becomes impossible to make the silly deduction:

> The fuse has blown.
> Therefore, the fuse has blown or the queen has abdicated.

But it remains possible to use the same rule to make the sensible deduction:

> If it is foggy or frosty, then the game will be canceled.
> It is frosty.
> Therefore, the game will be canceled.

A notational variation of this approach is simply to build the auxiliary rules into the schema of the major rules so that it is impossible to use the auxiliaries by themselves (Braine, 1978). A similarly prescriptive approach has been advocated by Sperber and Wilson (1982).

A quite different approach to restricting inferences can be based on the concept of semantic information. Psychologists are familiar with the statistical concept of information deriving from communication theory (Shannon & Weaver, 1949), but they often do not know that in some domains it is feasible to develop a measure of the amount of semantic information in a proposition. In general, it is reasonable to assume that the more possible states of affairs that a proposition rules out, the greater its semantic content. This assumption is readily put into practice with assertions built up out of propositional connectives such as *and, or,* and *if* (see Johnson-Laird, 1983). A conjunction, A & B, contains more information than one of its conjuncts, A, which in turn contains more information than a disjunction, A or B. It is easy to devise a measure of semantic information based on these considerations.

Although a valid deduction can never yield more semantic information than is contained in its premises, it can yield less. This asymmetry suggests a plausible hypothesis about the heuristics guiding the process of deduction: no conclusion should contain less semantic content than the premises on which it is based or should fail to express that information more parsimoniously (Johnson-Laird, 1983). Hence, what is wrong with the inference:

> The fuse has blown.
> Therefore, the fuse has blown or the queen has abdicated.

is that semantic content is radically reduced. And what is wrong with an inference that merely conjoins the premises is that it fails to express their content in a more parsimonious way.

The need to maintain semantic content — and to express it parsimoniously — is directly related to the tacit conventions of conversation (see Grice, 1975). There is at least one other conversational convention governing inference: there is no need to restate simple premises in a conclusion. For example, given the premises:

> If it is frosty or foggy then the game will be canceled.
> It is frosty.

the conclusion according to the heuristics is:

> Therefore, it is frosty and the game will be canceled.

Most reasoners, however, appreciate that it is not necessary to state the obvious and they do not repeat the premise. They draw the conclusion:

> Therefore, the game will be canceled.

The proposed heuristics impose constraints on the form of the conclusions that are deduced and predict (correctly) that reasoners will be loath to draw any conclusion whatsoever from a set of premises such as:

> My banker is prudent.
> Boys eat apples.

Most people untutored in logic are indeed inclined to suppose that there is no conclusion that follows validly from these premises. In fact, there are infinitely many valid conclusions that can be deduced, for example:

> My banker is prudent or girls like sweets (by a disjunctive rule)
> My banker is prudent and boys eat apples (by a conjunctive rule)

and so on. The point is that all of these conclusions are less parsimonious than the premises, and many of them contain less semantic information, too.

A constraint is not a mechanism, but there is an algorithm for making propositional inferences that automatically conforms to the heuristic principles, and it is this algorithm that provides the next clue to a psychology of reasoning that relies neither on formal rules nor on content-specific rules of inference.

### Propositional reasoning without rules of inference

The algorithm for reasoning with propositional connectives has been implemented in a computer program (see Johnson-Laird, 1982b). Its main feature is that it does not use formal rules of inference such as *modus ponens*. It has instead a knowledge of the meaning of the connectives, a procedure for making substitutions, and an ability to carry out compositional semantic interpretations. When the program is given premises, say, of the form:

> If A or B then C
> A

it first finds the maximally informative premise (in terms of the metric or semantic information). In this case, the most informative premise is the simple categorical assertion, A. It then searches for an occurrence of this premise as a constituent of another. It finds A as a constituent of the conditional premise and substitutes the value "True" for its occurrence there, since any premise is to be taken as true for the purposes of inference. This process of substitution transforms the conditional premise into:

> If True or B then C.

The truth conditions for inclusive disjunction guarantee that if one disjunct is true then the disjunction as a whole is true. Hence, the program carries out the corresponding piece of compositional semantics, leading to a simplified antecedent of the conditional:

> If True then C.

When both a conditional and its antecedent are true, then according to the truth conditions for conditionals, its consequent must be true, too. Hence, the final step is to reduce the conditional to the categorical conclusion:

> C.

The original premises are equivalent in semantic content to the conjunction:

> A and C

but the program automatically delivers a conclusion in accordance with the conversational convention. It does not repeat the premise that is the basis of the inference — a constraint that follows directly from the fact that the entire deduction is carried out on the conditional premise. The program draws a conclusion only if it is able to effect a compositional simplification; otherwise, like a human reasoner, it draws no conclusion at all.

Not all deductions can be made by substituting a truth value for a constituent of a complex premise. The following form of argument, for example, provides no such opportunity:

> A or B
> If A then C
> If B then D

In such cases, when the ordinary machinery has failed, the program splits a premise into separate constituents, determines what follows from each of them, and then combines these separate conclusions according to the connectives in the original premise. Thus, from the constituent A of the first premise, the ordinary compositional machinery operating on the second premise derives the conclusion C; from the constituent B of the first premise, the ordinary machinery operating on the third premise derives D; these two conclusions are then combined by means of the same connective, *or*, that joined their respective bases in the first premise. The result is the conclusion:

C or D

This process is handled by a recursive procedure so that a premise can be chopped up into several pieces before inferences are drawn from each of them.

The algorithm for making inferences by a process of compositional semantics depends on a representation of the meaning of the connectives — a representation that assumes that they are defined in a simple truth-functional way; for example, a conditional is true if and only if its antecedent is false or its consequent is true. In fact, the meaning of ordinary connectives does not match very readily with such a semantics — a phenomenon that has greatly exercised philosophers (e.g., Ramsey, 1950; Cooper, 1968; Stalnaker, 1968; Grice, 1975); linguists (e.g., Geis & Zwicky, 1971; McCawley, 1974; Gazdar, 1979); and psychologists (e.g., Johnson-Laird & Tagan, 1969; Wason & Johnson-Laird, 1972; Taplin & Staudenmayer, 1973; Rips & Marcus, 1977; Fillenbaum, 1978; Braine, 1979). There is, however, a natural generalization of the theory embodied in the algorithm: the inferential machinery, instead of interpreting merely the connectives, interprets the complete propositions. Inferences are made not by following either formal or content-specific rules of inference, but by constructing and evaluating mental models of the states of affairs described in premises (Johnson-Laird, 1975, 1980, 1983). According to this theory, there are three main components in the process of inference. First, the reasoner imagines how the world would be if the premises were true and takes into account any general information about their particular content even if it is not explicitly asserted. Second, a prudent reasoner abides by the fundamental semantic criterion of validity and searches for alternative models of the premises. Third, if all the models of the premises have something in common, then the reasoner formulates a corresponding conclusion; if there is no such state of affairs, then the reasoner draws no conclusion.

The chief advantages of this theory are that it makes sense of the otherwise disparate findings on the psychology of reasoning; that it replaces the vexatious puzzle of how formal rules of inference are acquired by children with the more tractable problem of how they acquire the semantic criterion of validity and the meaning of words; and that it leads to novel predictions that have been corroborated experimentally. The theory has been applied to spatial reasoning (Mani & Johnson-Laird, 1982) and to the inferences that underlie the interpretation of discourse (Garnham, Oakhill, & Johnson-Laird, 1982; Johnson-Laird, 1981). However, the next section deals primarily with its application to syllogistic reasoning.

## Syllogistic reasoning without rules of inference

Although psychologists have been studying syllogisms for over 70 years (cf. Störring, 1908), they have only recently proposed theories about the inferential mechanism. In the first such theory, Erickson (1974) argued that subjects encode the premises of syllogisms in a form that corresponds to Euler circles. This traditional pedagogical device uses circles to represent sets of entities. Thus, the premise "Some of the artists are bankers" requires four separate arrangements of circles (Figure 1). The first arrangement represents an overlap between the two sets, the second represents the set of bankers entirely included within the set of artists, the third represents an identity between the two sets, and fourth represents all the artists as bankers, though the actual premise is still true of it.

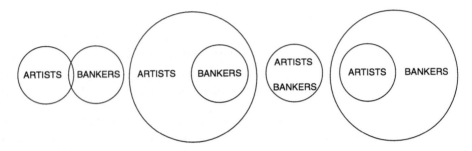

**Figure 1    The four Euler circle diagrams required for "Some of the artists are bankers."**

The premise "All the bankers are cooks" requires two Eulerian arrangements (Figure 2). There are many different ways to combine the representations of these two premises — many more than their simple product — and the combinations include cases where the artists are coextensive with the cooks, where they overlap, and where one set is included within the other. In all cases, however, the following conclusion holds:

Some of the artists are cooks.

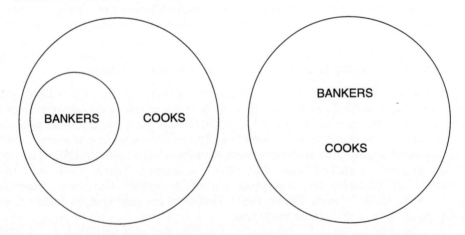

**Figure 2    The two Euler circle diagrams required for "All the bankers are cooks."**

Euler circles suffer from one severe problem as a basis for psychological theorizing: they can be combined in too many different ways. Erickson dealt with this combinatorial embarrassment by assuming that subjects do not always consider the full set of distinct ways in which an individual premise can be represented, and that subjects do not always form the complete set of combinations. Sternberg has recently proposed a theory of syllogistic reasoning based on strings of symbols corresponding to Euler circles, and he similarly limits the number of combinations that reasoners are supposed to construct (Guyote & Sternberg, 1981). Both theories accordingly render human beings intrinsically irrational with respect to syllogisms; and, like Euler circles, neither theory can be extended to cope with quantificational inferences of other sorts.

A different approach could be based on a mental logic for quantifiers, such as the quantificational calculus. No such proposal has been made, though it would at least preserve human rationality. It would also solve the problem of how reasoners make quantified inferences that are not syllogisms, such as:

> Some gourmets don't like every three-star restaurant.
> Therefore, not every gourmet likes some three-star restaurant.

The reluctance of psychologists to posit a quantificational calculus within the mind is strange, given their propensity for locating the propositional calculus there. One reason for their reluctance is perhaps that rules of inference for quantifiers, unlike those for connectives, are not intuitively obvious. One caution to be borne in mind in the framing of any such proposal is that certain inferences well within the competence of 7-year-olds do require a higher-order calculus in which quantifiers range over properties as well as individuals. For example, the following simple deduction:

> More than half the visitors in the room own cars.
> More than half the visitors in the room own houses.
> Therefore, some visitor in the room owns both a house and a car.

cannot be derived in the standard calculus (cf. Barwise & Cooper, 1980).

There is, of course, no need to espouse either Euler circles or mental logic to account for the ability to make such deductions. The theory of mental models readily explains both syllogistic inference and other deductions with quantifiers. First, the reasoner imagines how the world would be if the premises were true. Hence, with the premise, "Some of the athletes are bankers," the reasoner imagines some arbitrary number of athletes:

> athlete
> athlete
> athlete

to represent the relevant set of athletes and then mentally tags them in some way in order to indicate that some of them are bankers:

> athlete= banker
> athlete = banker
> (athlete) (banker)

The parenthetical items indicate that there may be athletes who are not bankers, and bankers who are not athletes. The information in the second premise, "All bankers are cooks," can then be added to this mental model to yield a combined model of both premises:

athlete = banker = cook
athlete = banker = cook
(athlete) (banker = cook)
(cook)

The new parenthetical item indicates that there may be cooks who are not bankers. Second, a prudent reasoner will attempt to construct other models of the premises. In the case of the present syllogism, there is no alternative model; but other syllogisms may yield two or three different models. Where there is only one possible model, an inference should be very easy — even subjects who fail to search for alternatives should be able to make the correct response; where there is more than one model, the task should be reliably harder. Table 1 summarizes the relevant results of three experiments. In Experiment 1, 20 American subjects were given all 64 possible pairs of syllogistic premises with a sensible everyday content and were asked to state what followed from each pair of premises (see Johnson-Laird & Steedman, 1978). Experiment 2 was a replication carried out with 20 students at the University of Milan; and Experiment 3 was a further replication with another 20 students who were given only 10 seconds in which to make their response to the problems (see Johnson-Laird & Bara, 1982). In each experiment, there was a highly reliable trend: the greater the number of models, the poorer the performance. Third, the reasoner formulates a conclusion that is consistent with the set of models. Our experiments have shown that there is a highly reliable bias in the form of conclusions. Over 80% of the conclusions to premises in which the terms had the following arrangement (as in the example above):

A — B
B — C

were of the form:

A — C

whereas over 80% of the conclusions to premises in which the terms had the arrangement

B — A
C — B

were of the form:

C — A.

The arrangement of terms is known as the *figure* of the syllogism, and this *figural effect* is most robust. No subject that we have tested has ever failed to show it. To a lesser extent, figure also affects the difficulty of a syllogism. Both the bias and the effect on accuracy can be explained as a result of the different mental operations required to form an integrated mental model (Johnson-Laird, 1983; Johnson-Laird & Bara, 1982). These operations, which have also been modeled in a computer program,

434

can be traced back through Hunter's (1957) classic account of three-term series problems to an idea originally put forward by William James (1890, Vol. 2, pp. 644–646).

**Table 1** **The percentage of correct valid conclusions in three experiments on syllogistic reasoning**[a]

|  | One model | Two models | Three models |
|---|---|---|---|
| Experiment 1 | 92 | 46 | 28 |
| Experiment 2 | 72 | 25 | 9 |
| Experiment 3 | 56 | 25 | 3 |

a The percentages are shown as a function of the number of mental models that have to be constructed to yield the correct conclusion.

The theory of mental models accounts for nearly all the erroneous conclusions that subjects draw — on the assumption that they fail to consider all the possible models of premises. The theory does not assume that subjects make illicit conversions of the premises (*pace* Chapman & Chapman, 1959; Revlis, 1975; Revlin & Leirer, 1978); it does not assume that there is an "atmosphere" produced by the premises favoring conclusions of the same superficial form (*pace* Woodworth & Sells, 1935; Erickson, 1974; Guyote & Sternberg, 1981). The theory predicts many of the same responses as these two hypotheses; in the crucial cases where the theories diverge, the evidence supports mental models (Mazzocco, Legrenzi, & Roncato, 1974; Johnson-Laird & Steedman, 1978; Johnson-Laird, 1983).

In daily life, many inferences occur so automatically that one is often unaware of making them. These inferences are particularly important in the interpretation of discourse, and they are so evanescent that their importance was discovered only when computer scientists attempted to program computers to understand texts. Consider the following passage, for example:

> The elevator took me to the fifth floor and Room 503. I knocked and went right in. Arthur lay slumped across his desk with an automatic in his hand and a pained look of surprise frozen on his face. He was very still. I eased him back in the chair and gently pried the gun from his hand. I balanced it on the end of a pencil and held it up to the light. I didn't know what I was looking for and I didn't find it.

In reading this extract, one inevitably makes a number of inferences, for example, that the narrator walked from the elevator to Room 503, knocked on its door, and entered it; that Arthur, sprawling across his desk, was in that room; that the narrator balanced the gun — not Arthur's hand — on the end of a pencil; and so on. The reader may also infer that Arthur is dead, and that the narrator is a man. These commonsense inferences are made by constructing a mental model based on the passage and general knowledge. They are rapid because, unlike deliberate deductions, the reader simply constructs a single representative model and makes no attempt to search for alternatives.

## Conclusions

The dominant tradition in the psychology of reasoning is that deduction depends on a mental logic consisting of formal rules of inference. The research described in this chapter presents a challenge to that view. The fact that content affects performance, so notably in Wason's selection task, argues against any purely formal approach to reasoning, and this thesis is perhaps strengthened by recent studies of expert thinking (e.g., Larkin, McDermott, Simon, & Simon, 1980). One reaction to the challenge is to propose that there are content-specific rules of inference. The problem with this proposal, however, is to explain how such rules could be set up without recourse to formal rules. Another reaction is to abandon rules of inference as the primary machinery of deduction in favor of the theory of mental models. According to this theory, the mind is equipped with a number of general procedures for constructing models, for searching for alternatives, and for formulating descriptions of what they have in common. The processes of construction and evaluation depend on a knowledge of the meanings of the premises and sometimes on general knowledge. The process of searching for alternatives depends on a grasp of the fundamental semantic criterion of validity. It is this principle, not a set of formal rules of inference, that underlies our deductive thinking.

## Acknowledgements

This research was supported by a grant from the Social Science Research Council of Great Britain.

## References

Barwise, J. & Cooper, R. (1980) Generalized quantifiers and natural language. In J. Barwise & I. Sag (Eds.), *Stanford working papers in semantics* (Vol. 1). Stanford, Calif.: Stanford University.

Beth E. W. (1971) *Aspects of modern logic.* Dordrecht, Holland: Reidel.

Beth, E. W. & Piaget, J. (1966) *Mathematical epistemology and psychology.* Dordrecht: Reidel.

Boole, G. (1854) *An investigation of the laws of thought, on which are founded the mathematical theory of logic and probabilities.* London: Macmillan.

Bracewell, R. J. & Hidi, S. E. (1974) The solution of an inferential problem as a function of stimulus materials. *Quarterly Journal of Experimental Psychology*, 26, 480–488.

Braine, M. D. S. (1978) On the relation between the natural logic of reasoning and standard logic. *Psychological Review*, 85, 1–21.

Braine, M. D. S. (1979) On some claims about if-then. *Linguistics and Philosophy*, 3, 35–47.

Brown, C., Keats, J. A., Keats, D. M. & Seggie, I. (1980) Reasoning about implication: A comparison of Malaysian and Australian subjects. *Journal of Cross-Cultural Psychology*, 11, 395–410.

Bryant, P. E. (1978) How stupid are we? *Times Higher Educational Supplement*. March 3.

Carnap, R. (1956) *Meaning and necessity: A study in semantics and modal logic* (2nd ed.). Chicago: University of Chicago Press.

Chapman, I. J. & Chapman, J. P. (1959) Atmosphere effect re-examined. *Journal of Experimental Psychology*, 58, 220–226.

Chomsky, N. (1965) *Aspects of the theory of syntax*. Cambridge, Mass.: MIT Press.

Church, A. (1936) A note on the Entscheidungsproblem. *Journal of Symbolic Logic,* 1, 40–41. (Reprinted [incorporating a subsequent correction] in M. Davis, Ed., *The undecidable: Basic papers on undecidable propositions, unsolvable problems and computer functions*. Hewlitt, N.Y.: Raven Press, 1965.)

Clark, H. H. (1969) Linguistic processes in deductive reasoning. *Psychological Review*, 76, 387–404.

Clark, H. H. & Clark, E. V. (1977) *Psychology and language: An introduction to psycholinguistics*. New York: Harcourt Brace Jovanovich.

Cohen, L. J. (1981) Can human irrationality be experimentally demonstrated? *Behavioral and Brain Sciences*, 4, 317–370.

Cooper, W. S. (1968) The propositional logic of ordinary discourse. *Inquiry*, 11, 295–320.

Covington, M. V., Crutchfield, L., Davis, L. & Olton, R. M. (1972) *The productive thinking program*. Columbus, Ohio: Merill.

Cox, J. R. & Griggs, R. A. (1981) *The effects of experience on performance in Wason's selection task*. Mimeo, Department of Psychology, University of Florida, Gainesville.

De Soto, C. B., London, M. & Handel, S. (1965) Social reasoning and spatial paralogic. *Journal of Personality and Social Psychology*, 2, 513–521.

Erickson, J. R. (1974) A set analysis of behavior in formal syllogistic tasks. In R. L. Solso (Ed.), *Theories in cognitive psychology: The Loyola Symposium*. Potomac, Md.: Erlbaum.

Evans, J. St. B. T. (1977) Toward a statistical theory of reasoning. *Quarterly Journal of Experimental Psychology*, 29, 621–635.

Evans, J. St. B. T. (1982) *The psychology of deductive reasoning*. London: Routledge & Kegan Paul.

Falmagne, R. J. (1980) The development of logical competence: A psycholinguistic perspective. In R. H. Kluwe & H. Spada (Eds.), *Development models of thinking*. New York: Academic Press.

Feuerstein, R., Rand, Y., Hoffman, M. B. & Miller, R. (1980) *Instrumental enrichment*. Baltimore: University Park Press.

Fillenbaum, S. (1978) How to do some things with IF. In J. W. Cotton & R. L. Klatzky (Eds.), *Semantic factors in cognition*. Hillsdale, N.J.: Erlbaum.

Finocchiaro, M. A. (1980) *Galileo and the art of reasoning*. Dordrecht: Reidel.

Frege, G. (1950) *Die Grundlagen der Arithmetik*. Translated by J. L. Austin as *The foundations of arithmetic*. Oxford: Blackwell. (Originally published, 1884.)

Garnham, A., Oakhill, J. & Johnson-Laird, P. N. (1982) Referential continuity and the coherence of discourse. *Cognition*, 11, 29–16.

Gazdar, G. (1979) *Pragmatics: Implicature, presupposition, and logical form*. New York: Academic Press.

Geis, M. & Zwicky, A. M. (1971) On invited inferences. *Linguistic Inquiry*, 2, 561–566.

Gillhooly, K. J. & Falconer, W. A. (1974) Concrete and abstract terms and relations in testing a rule. *Quarterly Journal of Experimental Psychology*, 26, 355–359.

Gödel, K. (1965) Uber formal unentscheidbare Sätze der Principia Mathematica und verwandter Systeme, I. *Monatshefte für Mathematik und Physik*, 1931, 38, 173–198. Translated by E. Mendelson as: On formally undecidable propositions of Principia Mathematica and related systems, I. In M. Davis (Ed.), *The undecidable: Basic papers on undecidable propositions, unsolvable problems and computable functions.* Hewlitt, N.Y.: Raven Press.

Golding, E. (1981) *The effect of past experience on problem solving.* Paper presented to the Annual Conference of the British Psychological Society, Surrey University.

Grice, H. P. (1975) Logic and conversation. In P. Cole & J. L. Morgan (Eds.), *Syntax and Semantics. Vol 3: Speech acts.* New York: Academic Press.

Griggs, R. A. & Cox, J. R. (1982) The elusive thematic-materials effect in Wason's selection task. *British Journal of Psychology*, 73, 407–420.

Griggs, R. A. & Cox, J. R. The effect of problem content on strategies in Wason's selection task. *Quarterly Journal of Experimental Psychology,* in press.

Griggs, R. A., Townes, K. J. & Keen, D. M. (1979) Processing numerical quantitative information in artificial linear orderings. *Journal of Experimental Psychology: Human Learning and Memory*, 5, 282–291.

Guyote, M. J., & Sternberg, R. J. (1981) A transitive-chain theory of syllogistic reasoning. *Cognitive Psychology*, 13, 461–525.

Henle, M. (1962) On the relation between logic and thinking. *Psychological Review*, 69, 366–378.

Henle, M. (1978) "Foreword" to R. Revlin and R. E Mayer (Eds.), *Human Reasoning.* Washington, D.C.: Winston.

Hewitt, C (1972) Description and theoretical analysis of PLANNER: a language for proving theorems and manipulating models in a robot. *MIT Artificial Intelligence Laboratory Report Number 258.*

Hughes, G. E. & Cresswell, M. D. (1968) *An introducnon to modal logic.* London: Methuen.

Hunter, I. M. L. (1957) The solving of three-term series problems. *British Journal of Psychology*, 48, 288–298.

Hutchinson, R. T. (Oct 1980) *Teaching problem solving to developmental adults: A pilot project.* Paper presented to the Conference on Thinking and Learning Skills. University of Pittsburgh.

Huttenlocher, J. (1968) Constracting spatial images: a strategy in reasoning. *Psychological Review*, 75, 550–560.

Inhelder. B. & Piaget, J. (1958) *The growth of logical thinking from childhood to adolescence.* New York: Basic Books.

James, W. (1980) *The principles of psychology* (Vol. 2). New York: Holt.

Johnson-Laird, P. N. (1972) The three-term series problem. *Cognition*, 1, 57–82.

Johnson-Laird, P. N. (1975) Models of deduction. In R. J. Falmagne (Ed.), *Reasoning: Representation and process.* Hillsdale, N.J.: Erlbaum.

Johnson-Laird, P. N. (1980) Mental models in cognitive science. *Cognitive Science*, 4, 71–115.

Johnson-Laird, P. N. (1981) Comprehension as the construction of mental models. *Philosophical Transactions of the Royal Society,* Series B, 295, 353–374.

Johnson-Laird, P. N. (1982) Ninth Bartlett Memorial Lecture: Thinking as a skill. *Quarterly Journal of Experimental Psychology*, 34(A), 1–29. (a)

Johnson-Laird, P. N. (1982b) Propositional representations, procedural semantics, and mental models. In J. Mehler, E. Walker, & M. F. Garrett (Eds.), *Perspectives on mental representation: Experimental and theoretical studies of cognitive processes and capacities.* Hillsdale, N.J.: Erlbaum.

Johnson-Laird, P N. (1983) *Mental models: towards a cognitive science of language, inference, and consciousness.* Cambridge, England: Cambridge University Press; Cambridge, MA: Harvard University Press.

Johnson-Laird, P. N. & Bara, B. (1982) *The figural effect in syllogistic inference.* Mimeo, Laboratory of Experimental Psychology, University of Sussex.

Johnson-Laird, P. N. & Steedman, M. (1978) The psychology of syllogisms. *Cognitive Psychology*, 10, 64–99.

Johnson-Laird, P. N. & Tagart, J. (1969) How implication is understood. *American Journal of Psychology*, 82, 367–373.

Johnson-Laird, P. N. & Wason, P. C. (1970) A theoretical analysis of insight into a reasoning task. *Cognitive Psychology*, 1, 134–148.

Johnson-Laird, P. N. & Wason, P. C. (Eds.). (1977) *Thinking: Readings in cognitive science.* Cambridge, England: Cambridge University Press.

Johnson-Laird, P. N., Legrenzi, P. & Legrenzi, M. S. (1972) Reasoning and a sense of reality. *British Journal of Psychology*, 63, 395–400.

Kneale, W. & Kneale, M. (1962) *The development of logic.* Oxford, England: Clarendon Press.

Larkin, J., McDermott, J., Simon, D. P. & Simon, H. A. (1980) Expert and novice performance in solving physics problems. *Science*, 208, 1335–1342.

Lipman, M. (1980) *Philosophy in the classroom* (2nd ed.). Philadelphia: Temple University Press, 1980.

Lunzer, E. A., Harrison, C. & Davey, M. (1972) The four card problem and the generality of formal reasoning. *Quarterly Journal of Experimental Psychology*, 24, 326–339.

Mandler, J. M. (1980) Structural invariants in development. In L. Liben (Ed.), *Piaget and the foundations of knowledge.* Hillsdale, N.J.: Erlbaum.

Mani, K. & Johnson-Laird, P. N. (1982) The mental representation of spatial descriptions. *Memory and Cognition*, 10, 181–187.

Manktelow, K. I. & Evans, J. St. B. T. (1979) Facilitation of reasoning by realism: Effect or non-effect? *British Journal of Psychology*, 70, 477–488.

Mayer, R. E. & Revlin, R. (1978) An information processing framework for research on human reasoning. In R. Revlin & R. E. Mayer (Eds.), *Human reasoning.* Washington, D.C.: Winston.

Mazzocco, A., Legrenzi, P. & Roncato, S. (1974) Syllogistic inference: The failure of the atmosphere effect and the conversion hypothesis. *Italian Journal of Psychology*, 2, 157–172.

McCawley, J. D. (1974) If and only if. *Linguistic Inquiry*, 5, 632–635.

Meltzer, B. (1973) The programming of deduction and induction. In A. Elithorn & D. Jones (Eds.), *Artificial and human thinking*. London: Elsevier.

Nickerson, R. (1980) Report on Phase I of Harvard's PROJECT INTELLIGENCE, a Venezuelan pilot program. *Human Intelligence International Newsletter*, 3, 1–2.

Osherson, D. N. (1975a) *Logical abilities in children, Vol. 3: Reasoning in adolescence: Deductive inference*. Hillsdale, N.J.: Erlbaum.

Osherson, D. N. (1975b) Logic and models of logical thinking. In R. J. Falmagne (Ed.), *Reasoning: Representation and process*. Hillsdale, N.J.: Erlbaum.

Pollard, P. (1981) The effect of thematic content on the "Wason selection task." *Current Psychological Research*, 1, 21–29.

Pollard, P. & Evans, J. St. B. T. (1981) The effects of prior beliefs in reasoning: an associational interpretation. *British Journal of Psychology*, 72, 73–81.

Popper, K. R. (1972) *Objective knowledge: An evolutionary approach*. Oxford, England: Clarendon Press.

Potts, G. R. & Scholz, K. W. (1975) The internal representation of the three-term series problem. *Journal of Verbal Learning and Verbal Behavior*, 14, 439–452.

Ramsey, F. P. (1950) General propositions and causality. In F. P. Ramsey (Ed.), *Foundations of mathematics and other logical essays*. London: Routledge & Kegan Paul.

Reich, S. S. & Ruth, P. (1982) Reasoning: Verification, falsification, and matching. *British Journal of Psychology*, 73, 395–405.

Revlin, R. & Leirer, V. O. (1978) The effect of personal biases on syllogistic reasoning: Rational decisions from personalized representations. In R. Revlin & R. E. Mayer (Eds.), *Human reasoning*. Washington, D.C.: Winston.

Revlis, R. (1975) Two models of syllogistic reasoning: Feature selection and conversion. *Journal of Verbal Learning and Verbal Behavior*, 14, 180–195.

Rips, L. J. & Marcus, S . L. (1977) Suppositions and the analysis of conditional sentences. In M. A. Just & P. A. Carpenter (Eds.), *Cognitive processes in comprehension*. Hillsdale, N.J.: Erlbaum.

Robinson, J. A. (1965) A machine-oriented logic based on the resolution principle. *Journal of the Association for Computing Machinery*, 12, 23–41.

Robinson, J. A. (1979) *Logic, form and function: Mechanization of deductive reasoning*. Edinburgh: Edinburgh University Press.

Rumelhart, D. E. (1979) *Analogical processes and procedural representations*. Technical Report No. 81. Center for Human Information Processing, University of California, San Diego.

Rumelhart, D. E. & Norman, D. A. (1981) Analogical processes in learning. In J. R. Anderson (Ed.), *Cognitive skills and their acquisition*. Hillsdale, N.J.: Erlbaum.

Shannon, C. E. & Weaver, W. (1949) *The mathematical theory of communication.* Urbana: University of Illinois Press.

Shaver, P., Pierson, L. & Lang, S. (1974) Converging evidence for the functional significance of imagery in problem solving. *Cognition,* 3, 359–375.

Sperber, D. & Wilson, D. (1982) Mutual knowledge and relevance in theories of comprehension. In N. Smith (Ed.), *Mutual knowledge.* London: Academic Press.

Stalnaker, R. C. (1968) A theory of conditionals. In N. Rescher (Ed.), *Studies in logical theory.* Oxford, England: Blackwell.

Sternberg, R. J. (Oct 1980a) *Instrumental and componential approaches to the nature and training of intelligence.* Paper presented to the Conference on Thinking and Learning Skills. University of Pittsburgh.

Sternberg, R. J. (1980b) A proposed resolution of curious conflicts in the literature on linear syllogisms. In R. Nickerson (Ed.), *Attention and performance* (Vol. 8). Hillsdale, N.J.: Erlbaum.

Störring, G. (1908) Experimentelle Untersuchungen über einfache Schlussprozesse. *Archiv Gesellschaft Psychologie,* 11, 1–127.

Taplin, J. E. & Staudenmayer, H. (1973) Interpretation of abstract conditional sentences in deductive reasoning. *Journal of Verbal Learning and Verbal Behavior,* 12, 530–542.

Trabasso, T., Riley, C. A. & Wilson, E. G. (1975) The representation of linear order and spatial strategies in reasoning: A developmental study. In R. J. Falmagne (Ed.), *Reasoning: Representation and process.* Hillsdale, N.J.: Erlbaum.

van Duyne, P. C. (1974) Realism and linguistic complexity in reasoning. *British Journal of Psychology,* 65, 59–67.

van Duyne. P. C. (1976) Necessity and contingency in reasoning. *Acta Psychologica,* 40, 85–101.

Wason, P. C. (1966) Reasoning. In B. Foss (Ed.), *New Horizons in Psychology.* Harmondsworth, Middlesex: Penguin.

Wason, P. C. (1983) Rationality and the selection task. In J. St. B. T. Evans (Ed.), *Thinking and reasoning.* London: Routledge & Kegan Paul.

Wason, P. C. & Johnson-Laird, P. N. (1972) *Psychology of reasoning: Structure and content.* London: Batsford; Cambridge, Mass.: Harvard University Press.

Wason, P. C. & Shapiro, D. (1971) Natural and contrived experience in a reasoning problem. *Quarterly Journal of Experimental Psychology,* 23, 63–71.

Wetherick, N. E. (1970) On the representativeness of some experiments in cognition. *Bulletin of the British Psychological Society,* 23, 213–214.

Whimbey, A. & Lochhead. J. (1980) *Problem solving and comprehension: A short course in analytical reasoning* (2nd ed.). Philadelphia: Franklin Institute Press, 1980.

Wickelgren, W. A. (1974) *How to solve problems: Elements of a theory of problems and problem solving.* San Francisco: Freeman.

Wilkins, M. C. (1928) The effect of changed material on the ability to do formal syllogistic reasoning. *Archives of Psychology,* 16(No. 102).

Winograd, T. (1972) *Understanding natural language.* New York: Academic Press.

Wittgenstein, L. (1922) *Tractatus logico-philosophicus*. Translated by C. K. Ogden. London: Roudedge & Kegan Paul.

Wood, D. & Shotter, J. (1973) A preliminary study of distinctive features in problem solving. *Quarterly Journal of Experimental Psychology*, 25, 504–510.

Woodworth, R. S. & Sells, S. B. (1935) An atmosphere effect in formal syllogistic reasoning. *Journal of Experimental Psychology*, 18, 451–460.

Youniss, J. (1975) Inference as developmental construction. In R. J. Falmagne (Ed.), *Reasoning: Representation and process*. Hillsdale, N.J.: Erlbaum.